Civil Liberties in Northern Ireland:

The CAJ Handbook

4th edition

edited by **Brice Dickson and Martin O'Brien**

Civil Liberties in Northern Ireland

This edition is dedicated to the memory of Gerry McAleer, who died on 8 June 2002.

Published by the Committee on the Administration of Justice
45-47 Donegall Street
Belfast
BT1 2BR

Tel: (028) 9096 1122
Fax: (028) 9024 6706

Website: www.caj.org.uk

British Library Cataloguing in Publication Data
        A catalogue record for this book is available from the
        British Library

ISBN 1 873285 34 5

Printed and bound by
Shanway Press
1-3 Eia Street
Belfast BT14 6BT
Tel: (028) 9022 2070

Cover design by Shanway Press
www.shanway.com

Contents

What is the CAJ?

The Committee on the Administration of Justice (CAJ) was established in 1981 and is an independent non-governmental organisation affiliated to the International Federation of Human Rights. CAJ takes no position on the constitutional status of Northern Ireland and is firmly opposed to the use of violence for political ends. Its membership is drawn from across the community.

The Committee seeks to ensure the highest standards in the administration of justice in Northern Ireland by ensuring that the government complies with its responsibilities in international human rights law. CAJ works closely with other domestic and international human rights groups, such as Amnesty International, the Lawyers Committee for Human Rights and Human Rights Watch, and makes regular submissions to a number of United Nations and European bodies established to protect human rights.

CAJ's activities include publishing reports, conducting research, holding conferences, monitoring, campaigning locally and internationally, individual casework and providing legal advice. Its areas of work are extensive and include policing, emergency laws, the criminal justice system, equality and advocacy for a Bill of Rights.

The organisation has been awarded several international human rights prizes, including the Reebok Human Rights Award and the Council of Europe Human Rights Prize.

Membership entitles you to receive the CAJ's monthly civil liberties newssheet *Just News*, to take part in the work of the sub-groups and to use the CAJ resource library and clippings service. If you would like to join CAJ or find out more about its activities, please contact:

CAJ, 45-47 Donegall Street
Belfast BT1 2BR
Tel: (028) 9096 1122 Fax: (028) 9024 6706
Website: www.caj.org.uk

Notes on Contributors

Maggie Beirne is Research and Policy Officer for the CAJ.

Brice Dickson is Chief Commissioner of the Northern Ireland Human Rights Commission, on secondment from his post as a professor of law at the University of Ulster at Jordanstown.

Eileen Evason is a professor in social administration at the University of Ulster at Jordanstown.

Neil Faris is a solicitor in Belfast and an adviser on public and commercial law.

Sharon Geary is the Information Officer for Housing Rights Service.

Anne Grimes is a solicitor employed by the Law Centre (NI) and a part-time Immigration Adjudicator.

Michael Hamilton is a teaching fellow at the School of Law, University of Ulster.

John Jackson is a professor of law at the Queen's University of Belfast.

Beverley Jones is a solicitor in Belfast and a former Chief Legal Officer at the Equal Opportunities Commission for Northern Ireland.

George Kilpatrick is a solicitor who formerly headed up the Disability Legal Team at the Equality Commission for Northern Ireland.

Stephen Livingstone is a professor of law at the Queen's University of Belfast.

Paul Mageean is a qualified solicitor and works as the Legal Officer at CAJ.

Anne McKeown is a social worker in Antrim Family Centre, Homefirst Community Trust.

Chris Moffat is education editor for Fortnight Educational Trust.

Rachel Murray is a lecturer in law at the University of Bristol.

Martin O'Brien is director of the CAJ.

Mary O'Rawe is a barrister and lecturer in law at the University of Ulster at Jordanstown.

Michael Potter is a barrister in Northern Ireland.

Mark Reid is a solicitor at the Western Area Office of the Law Centre (NI).

Ciaran White is a barrister and senior lecturer in law at the University of Ulster at Jordanstown.

Acknowledgements

Contributors to the fourth edition of this book have once again provided their services free of charge. We are extremely grateful to them for all their hard work in preparing their chapters. In addition to the writers there are a great many other people who have assisted in the book's production. At the heart of the production process is Liz McAleer, CAJ's administrator. Without her dedication to the task there would be no handbook. We are also indebted to a large number of individuals who assisted with proof reading and indexing: Dario Barsalini, Ciarán Fox, Peter and Moya Gahan, Aideen Gilmore, Eilis Haughey, Susanna Konner, Shelagh Livingstone, Vincent Mageean, Helen Martin, Conor McCarthy, Duncan McLaughlan, Deirdre O'Brien, Karen O'Connor, Anne Smith, Linzi Straghan, Mario Woldt and Michael Yim. We are also grateful to Liam Lynch for his advice and assistance in relation to relevant computer packages. Last but by no means least our appreciation goes to Lord Lester of Herne Hill QC for his Foreword. We are delighted that he has again agreed to identify himself with this work, as Lord Scarman, the writer of the Foreword for the first and second editions, did before him.

Brice Dickson and Martin O'Brien

FOREWORD

I am pleased to have been invited, once again, by the Committee on the Administration of Justice to provide the Foreword to the admirable handbook on civil liberties in Northern Ireland. Its subject matter is important to me. Indeed, as long ago as 1968, in a lecture on "Democracy and Individual Rights" to a Fabian audience, I drew attention to the importance for civil liberties in Northern Ireland of incorporating the European Convention on Human Rights into UK law. It was heresy at the time but is now conventional wisdom.

In my Foreword to the third edition I expressed regret at the length of time it had taken to make the Convention rights directly effective in UK courts. Since October 2000, when the Human Rights Act at last came into force, we have seen a gradual but significant shift in the way in which the judiciary, in Northern Ireland and Great Britain, have interpreted the law and official discretion to provide better protection against the misuse of state powers.

That protection has been further enhanced in Northern Ireland by the work of the Human Rights Commission, working alongside the Equality Commission, to develop a culture of respect for human rights. The Parliamentary Joint Select Committee, of which I am a member, has now recommended that either a single Equality and Human Rights Commission or two separate but linked Commissions should be set up in Britain. Once again, Northern Ireland has set an example to the rest of the UK.

One of the new additions to the handbook is the chapter on equality. Work is proceeding in Northern Ireland on a Single Equality Bill. Meanwhile, my own Equality Bill has been passed by the Lords and has won widespread support in the Commons. I very much hope that on both sides of the Irish Sea there will be equal protection of human rights (including equal treatment without discrimination) and, for that matter, that the Republic of Ireland will soon enact legislation to incorporate the Convention rights into Irish law.

This handbook provides accurate and practical help and advice to those who most need it. All who have contributed to its production should feel justifiable pride. It deserves a very wide audience and should serve as a model for similar handbooks for England, Wales and Scotland.

Lord Lester of Herne Hill QC

xi

Chapter 1

Introduction

Brice Dickson and Martin O'Brien

In all democracies the law is part and parcel of a wider notion called "the rule of law". By this is meant that no-one, whether an individual, a company, a private body or an organ of the government, can be above the law: the law must apply to everyone equally, without any unfair discrimination. Hand in hand with this principle runs the understanding that all individuals have certain basic rights – or fundamental civil liberties – which the state must not take away. It is those rights and liberties which form the subject-matter of this book.

The development of human rights law

After the end of the Second World War, which brought to light horrific violations of human rights in Germany and elsewhere, nations around the world were determined to take steps to guarantee protection to human rights in international and national law. The first concrete manifestation of this was the American Declaration of the Rights and Duties of Man, drawn up by the Organisation of American States in 1948. This was followed in the same year by the Universal Declaration of Human Rights, produced under the auspices of the newly-created United Nations. The Declaration was proclaimed on 10 December, which is now known worldwide as international human rights day. In 1950 the member states of the Council of Europe, meeting in Rome, adopted the European Convention for the Protection of Human Rights and Fundamental Freedoms.

All of these documents concentrated on protecting civil and political rights, such as freedom of expression, freedom of religion and freedom of association. But the American Declaration and the Universal Declaration also embraced, economic, social and cultural rights, such as the right to the preservation of health, the right to education and the right to work. In 1966, in order to supplement the general provisions of the Universal Declaration, the United Nations adopted two further International Covenants, one on civil and political rights, the other on economic, social and cultural rights. The gap in the European framework was filled by the adoption of the European Social Charter in 1961, another document prepared by the Council of Europe; it was issued in a revised form in 1996. The member states of the European Union also agreed their own Social Charter, as part of the Maastricht Treaty of 1992. In 1997 the Labour government of the UK said it would abide by this Charter. The Treaty of Amsterdam, also in 1997, strengthened the EU's commitment to human rights even further. Arising out of this, the Race and Ethnic Origin Directive and the Framework Employment Equality Directive were issued in 2000. These must be implemented by way of national legislation within the next few years and will result in strengthened protection of the right not to be discriminated against on the grounds of race, religion, age, disability or sexual orientation (for more details see Chapter 11).

In national legal systems there has been a comparable growth in human rights law. The vast majority of countries now have a written constitution with a Bill of Rights contained in it. The best known system is probably that of the United States of America, where the influence of the first 10 amendments to the Constitution – which were adopted in 1791 and are collectively known as the Bill of Rights – has been profound. In more recent years many other former colonies of the British Empire have marked their independence by adopting a constitution which includes guarantees for human rights. Even existing colonies, such as Gibraltar, are governed by legal provisions guaranteeing human rights.

The 1937 Constitution of the Irish Free State (now the Republic of Ireland) places Articles 40-44 under the general title of "Fundamental Rights" and includes such matters as the right to be held equal before the law, the right to one's life, person, good name and property, the right to liberty, freedom of expression, freedom of assembly and association, the right to education for children and the right to freedom from religious discrimination. The 1950 Constitution of India lays down similar legally enforceable fundamental rights. In Canada, a Bill of Rights was enacted in 1960 but this was supplanted in 1982 by a more far-reaching Charter of Rights and Freedoms. Australia – a federal state with a written constitution – does not yet have a Bill of Rights, but New Zealand – a unitary state with no written constitution and only chamber in Parliament – does. New Zealand's Bill of Rights, like that which operates in Hong Kong even after the handover to China, is based almost word for word on the United Nations'

International Covenant on Civil and Political Rights. The most advanced Bill of Rights in the world is now probably the one contained in the current Constitution of South Africa, in force since 1996. Nor is the tendency towards protection of human rights apparent only in countries which have an historical connection with English law. In France, the famous Declaration of the Rights of Man and of the Citizen (1789) was specifically incorporated into current law by the preamble to the 1958 Constitution of the Fifth Republic. In Germany, the 1949 Basic Law devotes the first 19 of its 146 Articles to basic rights. Moreover in both these countries the constitutional courts, or their equivalents, have gone to considerable lengths to develop the substance of these rights.

The enforcement of human rights

It is all very well to have laws on human rights, but if those laws are imperfectly enforced they may as well not exist. International agreements on human rights are especially difficult to enforce because there is, as yet, no supreme body to which governments of states can be made answerable; nor, usually, are there any sanctions which can be effectively imposed. The United Nations has tried to get round this problem by asking states to accede to what is called the Optional Protocol to the 1966 International Covenant on Civil and Political Rights. This allows citizens, in effect, to sue their own governments before the United Nations' Human Rights Committee. Likewise, the European Convention on Human Rights can be enforced against governments by individuals in the European Court of Human Rights in Strasbourg. However, none of these international judgments is backed by a system of effective penalties if the state concerned chooses not to comply. Enforcement ultimately depends on political pressure, which can often take years to exert. While every country in Europe has now agreed to be bound by the European Convention (with the exception of Serbia and Montenegro), as of 1 May 2003 only 104 countries worldwide had agreed to be bound by the United Nations' Optional Protocol (including Ireland, but not the United Kingdom).

At the national level, countries differ greatly in the ways in which they permit citizens to claim their rights and liberties. In the USA, any person can challenge the constitutionality of any law in any court. If the Supreme Court confirms that a law made by Congress (the US Parliament) is invalid, then that law can be ignored by everyone in the land. In France, MPs can challenge the constitutionality of a

Parliamentary statute before it is officially published but no challenge can be mounted after publication. In Ireland, both prior *and* subsequent court challenges are permitted.

Northern Ireland and the United Kingdom

The Human Rights Act 1998 represents a key development in ensuring respect for human rights throughout the United Kingdom. It was brought fully into force on 2 October 2000. From that date many of the rights provided for by the European Convention on Human Rights can now be relied upon directly in our courts. The Act makes it unlawful for any public authority to act incompatibly with the rights contained in the European Convention, unless a provision of primary legislation means that it could not act in any other way. It also requires all legislation to be interpreted and given effect as far as possible in a way which is compatible with the Convention rights. Courts now have to take account of European Court case-law and are bound to develop the common law compatibly with the Convention rights. All courts can invalidate subordinate legislation and the higher courts can issue a declaration of incompatibility for primary legislation. In response to such a declaration, government Ministers can make remedial orders to amend the offending legislation so that it conforms with Convention rights. To date 11 such declarations of incompatibility have been issued in England and Wales (although three have already been overturned on appeal and two others are the subject of appeal) and one in Northern Ireland (see Chapter 17).

Arising out of the Belfast (or Good Friday) Agreement in 1998 the Northern Ireland Human Rights Commission has been tasked with consulting on the scope for a Bill of Rights for Northern Ireland to supplement the rights contained in the European Convention on Human Rights. The Commission must then present its advice on the matter to the Secretary of State. It is expected that it will deliver its advice late in 2004 and the government has indicated that it will thereafter consult further on any proposals made.

The CAJ and a great many other groups and individuals are committed to securing a strong and inclusive Bill of Rights for Northern Ireland. As each of the chapters in this book will show, the law in Northern Ireland rarely confers positive rights on people but instead controls people's behaviour by placing all sorts of constraints on them: whatever is not affected by these constraints is deemed to be a liberty. The approach of the European Convention is not very different.

The constraints which at present exist are so far-reaching, and the rights conferred on government agencies so all-embracing, that the resulting liberty is at times very narrow in scope. A Bill of Rights could not only increase people's confidence in the administration of justice but also improve the content of the law and make people more physically and psychologically secure.

The role of non-governmental and statutory organisations

In practice, the educational and campaigning activities of non-governmental organisations may be more effective in improving the law on human rights than court actions. A large number of non-governmental organisations working in the field of human rights now exist, the best known probably being Amnesty International, which has its headquarters in London, national sections throughout the world and a regional office in Belfast. Within the United Kingdom the two most prominent organisations are possibly Justice (which is the British branch of the International Commission of Jurists) and Liberty (formerly known as the National Council for Civil Liberties).

In Northern Ireland much valuable work in this area was carried out in the 1960s and early 1970s by the Northern Ireland Civil Rights Association. In subsequent years a number of other organisations have been formed to work on a range of specific civil liberties issues. In 1973 the government itself set up the Standing Advisory Commission on Human Rights, to advise it on whether the law in Northern Ireland operates in a discriminatory fashion. This was replaced in 1999 by the Northern Ireland Human Rights Commission, which was given a wider remit and powers. Over the years a number of bodies were established to deal with various kinds of discrimination. In October 1999 a new Equality Commission was established, bringing together the existing equality bodies working on race, gender, disability and religion (see Chapter 11).

In 1981 the Committee on the Administration of Justice (CAJ) was formed as an independent voluntary organisation to carry out more general monitoring of the legal system in Northern Ireland. It has acquired a reputation for accuracy and thoroughness and the present book is a further demonstration of its wish to provide information about Northern Ireland's legal system to as wide an audience as possible.

The content of this book

The chapters in this book offer advice and information on a wide variety of common legal problems encountered by people living in Northern Ireland. Although they are ascribed to particular authors, they have been edited and cross-referenced so as to make the book more than a disparate collection of essays. The book tries to be reasonably comprehensive but inevitably there are some omissions. The fourth edition differs from the third in having additional chapters on the rights of the mentally ill, and environmental rights, but we have still not included matters such as consumer rights and patients' rights. All of the other chapters have been carefully revised and updated. Of course we have not been able to say as much as we would have liked about particular topics, but greater enlightenment can be obtained from the publications listed in the section on Further Reading.

The book begins with a description of how victims of denials of civil liberties can seek to obtain remedies through the courts and tribunals of Northern Ireland and with an explanation of the European dimension, public law remedies and legal aid. It then moves on to describe police and army powers, where the distinction between emergency and ordinary laws is most apparent. The next two chapters look more closely at the rights of detainees and at the system for handling complaints against the police, which has undergone considerable changes as a result of the move to independent investigations by the Police Ombudsman.

In Chapter 6 the position of prisoners is examined, an area which has given rise to a large amount of litigation in Northern Ireland. The impact of the European Convention on Human Rights has often been felt in prisons, although not always to the advantage of prisoners. Chapter 7 deals with issues related to the rights of immigrants. The next three chapters provide an exposition of people's rights to expression and information, whether through demonstrations, meetings, organisations or direct speech. These are followed by a general introductory chapter on equality rights which provides details on the work of the Equality Commission and the new statutory duty on public authorities to promote equality of opportunity across the nine grounds of gender, sexual orientation, age, religion, political opinion, disability, race, marital status and dependents. Five separate chapters then deal with religious discrimination, sex discrimination, racial discrimination, the rights of people with disabilities and the rights of people who are mentally ill. Chapter 17 outlines the law affecting family and sexual life and Chapter 18 provides information on children's rights.

The next five chapters are devoted entirely to the category known as social and economic rights, which many would argue are even more significant than civil and political rights. Respectively these deal with education, employment, housing, social security and the environment.

Each chapter aims primarily to explain the current law and is restrained in offering a critique. At times contributors have inevitably found it difficult to conceal their objections to some of the relevant legal provisions and the CAJ endorses the points they make in this regard. As far as possible contributors have sought to ensure that their chapters accurately state the law as of 1 March 2003. Occasionally more recent developments have been mentioned. If there are mistakes, please let us know.

Chapter 2

Victims' Rights

Brice Dickson

An important aspect of the law is the relief it provides for people who are victims of breaches of the law. The obtaining of remedies is a central element of justice and a right conferred by the law is an empty one if there are no means of effectively enforcing it. The law itself should provide procedures which are appropriate for remedying the different types of grievance which may arise.

To help convey how victims of illegal behaviour can get a remedy for the hurt and loss they may have suffered, this chapter first explains Northern Ireland's criminal and civil court system, together with the arrangements for tribunals and inquests. The European dimension, as provided by both European Union law and the European Convention on Human Rights, is also explained. Particular attention is paid to the remedying of grievances against public bodies, whether through the process of "judicial review" or through a complaint to the Ombudsman. Reference is then made to the schemes in place for the granting of legal aid to people who need financial assistance when dealing with their legal problems. Finally, some of the institutions created to help victims of the troubles in Northern Ireland, and some of the policy initiatives in this field, are described.

The criminal courts

Criminal offences in Northern Ireland divide into four broad categories:

- offences which must be tried summarily,
- offences which must be tried on indictment,
- offences which are triable either way – formerly called "hybrid" offences, and
- offences which are "scheduled" under the emergency laws.

Summary offences

Offences which must be tried summarily are the least serious offences. They are tried in a magistrates' court by a resident magistrate sitting without a jury. Illustrations of summary offences are to be found in the Public Order (NI) Order 1987, as amended (see Chapter 8). These include organising or taking part in a public procession in respect of which the required notice has not been given, trying to break up a lawful public procession or public meeting, committing riotous or disorderly behaviour in a public place or obstructive sitting in a public place. Other common examples include assault and many motoring offences. A person found guilty of a summary offence is liable to a sentence of imprisonment (of variable duration but usually not exceeding six months), to a fine or to both.

An appeal against a magistrates' court's decision can go either to a county court (on questions of fact and law) and/or to the Court of Appeal (on questions purely of law). From there an appeal can go to the House of Lords.

Indictable offences

These are serious offences which have to be tried in the Crown Court by a judge and jury. They include murder, manslaughter, rape, robbery and wounding or causing grievous bodily harm with intent to cause grievous bodily harm. The committal stage for these offences – i.e. the preliminary hearing into whether or not the accused person should be "committed" for trial – is heard in a magistrates' court. Appeals against decisions in the Crown Court go to the Court of Appeal and from there to the House of Lords.

Offences triable either way

An offence may be triable either summarily or on indictment in one of three situations. First, the legislation creating the offence may state that it can be tried either way. In this situation, the prosecution will decide how to proceed according to the seriousness of the offence. So, for example, under the Public Order (NI) Order 1987 a person who takes part in a prohibited procession may be tried either way depending on how grave his or her alleged misconduct was. Second, some offences normally triable on indictment, such as theft and indecent assault, may be tried summarily if the resident magistrate who hears the case at the committal stage considers that it is not a serious case and if both prosecution and defence have no objections. Third, a small number of statutory offences normally tried summarily (*e.g.* criminal damage) may be tried on indictment if the offence carries a potential sentence of more than six months and if the defendant asks to be tried on indictment.

Scheduled offences

The "scheduled" offences are those listed in Schedule 9 to the Terrorism Act 2000, being offences most commonly committed by persons engaged in politically motivated violence. The category cuts across the distinction between summary and indictable offences. Most of the scheduled offences are indictable, in which case they are tried before a "Diplock court", *i.e.* a single judge of the Crown Court, sitting without a jury. Some of the offences are stated by the Terrorism Act to be triable either summarily or on indictment, such as membership of a proscribed organisation or display of support in public for a proscribed organisation. A prosecution in respect of an offence under this part of the Terrorism Act cannot be instituted without the consent of the Director of Public Prosecutions for Northern Ireland (the DPP).

Some of the scheduled offences may be "de-scheduled" by the Attorney General if there is no element of "terrorism" involved in a particular case, but if he or she refuses to do this there can be no appeal against that decision. Some offences cannot be de-scheduled (or "certified out" as the process is sometimes called). Some offences are treated as scheduled offences only if committed in a particular way (*e.g.* robbery where a firearm is used).

The rights of victims in criminal cases

Under the current law, victims of crimes have surprisingly few rights before, during or after the criminal trial of a person who is prosecuted for the crime in question. They do not have the right, for example, to be told that the trial is about to commence, to be legally represented at the trial or to have a say in the sentence which is meted out if the person on trial is convicted. Nor can they insist on being told the reasons behind a decision of the DPP not to prosecute someone for the crime: the Report of the Criminal Justice Review, in March 2000, recommended that the presumption should shift to giving reasons, but the Justice (NI) Act 2002 does not implement this. Reasons will be given only in exceptional circumstances, at the discretion of the DPP.

A refusal to give reasons can, in theory, be challenged by making an application for judicial review (see p.16), but judges are very reluctant to interfere with the DPP's discretion in this regard (see *In re Adams*, 2000).

If the victim is to be a witness in the case and is deemed to be vulnerable (a category including all persons under 17 years of age), the Criminal Evidence (NI) Order 1999 allows for special measures to be taken to assist the witness during the trial. This may include permitting the witness to give evidence from behind a screen, out of the accused's sight. Evidence can in some instances be given by a video-link.

The Justice (NI) Act 2002 does confer some new rights on victims, as recommended by the Criminal Justice Review Report in March 2000. By section 68 the Secretary of State must make a Victim Information Scheme, by which information will be given to victims who wish to receive it about the release of prisoners who are serving sentences for crimes the victims have suffered. The first such scheme was announced in July 2002. In the case of temporary releases the victim can make representations to the Secretary of State to the effect that the release would threaten the safety or otherwise adversely affect the victim (s.69).

It is worth noting that section 71 of the Justice (NI) Act 2002 also requires the Secretary of State to devise a strategy for enhancing community safety in Northern Ireland. Moreover he or she is empowered (not required) to divide Northern Ireland into areas and establish for each area a body tasked with enhancing community safety in the area.

Inquests

The main legislation on inquests in Northern Ireland is the Coroners Act (NI) 1959, as amended, and the statutory rules made under it, in particular the Coroners (Practice and Procedure) Rules (NI) 1963, as amended. There are currently seven coroners and seven deputy coroners in Northern Ireland, all of whom must be solicitors or barristers of at least five years' standing.

The function of a coroner is to investigate unexpected or unexplained deaths, deaths in suspicious circumstances and deaths occurring as a result of violence, misadventure or unfair means. The coroner has a discretion whether or not to order a *post mortem* examination of the body but in practice a *post mortem* will be held in any case where the initial explanation of the death fails to satisfy the coroner. If the investigation indicates that death was due to unnatural causes an inquest is likely to be held; this happens in approximately 20% of investigations.

The inquest is held in public and usually takes place without the help of a jury, but a jury must be summoned where the death occurred in prison, where it was caused by an accident, poison or a notifiable disease, or where it occurred in circumstances which, if they were to continue or recur, would be prejudicial to the health or safety of the public. Unlike in England, there is no requirement to summon a jury where a death has occurred in police custody or by the action of the police in pursuance of their duty, although the coroner has a discretion to summon a jury in such a case. A jury at an inquest has between seven and 11 members.

The purpose of an inquest is to ascertain who the deceased was and how, when and where the deceased came by his or her death. However an inquest in Northern Ireland returns no verdicts as such. Prior to 1981 a coroner or a jury could return a verdict of death by "natural causes", "accident", "misadventure", "his (or her) own act", "execution of sentence of death" or an "open" verdict. Since 1981 a verdict has had to take the form of factual "findings" only. Neither the coroner nor the jury is permitted to express "any opinion on questions of criminal or civil liability" (rule 16 of the Coroners (Practice and Procedure) (NI) Rules 1963). In practice an inquest is not opened until the coroner has been informed that no criminal proceedings will be brought in relation to the death. Where a person is charged with a criminal offence, the coroner must adjourn any inquest, "in the absence of reason to the contrary" (rule 13 (1)), until after the completion of the criminal proceedings, including an appeal. This can obviously lead to long delays in the holding of an inquest. The coroner also has a discretion not to hold an inquest after criminal proceedings.

Procedures at inquests

The procedure for the conduct of an inquest is regulated by both statutory rules and the coroner's own discretion, the exercise of which may be subject to judicial review (see p.16).

The calling of witnesses at an inquest is a matter for the discretion of the coroner. Until recently a coroner was prohibited from compelling any person to give evidence "who is suspected of causing the death or has been charged or is likely to be charged with an offence relating to the death", but this prohibition (contained in rule 9(2) of the

1963 Rules) was removed early in 2002 in an effort to comply with four important judgments handed down by the European Court of Human Rights in May 2001 (*Jordan v UK* etc.). If such a person is called to give evidence, he or she does not have to answer a question if to do so would incriminate him or her.

Witnesses who give evidence may be questioned (but not cross-examined) by both the coroner and by other "properly" interested parties to the proceedings, either directly or through a barrister or solicitor (rule 7(1)). Evidence is given on oath. The questions must be confined to the remit of an inquest. Hearsay evidence is admissible. The relatives of the deceased are not entitled to call witnesses, although they may suggest the names of potential witnesses to the coroner.

Documentary evidence is also placed before the inquest. Relatives of the deceased may be given a copy of the *post mortem* report before the inquest begins. There is no general requirement, however, for other documentary evidence, such as forensic reports, photographs or witness statements, to be given to the relatives before then. But in cases where the death has occurred in police custody a Home Office Circular requires the police to make available to the family of the deceased all the evidence which they are making available to the coroner. In Northern Ireland this practice is now followed in relation to all cases where deaths have been caused by servants of the state. If the Secretary of State for Northern Ireland believes that a part of the written or oral evidence puts national security at risk, he or she can issue a Public Interest Immunity Certificate which may bar the disclosure of evidence to the inquest or control the way in which oral evidence is given (*e.g.* from behind a screen, hiding the witness from the general public: see *In re McNeill,* 1994). The coroner or court on judicial review may scrutinise the ambit of the term "national security" (see *In re McNeill* and *In re Toman,* 1994).

Before the inquest concludes relatives of the deceased may be allowed to make a statement. Once the inquest is over the coroner or the jury delivers their findings, which must be confined to "a statement of who the deceased was, and how, when and where" he or she died (rule 2(1)). No qualifications or additions are permitted, and no compensation can be ordered to be paid to any relative of the deceased. There can be no appeal against the decision of a coroner's inquest, although the proceedings may be subject to judicial review.

Although legal aid for inquests is contemplated by the Legal Aid, Advice and Assistance (NI) Order 1981 for those entitled to be legally represented at inquests, the relevant provision has never been implemented and legal aid is, therefore, not available at present for the inquest itself. However an *ex gratia* scheme has been established, administered by the Northern Ireland Court Service, whereby financial assistance can be granted in exceptional circumstances. Moreover, "green form" legal advice and assistance (see p.27) is available for those who meet the financial eligibility criteria and who want legal help prior to the inquest. Once the Access to Justice (NI) Order 2003 takes effect, there will be a power vested in the Lord Chancellor (or in the Minister of Justice in Northern Ireland once "justice" becomes a devolved matter) to make legal aid available in certain inquests.

At present a fundamental review of the inquest system in Northern Ireland (and in England and Wales) is on-going. Recommendations for change are expected to be made later in 2003. It is possible that they will recommend the introduction of a "two-tier" approach, whereby fairly routine cases will be examined much less rigorously than more controversial cases. One difficulty with this, of course, is that it is not always possible to say with confidence in advance which cases are going to be the controversial ones.

Juries

The law dealing with the qualification for jury service and the empanelling, summoning and balloting of juries is to be found in the Juries (NI) Order 1996. Some of its provisions apply to juries for inquests as well as to juries for criminal cases. In civil cases both the plaintiff and the defendant can each challenge the presence of up to six proposed jurors without giving any reason for the challenges; other proposed jurors can be challenged provided the judge thinks satisfactory reasons have been supplied (art.14). In criminal cases the prosecution can challenge proposed jurors only if reasons are given, whereas the defence can challenge up to 12 without giving reasons and only thereafter must they "show cause" for their challenges (art.15).

The civil courts

In general terms, the criminal law is primarily concerned with the punishment of those who have broken the law. The civil courts, however, are concerned with compensation and redress, with property matters and with questions of status, such as divorce and adoption. There are three types of court for civil proceedings in Northern Ireland: the magistrates' courts, the county courts and the High Court. Which court a civil matter first comes before depends largely on the seriousness of the issue, including the amount of money or the value of the property involved. Civil proceedings are often settled between the parties before the matter reaches the court.

Magistrates' courts

The powers of magistrates in civil matters are less extensive than their powers in criminal matters, on which they spend the greater amount of time. In civil matters, the procedure used in a magistrates' court is simple and speedy, and litigants are often represented by a solicitor rather than a barrister. The main civil powers of a magistrates' court relate to some domestic matters, such as financial provision orders, non-molestation orders and occupation orders (see Chapter 17). They also deal with small debts, including rent arrears (although there is some overlap with the small claims court: see below), some proceedings brought by landlords (including the Housing Executive and housing associations) to evict tenants, and licence renewal applications.

Appeals against a magistrates' court's decisions in civil matters go to a county court or (on questions purely of law) to the Court of Appeal.

County courts

The financial upper limit for most cases coming before the county courts is currently £15,000. The county courts can hear claims in "tort" (such as personal injury claims following an accident at work or on the roads), or for breach of contract, some undefended divorce petitions, equality of opportunity and discrimination claims other than in the field of employment (see Chapters 11 to 15) and applications to determine the proper rent for a protected tenancy under the Rent (NI) Order 1978 (see Chapter 21).

The county courts have a special "small claims" procedure for many claims not exceeding £1,000. This procedure is commonly employed by business and commercial organisations to claim payment of hire-purchase instalments or money owed for goods already delivered or services already rendered, but consumers can also use it if they wish to claim against shops or suppliers. Unlike in England and Wales, it cannot be used for road accident claims.

County courts also hear appeals against decisions of the Secretary of State for Northern Ireland on applications for compensation for criminal injuries and criminal damage or for compensation under the emergency powers legislation (see below).

Appeals against county court decisions in civil matters go to the High Court or (on questions purely of law) to the Court of Appeal.

The High Court

The jurisdiction of the High Court is not limited by the value of the claim. There are three Divisions of the High Court: the Queen's Bench Division, which deals principally with claims in tort and for breach of contract, the Chancery Division, which deals mainly with property matters, and the Family Division, which deals with petitions for divorce or nullity and matters affecting those who are mentally ill. The Queen's Bench Division (Crown Side) deals with applications for judicial review (see below). Appeals against High Court decisions can go to the Court of Appeal and from there to the House of Lords, but appeals in judicial review cases involving criminal matters go directly from the Queen's Bench Division to the House of Lords.

Judicial review

Judicial review is the main procedure which is available to challenge the validity of the decisions of public bodies. Where a solely contractual or other private relationship exists between an individual and the body, judicial review is not appropriate and other remedies must be sought. Similarly, where an alternative remedy such as an appeal to a tribunal, or to a body's internal review system, is both available and adequate, that procedure should be followed prior to the making of any application for judicial review. Public bodies which are susceptible to judicial review include the Northern Ireland government departments, government ministers, district councils, the Education and Library Boards, the health and social services boards, the Housing Executive, the lower courts and tribunals (including coroners) and in certain situations the Police Service.

Pieces of subordinate legislation (*e.g.* Rules, Regulations, even Acts of the Northern Ireland Assembly) can also be judicially reviewed if there is cause to believe that they were not properly authorised, but Acts of the Westminster Parliament can be subjected to judicial review only where it can be argued that they conflict with European Union law.

Judicial review is concerned with the procedures employed by a public body in reaching its decision and not with the merits of the decision itself, unless the decision is particularly outrageous, absurd or disproportionate. It is not a way of challenging an unwelcome decision; unless it can be argued that an unfair or unlawful procedure was employed in reaching it. The grounds on which a challenge may be made include these:

▪ the body has wrongly interpreted the relevant law,

▪ the body has taken into account irrelevant factors or ignored relevant factors,

▪ the body has failed to pursue the policy and objectives of the legislation in question,

▪ the body has unduly restricted its discretionary powers or followed an unfair or biased procedure,

▪ the body has taken a decision which no reasonable body in its position could have taken,

▪ the body has failed to act compatibly with the rights conferred by the European Convention on Human Rights, or

▪ the body has acted disproportionately when dealing with a certain problem (this is a fairly recent development, deriving from European Union law; it was applied by the House of Lords, for example, when striking down a new policy of the Prison Service in England regarding the searching of prison cells: *R v Secretary of State for the Home Department, ex parte Daly*, 2001).

In some instances a decision can be subjected to judicial review if the reasons behind it have not been conveyed to the affected persons.

An application for judicial review may be sought by a person or body with a sufficient interest in the matter who seeks the permission (or "leave") of the court promptly (in any event within three months of the challenged decision being made). The remedies which the court may grant to a successful applicant include *certiorari* (an order which quashes the public body's decision), *mandamus* (an order which compels a person or body under a duty to act to do so), *declaration* (an order which declares what the law is or what the rights of the parties are) and *prohibition* (an order which prevents the public body from proceeding with an unlawful decision). These remedies are available at the court's discretion and the court may, exceptionally, refuse to grant any of them if it believes that the applicant's conduct merits this or if it is in the interests of good administration to do so. Applications for judicial review are brought to court under Order 53 of the Rules of the Supreme Court (NI), so the application is sometimes referred to as an Order 53 application.

Compensation for personal injuries and property damage

If someone is injured, or has his or her property damaged, as a result of another person's negligent or deliberate act, it will usually be possible to claim compensation from that other person. If the person can be identified and has enough money, the claim can be taken through the civil courts: as explained above, a claim for up to £15,000 would usually be heard by a county court and a larger claim would usually be heard by the High Court. If the person cannot be identified but what he or she did amounts to a criminal offence, then it may be possible to claim compensation not from the perpetrator but from the state. These are called criminal injury or criminal damage claims. The Secretary of State makes the initial decision on the claim (which has to be notified to the police within two days in the case of an injuries claim and 10 days in the case of a damage claim) and appeals against that decision can be made to a county court. There is at present no limit to the amount of compensation a county court can order to be paid in these cases.

The Criminal Injuries Compensation (NI) Order 2002 has reformed the system by making it more tariff-based and reducing the involvement of lawyers. This is likely to reduce the overall amounts of compensation paid to claimants but to produce greater equality in the allocation of payments.

Appeals

In both criminal and civil matters, appeals can be taken against the decision of the original court. Although some other courts do have an appellate jurisdiction, the main appeal court is the Court of Appeal in Belfast. In criminal matters, a person convicted in the Crown Court may appeal to the Court of Appeal on a point of law, on a question of fact or against sentence. In some other situations the accused person will need the permission of the court before he or she can appeal. The prosecution cannot appeal against the acquittal of a person convicted in the Crown Court, although the Attorney General may refer a point of law to the Court of Appeal for its opinion. This does not affect the acquittal at all, but the opinion of the Court will guide the prosecution in future trials. The Attorney General also has the power to refer a case to the Court of Appeal where he or she believes that the sentence imposed by the Crown Court was too lenient.

The Criminal Cases Review Commission, the remit of which includes Northern Ireland, has the power to refer alleged miscarriages of justice to the Court of Appeal of Northern Ireland, and in some instances this has led to the quashing of a conviction (*e.g.* in the cases of William Gorman, Patrick McKinney, Ian Hay Gordon and Danny McNamee). The CCRC's address is Alpha Tower, Suffolk Street, Queensway, Birmingham B1 1TT (tel: 0121 623 1800).

The Court of Appeal also has jurisdiction in civil matters, particularly on points of law. In both criminal and civil matters an appeal may lie, with leave, to the House of Lords in London. Only two or three appeals from Northern Ireland are taken to the House of Lords each year.

The enforcement of civil judgments

A person who has lost litigation may be ordered by a court to pay money to the winner of the litigation. These people are known respectively as the judgment debtor and the judgment creditor. The judgment debtor is required to pay within a reasonable time. If he or she does not do so, the judgment creditor may ask the Enforcement of Judgments Office to send the debtor a document called a notice of intent to enforce. This orders the debtor to pay within 10 days. If the debtor still does not pay, the creditor may apply to the Office for actual enforcement of the judgment. As this can be an expensive procedure, it should be adopted only if the creditor is sure that the debtor has assets with which to pay. If the debtor does not have the means with which to satisfy the order, the creditor must accept that the original judgment in his or her favour may be worth nothing. The Enforcement of Judgments Office is at Bedford House, Bedford Street, Belfast BT2 7NR (tel: 028 9024 5081).

Tribunals

Tribunals are now very much a part of the legal system, dealing with thousands of cases every year. A tribunal is established (by legislation) where the intention is to provide a system of dispute resolution which is both specialised and also relatively speedy, cheap, informal and accessible. A tribunal is often composed of three people, of whom only one, the chairperson, is legally qualified. The best known tribunals are industrial tribunals (which deal with employment rights, including those relating to equality of opportunity: see Chapter 20), social security appeal tribunals (see Chapter 22) and the Mental Health Review Tribunal (see Chapter 16).

An appeal often lies on a point of law from a tribunal decision to the Court of Appeal, although there may also be an intermediate appeal before this stage is reached. Where the legislation provides an individual with recourse to an appeal tribunal, he or she should, as a general rule, follow that procedure rather than apply for judicial review. Tribunal decisions can also be subject to judicial review, but an applicant will be successful only if one or more of the factors mentioned above is present.

European Union law

The law of the European Union is also part of the domestic law of the United Kingdom. EU law deals with many matters concerning economic and social activity, most notably the free movement of goods, the free movement of workers and the Common Agricultural Policy. It also deals with matters designed to protect the enjoyment of these freedoms, such as the freedom to provide and to receive services, freedom of establishment, social security and discrimination (see more particularly Chapter 11). EU law is to be found in the Treaties of the European Community, including the Treaty of Rome, the Single European Act, the Maastricht Treaty and the Treaty of Amsterdam, in the Community's Regulations and Directives and in the decisions of the European Court of Justice and Court of First Instance. The former is the Community's main court and sits at Luxembourg.

If a matter involving EU law comes before a Northern Ireland court or tribunal, one of two procedures may be followed. If the EU law is clear, the domestic court must follow and apply it (and if necessary not apply any conflicting domestic law, even if it is part of an Act of the Westminster Parliament). If the meaning of the EU law is not clear, the domestic court may make a reference to the ECJ under Article 234 of the amended Treaty of Rome (see *e.g. Johnston v Chief Constable of the RUC,* 1987). While the reference is pending, the domestic proceedings are suspended. The ECJ gives its ruling only on the meaning of EU law (not on the domestic law), leaving the domestic court to apply the ruling on EU law to the facts before it. Lower courts and tribunals have a discretion whether or not to make an Article 234 reference, but domestic courts and tribunals against whose decisions there is no judicial remedy under domestic law *must* make a reference on questions concerning the interpretation or application of EU law. The Article 234 procedure cannot be invoked in those areas of domestic law not actually or potentially affected by EU law.

The European Convention on Human Rights

The European Convention on Human Rights (the ECHR) is an international treaty drawn up in 1950 which was ratified by the UK government in 1951 and which is binding upon it in international law. It guarantees protection of rights such as the rights to life, to liberty, to a fair trial and to respect for one's private and family life. It also seeks to protect fundamental freedoms, including freedom from torture or inhuman or degrading treatment or punishment, freedom of thought, conscience and religion, freedom of expression and freedom of peaceful assembly. The European Convention is not a product of the European Union but of the older and larger inter-governmental body known as the Council of Europe (now with 44 member states).

By virtue of the Human Rights Act 1998 most of the ECHR has been part of domestic law throughout the United Kingdom since 2 October 2000. This means that individuals in Northern Ireland can rely upon their Convention rights in any court or tribunal proceedings here. Anyone who is unhappy with the outcome of the local court or tribunal case – provided it has been taken as far as possible through the domestic court system (this is called "exhausting your domestic remedies") – can still take the issue to the European Court of Human Rights in Strasbourg. That Court, through a Committee of three judges, first decides whether the petition is admissible. It will be inadmissible if all domestic remedies have not yet been exhausted or if it is out of time (applications must usually be lodged within six months of the incident or decision being complained about), anonymous, substantially the same as a matter already examined by the Court, manifestly ill-founded or an abuse of the right of petition. The petition must also relate to a matter covered by the Convention, in terms of substance, location and time of the alleged violation.

If the petition is ruled to be admissible, the Court of Human Rights (normally sitting with seven judges) will undertake an inquiry and try to secure a "friendly settlement". This must, however, be compatible with the terms of the Convention. If it is not possible to secure a friendly settlement, the Court (sometimes after an oral hearing) will draw up a judgment indicating whether or not there has been a breach of the Convention. The Court's decision can be referred to a Grand Chamber of the Court (with 17 judges) if the state involved so requests. In practice most states delay before changing their law or administrative practice to bring it into line with the requirements of the Convention. The Council of Europe's Committee of Ministers has the role of ensuring that the Court's judgments are complied with in the state in question.

So far some 20 cases from Northern Ireland have led to judgments from the European Court of Human Rights, including *Dudgeon v UK* (1981, on homosexuality), *John Murray v UK* (1996, on access to a lawyer), *Jordan v UK* (2001, on the investigation of suspicious deaths) and *Devlin v UK* (2001, on challenging political discrimination). All of these have led to changes to the law or practice applying within Northern Ireland. In *Magee v UK* (2000) the European Court held that the applicant had not received a fair trial in Northern Ireland because of the conditions in which he had been kept at Castlereagh holding centre. Such a judgment does not itself quash the conviction, but Mr Magee then applied successfully to the Court of Appeal of Northern Ireland to have his conviction quashed on the ground that it was unsafe (*R v Magee*, 2001).

The need for a "victim"

Article 34 of the ECHR allows the European Court to consider applications only from "any person, non-governmental organisation or group of individuals claiming to be the victim of a violation by [a state] of the rights set forth in the Convention". This means that anyone who is not a direct victim cannot engage the Court's interest. The Committee on the Administration of Justice, or the Northern Ireland Human Rights Commission, for example, could not take an alleged breach of the Convention to court unless they themselves were allegedly the victims of the breach. When the UK Parliament incorporated the ECHR into its domestic law through the Human Rights Act 1998 it carefully preserved this rule (in s.7(7) of the Act). This means that there are organisations which might be eligible to make applications for judicial review (where the rules on "standing" are less demanding) but which could not take cases based directly on Convention rights.

The remedies available

The European Court of Human Rights may order the state to pay compensation − which it calls "just satisfaction" − to a successful petitioner, as well as his or her legal costs. The ECHR itself requires each state which has violated a person's rights and freedoms in the Convention to provide "an effective remedy before a national authority" (art.13). But this is one of the ECHR provisions which was not incorporated into UK law by the Human Rights Act 1998. Instead section 8 of the Act says that in relation to any act of a public authority which a court finds is unlawful because it breaches a Convention right, the court "may grant such relief or remedy, or make such order, within its powers as it considers just and appropriate". The section goes on to say that a court can award damages (*i.e.* compensation) only if it already has that power. Unfortunately this rules out criminal courts from giving such a remedy.

The Human Rights Act also makes it clear, in section 4, that if a public authority is found to have breached a Convention right when it was doing something that was required by an Act of the Westminster Parliament, the court cannot declare the Act, or any part of it, to be actually invalid. But the High Court can nevertheless issue a "declaration of incompatibility". This declaration leaves the domestic law unaltered for the time being, but in effect it serves as an invitation to the government to ask Parliament to pass an amending piece of legislation, or to approve a "remedial order" (see s.10 of the Human Rights Act 1998), in order to bring the domestic law into line with the ECHR requirements. So far there has been only one case in Northern Ireland where a judge declared part of an Act of Parliament to be incompatible with the ECHR (*In re McR*, 2002), regarding s.62 of the Offences Against the Person Act 1861: see p.367).

As far as Orders in Council are concerned, and legislation made by the Northern Ireland Assembly (whether as Acts, Rules, Regulations, etc), these laws *can* be declared invalid by a court (s.3(2) of the Human Rights Act 1998). The only exception is where these laws had to be worded in the way they were because of a requirement of an Act of the Westminster Parliament. Before any legislation is declared invalid the courts must strive, so far as it is possible to do so, to read and give effect to it in a way which is compatible with the Convention rights (s.3(1) of the 1998 Act).

The Ombudsman

In Northern Ireland the term "Ombudsman" covers two distinct offices, although they are in practice held by the same person. There is, first, the office of Assembly Ombudsman and, second, that of the Commissioner for Complaints. The relevant legislation is, respectively, the Ombudsman (NI) Order 1996 and the Commissioner for Complaints (NI) Order 1996, as amended.

The Assembly Ombudsman

The function of the Assembly Ombudsman is to investigate complaints of maladministration made against Northern Ireland government departments and some other bodies. The complaint must be made by a person who feels that he or she has suffered injustice as a result of the maladministration and the complaint should be made within 12 months of the action or inaction in question. "Maladministration" is not defined in the relevant legislation but it covers matters such as delay in responding to letters, incompetence in dealing with queries, perversity or arbitrariness in the taking of decisions and discrimination on irrelevant grounds.

The complaint should be made to the Ombudsman via a Member of the Legislative Assembly, who has a discretion whether or not to refer the complaint to the Ombudsman. The Member may decide to deal with the matter personally instead. If a person writes directly to the Ombudsman, the Ombudsman will, where the complaint merits further investigation, ask the complainant to refer the matter back through an MLA.

The Ombudsman is completely independent of government departments and the service provided is free of charge. He or she has full access to all files and records. The purpose of an investigation is to ascertain whether or not there has been maladministration; the Ombudsman has no jurisdiction to investigate the merits of decisions reached without maladministration. The Ombudsman does not usually investigate complaints where there is an alternative remedy available, particularly in a tribunal or by way of judicial review, although if an individual goes to a tribunal but still believes that the injustice remains unremedied, the Ombudsman may then investigate the complaint.

Once a preliminary investigation has been completed a decision is taken on whether a more in-depth investigation is required. When the investigative work finally comes to an end the Ombudsman sends a report to the complainant, the referring MLA and the relevant government department. If the Ombudsman upholds the complaint, he or she will try to effect a fair settlement, perhaps by securing appropriate redress for the complainant, such as an apology or the payment of compensation. In some cases, as a result of an Ombudsman investigation the department concerned will change its procedures. The Ombudsman cannot, however, compel the government department to provide any redress to a complainant.

The Ombudsman can also investigate complaints about personnel matters in the Northern Ireland Civil Service. His or her officials also investigate, on behalf of the Assembly, complaints of misconduct against Members of the Legislative Assembly.

The Northern Ireland Assembly Ombudsman is currently Mr Tom Frawley. He can be contacted at Progressive House, 33 Wellington Place, Belfast BT1 6HN (tel: 028 9023 3821).

The Commissioner for Complaints

The second office held by the Northern Ireland Ombudsman is that of Commissioner for Complaints. In that capacity he or she investigates complaints of maladministration made by an aggrieved individual against local or public bodies in Northern Ireland. These bodies include the district councils, the Education and Library Boards, the health and social services boards, the Housing Executive (although its own internal complaints procedure should be resorted to first), the Labour Relations Agency, the Council for Catholic Maintained Schools and the Equality Commission. The Commissioner can also now look at complaints against health service providers, including complaints about clinical judgments made by doctors, dentists and opticians.

There is direct access to the Commissioner for Complaints, whose services are again both free and independent, but the complaint usually needs to be made, at the latest, within 12 months. The Commissioner cannot question the merits of a decision taken without maladministration, nor will he or she usually investigate a complaint which could be the subject of legal proceedings or an alternative investigatory procedure. Certain matters also fall outside his or her jurisdiction, including the commencement or conduct of civil or criminal proceedings.

If the Commissioner's investigations disclose that there has been maladministration, he or she will try to secure a settlement, such as an apology or the payment of compensation. If this is unsuccessful, the complainant may apply to a county court for compensation. The Attorney General may also, at the request of the Commissioner, seek an injunction or a declaration from the High Court to restrain a public body from persistent maladministration.

Individuals who are dealing with a public body operating under the provisions of a "Charter", should note that the body itself may have introduced a complaints mechanism.

The contact details for the Commissioner for Complaints are the same as for the Assembly Ombudsman (see above).

The UK Ombudsman

Complaints against Westminster government departments are within the jurisdiction of the United Kingdom Parliamentary Commissioner, whose jurisdiction therefore includes the Northern Ireland Office, the Northern Ireland Court Service, the Inland Revenue, the Ministry of Defence and the Northern Ireland Human Rights Commission. The UK Parliamentary Commissioner is Ms Ann Abraham and her address is Office of the PCA, Church House, Great Smith Street, London SW1P 3BW (tel: 020 7276 3000; *www.ombudsman.org.uk*).

The Commissioner for Children and Young People

The Commissioner for Children and Young People (NI) Order 2003 makes provision for the creation of such a post for Northern Ireland. Mr Nigel Williams will take up the appointment in October 2003. He will have extensive powers to promote and protect the rights of children, especially those set out in the UN Convention on the Rights of the Child (1989). These will include the power to review complaint mechanisms, to support cases in court and to investigate alleged abuses of rights, although not in situations where the Commissioner has already looked more generally at the issues raised by a specific case or where some other statutory body has conducted an investigation.

Legal aid, advice and assistance

There are various types of legal aid schemes designed to provide financial assistance in legal matters. The controlling legislation is the Legal Aid, Advice and Assistance (NI) Order 1981 and the regulations made under it. The schemes are "means tested" in terms of both disposable income and disposable capital and in 1993 the financial limits were altered so as to make help available primarily to people who are on income support.

- The "Green Form" scheme (its popular name) allows a solicitor to offer advice on any area of law in Northern Ireland. The advice may be written or oral; it includes preparation of all types of documents but does not extend to representation at hearings. The assisted person may be required to make a financial contribution to the assistance, which in any event cannot exceed a value of £88.
- "ABWOR" – assistance by way of representation – is based on the green form scheme and is available for, amongst other things, proceedings before the Mental Health Review Tribunal.
- Civil legal aid covers most civil proceedings in the higher courts (excluding libel actions) but it is not available for either inquests or tribunals. The Department of Health, Social Services and Public Safety assesses financial eligibility for civil legal aid. The Law Society's Legal Aid Department also applies a "merits" test to determine whether or not it is reasonable for the party concerned to take or defend the proceedings in question. An assisted person may be required to make some financial contribution.
- Criminal legal aid is available for the defence of criminal proceedings by a solicitor or barrister. If granted by the court it is entirely free in Northern Ireland, unlike in England and Wales.

The system for delivering legal aid in Northern Ireland is about to be radically reformed as a result of the Access to Justice (NI) Order 2003. From September 2003 this will give responsibility for administering the system to a new body, the Legal Services Commission. Civil legal services will be provided out of a fixed annual fund and service providers will have to tender for the right to access that fund. The Commission will operate a Funding Code and will apply quality control measures to ensure that standards are being maintained. Criminal legal services will not be provided out of a capped budget. The existing ABWOR scheme will be absorbed into civil and criminal legal services and there will be a discretion to make funds available in some situations where they are not at present (*e.g.* at inquests).

Assistance from other bodies

As explained in Chapter 11 below, the Equality Commission for Northern Ireland will sometimes grant assistance to individuals who are seeking help with a claim based on discrimination. Likewise the Northern Ireland Human Rights Commission has the power to grant assistance to individuals (not organisations) who are taking legal proceedings concerning human rights. But the resources of both of these bodies are much less extensive than those of the Legal Aid Department, so very few applicants actually receive assistance in the end.

The Northern Ireland Human Rights Commission can also take human rights cases in its own name, although when doing so it cannot rely directly on Convention rights unless it has itself allegedly been the victim of a breach of the Convention. In June 2002 the House of Lords ruled that the Human Rights Commission can also apply to intervene in other people's court cases in order to bring a human rights perspective to the issues in question (*In re NIHRC*). The Commission welcomes approaches from individuals and lawyers who think that such interventions might be beneficial in their cases.

There are two government offices which focus on victims' rights. One is the Victims Unit within the Office of the First Minister and the Deputy First Minister at Stormont. Its responsibilities include:

- managing measures taken under the European Programme for Peace and Reconciliation (Peace II),
- developing a separate programme of activities designed to meet the strategic needs of victims, and
- ensuring the needs of victims are addressed within the devolved administration in Northern Ireland.

The Victims Unit's address is: Office of the First Minister and Deputy First Minister, Level A5, Castle Buildings, Stormont, Belfast BT4 3SR (tel: freephone, 080 8127 3333; *www.victimsni.gov.uk*).

The other office is the Victims Liaison Unit within the Northern Ireland Office. Its address is Room 123, Stormont House Annex, Stormont Estate, Belfast BT4 3ST (tel: 028 9052 7900; *www.nio.gov.uk*). Amongst other things this Unit:

- provides core funding to victims' support groups (of which there are already more than 50 in Northern Ireland),
- manages the Northern Ireland Memorial Fund, and
- addresses issues and needs arising in non-devolved areas such as compensation, criminal justice, security and the position of "the disappeared".

The address of the Northern Ireland Memorial Fund is Albany House, 73-75 Great Victoria Street, Belfast BT2 7AF (tel: 028 9024 5965).

As well as the numerous victims' groups in Northern Ireland there is a long-standing organisation called Victim Support (NI) which has been helping victims of all types of crimes for many years. It is to be given additional responsibilities under the Justice (NI) Act 2002. The address of Victim Support (NI) is Regional Office, Annsgate House, 70-74 Ann Street, Belfast   BT1 4EH (tel: 028 9024 4039); *www.victimsupport.org.uk.*

Chapter 3

The Powers of the Police and Army

Brice Dickson[*]

This chapter sets out those powers both of the Police Service of Northern Ireland (PSNI) and of the British army which people in Northern Ireland are most likely to encounter in everyday life. The specific topic of police questioning is dealt with in Chapter 4 and the system for dealing with complaints against the police is explained in Chapter 5. The system for complaining against the army – such as it is – is explained within this chapter at page 66. The general accountability roles of the Northern Ireland Policing Board and of the District Policing Partnerships are not covered in detail in this book, although see p.109. Nor is the role of the Police Oversight Commissioner (which will continue to at least 31 May 2005).

Much of the "ordinary" law on police powers is contained in the Police and Criminal Evidence (NI) Order 1989 – the PACE Order. This Order is similar in many respects to the Police and Criminal Evidence Act 1984, which governs the position in England and Wales. Books on the Act are therefore relevant to the law in Northern Ireland as well. Of course both pieces of legislation have been amended several times since they were first enacted. The position regarding police powers in relation to "terrorist" offences is now governed by the Terrorism Act 2000 and by the Anti-terrorism, Crime and Security Act 2001. Both of these Acts apply throughout the United Kingdom, but some of the provisions in the 2000 Act are special to Northern Ireland, not least because they apply to the army as well as to the police. Some provisions of the 2001 Act are part of the "ordinary" law, not of anti-terrorist law. Throughout this chapter the police powers are first described as they exist under the ordinary law and then as they exist under the anti-terrorist laws.

---

[*] I am grateful to Steven Greer for permission to use some of the material in his chapter on the powers of the army in the previous edition of this book.

The army's special powers exist only under the anti-terrorist laws. A soldier exercising any power when not in uniform must, if asked to do so by any person at or about the time of exercising the power, produce documentary evidence that he or she is a member of the army (s.95(10) of the Terrorism Act 2000). The army operates in Northern Ireland when called upon by the Chief Constable to assist in the maintenance of order. In that sense there is "police primacy". The army always acts under the direction and control of the police, but the police cannot interfere with the operational independence of the army. In practice this means that the police can tell the army *what* to do but not *how* to do it.

Special powers were conferred upon the army in Northern Ireland by the Stormont Parliament in the Civil Authorities (Special Powers) Act 1922, but in 1971 the legality of these powers was successfully challenged in the High Court by two Stormont MPs, on the grounds that the Government of Ireland Act 1920 reserved the making of laws concerning the armed forces in Northern Ireland to the Westminster Parliament (*R (Hume and Others) v Londonderry Justices*, 1972). Almost immediately the Westminster Parliament passed the Northern Ireland Act 1972, which bestowed new powers on Stormont to make laws concerning the armed forces, provided they were necessary for the maintenance of peace and order in Northern Ireland, and conferred retrospective validity on any actions taken before its enactment which would otherwise have been invalid because of the High Court's decision. Shortly thereafter Stormont was suspended and direct rule was imposed from Westminster.

The powers of the military police (the "red caps") used to be the same as those of police officers, but since 1991 they have been the same as those of other members of the army.

The anti-terrorist laws

Ever since the creation of Northern Ireland in 1920 there have been special powers conferred on the police. After the Northern Ireland Parliament was abolished in 1972, the Northern Ireland (Emergency Provisions) Act 1973 was passed (the EPA). In 1974 this Act was supplemented by the Prevention of Terrorism (Temporary Provisions) Act (the PTA), which was enacted for the whole of the United Kingdom but was designed to deal only with violence connected with the political affairs of Northern Ireland. The EPA and PTA would have lapsed if not renewed annually, and the EPA had to be completely re-enacted every five years. However, following a review by Lord Lloyd and Mr Justice Kerr in 1996, and a Government White Paper in 1998, both Acts were eventually replaced by the Terrorism Act 2000, most of which applies throughout the United Kingdom. This is a permanent Act; section 126 requires the Home Secretary to lay before each House of Parliament at least once in every 12 months a report on the working of the Act, but there is no guarantee of any debate on this report. At present the person appointed to prepare such reports is Lord Alex Carlile QC.

The only provisions in the Act which are not permanent are those in Part VII (*i.e.* ss.65-113), which sets out additional anti-terrorist powers just for Northern Ireland. In some respects these overlap with anti-terrorist powers conferred on the Police Service of Northern Ireland by other provisions in the same Act, but the former presumably take priority. The UK Government has said it will retain some or all of these additional powers in Part VII so long as the security situation in Northern Ireland requires this. Part VII was brought into force on 19 February 2001 and has to be renewed annually by an order of the Secretary of State (s.112). Following a report by Lord Carlile, such an order was indeed made in both 2002 and 2003. However, by section 112(4), Part VII will entirely cease to have effect after five years, *i.e.* in February 2006.

After the events in the United States on 11 September 2001, Westminster rushed through additional legislation in the form of the Anti-terrorism, Crime and Security Act 2001. Amongst other things this Act provides for the freezing of assets, regulates the security of pathogens, toxins, nuclear installations and airports and allows the retention of communications data. Changes to other aspects of civil liberties are noted throughout this chapter. The detention provisions in the Act are scrutinised each year by Lord Carlile and they will lapse completely, unless re-enacted, in November 2006. Moreover a committee of Privy Councillors is due to report on the whole Act by the end of 2003.

Statistics on the operation of the Terrorism Act 2000 in Northern Ireland are published on a quarterly basis, although somewhat belatedly, by the Statistics and Research Branch of the Northern Ireland Office's Criminal Justice Policy Division.

The definition of terrorism

"Terrorism" is defined in section 1 of the Terrorism Act 2000. It means the use or threat of action where three conditions are satisfied:
- the action must:
    - involve serious violence against a person,
    - involve serious damage to property,
    - endanger a person's life, other than that of the person committing the action,
    - create a serious risk to the health or safety of the public or a section of the public, or
    - be designed seriously to interfere with or seriously to disrupt an electronic system,
- the use or threat must be made for the purpose of advancing a political, religious or ideological cause, and
- the use or threat of action must be designed to influence the government or to intimidate the public or a section of the public (unless firearms or explosives are involved, in which case this condition does not need to be satisfied).

The offences in the Terrorism Act which require people convicted of them to be labelled as terrorists include:
- belonging to, or professing to belong to, a proscribed organisation,
- inviting support for, or arranging or addressing a meeting to further the activities of, a proscribed organisation (indeed s.1(3) makes it clear that *any* action taken for the benefit of a proscribed organisation is to be deemed to be an action taken for the purposes of terrorism),
- fundraising or using any property for the purposes of terrorism,
- laundering terrorist property,
- providing weapons training,
- directing a terrorist organisation,
- possessing articles or collecting information for a purpose connected with terrorism, and
- inciting terrorism overseas.

The power to stop and question under the ordinary law

Contrary to popular belief, the general rule is that the police do not have a general power to stop and question people. This is true not only of pedestrians but also of people in cars or any other form of transport. The police can, of course, *attempt* to stop and question people, and many of us will be content to comply with the police's request and will readily answer questions, but there is no legal obligation to stop when asked to do so or to answer questions put by a police officer. The PACE Order confers powers on the police to stop people for the purpose of searching them (these are dealt with below), but it does not remove a person's right not to be stopped for questioning.

To stop a person lawfully the police have to carry out an arrest. During the period of detention following an arrest the police can ask questions, but the person arrested is still under no legal duty to reply. In fact, when questioned at any time it is very often sensible to remain silent until a solicitor is present. As the then Lord Chief Justice for England and Wales put it in *Rice v Connolly* (1966): "the whole basis of the common law is the right of the individual to refuse to answer questions put to him by a person in authority". However, as explained more fully in Chapter 4, one of the consequences of the Criminal Evidence (NI) Order 1988 is that the silence of a detained person may later constitute corroborative evidence that that person is guilty of an offence. (As a result of the enactment of sections 34-38 of the Criminal Justice and Public Order Act 1994, the law on this point in England and Wales is now the same as in Northern Ireland.)

After the police have collected information from people who do allow themselves to be stopped and questioned, the police can store it, indefinitely if they wish and on computer if necessary. The Data Protection Act 1998 prevents people from gaining access to data which is "required for the purpose of safeguarding national security" or "held for the prevention or detection of crime". The latter phrase would cover most of the information held by the police. (See also Chapter 10.)

There are a number of important exceptions to the general rule that the police cannot lawfully stop people arbitrarily. These mainly concern road traffic situations and terrorism. The law on road traffic in Northern Ireland is virtually identical to that in England and Wales: it permits a police officer or traffic warden to control traffic and, provided the officer is in uniform, to require drivers to stop their vehicles (art.180 of the Road Traffic (NI) Order 1981). The law on terrorism is explained in the next section.

The power to stop and question under the anti-terrorist laws

The chief exception to the general rule in the context of alleged terrorist incidents is contained in section 89 of the Terrorism Act 2000. According to this, any police officer *or soldier* may stop and question any person for so long as is necessary to question him or her about his or her identity and movements, about a recent explosion or another recent incident endangering life or about a person killed or injured in any such explosion or incident. If a person fails to stop when required to do so under this section, or fails to answer to the best of his or her ability a question addressed under this section, he or she may be fined in a magistrates' court up to £2,000. Given that the compulsion to answer the questions exists under section 89 even if one thereby has to incriminate oneself, there is a doubt whether it is wholly compatible with Article 6(2) of the European Convention on Human Rights.

As yet there has been no authoritative ruling as to what exactly constitutes "stopping" within section 89. Knocking on a person's door and putting questions to the person who opens it may not qualify, but temporarily preventing someone from moving from his or her position in a queue or at a counter would probably be enough. Being approached while standing at a street corner would certainly constitute being "stopped" in this context. The power in section 89 can be used to stop pedestrians but is most frequently used at vehicle checkpoints (VCPs). There is no legal obligation to show a driving licence at a VCP, but it is an easy way of proving your identity.

There is also doubt over the exact scope of section 89. No-one knows for sure, for instance, whether in law the "identity" of a person includes his or her date of birth and address. The answer may depend on whether or not the person has a common name. The section also gives no indication as to how much detail a person must provide about his or her movements. However the duty to answer to the best of one's ability probably means that one must be as detailed as one can be. The general locality a person is coming from and going to must be disclosed, but it would probably be unreasonable to have to give the names of the people just visited or about to be visited. Nor is the meaning of "recent" in section 89 clear. But the questions asked do not have to be related to acts of "terrorism", so "any other incident endangering life" could refer, for example, to a fire or a car accident. There is no obligation to answer questions relating to one's occupation, family or friends.

Elsewhere in the United Kingdom soldiers have no power whatsoever to stop and question civilians. In Northern Ireland they can do so as often as they wish.

Port and border controls

Quite apart from the powers vested in immigration officers to question people who arrive in the United Kingdom from abroad (although the Republic of Ireland does not count as a place abroad for this purpose), section 53 and Schedule 7 of the Terrorism Act 2000 permit examining officers at ports (including airports) and in the border area in Northern Ireland to question people in order to determine if they are terrorists (whether or not the officers have any initial suspicions in that regard).

A person questioned in these circumstances must give the examining officer any information in his or her possession which the officer requests. He or she can be detained for up to nine hours to allow the questioning to be completed and during that time he or she can be photographed but not fingerprinted. Any interviews held will not be audio- or video-recorded unless they take place at a police station. The person detained has the same rights as other persons detained under the Terrorism Act (see p.55 below).

The Secretary of State may issue orders requiring people to complete and produce cards when embarking or disembarking at a port anywhere in the United Kingdom. Several such orders are currently in force. The Anti-terrorism, Crime and Security Act 2001 allows people who are suspected of being foreign international terrorists to be interned without trial in the United Kingdom if they do not agree to leave the country voluntarily (ss.21-32). These provisions are explained below (p.58).

Withholding information

Unlike its predecessors, the Terrorism Act 2000 did not originally contain a provision making it an offence to withhold information in one's possession about terrorism. But a new section 38B was inserted by the Ant-terrorism, Crime and Security Act 2001. This criminalises a failure to disclose to the police (unless one has a reasonable excuse for not doing so) information one has which one knows or believes might be of material assistance in preventing the commission by another person of an act of terrorism or in securing the apprehension, prosecution or conviction of a terrorist. The maximum penalty for the crime is five years in prison and an unlimited fine.

It is in any event a crime under section 5 of the Criminal Law Act (NI) 1967 to fail to give to the police information about an arrestable offence committed by some other person.

The power to stop and search people under the ordinary law

The police do not possess a general common law power to stop and search anyone at will. A person may, of course, consent to being stopped and searched, but if consent is withdrawn the search must cease immediately. The consent given may also be limited, for instance, to a search of a person's pockets or handbag. In this case any more extensive search will be an assault, for which compensation can be sought.

The police do possess limited stop and search powers conferred by legislation, in particular by the PACE (NI) Order 1989. For a useful list of other relevant legislation, see Annex A to the Code of Practice on this topic, referred to at p.63 below. As a rule, because it can be difficult to know whether the police are acting within their powers when conducting a search, it is better if the person being searched, rather than resisting the search and risking a prosecution for obstructing the police in the execution of their duty or for assault, submits to the search while informing the police that he or she is not consenting voluntarily. The police should be asked to name the exact power under which they are acting so that its terms can be checked later.

The PACE (NI) Order 1989 empowers police officers to stop, detain and search any person if they have reasonable grounds for suspecting that they will find stolen or prohibited articles. An article is prohibited if it is an offensive weapon or something intended for use in a burglary or theft. Any such item may be seized and need not be returned. The power can be exercised only in a public place. People who are in a garden or yard connected with a dwelling cannot be searched unless the police have reasonable grounds for believing that those people do not reside in the dwelling and are not there with permission.

A person can also be lawfully searched once he or she has been arrested and any weapon or evidence of a crime discovered can be seized. The person's home can be searched too, or the place where the arrest has occurred, provided that there is some connection between that place and the suspected offence.

If the police uncover evidence relating to a crime during the course of an unlawful search, that evidence is still admissible in a court of law but a civil action against the police for compensation can be begun. In *R v Khan* (1996) the House of Lords held that evidence obtained through a surveillance device illegally placed on private property used by the defendant was nevertheless admissible in court against him. When this case went to the European Court of Human Rights the judges held that there had been a breach of Article 8 (the right to respect for one's private life and home) but not of Article 6 (the right to a fair trial): *Khan v UK* (2000). The Regulation of Investigatory Powers Act 2000 has now provided statutory authority for surveillance in some situations and a Code of Practice has been issued on the use of "covert human intelligence sources" (CHISs).

Section 95 of the Anti-terrorism, Crime and Security Act 2001 inserts a new article 23A into the Public Order (NI) Order 1987. This permits a police officer of at least the rank of inspector, if he or she reasonably believes that activities may take place in any locality which are likely to involve the commission of offences and that it is expedient to prevent or control those activities, to authorise any constable in uniform, during a period of up to 24 hours, to require any person in that locality to remove any item which the constable reasonably believes that person is wearing wholly or mainly for the purpose of concealing his identity. Failure to remove the item is an arrestable offence punishable with up to a month in prison and a fine of £1,000.

Finally, section 96 of the Anti-terrorism, Crime and Security Act 2001 inserts a new article 23B into the Public Order (NI) Order 1987. This permits a police officer of at least the rank of inspector, if he or she reasonably believes that incidents involving serious violence may take place in any locality and that it is expedient to prevent or control their occurrence, or that people are carrying offensive weapons or dangerous instruments in any locality without good reason, to authorise any constable in uniform, during a period of up to 24 hours, to stop any pedestrian or vehicle and search the person or vehicle, or anything being carried, for offensive weapons or dangerous instruments. A dangerous instrument is defined as an instrument which has a blade or is sharply pointed. The constable does not need to have any suspicions in relation to the person or vehicle stopped. Again, failure to stop when asked to do so is an offence (although this time not an arrestable one), punishable with up to a month in prison and a fine of £1,000. Within

12 months of the event, a person stopped, or the driver of a vehicle stopped, is entitled to a written statement concerning the stop and search.

Safeguards for people being searched

Before a search is begun, a constable must prove that he or she is indeed a police officer (by displaying a card or giving his or her police number and station). The constable must also indicate the purpose of the proposed search, the reasons for making it and the fact that a written record will be made available to the person if requested within the next year. During the search a person cannot be required to remove any item of clothing in public, except an outer coat, jacket, headgear and gloves. Strip-searching is permitted at police stations in exceptional circumstances (see p.64). A person cannot be detained for longer than is reasonably required for the search to be carried out.

The duty to make a written record and the prohibition on requiring clothes to be removed do not apply to searches following an arrest, although an arrested person can be searched only if the custody officer considers it necessary to permit a record of the person's possessions to be taken. The search must be conducted by an officer of the same sex as the person searched and special conditions apply to "intimate" searches (see below). In any event, after a person has been arrested and taken to a police station, the station's custody officer must record everything which the person is carrying. Any of these things may be retained by the custody officer provided reasons are given, although clothes and personal effects may be seized only if the officer believes that the arrested person may use them to inflict injury, damage property, interfere with evidence or assist an escape, or if there are reasonable grounds for believing that the items may be evidence relating to an offence.

If the police act in a high-handed fashion during a search, or in breach of the powers conferred upon them, the person searched should lodge a complaint (see Chapter 5) or think about bringing a civil action for compensation (see Chapter 2). In 2001-2002 there were 2,782 civil actions initiated against the police (covering all sorts of issues); 717 cases were disposed of, with a total of £2.74 million agreed or awarded as compensation and legal costs of £1.78 million incurred.

Intimate searches

An intimate search is defined as "a search which consists of the physical examination of a person's body orifices". It requires the written authorisation of a police officer of at least the rank of superintendent, who must first have reasonable grounds for believing that an arrested person may have concealed on his or her body a "Class A" drug or anything which could be used to cause injury while in custody. "Class A" drugs include heroin but not amphetamines or cannabis and they can be searched for only by a registered doctor or nurse and not at a police station. Other intimate searches should also be conducted by a doctor or nurse unless a police officer of at least the rank of superintendent considers that this is not practicable, in which case they must be carried out by a constable of the same sex as the person searched; they can be conducted at police stations.

A written record must be kept by the custody officer of the parts of the body that have been searched, and why. Anything found during an intimate search may be retained only in the circumstances outlined above in relation to clothes and personal effects. In 2001-2002 the police in Northern Ireland conducted just one intimate search under these powers.

The power to stop and search people under the anti-terrorist laws

By virtue of section 84 and Schedule 10 of the Terrorism Act 2000 any police officer *or any soldier on duty* may stop any person in any public place and search him or her for explosives, firearms, ammunition or wireless apparatus. This power permits entirely random, and legally unchallengeable, searches: the police officer or soldier involved need not entertain any particular suspicions about the person searched. The power can also be exercised elsewhere than in a public place if the police officer or soldier has reasonable grounds to suspect the presence of these items. If a person fails to stop when required to do so he or she may be fined up to £5,000. A search cannot take place under this power for other items (see *Carlisle v Chief Constable of the RUC*, 1989). Under section 85 of the Terrorism Act 2000 explosives inspectors also have the power to stop a person in a public place and search for explosives. If any of the items mentioned are found during any search, they may be seized and retained.

A public place is defined as "a place to which members of the public have or are permitted to have access, whether or not for payment" (s.121). This includes such obvious public places as the street, a shop, a pub or a cinema but it also includes centres to which suspects arrested by the army are brought, as well as hotels, guest houses and hostels. In order to conduct a legal personal search somewhere other than in a public place the police or army must first lawfully gain entry to the premises.

Section 43 of the 2000 Act allows a police officer (but not a soldier) to stop and search anyone whom he or she reasonably suspects to be a terrorist in order to discover whether that person has in his or her possession anything which may constitute evidence that he or she is a terrorist. There must still be independent grounds for any subsequent arrest besides whatever is found during the course of such a search. People who have already been arrested under section 41 of the Act (see below) may also be searched (s.43(2)). In both instances the search must be carried out by a person of the same sex and anything found which constitutes evidence of terrorism can be seized and retained.

The power to stop and search vehicles under the ordinary law

Curiously, the exact legal position regarding the stopping of vehicles (a term which for present purposes includes vessels and aircraft) is unclear, even though the relevant powers are largely conferred by legislation – see article 180 of the Road Traffic (NI) Order 1981. In an English court case in 1982 (*Steel v Goacher*) it was held that the police had a power under the common law (*i.e.* not based on any statute) to stop traffic in order to prevent criminal activity. Failing to pull up when requested to do so by the police is therefore a more risk-laden thing for a driver to do than failing to stop walking when approached by the police, although it is uncertain what offence is being committed if one disobeys a police command to stop (other perhaps than obstructing the police in the execution of their duties).

The ordinary law already set out above in relation to searches of persons also applies to searches of vehicles. Thus, a car can be stopped, detained and searched if the police have reasonable grounds for suspecting that they will find stolen or prohibited articles in it. If a vehicle is parked on land connected to a dwelling, it may not be searched unless the police have reasonable grounds for believing that it is there without the permission of a person who resides there. The rules about the police having to identify themselves before making the search also apply, but no police officer can stop a vehicle unless he or she is in uniform. Persons inside a vehicle can be searched only if the conditions mentioned at pp.39-40 above are satisfied. Altogether 1,972 persons and vehicles were searched by the police in Northern Ireland under the PACE (NI) Order in 2001-2002; 278 people were arrested as a result of those searches.

Whenever the police search an unattended vehicle they have to leave a notice stating that it has been searched, the date of the search and the identity of the searching officer. The notice also has to indicate that a written record of the search can be requested within a year and that an application can be made for compensation for any damage caused. This duty does not apply to searches of vehicles at an airport, railway, dock or harbour, to searches of air cargo, or to searches conducted under the emergency laws (see below).

The PACE (NI) Order 1989 contains a second power relating to vehicle checks (art.6), but it deals with searches for wanted people rather than for stolen goods or weapons. It authorises a police officer to stop and check vehicles to see if they are carrying people who are unlawfully at large or who are intending to commit, have committed, or are witnesses to an offence (except a road traffic offence). The vehicles to be searched can be chosen in accordance with any criterion, *e.g.* the colour or age of the car, or the appearance of its occupants. The authorisation for a road check of this nature must come from a senior police officer and can last for no longer than seven days at a time.

The power to stop and search vehicles under the anti-terrorist laws

Under section 44 of the Terrorism Act 2000 a police officer in uniform (but not a soldier) can stop a vehicle in a specified area or at a specified place and can search the vehicle itself, the driver, any passengers and anything in or on the vehicle or carried by the driver or a passenger. However in Northern Ireland the use of this power must first be authorised by an assistant chief constable (s.44(3)(d)) and the authorisation can be given only if the assistant chief constable considers it expedient for the prevention of acts of terrorism and only for a maximum period of 28 days. The Secretary of State's approval of the authorisation must also be sought, although if it is refused this does not affect the legality of anything done up to that point.

The power under section 44 can therefore be used only to look for articles which could be used in connection with terrorism, but the searching officer does not need to have reasonable grounds for suspecting the presence of such articles. The vehicle and the people in it can be detained for such time as is reasonably required to permit the search to be carried out. If any article connected with terrorism is found, it can be seized and retained.

The Terrorism Act 2000 also allows the police to search premises (including vehicles) if a Justice of the Peace issues a warrant having first been satisfied that there are reasonable grounds for suspecting that a terrorist is to be found there (s. 42(1)).

By virtue of section 81 of the Terrorism Act 2000, a police constable in Northern Ireland may enter and search any vehicle if he or she has reasonable grounds for suspecting that it contains a person who could be arrested under the Act because he or she is reasonably suspected of involvement in terrorism. A similar power is conferred by section 82(2) in circumstances where a police officer wishes to search a vehicle for a suspected terrorist and section 82(3) allows the police to seize anything which they have reasonable grounds to suspect is being, has been or is intended to be used in the commission of a scheduled offence or an offence under the Act. By section 84 and Schedule 10 of the Terrorism Act 2000 a police officer, or a soldier on duty, may enter and search any vehicle to look for explosives, firearms, ammunition or wireless apparatus. Finally, to enable the police or army in Northern Ireland to look for people who may have been kidnapped, and whose lives are in danger, section 86 permits them to enter any place and search for the missing persons, although the authorisation of a police inspector or army officer is required in the case of searches of dwelling-houses (including caravans).

A power to search a vehicle brings with it a power to take the vehicle to any place for the purpose of carrying out the search (s.95(3)(b) of the Terrorism Act 2000). Moreover the person carrying out the search may, if he or she reasonably believes that it is necessary in order to carry out the search, require a person in or on the vehicle to remain with it or to go to and remain at any place to which the vehicle is taken to be searched (s.95(7)). Items found during any of the above searches may be seized and retained.

Generally speaking, anyone who fails to comply with an order to stop or with instructions concerning searches is guilty of an offence carrying a maximum penalty of six months' imprisonment and a fine up to £5,000.

The power to enter and search premises under the ordinary law

In Northern Ireland, under section 90 of the Terrorism Act 2000, the police and army can enter any premises if they consider it necessary in the course of operations for the preservation of the peace or the maintenance of order. This power can be exercised even when there is no question of terrorist activity at the time. Reasonable force can be used to effect an entry, if necessary (s.95(2)).

However neither the police nor the army have a general power to enter *and search* private premises in order to investigate criminal acts. Only in relation to some road traffic offences may they do so. Otherwise they may enter and search only if they have the permission of the occupier, if a breach of the peace is involved or if the requirements of the PACE Order are satisfied.

The relevant provisions of the PACE (NI) Order 1989 are articles 10-25. They deal only with searches of "premises", but this term is defined so as to include any place. It therefore covers outdoor as well as indoor premises, movable and stationary premises, occupied and unoccupied premises, and public and private places. The power to search carries with it the power to enter in order to conduct the search.

Entry with a warrant

The police will normally have to obtain a search warrant from a Justice of the Peace in order to enter and search premises and a JP can grant a warrant only if he or she is satisfied that a serious arrestable offence has been committed and that there is material on the premises which is likely to be relevant to its investigation. The JP must also be satisfied that it is not practicable for the police to obtain permission to enter the place, or that a search may be frustrated unless a police officer is allowed to enter immediately. Applications for warrants must specify the reasons for the proposed search, the premises to be searched and the articles to be looked for. The warrants themselves must be just as specific. They can authorise entry on one occasion only, which must occur within a month of the issue of the warrant and be at a reasonable hour unless this would frustrate the search.

If the police wish to search for personal medical records, documents dealing with counselling or with assistance given by a voluntary organisation, journalistic material or confidential business information, they must obtain either a production order or a warrant, not from a JP but from a county court judge. Before issuing such an order or warrant the judge must normally be satisfied that access to the material is in the public interest. Otherwise similar preconditions apply to the issue of a warrant as in the case of applications to a JP. The only material which is totally exempt from search is that which is subject to legal privilege; in the main these are communications between solicitors and their clients (art.12).

Entry without a warrant

Under articles 19 and 20 of the PACE (NI) Order, the only situations where a police officer is able to enter and search premises without a warrant are the following:

- where the officer wishes lawfully to arrest a person whom he or she reasonably suspects is present on the premises,
- where the police wish to search premises occupied or controlled by a person who has been arrested for an arrestable offence because they have reasonable grounds for suspecting that the premises contain evidence relating to that or some other connected arrestable offence,
- where entry is necessary in order to prevent serious personal injury or serious property damage,
- where entry is necessary in order to deal with or prevent a breach of the peace, or
- where any statutory provision so permits, *e.g.* the Food Safety (NI) Order 1991, article 33.

The power to seize objects

The police can seize and retain anything they are looking for during a lawful search. In addition, by virtue of article 21 of the PACE Order, an officer who is lawfully on any premises may seize anything found there (even if it is not being looked for) provided he or she has reasonable grounds for believing that it has been obtained as a result of an offence, or that it is evidence in relation to any offence, and that seizure is necessary in order to prevent it being concealed, lost, damaged, altered or destroyed. Even information accessible through a computer can be seized under this power.

Whenever anything has been seized, a written record must be provided, if requested, to a person who was the occupier of the premises or who had custody or control of the thing immediately prior to the seizure. Access to items seized, even if only in order to photograph or copy them, must be permitted by the officer in charge of the investigation unless he or she has reasonable grounds for believing that this would prejudice criminal proceedings. Otherwise items seized may be retained by the police for as long as is necessary. Under section 1 of the Police (Property) Act 1897 a person can apply to a magistrates' court for an order for the return of property or for a statement from the police as to why they think retention is still justified.

As explained above (p.38), anything seized during an unlawful search may nevertheless be used in court as evidence of an offence. Judges have a discretion to exclude the evidence because of the adverse effect on the fairness of the proceedings (art.76 of the PACE Order), but the person searched can seek compensation for infringement of his or her rights only by taking action in the civil courts (see Chapter 2). He or she can also lodge a complaint against the police (see Chapter 5).

The power to enter and search premises under the anti-terrorist laws

Under the Terrorism Act 2000, searches of any place can be made by the police as follows:

- to arrest a suspected terrorist (s.81),
- to arrest a person reasonably suspected of scheduled offences or offences in the Terrorism Act itself (s.82(2)),
- to look for explosives, firearms, ammunition or transmitters (s.84 and Sch.10), and
- to look for persons who have been kidnapped (s.86).

The last two of these search powers can also be exercised by soldiers on duty. Soldiers cannot enter and search premises to look for suspected terrorists or to arrest persons reasonably suspected of scheduled or Terrorism Act offences.

If the place to be searched is a dwelling-house then, as far as the section 84 and 86 powers are concerned, authority to conduct the search must be granted by a police officer not below the rank of inspector or by a commissioned army officer and there must be reasonable grounds for suspecting the presence of what is being sought. In 2001 (from the Act's commencement on 19 February) there were 347 searches conducted by the police under section 84 and 359 by the army, but there are no published figures on the quantities of weapons, ammunition or transmitters revealed by searches of homes. It has been held by the European Court of Human Rights that searches under the section 84 power are *not* a breach of the European Convention on Human Rights (*Murray (Margaret) v UK*, 1993).

Under paragraph 4 of Schedule 10 to the Terrorism Act 2000 the police or army may require any person who is in the place being searched for explosives etc. to remain in a part of it for up to four hours, although a police officer of the rank of superintendent or above may extend that period by a further four hours if he or she reasonably believes that it is necessary to do so. The police or army can use reasonable force to ensure that the requirement is complied with and anyone wilfully failing to comply runs the risk of two years' imprisonment and an unlimited fine. The police or army can arrest anyone reasonably suspected of committing this offence, which is triable without a jury. A challenge to the legality of detention during a house search was unsuccessful before the European Commission of Human Rights (*O'Neill and Kelly v UK*, 1992).

Although section 84 and Schedule 10 authorise the police to search only for explosives, firearms, ammunition and transmitters, if they find other incriminating items during the course of any search the person in possession of these items can be arrested and charged. Under section 57 of the 2000 Act it is an offence to have in one's possession *any article:*

> *in circumstances which give rise to a reasonable suspicion that [one's] possession is for a purpose connected with the commission, preparation or instigation of an act of terrorism.*

The items most likely to be involved in this offence are everyday things which can be used in the making of a bomb, *e.g.* rubber gloves, adhesive tape, bell-pushes, coffee-grinders and kitchen scales. It should also be noted that under section 58 of the Act it is an offence to have in one's possession, unless one has a lawful excuse, any information which is likely to be useful to a person committing or preparing an act of terrorism. The maximum penalty for the offences in sections 57 and 58 is 10 years' imprisonment and an unlimited fine.

When the police or army are searching premises for explosives, firearms, ammunition or wireless apparatus they can be assisted by specially appointed civilians such as forensic scientists and photographers.

Written records and compensation

Unless it is not reasonably practicable to do so, a written record has to be made of the search specifying the service number of the searching officer, the name of the apparent occupier of the premises, the address of the premises, the date and time of the search, any damage caused and any items seized during the search (para.8 of Sch.10). The apparent occupier must be supplied at once or as soon as is practicable with a copy of any such record (para.9 of Sch.10).

If, in the exercise of their powers under Part VII of the Terrorism Act (the part which confers additional powers on the security forces in Northern Ireland), the police or army take or damage any property, the Secretary of State must pay compensation provided a claim is submitted to the Northern Ireland Office no later than 28 days (or exceptionally six months) after the incident (s.102 and Sch.12 of the 2000 Act). An appeal against the size of a compensation award can be made within six weeks to a county court (para.5 of Sch.12). This right to compensation replaces any other legal right to claim compensation in the circumstances (see *Deehan v Chief Constable of the RUC*, 1990). Compensation can be denied if it is in respect of an act done in connection with a scheduled offence or a non-scheduled offence under the 2000 Act and the person applying for compensation has been convicted of that offence (para.9 of Sch.12).

The power to arrest under the ordinary law

The Police and Criminal Evidence (NI) Order 1989 contains provisions governing "arrestable" offences, a category which includes offences carrying a sentence (for those over 21) of five years or more, as well as some less serious offences for which Acts of Parliament provide a separate arrest power. The full list is in article 26 and Schedule 2 of the Order. It includes the following:
- smuggling offences under the Customs and Excise Acts,
- offences under the Official Secrets Acts 1911 and 1989,
- indecent assault upon a female,
- taking away a motor vehicle,
- "going equipped for stealing",
- loitering and importuning by a prostitute,
- impersonating a voter at a polling station,
- failing to provide a breath test, or being in charge of a motor vehicle while under the influence of drink or drugs, and

- public order offences under the Public Order (NI) Order 1987 (see Chapter 8).

The PACE Order also provides that the police can arrest without a warrant any person who is reasonably suspected of attempting or conspiring to commit any of the listed offences, or of inciting, aiding, abetting, counselling or procuring their commission. Article 27, moreover, makes it clear that the police may arrest someone for a non-arrestable offence if the service of a summons (*i.e.* a document requiring later attendance at court) is not practicable or appropriate. Service will not be practicable or appropriate if a person's name or address cannot be readily ascertained or is doubtful, if a child or other vulnerable person needs to be protected, or if the person to be arrested would otherwise suffer or cause injury or damage to property, commit an offence against public decency or cause an unlawful obstruction on a road. Altogether the police arrested 24,147 people under the PACE legislation between April 2001 and March 2002. This was a drop of 1.4% on the previous year's total.

There also exists a judge-made power to arrest someone for a breach of the peace. To be more exact, according to the leading case on the point (*R v Howell*, 1982), there is a power of arrest:
- where a breach of the peace is committed in the presence of the arresting officer,
- where the arresting officer reasonably believes that such breach will be committed in the immediate future by the person arrested, or
- where a breach of the peace has been committed and it is reasonably believed that a repetition is threatened.

The courts have even said that the police can arrest people who are not themselves threatening to commit a breach of the peace but whose conduct is likely to provoke others to do so. A breach of the peace was defined in *R v Howell* (1982) as:

an act done or threatened to be done which either actually harms a person, or in his presence his property, or is likely to cause such harm, or which puts someone in fear of such harm being done.

A person arrested for breach of the peace may be "bound over" by a magistrate. This means that he or she will not be further punished provided he or she commits no further breach of the peace, or some other crime, within a stipulated period. A challenge to the compatibility of these breach of the peace rules with the European Convention on Human Rights was unsuccessful in *Steel v UK* (1998).

The 1989 Order maintains the rule that the police may arrest any person so long as a warrant for that purpose has been issued to the police by a Justice of the Peace. The JP must be satisfied that the police reasonably suspect the person of a crime and that his or her voluntary co-operation is unlikely. Once a person has been dealt with by a court for the offence alleged in a warrant, the warrant ceases to be valid and cannot be used to justify a later arrest (*Toye v Chief Constable of the RUC*, 1991). Under the Justice (NI) Act 2002 Justices of the Peace are to become known as lay magistrates (s.10).

In all situations a police officer is entitled to use reasonable force when carrying out an arrest. The 1989 Order says that in exercising any power under the Order, the police "may use reasonable force, if necessary" (art.88). However, the use of unreasonable force, or of reasonable force in circumstances where it is not necessary, will not make the arrest unlawful. It will only make possible a claim for compensation, under the civil law, for assault. Using force to effect what is in any event an unlawful arrest may lead to the police having to pay so-called exemplary damages to the victim, as in *Carroll v Chief Constable of the RUC* (1988). In 1998 Mr David Adams was awarded £30,000 compensation for injuries sustained while being arrested by the police. In 2001 the RUC reportedly paid £100,000 in an out-of-court settlement to Bernard Griffin, who, after being arrested when he was 19, was beaten by police officers and falsely accused of possessing explosives. For their parts in this disgraceful episode two police officers were sent to prison, one for two years, the other for one year (*Irish News*, 25 August 2001).

An arresting officer must also indicate that the arrest is taking place and give a reason for it (unless the reason is very obvious). This was made clear in *Christie v Leachinsky* (1947) and confirmed by article 30 of the PACE Order. If it later turns out that the reason for the arrest was not a good one, the person arrested can claim compensation for "false imprisonment" and "malicious prosecution". But if the police show that they had "reasonable and probable cause" for acting as they did, perhaps because the person arrested had confessed to the alleged crime, no compensation will be awarded (*Cooke v Chief Constable of the RUC*, 1989).

It remains the case that an ordinary citizen has the power to make what is popularly known as "a citizen's arrest", although the extent of this power is not as great as in the case of the police. It does not permit a citizen to arrest someone who is *about to commit* an arrestable offence, and it does not allow an arrest for an arrestable offence which the citizen reasonably believes has been committed but which *in fact* has not been (*R v Self*, 1992). Given the difficulty of knowing which offences are arrestable and which are not, it is unwise for ordinary people to try to take the law into their own hands in this way.

The power to arrest under the anti-terrorist laws

The main arrest power of police officers

The main anti-terrorist arrest power conferred on the police in Northern Ireland is the same as that applying in Great Britain. It is conferred by section 41 of the Terrorism Act 2000. This provides that a constable may arrest without a warrant a person whom he or she reasonably suspects to be a terrorist. For this purpose a "terrorist" is defined by section 40 as a person who is, or has been, concerned in the commission, preparation or instigation of acts of terrorism or as a person who has committed an offence under a number of sections in the Terrorism Act itself. For the Act's definition of "terrorism" see p.33 above.

"Terrorism" itself, therefore, is not an offence, but persons reasonably suspected of being terrorists can be arrested. The Government claims that this arrest power is necessary because it helps to *prevent* terrorism. The arrest powers in the PACE Order, including the one which authorises arrest of any person reasonably suspected of being about to commit an arrestable offence, are deemed inadequate. It is clear, moreover, that, just as in the case of the PACE Order's powers, a police officer can be said to have "reasonable suspicion" for the purposes of section 41 if he or she is acting on information supplied and instructions issued by a superior police officer (see *O'Hara v Chief Constable of the RUC*, 1997). A challenge against this decision failed in the European Court of Human Rights (*O'Hara v UK*, 2001).

If the police arrest a person under the Terrorism Act, they still have to indicate why the arrest is occurring and under what power. If subsequent questioning – or the lack of it – shows that there were no real grounds for reasonably suspecting a connection with terrorism, an action in the civil courts for compensation for false imprisonment may succeed. It is a fact that, during the last 15 years, approximately 70%

of all the persons arrested in Northern Ireland under section 41 of the Terrorism Act or its predecessors have later been released without being charged. This might suggest that the arrest powers are being used not just for the legitimate purpose of rounding up genuine suspects but for the illegitimate purpose of harassing people or fishing for snippets of incriminating evidence about other people. Alternatively, it might mean that people who are arrested supply no evidence which the police can rely upon to found a charge.

The use of arrest powers just for the gathering of information is possibly a contravention of Article 5(1)(c) of the European Convention on Human Rights, which says that arrest or detention must be for the purpose of bringing the person "before the competent legal authority on reasonable suspicion of having committed an offence or when it is reasonably considered necessary to prevent his (*sic*) committing an offence". In *Brogan v UK* (1988), however, the European Court of Human Rights held that the definition of "terrorism" in what was then the Prevention of Terrorism (Temporary Provisions) Act 1984 ("The use of violence for political ends, including any use of violence for the purpose of putting the public or any section of the public in fear") was well in keeping with the Convention's notion of an "offence".

What is clear is that, when the police arrest someone under section 41, the grounds for the arrest must be notified at the time. This is a rule laid down by judges (see p.50 above) and it has not been expressly abolished by the Terrorism Act. Unfortunately, there is nothing to stop the police from arresting someone on reasonable suspicion of committing unspecified acts of terrorism (para.(b) of the definition of "terrorist" in s.40(1)), even though they may have enough suspicion of the person having committed particular offences (as listed in para.(a) of s.40(1)). But if a person disputes the lawfulness of his or her arrest the police must still supply details ("in general terms") of the matters which constituted reasonable grounds for the arresting constable's suspicion that the person was involved in terrorism (*Clinton v Chief Constable of the RUC*, 1991). Moreover the police power to enter and search premises if they reasonably suspect that a terrorist is to be found there (s.81 of the 2000 Act) applies only to suspected terrorists within s. 40(1)(b), not to terrorists reasonably suspected of particular offences.

In 2001, 234 people were arrested under the anti-terrorism laws in Northern Ireland; 50 of these were charged with an offence, including three who were charged with murder and nine with attempted murder. However some three-quarters of those arrested were released without charge.

The other arrest powers of police officers and soldiers

Under section 82 of the Terrorism Act 2000 a police officer may arrest without warrant any person whom he or she reasonably suspects is committing, has committed or is about to commit a scheduled offence or an offence under the Terrorism Act which is not a scheduled offence. When the list of scheduled offences (set out in Sch.9 to the Act) and other offences created by the Act is compared with the list of offences for which a person can be arrested without warrant under the PACE (NI) Order 1989 (see p.48 above), there is almost a complete overlap. There is therefore a good case for allowing section 82 to lapse. The annual statistics on its use show that it has not been resorted to since 1990 because the main arrest power in the anti-terrorist laws (now section 41 – see above) is much more wide-ranging.

The army's main arrest power in Northern Ireland is now conferred by section 83 of the Terrorism Act 2000. Rather alarmingly, this allows a soldier on duty who reasonably suspects that a person is committing, has committed or is about to commit *any* offence to arrest that person without a warrant and to detain him or her for up to four hours. The soldier need not give any reasons for the arrest other than to say that he or she is making the arrest as a member of Her Majesty's forces. There is an argument that these very extensive powers given to soldiers are disproportionate and that therefore they cannot be justified under Article 5 of the European Convention on Human Rights, but no such challenge has yet been successful in the courts. In practice the army hand over anyone who has been arrested to the police as soon as possible. They do not question the person arrested, this being a task for the police in accordance with the relevant Codes of Practice. In 2001 the army arrested 44 people in Northern Ireland.

The power to detain under the ordinary law

By article 32 of the PACE (NI) Order 1989 an arrested person has to be taken to a *designated* police station if it may be necessary to keep him or her in detention for longer than six hours. In Northern Ireland the 22 designated stations are in Antrim, Armagh, Ballymena, Banbridge, Belfast (Antrim Road, Grosvenor Road, Musgrave Street, Strandtown), Coleraine, Cookstown, Derry (Strand Road and Waterside), Downpatrick, Dungannon, Enniskillen, Larne, Limavady, Lisburn, Lurgan, Newtownards, Omagh and Strabane. Any other station may be used if detention is to be for less than six hours, or if otherwise there might be an injury caused to any person. Article 32(13), however, makes it plain that the duty to take an arrested person to a police station as soon as practicable after the arrest does not apply if the presence of the person is necessary elsewhere in order to carry out immediate and reasonable investigations.

Having been arrested and taken to a police station, a person can be arrested there for a further offence (art.33) but, if a person voluntarily attends a police station – to help the police with their inquiries – he or she must be allowed to leave whenever wanting to, unless first placed under arrest (art.31). An arrested person can be detained for questioning or released on bail. If the arrest took place under a warrant, the warrant itself may have been endorsed with a note authorising bail. Otherwise the police officer in charge of the station concerned may release the person on bail if satisfied that this will not lead to an injustice.

The maximum period of ordinary detention without charge is 24 hours (art.42(1)). Detention beyond 24 hours is possible only for "serious arrestable offences", a category defined in article 87. It comprises:

- offences which are always serious arrestable offences, such as manslaughter, kidnapping, most sexual offences, firearms offences and causing death by reckless driving (Sch.5 to the Order);
- offences for which a person can be arrested under the Terrorism Act 2000;
- arrestable offences which lead to, or are intended or likely to lead to, any of the following consequences: serious harm to the security of the state or to public order, serious interference with the administration of justice or with the investigation of an offence, the death of any person, serious injury to any person, substantial financial gain to any person or serious financial loss to any person; and
- arrestable offences consisting of making a threat which, if carried out, would be likely to lead to any of the above consequences (*e.g.* blackmail or intimidation).

In the case of these offences, a police officer of at least the rank of superintendent, and who is responsible for the police station concerned, may authorise detention for a further 12 hours, provided that there are reasonable grounds for believing that this detention is necessary to secure evidence and that the investigation is being conducted diligently and expeditiously (art. 43(1)). In relation to serious arrestable offences the police are therefore able to detain a person without charge for up to 36 hours. Between April 2001 and March 2002 only five persons were kept in police detention in Northern Ireland for more than 24 hours under this power and then released without being charged.

Detention beyond 36 hours is allowed only if authorised by a magistrates' court. The court can initially require further detention for up to 36 hours. A second court order can be applied for, but the total period of detention since the time of the arrest must not exceed 96 hours (arts.44 and 45). Before the 1989 Order came into force the maximum detention period was 48 hours. In 2001-2002 there were just 18 applications for extensions of detention, all of which were granted. Of the detainees involved, three were later released without being charged.

Throughout the period of detention the position of the arrested person must be reviewed. The first review must be carried out six hours after the detention begins and later reviews must be conducted at least once every nine hours. The review officer must be a police officer of at least the rank of inspector who has not been directly involved in the investigation up to that point. As soon as the grounds for detention cease to exist, the arrested person must be released or charged. Once charged, he or she must be released on police bail or brought before a magistrates' court on that day or on the following day. Until his or her release the arrested person is the responsibility of the station's "custody officer", who must have at least the rank of sergeant. It is this officer who must authorise the initial detention and any release.

While a person is in custody he or she may be visited by custody visitors, who are lay people appointed by the Northern Ireland Policing Board under section 73 of the Police (NI) Act 2000 (although they operated on a non-statutory basis, as "lay visitors", for nine years prior to 2000). Custody visitors can speak to detainees in private and can report on the conditions they find in the police stations' custody suites, but they cannot themselves investigate any complaints raised by detainees.

The power to detain under the anti-terrorist laws

The power to intern someone without trial, which was last exercised in Northern Ireland in 1975, was abolished altogether by section 3 of the Northern Ireland (Emergency Provisions) Act 1998. Persons arrested under section 41 of the Terrorism Act 2000 can be detained for up to 48 hours (s.41(3)). If the arrest occurs while the person is being examined at a port or border control, the 48 hour period is deemed to begin not at the time of the arrest but at the time the examination begins. The detainee's rights while in detention are set out in paragraphs 6 to 15 of Schedule 8 to the Terrorism Act.

The detainee can have one named person (who is known to the detainee) informed as soon as is reasonably practicable that he or she is being detained at a particular police station. The detainee also has the right to consult a solicitor as soon as is reasonably practicable, privately and at any time. But in certain circumstances – detailed in Chapter 4 – the exercise of both of these rights can be delayed if a police superintendent has reasonable grounds for so authorising (para.8 of Sch.8 to the 2000 Act). The rights must, however, be permitted to be exercised before the first 48 hours of detention have elapsed (para.8(2)). Moreover, an assistant chief constable can direct that a detainee's consultation with his or her solicitor must take place in the sight and hearing of a uniformed police officer of at least the rank of inspector who has no connection with the detainee's case (para.9 of Sch.8). In *Brennan v UK* (2001) the European Court of Human Rights held that there had been a breach of Article 6(3)(c) of the European Convention on Human Rights because a police officer had been within hearing during the applicant's first consultation with his solicitor after his arrest. But on the facts the Court awarded no compensation and it affirmed that, under the Convention, the right of access to a solicitor may be subject to restrictions for good cause. In 2001-2002, 10 requests to contact a friend or relative were delayed by a superintendent in Northern Ireland and in eight cases access to a solicitor was delayed.

Reviews of detention

Paragraphs 21 to 28 of Schedule 8 to the Terrorism Act 2000 provide for people arrested under section 41 to have their detention reviewed. The first review must be carried out as soon as is reasonably practicable after the person's arrest and thereafter at intervals of not more than 12 hours. The review officer has to be a police officer who has not been directly involved in the investigation of the matter in connection with which the person has been detained. The detention cannot continue unless authorised by the review officer and unless the person detained or his or her solicitor has been given the opportunity to make oral or written representations about the detention. The review officer must make a written record of the review in the presence of the detainee and inform him or her at that time whether and, if so, why detention is being continued.

Extensions of detention

Paragraphs 29 to 37 of Schedule 8 to the Terrorism Act 2000 regulate the extension of detentions beyond the initial maximum of 48 hours. Prior to the coming into force of these provisions the power to extend detentions vested in the Secretary of State and could lead to the detainee being kept in detention for a further five days in total. This necessitated the UK's "derogating from" (*i.e.* opting out of) Article 5 of the ECHR. In *Brogan v UK* (1988) the European Court of Human Rights held that detentions for longer than four days and six hours, without the authorisation of a judicial authority, were a breach of Article 5. However the validity of the derogation notice – *i.e.* whether it was made in accordance with Article 15 of the ECHR – was upheld by the European Court in *Brannigan and McBride v UK* (1993). With the commencement of the Terrorism Act 2000 this derogation notice has been withdrawn.

An extension is now possible only if a police officer of at least the rank of superintendent applies successfully to a county court judge or a designated resident magistrate for the issue of a warrant of further detention. The extension can be for any period provided that it does not end more than seven days after the date of the detainee's initial arrest (or the beginning of his or her examination at a port or border control if the arrest took place during such examination).

An application for an extension of detention can be made during the six-hour period following the initial maximum of 48 hours, but the application must then be dismissed by the judge or magistrate if he or she considers that it would have been reasonably practicable to make the application during that 48 hour period. Moreover an application cannot be heard unless the detainee has been given notice of it as well as an opportunity to make oral or written representations and to be legally represented at the judicial hearing, although the judge or magistrate can exclude the detainee and/or his or her legal representative from any part of the hearing. Such an exclusion *must* occur if the police officer applying for the extended detention asks for an order that specified information upon which he or she intends to rely be withheld from the detainee and his or her legal representative. Further applications for extended detention can be made provided that the total detention does not last longer than the seven day maximum.

Compensation for over-holding

Detention for a period longer than that permitted by the law will leave the police open to be sued in a civil action for false imprisonment (see Chapter 2). In one case, where a woman was detained from 9.30pm to 10.05pm simply so that she could then be medically examined (having already been at the police station all day), compensation of £300 was awarded (*Petticrew v Chief Constable of the RUC*, 1988). In *Moore v Chief Constable of the RUC* (1989), where Mr Moore was arrested early one morning and held for most of the rest of the day while being interviewed several times, the judge held that it was reasonable for the police to hold him from 6.30am to 8.00pm in order to dispel or confirm the arresting officer's reasonable suspicion that he was guilty of the attempted hijacking of a vehicle, but there were one or two hours' detention which the police had failed to justify and damages of £150 were awarded. Having ruled in 1992 (in *Oscar v Chief Constable of the RUC*) that the sum to be awarded for unlawful detention should be £600 per hour for up to the first 12 hours and usually a lesser hourly sum thereafter if the distress has lessened, the Court of Appeal of Northern Ireland has more recently ruled (in *Dodds v Chief Constable of the RUC*, 1998) that approximately £600 should be paid for the first hour of detention and that for a 24 hour period a sum of between £4,000 and £5,000 should be paid. The court stressed that this latter sum could be lower if the reason for the over-holding was a merely technical breach of the law and that it could be higher if the innocence of the defendant was very clear.

Detention of deportees

The Anti-terrorism, Crime and Security Act 2001 provides, very controversially, for the indefinite detention without trial of non-UK citizens who are not allowed to remain in the UK but who cannot be sent back to their home country because of the risk that they will be mistreated there (ss.21-23). Such detainees are free to leave for their home country if they so wish, and two or three of the persons so detained have done so, but a small group of other persons remain locked up with no prospect of any judicial hearing. An application for judicial review of the detention provisions was successful in the English High Court last year, but in October 2002 the Court of Appeal held that the detentions were not in breach of Article 5 of the European Convention on Human Rights because the deprivation of liberty was taking place in the context of immigration control, where the Article 5 standards do not bite so fiercely (*A and others v Secretary of State for the Home Department*, 2002). Lord Carlile conducts an annual review of how these detention provisions are operating in practice.

Watchdogs

Persons detained under the anti-terrorism laws in Northern Ireland may be visited while in custody by the Independent Commissioner for Detained Terrorist Suspects (Dr Bill Norris), a non-statutory office which has operated since 1993. The Commissioner must satisfy himself that the detainees are being properly looked after (he can pass on complaints, but cannot investigate them), but he can also – and does – sit in on interviews which the police hold with the detainees. He issues an informative annual report. Since 1 October 2002 the powers of custody visitors (see p.56 above) have been extended to allow them too to visit detainees who have been arrested under the anti-terrorism laws. But they cannot sit in on interviews. Since 6 May 2003 the custody visitors visit the "terrorist" detainees in that part of Antrim Police Station set aside for them.

The power to take photographs and fingerprints

As a person has no right in law to his or her own image, the police can photograph people as much as they want. This does not breach the European Convention on Human Rights (*Murray (Margaret) v UK*, 1993). Further regulation of the process was inserted as article 64A of the PACE (NI) Order 1989 by section 93 of the Anti-terrorism, Crime and Security Act 2001.

Article 61 of the PACE (NI) Order 1989 provides that fingerprints (and palm prints) may be taken without a person's consent if a police officer of at least the rank of superintendent authorises them to be taken or if the person has been charged with, or is to be reported for, an offence. In both of these situations the person must already have been detained at a police station. There is no power to fingerprint someone who has not been arrested and if an arrested person has not yet been charged or told that he or she is to be reported there must be reasonable grounds for suspecting that the person is involved in an offence and that the fingerprints will tend to confirm or disprove this involvement.

In the absence of consent, the police may use reasonable force to take fingerprints, but a written record must be kept of the reason for taking the prints.

If fingerprints have been given voluntarily and the person is no longer suspected of having committed an offence, the prints taken, and any copies, must be destroyed as soon as practicable, in the presence of the person involved if so requested. The person can even apply for a certificate to show that access to computer data relating to the fingerprints has been made impossible. But as a result of an amendment to article 64 of the PACE Order, inserted by section 83 of the Criminal Justice and Police Act 2001, prints taken in other circumstances can be retained, provided they are later used only for purposes related to the prevention or detection of crime, the investigation of an offence or the conduct of a prosecution. A challenge to this power of retention, arguing that it breached Articles 8 and 14 of the European Convention on Human Rights, was recently unsuccessful in the English Court of Appeal (*R v Chief Constable of South Yorkshire, ex parte Marper*, 2002)

Under the Terrorism Act – in Great Britain as well as in Northern Ireland – a police officer may take a detained person's fingerprints without his or her consent only if (1) the person is detained at a police station and a police officer of at least the rank of superintendent authorises it or (2) the person has been convicted of a recordable offence on or after 29 July 1996.

In terrorist cases fingerprints taken from the detainee may be used only for the purpose of a terrorist investigation, *i.e.* a check may not otherwise be made against the records of fingerprints taken under the PACE (NI) Order 1989. But they are not destroyed after the detained person has been released. Nor does a person have the right to know what photographs and other information the police possess in relation to him or her. In *In Re Gillen* (1990) the applicant was told that his photograph had gone missing from a police station. He sought further details about the loss but the court held that he had to be satisfied with the police's offer of advice on personal safety.

The power to take samples

Under the ordinary common law the police have no power to take samples from a person's body. To do so without the person's consent would be an assault. An important statutory exception is the Road Traffic (NI) Order 1981, under which it is an offence to refuse to supply a sample of breath, blood or urine in cases of alleged driving while under the influence of alcohol or drugs. The PACE (NI) Order 1989 creates further important exceptions in articles 62 and 63. The Order distinguishes between intimate samples, which can be taken only with the person's consent, and non-intimate samples, which can be forcibly taken.

"Intimate samples" are samples of blood, semen or any other tissue fluid, urine or pubic hair, or a swab taken from any of a person's body orifices except his or her mouth. "Non-intimate samples" are hair other than pubic hair, material taken from a nail or from under a nail, saliva, a mouth swab or any other body swab, a footprint or any other impression of a part of a person's body other than the hand. Curiously, mouth swabs are classified as non-intimate samples in Northern Ireland, but as intimate samples in England and Wales.

All samples require the written authorisation of a police officer of at least the rank of superintendent, who must have reasonable grounds for suspecting the involvement of the person in a serious arrestable offence and for believing that the sample will tend to confirm or disprove this involvement. A written record must be kept of the sampling. Intimate samples must be consented to in writing and (except for urine samples) be taken by a doctor. If a person refuses to consent to the taking of an intimate sample, then in any proceedings against that person the magistrate, judge or jury may "draw such inferences as appear proper" (art.62(10)).

Under the Terrorism Act 2000 the police powers in relation to samples are the same as in relation to fingerprints (see above). Again, no intimate sample may be taken without the detainee's consent.

The power to use force

Whenever they are carrying out their "ordinary" function of preserving the peace, the police are not entitled to use force. They must act with restraint, resisting pressure rather than applying it. Even when controlling crowds or patrolling a procession or parade they must not apply force in an active manner. If they do so, they can be sued for assault.

However, if the police are preventing crime or effecting a lawful arrest, they can use "such force as is reasonable in the circumstances" (s.3(1) of Criminal Law Act (NI) 1967). The burden of proving that the force used was reasonable lies on the police. For example, in *Wasson v Chief Constable of the RUC* (1987), since the police could not prove that their version of how Mr Wasson came to be injured by a plastic bullet was more likely to be true than Mr Wasson's version, they were held liable to pay compensation. But it seems that, even in the absence of any proof that the police knew that the person they fired at was committing an offence (such as driving a stolen car), a judge may still regard the use of real bullets as reasonable force whenever someone drives through a vehicle checkpoint.

In *Magill v Ministry of Defence* (1988) it was held that a soldier's act in firing at a 15-year-old driver was reasonable use of force in the prevention of crime. A police officer would probably enjoy a similar immunity in such circumstances, although much will depend on the particular features of each case. In *Kelly (John) v UK* (1993) a 17-year-old boy had been shot by the army while driving a stolen car which tried to evade a checkpoint. The European Commission of Human Rights held that an application by the boy's father was inadmissible because the force used was justifiable as an attempt to effect an arrest and any such arrest would have been lawful because the harm to be averted by preventing the escape of terrorists outweighed the harm likely to be caused by the shooting. However, in the light of the more recent decision by the European Court in *McCann and others v UK* (1998), the state may now be held liable for not planning vehicle checkpoints in such a way as to ensure that the security forces do not need to shoot to kill the occupants of a vehicle which fails to stop.

In relation to police powers expressly conferred by the PACE (NI) Order 1989, article 88 says that the police "may use reasonable force, if necessary, in the exercise of the power". The term "reasonable" suggests that the force used must be in proportion to the gain the police hope to achieve through exercising the power. The term "necessary" implies that other means of exercising the power must be attempted first. This would seem to impose a stricter test than that contained in the 1967 Act, but as yet no court has ruled on how the two provisions inter-relate.

As regards police powers conferred by the Terrorism Act 2000, section 114(2) says that a constable may if necessary use reasonable force for the purpose of exercising any of them except the power to question people at ports and in border areas. It is safe to assume that the army can also use reasonable force when exercising their powers under Part VII of the Act in Northern Ireland. But in both cases, under the Human Rights Act 1998, the force used would also have to be proportionate to the purpose behind the power.

For many years the police and army in Northern Ireland have used baton rounds (sometimes called plastic bullets) to help quell riots or other serious disturbances. Whether in any particular case the use of such a weapon is lawful will depend on the circumstances of its firing, and in particular on the dangers facing the officer in question. Under the European Convention, anyone is entitled to use proportionate force to protect his or her own life or the lives of others. The police and army have Guidelines for the use of baton rounds, but a failure to comply with those is not *per se* unlawful.

The power to interfere with property

Section 91 of the Terrorism Act 2000 is the provision which legalises the actions taken by the security forces whenever private property rights are interfered with in order to counter unlawful conduct. It permits any person, if authorised by the Secretary of State on the ground that it is necessary for the preservation of the peace or the maintenance of order, to take possession of any property, to defend any structure, to detain, destroy, or move any property, to carry out works on possessed land or to do any other act interfering with any public right or with any private rights of property. It is therefore perfectly lawful for the police to take over, say, a house for the purpose of keeping an eye on a nearby building. Farmland, too, can be requisitioned so that look-out posts or fences can be constructed.

Under section 92 of the 2000 Act a police officer, soldier or other authorised person may wholly or partly close a road, right of way or waterway if he or she considers this *immediately* necessary for the preservation of the peace or the maintenance of order. To permit more permanent measures to be taken, section 94 empowers the Secretary of State to order the closure of any highway.

Interference with any work undertaken pursuant to these powers is a crime, punishable by up to six months in prison and a fine of up to £5,000.

Codes of Practice

Article 65 of the PACE (NI) Order 1989 obliges the Secretary of State to issue codes of practice covering:
- searches of persons or vehicles without first making an arrest,
- the detention, treatment, questioning and identification of persons,
- searches of premises, and

- the seizure of property found on persons or premises.

Under article 60 a code must also be issued on the tape-recording of interviews at police stations. The codes are not themselves pieces of legislation – and are not therefore to be found in official collections of legislation – but they can be purchased in booklet form from the Stationery Office and they must be made available in all police stations for consultation by members of the public. The English codes (on which the codes in Northern Ireland are closely modelled) were issued in a revised form early in 2003, so it is likely that the codes in Northern Ireland will also be revised in the near future.

For the most part the codes simply repeat in clearer language the provisions of the main legislation, but occasionally they are more detailed. For instance, the code on searches of premises says that:

Searches must be conducted with due consideration for the property and privacy of the occupier of the premises searched, and with no more disturbance than necessary (para.5.9).

Likewise, the code on the treatment of detainees provides that:

A strip search may take place only if the custody officer considers it necessary to remove any article which a person would not be allowed to keep, and the officer reasonably considers that the person might have concealed such an article (para.10).

There are also special provisions dealing with the treatment in custody of vulnerable and mentally disordered people (see Annexes D and F to the code on treatment). If a national of another country is arrested and detained the code says that the police should give notice to the foreign consulate of that country.

A breach of the codes will not automatically render the police liable to criminal or civil proceedings (art.66). The only available penalty will be disciplinary proceedings. A court can, however, "take account" of a code's provisions when hearing any criminal or civil case, so it might refuse to admit a piece of evidence if it considers that it was obtained in breach of a code.

In both Great Britain and Northern Ireland there are separate codes of practice for the operation of the Terrorism Act 2000 (issued under ss.99 and 100). Before these are issued the Secretary of State has to publish them in draft form and consider any representations made to him or her about them. Generally speaking the current codes contain fewer safeguards for detainees than the equivalent PACE codes. Terrorist suspects do not have the right, for instance, to know the identity of their interrogators, nor can they obtain a copy of their custody record. As explained in Chapter 4, one of the codes governs the use of silent video-recorders at interviews with terrorist suspects.

Complaints against the army

Soldiers in the army are subject to the ordinary criminal law just like anyone else in society. In addition they can be dealt with under their own system of law, called military law, which means that for alleged offences that do not involve civilians they can be court-martialled. Very few soldiers have been prosecuted under the criminal law in Northern Ireland and those who have been tried and convicted have tended to receive sentences which, in practice, are not severe. After Private Lee Clegg was convicted of murder at a vehicle checkpoint, a successful campaign was mounted to have the conviction quashed even after it had been confirmed by the House of Lords (*R v Clegg*, 1995 and 2002). After two Scots Guards were convicted of the murder of Peter McBride in 1992 they were released from prison after serving just six years and were allowed to resume their places in the army even though soldiers found guilty of much lesser crimes have been ejected. Attempts to challenge in court the Army Board's determination in this case have so far failed (*In re McBride's Application*, 1999 and 2003).

Victims of alleged offences committed by soldiers can try to initiate a private prosecution, but this is extremely difficult in practice because of the problems involved in collecting sufficient evidence. Anyway, the Attorney General, who is a member of the UK Government, has the power to intervene in any private prosecution in order to terminate it on the ground that he or she thinks it is in the public interest to do so.

It is easier to bring a civil claim for compensation against the army, not least because the standard of proof required is "on the balance of probabilities" rather than "beyond a reasonable doubt". In several cases, even some involving the alleged misuse of firearms, the Ministry of Defence has settled out of court, although without an admission of liability. Occasionally cases have been fought to a successful conclusion in court.

If a breach of the law is suspected, notwithstanding attempts to prevent it, the victim should try to take note of what is happening and write down the details as soon as this becomes possible (times, exact locations, who was involved, etc). He or she should also ask for the names, numbers and units of the soldiers in question. Every army patrol is now required to carry cards identifying their regiment number with a phone number where complaints may be lodged. Soldiers are under orders to distribute the cards to anyone seeking to make a complaint against them.

A complaint should be lodged with the local army commander. It will then be investigated by the local "civil representative". A civilian official called the Independent Assessor for Military Complaints Procedures (currently Mr Jim McDonald) reviews the manner in which the army deals with complaints but cannot investigate complaints independently. His powers are now set out in section 98 of the Terrorism Act 2000. The Independent Assessor should be contacted if a complaint against the army is not dealt with satisfactorily by the army itself. The police should be involved if the complainant suspects that what has occurred amounts to a criminal offence, such as an assault. The Independent Assessor, unfortunately, has no official role to play in those cases. The latest annual report of the Assessor reveals that in 2001 there were 676 complaints made in Northern Ireland about army conduct. In December 2002 he issued a report on the use by the army in Northern Ireland of plastic baton rounds.

Further useful addresses

- British Army Headquarters (Northern Ireland)
  Thiepval Barracks
  Lisburn
  Co. Antrim
  tel: 028 9266 5111
  www.army.mod.uk/aroundtheworld/n_ire/

- Police Service of Northern Ireland
  Headquarters
  Brooklyn
  65 Knock Road
  Belfast BT5 6LE
  tel: 028 9065 0222
  www.psni.police.uk

- Northern Ireland Policing Board
  Waterside Tower
  31 Clarendon Dock
  Clarendon Dock
  Belfast BT1 3PG
  tel: 028 9040 8500
  www.nipolicingboard.org.uk

- Independent Commissioner for Detained Terrorist Suspects
  Hampton House
  47-53 High Street
  Belfast BT1 2QS
  tel: 028 9023 7181

- Independent Assessor for Military Complaints Procedures
  Hampton House
  47-53 High Street
  Belfast BT1 2QS
  tel: 028 9023 7181

- Statistics and Research Branch
  Criminal Justice Policy Division
  Northern Ireland Office
  Massey House
  Stoney Road
  Belfast BT4 3SX
  tel: 028 9052 7534
  www.nio.gov.uk

Chapter 4

The Rights of Detainees

John Jackson

The investigation of crimes was originally the responsibility of jurors, then of magistrates. During the nineteenth century the task was given to the police. As explained in Chapter 3, the police do not have a general power to stop a person for questioning unless he or she is placed under arrest. Nor do they have a general power to detain someone for the purpose of getting "help with police inquiries". There is no half-way house between voluntary co-operation with the police and arrest for a specific offence.

The absence of any duty to reply to police questions is usually referred to as "the right of silence". It also protects defendants (*i.e.* the persons accused of crimes) from having to give evidence at their trial. We shall see, however, that this right has been limited by the Criminal Evidence (NI) Order 1988. A person other than a defendant is protected by the right of silence at a trial only to the extent that he or she can claim the privilege to decline to answer a question which may incriminate him or her in a criminal offence.

The "voluntariness" principle

The police must conduct their questioning of suspects within the law and it is always open to a person who has been assaulted in the course of police questioning, perhaps for the purpose of extracting a confession, to bring a civil action against the police officers involved. A further question is whether ill-treatment of a detained person in the course of questioning renders his or her detention unlawful. In one case involving a man whose ear-drum was perforated, the High Court of Northern Ireland held that if a person is lawfully arrested for the purpose of questioning, but is subsequently assaulted during questioning, the detention becomes unlawful and the person is entitled to a writ of *habeas corpus* to secure release (*Ex parte Gillen*, 1988). But this decision was overruled by the Northern Ireland Court of Appeal in *Cullen v Chief Constable of the RUC* (1999) in the light of a

House of Lords decision expressing disapproval of the opinion that ill-treatment of a person detained makes the detention unlawful (see *R v Deputy Governor of Parkhurst Prison, ex parte Hague*, 1992).

For many years, the most significant restriction on the power of the police to question suspects was the rule that a statement could be used as evidence only if it had been made voluntarily. This meant that, when an accused person challenged the validity of a confession which he or she had allegedly made, the prosecution had to prove beyond a reasonable doubt that the statement had not been obtained "by fear of prejudice or hope of advantage held out by a person in authority". This test was later extended to require the prosecution to show that the statement was not obtained by "oppression". "Oppressive questioning" was defined by one judge as:

> *questioning which by its nature and duration or other attendant circumstances (including the fact of custody) excites hopes such as the hope of release or fears, or so affects the mind of the subject that his will crumbles and he speaks when otherwise he would have stayed silent.*

Whether there was oppression in an individual case depended on many elements, including the length of time intervening between periods of questioning, the length of any specific period of questioning, whether the accused had been given proper refreshment and the characteristics of the person who made the statement.

Article 74 of the PACE Order

In a major change brought about by article 74 of the Police and Criminal Evidence (NI) Order 1989 (known as the PACE Order), the prosecutor now has to prove that the statement was not obtained by oppression of the person who made it or in consequence of anything said or done which was likely to render it unreliable. The voluntariness principle, therefore, no longer applies.

The "admissibility" of a confession (*i.e.* whether it can be accepted as proper evidence in a court of law) is frequently tested at what is known as a "*voir dire*" or a "trial within a trial". This is when the judge asks the jury to withdraw so that it cannot be influenced by hearing evidence which the judge might rule to be inadmissible. If an alleged confession is ruled inadmissible by the judge, the prosecution may not adduce evidence given by the accused at the *voir dire* at a later stage of the trial, so long as the evidence in question was relevant to the issue at the *voir dire*. If what the accused says at the *voir dire* were to be admissible at the trial, it might significantly impair his or her right of silence at the trial.

For the purposes of article 74 of the PACE Order, "oppression" is defined to include torture, inhuman or degrading treatment and the use or threat of violence, whether or not amounting to torture (art.74(8)). This seems a narrower definition than at common law, but the word "includes" in article 74(8) entitles the courts to extend the categories of oppression to the kinds of conduct and circumstances considered oppressive at common law. In their interpretation of the equivalent English provision, the English courts have restricted oppression to the exercise of authority or power in a burdensome, harsh or wrongful manner, to unjust or cruel treatment and to the imposition of unreasonable or unjust burdens in circumstances which would almost always entail some impropriety on the part of the interrogator (*R v Fulling*, 1987).

The other kind of evidence which is wholly excluded under article 74 is a confession made in consequence of conduct likely to render it unreliable.   This extends the categories of behaviour which may exclude a confession beyond threats and inducements, but makes it clear that a confession will be excluded only where the conduct was *likely* to render unreliable any confession which the accused might have made as a result.   The question for the court is a hypothetical one: might what was said or done have been likely, in the circumstances, to make *any* confession by the defendant unreliable? Much therefore depends on what is considered by judges to make a confession unreliable.

Rules on police questioning

The conduct of police questioning used to be governed by what were known as the Judges' Rules, so called because they had their origin in a set of rules formulated and approved by senior English judges in 1912 and 1918. A second version of them was approved in 1964 and these were adopted in Northern Ireland in 1976. Appended to them was a set of Administrative Directions, which were concerned with affording persons questioned with reasonably comfortable conditions and adequate breaks and refreshment, and with creating special procedures for persons unfamiliar with the English language or of immature age or feeble understanding. It is important to realise, however, that neither the Judges' Rules nor the Administrative

Directions had the force of law; they were merely statements of good practice which judges were entitled to take into account when deciding whether a police officer had acted lawfully or not.

Guidance and Codes

A Code of Practice for the Detention, Treatment and Questioning of Persons by Police Officers, issued under article 65 of the PACE Order, now applies to all suspects, except those arrested and detained under the Terrorism Act. A separate Code of Practice issued under section 99 of the Terrorism Act deals with persons arrested and detained under that Act. There are differences in the degree of protection offered to suspects under each of these Codes.

The Code of Practice under PACE, in its current form requires all arrested persons, and all persons who are being questioned regarding their involvement or suspected involvement in an offence, to be cautioned in the following terms:

You do not have to say anything, but I must caution you that if you do not mention when questioned something which you later rely on in court, it may harm your defence. If you do say anything it may be given in evidence.

Suspects who are in custody must in addition be given a written notice setting out the terms of the 1988 Order so as to ensure that they are fully aware of the consequences of their action.

The Code contains detailed rules on how interviews are to be conducted. It requires that an accurate record be made of each interview with a person suspected of an offence and that the record be signed by the suspect as correct. Interviews in police stations cannot be conducted without the consent of the custody officer, who must be an officer not involved in the investigation of the offence but who has the responsibility for the treatment of detained persons.

In any detention period of 24 hours, a suspect must be allowed a continuous period of at least eight hours for rest. When an interviewing officer considers that there is sufficient evidence to prosecute a suspect and that the suspect has said all that he or she wishes to say about the offence, the officer must bring him or her before the custody officer, who is then responsible for considering whether he or she should be charged. On being charged the suspect should again be cautioned and given a written notice showing particulars of the offence and stating the terms of the caution. Questions relating to the offence should not be put to him or her after charge unless they are necessary to prevent harm to some other person or to clear up an ambiguity in a previous answer.

Audio-taping

A further Code of Practice has been issued under article 60 of the PACE Order requiring that interviews be taped in certain circumstances at police stations where approved tape-recording facilities exist. Under this Code, which became effective in July 1996, interviews should be taped where a person has been cautioned in respect of any indictable offence (including an offence "triable either way" – see Chapter 2), unless it is a driving offence. The only other exception is where the person is being questioned in respect of an offence under section 1 of the Official Secrets Act 1911. A uniformed officer not below the rank of inspector may also authorise an interview not to be taped where the equipment is faulty and the interview should not be delayed. This Code of Practice does not apply to persons arrested under the Terrorism Act but a system of audio recording in scheduled cases became formally operative from May 1999 and in February 2001 specific Codes of Practice were issued under the Terrorism Act requiring the audio-recording and video recording with sound of interviews. The effect of this is that all interviews by police officers of persons detained under the Terrorism Act 2000 must now be audio-recorded and video-recorded. A revised code on the video recording of interviews came into effect in Northern Ireland on 18 April 2003.

Young and mentally disordered persons

The PACE Code of Practice for the Detention, Treatment and Questioning of Persons by Police Officers requires that a person under the age of 17, or a person who is mentally disordered, whether suspected of an offence or not, must not be interviewed or asked to provide or sign a written statement in the absence of an "appropriate adult", unless an officer of the rank of superintendent or above considers that delay would involve an immediate risk of harm to persons or a serious loss of property, the alerting of other suspected persons or the hindering of the recovery of property. An "appropriate adult" means, in the case of a juvenile, the juvenile's parent or guardian, a social worker or a responsible adult over 18 who is not a police officer.

Article 58 of the PACE Order creates a new section 52 of the Children and Young Persons Act (NI) 1968, so that there is now a duty, where a juvenile is in police detention, to take such steps as are practicable to ascertain the identity of a person responsible for his or her welfare and to inform that person, unless it is not practicable to do so, why and where the juvenile is being detained.

Enforcement of the rules on questioning

Judges have discretion under the common law (*i.e.* non-statutory law) to exclude from court proceedings any statement which has been obtained unfairly. It is their duty to see that the accused has a fair trial according to law (*R v Sang*, 1979). In one Northern Irish case other matters which were considered relevant to the judge's discretion included the reason that led the accused to say what he or she did, whether the police had acted improperly in order to get him or her to crack under the strain, and the unlawfulness of the police conduct, but it was stressed that the "paramount criterion" was the fairness of the accused's trial (*R v McBrien and Harman*, 1984).

Article 76 of the PACE Order states that in any criminal proceedings the court may refuse to admit evidence on which the prosecution proposes to rely if it appears that, having regard to all the circumstances, including the circumstances in which the evidence was obtained, the admission of evidence would have such an adverse effect on the fairness of the proceedings that the court ought not to admit it. The effect of this is that, just as the courts have a broad common law discretion to exclude statements obtained unfairly, the courts have a broad statutory discretion to exclude statements obtained in breach of a Code issued under the Order. It is worth noting that the courts in England have been much more prepared to use their power to exclude statements under the statutory discretion (which has been in force there since 1986) than they have ever been prepared to do under their common law discretion. It is also important to note that as a consequence of the Human Rights Act 1998 courts are now required to give effect to European Convention rights, including the right to fair trial guaranteed by Article 6 of the Convention.

The Codes of Practice issued under the PACE Order, like the earlier Judges' Rules, do not have the full force of law. Article 66(7) states merely that a police officer will be liable to disciplinary proceedings for a failure to comply with any provision in a code. As regards whether a statement obtained in breach of a code can be used as evidence, article 66(10) states, in effect, that in all criminal and civil proceedings the courts may take such account of any breach as they think fit. In some cases this will mean excluding the statement.

Questioning under anti-terrorist legislation

A number of emergency powers were enacted for Northern Ireland in 1973 on the recommendation of the Diplock Commission and many are still enshrined in the Terrorism Act 2000. Rather than apply the voluntariness principle the Diplock Commission proposed that admissibility of confessions should depend on the much lower standard of the absence of torture or inhuman or degrading treatment, a standard derived from Article 3 of the European Convention on Human Rights. This was indeed the standard enshrined in the subsequent emergency laws, most recently in section 76 of the Terrorism Act 2000, for persons being tried on indictment (*i.e.* in the Crown Court) for a scheduled offence (*i.e.* one listed in Schedule 9 to the Terrorism Act 2000). If such a person wished to challenge the admissibility of a statement allegedly made by him or her, he or she had to adduce evidence which on the face of it showed that he or she had been subjected to torture, inhuman or degrading treatment, violence or the threat of violence in order to induce the making of the statement. The prosecution had then to satisfy the court that the statement was not obtained in this manner.

There were still difficulties over what exactly amounted to, say, degrading treatment. Statements made by a suspected member of a "terrorist" organisation after periods of searching questioning were admitted, notwithstanding that at the outset the suspect did not wish to confess and that the interrogation caused him or her to speak when otherwise he or she would have stayed silent (*R v Dillon and Gorman,* 1984). Such questioning would probably have constituted oppression at common law. However, the European Court of Human Rights has recently held that a suspect was denied a fair trial under Article 6 of the Convention where a statement was admitted into evidence after being obtained as a result of questioning conducted under conditions which were intended to be psychologically coercive and conducive to breaking down any resolve he or she may have manifested to remain silent (*Magee v UK*, 2000). The Court held that when the applicant was questioned under these conditions at the Castlereagh holding centre, he should have been given access to a legal adviser at the initial stages of interrogation in order to counterbalance the police's treatment of him.

Mr Magee's conviction was referred back to the Northern Ireland Court of Appeal by the Criminal Cases Review Commission and his conviction was quashed because it was unsafe (*R v Magee*, 2001).

Fortunately, in his report on the operation of the Terrorism Act 2000 in Northern Ireland during 2001, Lord Carlile recommended the repeal of section 76. After a period of consultation on this recommendation the Northern Ireland Office announced the repeal in August 2002. Since then the admissibility test laid down in article 74 of the PACE Order (see p.69 above) has applied even in Diplock cases.

The discretion to exclude evidence

Shortly after the enactment of the emergency legislation in 1973, the then Chief Justice explained that:

> there is always a discretion, unless it is expressly removed, to exclude any admissible evidence on the ground that (by reason of any given circumstance) its prejudicial effect outweighs its probative value and that to admit the evidence would not be in the interests of justice (R v Corey, 1973).

This discretion was then written into the emergency laws (*e.g.* s.76(6) of the Terrorism Act 2000), but now that article 74 of the PACE Order applies to questioning even in these cases the relevant judicial discretion is now that contained in article 76 of the PACE Order (see p.73 above).

The Codes of Practice compared

As mentioned above, the Code of Practice issued under the PACE Order for the Detention, Treatment and Questioning of Persons does not apply to persons detained under the Terrorism Act 2000. Instead their questioning is regulated by Codes of Practice issued under section 99 of that Act. As well as Codes of Practice on detention, treatment, questioning and identification, there are Codes of Practice on audio- and video- recording.

Like the Codes of Practice issued under the PACE Order, the Codes issued under the Terrorism Act lack the full force of law, but failure by police officers to comply with them (the Codes do not apply to arrests made by the army) may make them liable to disciplinary proceedings (unless criminal proceedings are pending against them) and the provisions of the Codes may be taken into account by the courts when deciding whether to admit confessions. The courts may also exercise their discretion to exclude statements obtained as a result of a breach of the Codes.

The latest Code on Detention, Treatment and Questioning issued under the Terrorism Act offers levels of protection which are an improvement upon those offered under the previous code, but they are still not as extensive as those in the Code of Practice issued under the PACE Order. There are still differences relating to the way in which access to legal advice is regulated (see below). Other differences worth noting are that, although all persons arrested and held in custody have rights of access to a lawyer and a right to have a person informed of their whereabouts (see below), persons detained under the Terrorism Act are not permitted to talk on the telephone with anyone, to have writing materials or to receive visits. While both Codes make provision for arrested persons to be medically examined by a Medical Officer, the Code of Practice under the Terrorism Act permits the detained person to be examined in addition by a medical practitioner from his or her practice only in the presence of the Medical Officer. In addition the Code under the Terrorism Act permits the custody officer to delay a medical examination requested by the detained person where he or she believes this would prejudice the investigation. No such restriction is allowed by the PACE Code.

From 2002 the Government has permitted the lay "custody visitors" to police stations (operating under a scheme first introduced in 1991) to monitor not only the treatment of PACE suspects held in custody but also suspects detained under the Terrorism Act. But since 1992 there has also been a non-statutory Independent Commissioner for Detained Terrorist Suspects (currently Dr Bill Norris) who, as well paying random visits to places where suspected terrorists are detained, can also sit in on police interviews with the suspects. He issues an informative annual report.

The right of access to a lawyer

Under article 59 of the PACE Order, a person arrested and held in custody is entitled to consult a solicitor privately at any time if he or she so requests. The police may delay in complying with the request only if the person is in detention for a serious arrestable offence and if an officer of at least the rank of superintendent authorises the delay. Delay is permitted only for up to 36 hours from the beginning of the person's detention. The allowable reasons for delay are that there are reasonable grounds for believing that the exercise of the right would be likely:

- to lead to interference with evidence or witnesses,
- to lead to serious loss of property,
- to lead to the alerting of other suspects, or
- to hinder the recovery of property or the proceeds of a crime.

In 2000-2001, of the 25,330 persons arrested under the PACE (NI) Order, 10,601 requested access to a solicitor and in no case was access delayed.

Article 57 also entitles a detained person to have someone informed that he or she has been arrested, subject to the same grounds of delay as in article 59. In 2000-2001 there were 5,290 requests for such information to be communicated and in only eight cases was communication delayed. Arrested persons have no absolute right to be told of these entitlements under articles 57 and 59, but the Code of Practice says that they *should* be told.

Articles 57 and 59 specifically exclude from their scope persons arrested or detained under the Terrorism Act 2000, but under paragraphs 6 and 7 of Schedule 8 to that Act such persons have a right to consult a solicitor privately and to have someone informed of the fact that they have been arrested if they make these requests. The detainee must be informed of these rights as soon as practicable after being arrested. The police may delay in complying with these requests only if such delay is authorised by an officer of at least the rank of superintendent and the delay must not extend beyond 48 hours from the beginning of the detention. The grounds of delay are broader than those allowed under article 59 of the PACE Order, extending to interference with the gathering of information about the commission of acts of terrorism and to alerting any person so that it will be more difficult to prevent an act of terrorism or to apprehend a person in connection with an act of terrorism. The Northern Ireland courts have held that it is sufficient that the police reasonably believe that there is a real risk of a legal adviser being used as an unwilling agent to convey information of use to "terrorists" (*R v Harper*, 1990; *R v Cosgrove and Morgan*, 1994).

The effect of a breach of the right

The right of access to a lawyer has been described in one English decision as "one of the most important and fundamental rights of a citizen" (*R v Samuel*, 1988). But the English courts appear to require some causal connection between any breach of the right and any resulting confession before they are inclined to exclude confessions on the grounds of denial of the right of access to a lawyer and the Northern Ireland Court of Appeal has approved of this approach (*R v Harper 1990; R v McWilliams*, 1996). The Northern Ireland courts have, however, recognised that the decision of a police superintendent to delay access to legal advice or to delay a suspect's right to have someone informed of detention is clearly one by an official which affects public rights and that it is therefore open to judicial review (*In Re Duffy's Application*, 1992; *In Re McKenna's Application*, 1992).

Under the Human Rights Act 1998 the courts now also have to give effect to Convention rights and the European Court of Human Rights has in recent years emphasised the existence and significance of the right to have access to legal advice during detention for questioning. In *Murray (John) v UK* (1996) the European Court of Human Rights held that the denial of legal advice for 48 hours, in combination with the right of silence provisions in the Criminal Evidence (NI) Order 1988 (see p.81), amounted to a violation of Article 6 of the European Convention on Human Rights. After being cautioned under the Order, the applicant had been interviewed 12 times without access to a solicitor. The Court held that, even though the restrictions on legal advice had been lawfully exercised, they were capable of violating the fair trial provisions in Article 6. The scheme contained in the 1988 Order, said the Court, was such that it was of "paramount importance" for the rights of the defence that an accused had access to a lawyer at the initial stages of police interrogation. In *Magee v UK* (2001) the European Court followed this decision in declaring that there is a right, implied by Article 6, to have the assistance of a lawyer from the initial stages of police questioning. The right can be restricted but only for good cause and, as mentioned above, the Court considered that the conditions of interrogation at Castlereagh holding centre were such that the applicant should have been allowed access to a solicitor from the outset in order to counterbalance those conditions.

Statistics illustrate that in recent years solicitors have increasingly been given access to suspects detained under the terrorism provisions when suspects have requested this. Legal challenges have instead centred on the refusal to allow solicitors to be present during police interviews. Over a number of years the Northern Ireland courts refused to recognise any right of legal access to police interviews in terrorist cases (*e.g. In re Russell's Application*, 1996). This approach was endorsed by the House of Lords in *Ex parte Begley* (1997), although their Lordships considered that the police had a discretion to allow solicitors to be present in exceptional circumstances and that the application of a fixed policy of refusing solicitors access to interviews would be unlawful. The latest Code of Practice under the Terrorism Act has finally recognised that the right of access to a solicitor extends, as it does for suspects arrested under the PACE Order, to a right to have a solicitor present during police interviews.

There remain, however, differences between the two Codes as regards other aspects of the right of access to a lawyer. The PACE Code, for example, states that where a person declines to speak to a solicitor in person, having been informed of the right to legal advice, the custody officer shall point out that the right to legal advice includes the right to speak with a solicitor on the telephone and ask him or her whether he or she wishes to do so. There is no mention of this practice in the Code of Practice under the Terrorism Act. Unlike the PACE Code, this Code also permits an officer of at least the rank of Assistant Chief Constable to direct that any consultation between the detained person and a solicitor must take place in the sight and hearing of a member of the uniformed branch of the police service not below the rank of inspector, so long as the authorising officer forms the view that the consultation may result in any of the consequences mentioned above as grounds for delaying access to a solicitor altogether for up to 48 hours. This practice may need to be reviewed in the light of a recent decision of the European Court of Human Rights that an accused's right to consult with his or her lawyer in private is part of the basic requirements of a fair trial, that it flows from Article 6(3)(c) of the Convention and that it may be restricted only where there is a "compelling reason" to do so (*Brennan v UK*, 2001). In this case the restriction was intended to prevent the solicitor passing information to other suspects at large but there was no allegation that the solicitor was likely to collaborate in such an enterprise. There was therefore no compelling reason for the restriction and, as it related to a consultation which was the first occasion on which the applicant was able to seek advice from his lawyer, the European Court found a breach of Article 6.

The right of silence before trial

Research indicates that only a minority of suspects in fact exercise their right to say nothing when questioned by the police, which suggests that the right may not be the valuable safeguard it is often claimed to be. One of the reasons for this is that there is nothing to stop the police asking questions and, even when a person indicates that he or she wishes to remain silent, there is no obligation on the police to stop asking questions until the point when the person is charged with an offence. The PACE and Terrorism Act Codes of Practice for Detention, Treatment and Questioning require police officers not to ask questions only once a suspect has been charged, unless the circumstances are exceptional. There are also a number of laws which impose a duty to answer questions or provide information. Section 26 of the Official Secrets Act 1939 provides that a policeman of at least the rank of inspector may be authorised to require a person to furnish information regarding an offence under section 1 of the Act. Under road traffic legislation, the police have a right to require the driver of a car to present his or her driving licence and, if the driver is alleged to be guilty of an offence under the legislation, to give his or her correct name and address and those of the owner of the car (Road Traffic (NI) Order 1981, arts.177 and 180).

As regards emergency legislation, section 89 of the Terrorism Act 2000 has already been explained in Chapter 3 (see p.35). Another exception to the right of silence is the offence of failing to disclose information without reasonable excuse about an act of terrorism or about people involved in terrorism, which has been inserted in the Terrorism Act 2000 by section 117 of the Anti-terrorism, Crime and Security Act 2001 (see p.36).

As a result of the Human Rights Act 1998, however, it is now open to citizens to challenge laws which impose direct duties on them to answer police questions, on the ground that they breach the European Convention on Human Rights. The European Court of Human Rights has held that the right to remain silent and not to incriminate oneself is an inherent part of the right to a fair trial (*Funke v France*, 1993). However, in a number of decisions the courts have recognised that the right is not absolute. In *Brown v Stott* (2001) the Judicial Committee of the Privy Council held that it was not a breach of a fair trial for a woman to be required to tell the police whether she had been driving her car at a certain time in accordance with road traffic legislation.

Enforcement of the right of silence

The citizen's right of silence in the face of police questioning has traditionally been enforced by two general rules. One was laid down in *Rice v Connolly* (1966), where the court held that silence cannot lead to a charge of obstructing the police in the execution of their duty. The second general rule states that, at a trial, the prosecution and the trial judge should not suggest to the jury that an adverse inference may be drawn from an accused person's silence when questioned by the police. The only common law exception to this rule is where two persons are speaking on even terms and one charges the other with something which the other says nothing to repel. In this instance the judge may make some comment, but even here he or she must be careful, for it has been held that to ask the jury to consider whether the person's silence in these circumstances indicates guilt or innocence is to short-circuit the intellectual process that has to be followed. Where the accuser is a police officer, the parties cannot normally be said to be on even terms, although everything depends on the circumstances.

Restrictions on the right of silence

The most serious dent in the general rule that adverse inferences should not be drawn from silence is created by the Criminal Evidence (NI) Order 1988, which defines three situations when adverse inferences may be drawn in court from an accuser's silence *before* trial. Article 3 provides that, when an accused relies in his or her defence on some fact which he or she failed to mention when questioned or charged by the police, then if the fact is one which the accused could reasonably have been expected to mention, the court or jury may draw such inferences from the failure as appear proper.

The other two situations when adverse inferences may be drawn are more limited. Article 5 provides that a court or jury may draw such inferences as appear proper where, after being arrested, a person fails to account to the police for the presence of an object, substance or mark on his or her person, or in a place where he or she was arrested, if the object, substance or mark is reasonably believed by the police to be attributable to the person's participation in an offence. Article 6 permits inferences to be drawn from a refusal by a person when arrested to account for his or her presence at a particular place at the time the offence was committed.

The Codes of Practice issued under both the PACE Order and the Terrorism Act require that persons who are questioned by the police be warned about the effect of article 3. In addition, the Codes require that, before a constable questions a person about the matters in articles 5 and 6, he or she must inform the person that there is reason to believe that what has been found is attributable to the person's participation in an offence or that the person's presence at the time of the alleged offence is attributable to his or her participation in it. The person must then be asked to account for what has been found or for his or her presence and warned that a failure to do so may result in a court deriving such inferences from the failure as appear proper.

The courts have in a number of decisions drawn adverse inferences against accused persons from their failure to respond to police questioning. In one of the first cases article 3 was invoked against the National Director of Publicity for Sinn Féin when he refused to reply to police questions after being arrested with seven others for unlawfully detaining a man suspected of being a police informant. The accused denied the charge and explained his silence on the ground that as a Sinn Féin spokesperson he had advised other people to remain silent and had to maintain this stance himself. But the Lord Chief Justice held that the failure to speak gave rise to very strong inferences against him that the innocent explanation which he offered in court was false (*R v Martin and others*, 1991).

One of the accused in this case subsequently claimed that the drawing of inferences from silence violated Article 6 of the European Convention on Human Rights, as it infringed his privilege against self-incrimination. In this case (*Murray (John) v UK,* 1996), the European Court of Human Rights held that the right to remain silent under police questioning and the privilege against self-incrimination were recognised international standards which lay at the heart of a fair procedure under Article 6. But the Court said that the right of silence was not absolute and it could not prevent a court taking into account an accused's silence in situations which clearly called for an explanation. On the facts of the case before it, the Court held that, having regard to the weight of the evidence against the applicant, the drawing of inferences from his refusal to explain his presence in the house where the alleged informer was being held captive was a matter of common sense and could not be regarded as unfair and unreasonable. As mentioned at p.79 above, however, the failure to grant the applicant access to legal advice before he was questioned by the police did constitute a violation of Article 6, as the effect of the Order makes it vital that an accused has access to a lawyer at the initial stages of police interrogation.

Subsequent decisions of the European Court have emphasised the limited impact which the drawing of inferences ought to have in contributing towards a defendant's conviction. In *Averill v UK* (2000) the court considered that the extent to which adverse inferences can be drawn from an accused's failure to respond to police questioning must be necessarily limited. The court ventured the view that, while it may no doubt be expected in most cases that innocent persons would be willing to co-operate with the police in explaining that they were not involved in any suspected crime, there may be reasons why in a specific case an innocent person would not be prepared to do so. In *Averill v UK* itself the prosecution case against the accused was strong and in the circumstances the court held that the applicant could have been expected to provide answers to questions put to him in custody.

But the European Court has been anxious to give particular weight to a solicitor's advice not to answer questions. In *Condron v UK* (2000), where the solicitor had advised the applicants not to answer questions because they were suffering from the symptoms of heroin withdrawal, the trial judge had nevertheless directed the jury that it was open to them to draw an adverse inference from their silence. The European Court held that this was a violation of the applicants' right to a fair trial because the judge's direction had left the jury at liberty to draw adverse inferences even if they were satisfied that the applicants remained silent because of the advice of their solicitor. The judge should have directed the jury that, if they believed the applicants' silence could not sensibly be attributed to their having no answer to the questions, or none that would stand up in cross-examination, they should not draw an adverse inference.

Questioning at the trial

The general rule, subject to an important exception in the case of an accused person, is that if a person is a "competent" witness, *i.e.* if his or her evidence may lawfully be admitted by the court, then that person may be lawfully *compelled* by the court to give evidence or to suffer the penalty for contempt of court. This means that he or she will be required to answer any questions put in court, unless some objection is taken by a party that the question cannot be answered on the ground that it would infringe the rules of evidence such as the hearsay rule, or the rule prohibiting opinion evidence, or the rules on character evidence.

Privileged communications

The witness can also object to answering a question if able to claim a "privilege". There are privileges connected with self-incrimination (see p.87), professional legal communications, and "without prejudice" negotiations.

Professional legal privilege extends to all communications passing between a client and his or her legal adviser in the course of seeking or giving legal advice. Also covered are communications between one party, or his or her legal adviser, and a third party which are made for the purpose of pending litigation. In addition, all good faith offers of compromise between parties are privileged (or "without prejudice") where litigation is pending or contemplated. A husband or wife could formerly also refuse to disclose any communication made to his or her spouse during the marriage, but this privilege ceased to have effect when article 79(8) of the PACE Order 1989 came into force.

One issue which Northern Ireland's courts have not yet had to face is whether communications between priests and penitents are privileged. The courts in England do not seem to recognise such a privilege but the Supreme Court in the Republic of Ireland has held that communications made in confidence to a parish priest by his parishioners are privileged.

Communications between doctors and their patients and between journalists and their informants are not privileged. Section 10 of the Contempt of Court Act 1981, however, states that no court may require a person to disclose the source of information contained in a publication for which he or she is responsible unless that disclosure is necessary in the interests of justice, or national security, or for the prevention of disorder or crime (see also Chapter 10).

Evidence through TV links

Article 81 of the PACE Order allows three categories of person, with the court's permission, to give live evidence through television links in the Crown Court. The three categories are witnesses outside Northern Ireland, witnesses aged less than 14 and witnesses who will not give evidence in open court through fear. The second category is restricted to cases involving certain offences of a sexual nature, cruelty and offences of assault or causing or threatening injury. The comparable English provision (s.32 of the Criminal Justice Act 1988) does not cover persons in the third category.

Children as witnesses

Since the general rule is that no testimony can be admitted as evidence unless it is given under oath, the common law position was that no child could give evidence unless he or she appreciated the solemnity of taking an oath and understood that taking an oath involved an obligation to tell the truth over and above the ordinary duty of doing so. However, Parliament has intervened over the years to make it possible for children to give unsworn testimony. Children under 14 may now give evidence unsworn and under article 3 of the Children's Evidence (NI) Order 1995 a child's evidence shall be received unless it appears to the court that the child is incapable of giving intelligible testimony. There is no minimum age below which a child cannot give evidence. Whether a child should give evidence or not is a matter for the judge's discretion depending upon the circumstances of the particular child.

Video-recordings of interviews with child witnesses are admissible as prosecution evidence in violent or sexual offences (art.5 of the Children's Evidence (NI) Order 1995). Children must be under 14 in the case of violent offences and under 17 in the case of sexual offences.

Accused persons and their spouses as witnesses

Accused persons have been competent to give evidence on their own behalf in Northern Ireland since 1923, but an accused person is not a competent witness for the prosecution in any criminal case. If the Crown wishes to rely on the evidence of an accused person who is prepared to give evidence against a co-accused, it has four options available to it. First, it can file a *nolle prosequi* with reference to his or her case, *i.e.* discontinue the prosecution. Second, it can state that no evidence will appear against the accused, in which case an acquittal will follow. Third, it can obtain an order for separate trials and, fourth, it can get the accused to plead guilty, in which case it is desirable that he or she be sentenced before being called on behalf of the prosecution.

Article 79 of the PACE Order changed the law by making the spouse of an accused competent to give evidence for the prosecution and for a co-accused and compellable for the prosecution and a co-accused where the offence charged involves an assault on the spouse or on a person under 17 or the offence charged is a sexual offence alleged to have been committed in respect of a person under 17.

Informers as witnesses

Informers are perfectly competent to give evidence against accused persons, but there is a rule that an accomplice (*i e.* an actual participant in the crime which the accused is alleged to have committed) must not be called on behalf of the prosecution unless the accomplice has already been prosecuted or it is made clear that a current prosecution will be discontinued. Without this rule a person against whom proceedings were pending would have every inducement to make his or her story sound as convincing as possible when giving evidence against co-participants. In fact, of course, even when an accomplice has been prosecuted, there may still be a considerable inducement to make his or her story sound convincing, such as when he or she has made a deal with the authorities ensuring an early release from prison, police protection on release or a financial reward. The trial judge has a discretion, which is rarely exercised, to exclude the evidence of an accomplice who is operating under "powerful inducements".

Some years ago a number of "terrorist" trials in Northern Ireland proceeded on the basis of accomplice evidence. The accomplices involved were called "supergrasses" in view of the large number of defendants implicated on their evidence. These trials caused a number of concerns, notably that many of the supergrasses were granted complete or partial immunity from prosecution or were given promises of having to serve only short sentences, and that their testimony was in a number of cases uncorroborated (*i.e.* not backed up by other evidence). There is no law which says that the testimony of suspects needs to be corroborated in this manner, and a number of defendants were convicted on the uncorroborated evidence of supergrasses. But these convictions were almost all overturned on appeal and there have been no major supergrass trials since 1983.

The accused's right of silence at the trial

Article 4 of the Criminal Evidence (NI) Order 1988 provides that the court or jury may, in determining whether the accused is guilty of the offence charged, draw such inferences as appear proper from the accused's failure to give evidence at the trial or from his or her refusal, without good cause, to answer any question. Before doing this, however, the court must at the conclusion of the evidence for the prosecution satisfy itself that the accused is aware that a failure to give evidence or to answer questions may result in this consequence. The effect of the article is to make it less attractive for accused persons to exercise their right of silence at the trial and to limit the right of an accused person to force the prosecution to prove the offence charged unaided by the accused. It should be noted, however, that the Order precludes the drawing of inferences where it appears to the court that the physical or mental condition of the accused makes it undesirable for him or her to give evidence.

In a number of cases the courts have drawn adverse inferences against accused persons who have not testified. In *Murray v DPP* (1994) the House of Lords upheld the view of the Court of Appeal in Northern Ireland that the 1988 Order changed the common law regarding the comments and inferences which could be drawn from an accused's silence at trial. The House of Lords held that once the prosecution has made out a *prima facie* case and the defendant refuses to testify, a judge or jury may draw such inferences from his or her silence as are dictated by common sense and may in a proper case draw the inference that he or she is guilty of the offence charged.

Article 78 of the PACE Order 1989 abolished the right of an accused person to make a statement from the dock without swearing an oath. The advantage to an accused of making an unsworn statement was that it permitted him or her to put a defence to the jury without having to submit to questions in cross-examination. The disadvantage was that the judge and jury were unlikely to be impressed by a defendant who did not submit to questioning.

The privilege against self-incrimination

One important occasion when a witness who is compelled to give evidence may refuse to answer a question is when there is, in the opinion of the court, a danger that the answer would expose the witness to prosecution for a crime. This privilege, known as the privilege against self-incrimination, extends to answers which would incriminate the witness's spouse. No adverse inference should be drawn by the judge or jury from the fact that the privilege is claimed.

A significant restriction on the privilege is imposed by section 1(e) of the Criminal Evidence Act (NI) 1923, which provides that any accused person who elects to give evidence may be asked any question in cross-examination notwithstanding that it could tend to make him or her appear guilty of the offence charged. Section 1(f)(ii) and (iii), however, prevent the defendant being asked about his or her previous misdeeds if the intention is to damage his or her credibility, unless the defendant gives evidence of his or her good character, or casts imputations on the character of the prosecutor, the witnesses for the prosecution or the deceased victim of the crime, or gives evidence against any other person charged in the same proceedings.

Further useful addresses

- Criminal Cases Review Commission
  Alpha Tower
  Suffolk Street
  Queensway
  Birmingham B1 1TT
  tel: 0121 623 1800
  www.ccrc.gov.uk

- Independent Commissioner for Detained Terrorist Suspects
  Hampton House
  47-53 High Street
  Belfast BT1 2QS
  tel: 028 9023 7181

- Police Service of Northern Ireland
  Headquarters
  Brooklyn
  65 Knock Road
  Belfast BT5 6LE
  tel: 028 9065 0222
  www.psni.police.uk

- Police Ombudsman for Northern Ireland
  New Cathedral Buildings
  St. Anne's Square
  11 Church Street
  Belfast BT1 1PG
  tel: 028 9082 8600
  www.policeombudsman.org

- Director of Public Prosecutions
  Royal Courts of Justice
  Chichester Street
  Belfast BT1 3JF
  tel: 028 9054 2444

Chapter 5

Complaints Against the Police

Mary O'Rawe

Although this chapter deals with the system for handling complaints against the police in Northern Ireland, it is important to remember that this is only one small aspect of police accountability. Some might argue that, in and of itself, even the best, most independent and impartial complaints system is a fairly ineffectual way of holding a police organisation to account. Complaint procedures tend to revolve around individual complaints against individual officers. The process is often lengthy and overly legalistic, with, at the end of the day, very few complaints being substantiated – not because the majority of such complaints are vexatious or groundless but because many of them concern institutional rather than individual failings. Complaint systems are also not designed to ensure that remedies are provided to the victims of police misconduct. A tendency to focus too exclusively on the efficacy of the complaint system can also lead to attention being diverted from the potential of other accountability mechanisms, such as that provided by the new Northern Ireland Policing Board.

This said, the complaint system merits close attention as it is still the area where individual members of the public are most likely to be personally affected by police accountability mechanisms. It is also an area where major changes have recently taken place in Northern Ireland – in part as a response to just the kind of failings outlined above. The changes were based on the government-commissioned "Hayes Report" of 1997 (*A Police Ombudsman for Northern Ireland?*), in which Dr Maurice Hayes recommended that complaints against the police should be investigated, not by the police themselves, but by a new and independent Office of the Police Ombudsman for Northern Ireland. The law relating to the handling of complaints against the Royal Ulster Constabulary – now, since November 2001, the Police Service of Northern Ireland (PSNI) – was altered very significantly by the Police (NI) Act 1998. This Act provided for the creation of the Police Ombudsman's Office, although the Office did not actually begin receiving complaints until 6 November 2000. The legislation also fell far short of implementing the system recommended by Hayes in a number of important respects.

The Report of the Patten Commission on Policing was published in September 1999 and despite that Report's call for the Hayes Report to be implemented in full, the Police (NI) Act 2000 added very little to the Ombudsman's powers. This is even more unfortunate, given that Patten viewed the success of this office as "key to the effective governance of Northern Ireland." The new Ombudsman system nevertheless marks a distinct (and, for the most part, very welcome) departure from previous failed systems for dealing with police complaints in Northern Ireland.

Several pieces of secondary legislation have been enacted making provision for specific aspects of the complaint system. They are:

- the Police and Criminal Evidence (Application to Police Ombudsman) Order (NI) 2000,
- the RUC (Conduct) Regulations 2000,
- the RUC (Unsatisfactory Performance) Regulations 2000,
- the RUC (Appeals) Regulations 2000,
- the RUC (Complaints etc.) Regulations 2000,
- the RUC (Complaints) (Informal Resolution) Regulations 2000, and
- the RUC (Conduct) (Senior Officer) Regulations 2000.

Most recently, further changes have been introduced by the Police (NI) Act 2003.

What constitutes a complaint?

The Police Ombudsman has the power to investigate any complaint from a member of the public about how police officers behave while doing their job. A complaint could involve anything from an allegation of criminal activity by a police officer down to a minor breach of the police's Code of Conduct. The Code of Conduct originally set out as Schedule 4 to the RUC (Conduct) Regulations 2000 was replaced by a new Code of Ethics on 14 March 2003. This new code is dealt with in more detail later.

The Ombudsman cannot investigate:

- conduct which has already led to criminal or disciplinary action, unless there is new evidence that was not available at the time of the original investigation,
- complaints about off-duty officers, unless the fact of being a police officer is relevant to the complaint,
- complaints about non-police officers acting with police officers (*e.g.* soldiers),
- complaints about traffic wardens or other civilian employees of the police,
- complaints about the direction and control of the police force by the Chief Constable,
- complaints which are not made by or on behalf of a member of the public,
- anonymous complaints,
- complaints made "out of time" (*i.e.* more than 12 months after the event),
- vexatious, oppressive or repetitious complaints,
- complaints where the complainant refuses to co-operate with an investigation,
- complaints where there is a lack of information necessary to conduct an investigation, and
- complaints which have been withdrawn by the complainant.

If a complaint is outside her legislative remit, the Police Ombudsman can, at her discretion, refer it to the Chief Constable, the Policing Board or the Secretary of State and notify the complainant accordingly. These bodies can then deal with the issue (or not) as they see fit.

The fact that a complaint can come to the Ombudsman only from a member of the public is problematic in that, historically, it has been complaints from other police officers that have stood the best chance of being substantiated and of having an officer disciplined. Complaints from other police officers are still investigated internally within the PSNI.

The Ombudsman expressed serious concern in her first annual report as to her role where alleged wrongdoing involves police officers acting with non-police officers. Currently she is only able to investigate the role of the police officer(s) concerned. Where the complaint concerns alleged criminal activity, this could result in the PSNI carrying out a parallel investigation into the matter in respect of the role of civilians or army personnel. The Ombudsman has recommended the creation of a power that would allow her to recommend the prosecution of persons engaged in joint criminal activity with police officers. In the meantime, such investigations will continue to prove ineffective as they cannot encompass all aspects of the behaviour complained about. With the powers to designate civilian staff as detention officers etc. under the Police (NI) Act 2003, there remains some doubt as to how far regulations to be issued under the new legislation will bring the behaviour of such individuals under the jurisdiction of the Ombudsman's office.

Another problem with the legislative definition of complaint is that it once again reduces the process to an examination of the conduct of an individual officer even though the alleged failings might well be symptomatic of an inappropriate police subculture, ineffective management, inadequate training or other organisational defects. Although individual responsibility is, of course, important, resources might be better allocated to acting on trends and patterns of complaints rather than indulging in a highly bureaucratic and legalistic procedure to discipline a series of individuals. Under the legislation, research by the Ombudsman's office is relegated to something discretionary rather than mandatory. Complainants whose concerns relate to policy or "operational" issues rather than specific wrongdoing by a given individual have been told by the office that it is outside the remit for investigation or action by the Ombudsman. This should change with the coming into force of the Police (NI) Act 2003. It should also be noted that the office's reports on plastic bullets and on the use of batons are very much set in an operational context.

A complaint must be made within 12 months of the behaviour complained of or it will generally not be investigated. The two exceptions to this are if there has been no previous investigation and if new evidence has come to light which was not reasonably available before. In both cases, an investigation will occur only if the Police Ombudsman considers the complaint to be "grave and exceptional".

If the behaviour or issue reported is deemed not to come within the definition of a complaint that can be investigated by the Police Ombudsman, the only way to challenge this is through an application for judicial review.

Complaints transferred from the ICPC

According to the Ombudsman's first annual report, on 6 November 2000, 2,124 complaints were transferred to that office from the now defunct Independent Commission for Police Complaints (ICPC). The decision was made to allow those investigations to progress under the old procedures, (*i.e.* police investigation) with reports simply being submitted to the Ombudsman's office. Six months later, 747 of these investigations had been completed. Around 50% of the total transferred cases were closed without further action; 604 were withdrawn, considered outside the remit of the Ombudsman's office or deemed incapable of investigation due to non-cooperation. A further 48 led to informal disciplinary action, with eight resulting in formal disciplinary action and eight closed following DPP charges and prosecutions. As of 31 March 2002, 330 investigations remained outstanding in respect of complaints transferred from the ICPC. A year or so later than figure stood at less than 100.

New complaints

Between 6 November 2000 and 31 March 2002, a total of 5,129 new complaints were received by the office. The vast majority of these related to incidents which had taken place since the office opened. In the first five months, allegations of oppressive behaviour (mainly assault) made up 50% of the total, while allegations of failure of duty accounted for a further 23%. The first annual report of the Ombudsman's office (covering the period 6 November 2000 to 31 March 2002) suggests a downward trend in the number of oppressive behaviour complaints, but these still account for 49% of the total received during this reporting period. 1,452 complaints (23%) related to failure of duty, 879 (14%) concerned incivility and 144 (2%) alleged malpractice. 89 (1%) referred to traffic issues and only 14 concerned racial discrimination. Some 636 (12%) are classified in the report as "other". Recent figures from the Ombudsoffice indicate that 49% of complaints received come from members of the Protestant community and 29% from Catholics.

How to make a complaint

The office of the Ombudsman has issued a pamphlet detailing, in accessible English, Irish, Chinese or Ulster Scots, how the complaint system works. This information can also be found on the office's website, *www.policeombudsman.org*. A complaint may be lodged in any of the following ways:

- by visiting the Police Ombudsman's office at New Cathedral Buildings, St Anne's Square, 11 Church Street, Belfast, between 9am and 5pm, Monday to Friday;
- by phone (0845 601 2931 or 028 9082 8600), although it is actually quite difficult to find a phone number for the office in the phone directory; (the Hayes Report recommended a freephone number);
- by fax on 028 9082 8659;
- by emailing to info@policeombudsman.org;
- by going to a solicitor, who can forward your complaint; legal aid may be available for legal advice from a solicitor, depending on your means;
- by visiting a Citizen's Advice Bureau or local advice centre where you will be told how to contact the Police Ombudsman;
- by making a complaint at a local police station, to the Northern Ireland Policing Board or the Secretary of State; in each of these cases your complaint should then be forwarded immediately to the Police Ombudsman's office; or
- by having a friend do any of the above on your behalf.

The complainant (*i.e.* the person making the complaint) should always keep a copy of any letter sent which sets out details of the complaint and any other relevant documentation. Ideally a note about what happened that gave rise to the complaint should be made as soon as possible after the event when details are fresh in your mind. This can then be drawn upon to write your letter or statement for the Ombudsman. Do not exaggerate detail or give information categorically if you are unsure about it. Any reliable witness will be a big help in proving your case, so do try to get contact details from any person at the scene who may have witnessed what happened and pass these on to the Ombudsman's office.

What happens to a complaint?

If the matter is classified as a complaint by the office of the Police Ombudsman, steps should be taken by the Chief Constable and by the Ombudsman's office to preserve any evidence relating to the conduct complained of.

A complaints investigator may arrange to meet with the complainant to take further details. This meeting should take place somewhere where the complainant feels comfortable. This might be at the office of the Police Ombudsman, an advice centre, a police station, a local hotel or some other suitable place. After this meeting a complainant should be told how the Police Ombudsman proposes to deal with the complaint and be given the name of the person responsible for dealing with the complaint.

A complainant should request a copy of any statement he or she makes to the Ombudsman's office and should check that the final version of any statement properly reflects what has been said. If there is anything he or she is unhappy with, a request should be made for the statement to be changed. Witnesses should similarly request a copy of their statements and ask for inaccuracies to be corrected.

At every stage of the proceedings the office should keep the complainant informed of progress and the complainant will also be provided with a written report on the decision as to whether a complaint is substantiated or not and what action (if any) is to be taken.

In *R v Chief Constable of West Midlands, ex parte Wiley* (1994) the House of Lords held that public interest immunity does not generally attach to statements obtained during a police complaint investigation. This means that, generally speaking, there is no automatic bar on the disclosure of such statements, even if the disclosure would reveal the identity of an informer, for example. The law recognises, however, that in exceptional cases, "where the Secretary of State perceives a real risk of intimidation…to persuade witnesses to change their evidence" (*R v Home Secretary, ex parte Hickey (No 2)*, 1995), there might be a reason for non-disclosure of witness statements to the complainant. At the same time, complainants do not, generally, have the right of access to statements or documents collected during the investigation into their complaint unless they can show that access to this material is "necessary for disposing fairly" of their civil claim for damages (*Lanigan, McCotter and Tumelty v Chief Constable of the RUC*, 1991).

In the English Court of Appeal case of *R (Green) v Police Complaints Authority* (2002) it was held that a complainant's legitimate interests under the European Convention of Human Rights are:

> *appropriately and adequately safeguarded by his (sic) right to a thorough and independent investigation, his right to contribute to evidence where he can, his right to be kept informed of the progress of the investigation…and his right to be given reasoned conclusions on its completion.*

This case laid down a general rule that complainants are not entitled to the disclosure of witness statements in the course of a police investigation until, at the earliest, its conclusion. The judgment did, however, refer favourably to the practice of Police Complaints Authority investigators in England of providing complainants with limited documentary evidence and an oral summary of witness evidence and the police officer's account of the incident on a confidential basis so as not to compromise any future criminal or disciplinary proceedings. At the time of writing a case taken by the Committee on the Administration of Justice against the Police Ombudsman for her refusal to release to the CAJ certain information obtained during an investigation of a complaint lodged by the CAJ is awaiting judgment.

Co-operation by the complainant

Around 60% of complaints are closed without full investigation, many (36%) because of the complainant's failure or unwillingness to co-operate with the office.

Some complainants are reluctant to co-operate because they fear that statements made by them might later be used against them by the police in related criminal or civil proceedings. The courts have held that complainants do not have the absolute right to have their statements kept secret (see *Ex parte Wiley*, 1994 at p.97 above). At present there is no legislative provision which protects statements made during formal investigations in the same way as those made during informal resolution or mediation (see below).

A complaint can be dealt with either by informal resolution or by investigation.

Informal resolution

The informal resolution process is governed by the Police (NI) Act 1998 and the RUC (Complaints) (Informal Resolution) Regulations 2000. The office of the Police Ombudsman has produced an information leaflet on informal resolution. It is currently available in English, Irish and Chinese.

The legislation provides for informal resolution of "suitable" complaints, *i.e.* where the matter is "not serious" and the complainant has consented. These will be cases where the behaviour complained of, even if proved, would not justify criminal proceedings. Such cases arise where "quality of service" is at issue – *e.g.* the behaviour is not unlawful or even manifestly unreasonable but might require an explanation or apology. In practice, complaints relating to children and vulnerable adults will not be dealt with in this way. The information leaflet from the Police Ombudsman states that a decision on whether informal resolution is appropriate will be given within three days of the complaint being lodged. At this point, the matter is handed over to the Chief Constable (or to the Policing Board in the case of senior officers) for the appointment of a police officer to carry out informal resolution procedures. The Police Ombudsman will simply monitor that this is done and receive a copy of the outcome in due course.

The police officer appointed by the Chief Constable or by the Policing Board to conduct the informal resolution procedure will seek the views of both parties, give the officer concerned an opportunity to comment orally or in writing on the complaint and try to resolve the matter to each side's satisfaction. An apology will not be forthcoming unless the officer concerned admits the behaviour which forms the substance of the complaint. A record will be made of the outcome of the procedure, and a complainant is entitled to a copy of this if he or she requests this from the Ombudsman's office within three months.

If informal resolution is successful, a complainant will be asked to sign a statement of satisfaction with the outcome. The complainant is not under any obligation to do this. If informal resolution is unsuccessful because agreement cannot be reached or it becomes apparent that the complaint is not suitable for informal resolution, the matter will be referred back to the Ombudsman. A complainant can unilaterally call a halt to informal resolution at any stage if he or she is dissatisfied with the progress being made.

No statement made by any person for the purpose of informal resolution can subsequently be used in any court or disciplinary proceedings unless it amounts to an admission of some conduct other than that which is being dealt with in the informal resolution procedure. As already mentioned, this contrasts with the rule which applies during investigations of complaints.

One of the obvious problems with the current legislative approach to informal resolution is that behaviour which might not appear serious in isolation could form part of a much more sinister pattern of harassment. Where this proves to be the case, one hopes that the matter would immediately be referred back to the Ombudsman. A complainant might also be concerned that the matter is handed back to the police instead of being dealt with by an independent arbiter. On the other hand, it can be argued that quality of service issues are much more appropriately addressed "in-house", with management learning lessons and taking responsibility for how its officers treat people on the streets. In any event, informal resolution cannot take place without the consent of the complainant. If any misgivings exist, a complainant can simply refuse to have the matter dealt with in this way.

The first annual report of the Ombudsman's office is, itself, critical of the current informal resolution procedures, deeming them "not good enough". The main concerns are that there is no requirement to mediate between officer and complainant and that officers tasked with attempting informal resolution are not trained to carry out this function. The report concludes that the current system is ineffective and needs to be replaced by a more flexible mediation system. The Police (NI) Act 2000 provides a power to mediate, but as of 31 March 2003 this had not been implemented.

Investigation

An investigation will occur where the complaint is not deemed suitable for informal resolution. If a complaint is deemed to be serious (*i.e.* involving death or serious injury) the Ombudsman *must* conduct an independent formal investigation. In other cases she can refer the matter to the Chief Constable for investigation by the police. She can continue to supervise this investigation if she deems it in the public interest to do so.

Where investigation is carried out by an investigator from the Ombudsman's office, he or she has the same powers and duties as any police officer of equivalent rank in respect of how the investigation is carried out (Sch.2 to the Police and Criminal Evidence (Application to Police Ombudsman) Order (NI) 2000). This includes the right to search, arrest and detain suspects and to use reasonable force where necessary. The office has arrested 12 police officers to date. The Police Ombudsman and her staff have a right of access to all PSNI information and documents deemed necessary for their investigation.

Investigation in the absence of a complaint

The Chief Constable must refer to the Ombudsman any matter which has resulted in death, even in the absence of complaint. Aside from this, if it appears to the Secretary of State, the Policing Board or the Chief Constable that a police officer may have committed a criminal offence or broken the police's Code of Ethics, they may refer the matter to the Police Ombudsman for her to investigate if they feel this is in the public interest. As of 31 March 2002, there had been 31 referrals by the Chief Constable. This figure has since risen to 81.

Even in the absence of a complaint or such a referral, the Police Ombudsman can herself decide, under section 55(6)(b) of the Police (NI) Act 1998, to investigate a matter formally if she has reason to think that a police officer may have committed a criminal offence or broken the Code of Conduct. This has happened 20 times. The Ombudsman has stated that she will undertake such an investigation only where her concern is serious and relates to possible criminal or disciplinary matters. On 12 December 2001, the Ombudsman presented a report on just such an investigation into matters preceding and following the Omagh bomb of 15 August 1998, in which 31 people, including two unborn children, were killed.

This investigation raised serious concerns as to how RUC Special Branch had handled information given to them prior to the bombing and how the investigation following the bombing had been hampered by the failure of Special Branch to hand over relevant information to the criminal investigation team. The report concluded, among other things that the leadership of Sir Ronnie Flanagan, then Chief Constable, was flawed. The report created enormous controversy, with the Chief Constable denouncing its findings as unfair and the investigation itself as less than rigorous. He claimed not to have been interviewed in relation to the Omagh investigation, or given a chance to respond prior to the report being published. Rather than accepting that mistakes were made and that systems were less than perfect, the Chief Constable's response attempted to deflect attention from the shortcomings of his force and to point the finger at the Ombudsman for her failure to understand how the police have to operate in the face of a terrorist threat.

The official government response to her report was far from satisfactory. While the bulk of her recommendations are now being implemented, there was initially resistance to acting on her report. A judicial review initiated by the Police Association following the report was eventually dropped in January 2003. This received little media attention so long after the original event – but resulted in a full vindication of the Ombudsman's findings in regard to Omagh.

Who investigates?

The Ombudsman's Investigations Directorate deals with all complaints made by members of the public or referred by the Secretary of State, the Policing Board or the Chief Constable. It also investigates when the Police Ombudsman decides to use her power to involve herself in an investigation even though no complaint has been made.

The Investigations Directorate is staffed by 16 complaints officers, who receive complaints and refer them on where appropriate, by around 30 investigators, who carry out all the investigations, and by a small team of professional standards officers, who deal with disciplinary matters arising from investigations.

In theory, the investigators are specially trained lay investigators. In practice, as with many such organisations throughout the world, investigators tend to be seconded or former police officers – eight of these, including the Director of Investigations, are currently from the Metropolitan Police Service in London. There are currently 17 seconded officers from around six different forces.

The Conduct Regulations lay down that, where the investigator is not from the Ombudsman's office, the investigating officer shall not be a member of the same sub-division or branch as the police officer subject to investigation. In the case of senior officers, the Chief Constable is also excluded from this role. The investigating officer must be of at least inspector rank (or Assistant Chief Constable in the case of a superintendent under investigation) and at least the same rank as the officer under investigation. The investigating officer should not have any other interest in the matter, and may come from another police force. The Ombudsman's office has to approve the investigating officer appointed.

The investigating officer must as soon as practicable (without prejudicing the investigation) give the police officer written notice of the investigation and provide a written copy of the complaint or report. He or she will be informed of his or her right to contact the staff association and to have another police officer present at any interview or hearing. The officer will be cautioned in accordance with Schedule 2 to the Conduct Regulations. This will allow an adverse inference to be drawn from silence in certain instances (see p.81).

At the end of the investigation, a written report will be furnished to the Ombudsman. The case may then be referred to a hearing. Where a case is not referred to a hearing, no mention of it will be made on the officer's personal record. This is an important safeguard in terms of unfounded allegations against an officer, but does have the potential to mask repeated complaints against an officer which, although falling short on proof of a specific incident, may indicate potential management issues around how that particular officer deals with members of the public generally.

Suspension from duty

Part II of the RUC (Conduct) (Senior Officer) Regulations 2000 deals with officers of the rank of Assistant Chief Constable and above. Part II of the RUC (Conduct) Regulations 2000 deals with suspension and investigation as regards all other officers. The Chief Constable (or Policing Board in the case of senior officers) has the power to suspend an officer where there is a report, allegation or complaint that he or she did not meet the required standard of conduct. There are further conditions, in respect of a senior officer, that the investigation would be prejudiced and that it is in the public interest that he or she be suspended. The approval of the Ombudsman is also needed for the suspension of a senior officer. At any time during an investigation, if it appears that the officer concerned did not meet the appropriate standard of behaviour, the Ombudsman's office should furnish the appropriate disciplinary authority with relevant information to allow it to consider whether the officer should be suspended. In respect of senior police officers of the rank of Assistant Chief Constable and above, the disciplinary authority is the Policing Board. For all other officers, the Chief Constable is the disciplinary authority.

Disciplinary investigation where possibility of criminal behaviour

Under the Conduct Regulations, whether or not an officer is suspended, no investigation into disciplinary matters can take place where there are outstanding criminal proceedings against the officer concerned, unless the Chief Constable considers that, in the exceptional circumstances of the case, it would be appropriate for the investigation to continue.

This means that, where there is a possibility that criminal proceedings might be recommended by the Ombudsman or commenced by the Director of Public Prosecutions (DPP), there will be no internal move to sanction the officer concerned until such criminal proceedings have come to an end. This can lead to the process being unsatisfactorily drawn out. Until relatively recently, if criminal proceedings were not initiated, under a gross misinterpretation of the "double jeopardy" rule – whereby a person cannot be tried twice for the same offence – many officers escaped any internal sanction at all. The legality of this practice was successfully challenged in England in *Ex parte Madden and Rhone* (1982) and it is now clear that each case should be considered on its own merits irrespective of the DPP's decision to prosecute or not in any given case.

Outcome of complaints

If there is no evidence to support the complainant's allegation, or for some other reason it is not substantiated (*i.e.* not proven), the complaint will not be investigated any further. The Police Ombudsman will give the complainant her reasons for this decision. This has tended to be by far the most common outcome in any system set up to investigate complaints against the police.

If the evidence shows that a police officer may have committed a crime, the Police Ombudsman will recommend to the DPP that he (or she) prosecute the officer. If the DPP decides to prosecute, the criminal proceedings will be conducted as they would be against any individual – in the magistrates' court if the offence is a fairly minor one (a *summary* offence), with the right of appeal to a county court and, if necessary to the Court of Appeal. In the case of a serious (*i.e.* indictable) offence, the case will begin in a magistrates' court prior to being transferred to the Crown Court, with a right of appeal to the Court of Appeal. Where the offence charged is one covered by anti-terrorist legislation, the officer may be tried by a judge sitting without a jury in a so-called "Diplock" court. (See also Chapter 2.)

A complainant may be called as a witness for the prosecution in any criminal trial. Aside from this, he or she will have no involvement in the process. Where the DPP decides not to initiate criminal proceedings, there is little that a complainant can do. Because the DPP is not obliged to give reasons for a decision not to prosecute (even under the new Justice (NI) Act 2002), a legal challenge, even by way of judicial review, is generally unlikely to succeed. A private prosecution is possible, but prohibitively expensive in most cases.

Under the Police (NI) Act 2000, if the investigation concludes that no criminal offence has occurred and the matter is not serious, mediation may be undertaken by the Ombudsman's office with the consent of both police officer and complainant. If mediation is not proceeded with in such circumstances, disciplinary action may be considered for recommendation. If the evidence shows that a police officer may have broken the police's Code of Conduct, the Police

Ombudsman will decide what disciplinary charges could be brought against the police officer and she will recommend disciplinary action. The conduct of the police officer in respect of attempts at mediation will be taken into account by the Ombudsman when deciding whether to recommend disciplinary action. To date, the mediation provisions have not been implemented as they are unworkable as currently drafted. The Police (NI) Act 2000 requires an investigation and an investigation report prior to mediation taking place. The Ombudsman is of the view that this defeats the purpose of mediation which should be both speedy and user-friendly. She has asked for these provisions to be amended, most recently on 19 March 2003.

If the Chief Constable does not accept the Ombudsman's recommendations regarding discipline, the Ombudsman can *direct* that he or she must do so. The problem with this, of course, is that, for all officers under the rank of Assistant Chief Constable, it will be the police who carry out the disciplinary proceedings and prosecute any disciplinary hearing. It cannot be ruled out that the Chief Constable's reluctance to institute such proceedings in the first place may have some influence on the final outcome.

If disciplinary charges are not preferred, a complainant can write to the Ombudsman's office requesting further explanation.

Disciplinary charges

The PSNI Code of Ethics sets out under a number of headings what is expected of a police officer in the performance of his or her duty. It can be accessed on the Policing Board's website: *www.nipolicingboard.org.uk.* Where the appropriate standard is not met under any of these headings, an officer may be subject to disciplinary action. The Code has detailed provisions organised under the following headings:

- professional duty,
- police investigations,
- privacy and confidentiality,
- use of force,
- detained persons,
- equality,
- integrity,
- property,
- fitness for duty,
- duty of supervisors.

Disciplinary hearing

If an officer accepts that his or her behaviour did not meet the appropriate standard, a sanction may be imposed without a hearing. Otherwise a disciplinary hearing may take place in accordance with the procedures outlined below. These are provided for by the Conduct Regulations and are also followed in respect of internal disciplinary matters, where a complaint has not been lodged by a member of the public. The standard of proof employed in disciplinary proceedings has historically been the criminal standard of "beyond reasonable doubt". The Hayes Report recommended that this be dispensed with in favour of a sliding scale depending on the seriousness of the behaviour alleged. The legislation establishing the Ombudsman's office was silent on this point, but the "balance of probabilities" standard has now been enshrined in regulations.

For officers below the rank of Assistant Chief Constable, the disciplinary panel consists of three police officers with an Assistant Chief Constable presiding. An officer must be given 28 days' written notice of a disciplinary hearing, and supplied with copies of any relevant statements, documents or other material obtained by the investigating officer. If there is a possibility that the officer could be dismissed, required to resign or demoted, the police officer may be legally represented. Otherwise he or she will be represented by another police officer. A verbatim record of the proceedings will be made. A complainant may attend any disciplinary hearing with a relative or friend. If called as a witness, he or she cannot attend the proceedings prior to giving evidence and may have to withdraw if sensitive material is to be presented to the panel which it is deemed the complainant should not hear. The complainant will then be subject to cross-examination. Other than this the hearing will be in private, although an authorised representative of the Ombudsman's office may be present. Adverse inferences may be drawn from the officer's silence in certain circumstances. The following sanctions may be imposed by the disciplinary panel:

- dismissal from the force,
- a requirement to resign from the force as an alternative to dismissal, taking effect one month from the date of the decision,
- a reduction in rank,
- a reduction in pay for such a period, not exceeding 12 months, as shall be specified in the decision,

- a fine of a sum representing not more than 13 days' pay recoverable over a minimum of 13 weeks,
- a reprimand, and
- a caution.

Under Part IV of the Regulations, an officer may request that the Chief Constable review the panel's decision.

In respect of senior officers, the disciplinary panel will consist of one person appointed by the Policing Board from a list nominated by the Secretary of State and one or more assessors, one of whom will be a former chief officer of police, will be appointed to assist this person. The case against the senior officer will be conducted by an independent solicitor and the senior officer may conduct the case in person or through a representative. Most of the procedures in respect of the attendance of the complainant are similar to those outlined above. In "special" cases of a serious nature, where an imprisonable offence may have been committed, the procedures may be modified in accordance with the Regulations.

Whether the officer is or is not a senior officer, the panel must find that the officer did not meet the appropriate standard if this is admitted by the officer or proved on the balance of probabilities. In the case of a non-senior officer, the panel will submit a copy of its report to the Chief Constable with (in the case of a complaint) a copy sent to the Ombudsman. The Chief Constable can record a finding of failure to meet the appropriate standard and either impose a sanction or take no further action. In the case of a senior officer, the disciplinary panel will submit a copy of its report to the Policing Board, again with a copy to the Police Ombudsman if the case has arisen out of a complaint. The sanctions for senior officers are dismissal, requirement to resign or reprimand.

Disciplinary appeals

An officer can appeal against a disciplinary sanction within 21 days. In the case of a senior officer (ACC and above), the Secretary of State appoints a panel of three, comprising one member of the Policing Board, one senior police officer and one legally-qualified presiding officer. For all other officers there will be a four-member panel, appointed by the Policing Board. This will include one member of the Policing Board, one legally qualified person to preside over proceedings, one senior police officer and one retired police officer.

The Appeals Regulations govern procedure and provide that the complainant can attend and may be allowed a friend or relative in view of age or other vulnerability. If giving evidence, attendance will not be allowed before the complainant gives evidence and the complainant may have to withdraw if sensitive material is to be put before the appeal panel. The appeal may be allowed, dismissed or a less severe punishment imposed. As far as is known, no complaint has ever been substantiated against a senior member of the RUC or PSNI.

Compensation

In a departure from the previous system, whereby a complainant had to initiate separate legal proceedings in a county court or the High Court, even where his or her complaint had been upheld, if a complaint is substantiated, the Ombudsman now has the power to recommend compensation. This does not affect a person's right to issue civil proceedings, but in the past it has often proved difficult to convince a judge that police maltreatment has occurred even though cases for assault, unlawful arrest and over-holding etc. have to be proved only on the balance of probabilities. Although several people have succeeded in obtaining compensation for such wrongs, generally such cases have been settled out of court with no admission of liability on the part of the police.

Research

The Ombudsman's office is required by law to supply statistical information regarding all complaints being handled. A small policy and research office reports monthly to the police in this regard and is currently developing a programme of analysing and profiling complaints and allegations made, together with other relevant data. It is hoped that this information will allow police managers to deal more effectively with conduct and practice issues which arise. The Policy and Research Directorate also carries out specific pieces of research and prepares policy papers on the work of the police and the Police Ombudsman's office as well as providing an information service for the public and a press and media service. The research department has also organised seminars with input from visiting speakers and is in the process of preparing a major international conference.

However, although the legislation also provides that the Police Ombudsman may monitor complaints against the police and check whether there are trends or patterns in police complaints, it stops short of according this function the status it requires to ensure that such trends and patterns are acted upon. This will change when the Police (NI) Act 2003 comes fully into effect, provided sufficient resources are allocated to this function. Section 13 inserts a new section 60A into the Police (NI) Act 1998, which allows the Police Ombudsman to investigate a current PSNI policy or practice if she believes this would be in the public interest. In the meantime the Ombudsman's office does what it can to alert the Chief Constable or relevant Assistant Chief Constable to trends and patterns and can point to Force Orders and policing practice already changed as result of its work.

Reports

The Police Ombudsman produces an annual report referring to the complaints she has dealt with during the previous year. She can also write a report on anything she thinks the Secretary of State should know about, in the public interest. In addition, the Secretary of State can ask the Police Ombudsman to carry out any necessary research and report on any matter. Any report that the Police Ombudsman makes to the Secretary of State under this power must also go before Parliament and be published. The Police Ombudsman must also send a copy of any report she makes to the Chief Constable and to the Policing Board and she must supply the Policing Board with any statistics which she thinks it should receive.

The Omagh report was presented to the Secretary of State under Regulation 20 of the RUC (Complaints) Regulations 2000. It is up to the Secretary of State to decide whether to publish any such report or not. The Ombudsman's statement in relation to this investigation was published under section 62 of the Police (NI) Act 1998.

Complaints against the Police Ombudsman

If there is a problem with how the Police Ombudsman has handled your complaint, you can further complain either directly to the Ombudsman's office or to the Secretary of State (Northern Ireland Office, Castle Buildings, Stormont, Belfast BT4 3SG).

Judicial review of decisions is also possible in limited circumstances. The judicial review applications made to date include that of the Police Association in connection with the Omagh report (withdrawn in January 2003) and that of the CAJ in connection with the police investigation into death threats received by Rosemary Nelson prior to her murder in 1999.

Powers of the Northern Ireland Policing Board

There is not scope within this chapter to look in detail at the powers and potential of the Northern Ireland Policing Board, which replaced the former Police Authority for Northern Ireland in November 2001. In respect of complaints and accountability generally, however, it is worth pointing out that the Board is designed to hold the Chief Constable to account. The Policing Board also remains the disciplinary authority responsible for the conduct of senior officers.

Under the Police (NI) Act 2000, the Policing Board can ask the Chief Constable for reports on any area of the activities of the Police Service. If not satisfied, the Board can begin an inquiry into the matter in question. Although the Chief Constable can appeal to the Secretary of State for permission to refuse to provide a report or to conduct an inquiry, the Chief Constable can do this only on very specific grounds and within a restricted timescale.

Other fora

District Policing Partnerships have recently been set up at a more local level. These should also provide a forum for concerns to be aired. They have, however, purely consultation status.

A further channel to raise policing concerns is provided in the shape of Community Police Liaison Committees (CPLCs) and Community Safety Partnerships in certain areas. The CPLCs have powers of their own but the Community Safety Partnerships have recently been awarded funds from the Northern Ireland Office to spend on a range of community safety initiatives, e.g. better street lighting at local level.

Chapter 6

Prisoners' Rights

Stephen Livingstone

Northern Ireland currently has three prison establishments. These are at Maghaberry (male and female prisons), Magilligan and Hydebank young offenders centre. As at 24 February 2003 the prison population was 1,085 (of which 1,068 were men and 17 women). Of these:

- 347 were on remand;
- 161 were young offenders;
- four were immigration detainees; and
- all women prisoners and immigration detainees were held at Maghaberry.

Prisons in Northern Ireland are under the authority of the Secretary of State, who appoints the governors, medical officers and all other officers. Since 1995 the Northern Ireland Prison Service has been an executive agency headed by a Director who has responsibility for "operational" matters. The Director reports to the Secretary of State, who in turn makes an annual report to Parliament on the working of the Prison Service. For each prison the Secretary of State must also appoint a Board of Visitors from members of the public. These Boards have two functions:

- to inspect the prison regularly and make an annual report to the Secretary of State; and
- to hear prisoners' complaints.

Legal rights of prisoners

In 1982, in the House of Lords case of *Raymond v Honey*, Lord Wilberforce said:

Under English law a convicted prisoner, in spite of his (sic) imprisonment, retains all civil rights which are not taken away expressly or by necessary implication.

This was certainly a great advance on earlier pronouncements, some of which had stated that the courts would not hear the claims of "disgruntled" prisoners. But it still left prison law in a state of uncertainty because in the absence of a Bill of Rights or written constitution it is not clear what "civil rights" *any* of us have. It is also unclear what rights are removed by "necessary implication". The introduction of the Human Rights Act 1998 has reduced some of this uncertainty. The European Court of Human Rights has long made clear that the European Convention on Human Rights applies to the circumstances of prisoners, and indeed some of the most significant cases to be decided by the Strasbourg Court relate to the circumstances of people in detention. However the Convention only sets out broad statements of rights and the European Court has made it clear that, where these are subject to limitation, the limitations may be more extensive in respect of those in prison than those at liberty.

Perhaps the first place to look for a more detailed indication of what rights and duties prisoners have is the Prison and Young Offenders Centre Rules (NI). These were extensively overhauled in 1995 and have been subject to further amendment in 1997, 2000 and 2001. These Rules relate to a wide range of matters such as letters, visits, medical treatment, food, religion and discipline. On entry to a prison a prisoner should be given information about these rules and may consult the rules at any reasonable time (rule 23). Families can obtain a copy of them from the Stationery Office. The rules, however, are very vague on many points and are normally amplified by Standing Orders issued by the Northern Ireland Office. Several of these have now been published.

The vagueness of the rules, and the secrecy which surrounds Standing Orders, obviously limits their usefulness as a source of prisoners' rights. Another limitation is the fact that courts have held on a number of occasions that a breach of the rules by the authorities does not of itself give a prisoner a right to sue. Advocates of prisoners' rights have consistently criticised this position and called for a legally enforceable code of rights.

Courts have nevertheless held that they will look at the Prison Rules when deciding whether a right asserted by a prisoner, such as to a fair hearing in a disciplinary procedure, or to privacy as regards correspondence, has been breached. Therefore a prisoner who feels that the authorities have done something that they have no right to do, or have prevented the prisoner from doing something that he or she has a right to do, might look at the Prison Rules when framing a legal claim. The 1995 Rules also contain (in rule 2) a set of general principles to guide their interpretation. Although the legal status of these principles is unclear, several of them (such as the requirements that all prisoners are treated equally and that reasons are given when a decision affects a prisoner) may be relevant to determining a prisoner's rights under the rules where a dispute arises. A claim might take one of a number of forms, *e.g.*:

- that the rules have nothing to say on the issue, *e.g.* where a prisoner is injured by another prisoner and claims compensation from the prison authorities;
- that the rules do cover the issue but are being interpreted wrongly, *e.g.* where the authorities claim that the rule entitling a prisoner to a fair disciplinary hearing does not entitle him or her to call a witness; or
- that the rules are themselves invalid because they contravene the Prison Act (NI) 1953 or the Human Rights Act 1998, *e.g.* where the authorities claim that they can intercept all correspondence with lawyers.

Asserting prisoners' legal rights is not therefore a simple business, as it may require reference to private law, public law or European law. In addition, nearly all cases will involve claims by the authorities that the right asserted must be denied on security grounds. Prisoners who feel that their rights have been infringed are thus well advised to seek legal advice, a topic discussed later in this chapter.

Rights automatically lost on conviction

Things have changed from the days when conviction for a felony automatically led to a prisoner forfeiting all his or her property. By section 9(1) of Criminal Justice Act (NI) 1953, legal restrictions on the property of convicted prisoners were abolished. Currently the most important rights lost by convicted prisoners are public rights:

- they are disqualified from voting in Westminster elections during the period of their imprisonment;
- they are disqualified from becoming members of the House of Commons if they are serving a sentence of a year or more in prison; this does not apply to prisoners on remand, who remain entitled to vote or stand for election at all times;
- there appear to be no express disqualifications from either voting or standing at local elections, but electoral law relating to proxy and

postal voting disables prisoners from casting votes they may be entitled to;

- any person sentenced to five years or more in prison or to detention at the Secretary of State's pleasure is permanently disqualified from jury service; and
- any person who serves a sentence of three months or more is thereafter disqualified from jury service for 10 years.

Internal grievance procedures

For a variety of reasons a prisoner may wish to complain about prison conditions or prison authorities' actions without resorting to legal proceedings. If so, he or she may wish to use the internal complaints procedure. This is an alternative procedure: there is no obligation to pursue a grievance internally before taking legal action.

Any prisoner with a grievance can request to see the governor, a member of the Board of Visitors or an officer of the Secretary of State. This request must be noted and reported to the governor as soon as possible (rule 74). The governor must see prisoners who have made such requests at a convenient hour every day, except at the weekends and on public holidays. Where a prisoner is not satisfied by the decision reached by the governor he or she may appeal this to the Secretary of State. Indeed all complaints about adjudications must be made to the Secretary of State. When members of the Board of Visitors or officers of the Secretary of State visit the prison, they must be told of any requests to see them and Board members must see any prisoner who has made such a request. A prisoner may also submit a written complaint in confidence to the prison governor under rule 78 or to the Secretary of State under rule 79. Although there is no clear indication in the Prison Rules or Standing Orders as to whether and how quickly a reply must be given to a prisoner's complaint, the prison service has indicated that, where possible, written complaints should be replied to within 15 days.

A prisoner may also wish to write to an MP, an MEP or the UK Ombudsman (the Northern Ireland Ombudsman's jurisdiction does not include prisons). Although complaints can, as noted above, be made in confidence where they allege misconduct by a specific member of prison staff, they will be disclosed to that member of staff in order for a full investigation to take place.

Since 1995 prisoners in England and Wales have been able to complain to a specific Prisons Ombudsman but the remit of this

Ombudsman does not extend to Northern Ireland and no similar institution exists in Northern Ireland. In England and Wales the Secretary of State must also appoint an Inspector of Prisons to investigate conditions and report to the Secretary of State. The Inspector's remit does extend to Northern Ireland. In 2002 the Inspector published a report on Hydebank young offenders centre and in February 2003 another was published on Maghaberry Prison.

Security classifications

All prisoners in Northern Ireland are classified into one of four security classifications. These are:

- Top Risk – prisoners whose escape would be extremely dangerous to the public, to the security forces or to the security of the state;
- High Risk – prisoners whose escape would be highly dangerous to the public, to the security forces or to the security of the state;
- Medium Risk – prisoners for whom escape must be made very difficult; or
- Low Risk – prisoners who do not have the motivation, ability or resources to make a determined effort to escape.

Currently there are no prisoners in the top risk category. In addition to the above, first offenders are classified as "star" prisoners, although this is a classification of diminishing importance as first time prisoners are increasingly integrated into the ordinary regime. Since the decision of the English Court of Appeal in *Ex parte Duggan* (1994) it would appear that the higher the security classification of a prisoner the greater his or her right to make representations and be given the gist of the reasons on which that classification was based.

Access to legal advice

The European Court of Human Rights has recognised that a prisoner's access to justice under Article 6 of the European Convention on Human Rights includes access to lawyers. A prisoner may therefore write to a legal adviser with a view to taking legal proceedings over any matter. Where this concerns an allegation of ill-treatment against a prison officer or the prison authorities, such a letter cannot be stopped on the grounds that the complaint has not been raised through normal channels. A prisoner may also write directly to the courts about a complaint and such a letter cannot be stopped.

When a prisoner writes to a lawyer in connection with any legal business this correspondence may not be read or stopped unless the governor has reason to believe it contains material which is not relevant to the legal business (rule 72(4)). Prison authorities are also required to provide reasonable facilities for lawyers to discuss pending proceedings with prisoners. A prisoner need give only 24 hours' notice that he or she wishes to discuss proceedings with a legal adviser and need only disclose that such a meeting relates to such proceedings.

Standing Orders indicate that all legal visits should be in the sight but not the hearing of a prison officer and rule 71(1) requires this where the prisoner is a party to legal proceedings (*i.e.* when a writ has been issued). Prisoners who are party to proceedings may also be examined by a doctor of their own choice in the sight but out of the hearing of a prison officer (rule 72 (5)).

The right to correspond and to read

Prisoners have a right to correspond with:
- their close relatives,
- their MP and MEP,
- the Ombudsman, and
- the European Court of Human Rights.

A prisoner can write to any other person or organisation but the governor may stop any letter where he or she thinks that such correspondence would constitute a genuine and serious threat to the security or good order of the prison.

A prisoner on remand has the right to send and receive as many letters as he or she wishes. Convicted prisoners may send and receive one letter after entering prison and thereafter one "statutory" letter a week. Postage on this letter will be paid for out of public funds and statutory letters cannot be withdrawn or withheld as a punishment. A prisoner can also send one extra letter a week on which the postage is paid at public expense. Subject to the discretion of the governor, a prisoner can write additional extra letters. Postage on these will normally be at the prisoner's expense but in a case of need a prisoner can apply to the governor to have these paid for out of public funds. The number of letters allowed in practice varies from prison to prison.

All letters to and from a prisoner (except those relating to legal proceedings) can be read by the prison authorities and may be stopped if a governor is of the opinion that they may offend a number of grounds, primarily drawn from Articles 8(2) and 10(2) of the European Convention on Human Rights. These include national and prison security, public safety and endangering good order and discipline in the prison. Governors are required to ensure that they have regard to whether the restriction imposed is proportionate to the prisoners' rights of privacy and free expression. Further guidance on when letters may be read or stopped can be found in Standing Order 5.3.3. The main grounds are that the letter contains:

- material relating to an escape;
- threats of violence to someone inside or outside the jail;
- coded messages;
- specific allegations of ill-treatment not previously raised with the governor, Board of Visitors or the Secretary of State (although complaints or comments about prison conditions should not be stopped); or
- material intended for publication for payment.

Where a letter is stopped, a prisoner should be told and given an opportunity to re-write it. Prisoners have the ability to make telephone calls, although these are subject to monitoring. Mobile phones are not permitted.

Books, newspapers and periodicals are all regarded as privileges. However, it is clearly arguable that denying a prisoner access to a particular document violates his or her right to receive information, as guaranteed by Article 10 of the European Convention on Human Rights, unless justified under the qualifications in Article 10(2) (see Chapter 10). According to Standing Order 4, prisoners can receive newspapers or periodicals from visitors or can order them by subscription directly from a newsagent or publisher. Subscriptions must cover a period of not less than two weeks for newspapers and not less than three months for periodicals. As the entitlement to newspapers and periodicals is regarded as a privilege, Standing Order 4 indicates that they may be removed as a punishment or if the governor feels that the content of the newspaper or periodical could prejudice the security, good order or discipline of the prison, could put at risk the lives of prison staff, is wholly or mostly in a language other than English or Irish (except where the prisoner is wholly unfamiliar with English) or in the medical officer's opinion could have an adverse affect on the prisoner from a medical or psychological point of view. A prisoner may obtain soft-backed books either from a friend or relative or directly from a newsagent or publisher, but he or she will not normally be allowed to retain more than six books in a cell in addition to a Bible, library books, a dictionary and approved texts issued by the prison education officer. Books are regarded as privileges and Standing Order 4 indicates that they may be removed on the same conditions as newspapers and periodicals.

Visits

Convicted prisoners are entitled to one statutory and three "privilege" visits per month. Remand prisoners are entitled to as many visits as they wish, but in practice they are normally allowed three per week. Visits usually last for 30 minutes. Where a prisoner is sentenced to solitary confinement as a punishment, the statutory visit should still be allowed unless the governor feels that the prisoner's behaviour and attitude are such that removal from solitary confinement would be undesirable or impracticable. If this happens the statutory visit should be postponed and a prisoner should receive all the missed statutory visits at the end of the period of solitary confinement.

Prisoners may receive visits from close relatives and any other person, subject to the Secretary of State's and governor's discretion. In *McCartney v Secretary of State for Northern Ireland* (1987), the courts upheld the Secretary of State's decision to prevent a Sinn Féin councillor from visiting a friend in prison on the basis of evidence of Sinn Féin's support for violence. A prisoner must give the name and address of each adult person whom he or she wishes to have as a visitor and must be informed if any application for a visiting permit is refused. Visits between close relatives where both are in prison will be permitted provided this does not pose a threat to the security or good order of the prison.

Up to three people will normally be allowed to visit a prisoner at each visit. Visits should take place with visitors seated at a table and will be in the sight of a prison officer, but for domestic visits they should be outside the hearing of a prison officer. Visits can be stopped if a visitor attempts to pass any unauthorised article to a prisoner and visitors cannot carry recording equipment, cameras or videos; they can make notes during a visit but these can be taken out of the prison only with the permission of the governor or of the prison officer instructed by the governor to decide upon such matters.

Clothes and food

Both remand and convicted prisoners are entitled to wear their own clothes. The governor may, however, prohibit the wearing of certain clothing if this is judged to be prejudicial to the good order or security of the prison. Limits on the amount of clothing a prisoner can possess are set by each prison, but generally prisoners are allowed up to three of each item of clothing. Clothes can be left for a prisoner as part of a parcel. Convicted prisoners are generally allowed one parcel every four weeks while remand prisoners can receive a parcel every fortnight. Parcels are restricted to clothing, footwear and musical instruments. Governors have a discretion in special circumstances to permit other items.

Prisoners on remand can be supplied with food at their own, friends' or relatives' expense. All prisoners should be provided with prison food which is wholesome, nutritious and well prepared (rule 82(1)). Prisoners with special dietary requirements should inform the prison medical officer, who is required to inspect prison food regularly. Standing Order 14 instructs governors to observe the relevant provisions of food and drugs laws.

Education

Educational classes have to be established at every prison and the prison authorities are required to encourage every prisoner able to profit from educational activities to do so. The prison authorities are also required to provide facilities for private study of correspondence courses, although the Secretary of State has power to determine what books and papers may be received from outside.

Religion

Where a prisoner belongs to a denomination for which no chaplain has been appointed to that prison, the governor is required to do what is reasonable, if requested by the prisoner, to arrange for visits by a minister or priest of that denomination.

A prisoner may also be allowed an occasional visit by a family priest or minister, or by the priest or minister of the area where he or she last resided. Such visits do not require a permit and should take place either in the sight but out of the hearing of a prison officer or in the presence of a prison chaplain.

Medical treatment and hygiene

A prisoner who feels unwell should be allowed to see the prison medical officer. Where the medical officer feels a prisoner's health is endangered by imprisonment, he or she should inform the governor and Chief Medical Officer. A prisoner can refuse any medical treatment unless it is an emergency and must give written consent before any major form of treatment is begun. Time spent in hospital counts as part of a prisoner's sentence.

The Prison Rules also contain a number of provisions relating to general hygiene, *e.g.* requiring every prisoner to have a hot bath or shower once a week and placing a duty on the prison authorities to provide prisoners with toilet articles necessary for health and cleanliness. Standing Orders instruct governors to observe the provisions of the Health and Safety at Work (NI) Order 1978 with regard to washing and bathing facilities.

Prisoners are entitled to one hour's outdoor exercise a day (weather permitting; if the weather is bad the exercise can be taken indoors). Prisoners segregated for punishment retain normal exercise privileges.

In law the Northern Ireland Office owes a "duty of care" to protect prisoners from injury. Therefore, if a prisoner is injured, *e.g.* while working, or as the result of an assault by another prisoner or a prison officer, he or she may be able to claim compensation from prison authorities.

Searches

Prisoners and their visitors can be searched by the prison authorities. Searches may be carried out at such times as the governor orders but must take place according to the directions of the Secretary of State (rule 16). The courts have ruled that there is no requirement to give reasons for a search. Where a prisoner is required to undress for a search it can be conducted only by and in the presence of officers of the same sex as the prisoner and must be conducted in as seemly a manner as is consistent with anything being discovered. Full or strip searches should be conducted only on reception, after contact with someone outside a prison or where the governor has grounds to believe that a prisoner is in possession of an unauthorised article which cannot be discovered by other means. The rules do not permit body cavity searches but a prisoner may be required to open his or her mouth for visual inspection (rule 16(8)). Searches should be conducted only on arrival, final departure or after the prisoner has left the prison and returned for whatever reason (such as to make a court appearance, go to hospital or visit a prisoner in another jail), although the governor has power to order a search on other occasions. Searches carried out in a way which violates these guidelines could constitute an assault.

Removal from association

The governor may segregate a prisoner from other prisoners where he or she feels it is in the prisoner's own interests or where it is desirable to maintain good order and discipline in the prison. Cases have suggested that failure to segregate some prisoners, such as known sex offenders, may breach the authorities' duty of care if they have no other policy for reducing risk to the prisoner and that prisoner is subsequently assaulted. However, a governor may not segregate a prisoner for more than 48 hours without the authority of a member of the Board of Visitors or the Secretary of State (rule 32(2)). If such authority is given, the position must be reviewed every month. Prisoners in segregation must be visited every day by the medical officer and if he or she so advises the governor must return a prisoner to association.

This type of individual segregation for security reasons is different from a policy of segregating prisoners from different religions or factions. Such a policy seems neither to be prohibited nor required by law. At present it does not officially occur in any Northern Ireland prison.

Women prisoners

Because the number of women prisoners in Northern Ireland's jails is declining (down from 75 in 1977 to 17 in 2003) and makes up a very small proportion (only about 2%) of the total prison population, their legal position is often ignored. Such small numbers may have a detrimental effect on women prisoners' access to work and education programmes. Failure to accord work and education facilities equal to those given to men may amount to unlawful sex discrimination.

In general, Prison Rules and Standing Orders apply equally to women as to men, but there are some differences. Rule 91(1) indicates that in matters of work, education, recreation or privileges governors may provide a different regime for female prisoners. However rule

91(2) indicates that this does not permit discrimination which would be unlawful if it occurred outside prisons.

The most significant difference relates to pregnancy and young children. Under rule 92(1), prisoners expected to give birth before the end of their sentence should be removed from the prison to a suitable hospital for whatever period the medical officer considers necessary. A mother and baby unit exists at Maghaberry Prison and prisoners may keep their babies with them in the unit until the baby is nine months old. But the courts have upheld a governor's discretion to remove a baby from the mother's custody, without giving her a hearing, where he or she considers it necessary for the welfare of the child or the good order of the prison.

Discipline

Prisoners may be subject to disciplinary punishment only for a limited and specific number of offences. These offences have a definable content and convictions on disciplinary charges may be challenged if a governor has misinterpreted the rule setting out an offence.

A prisoner should be given notice of the charges as soon as possible. The governor must normally inquire into the charge on the next day and at that inquiry give the prisoner a fuller account of what is alleged (rule 36). A prisoner must be given sufficient time to prepare a defence; if he or she feels that the time allowed was insufficient, an adjournment should be asked for at any subsequent hearing.

Unless the charge is thought so serious as to amount to a criminal offence and the police are called to investigate, the charge will be heard by a prison governor or assistant governor, who, if he or she finds the prisoner guilty, may impose a range of punishments including loss of up to 28 days' remission, loss of privileges for up to 28 days or solitary confinement for up to three days (rule 39(1)). The role of governors in disciplinary proceedings is currently under review as a result of the English case of *Ezeh and Connors v UK* (2002), where the European Court of Human Rights indicated that it would be a breach of Article 6 of the European Convention for a governor to lengthen a prisoner's sentence by imposing a penalty of added days or loss of remission. Since that decision in July 2002 governors have been instructed not to use the penalty of loss of remission in Northern Ireland. The *Ezeh and Connors* case is currently on appeal to the Grand Chamber of the Court.

If it upholds the earlier decision one would expect that some change will be made to the Northern Irish Prison Rules in this area.

Where a case comes before a governor, a prisoner is entitled to a fair hearing and to put his or her own case fully (rule 36(4)). He or she should be allowed to see all the statements made in the case, to call witnesses (except where these are called only to disrupt the proceedings), and to cross-examine witnesses who have given evidence (especially where hearsay evidence has been given, or there are inconsistencies in the evidence).

A prisoner can also ask for legal representation. Generally governors have been reluctant to grant this but they must consider carefully a number of factors (in particular the seriousness of the offence, whether any difficult points of law are involved and the prisoner's capacity to conduct his or her own defence) before deciding whether or not the prisoner should be legally represented. Court decisions have indicated that, if a governor unreasonably refuses representation, this may be a reason for overturning a disciplinary conviction. The European Court of Human Rights has indicated that legal representation will be required where the prisoner faces a potential penalty of loss of remission, although, as noted above, governors are currently indicating that they will not employ this penalty. If representation is granted, a prisoner will be entitled to free legal advice and assistance.

In deciding whether a prisoner is guilty, a governor must seek proof "beyond all reasonable doubt". A number of cases have come before the Northern Irish courts on the application of this standard to cases where an offence has been committed but is denied by two prisoners who share a cell. The courts appear to have ruled that the governor can convict both prisoners if there is evidence of collusion, *e.g.* an organised protest campaign, but may not do so where no such evidence exists. If a governor finds the standard of proof is not satisfied on a serious charge, he or she may not substitute a conviction on a less serious one. Any punishment given must be clearly set out in the decision of the governor; it cannot be added to by a subsequent action of the governor. In a recent case, for instance, it was held that a governor could not remove a prisoner's bedding while the prisoner was serving a disciplinary punishment in solitary confinement: removal of bedding was in effect an extra punishment which had not been awarded in the disciplinary proceedings.

If a prisoner feels that any of the above requirements have not been met and that he or she has been denied a fair hearing, he or she may seek to have the conviction quashed, although failure to comply with a procedural requirement does not automatically ensure that a conviction *will* be quashed on judicial review (see Chapter 2). Courts have generally refused to quash decisions by governors despite procedural errors where they feel the same result would have been arrived at even if the right procedure had been followed.

A prisoner may also petition the Secretary of State to quash or mitigate a disciplinary conviction where he or she feels that the conviction was unfair or the punishment too severe. The Secretary of State also has the power to review disciplinary convictions or punishments of his or her own volition (rules 44-45).

Early release under the Northern Ireland (Sentences) Act 1998

This legislation established a mechanism for the early release of a particular class of prisoners. Those included were prisoners convicted of scheduled offences and sentenced to between five years and life, who were not supporters of one of a range of terrorist organisations specified by the Secretary of State. The Act provided for prisoners to be eligible for release within a certain period of time after being sentenced and for all such prisoners to be eligible for release within two years of its coming into force. Once a prisoner was eligible for release his or her case was considered by persons known as the Sentence Review Commissioners, appointed by the Secretary of State. The Commissioners ordered release unless they were of the opinion that the prisoner would become involved in acts of terrorism or (in the case of a life sentence prisoner) that he or she would become a danger to the public.

All prisoners released were released on licence but each of them is subject to recall by the Secretary of State if he or she believes the prisoner has or is likely to break the licence conditions. Any recalls must be referred by the Secretary of State to the Sentence Review Commissioners for review.

Life sentence prisoners

Given the high proportion of Northern Ireland's prisoners serving life sentences (over 80 currently), the release procedures for such prisoners are of particular importance. Although there is provision for judges to recommend that prisoners should remain in jail for the rest of their lives, this power is very rarely used and nearly all prisoners sentenced to life are released after a number of years.

Life imprisonment is the mandatory sentence for the offence of murder, and is the maximum sentence available for a range of other crimes including attempted murder, manslaughter, causing an explosion and the most serious firearms and sexual offences. Those convicted of murder who were under 18 at the date of the commission of the crime can be sentenced to detention "at the Secretary of State's pleasure", and are commonly known as "SOSP" or "pleasure" prisoners.

Recently decisions on the release of all life sentence prisoners, apart from those governed by the early release procedure, have been placed in the hands of the Life Sentence Review Commission established by the Life Sentences (NI) Order 2001. Whenever someone is sentenced to life, the sentencing judge will normally make a recommendation (known as a "tariff") as to how long the prisoner should serve for the purposes of retribution and deterrence. In exceptional cases the judge can indicate the offence is so serious that no tariff should be set. Transitional provisions exist for prisoners sentenced before the 2001 Order came into force to have a tariff set by the Secretary of State after consultation with the Lord Chief Justice and trial judge, if available.

Once the tariff has expired the prisoner's case is considered by the Life Sentence Review Commission. This body consists of a range of people including lawyers, doctors and people "with knowledge and experience of the supervision or aftercare of discharged prisoners". The Commission should direct the prisoner's release if "it is satisfied that it is no longer necessary for the protection of the public from serious harm that the prisoner should be confined". In reaching its decision the Commission will hold a hearing in private and may take evidence from a range of people including the prisoner, the police and the Northern Ireland Office. The relevant rules provide for the Secretary of State to certify that certain evidence should not be disclosed to the prisoner and that the prisoner may be excluded from parts of the proceedings, provisions which may yet fall foul of the Human Rights Act 1998.

If a prisoner is refused release he or she should be reconsidered within two years (a period of time which may be too long to conform with Art.5(4) of the European Convention). All prisoners who are released are released on licence and may be subject to recall by the Secretary of State where it appears expedient in the public interest. After a prisoner has been recalled the Secretary of State must refer the decision to the Commission for ratification.

Transfer of prisoners

Where prisoners who originally come from Northern Ireland are imprisoned in Great Britain they may apply to be transferred to Northern Ireland. They have no legal right to transfer and the former European Commission of Human Rights stated that only in "exceptional circumstances" will failure to transfer breach the right to privacy and family life contained in the European Convention on Human Rights. Nevertheless there does exist a power to transfer prisoners between the rest of the United Kingdom and Northern Ireland in the Crime (Sentences) Act 1997.

The authorities must consider all transfer requests and they have indicated that they will grant them where the prisoner is sentenced and:

- has more than six months of his or her sentence still to serve;
- was ordinarily resident in Northern Ireland before imprisonment or has close relatives in Northern Ireland and it is reasonably believed that he or she has a firm intention of taking up residence there on release; and
- has no outstanding appeals or other criminal proceedings pending.

Transfer may take place on either a "restricted" or "unrestricted" basis. If the former applies the sending jurisdiction will continue to administer some aspects of release; if the latter applies the prisoner will be treated as though he or she had been sentenced in that jurisdiction. This is especially significant given that release arrangements in Northern Ireland generally grant greater remission of sentence than applies in other parts of the United Kingdom (one half rather than one third). Prisoners on restricted transfer can be returned if the Secretary of State is of the view that the purposes of the transfer are no longer being fulfilled. However, even prisoners on restricted transfer to Northern Ireland can apply for home leave and temporary release on the same basis as prisoners sentenced here.

The position of ex-prisoners

A prison sentence can continue to have a legal effect on someone even after he or she has left prison. Under the Rehabilitation of Offenders (NI) Order 1978 a person can be dismissed or a job offer withdrawn if he or she fails to provide information, when asked, about previous criminal convictions. However, there is no obligation to declare a conviction if the employer does not ask about previous convictions. There is also no obligation to declare a conviction and sentence if it has become "spent" under the terms of the 1978 Order. The Order contains a complex set of rules for determining when convictions are spent, especially in relation to those with several criminal convictions, and anyone applying for a job with a criminal record would be wise to seek advice on their application. Some basic guidelines, however, are as follows:

- a prison sentence, including a suspended sentence, of more than two-and-a-half years is never spent;
- a prison sentence of between six months and two-and-a-half years is spent only after 10 years where someone was over 17 at the time of the conviction (five years if under 18);
- a prison sentence of less than six months is spent after seven years (three-and-a-half if under 18 when convicted); and
- shorter time periods apply to those who were sentenced to a fine, community service, probation or received an absolute discharge.

Some forms of employment are deemed to be "excepted" and when applying for these a person with a criminal record is required to declare his or her convictions even if they are spent. These jobs include:

- jobs (including voluntary posts) which give substantial access to people under 18;
- certain professions (*e.g.* lawyers, doctors, nurses and accountants);
- certain occupations which are regulated by law (*e.g.* managers of insurance companies or nursing home owners); and
- appointments where national security may be at risk (*e.g.* some civil service posts, the police, the armed forces and some sensitive posts in the BBC or Post Office).

If the job is in the "excepted" category it should say this on the application form. In addition, those convicted of certain sexual offences are required to register with the police following conviction and are placed on the Sex Offenders Register. Specific advice on whether or not to declare a criminal conviction can be obtained from NIACRO (the Northern Ireland Association for the Care and Resetlement of Offenders).

Further useful addresses

- Northern Ireland Prison Service
  Prison Service Headquarters
  Dundonald House
  Upper Newtownards Road
  Belfast BT4 3SU
  tel: 028 9052 2922 (direct)   tel: 028 9052 5065 (general)
  www.niprisonservice.gov.uk

- HMP Maghaberry
  Old Road
  Ballinderry Upper
  Lisburn BT28 2PT
  tel: 028 9261 1888
  www.niprisonservice.gov.uk/maghaberry.htm

- HMP Magilligan
  Point Road
  Limavady
  Co Londonderry BT49 0LR
  tel: 028 7776 3311
  www.niprisonservice.gov.uk/magilligan.htm

- Hydebank Young Offenders Centre
  Hospital Road
  Belfast BT8 8NA
  tel: 028 9025 3666

- HM Inspectorate of Prisons
  1st Floor, Ashley House
  2 Monck Street
  London SW1P 2BQ
  tel: 087 0267 4298 (enquiries)   tel: 020 7035 2103 (reports)
  www.homeoffice.gov.uk

General Enquiries

- Northern Ireland Association for the Care and Resettlement of Offenders
  169 Ormeau Road
  Belfast BT7 1SQ
  tel: 028 9032 0157
  www.niacro.org

- Prison Reform Trust
  15 Northburgh Street
  London EC1V 0JR
  tel: 020 7251 5070
  www.prisonreformtrust.org.uk

- Extern
  1-5 Albert Square
  Belfast BT1 3EQ
  tel: 028 9024 0900

- Extern West
  10-12 Bishop Street
  Londonderry BT48 6PW
  tel: 028 7126 2104
  www.extern.org

- Coiste na n-Iarchimí
  10 Beechmount Avenue
  Belfast BT12 7NA
  tel: 028 9020 0770
  www.coiste.com

- EPIC
  33A Woodvale Road
  Belfast BT13 3BN
  tel: 028 9074 8922
  www.linc-ncm.org/epic.html

Chapter 7

Immigration and Asylum

Anne Grimes

Immigration law is the system of rules governing who can enter and live in the United Kingdom, under what conditions and for how long. It applies uniformly throughout the UK. It is currently a reserved matter, meaning that the relevant laws are enacted at Westminster. The Immigration Acts 1971 and 1988 set out the system of immigration control and provide for officials to enforce it. Section 3(2) of the 1971 Act empowers the Home Secretary to make Immigration Rules. The current Rules came into effect on 1 October 1994 (*House of Commons Paper 395*). There have been many amendments since then. The Immigration Rules set out in detail the circumstances in which "leave" (*i.e.* lawful permission) to enter or remain in the UK is to be granted or refused to persons who are subject to immigration control. The Rules are reproduced in full on the Home Office website at *www.homeoffice.gov.uk/ind*. The Immigration and Asylum Act 1999 largely governs the system for dealing with applications for political asylum and appeals. The Nationality, Immigration and Asylum Act 2002 has made further changes to the law.

Immigration control

No control

Certain categories of people are not subject to any immigration control and can freely enter and remain in the UK. These are:

- *British citizens*

  Before 1 January 1983 all people born in the UK were British citizens. Since that date, children born in the UK are British citizens only if one of their parents is "settled" in the UK (*i.e.* has permission to reside in the UK indefinitely) or if one parent was a British citizen at the time of the child's birth. People who are not British citizens by birth may be registered or naturalised as British citizens in certain circumstances.

- *People with the "right of abode" in the UK*
  Certain Commonwealth citizens have the "right of abode", *i.e.* those who (a) were born before 1 January 1983 and had a parent born in the UK or (b) are women who were Commonwealth citizens on 31 December 1982 and were married before 1 January 1983 to men who are British citizens or are Commonwealth citizens with a parent born in the UK.

- *Irish citizens travelling from Ireland*
  The Republic of Ireland, the UK, the Isle of Man and the Channel Islands form a Common Travel Area (CTA). No system of immigration control exists for nationals of these areas travelling within the CTA. Non-Irish citizens are governed by the Immigration (Control of Entry through Republic of Ireland) Order 1972. This provides that certain people travelling to the UK from Ireland are automatically given leave to enter for three months with a prohibition on employment. As there are no immigration officials at the border, this will not be stamped on their passports, but if they wish to stay longer they must apply to the Home Office for an extension of their leave to remain. This does not apply to visa nationals (see p.131) or to people who have previously entered or remained in the UK, who must obtain leave to enter the country. People who leave the UK for Ireland whilst having limited leave to remain in the UK and whose leave expires whilst in Ireland are automatically given leave to enter the UK for seven days upon their return. Children born in Northern Ireland are Irish citizens regardless of the status of their parents. These children will have the right to remain in the UK and Ireland, but the rights of their parents to remain in the UK are less clear.

Limited control

European Economic Area (EEA) nationals, *i.e.* citizens of the European Union (EU) and of three countries of the European Free Trade Association (EFTA), namely Norway, Liechtenstein and Iceland, are subject to limited control. They are free to enter the UK in order to exercise their EU rights to freedom of movement, *i.e.* to work or seek work, to enter into business or self-employment, to provide or receive services, to study, or if they are retired or self-sufficient. They can be refused entry or deported on the grounds of public policy, public security or public health. An EEA national may be accompanied by his or her family members no matter what their nationality. If such family members are coming to the UK from abroad they must obtain an "EEA Family Permit" from a British consular post before travelling. Dual nationals, for example Irish/British nationals (which includes most people in Northern Ireland), may elect to be dealt with as EEA nationals for the purpose of applying for a family member to join them in the UK. This can be advantageous, as the rules governing admission of family members of EEA nationals can be easier to meet than domestic immigration rules (see further below).

Full control

The following categories of people are subject to full immigration control and must, therefore, obtain leave to enter or remain in the UK:

- Commonwealth citizens without the "right of abode" (see p.130),
- British nationals who are not British citizens, *i.e.* British Overseas Citizens, British Dependent Territories Citizens, British Protected Persons, British Subjects and British Nationals (Overseas), and
- "aliens", *i.e.* all other nationalities.

Immigration control before entry

Prior to travelling, nationals of certain countries listed in the Appendix to the Immigration Rules ("visa nationals"- see below for the current list of visa nationals as this list is frequently updated it is worth checking the Home Office website for the current list), as well as people wishing to come to the UK for certain purposes (such as to settle as a spouse), are required to obtain entry clearance (often known as an entry certificate or visa) from a British consular post overseas. The list of visa national countries consists mostly of so-called developing countries and is regularly amended. Visa nationals who have already been granted leave to enter or remain in the UK for more than six months, or people who have been granted indefinite leave to remain and who are returning for settlement after an absence of two years or less, need not obtain visas when returning to the UK. In some circumstances the consular post abroad may, as well as granting entry clearance, also grant leave to enter the UK. The person need not then obtain leave to enter upon arrival in the UK.

Another form of immigration control imposed by the law is contained in the Immigration (Carriers' Liability) Act 1987, as amended. This provides for carriers to be fined for each passenger they bring to the UK who does not have the correct documentation, *i.e.* a valid passport and visa. The maximum fine is £2,000 per passenger. This means that employees of airlines, shipping companies, railways and hauliers act as unofficial immigration officials. The provision has particularly affected refugees who wish to come to the UK to seek asylum. Often they are unable to obtain passports from their own governments and checks by airline staff effectively stop many refugees from getting to the UK where they could claim asylum. Because of the numbers of people driven, by the carriers' liability legislation, to enter the UK illegally concealed in freight vehicles and railways, a penalty scheme was introduced in the 1999 Act to deter those intentionally or negligently allowing clandestine entrants into the UK.

In *Secretary of State for the Home Department v International Transport Roth GmbH & Others* (2002) groups of lorry drivers and haulage companies challenged the legality of the penalty scheme by way of judicial review. The Court of Appeal upheld the High Court's ruling that the legislation was incompatible with Article 6 of the European Convention on Human Rights, which protects the right to a fair trial, as well as Article 1 of Protocol 1 to the Convention, which provides for the protection of property, on the basis that the operation of the penalty scheme and the detention regime for seizing vehicles was unfair. In response to this judgment the government provided for a new civil penalty scheme in the Nationality, Immigration and Asylum Act 2002 (s.125 and Sch.8).

When many refugees have come to the UK from a particular country, the UK has named it a visa country. People cannot get visas as refugees, as they must be outside their own country in order to claim asylum.

Immigration control at time of entry

Immigration officers at the port of entry have the power to grant or refuse leave to enter the UK. Leave to enter is endorsed on the person's passport and may be limited in time and have all or any of the following conditions attached to it:

- a prohibition or restriction on employment,
- a condition requiring the person to maintain and accommodate him- or herself and any dependents without recourse to "public funds" (see below), or
- a condition requiring the person to register with the police.

Special rules apply to those who enter the UK through the Republic of Ireland. These are contained in the Immigration (Control of Entry through Republic of Ireland) Order 1972 (see p.133 above).

Immigration control after entry

After entry to the UK limited leave to enter may be extended or varied by the Secretary of State at his or her discretion. In practice, the power is exercised by staff at the Immigration and Nationality Department of the Home Office, Lunar House, 40 Wellesley Road, Croydon CR9 2BY, tel: 0870 606 7766. Applicants may apply for an extension of their "leave to remain" in the UK in the same category as their leave to enter was granted. They may also apply for a change of status. It is sometimes possible to switch from one category to another and to have time limits or other conditions changed. In certain circumstances applications may also be made for "settlement", *i.e.* a removal of all time limits and conditions attached to the applicant's leave.

Applications for variation of leave should be made to the Home Office before the expiry of existing leave, otherwise the applicant becomes an "overstayer" and can be liable to prosecution. In such situations, moreover, there is no right of appeal if the application is refused. Applications for leave to remain must be made on the mandatory application form and must include all documentation requested on the form. There is a different application form for each type of application. Application forms are available from the Application Forms Unit of the Home Office (tel: 0870 241 0645) and they are also available on the Home Office website (see address above). A failure to complete the form properly or to include all documentation without good excuse will lead to the form being returned; the application must then be resubmitted and may be late.

The Home Office will grant an application for variation of leave if the applicant satisfies all of the conditions for the particular category as set out in the Immigration Rules. The Secretary of State always has an overriding discretion to grant leave to remain despite the Rules. In practice, any request for the exercise of that discretion is dealt with by the Home Office.

Until June 2002 applications for extensions and variations of leave to remain could be made at the Public Enquiry Office at Belfast Immigration Office. The Belfast Office also carried out asylum and other interviews. This is no longer the case and applications are all now dealt with in Croydon. Moreover, asylum interviews are all now carried out in Liverpool; applicants must travel to Liverpool to be interviewed and, unless local representation can be arranged there, the applicant will attend without a legal representative.

The Immigration Rules

Full details of the conditions for entry and stay are set out in the Immigration Rules and these should be consulted before any application is made. Home Office guidance on the application of the Rules can be found on the Home Office website. The Rules set out conditions which apply to entry and stay, depending on whether the person comes to the UK for temporary purposes, to work, to join members of his or her family, to seek asylum or for other purposes.

Temporary purposes

Persons who are "visa nationals" (see p.131) require entry clearance from abroad to enter the UK in a temporary capacity. Persons in some other categories must also obtain entry clearance before travelling. All others must obtain leave to enter from an immigration officer upon arrival. Those entering in a temporary capacity may sometimes, but not always, switch to another category.

- *Visitors:* The maximum period of a visit is six months. Applicants must be able to support and accommodate themselves without working or claiming public funds (defined as income support, housing benefit, working families tax credit, income-based jobseeker's allowance, attendance allowance, severe disablement allowance, invalid care allowance, disability living allowance, disabled person's tax credit, child benefit or Housing Executive housing). They must intend to leave the UK at the end of their visit. Visitors may be permitted to stay to receive private medical treatment.

- *Students:* Students who are enrolled on a full-time course of day-time study at a publicly funded institute of further or higher education or a *bona fide* private education institution or an independent fee paying school must produce evidence of financial support without working or claiming public funds. They must also intend to leave the UK upon completion of their studies. Those granted leave to remain as students may undertake part-time or vacation work of up to 20 hours per week without seeking permission. Special rules apply to student nurses, doctors and dentists. It is also possible to apply to enter the UK as a prospective student in order to investigate courses of study.

- *Trainees:* Persons wishing to come to the UK for training or work experience may apply to enter on a temporary basis. Again there must be an intention to leave the UK at the end of the period. Training permits are obtained from Work Permits UK, Immigration and Nationality Directorate, Home Office, Level 5, Moorfoot, Sheffield S1 6PQ, tel: 087 0521 0224.

- *Au pairs:* Young people aged between 17 and 27 from certain countries (currently Andorra, Bosnia-Herzegovina, Croatia, Cyprus, Czech Republic, the Faeroes, Greenland, Hungary, Macedonia, Malta, Monaco, San Marino, Slovak Republic, Slovenia, Switzerland or Turkey) may come to live in the UK for a maximum period of two years from the date of first entry as *au pairs* in order to learn English.

- *Working holiday-makers:* Commonwealth citizens aged between 17 and 27 may come to the UK for a maximum period of two years from first entry on an extended holiday. They may work if it is incidental to their holiday. They must be in a position to support and accommodate themselves without claiming public funds. They must be unmarried or married to a person who also meets the working holiday-maker requirements and who intends to take a working holiday with his or her spouse. The applicant must not have any dependent children over five years old. He or she must obtain entry clearance before travelling and cannot switch to this category after entry. There are proposals to broaden the application of this scheme to include non-commonwealth countries and to relax some of the provisions.

- *Parents of a child at school:* A parent of a child under 12 years of age who is attending a private fee-paying day school can apply to enter or remain if he or she can show that he or she has funds to maintain a second home in the UK and is not seeking to make the UK his or her main home. Leave to enter or remain is granted for a maximum period of 12 months.

Work

- *Work permits:* These are obtained by the employer from Work Permits UK (see address above); the website is *www.workpermits.gov.uk.* They are granted only for certain categories of skilled employment where no other suitable candidates can be found in the UK or EEA. The potential employee should be outside the UK when the application is made. It is not usually possible for someone in the UK in another capacity to switch to a work permit. Work permits are initially granted for a period of up to four years. A permit entitles the holder to be employed in a particular job for a particular employer. The holder cannot switch job or employer without the permission of the Department of Employment and Learning. After four years, a work permit holder may apply for "settlement", *i.e.* permission to reside in the UK indefinitely without any time limits or restrictions. The 2002 Act has introduced fees for work permit applications.

- *Permit-free employment:* Certain jobs do not require a work permit, *e.g.* ministers of religion, missionaries or representatives of overseas newspapers, but applicants must obtain entry clearance from abroad before travelling.

- *Business people and the self-employed:* Such individuals need to have at least £200,000 available for investment in business in the UK and must show that employment will be created for at least two people already settled here. They must also obtain entry clearance before travelling.

- *Writers and artists:* If they can show that they will be able to support and accommodate themselves from their art, writing or savings and will not do any other work or claim benefits, writers and artists may be given entry clearance before travelling.

- *EU Association Agreements:* There are a number of agreements made between the EU and various countries which give nationals the right to set up a business in an EU country in certain circumstances without complying with the normal requirements. Currently agreements exist with Bulgaria, the Czech Republic, Hungary, Lithuania, Poland, Romania, Slovenia and Turkey. The relevant agreement should be checked before seeking to rely upon it.

- *Highly Skilled Migrant Programme (HSMP):* This was introduced in January 2002 as part of the government's new economic migration policy. People can be allowed to come to the UK to seek work if they obtain sufficient points under the scheme set out in the programme.

- *Family members:* Spouses and children under 18 years of age are normally permitted to enter or remain with persons qualifying in the above temporary categories of entry and stay.

Joining family

Family members may apply to come to the UK to "settle" here. "Settlement" or "indefinite leave to remain" in the UK means that the person is legally in the UK without any time limits or restrictions on working. People coming to settle must obtain entry clearance before travelling. Sometimes people who are here in a temporary capacity may be allowed to change to a category leading to settlement.

- *Spouses and fiancé(e)s:* Under the Immigration Rules a spouse of a British citizen or of someone settled here can obtain leave to enter or remain for an initial period of 12 months and thereafter indefinite leave to remain. It is proposed to increase this "probationary" period to two years. Both parties to the marriage must have met, they must be lawfully married and intend to live together permanently. The couple must be able to support and accommodate themselves without public funds. Similar principles apply in respect of fiancé(e)s, who must apply for entry clearance abroad and will be allowed to enter for six months during which period the couple should marry and then apply for leave to remain as a spouse.

  Many people born in Northern Ireland are dual Irish/British citizens. For the purpose of an application for leave to enter or remain by a spouse, an Irish/British national may elect to be dealt with as an Irish national, and therefore as an EEA national. If he or she does so any application to enter or remain made by his or her spouse is dealt with under European law. This means that if the Irish national is exercising an EU right in the UK, *e.g.* by working or studying here, his or her spouse is entitled to apply for an "EEA Family Permit" to join him or her in the UK. The application must be dealt with quickly, no fee is payable (unlike an application for entry clearance under domestic rules) and an application can only be refused if it is believed to be a "sham marriage". The Northern Ireland spouse may elect to have an application dealt with in this way even though he or she has not actually moved from one EEA country to another; simply having citizenship of another EEA country brings European law into play.

- *Other family members of an EEA national:* Individuals may also enter the UK if they are descendants of the EEA national or his or her spouse who are under 21 (or older if dependent), dependents in the ascending line of the EEA national or his or her spouse or other relatives who lived under the same roof in the country of origin.

- *Children:* Under the Immigration Rules children under 18 years of age who are unmarried (and in certain circumstances daughters under 21) will be allowed to settle in the UK if both parents have been accepted with a view to settlement in the UK or are already settled here. The rule prohibiting the claiming of public funds applies. In limited circumstances children may join one parent who is settled here. Specific rules apply to adopted children.

- *Parents and grandparents:* Under the Immigration Rules those over 65 years of age who are wholly or mainly financially dependent on a son, daughter, grandson or granddaughter who is a British citizen or settled in the UK may be granted indefinite leave to remain here. Applicants must show that they have no close relatives in their own countries to turn to. In the most exceptional compassionate circumstances a parent or grandparent under 65 may also be admitted in this category if living alone outside the UK.

- *Other relatives:* Other relatives must apply for entry clearance abroad and show that they are wholly or mainly financially dependent on their relative in the UK, that they have no other relatives in their own country to turn to, that they are living alone in the most exceptional compassionate circumstances and that they can be supported in the UK without claiming public funds.

- *"Common law" and same-sex relationships:* The current Immigration Rules were amended in October 2000 to incorporate provision for applications by so-called "common law" and same-sex partners of a person settled in the UK. A couple must show that they can be supported without public funds and have been living together in a relationship akin to marriage which has existed for two years or more. Leave will be granted for an initial period of two years and thereafter indefinite leave to remain will be granted if the couple remain together.

Seeking asylum

Political asylum is granted to those who can show that they have a well-founded fear of being persecuted for reasons of race, religion, nationality or membership of a particular social group or political opinion and that they are therefore unwilling or unable to return home. This definition is set out in the 1951 UN Convention on the Status of Refugees and its Protocol, to both of which the UK is a signatory.

Applications for asylum are made to the immigration officer at the port of entry or, after entry, to the Home Office if the refugee has come into the country in another capacity (such as a visitor or student) or has entered clandestinely. Anyone who applies for asylum is entitled to have his or her claim considered by the Home Office and to remain in the UK pending a decision. However, people who come to the UK through a "safe" third country may be refused asylum without their claim being considered and returned to that third country. This is a result of the Dublin Convention, agreed by member states of the EU on 15 June 1990. It entered into force on 1 September 1997.

Those who apply for asylum on entry may be detained or given temporary admission. The Home Office takes many months, often years, to make a decision. The Asylum and Immigration Act 1996 restricted access to benefits to asylum-seekers who claim asylum upon entry to the UK. The Immigration and Asylum Act 1999 changed the system of support for asylum-seekers again. It introduced a system of accommodation and support in the form of vouchers provided by the Home Office. In Northern Ireland the scheme is administered by the Northern Ireland Council for Ethnic Minorities (NICEM) on behalf of the National Asylum Support Service (NASS), which is part of the Home Office. NICEM are at 3rd Floor, Ascot House, 24-31 Shaftesbury Square, Belfast BT2 7DB (tel: 028 9023 8645). The NASS office is at 11B Merrion Business Centre, 58 Howard Street, Belfast, BT1 6PJ (tel: 028 9058 5971).

The Nationality, Immigration and Asylum Act 2002 introduced further changes to the system of support based on accommodation centres. It is intended that these will be in the form of induction, accommodation and removal centres with basic provisions on-site. Asylum-seekers living in the community will be required to report regularly and meet stringent residence requirements in order to continue to receive support. The Act denies support to those who do not claim asylum as soon as reasonably practicable after arrival in the UK. The refusal of support has been challenged by a number of asylum-seekers. In March 2003 the Court of Appeal ruled that the refusal of support in these cases was a breach of the ECHR. The test as to whether an asylum-seeker claimed as soon as is reasonable practical must depend on the circumstances of the applicant and the system must be operated fairly (*Q v Secretary of State for the Home Department*, 2003). It is proposed that people who have been granted refugee status or leave to remain in other EEA countries will not be entitled to any support from local authorities.

If the Home Office grants asylum the refugee is granted settlement in the UK. The refugee's spouse and children under 18 abroad can join the refugee. Sometimes refugees are not granted asylum but are allowed to remain in the UK anyway. This usually takes the form of a grant of "exceptional leave to remain", which is valid for a period of four years, after which indefinite leave to remain is normally granted.

Many applications for asylum are refused on the basis that the person's account is not believed by the Home Office. Appeals usually concentrate on establishing credibility, which can obviously be difficult in the absence of supporting evidence.

Some people who have been refused asylum have been granted exceptional leave to remain on the basis that even though they may not qualify for asylum they should not be sent back to their own country. As from April 2003 this policy has been ended. Instead two new categories of stay have been introduced. These are humanitarian protection, which will be granted in narrow circumstances where removal would be contrary to Articles 2 and 3 of the ECHR. It will normally be granted for three years followed by an active review. Discretionary leave may be granted in other cases, probably those where removal would breach Article 8 of the ECHR or some other Article 3 cases (*e.g.* some medical conditions which would make removal a breach of Article 3) or where the applicant is an unaccompanied child. Humanitarian leave will be incorporated into the Immigration Rules whereas discretionary leave will not.

Other purposes

- *UK born grandparents:* Commonwealth citizens who have a grandparent born in the UK can be granted leave to remain for four years, following which they can be granted settlement.
- *Returning residents:* A person with indefinite leave to remain in the UK will generally be allowed back for settlement if he or she returns within two years of leaving. People with limited leave to remain in the UK of at least six months will generally be allowed back into the UK subject to the same time limits and conditions after an absence abroad.
- *Retired persons of independent means:* A person with close connections with the UK, aged over 60, may come here if he or she has a guaranteed income of at least £25,000 a year. He or she must obtain entry clearance before travelling and is prohibited from claiming public funds and from doing any work or business. Settlement can be obtained after four years in this category.

- *Investors:* Investors who have £1 million and intend to invest £750,000 by way of government bonds, share capital or loan capital may come to the UK if granted entry clearance.
- *Access to a child:* A person with rights of access to a child resident in the UK may apply for entry clearance in order to enter the UK to exercise those rights. He or she must be able to support and accommodate him- or herself without working or having recourse to public funds and may stay for a maximum period of 12 months.
- *Home Office policies:* There are a number of well-established practices within the Home Office which are not written in the Immigration Rules but whereby, in appropriate circumstances, leave to remain is normally granted. For example, people who have been in the UK legally for a period of 10 years may apply for settlement, and settlement is also normally granted to those who have been here for more than 14 years, even if some of their stay has been unlawful. Also there are policies which apply to marriage breakdown, domestic violence and families where a child has been in the UK for seven years or more.

Enforcement of immigration law

There are a number of ways in which immigration laws are enforced. People may be removed or deported from the UK; they may also be detained at various stages of the process. In Northern Ireland enforcement is carried out by Belfast Immigration Office, which is based at Belfast International Airport (tel. 028 9442 2500).

Removal

The Immigration and Asylum Act 1999 extended the categories of people who can be removed from the UK. The removal procedure has more restricted rights of appeal than the deportation procedure. The following people can be removed from the UK:
- illegal entrants – people who entered the UK illegally by avoiding immigration control or by obtaining leave to enter by deception;
- overstayers – people whose leave to enter or remain has expired;
- people who have breached a condition of their entry or stay, *e.g.* by working when prohibited; and
- people who have been refused leave to enter at the port of entry to the UK.

The Nationality, Immigration and Asylum Act 2002 gives power also to remove children born in the UK where their parents entered the UK unlawfully and those who attempt to obtain permission to stay by deception.

An appeal against removal can be made only on the ground that there was no power in law to remove the appellant on the grounds given. This appeal can usually be exercised only after departure from the UK. An appeal against removal can be exercised within the UK in only two situations:

- where the removal would breach the UK's obligations under the UN's Convention on the Status of Refugees ("asylum grounds"), or
- where the removal would breach the UK's obligations under the European Convention on Human Rights (ECHR) ("human rights grounds").

Any appeal involving issues of national security is heard by the Special Immigration Appeals Commission (SIAC).

Deportation

Since the 1999 Act came into force, deportation can be initiated in the following circumstances:

- where an overstayer applied for leave to remain within the transitional regularisation period set up in the 1999 Act, *i.e.* before 1 October 2000;
- where the person is a family member of a person recommended for deportation;
- where a person's removal is deemed by the Secretary of State to be conducive to the public good; and
- where a criminal court recommends deportation following conviction of a crime punishable by imprisonment.

Where removal is on "conducive to the public good" grounds, or a family member is being deported, the Home Office follows a two-stage process. First, a decision to deport is issued. This carries a full right of appeal. The person to be deported may argue that the Home Office did not take account of all relevant factors as set out in the Immigration Rules.

Appellants may raise asylum grounds or claim that deportation would breach the ECHR. *In re T* (2000) an application for judicial review of a decision to deport was heard by Mr Justice Coghlin in the

High Court in Belfast. The case was decided prior to the coming into force of the Human Rights Act 1998, which incorporated the ECHR into domestic law. However, the judge took into account Article 2 of the ECHR, which protects the right to life, on the ground that it was also a fundamental right at common law, and decided that the Home Secretary did not take proper account of psychiatric evidence of the risk of the applicant committing suicide. The decision to deport was quashed.

The second stage of the deportation process is the issuing of a deportation order. There is no further right of appeal against a deportation order, except by way of an objection to removal to the destination named on the order. If an order is made, it is not normally revoked for at least three years. Until it is revoked the person subject to the order may not return to the UK. In certain circumstances the Home Office may also deport the person's spouse and children under 18.

Detention

The Home Office may detain people:
- who have entered the UK illegally,
- where their application for leave to enter is under consideration,
- against whom a decision to deport has been made,
- who are awaiting removal from the UK, or
- who have been charged with an immigration offence.

Immigration detainees in Northern Ireland are currently held in Maghaberry Prison, near Lisburn. They can apply for bail to the Chief Immigration Officer at Belfast Immigration Office and/or to an immigration adjudicator who sits in Belfast to hear immigration appeals (see below).

The English Court of Appeal considered the issue of the detention of asylum-seekers in Oakington Reception Centre in the case of *R v Secretary of State for the Home Department, ex parte Saadi,* (2001). Oakington houses asylum-seekers whose applications are being dealt with by the Home Office in a fast-track procedure. The Court of Appeal overturned the decision of the High Court that detention of asylum-seekers at Oakington violated the right to liberty enshrined in Article 5 of the ECHR. The Court of Appeal held that detention of asylum-seekers for a short period of about a week was lawful: the deprivation of liberty involved in this case fell at the bottom end of interference with that right and did not breach Article 5.

Criminal offences

The Immigration Act 1971, the Asylum and Immigration Act 1996, the Immigration and Asylum Act 1999 and the Nationality Immigration and Asylum Act 2002 all created criminal offences, *e.g.* overstaying or breaking conditions of leave. Suspected offenders can be arrested by immigration officers and the police. If convicted they can be fined, imprisoned and recommended for deportation. Offences introduced by the Asylum and Immigration Act 1996 include obtaining leave to enter or remain by deception, knowingly facilitating the entry of illegal entrants and employing immigrants who are not entitled to work. The Nationality, Immigration and Asylum Act 2002 also created offences connected with traffic in prostitution.

Challenging decisions

There are a number of ways in which immigration decisions can be challenged.

Appeals before entry to the UK

It is possible to appeal against the refusal of entry clearance on the grounds that the decision was not in accordance with the law or the Immigration Rules applicable or that discretion should have been exercised differently. The appeal is heard in the UK, generally at a venue close to the UK-based sponsor (*i.e.* the fiancé(e) or spouse in a marriage case, or the family member in a dependents case). The appeal is heard by an immigration adjudicator (see below). The appeal must be served on the relevant embassy within three months of the date of the refusal. People refused entry clearance after 2 July 1993 in the following categories no longer have a right of appeal:

- visitors – except those defined as "family visitors", whose right of appeal was restored in 2000 by the 1999 Act,
- prospective students,
- students for courses lasting less than six months,
- where a person has applied to enter or stay in the UK in a situation which is not permitted by the Immigration Rules ("mandatory refusals"); these situations are:
- where the applicant does not have a relevant document which is required by the Immigration Rules,

- where the applicant does not satisfy a requirement of the Immigration Rules as to age, nationality or citizenship,
- where the applicant is seeking entry, or an extension of stay, for a period longer than that permitted by the Immigration Rules, or
- where the Secretary of State certifies that exclusion is conducive to the public good; there is no appeal on human rights grounds in this category, but there can be an appeal to the SIAC.

Appeal upon entry to the UK

A person refused entry to the UK at a port of entry has a right of appeal against the refusal except where he or she falls into one of the following categories:
- visitors - except family visitors (see above),
- prospective students,
- students for courses lasting less than six months,
- mandatory refusals (see above), or
- where the Secretary of State certifies that exclusion is conducive to the public good.

People not in the above categories who have a valid entry clearance or visa upon entry have a right of appeal within the UK against a refusal of leave to enter and can stay in the UK while waiting for the hearing. Those without a valid entry clearance or visa have a right of appeal which can be exercised only after they have left the UK. In both cases the time limit for serving the appeal on the Immigration Service is 28 days. In all cases an appeal may be brought on asylum or human rights grounds if the asylum claim was made before the refusal of leave to enter.

Appeal after entry to the UK

A person has the right to appeal against a refusal of an application to extend or vary leave to enter or remain in the UK only in the following circumstances:
- where the application for variation or extension was made whilst the applicant still had leave to remain in the UK, *i.e.* before the expiry of the date on the last stamp in his or her passport, and was received by the Home Office on the correct form with all required documents before the expiry of the person's current leave to enter or remain;
- where the refusal is not a mandatory refusal (see above); or

- on asylum or human rights grounds (see below).

For most appeals the time limit for appealing in-country is 14 days and the appeal form must be served on the Home Office within the time limit. For asylum and human rights appeals the time limit is generally 10 working days. The time limit for appeal is set out on the notice of refusal.

Asylum and Human Rights Act appeals

Since 1993 all those refused asylum have a right of appeal against a refusal of asylum on the ground that removal would breach the UK's obligations under the UN Convention on the Status of Refugees. The current asylum appeal rights are set out in the Immigration and Asylum Act 1999, although some changes are included in the Nationality, Immigration and Asylum Act 2002. Since 2 October 2000 it has also been possible to appeal on the ground that a decision breaches the ECHR as incorporated into UK law by the Human Rights Act 1998. The most common provisions of the ECHR relied upon in immigration matters are Article 3, which prohibits torture, inhuman or degrading treatment or punishment, and Article 8, which protects the right to family and private life, but other Articles may also apply. A right of appeal on human rights and/or asylum grounds exists at the following stages:

- refusal of leave to enter,
- refusal of leave to remain, having entered the UK in another capacity, *e.g.* as a visitor or student,
- refusal of asylum after having overstayed – an appeal may be taken on asylum grounds against a decision to deport or a refusal to revoke a deportation order, and
- removal.

The 1999 Act introduced a new one-stop appeals procedure which means that appellants have only one opportunity to appeal and must raise all reasons for wishing to stay in the UK at the same appeal hearing. The Nationality, Immigration and Asylum Act 2002 restructures the appeals system to simplify and streamline the one-stop provisions. This involves restricting the types of immigration decisions which will attract a right of appeal, introducing a statutory closure date to prevent multiple adjournments of cases at the adjudicator stage, and narrowing the grounds of appeal to the Immigration Appeal Tribunal.

The Act also restricts access to judicial review of immigration decisions.

All appeals

Appeals are administered by the Immigration Appellate Authority, which is part of the Lord Chancellor's Department and is independent of the Home Office. For all appeals there is a two-tier system laid down in the Immigration Acts. An initial appeal lies to an adjudicator and a second appeal on a point of law, with leave, to an Immigration Appeal Tribunal (IAT). There is, however, no right to apply for leave to appeal to the IAT in certain asylum appeals where the appeal has been "certified" by the Secretary of State and the adjudicator agrees with the certification. An appeal lies, with leave, from the IAT to the Court of Appeal. The Special Immigration Appeals Commission (SIAC) deals with appeals involving national security.

The grounds for appeal to the adjudicator are narrow. The appellant must show one of the following:

- that the decision was wrong in law,
- that the decision was not in accordance with the Immigration Rules, or
- that the decision involved an exercise of discretion which should have been exercised differently.

Appeals in Northern Ireland are heard by an adjudicator sitting in Belfast. The 2002 Act makes legal aid available for representation before an adjudicator, the IAT and the SIAC. The Law Centre (NI) receives funding from the Home Office under the Immigration Act 1971 to provide representation at some appeal hearings. The Law Centre (NI) can be contacted at 124 Donegall Street, Belfast BT1 2GY (tel: 028 9024 4401).

Judicial review

Judicial review (see Chapter 2) is available against decisions of immigration officers, the Secretary of State or appellate bodies if such decisions are illegal or unreasonable. It is normally necessary to exhaust all immigration appeals first. The 2002 Act introduced a limitation to the availability of judicial review in immigration cases. Where the IAT refuses an application for leave to appeal, a decision which had been previously subject to judicial review, the 2002 Act introduced a procedure whereby a single High Court judge will determine an application for a review of the IAT's decision on the ground that the IAT made an error of law.

Representations to the Secretary of State

The Secretary of State has discretion to reverse a previous decision to refuse leave to enter or remain or to remove or deport someone and may direct the grant of entry clearance or leave to enter. The discretion is generally exercised only in exceptional or compassionate circumstances. However, where there is no right of appeal, for instance where an application for leave to remain is made after the previous leave expires, it is still worth asking the Home Office to reconsider the decision, particularly where there is further evidence or a change of circumstances.

Due to the limitations of the appeal procedures and judicial review, further representations to the Secretary of State are often the only remedy available to the applicant. It is possible to enlist the help of a Member of Parliament to take up the case with the Home Office Minister when all other appeals and reviews have been exhausted.

Regulation of immigration advisers

The 1999 Act set up a new scheme for the regulation of all those giving immigration advice. In order to provide immigration advice an individual or organisation must be:

- registered with the Office of the Immigration Services Commissioner (OISC), the regulator of the scheme; the address is 6th Floor, Fleetbank House, 2-6 Salisbury Square, London (tel: 020 7211 1500); the obligation to register applies to the for-profit sector (*e.g.* commercial immigration consultants) and a registration fee is payable;
- authorised to practise by a designated professional body – including the Law Society of Northern Ireland or the Bar Council for Northern Ireland; or
- exempted by either the OISC or the Secretary of State; this covers advisers from the not-for-profit or voluntary sector.

Those who need to register or to apply for exemption must comply with the requirements of the scheme in relation to competency and management issues.

Future developments

The Nationality, Immigration and Asylum Act 2002 was enacted in November 2002. Some of its provisions are not yet in force. It was preceded by a White Paper in February 2002. Some of the proposals contained in the White Paper have been introduced already without the need for primary legislation, whilst other changes can be effected by way of amendments to the Immigration Rules. The main changes and proposed changes can be summarised as follows:

Citizenship and nationality

Changes are proposed which tighten the application process and introduce an updated oath of allegiance and a formal "citizenship ceremony" at which the oath would be taken. Illegitimate children will have an entitlement to British citizenship in the same way as legitimate children.

Marriage and relationships

These proposals are not in the Act but will probably be made by way of changes to the Immigration Rules. It is proposed to increase the initial probationary period from one year to two, the probationary period is to be removed altogether for couples who have been together for five years or more, people who have been in the UK for less than six months will not be able to apply to remain on the basis of marriage and it will no longer be a requirement that unmarried partners be legally unable to marry.

Economic migration

The White Paper proposes limited measures to allow for more economic migration, including the introduction of a Highly Skilled Migrant Programme and expansion of the working-holidaymaker scheme which is currently limited to nationals of Commonwealth countries.

Asylum

A number of changes are being proposed including the introduction of an Application Registration Card, a network of induction, accommodation and reporting centres and cash payments by way of support for asylum-seekers to replace the voucher scheme.

Detention and enforcement

Changes have been introduced to increase detention facilities and make amendments to the bail procedures. Detention facilities will be re-designated as "removal centres".

Appeals

The "one stop" appeal process is to be simplified. Other proposed changes include the introduction of a statutory closure date to prevent multiple adjournments, limiting the jurisdiction of the Immigration Appeal Tribunal to appeals on a point of law, preventing judicial review of decisions of the Tribunal to refuse to grant leave to appeal by introducing a statutory review procedure and ending certification of asylum and human rights appeals which prevents further appeals to the Tribunal.

Criminal offences

New powers of search and arrest are to be given to immigration officials and new criminal offences are to be introduced including an offence of trafficking people into or out of the UK for the purposes of prostitution.

Border controls

Controls over entry to the UK are to be further tightened, for example by the introduction of an "authority to carry" scheme imposing penalties on carriers who bring people into the UK without having obtained prior authority from the Home Office.

Further useful addresses

- Joint Council for the Welfare of Immigrants
  115 Old Street
  London SE1V 9JR
  tel: 020 7251 8706
  www.jcwi.org.uk

- Law Centre (NI)
  124 Donegall Street   and   Western Area Office
  Belfast BT1 2GY   9 Clarendon Street
  tel: 028 9024 4401   Derry / Londonderry BT48 7EP
  www.lawcentreni.org   tel: 028 7126 2433

- Northern Ireland Council for Ethnic Minorities (NICEM)
  3rd floor, Ascot House
  24-31 Shaftesbury Square
  Belfast BT2 7DB
  tel: 028 9023 8645
  www.nicem.org.uk

- Chinese Welfare Association
  133 University Street
  Belfast BT7 1HP
  tel: 028 9028 8277

- The Multi-Cultural Resource Centre
  12 Upper Crescent
  Belfast BT7 1NT
  tel: 028 9024 4639
  www.mcrc.co.uk

- Northern Ireland Committee for Refugees and Asylum-Seekers
  c/o NICEM (see above)

- Refugee Action Group
  c/o Multi-Cultural Resource Centre (see above)

Chapter 8

Marches and Meetings

Brice Dickson and Michael Hamilton

Marches and meetings in Northern Ireland are not governed by a single piece of legislation. While there is a core of law which is relevant to all situations, there are several rules which are specific to particular sets of circumstances. The foremost statute for meetings is the Public Order (NI) Order 1987, as amended, but most of the rules concerning marches are laid down in the Public Processions (NI) Act 1998. This Act placed the Parades Commission on a statutory footing and gave to it the adjudicatory powers recommended by the report of the Independent Review of Parades and Marches in Northern Ireland (the North Report). Other relevant statutes include the Protection of Harassment (NI) Order 1997 and the Terrorism Act 2000.

The Human Rights Act 1998, which incorporated into Northern Ireland's law most of the European Convention on Human Rights (ECHR), further changed the context in which the rules governing marches and meetings operate. Before this Act, the "right" of public assembly in Northern Ireland was not expressly guaranteed by any law. Indeed for many years, the judiciary maintained that the "right" to assemble in public should be limited to activities incidental or ancillary to the right of passage along a highway. Any activity which exceeded those limits, even if peaceful and non-obstructive, amounted to trespass. In *DPP v Jones (Margaret)* (1999), however, Lord Irvine stated that such minimal protection was inadequate, especially because the Human Rights Act was due to come into force in October 2000:

> *Provided these activities are reasonable, do not involve the commission of a public or private nuisance, and do not amount to an obstruction of the highway unreasonably impeding the primary right of the general public to pass and repass, they should not constitute trespass. Subject to these qualifications, therefore, there would be a public right of peaceful assembly on the public highway.*

This "unreasonable use" test represented the first serious step towards establishing a positive right to assemble under domestic common law. Any court applying this test will be likely to consider factors which are similar, if not identical, to those arising under Article 11 of the European Convention.

European Convention law

Article 11 of the ECHR provides as follows:

(1) Everyone has the right to freedom of peaceful assembly and to freedom of association with others, including the right to form and to join trade unions for the protection of his (sic) interests.

(2) No restrictions shall be placed on the exercise of these rights other than such as are prescribed by law and are necessary in a democratic society in the interests of national security or public safety, for the prevention of disorder or crime, for the protection of health or morals or for the protection of the rights and freedoms of others. This Article shall not prevent the imposition of lawful restrictions on the exercise of these rights by members of the armed forces, of the police or the administration of the State.

Freedom of association

Most of the cases on Article 11 taken to the European Court of Human Rights have concerned the right to freedom of association rather than the right to freedom of peaceful assembly. A substantial number relate to a government's refusal to register a particular organisation (perhaps thereby denying it legal personality and any attendant benefits) because of a belief that its aims threaten national security or public order. An even greater proportion of cases, however, have involved the activities of trade unions. As with the right to peaceful assembly (see below), it is difficult to discern a definite pattern in the judgments handed down. On the one hand, the European Court has said that Article 11 "safeguards freedom to protect the occupational interests of trade union members by trade union action, the conduct and development of which the Contracting States must both permit and make possible". On the other hand, it has pointed out that the Article "does not secure any particular treatment of trade unions, or their members, by the State" (see, *e.g. Gustafsson v Sweden*, 1996). Nor does the Article guarantee the right to strike.

In the well-known GCHQ case, *Council of Civil Service Unions v Minister for the Civil Service* (1985), where workers at Government Communications Headquarters at Cheltenham were banned from belonging to certain trade unions, the unions involved were unsuccessful in persuading the English courts of the justice of their case.   They also lost at the European level, where the European Commission held that their complaint could not be considered because the ban was a "lawful restriction" necessary in the interests of national security (*CCSU v UK*, 1987).   In an earlier case (*Young, James and Webster v UK*, 1983) the European Court of Human Rights placed a general query over closed shop agreements between employers and one or more trade unions.   In *Sibson v UK* (1993) the Court held that an employer could require an employee belonging to a particular union to work at a separate site from that used by employees belonging to a different union.

Freedom of assembly

The European Commission and Court have not had to interpret the freedom of peaceful assembly clause in Article 11 very often.   When they have done so, national courts have usually been granted a wide "margin of appreciation".   This means that the European institutions have been prepared to defer to the national authorities' assessment of the necessity to restrict the right to assemble because of their presumed greater knowledge of local circumstances.   A local court will interfere by way of judicial review with the decision to restrict the right to freedom of assembly (*e.g.* by the police or Parades Commission) only if there is evidence that the authority concerned failed to consider proper matters, considered irrelevant matters, reached a decision which no reasonable person could make, or reached a decision which is incompatible with the European Convention.   Only on the last ground can the court examine the merits of the decision as opposed to looking merely at the processes used in reaching the decision (see, *e.g. In re Tweed*, 2001 and *In re Pelan*, 2001).

Other relevant ECHR rights

Marches and meetings often reflect the identity, culture, and politics of the participants and the communities to which they belong. In many cases, therefore, consideration of the right to freedom of assembly cannot logically be separated from that of the right to freedom of expression (Art.10 of the ECHR – see Chapter 9) or the right to freedom of religion (Art.9 of the ECHR). Where issues under all three Articles are raised, the Court will usually explore the substantive issues under the Article most relevant to the facts and treat the others as subsidiary.

Apart from the "rights and freedoms of others" which might be affected by an assembly, there are three other Convention rights which may be relevant to any case where restrictions have been placed on the right of peaceful assembly:

- Article 6 of the ECHR guarantees the right to a fair trial in the determination of a person's "civil rights or obligations". However, it is not yet clear whether in the eyes of the European Court the right to peaceful assembly falls within the definition of "civil rights". It is clear, though, that at common law the bodies which take decisions on whether assemblies should proceed or not must do so fairly and reasonably.
- Article 14 of the ECHR secures the enjoyment of the Convention rights and freedoms without discrimination on any ground.
- Article 17 of the ECHR says that the Convention must not be interpreted so as to give any state, group or person the right to engage in activities aimed at limiting other people's rights.

While the European Court has held there to have been unnecessary violations of the right to peaceful assembly on only two occasions (*Ezelin v France*, 1991 and *Stankov and the United Macedonian Organisation Ilinden v Bulgaria*, 2001), the European Commission and Court have outlined some general principles regarding the interpretation of Article 11:

- those who wish to exercise the right to peaceful assembly must have peaceful intentions;
- restrictions on the right to assemble should not be based solely on the impressions or perceptions likely to be created by the assembly; a demonstration may legitimately annoy or give offence to persons opposed to the ideas or claims that it is seeking to promote; and
- the right to counter-demonstrate should not be allowed to inhibit the right to demonstrate.

In *Christians Against Racism and Fascism v UK* (1980), the European Commission of Human Rights held that the right to assemble could not be taken away just because there was a possibility of a violent counter-demonstration. The thinking behind such a principle is that, in the long term, it is healthier for a society to allow all views to be expressed, even if their content is offensive to the majority of the general public. Ultimately, however, the European Commission held, that it *was* permissible for the United Kingdom to have a law which allowed the authorities to ban all public processions, or a class of public procession, for a period not exceeding three months. That is the power which now exists both in England (s.13 of the Public Order Act 1986) and in Northern Ireland for up to 28 days (art.5 of the Public Order (NI) Order 1987 in relation to open air public meetings, and s.11(2) of the Public Processions (NI) Act 1998 in relation to public processions). For some, it may be difficult to understand how blanket bans of this nature can, within the terms of Article 11(2) of the European Convention, be deemed "necessary".

In contrast to the *Christians Against Racism* case, the most recent Article 11 case decided by the European Court of Human Rights, *Stankov and the United Macedonian Organisation Ilinden v Bulgaria* (2001), found that the Bulgarian government *had* overstepped its margin of appreciation by preventing the applicant organisation (a Macedonian separatist group) from carrying placards, banners and musical instruments to, and from making speeches at, the historical sites where it wished to hold a protest. The Court ruled that even though the issues at stake touched on national symbols and national identity, that was not sufficient reason for the national authorities to be granted a wide discretion. The ban on the march was held by the European Court to have breached the applicants' Article 11 right.

Remaining questions

It is still unclear when exactly, under Article 11(2) of the ECHR, a march can be stopped, or re-routed, in order to prevent disorder or crime. Up to now, courts in the UK have generally not been prepared to distinguish between sources of disorder, so that restrictions on a procession are often upheld even if the disorder emanates from the opponents of a procession (see, *e.g.* the Scottish case of *Loyal Orange Lodge No. 493 v Roxburgh District Council*, 1979). Moreover, although antagonism between local inhabitants and participants in a parade does not of itself constitute sufficient reason for a parade to be re-routed, it has been held that if that antagonism will considerably increase the disruption to the life of the community, a re-routing may be justified (*In re Murphy*, 1991). However, two cases involving Orange parades in Scotland during 2001 indicate that an *unsubstantiated* fear that public disorder might result from the procession is not sufficient reason to impose a ban.

There is also a question over the meaning of the phrase "the rights and freedoms of others" in Article 11(2). None of the European cases involving freedom of peaceful assembly give any guidance as to what these rights might be in the context of parades and protests. The "rights and freedoms of others" which might conceivably be affected by the exercise of the right to peaceful assembly include the right to respect for a person's private and family life (Article 8), the right to peaceful enjoyment of one's possessions (Art.1 of Prot.1), and even, in some situations, the right to life (Art.2).

Associating with others

The effect of the various rules concerning freedom of association in Northern Ireland law is to confer upon individuals the right to associate with whomsoever they please. Of course, people who feel that they are being harassed or unduly annoyed by another person's company may well have a remedy in the law of trespass (which is an intentional interference with someone else's land, person or property), or they may qualify as the victims of other specific civil wrongs or crimes. These are all wrongs which can be committed just as much by individuals as by people acting in consort. Under the Protection from Harassment (NI) Order 1997 the victim or potential victim of harassment can claim damages for (among other things) anxiety and financial loss, as well as seeking an injunction to prevent the harassment from continuing. This Order also makes harassment a crime, punishable by up to six months in prison and a fine of up to £5,000 (see further p.163 below).

The chief exceptions to the right to freedom of association are as follows:

An association to plan the commission of a crime

Belonging to an association for the purpose of planning the commission of a crime would amount to the offence of conspiracy, which is committed (under art.9(1) of the Criminal Attempts and Conspiracy (NI) Order 1983):

> *if a person agrees with any other person or persons that a course of conduct shall be pursued which, if the agreement is carried out in accordance with their intentions, either (a) will necessarily amount to*

or involve the commission of any offence or offences by one or more of the parties to the agreement, or (b) would do so but for the existence of facts which render the commission of the offence or any of the offences impossible.

Under article 9A (inserted by s.6 of the Criminal Justice (Terrorism and Conspiracy) Act 1998), associating to plan a criminal act also includes conspiracy to commit offences outside the UK.

Under section 126 of the Trade Union and Labour Relations (NI) Order 1995 there is an exemption for acts that are to be done in contemplation or furtherance of a trade dispute, provided the offence is a minor one triable only before magistrates. Likewise, a husband and wife cannot alone be charged with conspiracy, nor can a person be charged with conspiring with a person who is under 10 (Criminal Justice (Children) (NI) Order 1998), but a person can be, and often is, charged with conspiracy with a person unknown. Incitement or attempt to conspire are not punishable as crimes. Conspiracies to commit a minor offence are punishable by an unlimited fine; conspiracies to commit a serious (*i.e.* "indictable") offence can be punished with the same maximum term of imprisonment as the indictable offence itself (art.11 of the 1983 Order above).

Actually associating in a crime, as opposed to a plan for a crime, makes a person guilty of aiding, abetting, counselling or procuring the crime. Where the actions of the principal offender are not contemplated by the accessory, the accessory cannot be held liable at all for the unforeseen crime. But where the actions of the principal *are* contemplated by the accessory and it is only the consequences of that action which the accessory does not foresee, then the accessory should be held liable for that which he or she did intend (*e.g.* for manslaughter rather than murder). This rule has been applied in several important cases in Northern Ireland (*e.g. R v Rules and Sheals*, 1997 and *R v Gilmour*, 2000).

Under the terms of the Northern Ireland Arms Decommissioning Act 1997, there is an amnesty for people charged with any of the offences listed in the Schedule to that Act. This includes a number of "inchoate" offences (*i.e.* attempting or conspiring to commit, or aiding, abetting, counselling, procuring or inciting the commission of, an offence) listed in the Schedule.

An association specifically banned by legislation

It must not be an association which has been specifically banned by legislation. In the UK, several associations are banned (or "proscribed") by section 3, and Schedule 2 of the Terrorism Act 2000. These are the Irish Republican Army, Cumann na mBan, Fianna na hEireann, Saor Eire, the Continuity Army Council, the Irish National Liberation Army, the Irish People's Liberation Organisation, the Red Hand Commando, the Ulster Freedom Fighters, the Ulster Volunteer Force, the Ulster Defence Association, the Loyalist Volunteer Force, the Orange Volunteers and the Red Hand Defenders. The Terrorism Act 2000 (Proscribed Organisations) (Amendment) Order 2001 further supplemented this list, but none of these additional organisations (which include Al-Qa'ida and ETA) are concerned with the affairs of Northern Ireland. Under the 2000 Act, the maximum penalty for belonging to a proscribed organisation, or for inviting support for it, is 10 years' imprisonment and an unlimited fine (s.12). If the support invited relates to money or other property, the maximum penalty is 14 years' imprisonment and an unlimited fine (s.15).

It is unlawful to be a member of a quasi-military organisation (s.7(1) of the Public Order (Amendment) Act (NI) 1970) and any person who takes part in the control of such an association is also guilty of an offence. There is an exemption for stewards employed by the organisers of any lawful public procession or meeting to assist in the preservation of order. The maximum penalty for membership of a quasi-military association is three months' imprisonment and a fine of £100 (s.7(8)); that for managing or training such an association is five years' imprisonment and a fine of £1,000 (s.7(9)(b)). See too the Unlawful Drilling Act 1819 (p.180).

Unlawful assembly

The association must not be an "unlawful assembly" under the common law. While the Public Order Act 1986 abolished the common law offence of unlawful assembly in England, this offence still remains in Northern Ireland. A person is guilty of it if he or she is a member of an assembly of three or more people which is either causing a disturbance or giving rise to a reasonable apprehension of a breach of the peace. "Breach of the peace" means conduct causing a reasonable apprehension (to someone present) of violence against persons or property (see further p.179). The offence can be committed both on private property and in public places, and the assembly need not be densely packed in order to be unlawful: persons illegally occupying 70 houses over a five week period have been held to constitute an unlawful assembly (*McKibben v Belfast Corporation*, 1936).

Association forbidden by order

Associating with others is illegal if it has been forbidden by administrative or judicial order. These orders are sometimes called exclusion orders. The type most relevant here (now called an occupation order) is that issued by magistrates in cases of domestic violence, for the purpose of excluding someone, usually a man, from premises occupied by that person's spouse or cohabitee (see Chapter 17). In Northern Ireland, unlike in England, it is not possible for a person to be given a court order excluding him or her from a local football match.

Controls on private meetings

When considering the law on meetings it is necessary to distinguish between private and public meetings. As regards the latter, it is also important to distinguish between public meetings in general and those held in the open air. Election meetings and council meetings are in a special position too.

Meetings on private premises which are restricted to a "private" group are virtually uncontrolled by the law. They are never unlawful, unless one of the exceptions mentioned at pp.157-160 above is relevant or unless certain offences are committed during the meeting. If, for instance, a breach of the peace is being committed, the police can enter private premises in order to break up a meeting. The police can also enter private premises in order to arrest a suspected criminal, which is why groups of after-hour drinkers in public houses are at risk.

Members of the public have no right to attend private meetings unless they are invited or given express permission to enter. "Gate-crashers" will be guilty of trespass, which is not normally a crime if it takes place on private premises but it allows the occupier of the premises to sue in the civil courts for compensation even if the trespassing has caused no damage. Even when permission to enter has been granted, it may later be withdrawn. If a club or society holds a meeting and tries to exclude certain members, those members, if they have the opportunity, are entitled to apply for a court order (called an "injunction") to compel the organisers to grant them admission.

Public meetings in general

As outlined in the first part of this chapter, there is now a qualified right to assemble peacefully in public under UK law. While all public meetings are subject to the rules set out below, while open air public meetings are subject to even further restrictions, and while meetings on public highways are particularly susceptible to controls, any restrictions must themselves be compatible with Article 11 of the ECHR (see pp.153-154).

A "public meeting" is defined by article 2 of the Public Order (NI) Order 1987 as including any meeting in a public place and any meeting (even in a private place) which the public or any section of the public is permitted to attend, whether on payment or otherwise. In turn, "public place" is defined as meaning any street, road or highway and any place to which the public or any section of the public has access, on payment or otherwise, as of right or by virtue of express or implied permission. "Meeting" is also defined in the same article: it means a meeting held for the purpose of discussing matters of public interest. A few points need to be made about these definitions.

- First, whereas "public place" and "meeting" are given exclusive definitions, "public meeting" is defined only so as to *include* certain categories of meeting. It is conceivable that a judge or law-enforcement officer could apply the term to other categories of meeting as well, such as meetings run by an organisation for its own members and their friends. In *McCartan Turkington Breen v Times Newspapers Ltd* (2000) the House of Lords, reversing the Northern Ireland Court of Appeal, decided that a press conference held in a private home was a public meeting.
- Second, in the definitions of "public place" and "public meeting", the phrase "public or any section of the public" is used. In English cases on race discrimination legislation this phrase has been interpreted so as not to cover clubs and societies with some form of membership system. To get round this interpretation Parliament had to amend that legislation in 1976 so that it could extend to many of those clubs and societies. It remains to be seen whether a court in Northern Ireland will take as restrictive a view of the meaning of this phrase as the English courts have done, although even if they do,

because of the point made in the preceding paragraph, it may not make the 1987 Order inapplicable.

- Third, the definition of "meeting" certainly excludes most of those meetings held merely for the purpose of discussing the internal matters of a particular group or association. The internal workings of a large political party may be a matter of public interest, but not perhaps the discussions of a parent-teacher association or a student society. Comparisons with other areas of the law, such as contempt of court and defamation, would suggest that virtually any matter could, in the proper circumstances, be of public interest.

- Fourth, a meeting can consist of as few as two people; there is no higher minimum number required, as there is for "assemblies" in England, where there have to be at least 20 people (s.16 of the Public Order Act 1986).

Note that the organisers of public meetings are generally under no legal obligation to notify the police that such a meeting is scheduled to take place. The exception to this concerns protest meetings which are "related" to a public procession. A protest meeting is "related" to a public procession if its purpose (or one of its purposes) is to demonstrate opposition to the holding of that procession on its route or proposed route (s.17(2) of the Public Processions (NI) Act 1998). The organiser of a related protest meeting must give 14 days' notice to the police unless it is not reasonably practicable to do so, whereupon notice must be given as soon as it is reasonably practicable (s.7 of the Public Processions (NI) Act 1998). The police are responsible for ensuring that those involved in public meetings do not break the criminal law.

Offences connected with public meetings

Needless to say, any behaviour which constitutes an offence in a private setting will not be any less criminal simply because it occurs at a public meeting. There are also some offences which can be committed only at public meetings (just as there are other offences, especially those concerning indecency and sexual relations, which can only be committed in public places).

Under article 7(2) of the Public Order (NI) Order 1987, a person is guilty of an offence, punishable in a magistrates' court by up to six months in prison and a fine of up to £5,000, if he or she at a lawful public meeting "acts in a disorderly manner for the purpose of preventing the transaction of the business for which the meeting was called together".

Two other offences currently regulated by the Public Order (NI) Order 1987 need to be mentioned. Under article 19, it is an offence "at or in relation to any public meeting" (or indeed in any public place) if a person:

(a) uses threatening, abusive or insulting words or behaviour, or (b) displays anything or does any act, or (c) being the owner or occupier of any land or premises, causes or permits anything to be displayed or any act to be done thereon, with intent to provoke a breach of the peace or by which a breach of the peace or public disorder is likely to be occasioned (whether immediately or at any time afterwards).

The House of Lords has said that behaviour does not qualify as threatening, abusive or insulting just because it gives rise to a risk that immediate violence will be provoked, nor is it enough that the behaviour gives rise to anger, disgust or distress: *Brutus v Cozens* (1972), where the defendant had merely run on to the No. 2 court at Wimbledon Lawn Tennis Club and distributed leaflets.

Under the Protection from Harassment (NI) Order 1997, a "course of conduct" amounting to harassment of another is both a crime and a civil wrong. In *Thomas v News Group Newspapers Ltd.* (2002) it was held that harassment must not be given an interpretation which restricts the right to freedom of expression, save in so far as this is necessary in order to achieve one of the legitimate aims contained in Article 10 of the ECHR. Two important cases heard before the Human Rights Act 1998 came into force – *Huntingdon Life Sciences Ltd. v Curtin and others* (1997) and *DPP v Moseley* (1999) – further suggest that the Protection from Harassment Act 1997 (the equivalent, in England and Wales, of the 1997 Order) was not intended by Parliament to be used to sanction restrictions on the right to peaceful assembly.

Outside the law of harassment, Northern Ireland has broader provisions in its Public Order (NI) Order 1987 in relation to acts intended or likely to stir up hatred or arouse fear, than currently exist in England. This is because definitions of fear and hatred in Northern Ireland are framed so as to include fear of, or hatred against, a group of persons defined by (amongst other things) reference to religious belief.

Although it did not become law, the Religious Offences Bill (2001-02) proposed that the Public Order Act 1986 in England be widened in scope so as to cover religious offences in addition to the already covered racial ones. In the Parliamentary debates on this Bill, the Northern Ireland law was highlighted as an obvious model to follow.

It is noteworthy, though, that Northern Ireland has no direct equivalent of the following:

- section 4 of the Public Order Act 1986, which makes it an offence to use "threatening, abusive or insulting words or behaviour" or to distribute or display "any writing, sign or other visible representation" with intent to cause a person to believe that immediate unlawful violence will be used against him or her;
- section 4A of the 1986 Act, which prohibits intentionally causing a person harassment, alarm, or distress by using threatening, abusive or insulting words or behaviour etc.; or
- section 5 of the 1986 Act, which provides that a person is guilty of an offence if he or she uses threatening, abusive or insulting words or behaviour etc. "within the hearing or sight of a person likely to be caused harassment or distress thereby."

These offences can be committed in private places but not private homes. Furthermore, significantly higher maximum penalties for these offences (and others including assault and criminal damage) were introduced by the Crime and Disorder Act 1998 where it can be shown that the offence was racially aggravated. The Anti-terrorism, Crime and Security Act 2001 does the same for religiously aggravated offences (s.39), and it increased the penalty for inciting racial hatred from a maximum of two years to seven years in prison. None of these provisions extend to Northern Ireland, but the government has recently consulted on whether they should.

Unlike the terms of the Protection from Harassment (NI) Order, the concept of harassment under the Public Order Act does not require "a course of conduct" to have occurred. It is interesting, therefore, that while section 5 of the latter was enacted to address, amongst other things, abusive and rowdy behaviour directed at older persons, ethnic groups, shoppers, and dwellers in housing estates, a 1994 Home Office Research Study into the application of this section revealed that in a significant number of cases the police used this section when they themselves were the subject of abuse.

Dressing up

Article 21 of the Public Order (NI) Order 1987 prohibits a person in any public place or at any public meeting from wearing a uniform signifying an association with any political organisation or with the promotion of any political object. The Chief Constable of the Police Service may, with the Secretary of State's consent, permit exceptions to this prohibition, but only for ceremonial, anniversary or other special occasions. There is no definition of "uniform" in the 1987 Order, so the courts will have to decide whether, for instance, wearing a beret or some kind of sash is enough to constitute a uniform. In the English case of *O'Moran v DPP* (1975) it was held that the wearing of dark berets, dark glasses, dark pullovers and other dark clothing, when escorting the coffin of an IRA supporter through London streets, could be regarded as a uniform.

Under section 13 of the Terrorism Act 2000 it is an offence for any person in a public place to wear an item of clothing or wear, carry or display an article in such a way as to arouse reasonable apprehension that he or she is a member or supporter of a proscribed organisation. The maximum penalty is six months' imprisonment and a fine of up to £5,000. Under the new article 23A of the Public Order (NI) Order 1987, inserted by section 95 of the Anti-terrorism, Crime and Security Act 2001, a police inspector can authorise any constable in uniform, during a period of up to 24 hours, to require any person in a specified locality to remove any item which the constable reasonably believes that person is wearing wholly or mainly for the purpose of concealing his identity. Failure to remove the item is an arrestable offence punishable with up to a month in prison and a fine of £1,000.

Public meetings on private premises

The definition in article 7 of the 1987 Order makes it clear that a meeting may constitute a public meeting even though it is held on private premises, whether outdoors or indoors. Police officers can attend such meetings in a purely private capacity, but their right to be there in a professional capacity is not certain. One well-known English case, *Thomas v Sawkins* (1935), suggests that the right exists in situations where the police reasonably apprehend a breach of the peace.

Council meetings

By law, all meetings of district councils in Northern Ireland, and all meetings of committees of those councils, are open to members of the public whether or not they reside in that council area (s.23 of the Local Government Act (NI) 1972). But by the same section, a council may decide by resolution to exclude the public when publicity would be prejudicial to the public interest because of the confidential nature of the business or for other special reasons. The power to exclude persons from a meeting in order to suppress or prevent disorderly behaviour also exists (s.27(a)). Newspapers can require copies of the agenda to be sent to them in advance of council meetings (s.24), but no person can insist on being allowed to take photographs at, or to record or relay, the proceedings (s.27(b)) (see too Chapter 10). Some other special rules apply to election meetings.

Open air public meetings

In some ways, controls on open air public meetings are stricter in Northern Ireland than in England. The Public Order Act 1986 allows the police in England to impose conditions on the holding of such meetings, but does not permit them to be banned. The one exception to this is if an assembly is a "trespassory assembly" as defined by section 14A of the Public Order Act 1986. Where such an assembly is anticipated, the chief officer of the police may apply to the council of the district for an order prohibiting the holding of all trespassory assemblies in the district or a part of it, for a specified period not exceeding four days, and covering an area with a radius not exceeding five miles. In Northern Ireland the powers of the police to impose conditions on open air meetings are contained in the Public Order (NI) Order 1987. Public open spaces are also usually regulated by bylaws issued by the relevant district council or public body. These bylaws may completely disallow public meetings in those spaces or require prior special permission. (See also p.178.)

Conditions

The power to impose conditions on open air public meetings (including protest meetings related to a public procession) is at present conferred by article 4(2) of the 1987 Order. This requires a senior police officer reasonably to believe that the meeting may result in serious public disorder, serious damage to property or serious disruption to the life of the community, or that its purpose is the intimidation of others with a view to compelling them not to do an act they have a right to do or to do an act they have a right not to do.

The police officer may then impose such conditions as to the place where the meeting may be held, its maximum duration, or the maximum number of persons who may constitute it, as appear necessary to prevent such disorder, damage, disruption or intimidation. The directions given by the senior officer must be in writing, except in cases where people are already assembling for the meeting. A person who knowingly fails to comply with a condition imposed under article 4 is punishable with up to six months in prison and a £5,000 fine. It is a defence for the accused to prove that the failure arose from circumstances beyond his or her control.

Bans

Only the Secretary of State can bar open air public meetings. This power is conferred by article 5(1) of the 1987 Order, as amended by the Public Processions (NI) Act 1998. This requires the Secretary of State to be of the opinion that the meeting is likely to:
- cause serious public disorder,
- cause serious disruption to the life of the community, or
- make undue demands upon the police or military forces.

The Secretary of State may then make an order prohibiting for up to 28 days the holding in that area of all or specified open air public meetings. It is strange that "serious damage to property" is expressly mentioned as one of the grounds for the police imposing conditions on meetings, yet not as one of the grounds for the Secretary of State imposing a ban, but the phrase "serious public disorder" could perhaps be interpreted as embracing serious damage to property.

The 1987 Order provides that a statement made by the Secretary of State as to the need to prohibit a meeting "shall be conclusive evidence of the matters stated therein" (art.5(3)). This probably means, alarmingly, that the reasonableness of the Secretary of State's opinion cannot be challenged in court by judicial review. There is no requirement that the Secretary of State must obtain the consent of the Chief Constable or of the Policing Board before issuing a banning order. In practice, however, the view of the Chief Constable will be accorded substantial weight. A person who knowingly organises or takes part in a banned open air public meeting is guilty of an offence for which the maximum penalty is six months in prison and a fine of £5,000 (Public Processions (NI) Act 1998, Sch.3, para.8).

While the North Report recommended (para.13.55) that the police should adopt and apply a set of guidelines and a Code of Conduct in relation to open air public meetings – similar to those which have now been published by the Parades Commission (see p.173) – this advice has not yet been followed. However the Code of Conduct issued by the Parades Commission does cover protest meetings which are related to public processions (even though the Commission has no power to act upon any breaches of that section of the Code).

Picketing

Some of the rules on picketing are described in Chapter 20. For the present, it is necessary to note that if two or more pickets are acting together they may well constitute a public meeting and so be subject to the rules set out above. In England and Wales this will be the case only if the numbers picketing are 20 or more, because only then will they constitute an assembly under English law.

One of the tests which the police must consider before deciding to impose conditions on an open air public meeting in Northern Ireland is whether its purpose is the intimidation of others (art.4(2)(b) of the 1987 Order). This is partly aimed at the control of picketing and in such a context "intimidation" will probably be interpreted as it has been under the Conspiracy and Protection of Property Act 1875, section 7 of which first imposed specific controls on picketing. That gives it a wider meaning than the one attributable to the same term in section 1 of the Protection of the Person and Property Act (NI) 1969 (see p.179). However, in a case arising out of the News International dispute at Wapping, an English court held that abuse, swearing and shouting did not of itself amount to intimidation (*News Group Newspapers Ltd v SOGAT '82*, 1986).

In 1998 a Code of Conduct for picketing was published by what was then the Department of Economic Development. Although its provisions do not impose any legal obligations, they are admissible as evidence in any relevant proceedings before the courts or industrial tribunals.

Street trading

The law governing street trading was changed by the Street Trading Act (NI) 2001. This repealed most of the provisions of the Street Trading (Regulation) Act (NI) 1929 and introduced a new licensing scheme with stronger enforcement powers. The Act was considered necessary because of an increase in recent years in the number of unlicensed street traders operating in Northern Ireland.

"Trading" is defined in the Act to include "supplying or offering to supply a service for gain or reward" (s.1) and the Act raises a presumption that any article or thing displayed in a street is there for the purpose of being sold or exposed for sale (s.17(2)). Only trading which takes place in a "street" can be regulated under the Act, but the definition of "street" is relatively broad. It includes any road or footpath (as defined by art.2(2) of the Road Traffic (NI) Order 1995), or any "public place." The latter is given a different meaning from that in the Public Order (NI) Order 1987, being defined as "a place in the open air within 10 metres of a road or footpath to which the public has access without payment, but which is not within enclosed premises or the curtilage of a dwelling" (s.25(4)). Significantly, the inclusion of land within 10 metres of a road means that a "public place" may cover land normally regarded as being private.

The licensing scheme enables district councils to designate specific streets as being suitable for street trading (s.3) and any such designation can specify that certain services or articles cannot be sold or supplied from street trading pitches in a particular street or that only certain services or articles can be sold or supplied. Street trading may be permitted in undesignated streets under the authority of a temporary licence or where the trader has been authorised to trade as a mobile trader (see below).

The Act requires all traders (subject to the exceptions in s.2) to have a licence regardless of their method of trading. Applications for a licence should be made in writing to the relevant council well in advance of the time for which the licence is required. However, both the fee and the exact procedure for granting, renewing or varying licences may differ between individual councils. There are essentially three categories of licence (s.5 and s.14):

- a licence to trade from a stationary "designated" pitch,
- a licence to trade as a mobile trader (this includes ice cream vans, hot food vans and mobile shops etc.), and

- a temporary licence to trade casually from a pitch for up to seven days.

Stationary or mobile street trading licences can be granted for a maximum of three years (s.6(4)) and only five temporary licences can be granted to any individual applicant in a year. No licence can be granted if the applicant is not an individual or if he or she has not reached the upper limit of compulsory school age (s.8). In addition, a council has the discretion to refuse an application on a number of grounds, including that trading in the space applied for would cause undue interference or inconvenience to persons or vehicles using the street, or that there are already sufficient traders trading in the street (s.9(1)).

An authorised council officer or police constable can seize any property, goods, receptacle, equipment, stall or vehicle if he or she has reasonable grounds for suspecting that the person using them is trading illegally (*i.e.* trading without a licence or in contravention of the conditions of a licence). Unlicensed traders are liable to prosecution, with a maximum fine of £1,000 (s.17(1)), and a court may order that any seized goods be disposed of (s.19). Notwithstanding this, certain specified breaches of a licence, or the failure to produce a licence on demand, may be dealt with instead by way of a fixed penalty notice (s.21, s.22 and Sch.1).

A comprehensive guide to the Act has been written by the Social Legislation Branch of the Department for Social Development and is available at: *www.dsdni.gov.uk/publications/documents/street_trading (1).pdf.*

Controls on public processions

The laws on public meetings will normally also be relevant to public processions. There are, though, a number of rules which are relevant only to processions. Most of these are contained in the Public Processions (NI) Act 1998.

Notice requirements

Section 6 of the Act requires the organiser(s) of a public procession to give 28 days' notice to the police. The Chief Constable must then immediately send a copy of the notification to the Parades

Commission (s.6(6)). According to the Chief Constable's annual report, there were 2,808 parades in 2001-2002. Of these, 23 were illegal.

While there is no obligation to advertise the procession in the press, the Code of Conduct issued by the Commission in accordance with s.3 of the Act states that it is important, where the parade route passes through a residential area or an area where there would normally be a high level of commercial activity, that the organiser gives local people, and those who carry out business in the area, the maximum notice possible of the intention to hold a parade. The Code suggests that this could be done by distributing flysheets with details of the parade and organisers around shopkeepers in the area and seeking agreement to have some posted prominently in shop windows, or placing a public notice in the local newspaper. Compliance with the Code of Conduct is a factor which the Parades Commission takes into account in deciding whether to impose conditions on a parade. That said, it has so far been cited by the Commission in only a relatively small proportion of its determinations.

The present notice requirement applies regardless of whether the procession consists of people walking, running, cycling or motoring. The notice must specify the following information:

- the date and time when the procession is to be held,
- its route,
- the number of persons likely to take part in it,
- the names of any bands which are to take part in it,
- the arrangements for its control being made by the person organising it, and
- the name and address of the organiser.

The obligation to give notice does not apply if the procession is a funeral procession (see p.175) or is of a description specified by the Secretary of State. There is no exemption just because the procession is one commonly held in the area in which it is proposed to be held, although this is one of the factors to which the Commission must have regard (see below). "Traditional" marches organised, for example, by the Orange Order, the Apprentice Boys or the Ancient Order of Hibernians still have to be notified. Less than 28 days' notice can be given only if it is not reasonably practicable to give the full notice. This means that spontaneous demonstrations *can* still be lawful.

A person who organises or takes part in an unnotified public procession, or in one which differs from the date, time or route notified, is punishable with up to six months in prison and a fine up to £5,000 (s.6(7) and (10) of the Public Processions (NI) Act 1998). It is, however, a defence to prove that the accused did not know of, and neither suspected nor had reason to suspect, the failure to satisfy the notice requirements (s.6(8)). If the alleged offence relates to a failure to keep to the notified date, time or route for the procession, it is also a defence to prove that the failure arose from circumstances beyond the accused's control.

The law is a little unclear as to when a gathering of people constitutes a parade, but it is safe to assume that the police are acting lawfully if they prevent individuals associated with a parade from doing separately what they are not permitted to do collectively. In *Broadwith v Chief Constable of Thames Valley* (2000) a man was convicted of breaching a re-routing order in England when he broke away from the demonstration and tried to go off on his own down one of the roads closed by the police. An appeal against the conviction was unsuccessful.

Conditions on processions

The power to impose conditions on public processions rests with the Parades Commission (although, as stated above, the power to impose conditions on open air public meetings, including those related to parades, remains with the police under the Public Order (NI) Order 1987). The Secretary of State can also revoke or amend a determination of the Commission following an application by the Chief Constable (s.9 of the Public Processions (NI) Act 1998), but this power has not yet been exercised. Conditions can relate to, for example, the route and timing of a parade, the numbers and bands notified to take part, the music to be played, or the banners to be carried by parade participants.

The Public Processions (NI) Act 1998 extended the statutory criteria for determining whether conditions should be imposed on a parade. This was done in an attempt to move away from decisions based solely on public order grounds. Section 8(6) provides that the Commission shall have regard to:

- any public disorder or damage to property which may result from the procession,
- any disruption to the life of the community which the procession may cause,
- any impact which the procession may have on relationships within the community,

- any failure of a person of a description specified in the guidelines to comply with the Code of Conduct, and
- the desirability of allowing a procession customarily held along a particular route to be held along that route.

In *In re Pelan* (1998), the Court of Appeal held that "community" in section 8(6)(c) could include the wider community in Northern Ireland and was not necessarily confined to those living in the vicinity of a particular parade. The court also held that the Commission could take into account any relevant factor in reaching its decisions, even if that factor is not contained in section 8(6).

In accordance with section 5 of the 1998 Act the Parades Commission has published guidelines setting out the factors which it will take into account when determining whether a procession should be made subject to conditions. The Commission has also published a set of procedural rules to explain how the Commission will exercise its functions (s.4) and a Code of Conduct providing guidance to persons organising a public procession and regulating the behaviour of persons taking part in it (s.3). This Code deals with matters such as the stewarding of parades and protests, the consumption of alcohol and respect for places of worship, memorials and cemeteries. The Parades Commission does not have the power to impose fines for breaches of the Code. These three documents were revised in July 1999.

It is an offence, punishable summarily up to a maximum of six months in prison and a fine of £5,000, for a person knowingly to fail to comply with a condition imposed by the Parades Commission on a parade, or to incite another person to do so (s.8(7) and (8)). Section 13 of the 1998 Act permits the police to confiscate alcohol being carried by those marching, about to march or about to view a march. Anyone who refuses to surrender alcohol will be liable to a fine of up to £500 (s.13(6)).

According to the Parades Commission's 4th Annual Report, in 2001-2002 parades were rerouted on 130 occasions and a further 22 parades had other conditions imposed upon them.

Hindering a procession

People taking part in a public procession in Northern Ireland are given a certain amount of protection by section 14 of the Public Processions (NI) Act 1998:

A person who for the purpose of preventing or hindering any lawful public procession or of annoying persons taking part in or endeavouring to take part in any such procession –

> *(a) hinders, molests, obstructs those persons or any of them,*
> *(b) acts in a disorderly way towards those persons or any of them, or*
> *(c) behaves offensively and abusively towards those persons or any of them,*

shall be guilty of an offence.

This offence is punishable, in a magistrates' court only, with a maximum of six months in prison and a fine up to £5,000. However, statistics from the Director of Public Prosecutions show that only five prosecutions were brought under this section between 1998 and 2001, and all of these were in 1999. There have, however, been a greater number of prosecutions brought under article 20 of the Public Order (NI) Order 1987, which makes it an offence for a person in a public place to wilfully obstruct traffic or seek to hinder any lawful activity (see below at p.177). It is impossible, however, to say what proportion of these prosecutions are connected with parades. The Protection from Harassment (NI) Order 1997 may provide an additional legal mechanism for dealing with disruptive influences at or near parades, but these are directed at persons who have pursued a "course of conduct", meaning conduct on at least two occasions (see p.164).

Bans

As with open air public meetings, only the Secretary of State can ban processions in Northern Ireland, and only if he or she considers that it is necessary in the public interest to do so (s.11 of the Public Processions (NI) Act 1998). This power was last exercised in 1996 (then under art.5 of the Public Order (NI) Order 1987) to prohibit all parades in Derry/Londonderry along the stretch of the city walls overlooking the Bogside between 7 and 31 August. Under the 1998 Act, the Secretary of State must have regard to:

- any serious public disorder or serious damage to property which may result from the procession,
- any serious disruption to the life of the community which the procession may cause,
- any serious impact which the procession may have on relationships within the community, and

- any undue demands which the procession may cause to be made on the police or military forces.

The Secretary of State can ban any individual parade or, should that be considered insufficient having regard to the above factors, all parades in a particular area for a period not exceeding 28 days. This is a shorter period than was previously specified in the Public Order (NI) Order 1987 (which permitted bans of up to three months). It is significant that in England, while public meetings cannot be banned unless they constitute a "trespassory assembly" (s.70 of the Criminal Justice and Public Order Act 1994), all public processions in an area can be prohibited for up to three months following an application by a chief officer of the police to the relevant local council (s.13 of the Public Order Act 1986). A significant number of these bans have recently been put in place to prevent National Front marches from taking place in cities where there are clear racial tensions, including Burnley and Bradford.

In Northern Ireland it is an offence, punishable summarily up to a maximum of six months' imprisonment and a fine of £5,000, for a person to organise or take part in a public procession which he or she knows to be banned (s.11(9) of the 1998 Act).

The Parades Commission

The Parades Commission comprises seven members (currently all male) and has an information-giving role as well as an adjudicatory one. At the time of writing, the recently published report of an independent review of the Commission, conducted by Sir George Quigley, is still open for consultation. This follows two earlier reviews – one by the Northern Ireland Office and another by the Northern Ireland Affairs Select Committee – neither of which recommended extensive changes to the Public Processions (NI) Act 1998.

The Parades Commission can be contacted at: 12th floor, Windsor House, 9-15 Bedford Street, Belfast BT2 7EL; tel: 028 9089 5900; *www.paradescommission.org*

Funerals

Funeral processions have been exempted from the notice requirements of the Public Processions (NI) Act 1998. Nevertheless, under regulations made in 1991, the police can require mourners to travel in vehicles. However, at the point where, or when, a funeral procession loses its connection with the interment or cremation of a body, it will be liable to the controls laid down in the 1998 Act for other types of public processions.

Bands

Northern Ireland also has a unique provision for the control of bands, which are defined as "a group of two or more persons who carry for the purpose of playing or sounding, or engage in the playing or sounding of, musical or other instruments" (s.17 of the Public Processions (NI) Act 1998). Section 12 of the 1998 Act allows the Secretary of State to require bands to be registered and anyone knowingly parading with an unregistered band would be guilty of an offence punishable with up to six months' imprisonment and a fine up to £5,000. In fact, no registration requirement has yet been made and there may be difficulties in creating one which could not be easily evaded. Even if section 12 were to come into effect, it would not apply to bands playing at a public meeting rather than in a public procession.

Additional public order offences

Many of the offences which might be committed during the course of meetings or processions have already been referred to. It is now necessary to describe some further offences.

Riot (or riotous assembly)

In Northern Ireland this is still a common law offence committed whenever three or more people, in execution of a common purpose, use force or violence which alarms or terrifies at least one person "of reasonable firmness", and with an intent to assist one another, by force if necessary, against any person who may oppose them. The maximum penalty is life imprisonment.

Affray

This common law offence consists of unlawful fighting, or a display of force, in such a manner as to terrify a person "of reasonable firmness" (who does not have to be present at the scene). It can be committed by one person acting alone, but is commonly charged whenever the police break up street fights or pub brawls. The maximum theoretical penalty is life imprisonment, although the Northern Ireland courts may follow the sentencing guidelines issued by the English Court of Appeal in *R v Keys and Others* (1986), where it was said that the leaders and organisers of serious affrays can anticipate sentences of at least seven years in prison.

Riotous, disorderly or indecent behaviour

It is an offence under article 18 of the Public Order (NI) Order 1987 for a person in any public place to use behaviour which is riotous, disorderly or likely to occasion a breach of the peace. The maximum penalty is six months in prison and a fine of £5,000. In *Clinton* v *Watts* (1992) the Northern Ireland Court of Appeal held that words alone can constitute disorderly behaviour (*e.g.* swearing and shouting) and that it is enough if the behaviour is seen by a police officer: the behaviour does not have to be directed towards any particular person provided it at least seriously infringes the values of orderly conduct held by right-thinking people. Section 9 of the Criminal Justice (Miscellaneous Provisions) Act (NI) 1968, as amended, criminalises, in addition, indecent behaviour in any public place and behaviour, on premises where intoxicating liquor is sold, which is riotous, disorderly, indecent or likely to occasion a breach of the peace.

PSNI statistics reveal that, in 2001-2002, disorder occurred at 28 of the 2,808 parades which took place in Northern Ireland.

Obstructive sitting etc. in public places

Under article 20 of the 1987 Order a person is guilty of an offence – maximum penalty one month's imprisonment and a fine of £1,000 – if he or she sits, stands, kneels, lies down or otherwise conducts him- or herself in a public place so as wilfully to obstruct traffic or to hinder any lawful activity. There is also the offence known as obstruction of the highway (see art.88 of the Roads (NI) Order 1993):

Any person who, without lawful authority or reasonable excuse, in any way intentionally or negligently obstructs the free passage along a road shall be guilty of an offence and liable on summary conviction to a fine not exceeding £500.

These offences can obviously be committed not just by people opposing a march but also by those taking part in it. Just because a march has not been rerouted or banned does not mean that the people taking part in it have complete freedom to cause any obstruction they like.

Breach of council bylaws

District councils and some other authorities have power to issue bylaws (which require confirmation by the Secretary of State) to regulate activities in public places. Council bylaws can be inspected free of charge at council premises and generally speaking the maximum penalty for contravening them is a fine of £20, plus £2 for each day that the offence continues after conviction (s.92 of the Local Government Act (NI) 1972).

Persons employed by the district council and police officers may be authorised by the council to secure the enforcement of bylaws. Under section 21 of the Town Police Clauses Act 1847, still in force in Northern Ireland, it is an offence (now punishable with a fine up to £1,000) wilfully to breach an order made by a local authority "for the route to be observed by all...persons, and for preventing obstruction of the streets,...in all times of public processions, rejoicings or illuminations".

Offences in relation to public buildings

Under article 23 of the 1987 Order, it is a criminal offence to be a trespasser in a public building (a term which is widely defined and includes the Stormont Estate) or knowingly to interfere with the carrying on of any lawful activity in any public building. The maximum penalty is two years' imprisonment and an unlimited fine.

Obstructing a police officer

Assaulting, resisting, obstructing or impeding a police officer in the execution of his or her duty is an offence under section 66 of the Police (NI) Act 1998. The obstruction must be intentional, but nearly any act qualifies if it makes the job of the police more difficult to carry out. A police officer can him- or herself be guilty of the offence, especially if he or she colluded with a suspect to mislead an investigation (*Clinton* v *Kell*, 1991). However, a refusal to give information is not obstruction (although it may amount to a separate offence: see Chapter 3). If a police officer is exceeding his or her duty at the time, no obstruction can occur in law. The maximum penalty is two years in prison and an unlimited fine.

Intimidation

By section 1 of the Protection of the Person and Property Act (NI) 1969 it is an offence if a person unlawfully causes another in any way whatsoever to do or refrain from doing any act. This widely worded provision carries a maximum penalty of five years' imprisonment and an unlimited fine. Participants in a provocative and disorderly demonstration can be prosecuted under it if, for instance, their actions cause someone to stay indoors for a prolonged period. As with so many of these offences, the impact of the section depends greatly on the prosecution policies of the police and the Director of Public Prosecutions.

Breach of the peace

According to Lord Justice Watkins in *R v Howell* (1982), a breach of the peace arises:

whenever harm is actually done or is likely to be done to a person or in his (sic) presence to his property or a person is in fear of being so harmed through an assault, an affray, a riot, unlawful assembly, or other disturbance .

The breach can occur on private premises even though no member of the public outside the premises is involved: *McConnell v Chief Constable of the Greater Manchester Police* (1990).

A speaker at a meeting may well say things which others find offensive, but so long as he or she does not "interfere with the rights of others so as to make a violent reaction not wholly unreasonable" his or her conduct should not be restricted (*Redmond-Bate v DPP*, 1999). In this case, three women, preaching on the steps of Wakefield Cathedral, were arrested for a breach of the peace when some members of the gathered crowd became hostile towards them. The Court of Appeal held that if the threat of disorder came from passers-by, then it was the passers-by and not the preachers who should have been asked to desist and arrested if they would not.

A breach of the peace is not itself a criminal offence, but it can very easily constitute some other offence and therefore the police and courts have significant powers to prevent breaches of the peace. A magistrate has power under article 127 of the Magistrates' Courts (NI) Order 1981 (and under the Justices of the Peace Act 1361) to "bind over" any person to keep the peace and/or be of good behaviour for a period up to two years, on pain of paying a sum of money if he or she fails in this duty. If this sum is not paid, the court may send the person to prison for up to six months. The time and money specified in a binding-over order must be reasonable (usually the time period is 12 months). Appeals can be made to the Crown Court and judicial review proceedings may be taken in the High Court.

There have been many attempts to have the law on breach of the peace abolished or reformed, because it represents a grave risk to basic freedoms. As yet all such attempts have been unsuccessful. Furthermore, the European Court on Human Rights has ruled that "breach of the peace" is sufficiently defined so as to be "prescribed by law" within the terms of the European Convention on Human Rights (*Steel and others v UK*, 1998).

Unlawful drilling

Parts of the Unlawful Drilling Act 1819 are still in force in Northern Ireland. Section 1 prohibits:

> *...all meetings and assemblies of persons for the purpose of training or drilling themselves, or of being trained or drilled to the use of arms, or for the purpose of practising military exercise, movements, or evolutions, without any lawful authority from His Majesty, or the lieutenant, or two justices of the peace of any county.*

The maximum penalty for persons conducting the training is seven years in prison; for those being trained it is two years. Prosecutions have to be brought within six months of the commission of the offence (s.7). Training in the making or use of firearms or explosive substances is also an offence under section 54 of the Terrorism Act 2000, the maximum penalty being 10 years in prison and an unlimited fine.

Chapter 9

Freedom of Expression

Paul Mageean[*]

The right to freedom of opinion and expression is one of the cornerstones of a properly functioning democratic society. It has featured in all of the key international and regional human rights instruments. Article 19 of the Universal Declaration of Human Rights states that:

Everyone has the right to freedom of opinion and expression; this right includes freedom to hold opinions without interference and to seek, receive and impart information and ideas through any media and regardless of frontiers.

The United Kingdom and Ireland are both signatories to the Universal Declaration, although it has no standing in domestic law.

Article 10 of the European Convention on Human Rights states that:

1. Everyone has the right to freedom of expression. This right shall include freedom to hold opinions and to receive and impart information and ideas without interference by public authorities and regardless of frontiers. This Article shall not prevent States from requiring the licensing of broadcasting, television and radio.

2. The exercise of this freedom, since it carries with it duties and responsibilities, may be subject to such formalities, conditions, restrictions or penalties as are prescribed by law and are necessary in a democratic society, in the interests of national security, territorial integrity or public safety, for the prevention of disorder or crime, for the protection of the reputation or rights of others, for preventing the disclosure of information received in confidence, or for maintaining the authority and impartiality of the judiciary.

Article 10 is of course now part of domestic UK law, by virtue of the Human Rights Act 1998. Before incorporation, a number of aspects

---

[*] A lot of the material in this chapter derives from that produced for the third edition of this handbook by Steve McBride.

of British and Irish law had been successfully challenged at the European level under Article 10, including the rules on telephone tapping and contempt of court. Since 2 October 2000 the press has lost several cases in the English courts despite section 12 of the 1998 Act, which states that courts must have particular regard to the importance of the Convention right to freedom of expression.

The law within Northern Ireland relating to freedom of expression must be sought in a wide variety of sources besides the Human Rights Act:

- The criminal law punishes various offences which involve threatening or inciting comments, comments deemed to be offensive to public morals, breaches of official secrecy or the prejudicing of court proceedings.
- The civil law, through the rules on defamation *(i.e.* libel and slander), allows an individual to protect his or her reputation and also provides remedies for, amongst other things, breach of confidence and breach of copyright.

Not only individuals but also the mass media are subject to most of these restraints, and the mass media are in some cases subject to others also.

Criminal offences

Incitement

It is an offence under judge-made law to incite another person, whether by threats or encouragement, to commit any criminal offence. The incitement can be by words or conduct. There must be an intention that the other person commit the offence, but it is irrelevant whether or not the offence is actually committed.

Conspiracy

It is an offence under article 9 of the Criminal Attempts and Conspiracy (NI) Order 1983 to agree with any person to commit any criminal offence. Conspiracy is committed as soon as there is such an agreement; it need not be formal, explicit or detailed.

Threats

A threat to kill someone, communicated to that person or another, is a criminal offence, carrying a sentence of up to 10 years' imprisonment. It is also a crime, carrying the same maximum sentence, to threaten without lawful excuse to damage or destroy the property of another. There are specific criminal offences of procuring sexual intercourse by threats or false pretences, and of obtaining entry into any premises by violence or the threat of violence.

Intimidation

Section 1 of the Protection of the Person and Property Act (NI) 1969 provides that a person shall be guilty of an offence if he or she:

> *unlawfully causes, by force, threats, or menaces or in any way whatsoever, any other person (a) to leave any place where that person is for the time being resident or in occupation; or (b) to leave his employment; or (c) to terminate the services or employment of any person; or (d) to do or refrain from doing any act.*

There is a penalty of up to five years' imprisonment for such intimidation (see also p.179).

Incitement to hatred

Article 9 of the Public Order (NI) Order 1987 makes it an offence to use or display threatening, abusive or insulting words or behaviour, with intent to stir up hatred or fear of a section of the Northern Ireland community, or where such fear or hatred is likely to be stirred up. The fear or hatred must be directed against a group of persons defined by religious belief, colour, race, nationality or ethnic or national origins. It is not an offence to use such words or behaviour in a private dwelling, provided that the person concerned has no reason to suppose that the words or behaviour will be seen or heard outside.

Prosecutions under this section are extremely rare. Indeed the CAJ has referred some matters to the police with a view to prosecution under this section, but none has actually resulted in prosecutions.

It is similarly an offence under articles 10 and 11 of the Public Order (NI) Order to publish, distribute, play or show written or taped material which is threatening, abusive or insulting, with the intention of stirring up fear or hatred or where such fear or hatred is likely to be aroused. It is an offence under article 13 to possess such material with a view to publishing, displaying or distributing it.

As of 1 March 2003 the Northern Ireland Office was considering responses made to its consultation paper on reform of the race and sectarian crime legislation in Northern Ireland. It is considering the creation of new offences and changes to the rules on sentencing.

Rumours

Article 14 of the Public Order (NI) Order 1981 makes it an offence to publish or circulate any statement or report likely to stir up hatred or fear of any section of the public in Northern Ireland on the basis of race, religion or national origin, knowing that report or statement to be false and intending to provoke a breach of the peace at any time.

Poison pen letters

The Malicious Communications (NI) Order 1988 makes it an offence to send or deliver articles with the intention of causing distress or anxiety. The maximum penalty is a fine of £2,500.

Bomb hoaxes

It is an offence under article 3 of the Criminal Law (Amendment) (NI) Order 1977 intentionally to cause or communicate a false bomb warning. The maximum penalty is five years' imprisonment.

Support for proscribed organisations

It is an offence under section 12 of the Terrorism Act 2000 to invite support for a proscribed organisation, to manage, arrange or speak at a meeting which the person knows is to support a proscribed organisation, further the activities of such an organisation or to be addressed by a person who belongs to (or professes to belong to) a proscribed organisation.

Public order offences

These are dealt with in Chapter 8.

Sedition

The old offence of sedition (also called seditious libel) makes it a crime to speak or publish words which are likely and intended to provoke public disorder and violence against the monarch, government or constitution of the United Kingdom. In practice, conduct which might once have been charged as sedition is now likely to be dealt with under one of the other headings mentioned here.

Incitement to disaffection

The Incitement to Disaffection Act 1934 makes it an offence punishable by two years' imprisonment to endeavour to seduce any member of the armed forces from his or her duty or allegiance to the Crown, while the Mutiny Act 1797 makes it an offence punishable by life imprisonment to incite any member of the armed forces to mutiny or commit traitorous acts. The 1934 Act also criminalises possession of a document inciting disaffection with the intention of using it for that purpose.

Defamation

The law of defamation causes a great deal of difficulty for journalists and others making public comment.   Defamation is essentially the publication of a statement about someone which is both untrue and likely to be damaging to his or her reputation. Publication simply means the communication of the statement to another person (other than the person defamed) and the statement need not be in words; a drawing or cartoon may suffice.

Defamation may be either libel or slander; libel is defamation in a permanent form, notably in printed form, but also including film, tape, television and theatre. Slander is defamation in non-permanent form, usually unrecorded speech. There is only one important difference between the two forms of defamation: for slander, but not for libel, there is a need to prove financial loss. The exceptions are slanderous words concerning a person's competence in his or her trade or business, or suggesting that a woman is "unchaste" or that a person has a contagious disease or has committed a criminal offence. In these cases financial loss need not be proved.

Two particular aspects of suing for defamation discourage the making of such claims and encourage the settlement of those that are made. First, legal aid is not available either to take or to defend a defamation action. Second, defamation is one of the very few civil issues which must be tried by a jury (unless both parties agree to trial by judge only). The jury (consisting of seven people in Northern Ireland) has to decide whether the plaintiff (*i.e.* the person bringing the action) has been defamed and, if so, the amount of damages to be awarded. The issues involved may be very complex, making for an uncertain outcome and a long and expensive trial. The amounts awarded by juries for defamation may vary from the colossal (£1.5 million in one recent case) to the contemptuous (1p in Albert Reynolds' clash with the Sunday Times in 1999). Defamation actions are usually a risky business for all concerned.

Proving defamation

A person who alleges defamation must show that the comments in question diminish his or her reputation in the eyes of "right thinking members of society". The judge must decide whether the statement is capable of bearing a defamatory meaning, but the jury must decide whether it actually does carry such a meaning and whether it could reasonably be taken to apply to the plaintiff.

The intentions of the person making the statement are normally irrelevant; in most circumstances it will be no defence to say that no defamatory meaning was intended, or that the statement was not intended to be taken as referring to the plaintiff. Nor need the plaintiff show that anyone did in fact read such a meaning into the statement, or thought any less of the plaintiff because of it. It is enough if they might have done.

The court is entitled to consider innuendoes and hidden meanings, and it is not necessary for the defamation to be obvious to the general public: it is sufficient if some other person with particular knowledge is able to identify the plaintiff as the subject of a defamatory statement. A statement about a broad group, such as a racial grouping, will not normally be actionable, but a statement about a specific grouping, or an unidentified member of such a grouping (such as a committee) will be actionable by any member of that group.

Defences to defamation

It is a defence to prove that on the balance of probabilities the statement was true (this is known as the defence of "justification"). But it is not enough that the defendant believed that the statement was true, or had reasonable grounds for believing that it was true, or was merely repeating what he or she had been told by someone else. It is also a defence to prove that the statement was fair comment, *i.e.* that it was the expression of an opinion held honestly and without malice by the defendant on a matter of public interest. The statement must be an expression of opinion, not of fact, and the facts on which it is based must be substantially correct. Matters of public interest include politics, books and plays.

The defence of "privilege" exists so that people may be free, in appropriate circumstances, both public and private, to communicate without fear of being sued for defamation. "Absolute" privilege covers statements made in Parliament, in parliamentary papers or in court, and extends to fair, accurate, and contemporaneous newspaper reports of judicial proceedings. The makers of such statements and reports cannot be sued for defamation. In a recent case before the European Court of Human Rights, *A v UK* (2002), the Court held that a woman's rights under the European Convention had not been violated just because she was not able to sue her MP for libel in relation to statements he had made about her in Parliament. A number of governments intervened in the case to defend the principle of parliamentary privilege. The Court held that such privilege was justifiable and proportionate in a democratic society.

"Qualified" privilege, which means that the maker of a statement cannot be sued provided that the material is published without malice, attaches to a wide variety of other situations, including reports of parliamentary proceedings and non-contemporaneous reports of judicial proceedings. Fair and accurate reports of public meetings or meetings of a range of public or semi-public bodies, including local authorities, and reports of the decisions of trade, professional, religious, educational and sporting bodies are protected by qualified privilege, provided that anyone aggrieved by such a report is given a reasonable right of reply. The House of Lords has held, overruling the Court of Appeal in Northern Ireland, that a press conference is a public meeting for these purposes (*McCartan Turkington Breen v Times Newspapers Ltd*, 2000). Qualified privilege also covers situations where one person is under a moral or legal duty to give information and another to receive it. This might cover complaints to the police, to social workers or to an employer about an employee.

In 1991 the Neill Committee Report recommended a number of amendments to the law aimed at simplifying and speeding up defamation actions. The Defamation Act of 1996 enacted some of these recommendations, and in particular established a procedure whereby the publisher of a defamatory statement can offer to publish a correction and apology and, if necessary, have damages set by a judge rather than by a jury. The Act provides that anyone who may be associated with a defamatory statement, but is not the author or publisher of that statement – such as a printer, distributor or live broadcaster – has a complete defence provided that he or she took reasonable care and had no reasonable notice of any defamatory content. The Act also reduces the time limit for bringing an action to one year in most cases, and provides a summary procedure for dealing with some cases where there is no prospect of success or where no realistic defence can be offered.

Injunctions

Anyone who anticipates that a defamatory statement will be published about him or her may apply for an injunction to prevent publication. The courts, however, acknowledge the importance of protecting free speech and will not normally grant such an injunction where the defences of justification or fair comment are likely to be pleaded.

Malicious falsehood

There may be occasions when people suffer damage through incorrect statements being made about them, even though those statements do not strike at their reputation and hence are not defamatory. For example, a professional person may lose business through an incorrect report that he or she has retired or gone on a long holiday. Anyone in such a position may be able to sue for malicious falsehood where it can be shown that the person making the statement acted from malicious or improper motives. In *Kaye v Robertson* (1991) an injured actor successfully sued a tabloid newspaper under this heading.

Criminal libel

Libel may also be a crime if it is so serious as to require criminal prosecution in the public interest. Proceedings against a newspaper or periodical can be initiated only with the consent of a High Court judge, and such consent is likely to be granted only in exceptional circumstances.

Broadcasting and television

Broadcasting in the UK, and hence in Northern Ireland, requires a government licence under the Wireless Telegraphy Acts. All television broadcasting in Northern Ireland is under the authority of either the BBC or the Independent Television Commission (the ITC), a regulatory and supervisory body which grants the franchises under which all independent television companies operate, and which was set up in 1990 to replace the former Independent Broadcasting Authority. The Independent Radio Authority has a similar role in respect of independent radio stations, and the Cable Television Authority deals with cable television. Satellite television based in the UK is subject to the authority of the ITC, with the Home Secretary having a power to proscribe any unacceptable foreign satellite service.

The BBC was established by Charter and the ITC by the Broadcasting Acts of 1990 and 1996. Both have ultimate responsibility for programmes broadcast under their authority. The ITC is under a statutory duty to ensure that news reporting is fair and impartial and that nothing is broadcast which offends against good taste or decency or which is likely to incite crime or disorder or be offensive to public feelings. The BBC has bound itself to a similar standard. Unlike its predecessor, the ITC does not have the right to call in programmes for pre-transmission vetting, but it does have significant sanctions in respect of independent television companies, including the power to impose financial penalties.

The 1990 Act makes the Obscene Publications Act and, in Northern Ireland, the incitement to hatred laws (p.187 above), applicable to broadcasting. In Northern Ireland a senior police officer, suspecting that an offence has been or is likely to be committed under the incitement to hatred laws, has the right to demand access to any relevant scripts, films or tapes.

The Broadcasting Standards Commission

The Broadcasting Standards Commission was established by the Broadcasting Act 1996, replacing the Broadcasting Standards Council and the Broadcasting Complaints Commission. It has a statutory duty to monitor broadcasting and to draw up codes of practice in respect of sex, violence, good taste and decency in broadcasting, and also in respect of the avoidance of unjust and unfair treatment and the unwarranted infringement of privacy. Broadcasting bodies are under an obligation to take account of the Commission's codes when establishing their own practices. The Commission has the power to receive complaints about standards in broadcasting and can require broadcasting bodies to publicise its findings in respect of such complaints. The BSC can be contacted at 7 The Sanctuary, London SW1P 3 JS (tel: 020 7233 0544).

Broadcasting bans

Both the BBC and the ITC are subject to reserved government powers. These include the power, vested in the Home Secretary, to order both bodies to include or exclude specific matters in their broadcasts. This power was invoked in October 1988 when Douglas Hurd, the then Home Secretary, instructed the BBC and the IBA to:

refrain at all times from sending any broadcast matter which consists of or includes any words spoken, whether in the course of an interview or discussion or otherwise, by a person who appears or is heard on the programme in which the matter is broadcast (a) where the person speaking the words represents or purports to represent an organisation specified below, or (b) the words support or solicit or invite support for such an organisation.

The notice then specified eight organisations proscribed under emergency legislation including the Irish Republican Army, the Irish National Liberation Army, the Ulster Volunteer Force, the Ulster Freedom Fighters, and the Red Hand Commandos, as well as three otherwise legal organisations – Sinn Féin, Republican Sinn Féin and the Ulster Defence Association (eventually made illegal in 1992).

The notice stated that the ban did not apply during election campaigns or to words spoken in Parliament. The Home Office also indicated that it did not prevent the showing of pictures of an affected speaker while a reporter read a paraphrase or even a word-for-word report of what the speaker was saying. Nevertheless the ban was still broad-ranging and, because it was imposed by the Home Secretary exercising powers under existing legislation, it was not readily subject to legal challenge or clarification. One legal challenge was rejected by the House of Lords (*R v Secretary of State for the Home Department, ex parte Brind*, 1991), and again by the European Commission of Human Rights. Decisions on implementation of the ban were in the final analysis a matter for the broadcasting authorities. Members of the public, persons affected by the ban and even journalists and programme makers had very little means of redress over any particular decision.

The ban was rescinded shortly after the declaration of the IRA ceasefire in September 1994. Legally, it could be re-imposed at any time, although arguably the Human Rights Act may impact on the legality of such a move.

Newspapers and periodicals

Complaints against newspapers can be made to the Press Complaints Commission (the PCC), which was set up in 1991 following the Calcutt Report of 1990. The PCC has published a code of practice covering issues such as accuracy, the right to reply, invasion of privacy, harassment and misrepresentation, but its real powers are very limited and essentially the code of practice relies on self-regulation. The PCC does not provide financial compensation for complainants. It tries instead to find an amicable agreement between the parties involved or, in other cases, provides critical adjudications in the resolution of complaints. It receives about 3,000 complaints every year, the majority of which relate to accuracy in reporting and intrusion into privacy. The PCC can be contacted at 1 Salisbury Square, London EC4Y 8JB (tel: 020 7353 1248; helpline: 020 7353 3732).

Advertising

Complaints about advertisements may be made to the Advertising Standards Authority (the ASA). This is an independent body sponsored by the advertising industry itself. It has published a Code of Advertising Practice, among the requirements of which are that advertisements should be legal, decent, honest and truthful. The ASA rules on complaints and in extreme cases may instruct subscribing media organisations not to accept an advertisement. The ITC (see p. 189) applies similar rules in respect of advertising on commercial television and radio. The ASA can be contacted at 2 Torrington Place, London WC1E 7HW (tel: 020 7580 5555).

Films and videos

The British Board of Film Classification censors and classifies films and video tapes. In respect of video tapes it has statutory powers under the Video Recordings Act 1985, which allows massive fines for selling or distributing videos which have not obtained a Board classification. Most local authorities, which have a licensing role in respect of cinemas in their areas, make it a licensing requirement that no film can be shown which does not have a BBFC certificate but they have the right to ban even films which do have a classification. Local authority licensing requirements do not apply to private cinema clubs.

Copyright

Copyright law prevents the use of protected material without the copyright owner's consent. Material protected may include original literary works (very broadly defined and including almost anything written down), artistic and musical works, photographs, films, sound and video recordings, and television and radio broadcasts. It is not a breach of copyright to make fair use of a copyrighted work for the purposes of criticism or reporting of current events, provided that the author of the work is properly acknowledged. Use of copyright material may also be justified where the public interest is best served by publication. Breach of copyright is not a crime, but it allows the copyright owner to sue for compensation.

The internet

A developing area in relation to freedom of expression is of course the internet. Governments are increasingly interested in subjecting the internet to restrictions. The reasons for this may be legitimate, such as tackling child pornography and hate speech, but also some governments may be interested in restricting criticism of the government. It is important that in trying to deal with these difficult issues government bears in mind the important role the internet plays in providing important information to ordinary citizens. In addition, of course, any attempts to restrict access to the net or what is on the net will need to be tested against the provisions of the Human Rights Act.

However it is clear that the Regulation of Investigatory Powers Act 2000 gives the security services extensive powers not only to intercept email communications but also to get access to details of internet access by a particular user including sites visited and chat rooms used. Human rights groups, including Amnesty International, have expressed the view that these powers are excessive and not subject to sufficient judicial scrutiny.

It is also the case that governments can find attempts to impose restrictions on what is on the net to be difficult, particularly because many ISPs (Internet Service Providers) are outside the UK. In relation to the issue of child pornography and chat rooms the government has set up a voluntary scheme involving those in the industry to try and ensure protection for children. It is likely, however, that legislation dealing with the internet will be passed in future years.

Obscenity

In England and Wales the judge-made law on obscenity was largely superseded by the Obscene Publications Act 1959, but that legislation has never been extended to Northern Ireland. The common law still applies here, making it a criminal offence to publish what is technically called "an obscene libel."

The common law test of obscenity is whether the material in question has a tendency to "deprave or corrupt" those who are likely to see it. Whether a particular publication is obscene is for the jury (if there is one) or the judge to decide, applying the current standards of ordinary decent people. "Deprave or corrupt" means something which is more than merely shocking or offensive. Although obscenity is normally taken to apply to pornographic matter, it can cover other material as well, such as publications advocating drug-taking or glorifying violence.

To break the law it is sufficient, as in defamation, to "publish" the material to one other person, but it is not necessary to prove that any person has actually been depraved or corrupted. Having an intention to publish, knowing that the material would have a tendency to deprave or corrupt, is enough. The Obscene Publications Act provides a specific defence for publications if they are for the public good in that they are in the interests of science, literature, art or learning, or are other objects of general interest. The common law position is less clear, but there is probably a basis for an essentially similar defence. The Human Rights Act 1998 may, of course, have an impact on such prosecutions.

Indecency

A variety of statutes and local by laws deal with indecent behaviour, publication or display. "Indecent" lacks any clear legal definition but would seem to include anything offensive to the standards of ordinary reasonable people, though lacking the element of depravity necessary for obscenity (see too Chapter 17).

The customs and excise authorities have wide powers to seize indecent or obscene material brought into the United Kingdom, though the effect of a ruling by the European Court of Justice has been to restrict these powers to material which would be deemed obscene rather than merely indecent. The Post Office Act 1953 makes it an offence to send any indecent or obscene article through the post, while the Unsolicited Goods and Services (NI) Order 1976 prohibits the posting of unsolicited sexual publications. The British Telecom Act 1981 criminalises telephone calls which are grossly offensive, indecent, obscene or menacing. The Protection of Children (NI) Order 1978 makes it an offence to take, distribute or possess indecent photographs of children.

Blasphemy

The judge-made law on blasphemy once made it a crime to deny the truth of the Christian religion. In its modern form, however, blasphemy simply covers comment which amounts to an insulting or abusive attack on the Christian religion. The intention of the person making or publishing the comment is irrelevant; it is only necessary to show that he or she is responsible for comments which the court deems to be sufficiently offensive.

The offence remains extremely vague and unsatisfactory. As has been confirmed by a case arising out of the Salman Rushdie affair (*Ex parte Choudhury,* 1990), it does not protect non-Christian religions, and there is even doubt as to whether it extends beyond protecting the doctrines of the Church of England. With modern legislation now providing racial and religious groups with some measure of protection against abuse and discrimination, it would be best if the crime of blasphemy were either abolished altogether or limited, as the Law Commission has recommended, to disruptive or abusive behaviour at a religious service or on church premises.

The Elected Authorities Act

The Elected Authorities (NI) Act 1989 provides that any candidate for election to a district council or to the Northern Ireland Assembly (but not to the Westminster Parliament) must sign a declaration when submitting his or her nomination papers, and again, if elected, before taking his or her seat. The declaration states that:

> *if elected, I will not by word or deed express support for or approval of (a) any proscribed organisation or (b) acts of*

terrorism (that is to say, violence for political ends) connected with the affairs of Northern Ireland.

The declaration covers comments at public meetings or in circumstances where the person concerned can reasonably be expected to know that his or her comments will become public knowledge. The relevant test is whether the comments can reasonably be understood to express support or approval for an illegal organisation or for acts of terrorism.

The Act states that a district council, or any member of that council or any elector for that council, may take legal proceedings in the High Court for a judicial determination that a member of that council is in breach of the declaration. If such a ruling is granted, that member will be disqualified from holding office and will not be permitted to stand again for election for a period of five years. No such proceedings have yet been taken.

Contempt of court

The law on contempt of court seeks to protect the fair and impartial administration of justice. It is particularly concerned with preventing juries from being exposed to prejudicial comment. The modern law is largely to be found in the Contempt of Court Act 1981, which was passed after criticism of existing UK law by the European Court of Human Rights in the *Sunday Times* case (1979).

The 1981 Act makes it an offence to publish anything which creates a substantial risk that the course of justice in any particular case will be substantially impeded or prejudiced. This covers any speech, writing or broadcast addressed to the public or any section of it, and the rule applies when any proceedings are "active" (*i.e. sub judice*, to use the old phrase). Criminal proceedings are active from the time when someone is arrested or an arrest warrant or a summons has been issued. Civil proceedings are active from the time when a date is set for trial. Appeals are active from the time when leave to appeal is applied for or notice of appeal lodged.

Liability is "strict", *i.e.* the intention of the publisher is not normally relevant. It has been held, however, that the 1981 Act has not affected the common law position concerning material published with the intention of prejudicing or interfering with court proceedings: it can still be contempt to publish such material, even when no proceedings are active (*Attorney General v News Group Newspapers*, 1988).

Publication of an accused's criminal record or comment on his or her character or that of a witness, or linking an accused to other offences, would probably constitute a substantial risk of prejudice, as would publication of a photograph of an accused where identification may be an issue. But fair, accurate and contemporaneous reports of proceedings in court cannot be contempt and discussion in good faith of public affairs or matters of public interest is not contempt if any risk of prejudice to particular proceedings is only incidental to the discussion.

There is also some disagreement as to whether the *sub judice* rule applies to those cases which would be dealt with in Northern Ireland's Diplock courts, with some arguing that because juries do not sit in those courts, the rule does not apply. It is also a fact that in recent cases in both Britain and Northern Ireland high levels of arguably prejudicial material have appeared in the media with no action being taken under the Contempt of Court Act.

Any attempt to bribe, intimidate or otherwise improperly influence witnesses, jurors or judges would be contempt of court. Abusive criticism of judges, or accusations of prejudice or partiality against them, may amount to the old form of contempt known as "scandalising the court", although the Court of Appeal has said that criticism in good faith of a judgment, however vigorous, should not constitute contempt.

Section 8 of the 1981 Act completely outlaws any approaches to jurors, however innocuous. It declares it to be contempt of court to obtain, disclose or solicit any particulars of statements made, opinions expressed, arguments advanced or votes cast by members of a jury during their deliberations.

Contempt of court also covers disorderly behaviour in court, failure to comply with court orders or to observe an undertaking given to the court, and obstructing court officers in the course of their duties. It was held in the course of the "Spycatcher" litigation that a newspaper could be in contempt of court for publishing material which was the subject of injunctions preventing publication by other newspapers. In *Harman v Secretary of State for the Home Department* (1983) a solicitor allowed a journalist to see some documents concerning prisons which the court had ordered the Home Office to disclose to the court. The House of Lords decided that this behaviour was contempt, but when the solicitor took the case to the European Commission of Human Rights the government agreed to settle it. Under the terms of this settlement the government promised to change the law so that it would no longer be a contempt to disclose documents already produced in court pursuant to a court order. Despite this, in *McShane v UK* (2002) the RUC lodged a formal complaint with the Law Society of Northern Ireland against a solicitor whom the RUC alleged had disclosed to a third party (so that this party could submit them to the European Court) documents which she had access to by way of pre-inquest disclosure. The European Court of Human Rights ruled that this RUC action was a breach of Article 34 of the Convention, which guarantees free and unhindered access to the Convention system.

Other restrictions on court reporting

Most legal proceedings in Northern Ireland take place in open court, and can be reported by the press. The press and public can be excluded from prosecutions taken under official secrets legislation and in a number of circumstances where publicity would defeat the interests of justice, such as blackmail cases. Similarly, the Contempt of Court Act 1981 allows courts, in exceptional circumstances, to order that the names of parties or witnesses, or other relevant information, must not be mentioned in open court or the press.

There are a number of other circumstances where press reporting of court proceedings is subject to limitations. The names of rape victims are protected from publication by the Sexual Offences (NI) Order 1978 (see Chapter 17). Only very limited factual information can be published about committal proceedings in magistrates' courts (which precede criminal trials), unless the defendant asks for reporting restrictions to be lifted. In a jury trial the press cannot report legal arguments heard in the absence of the jury. Juvenile court proceedings can be reported on condition that the identity of the defendant or witnesses is not revealed (see Chapter 18). Most matrimonial proceedings are held in private and are subject to substantial reporting restrictions.

It should also be noted that a recent review of criminal justice (by Lord Justice Auld) recommended that the name of a person arrested should not be published until the prosecutor had determined whether to proceed with the remand application. While the UK government indicated that it accepted this recommendation, it is not clear to what extent it will be implemented and whether it will affect current practice.

Journalists' sources

The Contempt of Court Act 1981 provides a measure of protection for journalists' sources. Section 10 says that a court can order a journalist or editor to disclose a source only where such disclosure is necessary in the interests of justice or of national security, or for the prevention of disorder or crime.

The police may in some circumstances seize documents and other journalistic material. Under the Police and Criminal Evidence (NI) Order 1989 they may obtain a court order granting access to such material where they can satisfy a judge that the necessary conditions have been met (see Chapter 3). They may also be able to obtain such material, including films and photographs, under section 39 of the Terrorism Act 2000 (see also s.19 and Sch.5), which requires the disclosure of any information which may be of assistance in preventing terrorism. In 1999 Ed Moloney, the Northern Editor of the Sunday Tribune, was issued with a court order under the equivalent provisions of the previously applicable Prevention of Terrorism Act to hand over his notes from a 1990 interview with William Stobie, a suspect in the murder of Pat Finucane in 1989. Moloney refused to comply with the order and sought judicial review. He was successful, but only on the limited ground that the police had not sufficiently made the case that the documents in question would be of substantial value to the investigation. However, the law under which the original order was sought remains largely unaltered.

In the recent case of *Ashworth Hospital Authority v MGN Ltd* (2002) the House of Lords held that the Daily Mirror could be required to disclose the source of its information about the private medical records of the moors murderer Ian Brady. The Lords said it was enough if the source had been "involved" in wrongdoing, but they stressed that disclosure should be ordered only exceptionally and that there had to be both a pressing social need and a legitimate aim which was being proportionately pursued.

Official secrets

Official secrecy has often been the subject of very considerable controversy. Section 1 of the Official Secrets Act 1911, which is still in force, makes what would commonly be called spying an offence; it deals with collecting or revealing information likely to be useful to an enemy, for any purpose prejudicial to the safety or interests of the state. The Official Secrets Act 1989 essentially creates two kinds of offence:

- It makes it an offence for any member or former member of the security services, or anyone associated with security or intelligence activities, to disclose any information about such activities. The Home Secretary may by notification make anyone who comes into contact with intelligence activities subject to this restriction. Journalists who assist or encourage such disclosure, or who publish such information with grounds for believing that it has been disclosed without permission, may be prosecuted as accomplices.

- It is an offence to disclose other kinds of government information where damage is caused or likely to be caused by unauthorised disclosure. The categories of information covered include anything which would endanger British interests abroad, prejudice the capabilities of the armed forces, or impede the work of the police. Confidential information obtained from another state or international organisation is also protected. Where information about intelligence, security, defence or international issues has been communicated to other governments or international organisations and has been leaked abroad it is an offence to repeat it in the United Kingdom.

Section 5 of the 1989 Act also makes it an offence for journalists or editors to publish information where they know it to be protected by the Act and have cause to believe that publication would be damaging to the national interest. The Act does not allow any defence of acting in the public interest: unauthorised disclosure, and in some cases publication, of protected information is a criminal offence even though it may expose criminal activities, corruption or serious government malpractice. The absence of such a public interest defence is a particular cause for concern, even though there was no such defence in the old Act of 1911, but it may be that scrutiny in the courts and the common sense of juries will tend to keep a check on any abuse of the 1989 provisions.

David Shayler, a former employee of MI5 who disclosed information to the press detailing an alleged plot to murder Colonel Qaddafi of Libya, recently lost his appeal against being convicted for breaching the Act (*R v Shayler*, 2002). His disclosure had supposedly put secret agents' lives at risk. He has lodged an application with the European Court of Human Rights alleging that his Article 10 rights have been violated by the criminal action taken against him.

Unauthorised disclosure of government information outside the areas specified in the Official Secrets Act 1989 is not a criminal offence, but it may well expose the culprit to internal disciplinary procedures. The government may also use the civil law to obtain injunctions against publication or to claim damages for breach of confidence.

"D Notices"

The "D Notice" system is an informal system which acts as a restraint on press coverage of sensitive defence and security topics. The notices are issued by the Defence, Press and Broadcasting Committee, a body composed of officials from government departments concerned with national security and representatives of broadcasting organisations and the press. The Committee gives guidance on the publication of material which is sensitive on national security grounds, and from time to time issues notices warning that publication of certain stories may be harmful to national security. The system lacks legal force: the Committee cannot prevent publication and prior clearance from the Committee is no defence to prosecution under the Official Secrets Acts.

In a recent case the journalist Tony Geraghty, who was served with a D notice requesting him to hand over the manuscript of his pending book, refused to do so. He was subsequently charged under the Official Secrets Act but eventually the charges were dropped.

Further useful addresses

- Article 19
  Lancaster House
  33 Islington High Street
  London N1 9LH
  tel: 020 7278 9292
  www.article19.org

Chapter 10

Information and Privacy Rights

Brice Dickson [*]

This chapter outlines the legal position in Northern Ireland concerning the right to obtain information. It explains when each of us can obtain information about others and when each of us is entitled to keep information about ourselves private. It is an area of law which is undergoing considerable change at the moment, partly because of the passing of the Freedom of Information Act 2000 and partly because the Human Rights Act 1998 has created a right to a private life which did not previously exist in any part of the United Kingdom. The chapter overlaps to some extent with Chapter 9 on the right to freedom of expression; in particular, three of the matters dealt with there – the rules on contempt of court, disclosure of official secrets and "D" notices – are particularly relevant to the subject of this chapter also.

In general, giving people access to information held by others is important because informed citizens are the basic ideal upon which a free and democratic society is premised. If public authorities were allowed to operate in secrecy there is a danger that they would abuse the powers entrusted to them and that officials would become corrupt. Allowing people access to official information enables them to participate more effectively in law-making and administration. Moreover people need to be able to check the accuracy of information which is held about them; otherwise they could be denied basic entitlements.

The Open Government Code

At present access to information held by official bodies is regulated not by a fully enforceable law but by a Code of Practice on Access to Information (sometimes called the Open Government Code).

---

[*] Some of the material in this chapter is derived from that written for earlier editions by Gerry McCormack.

A copy of this is available on the website of the Lord Chancellor's Department (*www.lcd.gov.uk*). In Northern Ireland the Code applies to public bodies under the jurisdiction of the Assembly Ombudsman. Some Northern Ireland departments and bodies are expressly subject to the jurisdiction of the UK Parliamentary Commissioner for Administration (see Chapter 2).

The Freedom of Information Act 2000

By tradition the United Kingdom has run its affairs in relative secrecy. Many years of strong campaigning for a Freedom of Information Act came to fruition only in 2000. By then many other countries already had quite a history of open government. Sweden's system for granting the public access to information dates back to its Constitution of 1766 and in the USA the Administrative Procedure Act was passed in 1946, giving a right of access to government records in relation to proceedings taking place before an administrative body. A more far-reaching Freedom of Information Act was passed there in 1966 and it has given rise to a great deal of litigation. Canada, Australia and New Zealand each enacted a Freedom of Information Act in 1982 and the Republic of Ireland did so in 1997. The Irish Act currently applies to some 360 public bodies and all remaining public bodies (with the exception of the police and schools) are to be covered by the end of 2005.

A number of schemes were proposed in the United Kingdom for affording the public a right of access to government-held information. A Green Paper in 1979 concluded that a major step forward would be the production of a Code of Practice to guide Ministers in reacting to requests for information and as a result the Open Government Code referred to above was produced. Mr. David Steel MP put forward a private members' Bill in 1984, but it failed to gain enough Parliamentary support. Since then the main group lobbying for reform has been the influential Campaign for Freedom of Information, based in London. The Labour Party was elected to power in 1997 with a commitment to introduce appropriate legislation.

The Freedom of Information Act 2000 gives a general right of access to all types of "recorded" information held by public authorities (s.1). It therefore extends the rights conferred by the Data Protection Act 1998, which are confined to allowing individuals to access information about themselves. "Public authority" in this context includes all government departments, all "non-departmental public bodies" (such as the Equality Commission for Northern Ireland and the Northern Ireland Human Rights Commission), all National Health Service bodies (including GPs and dentists), all schools, colleges and universities and all police forces. A full list is contained in Schedule 1 to the Act. Individuals will be able to demand to be told "promptly" (and certainly within 20 days) whether certain information is held by the public authority and to inspect or receive a copy or summary of the information if it is held. The right applies even to information collected before the Act was passed but individual requests cannot be made until 1 January 2005 and they will have to be made in writing (e-mails will suffice).

Public authorities must produce a "publication scheme", which (by s.19) has to be approved by the Information Commissioner (see below). The deadline for submitting schemes for approval differs depending on the type of public authority in question. For central government organisations, or public bodies sponsored by these, the deadline was 30 September 2002; for local authorities it was 31 December 2002; for police and prosecution services and the armed forces it is 30 June 2003; for the NHS it is 31 August 2003 and for education bodies it is 31 December 2003. The schemes must set out the range, format and location of information which is held by the authority and which will be made available. If "significant" time will be spent searching for or producing the information requested, a fee is chargeable by the authority in advance (in accordance with Fees Regulations yet to be published) and the time for releasing the information is then extended to three months.

Certain types of information (23 in all) are exempt from having to be made available, including information which relates to national security, defence, international relations, law enforcement, legal professional privilege, commercial interests or personal data (ss.21-44). In most of these cases the authority must first ask itself whether the supposedly exempt information would, if released, prejudice those considerations and, if so, whether the public interest in withholding the information outweighs the public interest in releasing it. If exempt information forms part of a generally non-exempt document the document must still be released but with the exempt parts obscured. Information is exempt if it was supplied to the public authority by a body such as the Security Service or the National Criminal Intelligence Service (s.23), provided a certificate to that effect has been signed by a government Minister. The Information Commissioner or any applicant whose request for information is affected by this certificate can then appeal to the Information Tribunal (see below) against any such certificate.

Public authorities will not have to provide information if the request is "vexatious" (s.14). If the information sought has already been transferred to the Public Record Office of Northern Ireland, the request will be passed on to that Office (s.15). Public authorities have a statutory duty to provide advice and assistance, so far as is reasonable, to persons making requests for information (s.16) and the Lord Chancellor has issued a code of practice providing guidance to public authorities as to the practice which they should follow in this regard ("the section 45 Code"). Another code gives guidance on good practice in the management of records within organisations ("the section 46 Code").

The Information Commissioner

The Freedom of Information Act 2000 will be enforced by the Information Commissioner, a new post created in 2001 which subsumes the previous role of the Data Protection Registrar. The Commissioner reports directly to Parliament and in addition to approving and advising on publication schemes and enforcing the Act, his or her role is to promote good practice in this area and to provide information to the general public about the Freedom of Information Act. Under Schedule 3 to the Act the Information Commissioner can apply to a county court judge for a warrant to enter and search premises in order to inspect and seize any material there which may be evidence that a public authority is failing to comply with the Act. He or she can even obtain information from the Ombudsman.

If the Information Commissioner is satisfied that a public authority has failed to comply with the Act he or she can issue an enforcement notice requiring the authority to take specified steps (s.52). Failure to comply with an enforcement notice allows the Information Commissioner to certify this to a judge, who can then deal with the authority as if it had committed a contempt of court (s.54) (see Chapter 9). The Act makes it clear that no claim for compensation can be made in respect of a failure to comply with the Act (s.56).

Appeals against decisions of the Information Commissioner (*e.g.* that a request for information has not been dealt with properly) can be taken to the Information Tribunal (s.57), which has replaced the former Data Protection Tribunal, and in Northern Ireland a further appeal on a point of law can then be taken to the High Court (s.58).

The current Information Commissioner is Mr Richard Thomas. In 2003 three additional Assistant Commissioners will be appointed to run branch offices of the Commission in Scotland, Wales and Northern Ireland.

Each year the Lord Chancellor lays before Parliament a Report on the Implementation of the Freedom of Information Act. The second such report, laid on 29 November 2002 and available from the website of the Lord Chancellor's Department, reproduces all the documents which currently constitute the framework for governing access to government information, including the Open Government Code, the Code of Practice on Openness in the NHS and a summary of the Environmental Information Regulations. (For rights concerning access to environmental information, see Chapter 23. It is anticipated that new regulations covering that area will be brought into effect in 2003 and that the Information Commissioner will then be appointed as the supervising authority there too.)

The Constitution Unit, based in University College London, publishes a very useful quarterly newsletter on freedom of information.

Article 10 of the ECHR

It is often overlooked that Article 10 of the ECHR protects not just the right to freedom of expression but also the right to receive information and ideas without interference by a public authority. But the right to (passively) receive information is not the same thing as the right to (actively) seek information and the European Court has not yet interpreted Article 10 to include the latter. An example of how Article 10 has been used to protect the right to receive information is the case of *Open Door and Dublin Well Woman v Ireland* (1993), where Ireland was held to have violated the Article by restricting the provision of information to Irish women about abortion facilities in other countries.

As mentioned below, Article 8 of the ECHR has also sometimes been interpreted in a way which gives access to information. For example, in *McGinley and Egan v UK* (1998) the European Court held that ex-servicemen stationed on or near Christmas Island at the time of British nuclear tests there 40 years earlier were entitled to all relevant and appropriate information about the potential consequences of the tests (although on the facts the case was lost because the information had been accessible but had not been applied for).

The Data Protection Act 1998

In 1984 a Data Protection Act was passed in order to comply with the Council of Europe's 1981 Convention for the Protection of Individuals with regard to Automatic Processing of Data. It compelled users of computerised data to register with the Data Protection Registrar (now the Information Commissioner), non-registration being a criminal offence. A second Data Protection Act was passed in 1998, replacing the first Act and extending its provisions to non-computerised records. It was prompted by the European Union's Data Protection Directive 95/46/EC and it came into force on 1 March 2000. The Commissioner can issue enforcement or de-registration notices against registered users who violate the Act's data protection principles. To check whether these principles are being maintained the Commissioner has powers of entry and inspection. Appeals against decisions taken by the Commissioner can go to the Information Tribunal (see above).

A user of data is defined by the Act as a person who "controls the contents and use of the data" which are part of a collection processed or intended to be processed by that person or by someone on his or her behalf. The core of the Act is the part giving "data subjects" the right of access to stored data. Upon request in writing (for which a charge of up to £10 can be made) a data user must within 40 days state whether he or she has any personal data relating to the person making the request and must supply that person with a copy of such data. The data subject must be an identifiable living person, not a company. If damage or distress is caused as a result of an inaccurate entry, compensation is payable by the data user unless he or she can prove that such care was taken as was reasonably required in all the circumstances to ensure the accuracy of the data at the time. A court can order inaccurate data to be rectified, erased or supplemented.

Exemptions

Three important matters are exempt from registration:
- personal data required for the purpose of safeguarding national security,
- payroll and accounting data, and
- data held for domestic or club purposes.

In addition, five other types of data are exempt from the subject access provisions:

- personal data held for the prevention or detection of crime,
- personal data held for the assessment or collection of any tax or duty,
- personal data relating to the physical or mental health of the subject,
- data held subject to legal professional privilege or for the making of judicial appointments, and
- data held in confidence for statistical or research purposes.

Data protection principles

The data protection principles which all data users must adhere to are laid out in Schedule 1 to the 1998 Act:

- The information to be contained in personal data must be obtained and processed fairly and lawfully.
- The personal data must be held only for one or more specified and lawful purposes.
- Personal data held must not be used or disclosed in any manner incompatible with the purpose(s) for which it is held.
- Personal data held must be adequate, relevant and not excessive in relation to the purpose for which it is held.
- Personal data must be accurate and, where necessary, kept up to date.
- Personal data must not be kept for longer than is necessary.
- An individual is entitled at reasonable intervals and without undue delay or expense to be informed by any data user whether he or she holds personal data about that individual, and to have access to any such data.
- An individual is entitled, where appropriate, to have personal data corrected or erased.
- Computer bureaux must take appropriate security measures against unauthorised access to or alteration, disclosure, loss or destruction of personal data.

The Information Commissioner is currently drawing up an Employment Practices Data Protection Code to provide best practice guidance to allow employers to comply with the 1998 Act. Parts I and II, dealing respectively with recruitment and selection and with the regulation of employment records, were issued in 2002.

Special situations

The Access to Personal Files and Medical Reports (NI) Order 1991 gives power to the Secretary of State to make regulations conferring on people a right of access to information about themselves on local authority records. To date regulations have been made covering housing, social work and education records. The Act does not, however, permit access to employment records, government benefit and immigration records, or bank, building society and credit records.

The Companies (NI) Order 1986 requires companies incorporated in Northern Ireland to supply certain information to the Companies Registry. This may then be examined by members of the public on payment of a fee. The companies must also disclose certain facts and figures in their annual reports (and any prospectuses issued prior to the issue of shares to the public).

The Land Registration Act (NI) 1970 provides for the registration of the ownership of property in the Land Registry, details of which may be consulted by the public. This scheme applies principally to rural property. The Registration of Deeds Act (NI) 1970 provides for the registration of "memorials" (*i.e.*, shortened versions of certain documents of title to land), a scheme which particularly covers urban property and which again allows for public access.

The registration of births and deaths is provided for under the Births and Deaths Registration (NI) Order 1976. Article 34 requires the Registrar General to keep an index for each register and this is open for inspection by the public. Any individual may obtain a certified copy of an entry in the register upon payment of a fee. The picture regarding marriages is similar. All marriages, with the exception of Roman Catholic marriages, are governed by sections 68-71 of the Marriages (Ireland) Act 1844, which permit searches in the registers. Much the same effect is achieved for Roman Catholic marriages by section 19 of the Registration of Marriages (Ireland) Act 1863, as amended.

Section 23 of the Local Government Act (NI) 1972 requires meetings of a local authority to be open to the public, a right of access which extends to the Fire Authority of Northern Ireland but not to Education and Library Boards or to Health and Social Services Boards. A copy of the agenda at local authority meetings must be supplied on request to any newspaper and the minutes of council meetings during any of the previous six years can be inspected. The 1972 Act permits a council to pass a resolution excluding the public from a meeting whenever publicity would be prejudicial to the public interest by reason of the confidential nature of the business to be transacted or for such special reasons as may be specified (*e.g.* the need to receive advice from a non-council source in private). There is also a power to exclude disorderly or misbehaving members of the public and to ban photographs or recordings (s.27).

Public records relating mainly to Northern Ireland are stored at the Public Records Office (NI), which was established under an Act of Parliament in 1953. By section 3, records are to be delivered to the office 20 years after their making. Access to members of the public is possible 30 years after a document has been made, but this period may be extended in three situations:

- if the papers are exceptionally sensitive, their disclosure being contrary to the public interest on security or other grounds;
- if the documents contain information supplied in confidence, the disclosure of which might constitute a breach of faith; or
- if the documents contain information about individuals, the disclosure of which would cause distress or danger to living persons or their descendants.

Discovery of documents

Parties to a court action can be compelled to disclose the existence and contents of certain documents, a process known as "discovery". For county court actions, discovery is regulated by Order 15 of the County Court Rules (NI) 1981, while for High Court actions the relevant provision is Order 24 of the Rules of the Supreme Court (NI) 1980, as amended. A court order for discovery is required only if the parties do not volunteer the information themselves and the court would need to be convinced that production of the documents in question is necessary for disposing fairly of the case or for saving costs. In practice discovery of documents is not ordered during applications for judicial review.

Generally speaking, there is no power to order discovery against someone who is not a party to the proceedings. The correct procedure is to call that person as a witness to give oral testimony. But the House of Lords held in *Norwich Pharmacal Co. v Customs and Excise Commissioners* (1974) that, where a person through no fault of his or her own gets mixed up in another person's wrongdoing, he or she may incur no personal liability in law but is under a duty to assist the victim of the wrongdoing by giving him or her full information. In a further decision, *British Steel Corp. v Granada Television Ltd* (1980), the House of Lords stressed that an applicant's interest in obtaining information so as to detect and punish wrongdoing must be shown obviously to outweigh the public interest in protecting the source and ensuring the free flow of information to the media. Moreover, no order can be issued against a stranger who is completely uninvolved in the suspected wrongdoing. In an important recent case, *Ashworth Hospital Authority v MGN Ltd* (2002), the House of Lords held that a newspaper could be forced to disclose its source for a story if it came by that story as a result of someone else's wrongdoing; the wrongdoing in this case took the form of an employee at a secure hospital releasing the medical records of Ian Brady, one of the moors murderers (see too Chapter 9).

A further important provision is section 31 of the Administration of Justice Act 1970, which permits what is called "pre-trial" discovery when a person who is likely to be a party to legal proceedings concerning injury or death can apply for an order of discovery against another likely party. The disclosure of documents might then enable the applicant to discover whether he or she has a case worth starting in the courts. Section 32 enables a claimant in a personal injury or fatal accident case to obtain discovery of, for instance, medical records. This provision is to be generously interpreted in the plaintiff's favour (see *O'Sullivan v Herdmans Ltd*, 1987). The European Court of Human Rights has ruled that if a court's refusal to grant disclosure significantly disadvantages one party to proceedings this could be a breach of Article 6 of the ECHR (*De Haes and Gijsels v Belgium*, 1998).

There are two important limitations to the right to obtain discovery of documents:

- the claim of legal professional privilege protects all confidential communications between a client and his or her lawyer, as well as some confidential communications between either of these people and a third party; and

- public interest privilege allows the Minister who is at the head of a relevant government department to contend that disclosure of the documents in question would be injurious to the public interest, either because of their contents or because of the class of documents to which they belong; in recent years the courts have made it clear that, if such a "public interest immunity" claim is asserted by the government, judges can inspect the documents to see whether in fact the public interest does lie in their being kept secret.

The right to privacy

Prior to the commencement of the Human Rights Act 1998 in October 2000 the law of Northern Ireland (and of England), notoriously, did not protect the right to privacy as such. If a person wanted to prevent, or claim compensation for, an intrusion into his or her private life, he or she had to seek to do so by indirect legal means. Thus, suing someone for a breach of confidence was possible provided that some private information had been misused, and it was at times possible to succeed in a claim of trespass or nuisance, particularly if private property had been invaded or the intrusion had been insistent and repeated. For instance, if a private detective posing as a post office engineer were to obtain entry to a building and place a bugging device in a telephone receiver, this would be trespass to land as well as trespass to goods. The persons in possession of the land and telephone could sue for compensation and the damages awarded would be increased in cases of insolent or oppressive behaviour, particularly if the trespasser was an officer of the state ("aggravated" and "exemplary" damages). An owner of land does not possess all of the air above the land, so he or she cannot sue an aerial photographer who flies over the land to take pictures of it, but constant overhead surveillance might constitute, in law, a nuisance, or harassment, as would the making of persistent telephone calls to a person's home or office.

As regards invasions of privacy by the press, it has for many years been possible to complain to the industry's own regulator, now called the Press Complaints Commission (see Chapter 9). This body was first set up in 1953 and now consists of an independent chairperson and 15 members, a majority of whom have no connection with the press. The Commission may censure a newspaper or journalist and can even require its adjudication to be published by the offending paper, but it has no power to fine an offender or to award damages to a complainant. When the actor Gordon Kaye was duped by a journalist into giving an interview and allowing photographs to be taken when he was in hospital after being injured in an accident, he was able to win a court case based on the concept of "malicious falsehood" (*Kaye v Robertson*, 1991).

The European Commission of Human Rights (which of course has since been merged with the European Court) held, on at least three occasions, that the failure of UK law to provide a direct action for breach of privacy was not a violation of Article 8 of the ECHR. In

Winer v UK (1986) the applicant was complaining about allegations made against him in a book about the South African Bureau of State Security (BOSS), in *Stewart-Brady v UK* (1997) the moors murderer Ian Brady claimed that a newspaper article had breached his privacy, and in *Spencer v UK* (1998) the brother and sister-in-law of Princess Diana complained about a newspaper article and photograph concerning the sister-in-law's attendance at an eating-disorder clinic; in each of these cases the European Commission said that there were enough remedies available in English law to ensure that breaches of the right to respect for private life were not ignored.

The effect of the Human Rights Act 1998

With the incorporation of the ECHR into UK law by the Human Rights Act 1998, the right to a private life has become part of the law of Northern Ireland. The principles already laid down by the European Court of Human Rights therefore apply and already in the first two years of the Act's operation there have been several high-profile cases in England where, in effect, the right to privacy has been protected, at least to some extent. In *Douglas and others v Hello!* (2001) Michael Douglas and Catherine Zeta-Jones sought to prevent Hello! Magazine from publishing unauthorised photographs of their wedding. Although the Court of Appeal did not grant the injunction, it came to this conclusion because it felt that the film stars could be adequately compensated by an award of damages, an explicit recognition that privacy (or at any rate confidence) is now protected by law. In the eventual trial of the claim for damages the High Court judge found the magazine liable only for breach of confidence (11 April 2003). Similarly, in *Venables and Thompson v News Group Newspapers Ltd* (2001) the two boys who killed the toddler Jamie Bulger were able to obtain lifetime world-wide injunctions against a newspaper to stop it publishing details of the young men's identity after their release from detention. Lawyers for Mary Bell, another child-killer, obtained a similar injunction in May 2003.

In *Campbell v Mirror Group Newspapers Ltd* (2002) the model Naomi Campbell initially won £3,500 damages for breach of confidence and of the Data Protection Act 1998 when a newspaper published articles about her attendance at Narcotics Anonymous. But the *Mirror* won in the Court of Appeal on the basis that the claimant had not satisfied the test of showing that the disclosure "would be highly offensive to a reasonable person of ordinary sensibilities". In *A v B plc and another C* (2002), a case involving revelations about the extra-marital affairs of a professional footballer, the English Court of Appeal set out no fewer than 15 guidelines to help courts strike a balance between the competing rights of privacy and freedom of expression. In *Theakston v MGN Ltd* (2002) a High Court judge in England said that the Human Rights Act had not created a new tort of breach of privacy but had imposed a duty on courts to develop the tort of breach of confidentiality. He added that no duty of confidence arises *per se* from acts of sexual intimacy (although on the facts he prohibited publication of photographs of the plaintiff in a brothel). Some commentators therefore maintain that the Human Rights Act has not yet had the effect of allowing individuals to sue other individuals or private companies for breach of privacy (because the Act expressly applies only to public authorities) but others maintain that the trend is definitely in favour of this so-called "horizontal" application of the legislation.

What is clear, however, is that, according to the European Court of Human Rights, Article 8 of the ECHR, which protects the right to respect for one's private life, protects much more than a person's right to have personal information kept private. It also protects a person's "autonomy". This can be useful, for example, when a person with a disability or with a particular sexuality wishes to seek the right to live as independently as possible. It was part of the basis for the European Court's decisions on the rights of homosexuals in the British armed forces (*Smith and Grady v UK*, 1999 and *Lustig-Prean and Beckett v UK*, 1999, where the investigations and report into the applicants' sexual orientation were held to be a breach of Article 8) and it was used most recently in decisions protecting the rights of transsexuals in the UK (*Goodwin v UK*, 2002 and *I v UK*, 2002). Similarly, the European Court has stressed that Article 8 imposes positive obligations on the state (*X and Y v Netherlands*, 1985). In *Gaskin v UK* (1990) the Court held that the UK government had a duty to allow people to get access to the records of their foster care during childhood.

Breach of confidence

Whatever the current legal position concerning the right to privacy, it is clear that Northern Ireland law does protect confidences. There may, for example, be a contract in existence, one of whose terms prevents a contracting party from disclosing information to a non-contracting party. This is common in employment contracts, which often prohibit employees from revealing information acquired during the course of their employment. It also exists in contracts between banks and account holders. At times the courts are prepared to infer such a duty of confidence from the circumstances, even though it was not expressly mentioned in the written contract.

In certain circumstances the law imposes an obligation not to disclose information received in confidence even in the absence of any contract. It is generally necessary that the recipient has expressly or impliedly acknowledged the obligation, but he or she will not be held to it if the information is already in the public domain. This defence was upheld in a 1978 case where John Lennon tried unsuccessfully to prevent the *News of the World* from publishing an article by his former wife about their married life. Lord Denning said that the relationship of the parties had ceased to be their private affair. Similar arguments prevailed in the "Spycatcher" case, where the House of Lords concluded that publication of Peter Wright's memoirs in Britain could not be prevented because they had already been published and much publicised throughout the world (*Attorney General v Guardian Newspapers Ltd (No.2)*, 1990).

A second possible defence to an action for breach of confidence is the public interest. The courts take this to mean that no-one can be prevented from disclosing information which indicates the commission of a crime. Thus, if a journalist wishes to reveal details of misconduct confided to him or her by someone involved in the misconduct, he or she cannot be prevented from doing so (see *British Steel Corp. v Granada Television Ltd*, 1980).

Telephone tapping, tampering with mail and surveillance

In *Malone v Metropolitan Police Commissioner (No.2)* (1979) an English court confirmed that a person had no right not to have his or her telephone tapped by state authorities. There was nothing to make the practice unlawful, therefore it had to be tolerated. Mr. Malone then took his case to Strasbourg, where the European Court of Human Rights decided in 1984 that the United Kingdom's law was in breach of Article 8 of the ECHR. Article 8 guarantees the right to respect for everyone's private and family life, home and correspondence. The Court said that the United Kingdom's law did not indicate with sufficient clarity the scope and manner of exercise of the relevant discretion conferred on the public authorities.

The Interception of Communications Act 1985 was passed in order to comply with the European Court's judgment in the *Malone* case. It is now an offence for anyone to intercept communications sent by post or by means of a public communications system. However, interception remains permissible if it is consented to (*e.g.* when someone wishes to trace offensive telephone calls) or if it is carried out under a warrant issued by the Secretary of State, who must not issue one unless he or she considers it to be necessary in the interests of national security, for the purpose of preventing or detecting serious crime or for the purpose of safeguarding the economic well-being of the United Kingdom.

The Prime Minister appoints an Interception of Communications Commissioner to supervise the issuing of warrants and an Intelligence Services Commissioner to (amongst other things) keep under review the performance by members of the intelligence services of their powers and duties under the Act. There is a tribunal to investigate complaints. If the tribunal finds that the Act has been violated it must inform the complainant and the Prime Minister and it may cancel the warrant, order the intercepted material to be destroyed and direct compensation to be paid. If the tribunal finds no violation of the Act, the complainant is told this, but not whether interception has in fact been carried out. There is therefore still no absolute right to know whether your telephone is being tapped and no figures have ever been released on the number of taps authorised in Northern Ireland.

The 1985 Act did not deal with surveillance by electronic bugging devices. The use of such devices is not of itself a crime, although physically placing an electronic bug may give rise to a civil action for trespass and it could be a breach of Article 8 (*Khan v UK*, 2000). In any event, more sophisticated modern devices are capable of listening in on conversations from a considerable distance. These matters are now governed by the Regulation of Investigatory Powers Act 2000, which was passed in order to ensure that when the Human Rights Act 1998 came into force the current domestic law on surveillance would be compatible with the ECHR. The 2000 Act permits directed and intrusive surveillance, and also the use of covert human intelligence sources, provided these are expressly authorised by designated persons such as the police or the security services (*i.e.* those bodies listed in Sch.1 to the Act).

The authorising persons must believe that the authorisation is necessary in the interests of national security, for the purpose of preventing or detecting serious crime or in the interests of the economic well-being of the United Kingdom (ss.28(3) and 32(3)). Directed and covert surveillance can also be authorised in the interests of public safety, for the purpose of protecting public health, for the purpose of assessing any tax or for any other purpose specified in an order made by the Secretary of State (s.28(3)). In Northern Ireland, the Office of the First Minister and Deputy First Minister is amongst those who are designated to authorise directed or covert surveillance but not intrusive surveillance (s.31) and there is an Investigatory Powers Commissioner for Northern Ireland to keep this function under review (s.61). Authorisations of intrusive surveillance granted to the police or customs officers have to be approved by a Surveillance Commissioner (s.36), and appeals against the decisions of that Commissioner can be taken to the Chief Surveillance Commissioner (s.38).

Codes of practice have been issued to cover many of the powers conferred by the Regulation of Investigatory Powers Act. As yet there does not seem to be any examples of the powers being challenged in Northern Ireland and there is little case-law on the area anywhere in the United Kingdom.

Entitlement cards

In 2002 the British Government published proposals for an "entitlement card", supposedly to help prevent fraud. A copy of the paper is available on the website of the Home Office (*www.homeoffice.gov.uk*). There are obviously concerns in civil liberty circles that such a card would allow the government to establish a national database on everyone who lives in the United Kingdom and to link this database to existing databases so that more intrusive surveillance can be conducted of certain individuals. In May 2003 the Home Secretary stated that he hoped to introduce legislation on these cards within two months.

Further useful addresses

- Campaign for Freedom of Information
  Suite 102
  16 Baldwins Gardens
  London EC1N 7RJ
  tel: 020 7831 7477
  www.cfoi.org.uk

- Information Commissioner
  Wycliffe House
  Water Lane
  Wilmslow
  Cheshire SK9 5AF
  tel: 01625 545745
  www.informationcommissioner.gov.uk

- Privacy International
  2nd floor, Lancaster House
  33 Islington High Street
  London N1 9LH
  tel: 07947 778247
  www.privacyinternational.org

- Public Record Office of Northern Ireland
  66 Balmoral Avenue
  Belfast BT9 6NY
  tel: 028 9025 1318
  www.proni.gov.uk

Chapter 11

General Equality Issues

Maggie Beirne

A number of chapters following immediately on from this relate directly to areas where Northern Ireland has detailed anti-discrimination legislative protections. This chapter, however, will give a more general background to the legislative and policy developments that exist to address discrimination and/or equality issues across a range of social groups, and in particular social groups that do not have Northern Ireland legislation explicitly devoted to their protection.

The Northern Ireland Act 1998

The Northern Ireland Act 1998 puts on to a legal basis many of the decisions made by the parties to the Belfast (Good Friday) Agreement and subsequently endorsed in referenda. The Act, in sections 73 to 78, explicitly addresses non-discrimination and equality of opportunity.

Sections 73 and 74

These sections establish "a single body corporate to be known as the Equality Commission for Northern Ireland". This body (to consist of not less than 14 and not more than 20 Commissioners appointed by the Secretary of State) takes over, amongst other things, all the functions previously performed by the Fair Employment Commission, the Equal Opportunities Commission for Northern Ireland, the Commission for Racial Equality for Northern Ireland and the Northern Ireland Disability Council. In addition, provision was made (s.74(4)) for the new Equality Commission to create Consultative Councils, although to date no such Councils have been created.

The Equality Commission has since its formal establishment on 1 October 1999 moved the different Commission staff to a single site office (Equality House, in the centre of Belfast), prepared annual reports for the Assembly, taken on new and pursued outstanding anti-discrimination cases, and initiated a major programme of work with regard to section 75 of the Northern Ireland Act. A more detailed explanation of the work of the Equality Commission begins on p.231.

Section 75

Section 75(1) imposes a duty on public authorities, when carrying out functions with reference to Northern Ireland, to have due regard to the need to promote equality of opportunity (a) between persons of different religious belief, political opinion, racial group, age, marital status or sexual orientation; (b) between men and women generally; (c) between persons with a disability and persons without; and (d) between persons with dependents and persons without. The section then goes on (in s.75(2)) to say that:

> *without prejudice to its obligations under subsection (1), a public authority shall in carrying out its functions relating to Northern Ireland have regard to the desirability of promoting good relations between persons of different religious belief, political opinion or racial group.*

Taking in turn each of the elements of what has come to be known as the "section 75 duty" or "the equality duty", it should be noted that:

- *Public authorities* are defined in section 75(3) of the Act largely by reference to other statutory instruments. A full listing of all the public authorities automatically required to comply with the section 75 duty is to be found in the Equality Commission's guidelines (Guide to the Statutory Duties – Appendix 3). The listing is very extensive and, by way of example, it includes government departments, Education and Library Boards, Health and Social Service Boards, and a wide variety of perhaps lesser known but important agencies (either in their own right, or as part of a wider public authority) – for example, the Labour Relations Agency, the European Union Special Support Programme Body and the Community Relations Council.
- *Designation of further public authorities:* Most public authorities are automatically required to comply with the equality duty because they fall within the definition of a public authority in one or other statutory instruments mentioned explicitly in section 75(3) of the Northern Ireland Act. However, it is also (under s.75(3)(d)) open to the Secretary of State to designate "any other person" who then is required to comply with the equality duty. In order to conform with

this provision, the Secretary of State decided to consult with a wide range of public bodies not explicitly covered by the Act to seek their advice on the appropriateness or otherwise of their being designated under this provision. Consequently, three Designation Orders have since been issued, adding further public bodies to the list of those automatically covered.

- It is also the case that, as and when new public bodies are created, specific designations may be required to clarify their obligation to comply with section 75. This can be done either in the context of the legislation establishing the body itself, or by way of inclusion in a list of newly designated bodies. Thus, the passage of the Police (NI) Act 2000 (Sch.6, para.24(2)) rendered the Chief Constable of the Police Service of Northern Ireland, the Northern Ireland Policing Board and the Police Ombudsman for Northern Ireland subject to the equality duty. In other situations, the new body can simply be added to the next appropriate Designation Order.

- Further Designation Orders can be expected and a full list of all current public authorities obliged to comply with the section 75 duty can be requested from the Equality Commission.

- *In carrying out its functions in relation to Northern Ireland:* The equality duty is part of the Northern Ireland Act and, as such, applies only to Northern Ireland. It is not UK-wide. This would normally mean that section 75 would not apply to the work of public bodies based in Britain, but the legislation is clear that public authorities, when carrying out functions in relation to Northern Ireland, *are* eligible to be covered. The Secretary of State has already designated bodies such as the Department of Trade and Industry and the Department of Culture, Media and Sport. Moreover, consideration is being given to the appropriateness or otherwise of designating bodies such as the Treasury, the Ministry of Defence and the British Broadcasting Corporation, but no such designation has yet been forthcoming.

- *Due regard to the need to promote equality:* The term "due regard" is stronger in law than "regard" and the expectation is therefore that public authorities must do more than simply take equality of opportunity into account. At the same time, the duty does not override other statutory duties with which the public body might have to comply. In the words of one leading academic in this area, Professor Christopher McCrudden, due regard at least imposes a requirement:

that any function exercised by the public body must be exercised giving considerable weight to the importance attached to equality of opportunity in the (Northern Ireland) Act. This duty is not just a statutory duty; it is a constitutional duty and should therefore be accorded considerable weight. The body, must, of course, act reasonably. Perhaps most importantly, it must also act in a proportionate manner. By this is meant, to put it simply, that the public authority accord weight not only to administrative considerations but also the strength of the interest in equality.

- *Specified section 75 categories:* It is important to note that the listing in the legislation of nine social categories (religious belief, political opinion, racial group, age, marital status, sexual orientation, gender, disability and existence or not of dependents) has its roots in the Policy Appraisal and Fair Treatment (PAFT) guidelines. These guidelines were discretionary and were issued by way of an inter-departmental circular on 22 December 1993. They were extensively criticised as being ineffective. When it was decided that the only way to secure equality outcomes was to transform the discretionary guidelines into a legislative requirement, lobbying efforts were undertaken to encourage the government to extend the listing of social categories beyond the nine categories named in the PAFT guidelines, but these efforts proved unsuccessful. The equality concerns of ex-prisoners, of people of differing social classes, of rural and urban dwellers etc. cannot therefore be argued on the basis of the section 75 duty. At the same time, it is worth noting that campaigners around these and other such issues have drawn sustenance from the good practice imposed on public authorities by the section 75 duty. They have argued that if authorities are examining how best to promote equality of opportunity across a whole range of social groups, why would they choose to ignore concerns brought to their attention by groups other than those referred to explicitly in the section 75 duty?

- *Have regard to the desirability of promoting good relations:* As noted above, "regard" is a weaker stricture than "due regard", so there is a clear hierarchy in the legislation between the obligation to promote equality and the obligation to promote good relations, with the former having precedence. However, to quote the Secretary of State at the time:

> *[W]e regard equality of opportunity and good relations as complementary. There should be no conflict between the two objectives. Good relations cannot be based on inequality between different religions or ethnic groups. Social cohesion requires equality to be reinforced by good community relations ....I repeat that we see no conflict between these two objectives. (Hansard, vol.317, no. 215, 27 July 1998, col.109)*

The two duties are also treated somewhat differently in the Schedule to the Act, which sets out different methods of enforcement for the equality and the good relations duties.

Schedule 9

The Northern Ireland Act 1998 contains a number of Schedules, Schedule 9 of which is entitled "Equality: Enforcement of Duties". Under this Schedule:

- The Equality Commission must keep under review the effectiveness of the equality duty imposed by virtue of section 75 of the Northern Ireland Act; offer advice to public bodies on these issues, carry out such other functions as the Schedule lays down, receive and investigate complaints, and carry out investigations.
- Public authorities must develop an Equality Scheme and submit it to the Equality Commission within six months of the commencement of the Schedule or, if later, the establishment of the public body, and must review the Scheme within five years.
- Equality Schemes must show how the public authority concerned proposes to fulfill its section 75 obligations and, in particular, conform to any guidelines prepared by the Equality Commission. Such Schemes must be approved by the Commission or referred to the Secretary of State, who shall either approve, request revisions, or make a Scheme for the public authority concerned.
- Any guidelines prepared by the Equality Commission must include instructions to the public bodies to make reference to: the aims of the policies which are covered by the Equality Schemes, measures which might mitigate any adverse impact of those policies, alternative policies which might better achieve the promotion of equality of opportunity and the need to make policy decisions by taking into account any such assessment or consultation carried out in relation to the policies.

Since the passage of the Northern Ireland Act 1998, the Equality Commission has sought to assist public bodies to comply with their section 75 duties by issuing two major documents. The first is entitled *Guide to the Statutory Duties: A guide to the implementation of the statutory duties on public authorities arising from section 75 of the Northern Ireland Act 1998* (called the "Guide"). This Guide explains the background and importance of the section 75 duty, explains the scope of the legislation, sets out the procedures for preparing, implementing and getting approval for Equality Schemes and indicates how complaints and investigations of failure to comply with an approved Scheme can be initiated. The main purpose of the Guide, however, is to provide guidelines on the form and content of Equality Schemes and in this respect it constitutes part of the legal obligation imposed on public authorities to ensure their compliance with the section 75 duty.

Accordingly, the guidelines on form and content are very explicit about the key elements of an Equality Scheme. Definitions for "the promotion of equality of opportunity" – and its relation to affirmative action, positive action, and the government's commitment to target disadvantage and social need – are explored, as are the definitions to be used for the legislative reference to "functions and policies".

Equality Schemes must include:

- a general introductory statement specifying the purpose of the Scheme and the public authority's commitment to the statutory duties;
- the authority's arrangements for assessing compliance with section 75 duties, and for consulting on matters to which a duty under that section is likely to apply;
- arrangements for assessing and consulting on the impact of policies adopted or proposed;
- arrangements for monitoring any adverse impact;
- arrangements for publishing the results of equality impact assessments and monitoring any adverse impact;
- commitment to take into account the results of the equality impact assessment and consultation carried out in relation to the policy;
- staff training arrangements;
- plans for ensuring and assessing public access to information and services;
- the timetable for measures proposed in the Scheme;
- details of how the Scheme will be published;
- arrangements for dealing with complaints; and

- a commitment to hold a review of the Scheme within five years.

The *Guide to the Statutory Duties* considers each of these elements in turn and provides detailed guidance on them.

The Guide includes by way of appendices the relevant legislative texts (s.75 of the Northern Ireland Act, and Sch.9 to the Act), but also has a list of public authorities to whom the duty applies (App.3), a list of groups and organisations working in the areas covered by section 75 (App.4), and a variety of other bibliographic references which may be of interest and use. Appendices 3 and 4 are no longer current, but the Commission can make available on request up-dated address lists both for relevant public bodies and "section 75" groups. The legislation is clear that:

> *before submitting a scheme, a public authority shall consult, in accordance with any direction given by the Commission, (a) representatives of persons likely to be affected by the scheme and (b) such other persons as may be specified in the directions* (Sch.9, para.5).

While the Guide does include an annexe on "the procedure for the conduct of equality impact assessments", the Commission has issued a second major explanatory text specifically on this topic. Entitled *Practical Guidance on Equality Impact Assessment* (or *the Guidance*), this document does not have the same statutory significance as the Guide. It constitutes "practical guidance" to public authorities which will carry out equality impact assessments and to the consultees who will be engaged in consultations during those assessments. The Guidance discusses the purpose of equality impact assessments and the need to define the aims of any policy prior to undertaking the detailed seven steps required to undertake an impact assessment. The seven steps are listed as (1) consideration of available data and research; (2) assessment of impacts; (3) consideration of measures which might mitigate adverse impact and alternative policies which might better achieve the promotion of equality of opportunity; (4) formal consultation; (5) decision by the public authority; (6) publication of the results of the assessment; and (7) monitoring for adverse impact in the future and publication of the results of such monitoring.

In an appendix, the document includes examples of what should be understood by the different social categories cited in section 75 – "age", "marital status", "men and women generally", "persons with a disability", "persons with dependents", "political opinion". "racial group", "religious belief" and "sexual orientation". Another appendix, provided by the Northern Ireland Statistics and Research Agency, contains a list of key sources of data within Northern Ireland departments.

With regard to consultation, it is important to note that, whilst Equality Schemes can be submitted only after consultation with "representatives of persons likely to be affected by the Scheme", and others explicitly directed by the Commission, an equality impact assessment requires consultation also with "those directly affected by the policy to be assessed, whether or not they have a direct economic or personal interest".

Both the Guide and the Guidance are currently being reviewed by the Equality Commission to see if they need revision and adaptation in the light of experiences to date.

Section 75 and the mainstreaming of equality

It is worth noting that the equality duty introduced by way of the Northern Ireland Act 1998 is quite distinct from all the earlier efforts to counter discrimination – much of the detail of which is spelled out in subsequent chapters in this book. There are three key ways in which this positive equality duty can be distinguished from earlier non-discrimination initiatives.

First, the new equality duty, unlike anti-discrimination legislation, is anticipatory in that it tries to avoid, rather than retrospectively punish, inequality of treatment. Rather than penalising illegal behaviour after the event, section 75 encourages public bodies to think in advance about their action with a view to avoiding behaviour that will have an adverse impact on certain social groups and/or taking steps that will better promote equality of opportunity for different social groups.

Second, the focus moves from discrimination *per se* to acts or behaviour which have or might have an adverse impact. The existence of an adverse impact is much easier to admit than would be discriminatory behaviour, since it does not make anyone amenable to legal action and requires only an examination of possible mitigating or alternative approaches on the part of the authority concerned.

Third, determining whether there is a possible adverse impact, examining alternatives or possible mitigating measures, and indeed complying with Schedule 9, requires direct consultation with those likely to be most affected. In so doing, policy making itself is changed, since the people most affected by decisions are drawn into the decision-making process itself, rather than being left to cope with the exclusion and the adverse impact the decisions might have – able only to seek redress after the fact.

For all these reasons, many who are working to end discrimination and promote equality have embraced the new equality duty enthusiastically. As a result of lobbying efforts around the Policy Appraisal and Fair Treatment (PAFT) guidelines, and then subsequently the passage of the section 75 duty, groups working actively on issues of age, disability, fair employment, and other equality agendas came together in a loose-knit coalition of groups. The Equality Coalition (as the group came to be known) numbers among its long-standing members organisations such as Disability Action, the Northern Ireland Council for Ethnic Minorities and the Coalition on Sexual Orientation, and has as its mission statement that it is "an alliance of non-governmental groups that work to ensure the equality duty is put into practice, and to increase the public profile of the equality agenda in Northern Ireland". The Coalition, and its individual member groups, can be approached by anyone wishing to understand better the importance of the section 75 duty and, more importantly, how it can be used to promote greater equality of opportunity for individuals and groups suffering inequality or disadvantage.

The equality duty does, however, have its critics, and even its proponents would accept that it offers weaker enforcement options for individuals seeking a remedy than does the anti-discriminatory legislation described in detail in the following chapters. Precisely because the onus of the equality duty is on avoiding adverse impact, seeking ways in which to better promote equality of opportunity, and on the policy changes needed to bring this about, the duty is essentially geared to bringing about a fundamental cultural change within the policy making process. There is a complaint mechanism built into the section 75 duty, and all public authorities must include in their Equality Scheme how they intend to process any complaints made to them. Accordingly, individuals do have a remedy if they believe that a public authority's Equality Scheme has not been complied with, and they can institute a formal complaint via the Equality Commission to this effect, but they are somewhat constrained in bringing a complaint about a general failure to comply with the section 75 duty. The Commission is currently establishing detailed procedures governing the handling of such complaints, and the decision-making process regarding its section 75 investigatory functions.

Single Equality Bill

When the unified Equality Commission was created, the government gave no corresponding commitment to create a single piece of equality legislation. Indeed, the White Paper "Partnership for Equality" (March 1998) which proposed the creation of a single Equality Commission indicated that "It is not proposed that the separate anti-discrimination laws currently in force should be brought together in one statute" (para.4.13). The devolved administration, however, took a different approach. In May 2001 a discussion document issued by the Office of the First Minister and Deputy First Minister (OFMDFM) committed the Office to a new Single Equality Bill which would "enable us to harmonise our anti-discrimination laws as far as practicable and to consider the extension of protection to new categories". In particular, the OFMDFM said that the Bill "will not involve a reduction in protection offered by current laws". Little progress has been made towards this goal following the Assembly's suspension in October 2002 this matter is being pursued by officials under direct rule.

The fairly consistent message from non-governmental groups working on the equality agenda has been that the legislation, when drafted, should:

- harmonise current provisions upwards,
- simplify and streamline procedures,
- conform to EU law and to good international practice, and
- seek to achieve measurable and real equality outcomes.

The legislation should be broad in scope, clarify exemptions, develop clear definitions, encourage positive action and establish clear structural and procedural remedies. Organisations and individuals working on equality will measure the eventual draft legislation against all of these criteria.

Bill of Rights

Another crucial document still in the making at the time of writing is a Bill of Rights for Northern Ireland. The Northern Ireland Human Rights Commission established equality as one of the nine themes on which it sought expert help when consulting on the Bill of Rights and for which it created a working group. In fact, whereas the Belfast (Good Friday) Agreement is arguably ambiguous about the overall nature and remit of any Bill of Rights for Northern Ireland, it makes very clear that the Commission must consider equality in the course of the debate. To quote the Agreement directly:

> *The new Northern Ireland Human Rights Commission is invited to consult and advise on the scope for defining, in Westminster legislation, rights supplementary to those in the European Convention on Human Rights. Among the issues for consideration by the Commission will be:*
>
> - *the formulation of a general obligation on government and public bodies fully to respect, on the basis of equality of treatment, the identity and ethos of both communities in Northern Ireland; and*
> - *a clear formulation of the rights not to be discriminated against and to equality of opportunity in both the public and private sectors.*

There seems to be general agreement that any eventual Single Equality Bill and Bill of Rights must be complementary and not contradictory. Moreover, the eventual definitions used must allow for growth and better understanding of equality over time, but must not be so vague as to be anodyne. Much may depend on which of these foundational initiatives comes to fruition first.

It is worth noting that there is no domestic legislation giving stand-alone protection against discrimination. The comprehensive UN Covenant on Economic, Social and Cultural Rights commits states:

> *to guarantee that the rights enunciated in the present Covenant will be exercised without discrimination of any kind as to race, colour, sex, language, religion, political or other opinion, national or social origin, property, birth or other status.*

There is, however, no domestic remedy for individuals experiencing such discrimination. A similar provision exists in the UN Covenant on Civil and Political Rights and is arguably even stronger in that it requires the states:

> *to ensure to all individuals within its territory and subject to its jurisdiction the rights recognised in the present Covenant, without <u>distinction</u> (emphasis added) of any kind, such as race, colour, sex, language, religion, political or other opinion, national or social origin, property, birth or other status.*

The Covenant, however, is not directly enforceable in our domestic courts.

The Human Rights Act 1998, which incorporates the European Convention on Human Rights (ECHR), provides certain protections against discrimination, given that Article 14 of the ECHR prohibits discrimination. However, the right not to be discriminated against applies only in relation to rights in the Convention and is not free-standing. A large number of other economic rights, for example, would fall outside of this anti-discriminatory measure. Protocol 12 to the Convention will remedy this and make the anti-discrimination provisions free-standing, but this has not yet received sufficient governmental support (including from the UK government) to be binding on any state.

European legislation

In part because of the limited equality provisions in domestic legislation, much has depended on the European jurisprudence and practice in this area. The incorporation of the ECHR via the Human Rights Act was a particular advance, but the Council of Europe and the European Court of Human Rights have had arguably less relevance for local equality developments than the European Union and the European Court of Justice.

In particular, it is worth exploring the potential of one of the most recent European Union Directives which, when implemented in full, offers great potential for greater equality of treatment for all. Council Directive 2000/78/EC of 27 November 2000 establishes a general framework for equal treatment in employment and occupation. Its significance lies in the fact that:

- it must be complied with by 2 December 2003 or, at latest – in terms of age and disability — by December 2006; the UK Government has no discretion in the matter;
- some of the obligations touch on areas of discrimination and inequality (*e.g.* age and sexual orientation) not currently covered by any UK or Northern Ireland legislation (apart, indirectly, from the section 75 duty commented on above); and
- some of the obligations go beyond what is currently on offer in UK legislation in, for instance, giving a clear role to "representative groups".

The Framework Directive lays down a general framework for combating discrimination on the grounds of religion or belief, disability, age or sexual orientation as regards employment and occupation, "with a view to putting into effect in the member states the principle of equal treatment". The Directive defines the "principle of equal treatment" to encompass a prohibition of both direct and indirect discrimination, a prohibition of harassment (which is to be deemed a form of discrimination) and a prohibition of victimisation. The Directive also makes it clear that positive action is acceptable "with a view to ensuring full equality in practice" and that the principle of equal treatment "shall not prevent any member state from maintaining or adopting specific measures to prevent or compensate for disadvantages linked to any of the grounds referred to". While a variety of possible exemptions with respect to occupational requirements, reasonable accommodation for disabled persons and differences of treatment on grounds of age are set out (arts.4, 5 and 6 respectively), the importance of the Directive lies in its breadth of coverage in terms of categories of person not previously protected from discrimination.

The Directive also places an obligation on member states to ensure that there are appropriate judicial and/or administrative procedures to ensure that the rights can be vindicated and that "associations, organisations or other legal entities …[with]…a legitimate interest …may engage, either on behalf of or in support of the complainant". This greatly strengthens the hand of individuals who may feel unable to bear the burden of single-handedly pursuing a remedy for unequal treatment. Furthermore, member states are required to take adequate measures "to promote dialogue between social partners with a view to fostering equal treatment" and similarly are required to "encourage dialogue with appropriate non-governmental organisations which have…a legitimate interest in contributing to the fight against discrimination".

Uniquely, this EU Directive, binding on all EU states, refers in Article 15 specifically to Northern Ireland. Particular provision is made to allow measures to be taken which will "tackle the under-representation of one of the major religious communities in the police service of Northern Ireland". The EU has therefore agreed that "differences in treatment regarding recruitment into that service, including its support staff, shall not constitute discrimination insofar as those differences in treatment are expressly authorised by national legislation". Moreover, Article 15.2 notes that:

in order to maintain a balance of opportunity in employment for teachers in Northern Ireland, while furthering the reconciliation of historical divisions between the major religious communities there, the provisions on religion or belief in this Directive shall not apply to the recruitment of teachers in schools in Northern Ireland in so far as this is expressly authorised by national legislation.

Both of these are provisions are formulated in a manner which would allow the UK to change domestic legislation in such a way, and at such a time, as to end them.

Enforcement by the Equality Commission

The Equality Commission for Northern Ireland is the independent public body established under the Northern Ireland Act 1998 to fulfill a range of statutory duties related to equality. The Commission now carries out all the functions previously performed by the Equal Opportunities Commission for Northern Ireland, the Fair Employment Commission, the Commission for Racial Equality for Northern Ireland and the Northern Ireland Disability Council.

The Commission's Mission Statement is to "combat discrimination and promote equality of opportunity through advice, promotion and enforcement". Its key duties include the promotion of equality of opportunity, the elimination of unlawful discrimination, the promotion of good relations, the oversight of the effectiveness of statutory duties on public authorities and the keeping of relevant legislation under review.

This simple listing may give the impression that there is a single body of legislation that lays down the powers and remit of the Commission. This is not the case. The Equality Commission has different powers according to the relevant legislation being relied upon, so that an individual concerned about sex discrimination cannot have the same expectations of the Commission as someone concerned about religious discrimination or discrimination on grounds of race or disability. The legislation around the promotion of equality of opportunity, as set out in section 75 of the Northern Ireland Act, gives the Commission different powers again (see p.219 above).

Much of the detail about the powers of the Commission is explored in the following chapters. While there are some variations between each of the different anti-discrimination regimes, there is also much that they have in common. For instance, whatever the alleged type of unlawful discrimination, the Commission's duties are:

- to work towards its elimination,
- to promote equality of opportunity and
- to keep the working of the relevant legislation under review.

There are also broadly comparable powers regarding the obtaining of information, the carrying out of investigations, the issuing of non-discrimination notices and the prohibiting of discriminatory advertisements. Moreover the criteria which the Commission has to apply when deciding whether to grant assistance to prospective litigants are broadly the same across the various categories of discrimination. These criteria are:

- is there is a question of principle at stake,
- is it unreasonable to expect the litigant to deal with the case unaided, and
- are there any other special circumstance which make it appropriate to grant assistance?

In theory assistance can be granted even if only one of these three criteria is satisfied.

Sex discrimination

The Equal Opportunities Commission for Northern Ireland (EOC-NI), set up by the Sex Discrimination (NI) Order 1976, has now been subsumed into the Equality Commission for Northern Ireland. In addition to the common powers already mentioned the Commission may undertake, or assist (financially or otherwise) the undertaking by other persons of, research and educational activities and in very limited circumstances it is empowered to take legal action in its own name (arts.38-42). So far the bulk of the enforcement work in this area has been in the realm of litigation (art.75). The complex provisions and the lack of resources required for formal investigations have meant that only a few of these have been undertaken. A radical change in the powers of the Commission in this area is required if it is to have the necessary tools to combat discrimination. It should be given wider investigative powers together with greater scope to pursue legal actions. Since discrimination affects groups of people, class or representative actions are also necessary to combat unlawful sexual discrimination.

Religious and political discrimination

The Fair Employment and Treatment (NI) Order 1998 (FETO) sets down in article 7 not just the three common duties mentioned above but also the additional duty to promote affirmative action. In order to assist the Commission carry out these functions, a number of more detailed functions are also set down in the Order. The Commission has an educational and advisory function (art.8), which includes establishing advice-giving services, providing training, holding conferences, undertaking research and disseminating information about the Commission and its work. The Commission is also expected to maintain a code of practice containing such practical guidance as the Commission thinks fit for the promotion of equality of opportunity, including the elimination of unlawful discrimination in the employment field. The Commission may in addition issue a code of practice giving practical guidance on the elimination of discrimination in other spheres (art.9)

The 1998 Order makes it a duty of the Commission "to identify and keep under review patterns and trends of employment and of occupations in Northern Ireland" and requires it to keep itself informed about complaints to the Fair Employment Tribunal (art.10).

Article 11 authorises the Commission to conduct investigations for the purposes of considering what action, if any, ought to be taken to promote equality of opportunity. The investigation may be addressed to any employer, any person with authority to select or nominate another person for employment by a third person, any employment agency, any vocational organisation, any person providing services relating to employment training, and any person with power to confer a qualification that is needed for, or facilitates, engagement in employment in any capacity. A detailed Schedule to the Act lays out how such investigations should be conducted.

Pursuant to an investigation under article 11 of FETO, the Commission may determine that the person or entity being investigated ought to take action to promote equality of opportunity. In such cases, the Commission "shall use its best endeavours" to ensure that the person concerned takes such action "as is, in all the circumstances, reasonable and appropriate" and, where appropriate, "secure a satisfactory written undertaking by him that such action will be taken" (art.12(2)). If the undertaking is not given, or if an undertaking is given but not complied with, the Commission must serve a notice containing directions, or (in the latter case) may apply to the Tribunal for enforcement of the undertaking.

Under article 13, persons or entities may give a voluntary undertaking to the Commission to take action to promote equality of opportunity. If, however, this undertaking is not complied with, the Commission must either serve a notice containing directions to supersede the undertaking or apply to the Fair Employment Tribunal for enforcement of the undertaking.

Article 14 of FETO sets down the parameters of the directions to be issued by the Commission. Directions may include directions for the abandonment or modification of any practice or for the substitution or adoption of new practices specified by the Commission. With some qualifications, any such directions are binding on the person concerned and are enforceable in accordance with a Tribunal Order (the procedures for which are also laid out in the legislation).

The Commission can seek a court injunction to counter a person's "persistent" discrimination (art.41) or to restrain the publication of discriminatory advertisements (art.42). Article 45 of the 1998 Order goes further than other comparable anti-discrimination legislation in that it *requires* the Commission to give advice to complainants requesting it, "unless it considers that the request is frivolous".

Racial discrimination

The role of the Commission in this field is laid down in the Race Relations (NI) Order 1997. As well as imposing the duties common to other areas of anti-discrimination legislation, the Order provides detailed regulations regarding the conduct of investigations, the giving of undertakings not to discriminate and persistent discrimination.

Disability discrimination

The Equality Commission was granted powers under the Equality (Disability, etc.) (NI) Order 2000 to enforce rights under the Disability Discrimination Act 1995. As well as the common duties mentioned above it must take such steps as it considers appropriate to encourage good practice in the treatment of disabled people. The Commission also has the powers in this context:

- to assist disabled people by offering information, advice and support, including funding cases under Parts II and III of the 1995 Act,

- to provide information and advice to employers and service providers,
- to undertake formal investigations,
- to prepare statutory codes of practice and practical guidance on how to comply with the law, and
- to arrange for independent conciliation between service providers and disabled people as service users.

Age discrimination

There is currently no legislation in Northern Ireland that people can rely upon when challenging alleged discrimination on grounds of age. Indeed, there are extensive legislative provisions and/or administrative arrangements which differentiate between people of different ages. For example, criminal law and electoral provisions differentiate between children and adults, and often vary as between children of different ages. At the other end of the age spectrum, compulsory retirement (at different ages) cannot currently be challenged on the grounds of discrimination. The Human Rights Act 1998 outlaws discrimination in relation to the rights guaranteed by the European Convention, but makes no explicit reference to age as one of the grounds of complaint.

The rights of children and young people are addressed separately in this book (see Chapter 18). As to older people, the only protection that currently exists is the section 75 duty, which requires all public authorities to promote equality of opportunity "regardless of age". The equality duty imposes a duty on authorities to consult with older people about policies which affect them, and requires authorities to consider alternative options, or mitigating factors. In practice, however, this will not automatically require authorities to over-turn policies or practices that some might consider discriminatory.

The coming into force of the EU's Framework Directive (see p.229) will make an important advance in this direction, in that it will outlaw discrimination on grounds of age unless any:

differences of treatment on grounds of age are objectively and reasonably justified by a legitimate aim, including legitimate employment policy, labour market and vocational training objectives, and if the means of achieving that aim are appropriate and necessary (art.6)

Article 6 indicates that the differences of treatment that can be considered justifiable may include: the setting of special conditions on access to employment and vocational training, employment and occupation, including dismissal and remuneration conditions; the fixing of minimum conditions of age, professional experience, or seniority in service for access to employment or to certain advantages linked to employment; the fixing of a maximum age for recruitment which is based on the training requirements of the post, or the need for a reasonable time for employment before retirement; and the fixing of occupational social security schemes.

With regard to age, the EU Directive's provisions do not have to be implemented in member states until 2 December 2006.

Sexual orientation discrimination

As with age discrimination, there is no stand-alone legal provision in UK domestic legislation outlawing discrimination on grounds of sexual orientation.   There is no reference in the ECHR (or in the Human Rights Act 1998) specifically to sexual orientation.   "Sex", however, is mentioned explicitly as one of the grounds and there are a number of cases of direct relevance to the rights of people of differing sexual orientation which have been pursued successfully to the European Court on Human Rights under this rubric. (See also Chapter 17.)

As with age, therefore, the key legislative provisions in Northern Ireland relevant to remedying discrimination or promoting equality of opportunity on grounds of sexual orientation are the section 75 duty in the Northern Ireland Act 1998 and the EU Framework Directive.   The particular significance of the Directive is its explicit recognition of the need to combat discrimination on the grounds of sexual orientation as regards employment and occupation.   As with other grounds, it is recognised (introductory para.23) that:

in very limited circumstances, a difference of treatment may be justified where a characteristic related to religion or belief, disability, age or sexual orientation constitutes a genuine and determining occupational requirement, when the objective is legitimate and the requirement is proportionate.   Such information should be included in the information provided by the Member States to the Commission.

The exact significance of terminology such as "genuine", "determining", "occupational requirement", "legitimate objective" and "proportionate requirement" may come under close scrutiny as the courts seek to give effect to the Framework Directive when it comes into force (with regard to sexual orientation) by 2 December 2003 at the latest. Already, for example, some have questioned whether the protections afforded to people of differing sexual orientation in this Directive are reinforced, or undermined, by the clarification in introductory paragraph 24 of the same Directive, that the EU:

> *respects and does not prejudice the status under national law of churches and religious associations or communities in the member states and that it equally respects the status of philosophical and non-confessional organisations. With this in view, member states may maintain or lay down specific provisions on genuine, legitimate and justified occupational requirements which might be required for carrying out an occupational activity.*

Further useful addresses

- Equality Commission
  Equality House
  7-9 Shaftesbury Square
  Belfast BT2 7DP
  tel: 028 9050 0600
  textphone – 028 9024 0010
  www.equalityni.org

- Equality Coalition
  45-47 Donegall Street
  Belfast BT1 2BR
  tel: 028 9096 1120

- Coalition on Sexual Orientation (CoSO)
  2-6 Union Street
  Belfast BT1 2JF
  tel: 077 885 7007
  www.coso.org.uk

- Help the Aged
  Ascot House
  24-30 Shaftsbury Square
  Belfast BT2 7DB
  tel: 028 9023 0666
  www.helptheaged.org.uk

- Age Concern
  3 Lower Crescent
  Belfast BT7 1NR
  tel: 028 9024 5729
  www.ageconcern.org.uk

- Community Relations Council
  6 Murray Street
  Belfast BT1 6DN
  tel: 028 9022 7500
  www.community-relations.org.uk

Chapter 12

Religious and Political Discrimination

Stephen Livingstone[*]

D iscrimination on grounds of religion or political belief has been a central civil liberties issue in Northern Ireland's history. From the beginnings of the Northern Ireland state a public commitment was given to preventing religious discrimination, in that section 5(1) of the Government of Ireland Act 1920 provided that the Parliament of Northern Ireland could not "give a preference, privilege or advantage, or impose any disability or disadvantage, on account of religious belief."

However, expressing a commitment to the absence of discrimination is one thing, devising the mechanisms to eradicate it is another. By the 1960s the civil rights movement and a number of studies, notably the government-appointed Cameron Commission, had established the existence of significant discrimination in housing and employment. Most legislative action to counter this has been in the area of employment, where Northern Irish legislation is shortly to be supplemented by the EU Employment Directive (see p.229 above), but there have been significant anti-discrimination measures in other fields too.

Complaints of employment discrimination

If people feel they have not been selected for an interview, job or promotion because of their religion or political views, they will succeed in a claim of discrimination if they can prove a number of points:
- that they have been the victim of either direct or indirect discrimination,
- that the discrimination was carried out by a "relevant body",

---

[*] Some material written by Austin Magill for the equivalent chapter in the first edition of the handbook is still included.

- that the discrimination related to a "relevant matter", and
- that the discrimination is not protected by any of the exceptions in the legislation.

Each of these points is considered in more detail in the following paragraphs.

Direct discrimination

The legislation defines direct discrimination as occurring where a relevant body treats a person less favourably than other persons would be treated on grounds of religion or political opinion (art.3(2) of the Fair Employment and Treatment (NI) Order 1998). This is probably what most people think of when they consider what discrimination is, namely deliberately refusing a job or promotion to someone because he or she is a Catholic or Protestant. However, direct discrimination is not limited to such malicious or deliberate action: an employer will still be liable even if the discrimination is applied out of concern for the person or the views of others. In the case of *Neilly v Mullaghboy Private Nursing Home* (1991) the employer was found to have discriminated where she dismissed a cook from her nursing home job because the residents of the home said they did not want a Catholic cook from the Irish Republic. This was discrimination even though the employer did not share the residents' views. Employers will also be liable under this head of discrimination if they fail to protect employees from sectarian harassment, whether by other workers or customers, when they are aware of such harassment (and arguably when they reasonably ought to be aware of it).

Direct discrimination also occurs where decisions are based on generalised assumptions about people of a particular religion or political opinion, *e.g.* where a brewery refuses to employ a member of the Free Presbyterian Church because of an assumption that the abstentionist policy practised by that church would mean that its members would not be loyal and enthusiastic brewery employees. The employer would need to establish that the attitudes of that particular applicant would be likely to make him or her a bad employee. The fact that the definition states that less favourable treatment need only be based on "grounds of religion or political opinion" means that discrimination occurs whenever religion or political opinion becomes one factor in the decision. It would therefore be discrimination to dismiss an employee because his wife was a Catholic, even though the employee was not. It will also be discrimination to treat someone

differently because of his or her supposed religion or political belief. The Fair Employment Tribunal has indicated that the term "political opinion" is not limited to opinions about the constitutional position of Northern Ireland (*McKay v NIPSA*, 1994), but the Court of Appeal has stated that the political opinion must relate to the government of the state or public policy (*Gill v NICEM*, 2002).

The number of cases in which religion or politics is explicitly given as a reason for a decision is likely to be small. However, a person may feel that, although he or she has been refused a job or promotion on grounds that do not obviously involve religion or politics, the "real" reason for the decision was his or her religion or political opinions. The courts have recognised that deciding claims of discrimination will often involve making inferences and attempting to unearth facts not immediately available. A number of things may help a person claiming direct discrimination to bring these facts into the open:

- Where an application is made to the Fair Employment Tribunal (discussed below) the rules on "discovery" of documents applicable to county court actions will apply (see p.209). The Tribunal has indicated that even confidential documents relating to interviews and selections can be discovered where it is in the public interest that they be available for the applicant's case. In addition, the applicant may serve a prescribed form on those alleged to be discriminating which contains questions about their reasons for doing any act or about any other relevant matter. The replies can be used in evidence in any tribunal hearing. If the alleged discriminator fails to reply within a reasonable time, or if the Tribunal finds the reply to be evasive, it may draw whatever inferences it considers just and equitable.

- The courts and the Tribunal have indicated that it will be legitimate to infer discrimination where a better qualified person of a different religion is not shortlisted, appointed or promoted. At this point the employer is called upon to explain the non-discriminatory reasons why this person was not shortlisted, etc. (*Fair Employment Agency v Craigavon Borough Council*, 1980). Indeed, in *Department of the Environment v Fair Employment Agency* (1989) the Northern Ireland Court of Appeal indicated that this inference could be drawn where the applicants were equally qualified. Other cases show that, if the reasons the employer puts forward to explain the different treatment of the person complaining from that of someone of a different religion are vague or subjective, the Tribunal is entitled to

conclude that the "real" reason was discrimination. In one case the Tribunal was satisfied there was discrimination when a better qualified person was passed over for a job and there was no evidence as to what criteria were adopted in shortlisting and making appointments. The Tribunal decisions to date indicate that an employer's case will be greatly weakened if he or she has failed to adhere to the Fair Employment Commission's Code of Practice (see p.233). Failure to use objective criteria, train interviewers, retain notes or remove the display of sectarian emblems have all been referred to by the Fair Employment Tribunal as factors which have been taken into account in the process of drawing inferences. In general, compliance with the Code of Practice is regarded by the Tribunal as central to determining whether discrimination has occurred or not. In one case it stated:

> *this Code is the employer's sword in the affirmative action road to equality of opportunity and the employer's shield when he is attacked for alleged discrimination.*

The EU Employment Directive (which applies to discrimination on grounds of religion or belief, amongst others) reinforces this by providing that, where facts are established from which it may be presumed that there has been direct or indirect discrimination, "it shall be for the respondent to prove that there has been no breach of the principle of equal treatment."

Indirect discrimination

This occurs where one of the "relevant bodies" applies a "condition or requirement" equally to all applicants or employees but the proportion of persons of a particular religious belief or political opinion who can comply with this condition or requirement is "considerably smaller" than those not of that belief or opinion. The condition or requirement must be to the detriment of the person complaining of discrimination because he or she cannot comply with it and the person or body applying the condition or requirement "cannot show [it] to be justifiable irrespective of the religious belief or political opinion of the person to whom it is applied."

What this rather convoluted formulation means is that employers may be liable for discrimination where their employment decisions are based on criteria which may have nothing to do with religion or political opinion but whose effect is to reduce substantially the number

of members of a particular religious or political group who could be considered for the employment in question. If the use of such criteria does have this effect the employer will be liable for discrimination unless he or she is able to show that the criteria are important for the job in question.

Examples of indirect discrimination are:

- an employer requiring all employees to live in East Belfast;
- recruiting all employees from a particular youth club which is run by the Catholic church;
- recruiting on the recommendation of current employees where the current workforce is overwhelmingly of one religion; and
- promoting only people with particular qualifications which are generally unavailable to people from one community, or promoting only people with a certain length of service where members of a particular religious group are under-represented among those with that length of service.

This notion of indirect discrimination was introduced into Northern Ireland's fair employment law for the first time by the Fair Employment (NI) Act 1989. However, it has been employed for some time in sex discrimination law throughout the United Kingdom and in race discrimination law in Great Britain. Its use there has given rise to certain areas of doubt:

- The first of these concerns is the use of the phrase "condition or requirement". The Northern Ireland Court of Appeal in *Hall v Shorts Missile Systems* (1997) endorsed the view that the condition or requirement in question had to be a "must", *i.e.* that a person would be entitled to the job etc. only if he or she complied with it.
- The second issue is the reference to "can comply". This appears to mean "can comply in practice", so it would not be a valid argument for an employer to say that Catholics could comply with a requirement that employees must live in East Belfast.
- Thirdly, the proportion in question must be "considerably smaller". There is no clear indication as to what proportion is sufficient. In an English case the Employment Appeal Tribunal indicated that 95.3% of men in the economically active population who are not in receipt of an occupational pension is a considerably smaller proportion than the 99.4 % of women who are similarly situated. In *McCausland v Dungannon District Council* (1992) the Fair Employment Tribunal stated that a difference of 2% of Protestants compared with 1.5% of Catholics being able to be appointed via an internal civil service

trawl was not "considerably smaller". In the gender discrimination context the Court of Appeal in England, in *Edwards v London Underground (No.2)* (1998), has indicated that there is scope for a "common sense" approach to this question where limited statistics are available. There is also little law on the question of what "pool" of employees or potential employees is relevant for comparison. It seems that one looks to the pool of people from the complainant's community who are qualified for the job in question on all the criteria the employer uses, apart from those challenged as indirectly discriminatory. Thus, if the job is a relatively low skill one, the pool might be the entire Protestant or Catholic population. If it requires high skill, the pool might be Protestant or Catholic workers with a particular qualification (where the requirement of that qualification is not itself being challenged as discriminatory).

- The fourth issue is what employers must show if they argue that a condition or requirement is "justifiable". The Fair Employment Tribunal has adopted the approach developed in the race discrimination context. This indicates that there has to be an "objective balance between the discriminatory effect of the condition or requirement and the reasonable needs of the party who applies the condition" (*Hampson v Department of Education and Science,* 1990). These reasonable needs may include economic or administrative needs. This suggests that it is not enough for an employer to produce just any reason, but nor must the employer prove that the condition or requirement was necessary for performance of the job. The Tribunal must carry out a balancing test.

The current test for indirect discrimination may be revised when the EU Employment Directive comes into effect. This provides that it shall be unlawful discrimination where an "apparently neutral provision, criterion or practice" (this is wider than a "condition or requirement") puts people of a particular religion or belief "at a particular disadvantage" compared with other persons (there is no need to show it affects a "considerably smaller" pool). The justification test is also more exacting, requiring that the employer demonstrate that the provision, criterion or practice is "objectively justified by a legitimate aim and that the means of achieving that aim are appropriate and necessary."

"Relevant bodies"

Employers are the main body against whom claims of discrimination may be brought. But five other bodies are mentioned in the Fair Employment and Treatment (NI) Order. These are:

- persons with statutory power to select employees for others;
- employment agencies (at least as regards acts done as an employment agency);
- vocational organisations;
- persons providing training services; and
- persons with power to confer qualifications which might facilitate employment; in *Bone v Department of the Environment for NI* (1993) the Court of Appeal indicated that the term "qualification" was limited to a status conferred on someone relating only to their work or trade and which was either necessary for the work or trade or an advantage in the work or trade; therefore a pilot's licence would appear to be a qualification but not planning permission for a property developer or a bank loan for a business.

Employers are prohibited from discriminating against not only applicants for employment but also those they already employ, including "contract workers" supplied by someone else.

"Relevant matters"

Complaints may be made in respect of:

- refusal of a job or promotion;
- dismissal or redundancy arrangements;
- the terms on which employment is offered;
- "the arrangements made for determining employment" (which includes shortlisting, interview procedures, and application forms);
- "access to benefits"; or
- being "subjected to any other detriment"; the courts have indicated that someone will be subject to a "detriment" if a "reasonable worker would or might take the view that they had been disadvantaged" (*Shamoon v Chief Constable of the RUC,* 2003).

The Fair Employment and Treatment (NI) Order gives the Equality Commission for Northern Ireland (see Chapter 11) power to seek "injunctions" (*i.e.* prohibitions) against advertisements which indicate an intention to discriminate directly against someone.

Under article 3(4) of the 1998 Order it is unlawful to discriminate against anyone because he or she is or has been involved in fair employment proceedings, either as complainant or witness ("victimisation").   It will not be unlawful, however, where the allegations in question are false and not made in good faith.

Exemptions

There are three general exemptions from unlawful discrimination.

- Article 78 of the 1998 Order exempts acts done to comply with a statutory requirement passed before the 1998 Order came into force.
- Article 79 of the 1998 Order indicates that an act will not be unlawful where it is done for the purposes of safeguarding national security. The Secretary of State may issue a certificate indicating that an act was done for the purpose of safeguarding national security, public safety or public order, and in that event the act done is exempt from challenge as discriminatory. However, following a number of successful applications to the European Court of Human Rights (most recently *Devlin v UK,* 2001, and *Devenney v UK,* 2002), the validity of such certificates may now be challenged before a special tribunal.
- Article 2(4) of the 1998 Order states that discrimination on the ground of a person's political opinion will not be unlawful where that opinion includes approval or acceptance of the use of violence for political ends connected with Northern Ireland.

There are also specific exemptions for particular jobs:

- employment or occupation as a minister or priest,
- employment for the purposes of a private household, and
- employment as a teacher in a school (though the Equality Commission wants this removed).

Actions by employers may in addition be exempt if they are part of the *affirmative action* provisions provided for in the fair employment legislation; these are discussed below (see p.254).

The Fair Employment Tribunal (FET)

If someone feels that he or she has been the victim of direct or indirect discrimination an application should be made within three months to the Fair Employment Tribunal. The Tribunal will send a copy of the application to the Labour Relations Agency, which is under a duty, if requested by both the applicant and the body being complained against, to try to achieve a settlement without the application being heard by the Tribunal. The Agency can also intervene of its own accord if, after considering the application, it feels it could achieve a settlement with a reasonable chance of success.

If a Labour Relations Agency settlement is not attempted, or if it proves unsuccessful, the application will be heard by the Fair Employment Tribunal. Currently there is an average of two years between the issuing of proceedings and a case being heard by the Tribunal. The FET is organised along the same lines as an industrial tribunal and the President of the industrial tribunals is also President of the Fair Employment Tribunal. The applicant may represent him or herself in person before the Tribunal or may be represented by a lawyer, but legal aid is unavailable. The applicant may, however, apply to the Equality Commission both for initial advice on making an application and for free representation before the Tribunal (see Chapter 11).

The Tribunal hearings will normally take place in public but the Tribunal can sit in private to hear certain categories of evidence. These include:

- evidence which the Tribunal feels it may be against the interests of national security or public order to be heard in public;
- evidence which consists of information given in confidence;
- information which might cause substantial injury to the undertaking which employs the person giving it; and
- evidence which would create a substantial risk of exposing someone to physical attack or sectarian harassment.

Remedies

If the claim of discrimination is accepted by the Tribunal, various remedies are available. The Tribunal may:

- make a declaration of the parties' rights;
- recommend that the discriminating party should take specified action within a prescribed period to eliminate the effects of the discrimination; in one case the Tribunal ordered the employer to put up a sign to the effect that the applicant had been discriminated against; or
- award damages; awards may include compensation for injured feelings, or aggravated damages where a person has been treated in an especially arrogant or callous manner; in the case of *Duffy v*

Eastern Health and Social Services Board (1991) both categories were invoked and a total of £25,000 was awarded; in this case the Tribunal also awarded exemplary damages, but it has subsequently decided that these are punitive and not permissible within the terms of the legislation.

Since 1995 there has been no upper limit on the total compensation the Tribunal may award in respect of any one complaint. However damages will be available for unintentional indirect discrimination only if the Tribunal feels that it is just and equitable to award them. If the Tribunal makes a recommendation for specific action which the employer must take and the employer fails to comply within a reasonable period, the Tribunal may subsequently make an award of damages if it did not do so before, or increase the damages awarded. An appeal on a point of law can be made against any aspect of the Tribunal's decision to the Court of Appeal.

Actions to ensure equality of opportunity

The measures already explained are all targeted at preventing employers and other relevant bodies from using discriminatory criteria in respect of jobs, promotions, benefits and qualifications. However, they are of limited effectiveness, as they begin to "bite" only when employers receive applications for jobs, promotions, etc. In Northern Ireland, for a variety of historical reasons, the perception has grown up that certain jobs are essentially reserved for one religion and that there is little point in people from another religion bothering to apply for them. Hence applications are not forthcoming from the under-represented group and substantial imbalances in workforces remain. Anti-discrimination provisions are unlikely alone to achieve the aim of the legislation that employment, qualifications and promotions are genuinely open to all, regardless of religion or political opinion. For this reason the legislation contains other measures aimed at ensuring "equality of opportunity" and "fair participation".

The definition of "equality of opportunity" is given in Article 5 of the 1998 Order. This states that a person has equality of opportunity with a person of any other religious belief if he or she has:

in any [employment] circumstances the same opportunity ... as that other person has or would have in those...circumstances, due allowance being made for any material difference in their suitability.

This definition is similar to that previously contained in section 3 of the Fair Employment (NI) Act 1976. The Standing Advisory Commission on Human Rights (the predecessor of the Northern Ireland Human Rights Commission) observed that the Fair Employment Agency (the body replaced first by the Fair Employment Commission and then by the Equality Commission) interpreted section 3 to mean that equality of opportunity was denied if practices adopted by employers operated to exclude members of a community under-represented in the workforce or discouraged applications from that community. Such practices include those now described as "indirect discrimination", *e.g.* word-of-mouth recruiting. But the Agency's interpretation seemed to go further. It included practices, such as displaying sectarian symbols at workplaces or advertising only in newspapers not generally read by the under-represented community, which had the effect of discouraging applications from that community.

On some occasions the Agency also recommended the taking of positive steps to remedy past under-representation, such as setting goals and timetables for minority representation in the workforce or establishing training programmes targeted at the under-represented community. There remained some doubt as to whether recommending positive steps, as opposed to recommending the removal of barriers to recruitment, was within the definition of equality of opportunity. Some ambiguity about the scope of the concept remains. However the 1989 Act (the predecessor of the 1998 Order) introduced a new ideal, "fair participation", which employers can in some circumstances be required by the Equality Commission to attain. "Fair participation" is not defined in the legislation, but the Code of Practice issued by the Fair Employment Commission indicates that what is fair depends on the circumstances and that:

> *employers should be making sustained efforts to promote [fair participation] through affirmative action measures and, if appropriate, the setting of goals and timetables. It does not mean that every job, occupation or position in every undertaking in Northern Ireland must reflect the proportionate distribution of Protestants and Roman Catholics in the province.*

What this appears to be aiming at is that if the employer is or should be aware (through monitoring) of significant under-representation of one community in the workforce, and is not taking steps to counteract this, a failure to ensure fair participation exists.

The legislation does not place employers under a specific duty to ensure equality of opportunity or fair participation but does give the Equality Commission powers to require action where an employer is failing to ensure either. It also places a number of other specific duties on employers which are designed to assist the ensuring of equality of opportunity.

Monitoring

The Fair Employment and Treatment (NI) Order 1998 now requires all employers with a workforce of more than 10 employees to register with the Equality Commission. Failure to register exposes an employer to a fine not exceeding £2,000. Any new employer taking over a registered concern must apply within one month to the Commission to change the registration. To any proceedings in respect of non-registration there is a statutory defence of having a reasonable excuse for failing to make an application.

The OFMDFM has power to certify a body as a public authority in a number of specified circumstances – if they are a Westminster or Northern Ireland Department, a body created by statutory provision or "a person appearing to the Department to exercise functions of a public nature". Lists of bodies already certified can be found in the Fair Employment (Specification of Public Authorities) Order (NI) 1989. Although public authorities are exempt from registration requirements they are not exempt from the requirements placed on registered concerns to provide information.

Registered employers (and public authorities) are required to monitor the composition of their workforce by religion. As the Code of Practice states, such monitoring is less concerned with a person's religious beliefs than with ascertaining his or her "community background", Protestant or Catholic. The exact information which the employer has to collect and the methods by which it is to be collected are spelt out in the Fair Employment (Monitoring) Regulations (NI) 1999. Guidance for employers is also provided in the Code of Practice.

To ascertain a person's community background an employer can use the "principal method" of directly asking the employee. Often this question will be asked as part of the application process on a separate form. If this method does not establish to which community an employee belongs, an employer can fall back on the "residuary method". This allows an employer to use a variety of information about an employee or applicant, including his or her name, the school he or she attended, the school or religious organisation from which a reference was sought or membership of clubs or societies and sporting or leisure pursuits, to determine to what community he or she belongs. The OFMDFM has published a schools list, "The Classification of Schools for Monitoring Purposes", which is to be used along with questions about schools attended to classify an employee's community background. Employers must inform employees which community they have been classified as belonging to. After being so informed, employees have seven days to challenge what they see as inaccuracies.

Registered concerns (and public authorities) are required to submit a monitoring return each year to the Equality Commission on the composition of their workforce. The information must be broken down by sex and job category. Employers of over 250 people, and public authorities, are also required to produce monitoring returns (similar to those for employees) regarding *applications* for employment and information on those who have ceased to be employed by the employer. All registered employers must obtain information regarding the community background of applicants for employment and retain this for three years. Failure to produce a monitoring return without reasonable excuse exposes an employer to a fine of up to £5,000, while sending in a monitoring return which is not prepared in accordance with the regulations can lead to a fine of up to £10,000. Employees or anyone else who provides false information, knowing it will be used for a monitoring return, also commit an offence.

Information provided for the purposes of monitoring is confidential and anyone who discloses it is guilty of an offence and liable to a fine up to £5,000. There are exceptions for disclosure which is necessary for legal proceedings, disclosure to the Equality Commission and disclosure to someone else in the business or public authority whose duties reasonably require such information.

Periodic reviews

Employers are required to carry out reviews of workforce composition at no more than three year intervals after registration. These are directed at discovering whether members of each community have fair participation in the workplace. If the employer determines that they do not then the employer should determine what affirmative action, if any, would be appropriate. Affirmative action may include the setting of goals and timetables regarding the composition of the workforce and applicants.

General affirmative action measures

Article 4 of the 1998 Order defines affirmative action as "action designed to secure fair participation in employment by members of the Protestant or Roman Catholic community in Northern Ireland". This may include abandonment of practices which discourage participation and adoption of practices which encourage participation.

Modifying or abandoning restrictive practices means dealing with the kinds of things that the provisions on indirect discrimination are aimed at, *e.g.* looking at the educational qualifications normally set for a job and deciding whether these are really necessary for that job and whether they are likely to have a discriminatory effect. It could include considering the means by which jobs are advertised or abandoning informal methods of recruitment, such as by word-of-mouth.

As regards measures to encourage participation, the basic rule is that an employer can do anything which does not itself turn out to constitute either direct or indirect discrimination (unless it is specifically exempted as discussed below). Thus, an employer cannot, under the guise of an affirmative action programme, set aside a certain percentage of jobs for members of a particular religious group. The provisions do not allow for "quotas" or for "preferential hiring", with the exception of the specific areas of police recruitment as provided for in the Police (NI) Act 2000 (50% of new recruits have to be Catholics and 50% non-Catholics). However, an employer may establish a target and timetable for improving the participation of a certain section of the community in the workforce, or apply a monitoring scheme even where this is not required by the legislation.

Specifically exempted affirmative action

The legislation specifically exempts certain actions from being challenged as directly or indirectly discriminatory if they are taken as part of an affirmative action programme. These actions are:

- provision of religion specific training facilities,
- provision of training in pursuance of affirmative action,
- redundancy;
- encouraging applications from an under-represented community, and
- selection from the unemployed.

Provision of religion specific training facilities

The first of the exemptions is provided for in Article 76 of the 1998 Order. It exempts the provision of training facilities in a particular place by an employer or person providing training services where this is provided only to persons of a particular belief. Such training schemes require the approval of the Equality Commission, which can be given if at any time within the 12 months prior to the provision of the training it appears to the Commission either that there are no people of the religious belief in question employed by this employer or that the proportion is small in comparison with what might reasonably be expected.

Provision of training in pursuance of affirmative action

In addition to the provision on religion-specific affirmative action, the 1998 Order retains the provision which permits an employer to provide specific training to a group "not framed by reference to a religious belief or political opinion". Such training is protected against any claims that it is directly or indirectly discriminatory

Redundancy

A further exempt form of affirmative action, contained in Article 73 of the 1998 Order is any affirmative action practice adopted with regard to redundancy. In *Hall v Shorts Missile Systems* (1997) a majority of the Court of Appeal appeared to take the view that such a policy would not amount to unfair dismissal of such employees even where it had not been agreed with trade unions.

Encouraging applications from the under-represented community

A fourth exempt form of affirmative action, allowed by Article 74 of the 1998 Order, are measures taken to encourage applications from an under-represented community for employment or training. This permits employers to strengthen contacts with minority schools with a view to encouraging applicants or to advertise primarily (or perhaps even exclusively) in one sector of the press. It would seem lawful for employers to advertise the fact that they have set goals and timetables for minority representation in their workforce as a means of encouraging minority applicants to apply. What the section would not seem to permit is "encouraging applications" by actually discriminating in favour of the under-represented community when selecting people for employment or training. However, if merely having a "preference" for people from a particular locality or with particular qualifications or experience (even where this is not shown to be job-related and can be complied with by a substantially smaller section of one community) is not indirectly discriminatory (assuming that a "preference" would not be a "condition or requirement") then it would appear to be lawful to advertise such a preference as part of an affirmative action programme.

Selection from the unemployed

The 1998 Order introduced a new form of affirmative action, by providing that a criterion for selection to the effect that someone has not been in employment for a specified period would not be unlawful (art.75). Without this specific provision such measures could be challenged as indirectly discriminatory in some parts of the country.

Affirmative action directed by the Equality Commission

The above discussion concerns circumstances where an employer voluntarily adopts an affirmative action plan. In some circumstances the Equality Commission may impose an affirmative action plan on an employer. Article 12 of the 1998 Order empowers the Commission to issue directions to employers if, after a formal investigation (see p. 254), the Commission concludes that an employer is not affording equality of opportunity and is unable to secure an undertaking from the employer that it will take steps to ensure equality of opportunity. Such directions may include the setting of goals and timetables.

If the directions have not been complied with "within such period as the Commission considers reasonable" the Commission can apply to the Fair Employment Tribunal (FET) for an enforcement order. If the FET upholds the application it may make an order setting out what steps should be taken to give effect to the directions and specifying that the employer must report what action has been taken to the FET within a certain time. Failure to comply with any part of this order renders the employer liable to pay a fine of up to £40,000. Employers have a right of appeal to the FET when the Commission's directions are issued on the grounds that they are already affording equality of opportunity or that the directions are inappropriate. A right to appeal to the Court of Appeal on a point of law also exists regarding any of the FET's decisions.

The Equality Commission also has power to make recommendations of affirmative action where an employer's review discloses that members of a particular community are not enjoying or are not likely to continue enjoying fair participation in employment. However, it does not appear that the recommendations are themselves legally enforceable.

Contract compliance

The term "contract compliance" is borrowed from the American experience of government contracting. There, however, it works as an incentive system whereby government grants and contracts are made more available for those with affirmative action programmes. The Northern Irish provisions are more like a penalty scheme, where grants and contracts may be lost if there is a proven failure to afford equality of opportunity.

The provisions allow for limits to be placed on the award of public grants and contracts. This is significant because more than 40% of private sector concerns in Northern Ireland are in receipt of some form of public funds. The Order indicates that public authority contracts and government financial assistance should be denied to "unqualified people" and there are four circumstances in which a concern can become unqualified:

- after conviction of an offence relating to failing to register,
- after conviction for failing to rectify the register when a new employer has taken over the concern,
- after conviction of an offence relating to failure to return a monitoring return, or
- as a result of receiving a penalty after failing to comply with a Tribunal order to enforce an employer's undertaking or Equality Commission directions.

Where any of these conditions is satisfied, the Equality Commission may issue a notice stating that such a person is unqualified and it can take all reasonable steps to bring this to the attention of public authorities. Employers have rights of appeal against this notice, first to the Commission itself, then to the FET and eventually to the Court of Appeal on a point of law. Public authorities are disbarred from entering into contracts with or accepting tenders from unqualified persons. Northern Ireland government departments may also refuse to pay any grant or discretionary assistance to unqualified persons. The Equality Commission can obtain an injunction from the High Court if it feels that a public authority is likely to breach its duty not to give contracts to disqualified persons, but no such powers exist in respect of government grants.

The Secretary of State may exempt contracts if he or she certifies that the work is necessary or desirable for the purposes of safeguarding national security, public safety or public order. A Northern Ireland department may also exempt a contract if it certifies that the work could not otherwise be done without disproportionate expense.

Non-employment situations

Northern Ireland has had fair employment legislation since 1976. However religious and political opinion discrimination in the non-employment sphere was prohibited for the first time only in 1998. The Order of that year prohibits discrimination in respect to the provision of higher and further education, the disposal and management of premises and the provision of goods, facilities and services. This last category includes things like the provision of credit or grants, accommodation in a hotel or access to places the public are permitted to enter. There are exemptions in respect of small premises where the owner resides in them and in respect of goods, facilities and services when their essential nature require that they be delivered to people of a particular religious belief or political opinion (*e.g.* a religious society or political party). Goods, facilities and services provided by a school are also exempt.

The Equality Commission

The role of the Equality Commission is explained in Chapter 11.

Other provisions against discrimination

Northern Ireland Act 1998

Section 75(1) of the Northern Ireland Act 1998 places public authorities under a duty to have due regard to the need to promote equality of opportunity on a range of grounds, including religious belief and political opinion. They also have a duty to have regard to the need to promote good relations between persons of different religious belief or political opinion (s.75(2)). The full significance of section 75 is discussed in Chapter 11.

By section 76(1) of the Northern Ireland Act 1998, acts by government and public bodies which are discriminatory on political or religious grounds are made unlawful and actionable in the courts. This is a re-enactment of section 19(1) of the Northern Ireland Constitution Act 1973. Orders in Council can be challenged under this heading and Assembly legislation which discriminates on the grounds of religion or political belief may also be ruled invalid by the courts. Only a small number of cases have so far invoked it, perhaps because it is generally assumed that here "discrimination" refers only to "direct discrimination".

Human Rights Act 1998

The Human Rights Act 1998 makes Article 14 of the European Convention on Human Rights part of the law of Northern Ireland. This prohibits discrimination in the "enjoyment of the rights and freedoms set forth in the Convention", on a range of grounds including "religion, political or other opinion". The scope of this provision is therefore limited, as the discrimination must be linked to another right contained in the Convention, such as fair trial or free expression. As the Convention contains no right to work, for example, employment discrimination is not covered by it. In addition, the European Court of Human Rights has made it clear that different treatment on religious grounds may be justified if it has a legitimate aim and the means adopted are proportionate to the aim pursued (*In re Parsons*, 2002). Affirmative action is one example of a legitimate aim. Although the Northern Ireland Act 1998 and the Fair Employment and Treatment (NI) Order 1998 are likely to provide a remedy in most cases of discrimination on grounds of religion and political opinion, the Human Rights Act 1998 may still be of relevance where something is not clearly covered by either, for example, policy decisions by UK government departments in Northern Ireland.

Article 14 provision is arguably at its most relevant in relation to certain grounds of discrimination, such as age or sexual orientation, which are not currently covered by specific legislation in Northern Ireland. Although the Act cannot be invoked against private employers or service providers, it may provide a remedy in respect of discrimination in the public sector, at least where it can be related to another protected Convention right, for example if a gay man or lesbian was automatically denied the opportunity to adopt a child. The Act is also relevant to discrimination in the public sector on grounds of sex, race or disability as these do not enjoy the additional protection of the anti-discrimination provisions of section 76 the Northern Ireland Act 1998. If the Northern Ireland Assembly were, for example, to pass legislation providing for childcare grants to be paid only to mothers, this could be challenged by fathers under the Human Rights Act 1998.

The Ombudsman

As explained in Chapter 2, the function of the Ombudsman is to deal with complaints from members of the public who claim to have suffered injustice by reason of "maladministration" by those bodies which fall within his or her jurisdiction. Maladministration includes discrimination and since the fair employment legislation largely covers issues of employment discrimination the Ombudsman tends to restrict his or her attention to cases falling outside the remit of the Equality Commission (*e.g.* cases where a national security certificate has been issued, or complaints of discrimination in the provision of public services).

Chapter 13

Sex Discrimination

Beverley Jones

L egislation to eliminate discrimination between the sexes was introduced into Northern Ireland in the mid-1970s. It followed developments in Great Britain, which were in turn influenced by the American civil liberties movement of the 1960s. In addition, the United Kingdom was seeking membership of what is now called the European Union (EU) and the Treaty of Accession required the introduction of equal pay for equal work between men and women.

European Union law

EU law plays a crucial role in the interpretation of the domestic legislation governing equal treatment between men and women in Northern Ireland. It takes precedence over conflicting provisions in our domestic law, just as it does in all other member states. It is interpreted and enforced by the European Court of Justice (ECJ) in Luxembourg through cases brought before that Court by the EU's Commission or referred to it by the national courts of member states.

Article 141 of the Treaty of Amsterdam 1997 (which amended Article 119 of the Treaty of Rome 1957) requires equal pay for men and women engaged in equal work. "Equal pay" means that pay for the same work at piece rates must be calculated on the basis of the same unit of measurement, and pay for work at time rates must be the same for the same job. In 1975 the Equal Pay Directive (75/117/EEC) further defined the concept as meaning:

> *...for the same work or for work to which equal value is attributed, the elimination of all discrimination on grounds of sex with regard to all aspects and conditions of remuneration. In particular, where a job classification system is used for determining pay it must be based on the same criteria for both men and women and so drawn up as to exclude any discrimination on grounds of sex.*

In 1976 another Directive was passed, called the Equal Treatment Directive (76/207/EEC), which aimed to achieve equality in respect of access to employment, vocational training, promotion and other working conditions. Similar Directives have since been passed concerning social security, occupational pension schemes and the protection of self-employed women and spouses who work for the self-employed during pregnancy and motherhood. In 1994 a Directive setting out minimum standards for the protection of pregnant and breast-feeding workers was implemented (92/85/EEC). Further Directives in respect of part-time and fixed-term workers, passed as framework agreements between the social partners at EU level, are likely to have a significant impact on the elimination of sex discrimination for such workers who are predominantly female.

Equal pay law

The Equal Pay Act (NI) 1970 was amended by the Sex Discrimination (NI) Order 1976 and both pieces of legislation came into effect in July 1976. The two laws are supposed to be read as a "harmonious code", although such a reading is difficult since their language is different and they cover mutually exclusive areas. The 1970 Act, which was further amended in 1984, governs only sex discrimination arising in terms and conditions of individual contracts of employment concerning pay. The Sex Discrimination (NI) Order 1976, which has been amended by several further Orders, was intended to eliminate discrimination in other aspects of employment. In addition, the Order outlaws discrimination on the grounds of sex in the field of education and in the provision of goods, facilities and services to the public.

Between 1976 and 1984 a woman (or a man) was entitled to equal pay only where she was employed on "like work" with, or work rated as equivalent to, that done by a colleague of the opposite sex. In the case of *Commission of the European Communities v UK* (1982) the ECJ held that the Equal Pay Act (NI) 1970 did not comply with the requirements of what was then Article 119 of the Treaty of Rome nor with the Equal Pay Directive, since there was no provision in the Act enabling a woman doing work of *equal value* to a man undertaking a different job to claim equal pay. The government was held to be in breach of its European obligations and was required to introduce amending legislation, namely the Equal Pay (Amendment) Regulations (NI) 1984. These provide a statutory right for women undertaking work of equal value to that done by men to claim equal pay. However, the procedure for such a claim is complex, costly and lengthy. Concerns remain as to whether the government has properly complied with its obligations under EU law.

Making an equal value claim

Claiming is regulated by the Industrial Tribunal (Constitution and Rules of Procedure) Regulations (NI) 1996. First, at a preliminary hearing the tribunal considers whether it is reasonable to compare the applicant's job with the male job with which she wishes it to be compared. It is the applicant who chooses the comparator, who must work either at the same place or for the same employer at a different place but under the same terms and conditions. The tribunal will also consider at this stage whether the claim should be dealt with as a "like work" or "rated as equivalent" claim. The ECJ has confirmed that equal value means *at least* equal value (*Murphy v Board Telecom Eireann,* 1988).

The fact that there are men doing the same work as an applicant, and who are paid the same, does not preclude an equal value claim with comparators engaged in different jobs (*Pickstone v Freeman's Mail Order Ltd,* 1988). It may, however, be relevant at a later stage of the proceedings, when the employer is entitled to raise the defence that the difference in pay is due to a "genuine material factor" not based on sex. At the same time, where the employer is alleging that the jobs being compared are the subject of a job evaluation scheme, the tribunal will consider whether such a scheme is properly "analytical" and whether it is tainted with sex discrimination. An analytical scheme is one which compares jobs under headings such as skill, effort, responsibility and decision-making, rather than making whole-job comparisons. In the case of *Bromley v H & J Quick Ltd* (1988), the Court of Appeal in England set out guidelines for the requirements which must be met if the scheme is to preclude an equal value claim. In *McAuley and others v EHSSB* (1990) the Court of Appeal of Northern Ireland held that the job evaluation scheme which applied to all health service ancillary workers in Great Britain could not preclude an equal value claim in Northern Ireland, because the GB scheme had never been applied to Northern Ireland.

In a raft of cases currently before the ECJ the restrictive scope under national law for challenging inequality in pay is under scrutiny. In *Lawrence and others v Regent Office Care Ltd* (2002), however, the

ECJ did not permit a cross-employer comparison where the differences in pay could not be attributed to a single source and there was no body which was responsible for the inequality and could restore equal treatment. In this case the employer of the applicants, who were female catering assistants and cleaners, was a private contractor to a local council. Previously the applicants had been employed directly by the council. The male comparators were manual staff who remained employed by the local council. In *Allonby v Accrington and Rossendale College* (2001) female part-time lecturers contracted to the College by their employer, the Education Learning Service, are awaiting a decision from the ECJ on whether they can compare with full-time male lecturers employed within the College. The applicants may be in a slightly stronger position than those in *Lawrence* since they are employed in the same jobs as their male comparators but the reasoning in *Lawrence* may still preclude their claims.

Recently the Court of Session in Scotland held in *South Ayrshire Council v Morton* (2002) that a female applicant employed as a primary school head-teacher can compare her terms and conditions to those of male secondary school head-teachers employed in a different councils but whose terms and conditions are governed by the same national agreement. This would appear to be in line with the ECJ's view in *Lawrence* in that the national agreement constitutes the single source from which any inequality and restitution flows.

Independent experts

Once the tribunal is satisfied that the claim is reasonable and has excluded the application of a job evaluation scheme, the matter is referred to an independent expert who prepares a report on whether the jobs compared are of equal value. There is a small panel of independent experts who are appointed by the Labour Relations Agency in Northern Ireland specifically for this purpose. Once the independent expert's report is completed the tribunal is reconvened. If the tribunal decides to admit it as evidence, the facts on which it is based cannot be disputed. If the report is not admitted as evidence, the tribunal must appoint a second expert to prepare a report. A tribunal can accept or reject an expert's findings and the parties themselves are entitled to call their own expert evidence to refute the independent expert's report. In practice this is a hard task, although not impossible.

Defences

During the independent expert's investigation the employer may raise any matters which he or she believes constitute "a genuine material factor" defence. The House of Lords in *Rainey v Greater Glasgow Health Board* (1987) held that a difference in pay which was objectively justified would defeat a claim for equal pay. At a European level, in *Von Hartz v Bilka Kaufhaus GmbH* (1986), the ECJ underlined the need for objectivity in justifying differential access to pay and benefits. The tribunal can accept, reject or adjourn consideration of the "genuine material factor" defence. If the defence is accepted, the claim fails. If it is rejected or adjourned, the independent expert prepares a report for the tribunal. The average time required for the preparation of reports is approximately two years, even though the original Regulations contemplated a much shorter period (seven weeks). With a view to reducing delays in the procedure for equal value claims the 1996 Regulations include provision for progress reports to be provided by independent experts.

Further recent decisions of the ECJ have clarified the standard required for defending differences in pay. Article 141 of the Treaty of Amsterdam 1997 outlaws differences in pay only if they are due to a sex difference. In *Brunhoffer v Bank der Österreichischen Postsparkasse AG* (1999) the ECJ confirmed that the onus of proving the presence of sex discrimination in the pay system shifts only when the applicant has established a *prima facie* case that she is a victim of less favourable treatment which can be explained only by the difference in sex. Hence, once it is established that the difference in pay is not due to sex discrimination there is no requirement to provide any objective justification for pay difference. In the case of *Strathclyde Regional Council v Wallace* (1998), once it had been held that none of the factors which explained the difference in pay were tainted by sex discrimination, there was no requirement for the employer to objectively justify the differences. A similar decision was reached by the House of Lords in *Barry v Midland Bank Plc* (1999).

Once the statistics suggest that a difference in pay may be due to sex discrimination the ECJ will require the employer to justify objectively the difference by factors unrelated to sex. The decision in *Jamstlldhetsombudsmannen v Orebro Lans Landsting* (2000) has reinforced the position as outlined by the ECJ in *Enderby v Frenchay Health Authority and Secretary of State for Health* (1994). *Enderby* required an objective justification of the pay differential where two jobs of equal value were carried out, "one almost exclusively by women and the other predominantly by men". It was not sufficient merely to explain the way in which the difference had arisen if statistics showed that women were more likely to earn lower pay than their male comparators.

The ECJ has given consideration to the types of justifications put forward by employers to explain pay differences. It has not accepted different collective bargaining structures as explaining differences in pay where they are based on gender-segregated jobs. An allegation of poor performance, unless it is specifically linked to individual performance, is also unlikely to be acceptable. In *Angestellten-Betriebsrat der Wiener Gebietskrankenkasse v Wiener Gebietskrankenkasse* (1999) the ECJ appeared to accept as a material factor justifying pay difference different professional qualifications, even though the jobs performed were the same. This decision has been criticised, since it did not consider the extent to which the different qualifications were required to perform the work.

In *Hayward v Cammell Laird Shipbuilders Ltd* (1988), the employer argued that, even though the applicant did work which was of equal value to her male comparators, she was not entitled to an increase in pay because her overall terms of employment were no less satisfactory than those of the men, since she enjoyed access to pension rights and sick pay which they did not. The House of Lords ruled that she was nevertheless entitled to the increase in pay, as she could compare a specific less favorable term of her contract with a similar term contained in the men's contracts. The court ruled that it was not required to consider the value of the overall package of terms and conditions enjoyed by the applicant and her male colleagues. In 1991 the ECJ upheld this approach in *Barber v Guardian Royal Exchange Assurance Group*. Later cases have stressed the employer's obligation to ensure "transparency" in pay structures.

Equality clauses

If the "genuine material factor" defence fails, the applicant will be entitled to an equality clause to be inserted into her contract of employment. She will then be entitled to equal pay. It is important, however, for an applicant to note the limitations of the equality clause. Following the ECJ decision in the case, *Enderby* returned to the tribunal under the name *Evesham v North Hertfordshire Health Authority* (2000) and the tribunal ruled that the applicant was entitled to equal pay with her comparator. Unfortunately her comparator had been employed in his post for only one year, while the applicant had been employed for five years. She believed she was entitled to £4,000 more than her comparator but the tribunal, and subsequently the Employment Appeal Tribunal, held that this was more than was required under the Equal Pay Act, as amended. Thus the applicant was entitled only to an amendment to her contract to make it no less favourable than that of her male comparator.

Under national law the equality clause can include an element of up to two years' back pay. However, in light of the ECJ's decisions in *Preston v Wolverhampton Healthcare NHS Trust* (2001) and *Levez v T H Jennings* (1999), this remedy has been found deficient in that it fails to provide a level of damages equivalent to that allowed for other similar complaints, such as racial discrimination.

Difficulties with the legislation

It is clear that the amended legislation still does not comply with EU law in a number of important respects, as outlined above. In addition, the processing of cases remains inordinately lengthy, despite almost 18 years of the operation of the legislation. Without expert advice and legal representation throughout, it is unlikely that any claim will succeed. Absolute bars to claims, under the job evaluation and genuine material factor provisions, may contravene individual rights of review. Given the substantial differentials in pay between men and women, employers have every incentive to seek to defeat equal pay claims, particularly where industries employ predominantly female workers. There are instances of employers changing the duties of applicants or comparators in order to circumvent the law, as well as threats of dismissal or redundancy if claims are pursued. The Confederation of British Industry has called for the repeal of the legislation, arguing that it places too heavy a burden on industry.

In 1996 the European Commission published its code of practice in this area. There is, however, little evidence of employers reviewing their pay structures to ensure implementation of the principle of equal pay. Indeed, many employers continue to adopt a policy of doing nothing until faced with a claim. Despite all the difficulties with the equal value procedures, the Equality Commission for Northern Ireland continues to receive a significant number of equal pay complaints.

Sex discrimination legislation

The Sex Discrimination (NI) Order 1976, as amended, provides limited protection against unequal treatment of men and women in the fields of employment, education and the provision of goods, facilities and services to the public. There are a number of important exclusions which restrict the scope of the legislation, but unlike the equal pay legislation the Order contains definitions of what constitutes discrimination: while the terms are not specifically used, the Order distinguishes between "direct" and "indirect" discrimination (see below). The 1976 Order also set up the Equal Opportunities Commission for Northern Ireland, now subsumed into the Equality Commission for Northern Ireland by virtue of the Northern Ireland Act 1998 (see Chapter 11).

In 1999 the government introduced new legislation to ensure compliance with EU law in the form of the Sex Discrimination (Gender Reassignment) Regulations (NI) 1999. These expand the scope of the 1976 Order to protect individuals from discrimination on grounds that they are contemplating, undergoing or have undergone gender reassignment. However they do not address the issue of sexual orientation. A decision of the House of Lords in *Pearce v Governing Body of Mayfield Secondary School* (2002) is awaited to provide an authoritative decision on whether the sex discrimination legislation can be interpreted as prohibiting homophobic discrimination. The government must, however, take steps to implement such protection by December 2003 in order to comply with the Framework Employment Equality Directive of 2000 (see Chapter 11).

Direct discrimination

Direct discrimination means treating an individual less favorably than a person of the opposite sex (and, at work, a married person less favourably than a single person). For example, if girls have to obtain higher marks than boys to secure a grammar school place, a *prima facie* case of unlawful discrimination arises under the education provisions of the 1976 Order. Unless it can be shown that the reason for the less favourable treatment is unrelated to the sex of the children, it will be unlawful. The motive for the treatment is irrelevant, even if it is intended for perceived good reasons (*In re EOC for Northern Ireland*, 1988).

It is for the court to determine whether the reason provided for the less favourable treatment is not based on sex. In *Wallace v South-Eastern Education and Library Board* (1980), the Northern Ireland Court of Appeal recognised that there was rarely clear evidence of sex discrimination and that unless the court was able to draw an inference of unlawful discrimination from the circumstances of the complaint the purpose of the legislation would be largely defeated. Significantly, sex discrimination legislation departs from the traditional burden of proof rule in other discrimination law in that to comply with EU obligations the Sex Discrimination (Indirect Discrimination and Burden of Proof) Regulations (NI) 2001 require tribunals and courts to draw an inference of sex discrimination in the absence of a clear and specific explanation. This inference is required only in the area of employment, not in the area of goods, facilities, services or education.

Indirect discrimination

Until the Sex Discrimination (Indirect Discrimination and Burden of Proof) Regulations (NI) 2001 the requirements for indirect sex discrimination were the same as for racial, religious or political discrimination. The Regulations now require a different test to be applied in employment cases: indirect sex discrimination arises if an employer applies to a woman a provision, criterion or practice which (1) is applied equally to a man but is such that it would be to the detriment of a considerably larger proportion of women than men, (2) cannot be shown to be justifiable irrespective of the sex of the person to whom it is applied and (3) operates to the woman's detriment. It remains to be seen how these relatively new provisions will be interpreted by the national courts in the light of previous case-law. The Regulations appear consistent with the EU standard applied in the equal pay case of *Enderby* (1994), in that they adopt a result-orientated approach which aims to remove barriers to equality of opportunity rather than erecting complex technical hurdles preventing change.

Victimisation

The Sex Discrimination (NI) Order 1976 defines and prohibits victimisation. It aims to protect a person from being less favourably treated because he or she has asserted a right under the equality laws. In a race relations case before the Employment Appeal Tribunal in England (*Aziz v Trinity Street Taxis Ltd*, 1988), it was held that the appellant had failed to show victimisation since he had produced no evidence to suggest that he would have been treated any differently had he complained under other legislation. However, in a fair employment case the Northern Ireland Court of Appeal appeared to reject the approach in *Aziz*, holding that a complainant did not have to prove that the victimisation was solely or predominantly due to the earlier complaint (*Northern Health and Social Services Board v Fair Employment Commission for Northern Ireland*, 1994).

Until recently, under national law an applicant in a sex discrimination case could not claim any form of unlawful discrimination after the expiry of the employment relationship. This approach was challenged in *Coote v Granada Hospitality* (1998), where the ECJ held that national law was deficient in failing to provide protection from victimisation where the applicant was refused a reference following termination of employment. As a result, in the field of sex discrimination only, it is now unlawful to discriminate by way of victimisation in the post-employment relationship between a former employer and ex-employee. It should be noted, however, that an ex-employee cannot claim in respect of any other form of sex discrimination.

Sex discrimination in education

Articles 24-29 of the 1976 Order make it unlawful for a body responsible for the provision of education to discriminate against girls or boys. This applies to both schools and the Education and Library Boards, but the Order does not cite the Department of Education of Northern Ireland as a "body responsible". The reason for this appears to be that the Department is expected to ensure that schools and Boards do not offend the legislation. In *In re EOC for Northern Ireland* (1988) the Department marked "11-plus" papers, adjusting the scores for boys and girls differentially. It then separated the sexes, taking the top 27% of boys and the top 27% of girls as eligible for free grammar school places. The effect of this practice was to exclude from free places some girls who had better marks than some boys. The High Court held that the practice constituted unlawful discrimination and that the Boards had contravened the Order by implementing the Department's decision. The Department itself was found to have contravened article 40 of the Order, which prohibits the issuing of unlawful instructions. It should be noted, however, that the 1976 Order contains special exemptions for single sex schools.

Sex discrimination in the provision of goods, facilities and services

Article 30 of the 1976 Order requires that goods, facilities and services must be available to both sexes "in the same manner and on the same terms as are normal in relation to men". Whilst there are no definitions of "goods", "facilities" or "services" in the Order, access to loan facilities and service in a public bar have been held to fall within these provisions, but in *R v Entry Clearance Officer, Bombay, ex parte Amin* (1983), the House of Lords held that the provision of vouchers allowing entry into the United Kingdom did not constitute a "facility" under the English section equivalent to article 30 in Northern Ireland's law.

The court also held in *Amin* that the section applies only to "market-place activities", *i.e.* activities which can be undertaken by a private individual. To a large extent this appears to exclude the state from liability for discrimination and to prevent scrutiny of the operation of government policies in the areas of social security and taxation. However, EU law can in some instances provide protection from state discrimination. The failure to pay invalid care allowance to a married woman who gave up work to nurse an infirm relative owing to discriminatory assumptions made by the Department of Health and Social Security was found to be contrary to the European Social Security Directive in *Drake v Chief Adjudication Officer* (1985). This case led to many married women becoming eligible for the benefit. This extensive area of exclusion from the scrutiny of anti-discrimination law is currently under review, particularly in the area of race discrimination, and is likely to be narrowed significantly in the future.

Another exemption which limits the scope of article 30 is that governing private clubs. Under this, women are often denied equal access to sporting facilities, and the denial can extend to the use of public facilities, such as at golf clubs. In *Bateson v YMCA* (1980) the Northern Ireland High Court held that a temporary day membership card, which allowed access to a snooker table, did not make the facility a private club, so to deny women access to it amounted to unlawful discrimination.

Sex discrimination in employment

The 1976 Order makes it unlawful for employers to discriminate in the selection of employees and in the treatment of their workforce. This covers training and promotion opportunities, benefits, facilities, services, dismissals or "any other detriment" (art.8). Only if there is a "genuine occupational qualification" is it lawful for an employer to seek specifically to employ a man (or woman), or to consider one sex only for training or promotion (art.10). In some circumstances, however, employers and training bodies can provide under-represented groups with the skills necessary for work which they may not have done traditionally (arts.17, 48 and 49). Courses can be run in companies trying to encourage applications for particular posts where there have been few or no women (or men) in the previous 12 months. Training bodies can provide courses limited to one sex or to persons who may have been away from employment because of domestic responsibilities.

Firms employing less than six employees, and private households, used to be excluded from the 1976 Order. But in *Commission of the European Communities v UK* (1983), the ECJ held that these exclusions were unjustified. It did, however, recognise that there might be instances when an employer could seek a person of a particular sex for employment in a private household. The Sex Discrimination (NI) Order 1988 (which parallels the 1986 Act in Great Britain) implemented the European Court's ruling.

Sexual harassment

"Sexual harassment" is now recognised as behaviour which can amount to unlawful discrimination. It encompasses unwelcome sexual advances and sexually explicit comments as well as physical assault. An industrial tribunal in Belfast upheld the first claim in the UK in the case of *M v Crescent Garage Ltd* (1982). Subsequently, in *Porcelli v Strathclyde Regional Council* (1984) the House of Lords established conclusively that a campaign of unpleasant and lewd comments by the applicant's male work colleagues, which resulted in her seeking a transfer, constituted unlawful sex discrimination. The fact that the behaviour was not sexually motivated was not considered relevant, since the complainant was subjected to treatment to which a man would not have been subjected.

Pregnancy

Employers are allowed to provide preferential treatment for women in connection with pregnancy and maternity but the 1976 Order provides no specific protection against *less* favourable treatment on these grounds. Because the legislation compares like with like in determining "less favourable" treatment, an early claim of unlawful discrimination on the ground of pregnancy failed (*Turley v Allders Department Stores Ltd*, 1980). As a man could not become pregnant, the failure to promote, or the dismissal of, a pregnant woman was held not to be unlawful. An industrial tribunal in Northern Ireland was the first in the UK to disagree with this interpretation. In *Jordan v Northern Ireland Electricity Service* (1984) the tribunal, appreciating the inadequacy of the Order in dealing with one of the fundamental grounds for discrimination against women, held that the reason for the failure of the employer to promote Mrs Jordan was that she was pregnant and that this amounted to sex discrimination. The tribunal did not address the question of the need for a comparison. In England the approach to such claims was, generally, to compare pregnant women with sick men in order to bring the claim within the scope of the Order. In the *Dekker* and *Hertz* cases (1991) the ECJ adopted the approach taken by the industrial tribunals in Northern Ireland and in *EMO Air Cargo (UK) Ltd v Webb* (1995) the House of Lords finally accepted that there was no need for a male comparison in order to provide protection from pregnancy discrimination. The Employment Rights (NI) Order 1996, which consolidated employment rights, and the Employment Relations (NI) Order 1999, implemented proper maternity rights and protection from dismissal on grounds of pregnancy.

It remains the position, however, that the failure to pay a woman full pay during maternity leave does not amount to unlawful discrimination. In *Gillespie and others v Various Health Boards* (1996) the ECJ held that a maternity allowance should be "adequate" but that, provided such allowance was no less favourable than statutory sickness benefits, it would meet the test of adequacy. However, failure to pay a woman her pay rise during pregnancy was held to be discriminatory.

An on-going concern following the decision in *Webb* was whether an employer can discriminate against an applicant for a fixed-term contract who is pregnant. In the cases of *Tele Danmark v Handels-Og Kontorfunktionaerernes Forbund I Danimark* and *Jimenez-Melgar v Ayuntamiento de los Barrios* (2001) the ECJ has clarified the obligations facing employers in these circumstances. First, a prospective employee has no obligation to advise of her pregnancy in order to obtain maternity protection, since maternity protections do not depend on an ability to be present at work. Second, the same maternity protection exists for both permanent and fixed-term workers. Thus, any attempt to avoid, end or not renew a fixed-term contract in order to preclude the employment of a pregnant woman amounts to unlawful discrimination. Third, it would not be unlawful where an employer avoids, ends or does not renew a fixed-term contract if the reason is unconnected with pregnancy or maternity.

Further clarification of the extent of maternity protections is still required. For example, it would appear on the basis of current case-law that any refusal to grant performance pay due to the absence of the employee on maternity leave would amount to unlawful sex discrimination. In addition it would appear that national employment law in relation to maternity rights is ambiguous on the question of whether a woman can be dismissed, in circumstances where she is treated no less favourably than a male on sick leave, due to pregnancy related illness which continues beyond the expiry of maternity leave (see *Caledonia Bureau Investment v Caffrey*, 1998).

Work / life balance

Increasingly, mainstream employment law requires employers to consider requests for flexible working arrangements to address the work/life balance necessary for many employees. Whilst this is in general terms a recent development, commencing with part-time workers' rights to pro-rata benefits introduced in August 2001 and with additional obligations on employers proposed for introduction in 2003, sex discrimination provisions have enshrined this obligation since the late 1970s.

In essence, where a request for flexible or reduced hours is refused, *potential* indirect sex or marital status discrimination arises, since the courts accept that women and parents are less able to comply with a full-time work requirement due to family responsibilities. If an employer is not in a position to grant a request for flexibility, he or she will be required to justify the refusal where this would result in a detriment to the applicant. Given this obligation, it is unlikely that a policy which opposed flexible work would provide the justification necessary for refusal of flexible work for domestic reasons. However, it must be stressed that there is no automatic right under sex discrimination provisions, nor indeed under mainstream employment provisions in this area, to flexible work because of domestic responsibilities. The obligation resting on the employer is to balance the needs of the organisation with the equality issues. Hence, whether an employee can be granted flexible work will depend on the individual facts of the case and the precise nature of any flexible arrangement will be the subject of negotiation since the employer may not be in a position to grant the employee's specific request but may be in a position to meet the request half-way.

Retirement and pensions

Matters relating to death or retirement fall outside the scope of the 1976 Order. However, in *Marshall v Southampton and South-West Hampshire Area Health Authority* (1986) the ECJ held that, whilst discrimination in the state pension age was lawful, the domestic legislation could not preclude protection against *dismissal* at different ages for men and women, even though they were based on the age at which people became entitled to the state pension. Although the Sex Discrimination (NI) Order 1988 limits the scope of this exclusion, successful challenges to the exclusion which commenced with *Barber v Guardian Royal Exchange Assurance Group* (1991) still continue. However member states of the EU took steps to limit the impact of the *Barber* case by adopting a Protocol to the Treaty of Rome precluding redress for discrimination occurring prior to the *Barber* judgment.

Thousands of cases concerning discrimination in pension benefits for part-time workers have been lodged before tribunals in Great Britain and Northern Ireland. These part-time workers were excluded from pension benefits and they are seeking to protect pensions by claiming previous years' benefits. In *Magorrian and others v EHSSB* (1996), referred from a tribunal in Belfast, the ECJ held that part-time workers excluded entirely from a particular pension benefit were entitled to claim pension rights back to 1976, provided they were willing to repay any contributions owed. This position was reiterated in a consolidated case from a tribunal in Birmingham, *Preston and others v Wolverhampton Healthcare NHS Trust and others* (2001). Currently, tribunals nationally are considering how best to apply these judgments to the thousands of claims. Complex issues in respect of interest and tax liabilities are raised in them.

Collective agreements

In *Commission of the European Communities v UK* (1983), the failure to provide a remedy against discrimination appearing in non-binding collective agreements between unions and employers was found to be contrary to European law. The government argued unsuccessfully that, since the agreements were unenforceable, there was no necessity to provide a remedy. It was held that, irrespective of the legal effect of these agreements, they did in fact regulate working conditions and industrial relations. The 1988 Order accordingly makes void any term of a contract of employment which arises from discrimination in a collective agreement, but does not provide a mechanism to challenge the actual agreement.

National security certificates

Until 1988 there could be no consideration of matters covered by the 1976 Order whenever a certificate asserting that a question of national security was involved had been issued by the Secretary of State. In *Johnston v Chief Constable of the RUC* (1986), the applicant was one of 39 female reservists in the RUC whose three-year contracts of employment were not renewed, whilst those of male colleagues were. When the women challenged the decision, the Secretary of State issued a national security certificate. The case was referred to the ECJ, which held that the failure to allow for judicial review of the issue of a national security certificate in Northern Ireland was a breach of European law. The Sex Discrimination (Amendment) (NI) Order 1988 implemented the Court's ruling.

Protective legislation

Article 52 of the 1976 Order allows for the retention of many discriminatory pieces of legislation on grounds of health and safety. Much of the discriminatory protective legislation was in fact repealed early in 1990.

Remedies

In a claim of sex discrimination an industrial tribunal can issue a declaration that the employer has unlawfully discriminated against the applicant. It can also recommend that the employer should reduce the effect of the discrimination on the applicant. Finally, the tribunal can award unlimited compensation. However, there are no powers to issue injunctions (*i.e.* orders to do or not do something) and this means that the remedies of the court are often inappropriate, especially in sexual harassment cases. In addition, the powers of the tribunal to recommend means of redressing the impact of discrimination are very limited.

Conclusion

Irrespective of any new Equality Act containing harmonised anti-discrimination law (see Chapter 11), a comprehensive piece of legislation on sex discrimination and equal pay is urgently needed in Northern Ireland. It should require positive action by employers and state institutions, as the mere prohibition of discrimination is insufficient to secure equality. The failure of the state to provide a comprehensive system of child-care facilities means that the burden of domestic responsibilities continues to rest upon women's shoulders. Stereotypical attitudes persist. Equal pay will not be won until sex segregation in employment is removed and women have equal representation in higher managerial grades. Strengthening the law to provide a coherent enforceable set of rights would manifest the commitment of the state towards the principle and practice of equality. Its importance is in setting the standard to be followed by society.

Chapter 14

Race Discrimination

Ciaran White

International and European law

International law prohibits racial discrimination in Article 26 of the UN's International Covenant on Civil and Political Rights (1966). Neither the International Covenant on Economic, Social and Cultural Rights (1966) nor the European Convention on Human Rights (1950) prohibits racial discrimination in so many words, but they do require states to guarantee that the rights protected by those treaties will be exercised without discrimination based on race. (The latter treaty has now been incorporated into domestic law by the Human Rights Act 1998, which means that it is a remedy that may be availed of in the domestic courts: see Chapter 1). Protocol 12 to the European Convention on Human Rights does prohibit discrimination generally, but the UK has not yet even signed this.

However, the most significant international legal treaty dealing with racial discrimination is the UN's Convention on the Elimination of All Forms of Racial Discrimination (1965). This obliges the UK to pursue, by all appropriate means, and without delay, a policy of eliminating racial discrimination in all its forms and to promote understanding amongst all races. The government's success in meeting these obligations is examined periodically, every two years or so, by the Committee on the Elimination of Racial Discrimination. This Committee's criticism of the UK for failing to enact anti-racism legislation for Northern Ireland was instrumental in securing the enactment of the Race Relations (NI) Order 1997. The next Committee examination of a UK report is due to occur in the summer of 2003.

As explained in Chapter 11, the law of the European Union, especially its Directives, will also have a significant influence on the shape and content of anti-discrimination legislation in Northern Ireland in the near future. In particular, the Office of the First Minister and Deputy First Minister has committed itself to implementing two Directives in 2003 – the Race and Ethnic Origin Directive (Council

Directive 2000/43/EC) and the Framework Employment Equality Directive (Council Directive 2000/78/EC). Furthermore, there is an undertaking to harmonise the various anti-discrimination statutes into one Single Equality Act.

The net effect of these developments will be that eventually one Act will contain all the anti-discrimination and equality law for Northern Ireland, and its content, particularly the definitions of direct and indirect discrimination and the rules on discharging the burden of proof, will have been greatly influenced by European Union Law. However, for the time being we must look to the Race Relations (NI) Order 1997 to establish the applicable anti-racism law.

Race and the "statutory duty"

Before examining the 1997 Order, it is worth mentioning the new statutory duty created by section 75 of the Northern Ireland Act 1998. It requires specified public bodies to have due regard, in the performance of their functions, to the need to ensure equality of opportunity between – amongst others – persons of different racial or ethnic origin. The net effect of this duty is to require those bodies to assess the impact of their policies and administrative activity on persons of minority ethnic status, ameliorating or eradicating any adverse impacts where they occur. The duty is enforced by the Equality Commission for Northern Ireland (see Chapter 11). Over time it should have the impact of tackling racial discrimination and racial disadvantage at an institutional level.

The 1997 Order

The Race Relations (NI) Order 1997 is the main anti-racism legislation in Northern Ireland and it is very similar to the Race Relations Act 1976 applying in Great Britain, although there are some key differences which will be noted where appropriate. The Order outlaws racial discrimination in the workplace, in education, in the provision of goods, facilities and services, and in the disposal and management of premises. It also provides a mechanism for victims of discrimination to obtain redress and established the Commission for Racial Equality for Northern Ireland (CRE(NI)). The CRE(NI) has since been merged, by section 74 of the Northern Ireland Act 1998, with other equality bodies to form the Equality Commission for Northern Ireland.

It is worth noting that the Race Relations (Amendment) Act 2000, a more recent anti-racism statute that had its origins in the MacPherson report into the killing of Stephen Lawrence, does not apply in Northern Ireland, although elements of it have been incorporated by means of other legislation. The responsibility for equality legislation is a devolved one, so the onus is primarily on the Northern Ireland Assembly to adopt the additional elements of the 2000 Act to ensure that the code of anti-discrimination law in Northern Ireland is comparable to that in Great Britain. Of course while the Assembly is suspended the responsibility reverts to Westminster.

As with all anti-discrimination legislation, there are important concepts which require explanation in order to appreciate the manner in which the legislation operates.

Direct discrimination

The courts have formulated a very simple test to act as a guide in establishing whether direct discrimination has taken place: "Would the complainant have received the same treatment from the defendant but for his or her [race]?" (*James v Eastleigh Borough Council,* 1990). Motives or intentions are irrelevant: if, for instance, an employer refuses to employ a person because he or she fears that that person will be harmed by other racist employees, that still amounts to unlawful discrimination, notwithstanding the fact that it is done with the best of intentions. "Race" need not be the only ground on which a decision was made. It will still be unlawful if race was an important factor in the decision, even though other considerations also influenced it (*Owens and Briggs v James,* 1982).

Because discrimination occurs where, on racial grounds, a person treats another less favourably than he or she treats, or would treat, other persons, the victim need not suffer less favourable treatment because of his or her own racial origins. A person who is dismissed because he or she refuses to comply with management's instructions to expel black youths from the workplace, for example, will be a victim of racial discrimination despite the fact that he is white (*Showboat Entertainment Centre v Owens*, 1984). Similarly, in *R v CRE, ex parte Westminster City Council* (1984) the High Court found that discrimination occurred when the Council, under pressure from an all-white workforce, refused to employ a black man in its refuse collection section.

It is also discrimination for someone to "knowingly aid" (art.33) another in the commission of an unlawful act under the legislation. In two recent cases the House of Lords has had to consider the application of this concept (it appears in s.33(1) of the Race Relations Act 1976). In *Anyanwu and another v South Bank Student Union and another* (2001) the complainants were officers of the Students' Union who were expelled from the South Bank University. This had the effect of requiring their contracts of employment with the Students' Union to be terminated. The complainants alleged that the Students' Union had subjected them to racial discrimination and that the University had "knowingly aided" them in this. The House of Lords considered that the University's actions were capable of infringing section 33 and remitted the matter back to the employment tribunal for a re-hearing. Their Lordships rejected the Court of Appeal's view that the party aiding the discriminator needed to be a "prime mover" in order to attract liability. The Tribunals should, they said, give an ordinary view to the meaning of "aids".

The concept was also considered in *Hallam v Avery* (2001) when the culpability of the police for a discriminatory action of a local authority was in issue. The plaintiff was an English Romany who booked the council property for her wedding reception. The police informed the council that it was a "gypsy wedding" and that large numbers might attend and public disorder might ensue. The council's reaction, in imposing additional conditions on the plaintiff, was a discriminatory act. The more difficult issue, however, was whether the involvement of the police was also an unlawful act because the police could be considered to have knowingly aided the council in performing a discriminatory act. The House of Lords accepted that it was open to the trial judge to conclude that the police were alerting the council to what they considered a potential problem, that there were a number of ways the council could have reacted and that the plaintiff had not demonstrated that the police had knowingly aided the council in discriminating.

Indirect discrimination

Indirect discrimination occurs where conditions or requirements are imposed which, while superficially free from racial bias, operate in a disproportionately disadvantageous way upon persons of a particular racial group. The definition of indirect discrimination, in article 3(b) of the 1997 Order, has four elements:

- a requirement or condition is applied equally to all,

- the proportion of persons from the same racial group as the alleged victim who can comply with the requirement or condition is considerably smaller than the proportion of persons not belonging to that racial group,
- the requirement or condition cannot be shown to be justifiable, and
- the requirement or condition operates to the detriment of the alleged victim because he or she cannot comply with it.

For example, a refusal to employ a person because he or she is of an ethnic minority origin would be direct discrimination, whereas a refusal to employ someone because he or she was not born in Northern Ireland could amount to indirect discrimination. This is because a significantly smaller proportion of persons of minority ethnic origin could comply with such a requirement. Charging "overseas" students significantly higher fees than "home" students has been deemed by the House of Lords to be indirect discrimination (*Orphanos v Queen Mary College*, 1985), although such fees are now justified by legislation (Education (Fees and Awards) Act 1983).

The adverse effect of the requirement or condition does not amount to unlawful discrimination if it can be shown to be justified. In deciding this the courts will balance the degree of discrimination against the need for the requirement. In *Hampson v Department of Education and Science* (1990) a judge said that "justifiable" requires an objective balance between the discriminatory effect of the conditions and the reasonable needs of the party who is applying the condition. The difficulty with this test, however, is that it appears to equate "justifiable" with "reasonable", rather than with "necessary" or "extremely important". Nevertheless the statement has since been approved by the House of Lords in *Webb v EMO Air Cargo (UK) Ltd (No. 2)* (1995). An example of a justifiable condition can be found in *Panesar v Nestlé Co. Ltd* (1980), where employees in a confectionery factory were prohibited from wearing beards for hygiene reasons. This condition was held not to be a discriminatory one even though it impacted adversely on Sikhs, because it was a justifiable requirement in the context of that business.

Racial groups and racial grounds

As we have seen, discrimination on racial grounds, or against racial groups, is unlawful. However, what are "racial grounds" and how does one ascertain what is a "racial group"? "Racial grounds" are defined, in article 5(1), as meaning colour, race, nationality or ethnic or national origins and a racial group is one composed of persons defined by reference to any of these grounds. It has been left to the courts to provide further guidance on defining what groups are protected by the legislation. This was done by the House of Lords in *Mandla v Dowell Lee* (1983). In that case a young Sikh boy, who wished to attend a private school, was denied admission on the basis that he could not comply with the school policy on uniforms, because he wore a turban over his unshorn hair, in accordance with the tenets of his religion. Religious discrimination legislation does not apply in Great Britain and his complaint was that he had suffered racial discrimination. It was thus vital to establish whether Sikhs were an ethnic group protected by the legislation. In holding that they were, Lord Fraser set out what he considered were the criteria to judge whether a group was an ethnic one. There are two essential criteria which a group must possess:

- a long-shared history, of which the group is conscious as distinguishing it from other groups, and the memory of which it keeps alive; and
- a cultural tradition of its own, including family and social customs and manners, often but not necessarily associated with religious observance.

There is also a range of non-essential criteria. Compliance with these is not crucial, but it does serve to reinforce the view that the group is an ethnic one. They are:

- a common geographical origin or descent from a small number of common ancestors,
- a common language not necessarily peculiar to that group,
- a common literature peculiar to that group,
- a common religion, different from that of neighbouring groups or from the general community surrounding it, and
- being a minority, or being an oppressed or dominant group, within a larger community.

In *Mandla v Dowell Lee* (1983) Sikhs were considered to be an ethnic group and the requirement regarding school uniforms was therefore held to be indirectly discriminatory. As a result a number of legislative amendments had to be made to accommodate Sikhs. One of these makes Sikhs exempt from the requirement to wear safety helmets on construction sites (art.13 of the Employment (Miscellaneous Provisions) (NI) Order 1990).

Jews have also been considered an ethnic group (*Seide v Gillette Industries Ltd.*, 1980), as have English Romanies (*CRE v Dutton,* 1989) and Welsh people (*Griffiths v Reading University Students' Union,* 1997). In *BBC Scotland v Souster* (2001) it was held that English and Scottish persons could benefit from protection of the Race Relations Act 1976, on the basis that discrimination against them would be on the basis of their "national origins". However, Rastafarians do not qualify for protection (*Crown Suppliers (PSA) v Dawkins,* 1991). A significant difference between the English Act and the Northern Ireland Order is that, in article 5(2)(a) of the 1997 Order, Travellers are specifically included as an ethnic group protected by the legislation. They are defined as:

> *the community of people commonly so called who are defined (both by themselves and by others) as people with a shared history, culture and traditions including, historically, a nomadic way of life on the island of Ireland.*

Because of the existence of the Fair Employment (NI) Acts 1976-89, the Race Relations (NI) Order specifically withheld protection from groups defined by reference to religious belief or political opinion. This means that Catholics and Protestants, for example, are not in a position to use the 1997 Order where they allege discrimination on the basis of their religious identities. Instead they must bring a complaint under the fair employment legislation, if possible. However, if they can prove that the discrimination was on the basis of their "Irishness" or "Britishness", they may be protected by the 1997 Order.

Complaints assisted by the Equality Commission in recent years have involved a wide range of racial groups, including Thai, Indian, German, Ghanaian, Algerian, English, Irish and Traveller applicants.

Segregation

Segregating persons on racial grounds is "less favourable treatment" (art.3(3)) and therefore always amounts to direct discrimination. This ensures that those of a racist mentality cannot escape the effect of the legislation by arguing, for example, that they have provided facilities of an identical, but segregated, nature for different racial or ethnic groups and that therefore no group has been less favourably treated. Thus, if an employer has separate toilets for Asian and white employees this will amount to unlawful racial segregation (*Qadus v Henry Robinson (Ironfounders) Ltd*, 1980).

Victimisation

Victimisation occurs where a person is subject to less favourable treatment because he or she has:
- brought a case under the 1997 Order,
- given evidence or information in connection with a case brought by someone else,
- alleged that a person has contravened the Order, or
- done anything under the legislation.

Victimisation occurs where the victim is treated less favourably merely because the discriminator believes, or suspects, that the victim has done, or intends to do, any of these acts (art.4). However, in two cases the victimisation provisions in England have been narrowly interpreted, presenting difficulties for future complainants. In *Kirby v Manpower Service Commission* (1980), an employee in a Job Centre was transferred to less desirable work after he reported incidents of alleged racial discrimination on the part of employers to the local Community Relations Council. His employers considered his actions to amount to a breach of confidence and justified his transfer on that basis. The industrial tribunal considered that the transfer did not amount to victimisation because any employee disclosing confidential information would have been treated in this way. In *Aziz v Trinity Street Taxis* (1988) an Asian taxi driver, who felt that he was unfairly discriminated against in the fee he was being charged by the organisation to operate another taxi, made a complaint to an industrial tribunal. In the course of the proceedings it was disclosed that Mr Aziz had secretly recorded conversations with other members of the organisation to support his claim. He was subsequently expelled from the organisation. His complaint of victimisation failed because the Court of Appeal accepted the organisation's assertion that it had expelled Mr Aziz because he had breached the trust of the other members of the organisation. The victimisation provisions therefore protect a person only if the action taken against him or her follows because it is known, or believed, that he or she has made use of the Order and not because of some other reason.

However, some more recent cases have shed light on the operation of the victimisation provisions. In *Nagarajan v London Regional Transport* (1999) the complainant had taken action against the respondents, his employers, on previous occasions. He then applied for another position within the company but was unsuccessful. In the course of proceedings it emerged that the company considered that his attitude was too "anti-management". The Tribunal considered that the company's view on this was influenced, consciously or subconsciously, by the earlier complaints he had made and accordingly the company was guilty of victimisation. The House of Lords confirmed that in establishing victimisation the complainant does not have to prove that the respondent was motivated by a conscious or deliberate desire to treat the complainant less favourably because he had made complaints previously. It was enough that the evidence allowed the Tribunal to infer from the evidence that the respondent had been influenced, even subconsciously, by the previous discrimination complaints.

In *Chief Constable of the West Yorkshire Police v Khan* (2001) it was alleged that the Chief Constable's decision not to issue Khan with a reference in respect of his application to join another police force because the police officer had lodged a discrimination complaint against the Chief Constable, which complaint was still pending, was victimisation. The Chief Constable argued that he would ordinarily issue references but not where there were proceedings pending against him. The House of Lords considered that because the Chief Constable was seeking to preserve his position, and because the decision had been taken because of the existence of proceedings, not "by reason of" them, he was not guilty of victimisation. However, had it not been for this distinction, the Chief Constable would have been guilty of victimisation as the House of Lords considered that the complainant had been less favourably treated in the refusal to issue him a reference.

These two cases show that motive is also irrelevant in establishing victimisation and that it can be inferred from the circumstances, unless the respondent can show that some reason other than the commencement of the proceedings motivated the treatment of the complainant.

Employment

Discrimination in the recruitment of new employees or in the treatment of existing employees is outlawed. There is no limit to the size of firm, company or organisation to which the legislation applies. Trade unions and employers' organisations may not discriminate when considering applications for membership or when affording members access to benefits, facilities or services. Bodies which confer qualifications which are necessary to allow persons to engage in a particular trade or profession are also covered by the Order. Those involved in vocational training which would equip a person for employment are prohibited from discriminating in the terms on which it provides access to that training or to the facilities concerned with that training.   Partnerships are also included within the ambit of the legislation, so that partners may not discriminate when selecting a new partner, when setting the remuneration for an existing partner or when treating existing partners. Barristers may not discriminate when choosing a "pupil" *(i.e.* trainee barrister) and it is also unlawful for any person to discriminate when instructing a barrister. Recruitment to the police must also be conducted in accordance with the legislation.

The legislation extends protection to contract workers, so that a builder who has a contract with Northern Ireland Electricity, for example, which pays considerably more than other work which he is contracted to do, is guilty of discrimination where he denies an Indian man the opportunity to work on that contract.

If it is a "genuine occupational qualification" (GOQ) that a person be of a particular ethnic group then an employer will have an effective defence (art.8). This means that if it can be demonstrated that it is a *bona fide* requirement that the post-holder be of a certain ethnic origin, it is not unlawful discrimination to prefer such a person. This exception applies only in respect of certain prescribed occupations where such a person is required for reasons of authenticity. These occupations are:

- dramatic performances or other entertainments,
- modelling as an artist's or photographer's model, and
- working in a place where food and drink are provided to and consumed by the public.

The defence also applies where a person is needed to provide personal services promoting the welfare of a particular group and these services can most effectively be provided by a person of that racial group. Employing a Chinese person, therefore, to act as a health visitor to the Chinese community is not unlawful provided that a person of that ethnic origin is best placed to deliver those services to the Chinese community. However, an employer cannot avail of this defence where he or she already has employees of the racial group in question who are capable of carrying out the relevant duties, whom it would be reasonable to employ on those duties and whose numbers are sufficient to meet the employer's likely requirements without undue inconvenience (art.8(4)).

Employers are liable for acts of discrimination committed by employees in the course of their employment, whether or not done with the employer's knowledge or approval (art.32(1)). They do have a defence if they can prove that they took such steps as were "reasonably practicable" to prevent the employee from either doing a particular act or doing similar acts (art.32(5)). If the employer does avail of this defence (*e.g.* because he or she has provided anti-racism training) then the only other option open to the victim is to bring proceedings against the employee alone. However, the employee is often unlikely to be in a position to afford to pay damages.

Affirmative action measures

Positive discrimination – *e.g.* preferring a black person to a white person for a vacant position because black persons are under-represented in the workforce – is unlawful. It could be lawful only if it were a "genuine occupational qualification" (see above) that the person be of Afro-Caribbean origin. But although the legislation does not authorise positive discrimination, it does allow for what are generally termed "affirmative measures". These provide exemptions from the Order where access to training facilities is provided for, or encouragement directed at, members of a particular racial group only. They apply, however, only where that group has "special needs" or where there has in the past 12 months been an under-representation of persons from that group in a particular sector of the workforce. English language instruction may be a "special need".

Education

Discrimination by either public or private educational establishments in relation to an application for admission to a school, college or university, or in the treatment of existing pupils in those establishments, is prohibited by article 18 of the 1997 Order. This prohibition applies to all levels of education, from primary to tertiary. Education and Library Boards and the Council for Catholic Maintained Schools (CCMS) are under a further duty not to discriminate (art.19). There is also a general duty on public sector educational establishments to "secure that facilities for education, and any ancillary benefits or services are provided without racial discrimination" (art.20). This general duty therefore should persuade educational establishments to "equality-proof" their provision.

The enforcement of provisions relating to education is slightly different from that for other provisions. For instance, the Department of Education can intervene to issue directions to an educational establishment or authority which has failed to observe articles 18, 19 or 20 (art.21). An individual's right to bring a complaint to a county court where the discrimination is related to an admission decision, the treatment of a pupil or the discharge by an Education and Library Board, or the CCMS, of its statutory duties, is not affected. However, the general duty on the public sector to ensure that facilities for education are provided without racial discrimination can be enforced only by the Department (art.21). If the Department refuses to enforce it, an individual might be able to obtain a judicial review of that refusal.

The duty of education authorities to comply with parental preference about the school at which they wish their child to be educated (see Chapter 19) is not limited by the racial discrimination legislation. In *R v Cleveland County Council, ex parte CRE* (1990) the Court of Appeal had to interpret the relationship between these two laws. A mother wished to have her daughter (who was of mixed English and African descent) moved from a primary school with nearly all Asian pupils to one that was predominantly white. The request was made because the mother feared her child would learn Pakistani at the expense of English. The court concluded that the local education authority had not committed an unlawful act in acceding to the mother's request.

Goods, facilities and services

Goods, facilities and services made available to the public, or to a section of it, whether for payment or not, cannot be provided or made available in a discriminatory manner. The legislation helpfully provides examples of what amounts to "facilities" and "services". These are:

- access to public places,
- availability of accommodation in hotels, boarding houses or similar establishments,
- facilities by way of banking or insurance for grants, loans, credit or finance,
- entertainment, recreation or refreshment facilities,
- education facilities, transport or travel services, and
- services provided by a profession or trade, or by a local or public authority.

The services of a "local or public authority" are not further defined. However, the courts in Great Britain have had occasion to interpret this part of the equivalent legislation there. In *R v CRE ex parte Hillingdon* (1982) it was accepted that housing provision is a service for the purposes of this legislation, although housing allocation by a public authority is also covered by the provisions relating to premises (see below). Presumably health and social services provision would similarly be categorised as a "service", but the courts have yet to consider this matter.

This form of discrimination makes up a considerable portion of the Equality Commission's race equality caseload and often takes the form of denial of service to Travellers in shops and pubs. The first case of this kind, *Ward v The Olive Grove*, was heard in a county court at the end of 1999, with each of the four Traveller applicants being awarded £2,500 compensation.

A major limitation on the applicability of the provision resulted from a House of Lords decision in *R v Entry Clearance Officer, Bombay, ex parte Amin* (1983), where their Lordships decided that a refusal by an immigration officer in Bombay to issue a special voucher to an Indian woman to enable her to settle in the UK, on the ground that a woman could not be a head of household, was not in relation to a service provided by a public authority. "Goods, facilities and services" was to be interpreted as applying to acts which were at least similar to acts which could be done by private persons and the Entry Clearance Officer was not providing a service but performing the duty of controlling would-be immigrants. This suggested that there was a range of governmental activities that would not be covered by anti-racism legislation and that government could discriminate with impunity in those areas. As a result of this case an amendment was made to the 1976 Act (by s.5 of the Housing and Planning Act 1986) ensuring that the 1976 Act applies to the planning process in Great Britain. An equivalent provision is not included in the 1997 Order, so it is unclear whether planning is a service of a public authority for the purposes of the law in Northern Ireland.

The scope of this provision was further confused by *Savjani v Inland Revenue Commissioners* (1981), where the Court of Appeal held that the IRC, in complying with their duty to collect tax, also provided a service for the purposes of the Race Relations Act because they determined the manner in which a person demonstrated that he or she was entitled to tax relief. Mr Savjani had therefore suffered discrimination because he was required to produce a full birth certificate for his child before obtaining relief, whereas non-Indians were required to produce only a short birth certificate. The CRE in Great Britain has argued that an appropriate amendment should be made to the race relations legislation to ensure that it applies to all governmental activities.

Clubs

Most private clubs are now covered by the race relations legislation. Associations with more than 25 members may not discriminate in admitting a person as a member or in allowing him or her to avail of any of the benefits offered to members. But some clubs remain exempt. Associations whose main object is "to enable the benefits of membership to be enjoyed by persons of a particular racial group, defined otherwise than by reference to colour" are not subject to the legislation. Thus a Zimbabwean Students' Association, for instance, although restricting membership to one racial group, would not be guilty of discrimination because non-Zimbabweans are not permitted to join. However, such an association would be guilty of discrimination if it refused to admit white Zimbabweans.

Premises

Landlords, estate agents, rental agencies and anyone selling, letting or in any way disposing of premises in Northern Ireland, may not discriminate on racial grounds (art.22). This prohibition extends to both the public and private sectors. Private individuals selling their homes escape the effects of the legislation only if they do not use the services of an estate agent and do not publish adverts indicating that the property is for sale. Otherwise, refusing to sell property to a minority ethnic person would amount to discrimination, as would charging a higher price. Where premises are "small" and the person selling or renting the property or a near relative (*e.g.* spouse, parent, child or grandchild) continues to live in the residential accommodation, sharing it with the other persons, the legislation will not apply. "Small premises" are those where (a) the residential accommodation comprises no more than two other households and (b) the premises cannot accommodate more than six persons, excluding the relevant occupier and his or her near relatives.

Exemptions

There are a number of circumstances where the 1997 Order is deemed not to apply. These are briefly set out here:
- any action carried out in accordance with legislation is not covered by the Order (art.40(1)) – see the exemption for Sikhs in relation to safety helmets mentioned at p.281 above;
- an act of discrimination based on a person's nationality, place of residence or length of residence inside or outside the United

Kingdom is not unlawful if it is done to comply with any arrangement approved, or condition imposed, by a Minister or government department (art.40(2));

▪ acts which are done for the purpose of safeguarding national security, or protecting public safety or public order, are not unlawful (art.41). This exemption is wider than that found in the 1976 Act in Great Britain; in that statute only acts deemed to safeguard national security are exempt.

Sports associations or competition organisers are not guilty of discrimination where nationality, place of birth or length of residence requirements are imposed in order to determine whether a person is eligible to represent some area or to compete in any sporting competition.

The duty on district councils

Every district council is under a duty to:

make appropriate arrangements with a view to securing that its various functions are carried out with due regard to the need to (a) eliminate unlawful racial discrimination and (b) promote equality of opportunity, and good relations, between persons of different racial groups (art.67).

This is a duty to be pro-active about eliminating racial discrimination and in that sense is similar to, though more extensive than, the general duty on public sector education establishments found in article 20. It differs from almost all of the provisions examined so far in that, whereas they prevent unlawful discrimination, this duty obliges councils to consider how they might go about eliminating it, and how they might promote good relations. On the other hand, given that district councils in Northern Ireland are responsible for a narrower range of activity than their counterparts in Great Britain, this duty is not as significant in Northern Ireland as it might be there. In any event the duty has largely been superseded by section 75 of the Northern Ireland Act 1998 (see Chapter 11).

The equivalent duty in the 1976 Act – section 71 – has been interpreted by the courts in a number of cases. In *Wheeler v Leicester City Council* (1985) the Council had imposed a ban on Leicester City Rugby Football Club prohibiting it from using council property. It had done this because three club members had played on the English Rugby Football Union's 1984 tour of South Africa. The council defended its action on the basis that it was acting in accordance with its duty to promote good race relations having regard to the significant number of persons of Asian or Afro-Caribbean ethnic origin in its area. The House of Lords considered the ban unreasonable and that the club was being punished although it had done no wrong.

The Order allows local authorities to adopt a limited "contract compliance" policy *(i.e.* ensuring that contractors are "fair" employers before awarding them contracts) when exercising their contractual powers (Sch.2, para.6). Generally they must not have regard to "non-commercial matters" when awarding contracts. Matters which are "non-commercial" include:

- political interests of contractors, directors, partners or employees,
- financial support by contractors of any institutions to or from which the council gives or gets support, and
- the country of origin of supplies or the locations in any country of the business interests of the contractors.

Local authorities are, however, permitted to ask questions, which will be approved by the Department of Enterprise, Trade and Industry, seeking information or undertakings relating to workforce matters, provided these matters are "reasonably necessary" to secure compliance with article 67.

Criminal justice

The application of anti-race discrimination legislation to the criminal justice service is at present quite patchy. The Northern Ireland Prison Service, for example, is not subject to the Race Relations (NI) Order as a result of the *Amin* case (see p.288). However, racial harassment by a police officer would amount to a disciplinary offence and a complaint can be made to the Chief Constable or to the Police Ombudsman (see Chapter 5). The Race Relations (Amendment) Act 2000 has, in light of the MacPherson report into the murder of Stephen Lawrence, extended the 1976 Act to the police in England and Wales and a similar amendment has been made in Northern Ireland by the Police (NI) Act 2000 (Sch.5 para.2).

Information on ethnic minority status and the criminal justice system should be made available to criminal justice service agencies as well as to the public. Under article 56(1)(b) of the Criminal Justice (NI) Order 1996 the Secretary of State is required to publish such information as he or she considers expedient for the purpose of:

facilitating the performance by...persons [engaged in the administration of criminal justice] of their duty to avoid discriminating against any person on any improper ground.

The police in Northern Ireland recorded 237 racial incidents in 1999-2000, of which 40% were directed at the Indian community and almost a third at Chinese persons. This figure increased to 260 in 2000-2001, though it fell to 185 in 2001-2002 (last year for which figures available)

Race hate crime

At present the existing law on race hate crime in Northern Ireland is found in the Public Order (NI) Order 1987. An offence is committed if a person uses:

threatening, abusive or insulting words or behaviour, or displays any written material which is threatening, abusive or insulting, ...

if – (a) he intends thereby to stir up hatred or arouse fear; or

(b) having regard to all the circumstances hatred is likely to be stirred up or fear is likely to be aroused thereby. (art.9)

Whilst there is no specific racially motivated offence in Northern Ireland, racial motivation will be a key factor influencing the appropriate sentence for an offence which has been motivated by racial hatred. The government, in November 2002, launched a consultation process on this topic, with a view to considering changes to the law in Northern Ireland. Options being considered include legislation directing the judiciary to have regard to the racial motivation of the offender when sentencing and legislation to place specific racially motivated offences on the statute book.

Equality Commission for Northern Ireland

The general work of this Commission is described in Chapter 11. As far as racial discrimination is concerned, the first Code of Practice for Employers on the Elimination of Racial Discrimination and the Promotion of Equality of Opportunity in Employment was issued in August 1999. The Commission is currently finalising a Code of Practice on Racial Equality in Housing and Accommodation. Failure to adhere to any provision of the Codes is not itself an unlawful act but, in any cases taken under the Order, such failure could be used as evidence in a court or tribunal. The Equality Commission has also issued a good practice guide on racial equality in education and a good practice guide to promote racial equality in planning for Travellers.

In 2000-2001 the Commission granted assistance to 195 of the 244 race complaints made to it. The majority of these supported complaints related to non-employment matters (which are dealt with in county courts).

Formal investigations

Formal investigations can be conducted under article 46 of the Race Relations (NI) Order 1997 to ascertain whether equality of opportunity operates in particular workplaces and spheres of life or because it is suspected that unlawful acts of discrimination are being perpetrated. Before commencing a formal investigation the Commission must draw up terms of reference and give general notice of the investigation, unless it is confined to "named persons" (*i.e.* a specific individual or firm), in which case notice is given to those persons only.

Before embarking on a "named person investigation" the Commission must have a belief, however tenuous, that the named person has been guilty of performing a discriminatory act and that belief must be stated in the proposed terms of reference (*In re Prestige Group plc,* 1984).

General investigations are more exploratory in nature and may relate, for example, to a particular industry in a locality. They can be commenced without a belief that a particular discriminatory act has taken place, but no person, firm or organisation can be mentioned in the terms of reference. The power to require disclosure of documents and attendance of persons cannot be exercised in regard to general investigation without the permission of the Office of the First Minister and Deputy First Minister (art.48(1)).

Non-discrimination notice

A non-discrimination notice prohibits the person to whom it applies from doing any of the specified acts again and, if necessary, requires that the Commission be notified of consequential alterations to any existing practices or arrangements. However, a non-discrimination notice cannot be served until the person named in it has been given the opportunity to make oral or written representations within 28 days. A right of appeal against a non-discrimination notice lies to an industrial tribunal, if the matter involved concerns employment matters, or to a county court if the matter relates to the provision of goods, facilities, services or premises.

Where the complaint is one of racial discrimination relating to an admission decision made by an educational establishment, the treatment of existing pupils or the performance of statutory duties by Education and Library Boards, or the Council for Catholic Maintained Schools, then a slightly different procedure applies.

There are a number of options open to an industrial tribunal if it finds the allegation of discrimination proven (art.53). It may:

- make a declaration as to the legal rights of the parties,
- make an order requiring the respondent to pay such compensation to the victim as would be obtainable in a county court,
- recommend that the respondent take, within a specified period, action which would reduce or eliminate the adverse effect of the act of discrimination; a failure to comply with such a recommendation allows the tribunal at a later stage to award damages or to increase the amount already awarded.

Successful complainants in a county court can be awarded damages, which may include an amount for injured feelings. However, no damages are available for indirect discrimination if the service provider can show that discrimination was not intended by the imposition of the condition or requirement in question.

The Commission alone has enforcement powers in relation to a number of specific activities, namely discriminatory advertisements and pressurising or instructing others to discriminate. If it considers that either of these events has occurred, it may bring proceedings to have it confirmed that the alleged discriminatory act occurred (art.60).

Monitoring workforce composition

While there is no legal obligation on employers to monitor the ethnic composition of their workforces, such monitoring constitutes good practice and is quite useful to the employer when endeavouring to establish equality of opportunity in the workplace. This monitoring could be dovetailed with that undertaken for the purposes of complying with the fair employment legislation (see Chapter 12). The CRE in Great Britain has long campaigned for the introduction of such monitoring and it may become a feature of the legal regime for combating race discrimination in the future.

Chapter 15

Disability Discrimination

George Kilpatrick

Disability Discrimination Act 1995

The Disability Discrimination Act 1995 (DDA) aims to deal with the discrimination which disabled people face every day regarding employment, membership of trade organisations and access to goods, facilities, services, premises, education and transport. There are, however, serious shortcomings in the legislation which will be touched on below. In 1999 the Disability Rights Task Force (DRTF) made 156 recommendations for changes to the Act. The Stormont Executive and the Westminster Government have undertaken consultation exercises with a view to amending it.

In addition to the DDA itself, which applies throughout the UK although Northern Ireland modifications are contained in Schedule 8, there are many pieces of delegated legislation made under the authority of the DDA. Further helpful publications are available from The Stationery Office (16 Arthur Street, Belfast BT1 4GD). These include the following:

- Guidance on Matters to be Taken into Account in Determining Questions Relating to the Definition of Disability ("the government Guidance").
- Code of Practice for the Elimination of Discrimination in the Field of Employment Against Disabled Persons or Persons Who Have Had a Disability ("the Employment Code").
- Code of Practice Relating to Duties of Trade Organisations to their Disabled Members and Applicants.
- Code of Practice on the Rights of Access to Goods, Facilities, Services and Premises ("the Part III Code").

These publications do not impose any legal obligations themselves but industrial tribunals and courts must take them into account when they appear relevant. Anyone wanting further advice in relation to disability discrimination should contact the Equality Commission for Northern Ireland (see Chapter 11). With regard to the rights of disabled people more generally, further advice should be sought from Disability Action, 189 Airport Road West, Belfast BT3 9ED (tel: 028 9029 7880; textphone: 028 9029 7882).

A number of amendments will have to be made to the DDA as a result of the EU Framework Directive on Employment. The changes are required by 2006, but the UK government has indicated an intention to implement these by October 2004.

Who is protected by the DDA?

With the exception of the victimisation proceedings (see below), to take advantage of the rights conferred by the DDA, a person must have: -

> *a physical or mental impairment which has a substantial and long term adverse effect on his (sic) ability to carry out normal day-to-day activities* (s.1).

Schedule 1 of the DDA expands on this definition, as does the government Guidance.

The leading authority of *Goodwin v The Patent Office* (1999) emphasised the importance of adopting an inquisitorial and purposive approach when ascertaining whether a person meets the statutory definition of disability. The elements of the statutory definition of disability will now be discussed.

Physical impairments

According to the English Court of Appeal in *McNicol v Balfour Beatty Rail Maintenance Ltd* (2002), an "impairment" "may result from an illness or it may consist of an illness".

There is no definition of what amounts to "a physical impairment". The Disability Discrimination (Meaning of Disability) Regulations (NI) 1996 ("the Meaning of Disability Regulations") exclude certain impairments which might otherwise be regarded as physical impairments. An example is "seasonal allergenic rhinitis", more commonly known as hay fever. However, this exclusion does not apply if, for example, the hay fever activates another condition, such as asthma. The Regulations also exclude addictions to nicotine, alcohol or another substance, unless the addiction arises as a result of medical treatment or administration of medically prescribed drugs.

Mental impairments and sensory disabilities

According to Schedule 1 of the DDA, a mental impairment includes an impairment resulting from or consisting of a mental illness, but only if the mental illness is clinically well recognised. According to *Goodwin* and also the government Guidance, an illness is likely to be regarded as clinically well recognised if it is mentioned in the World Health Organisation's International Classification of Diseases. Mental impairments that are excluded by the Meaning of Disability Regulations include exhibitionism, voyeurism and a tendency to set fires, steal or physically or sexually abuse other persons. In *Power v Panasonic UK Ltd* (2003), the Employment Appeal Tribunal (EAT) emphasised the distinction in the DDA between alcohol dependency and impairments, such as depression, that arise from such conditions. The former will be excluded, the latter may not be.

Parliamentary debates make it clear that sensory impairments were intended to be covered by the legislation. Indeed the government Guidance refers specifically to some of these. However, there have been difficulties for partially sighted individuals establishing that they are disabled for the purposes of the legislation. Change in this regard is imminent at the time of writing so that those certified as blind or partially sighted will be regarded as disabled.

"Substantial effect"

The government Guidance makes it clear that a substantial effect is more than a minor or trivial one. In ascertaining the degree of the effect, it is possible to consider the cumulative effects of two or more disabilities.

Schedule 1 to the DDA makes provision for conditions such as cancer, multiple sclerosis, muscular dystrophy and the HIV virus. An individual with such a progressive condition, with an effect on his or her ability to carry out normal day-to-day activities but not yet a substantial adverse effect, will be deemed to satisfy the definition. However, the individual will need to show that the condition is more likely than not to result in such impairment. Moreover the progressive condition definition fails to address certain conditions. For example, someone who declares to an employer that he or she is HIV positive, but asymptomatic, would not be entitled to the protection of the DDA, as there is no effect on his or her ability to carry out normal day-to-day activities. This definition of the DDA is likely to be amended to ensure that such progressive conditions are always covered.

Individuals who have a severe disfigurement are not required to satisfy the various ingredients of the statutory definition of "disability". Rather, Schedule 1 makes it clear that a severe disfigurement is to be treated as having a substantial adverse affect on the ability of the person concerned to carry out normal day-to-day activities.

"Long term effect"

According to Schedule 1, an impairment will be regarded as having a long term effect only if it has lasted (or is likely to last) at least 12 months or for the rest of the person's life. An impairment which no longer has a substantial adverse effect, but did so in the past and which is likely to recur, is still to be treated as falling within the definition if the effects are likely to recur beyond 12 months of the first occurrence. This should cover people with recurring disabilities, such as epilepsy, and conditions that go into remission, such as rheumatoid arthritis.

There is conflicting case-law as to the relevant point of time for deciding whether or not impairment has a substantial and long-term adverse effect on normal day-to-day activities. In *Greenwood v British Airways plc* (1999) the EAT held that in determining whether or not the effect was "likely" to last for at least 12 months the tribunal should consider the adverse effects of the impairments right up to and including the tribunal hearing. However, another division of the EAT in *Cruickshank v VAW Motorcast Ltd* (2002) held that the material time to assess the disability is at the time of the alleged discriminatory act. The latter decision is probably the correct one. The question that should really be asked is, "at the time of the act of discrimination, was it more likely than not that the effect would last at least 12 months?"

"Normal day-to-day activities"

Schedule 1 indicates that an impairment is to be taken to affect the ability of the person concerned to carry out normal day-to-day activities only if it affects one or more of the following:
- mobility,
- manual dexterity,
- physical co-ordination,
- continence,

- ability to lift, carry or otherwise to move everyday objects,
- speech, hearing or eyesight,
- memory or ability to concentrate, learn or understand, or
- perception of the risk of physical danger.

In *Goodwin v The Patent Office* (1999) the EAT emphasised that the important focus is on what the person cannot do, or can do only with difficulty. In Schedule 1 there is no mention of "work". This leads to scenarios arising where individuals may be disabled in laypersons' terms and therefore liable to dismissal, but not disabled enough to fall within the definition of a disabled person for the purposes of the DDA. As a result, they would be without a remedy despite the fact that they cannot work because of the severity of their impairment. So, for example, those individuals with back injuries, who may not be able to lift heavy weights, may not satisfy the definition of a disabled person and therefore are liable to dismissal, and will have no redress if employers fail to make adjustments, such as transferring them to lighter duties.

In *Ekpe v Commissioner of Police for the Metropolis* (2001) the EAT said that if one of the capacities listed in Schedule 1 has been affected "then it must be almost inevitable that there will be some adverse effect upon normal day-to-day activities". The next stage in the test is for the tribunal to establish whether or not this effect is substantial and long term. What is a normal day-to-day activity must be addressed without regard to whether it is normal to the particular applicant. In *Abadeh v British Telecommunications plc* (2001), the EAT regarded travelling by underground as a day-to-day activity, despite the applicant not living in London.

A person may fall within the definition of a disabled person if he or she is receiving medical treatment to correct the impairment or to have a prosthesis in order to alleviate his or her condition. In *Kapadia v London Borough of Lambeth* (2001) counselling sessions were held to amount to medical treatment for someone with a mental illness such as depression.

Past disability

Individuals who have had a disability in the past can complain of an act of discrimination if they believe that they have been discriminated against on the grounds of this past disability. This is irrespective of whether the DDA was in force or not at that time. But they will still need to show that the constituent factors of the definition of disability are met. Therefore, the individual whose condition has been permanently improved, for example after counselling has ended, may still be able to initiate a discrimination complaint, if, for example, he or she is refused employment because there is a history of depression.

Medical evidence

In *Vicary v British Telecommunications plc* (1999) the EAT made it clear that it is for the tribunal and not medical experts to decide what a normal day-to-day activity is and whether the effect of a person's impairment is substantial. However, medical evidence can be helpful in securing an assessment of an applicant's ability to carry out normal day-to-day activities. Additionally, medical experts will be able to give a prognosis on the condition and provide an opinion as to the effect of medication.

Discrimination in employment

The employment provisions of the DDA are contained in sections 4-18 and they are supplemented by the Disability Discrimination (Employment) Regulations (NI) 1996 (the Employment Regulations). The government has also published the Employment Code, which is admissible in evidence before an industrial tribunal and must be taken into account where relevant.

Excluded employment

Various employees are excluded from the DDA by sections 64-68. They include members of the armed forces, prison officers, fire fighters, employees who work wholly and mainly outside the United Kingdom and employees who work on board ships, aircraft or hovercraft. While there are no express provisions dealing with police officers, the Employment Code indicates that police officers will not be covered.

Small employers

Currently the employment provisions do not apply to an employer with fewer than 15 employees. But as a result of the EU Framework Directive on Employment (2000) the threshold exemption will have to be removed completely by December 2006. It will, in all likelihood, be removed in October 2004. According to the decision in *Hardie v C D Northern Ltd* (2000), when calculating the number of employees the definition of an employee as contained in the DDA must be used. This extended definition covers those working under a contract of services, apprentices and those who contract personally to do any work.

Contract workers

The EAT in *Abbey Life Assurance Ltd v Tansell* (2000) confirmed that contract workers are also protected against discrimination. Therefore, the end user of the individual services, as well as the recruitment agency placing them with the end user, has obligations under the DDA not to discriminate against disabled employees. It is likely that the government will in October 2004 bring within the ambit of the legislation the following:

- partners and prospective business partners in business partnerships of any size,
- police officers – required to comply with the EU Framework Directive
- prison officers – required to comply with the EU Framework Directive
- fire fighters – required to comply with the EU Framework Directive
- barristers and their pupils, and
- employees on a ship, airplane or hovercraft registered in the jurisdiction.

When is discrimination unlawful under the DDA?

The DDA sets out three separate forms of unlawful discrimination:

- unjustifiable less favourable treatment for a reason relating to a disability,
- unjustified failure to make reasonable adjustments, and
- victimisation.

Section 4 makes it clear that it is unlawful for an employer to discriminate against a disabled person (or person who has had a disability) in the following circumstances:

- in the arrangements which are made for the recruitment and selection of employees,
- in refusing or deliberately not offering employment,
- in the terms and conditions of employment offered or afforded,
- in opportunities for promotion, transfer, training or receiving any other benefit, service or facility, and
- in dismissal from employment or any other detriment.

Section 11 permits a tribunal to assume disability discrimination if an advertisement for a post suggests that the employer will discriminate against disabled people.

"Less favourable treatment"

Section 5(1) of the DDA sets out the definition of less favourable treatment:

an employer discriminates against the disabled person if –

> a) *for a reason which relates to the disabled person's disability, he treats him less favourably than he treats or would treat others to whom that reason does not or would not apply; and*
>
> b) *he cannot show that the treatment is justified.*

This wording is very different from that contained in the equivalent sections in other equality legislation, where the focus is on the fact that less favourable treatment is "on grounds" of, for example, religion. However, within the DDA the less favourable treatment must still be for a reason related to the disabled person's disability, not just because of the mere fact of the disability.

The case of *Clark v TDG Ltd t/a Novacold* (1999) saw the English Court of Appeal providing useful guidance on this aspect of discrimination. It concerned an individual with a back disability who was dismissed due to his absenteeism. The question was with whom should Mr Clark be compared for the purposes of establishing less favourable treatment? One possibility was a comparison between the disabled employee and an employee who has been absent from work for the same length of time but for a reason which is not disability-related. The second option was to compare Mr Clark's treatment with that of someone who was not disabled, who was working and therefore had not been absent for a disability-related reason. The Court of Appeal adopted this second approach. It indicated that the test of less favourable treatment is based on the reason for the treatment of the disabled person and not on the grounds of disability.

Knowledge of the disability

As is well established in other areas of discrimination law, intention, purpose or motive is irrelevant in establishing whether unlawful discrimination has occurred. However, there must be a connection between the discriminatory treatment and the applicant's disability. The question then arises as to whether or not the employer's knowledge of the disability is crucial for the employee to establish that he or she has been less favourably treated for a reason relating to disability.

Although there is still some uncertainty, tribunals tend to follow the decision of the EAT in *HJ Heinz & Co Ltd v Kenrick* (2000). The EAT held that knowledge either of the disability or its material features is irrelevant. The test of the relationship between the alleged act of discrimination and the disability is an objective one. Therefore the question to ask is simply "is there a connection between the discriminatory treatment and the disability?" Whether or not the employer was aware of the existence of the disability is irrelevant. The EAT did indicate, however, that knowledge may be important when addressing the defence of justification (see below).

London Borough of Hammersmith and Fulham v Farnsworth (2000) went further than *Heinz*, suggesting that knowledge was irrelevant even to the issue of justification. As a result of this decision, it is clear that employers will not be able to hide behind issues of doctor/patient confidentiality in relation to the preparation of medical reports etc. when claiming they had no knowledge of a complainant's disability. The case concerned an employer who had received an adverse report on Mr Farnsworth from an Occupational Health Physician. The employer then failed to inquire into the details of the applicant's disability on the grounds of confidentiality. However, the EAT held that the physician was not bound by any duty of confidence owed to the employee as the physician had been acting on behalf of the employer and the applicant had consented to the provision of medical information to the employer.

The employer's defence of justification

Assuming that the applicant establishes less favourable treatment, the burden of proof then passes to the employer to justify the alleged unlawful discrimination. This occurs, according to section 5(3) of the DDA. *"If, but only if, the reason for it is both material to the circumstances of the particular case and substantial."*

The early authority of *Baynton v Saurus General Engineers Ltd* (1999) suggested that tribunals had to carry out a balancing exercise between the interests of the disabled employee and the interests of the employer. However, the *Heinz* decision held that the threshold the employer needs to satisfy when raising the defence is "very low". So if the reason for the treatment is material, *i.e.* relates to the individual circumstances of the particular case, and is substantial, then justification has to be held to exist. This does not mean that all that employers have to do is show that they believed that the reason for the treatment was material and substantial. They must show that the reason for the treatment was in fact material and substantial.

Factors relied upon to justify the treatment of the employee must be material to the circumstances of the particular case. The *Baynton* decision confirms that the particular circumstances of the case relate to both those of the employer and those of the employee. In the English Court of Appeal decision of *Jones v Post Office* (2001) there was a suggestion that there must be a reasonably strong connection between the employer's reason for the treatment and the circumstances of the individual case. This part of the defence is important, because it means employers will not be able to rely upon stereotypes of disabled people. The Employment Code gives the example of a blind person not being short-listed for a computer job because the employer thinks that blind people cannot use computers. Such a general assumption would not in itself be a material reason: it is not related to the particular circumstances of the disabled person in question.

According to Arden LJ in *Jones*, the "substantial" reason that the employer puts forward for his or her treatment of the disabled person "must carry real weight and be of substance". The decision made by the employer need not be the one the tribunal regards as correct, provided it is "substantial". The test of justification as laid down by the Court of Appeal in *Jones* therefore involves asking three sequential questions:

▪ What was the reason for the treatment of the employee?

- Is there a sufficient connection between the reason for the treatment and the circumstances of the particular case?
- Is that reason, on examination, a substantial reason?

According to *Callaghan v Glasgow City Council* (2001), an employer can still rely on the defence of justification even if he or she had no knowledge of the disability. The duty to make reasonable adjustment is considered in more detail below. However, less favourable treatment cannot be justified where an employer under a duty to make or adjust fails unjustifiably to make that adjustment, unless the less favourable treatment would have been justified even if the reasonable adjustment duty had been complied with.

The tribunal's role

The Court of Appeal in *Jones* indicated that tribunals, in considering an employer's justification, are undertaking a similar task to that which already occurs in unfair dismissal cases. In such cases tribunals apply the so-called "band of reasonable responses" test to establish whether the dismissal was reasonable. This means that, whilst members of the tribunal might have reached a different conclusion from the employer in deciding whether or not to dismiss an employee, they cannot substitute their opinion for that of the employer. *Jones* is a move towards a similar approach in addressing the justification defence, but rather than considering the reasonableness of the event, as occurs in unfair dismissal, tribunals, once they have established the reason for the treatment, must consider the materiality and substantiality of that reason. If these criteria are met, even if the tribunal would have reached a different conclusion, the tribunal must still respect the employer's decision.

The effect of *Jones* means that tribunals cannot, for example, evaluate medical evidence, or conduct their own risk assessment to substitute their opinion for that of the employers. The focus of the tribunal is to decide whether the reason for the treatment is justified, not the correctness of the employer's decision. So, provided that appropriate and competent medical advice is taken on the facts of that particular case, and provided the employer follows that advice, the employer is well on the way to justifying the treatment. *Jones* therefore highlights a shortcoming of the DDA when compared with the other concepts of justification within domestic and European indirect discrimination law. The new Framework Directive allows for an objective justification standard for indirect disability discrimination to be introduced into domestic legislation. However, it is unlikely that the government will introduce such an amendment, as the terms of the Directive permit indirect discrimination to be addressed via reasonable adjustments (see below).

The Directive will also require the justification defence to be removed in relation to cases of less favourable treatment on the grounds of disability. Additionally, changes to the rules on justification in relation to pension and insurance benefits (see below) are likely to occur in October 2004 as a result of the Directive.

Pensions

Less favourable treatment for disability-related reasons such as denial of access to occupational pension schemes is likely to be unlawful under section 4 of the DDA unless justifiable. The reasonable adjustment duty does not currently apply to such schemes. However, with effect from October 2004, in order to comply with the Framework Directive, employers will be obliged to make reasonable adjustments for individual employees where they are responsible for setting scheme rules and the rules cause substantial disadvantage. Pension managers, trustees and insurance companies will have to justify their responsibilities under schemes objectively, for example by reliance upon actuarial evidence. They will also be required to make reasonable adjustments in how they provide information about the scheme to disabled people.   Section 17 of the DDA provides that every occupational pension scheme will have a non-discrimination rule. This rule relates to the terms on which persons become members and how they are treated as members.   The trustees and managers of such schemes must not do anything which, if done by an employer, would be unlawful under the DDA. The usual justification defence applies in such cases.

The Employment Regulations address employment benefits under occupational pension schemes in respect of termination of service, retirement, old age, death, accident, injury, sickness or invalidity. If the costs of providing such benefits under such schemes to a disabled person are (or are likely to be) substantially greater compared with someone without that disability, justification of less favourable treatment in the application of eligibility criteria for receiving such benefits might exist. However, the employer will need to show on the basis of actuarial and/or medical advice that the costs would be substantially greater. In the event that an employer is justified in refusing a disabled employee access to some benefits, but not others, the Employment Regulations provide that an employer will be justified in setting a uniform rate of contributions for all staff, despite the fact that a disabled employee is ineligible for all the benefits.

Insurance benefits

Under section 18 of the DDA insurance providers who provide insurance benefits to an employer's workforce as a result of an arrangement with the employer must not discriminate against disabled employees. If, in the way it provides such services to a disabled employee, such an organisation committed an act of discrimination against a disabled member of the public in the provision of similar insurance services, that would be unlawful (see below).

The employer's duty to make reasonable adjustments

The second form of disability discrimination arises from the employer's failure to make reasonable adjustments to working arrangements and the working environment in order to accommodate disabled persons. It is provided for in section 6 of the DDA. As is made clear by section 6(7), this is not an obligation to discriminate positively in favour of disabled persons at large. Nevertheless, there is nothing within the employment provisions to prevent employers from treating a disabled person more favourably than a non-disabled person.

When is the duty triggered?

Section 6(1) indicates that where any physical feature of premises occupied by the employer, or any other working arrangements made by or on behalf of the employer, causes a substantial disadvantage to a disabled person compared with a non-disabled person, the duty is activated. If either of these scenarios arises, the employer must take such steps as are reasonable in all the circumstances to prevent that disadvantage, *i.e.* make a reasonable adjustment.

The reasonable adjustment duty in the employment provisions is different from that in the goods, facilities and services provisions. In the latter provisions, the duty to make reasonable adjustments is owed to disabled persons at large. The duty within the employment provisions is owed to "the" particular disabled person who is placed at "a substantial disadvantage".

Exceptions to the duty

Section 6(11) indicates that there is no duty to make adjustments in relation to any benefits under an occupational pension scheme, or any other benefits under a scheme or arrangement for the benefit of employees, in respect of termination, retirement, old age, death, accident, injury, sickness or invalidity. However, in *London Clubs Management Ltd v Hood* (2001) it was held that payment of sick pay can be a reasonable adjustment within section 6.

The Employment Regulations permit performance related pay (PRP) schemes to be justified, so long as they apply equally to all employees or a particular class of employees. Such schemes are deemed not to place a disabled person at a substantial disadvantage; therefore the duty to adjust a PRP scheme will not arise. However, employers are still under a duty, for example, to provide additional training or equipment which would aid the performance of a disabled employee, which may then have a positive knock-on effect in relation to that employee's PRP entitlement. Changes to the DDA in regard to the justification of PRP schemes will be required to comply with the EU Framework Directive. This is likely to occur in or around October 2004, with the expansion of the reasonable adjustment duty to such schemes, pensions and insurance schemes (see above). The other alternative will be the introduction of indirect discrimination in such schemes with an objective discrimination defence.

Knowledge

Section 6(6) highlights the difference between the reasonable adjustment duty and less favourable treatment provisions in relation to the question of knowledge. It is clear from this sub-section that, "if the employer does not know and could not reasonably be expected to know" of the person's disability and the likelihood of a substantial disadvantage arising, the duty is not activated. As pointed out in *Farnsworth* (above, p.303), employers will be unable to deny knowledge of disability if their occupational health department, or a doctor on their behalf, has examined the disabled person and the individual has consented to providing the information to the employer.

However, the duty to make reasonable adjustments can be a difficult line for employers to tread. The Employment Code recommends that employers should be positive in welcoming applications from disabled persons and asking about the disability or the effects of it. This could aid employers to comply with their duties to make reasonable adjustments. However, as the Code indicates further, employers should ask disability-related questions only if a disability is or may be relevant to an individual's ability to perform the functions of a job.

It is often in a disabled person's interest to advise employers of his or her disability and possible disadvantage. This puts the employer on notice to make reasonable adjustments. But the employer can do so only if the disabled person provides sufficient information.

In *British Gas Services Ltd v McCaull* (2001) the EAT held that the test under section 6 is objective, *i.e.* did the employer take such steps as it is reasonable in all the circumstances of the case for him or her to have to take in order to prevent the arrangements by the employer from placing the disabled person at a substantial disadvantage compared with those who are not disabled? The EAT indicated that there would be no automatic breach of the duty to make reasonable adjustments simply because an employer was unaware that that duty existed. The question is what steps the employer took or did not take. It is very possible that an employer might take reasonable steps, as contemplated by the legislation, whilst being blissfully unaware of the fact that the provisions even exist. However, it is important to note that the EAT indicated in *McCaull* that:

> the reason for the employer's failure to comply with his section 6 duty may come into play under section 5(4) and it will no doubt be very difficult for an employer to justify the failure to take reasonable steps if he has not considered what steps should be taken.

"Arrangements"

Arrangements covered by the legislation include recruitment arrangements and any term, condition or arrangements on which employment, promotion, transfer, training or any other benefit is offered. Case-law suggests the term will be interpreted narrowly. *Kenny v Hampshire Constabulary* (1999) concerned a successful candidate for a computer position. He needed assistance going to the toilet due to the nature of his disability. The offer was withdrawn when the respondent was unable to find volunteers to assist in this role. The EAT held that such assistance could not amount to "an arrangement" related to the job.

In *Kent County Council v Mingo* (2000), a redeployment policy gave preference to redundant and potentially redundant employees above those who were unable to work due to capability reasons. This policy put Mr Mingo, who had been off work for disability-related reasons, at a substantial disadvantage and he was unsuccessful in seeking redeployment. Such procedures should have been adjusted to give priority to disabled people. The only other individuals who should take preference over those with disabilities are those returning to work from pregnancy, who are entitled to return to suitable vacancies under the terms of the Maternity and Parental Leave etc. Regulations (NI) 1999.

"Physical features of premises"

There is no definition of what the term "physical feature of premises" means. The Employment Regulations highlight the following as being physical features:

- any feature arising from the design or construction of a building on the premises,
- any feature on the premises or any approach to, exit from or access to such a building,
- any fixtures, fittings, furnishings, furniture, equipment or materials in or on the premises, and
- any other physical element or quality of any land comprised in the premises.

It is never reasonable, under regulation 8(2), for an employer to have to take the step of altering any physical characteristics which have been adapted with a view to complying with Part R of the Building Regulations in force at the time.

Substantial disadvantage

The employee must show that he or she is being placed at a substantial disadvantage in comparison with persons who are not disabled by the arrangements or the physical features concerned, but there has been no authoritative case-law on this particular point as to how the comparison should work in practice. The Employment Code permits hypothetical comparisons. It is clear from the Code that "substantial" has the same meaning as in the definition of disability and justification, *i.e.* more than a minor or trivial weight.

What are reasonable steps?

Section 6(3) and the Employment Code set out examples of steps that an employer might make. They include:

- making adjustments to premises,
- allocating some of a disabled person's duties to another person,
- transferring the disabled person to fill an existing vacancy,
- altering a disabled person's hours,
- assigning a disabled person to another workplace,
- allowing absences during working hours for treatment, rehabilitation or assessment,
- giving or arranging appropriate training,
- purchasing or modifying equipment,
- modifying instructions or reference manuals,
- changing procedures for testing or assessments,
- providing a reader or an interpreter, or
- providing supervision.

As well as assessing what steps the employer might have taken to prevent the substantial disadvantage arising for the disabled employee, a tribunal will consider whether it was reasonable for an employer to take that particular step. Pursuant to section 6(4), various matters will be taken into consideration by the tribunal in determining reasonableness in this context. They include the following:

- the effectiveness of the step in preventing the disadvantage,
- the practicability of the step,
- the financial and other costs in taking action,
- the subsequent disruption caused,
- the employer's financial and other resources, and
- the availability of financial or other assistance to assist in taking action.

Government assistance in relation to funding might be available for the purchase of special equipment or the protection of salary. This is through the Access to Work Scheme, which is administered by the Training and Employment Agency.

The more active employers are in considering and making adjustments, the stronger their case will be when defending an applicant's case. Failure to be pro-active can have fatal consequences in any tribunal case. In *Cosgrove v Caesar and Howie* (2001) a clinically depressed former secretary was unable to put forward evidence as to what reasonable adjustments would have facilitated her return to work from depression and therefore prevented her dismissal. The EAT held in these circumstances that this failure on the applicant's part did not mean that the employer could be taken to have satisfied the section 6 duty.

Justification of failure to make reasonable adjustments

This defence will be removed, in all likelihood in October 2004, in order to comply with the EU Framework Directive. Currently, in effect, an employer has two defences in relation to any failure to make reasonable adjustments. The first is to argue that the adjustment was not reasonable. If he or she fails to persuade the tribunal on this front, it is then open to the employer to argue that he or she was justified in not making the adjustment. As with less favourable treatment, a failure to comply with the adjustment duty can be justified only if the reason for the failure is both material to the circumstances of the particular case and substantial. The decision in *Jones* (p.304 above) confirms that a tribunal cannot substitute its own judgment for that of an employer's. In *McCaull* (p.309 above) the EAT held that failure to consider what reasonable adjustments could be made would make it very difficult for an employer to justify his or her actions.

Enforcement

The enforcement procedures are set out in section 8 of the DDA. Individual complaints against employers can be taken to an industrial tribunal. The application must be presented within three months of the act of discrimination, although the tribunal has discretion to hear a claim out of time if it considers it "just and equitable" to do so. There may be more room for arguing that this discretion should be applied in disability cases because someone's disability may have prevented him or her from being able to access legal advice or to submit the complaint.

Section 56 provides for the use of a statutory questionnaire to secure additional information from the respondent. As with sex discrimination legislation, restricted reporting orders to restrain publicity are available on application to the tribunal.

Section 9 makes void any contract, term or agreement which involves an employee contracting out of any part of the employment provisions or which limits or excludes the operation of the DDA or prevents any person from presenting a complaint to an industrial tribunal. The DDA has the usual exception to this which permits the settling of complaints through the Labour Relations Agency or through the compromise agreement process.

The remedies available at tribunal are:

- a declaration,
- compensation, including damages for injury to feelings and interest, and
- recommendations requiring "reasonable" action (as opposed to practicable actions as found in other equality legislation) to obviate or reduce the adverse effect of the discrimination; there may be room to secure a recommendation for reasonable adjustments to accommodate those who remain in employment and disabled.

Victimisation

This is the final form of discrimination provided for under the DDA and it applies in both employment and goods, facilities and services cases. As in other areas of law, those who have taken "protected acts" under the DDA, and who are victimised as a result, have further grounds for complaint under section 55. The "protected acts" (where "A" is the alleged victim) are as follows:

- A has brought proceedings against B or any other person (C) under the Act;
- A has given evidence or information in connection with the proceedings brought by another person (D) against B or C under the Act;
- A has otherwise done anything under the Act in relation to B or any other person (C);
- A has alleged (expressly or impliedly) that B or C has contravened the Act; or
- B believes or suspects that A has done or intends to do any of the above things.

Additionally, it is essential that any allegation made by A is made in good faith and not false. The question of whether or not A is

Discrimination in relation to goods, facilities, services and premises

A service provider's responsibilities under the DDA are laid out in sections 19-21. The provisions relating to premises are contained in sections 22-24.

It is unlawful for a service provider to treat disabled people less favourably for a disability-related reason:

- by refusing to provide, or deliberately not providing, any service which it offers to members of the public,
- in the standard or manner of the services which it provides, or
- in the terms to which it provides a service.

It is also unlawful for service providers to fail to comply with the duty to make reasonable adjustments, if that failure has the effect of making it impossible or unreasonably difficult for a disabled person to make use of any service provided. From 1 October 2004 further duties to remove, alter or avoid physical barriers will be implemented.

Regulations have been issued dealing with this part of the DDA and the Part III Code (see p.295) gives practical advice as to how to comply with the responsibilities under the legislation. The Part III Code may be used in evidence and a court must take it into consideration where relevant.

Who is a service provider?

Under section 19(2) a service provider is a person concerned with the provision, in the United Kingdom, of services to the public or a section of them, regardless of whether payment is made. This is a wide definition and will apply across the private, public and voluntary sectors. However, a number of potential service providers are excluded from the remit of sections 19-21. They include providers of education and certain closely related services (but ancillary services such as college welfare services are covered). Nor do the sections apply to manufacturers and designers unless they supply goods or services directly to members of the public. Private members' clubs are also outside the ambit of this part of the DDA unless they make their services available to the public by, for example, hiring out their premises for wedding receptions or jumble sales. Additionally, services provided under statutory authority are not services for the purposes of the DDA.

"Less favourable treatment"

Section 20(1) states that a provider of services discriminates against a disabled person if:

(a) for a reason which relates to the disabled person's disability, he treats him less favourably than he treats or would treat others to whom that reason does not or would not apply; and

(b) he cannot show that the treatment in question is justified.

Direct parallels can be drawn here with the DDA provisions on employment, but there is nevertheless case-law which appears to run contrary to the *Clark* decision (see p.302 above) in this context. In *R v Powys County Council, ex parte Hambridge (No.2)* (2000) the English Court of Appeal addressed the issue of less favourable treatment in a case concerning the charging for home-care services according to how much individuals received in terms of benefit income. Mrs Hambridge was regarded as being in bed and breakfast accommodation and was thus subject to a charge for the home-care services. She sought a judicial review of the banding structure following the introduction of the charges. As she was in receipt of income support and disability living allowance (DLA) she was charged for the provision of home-care services, whereas someone only on income support was not so charged. She argued that this amounted to less favourable treatment for a reason relating to her disability, as the only reason she was in bed and breakfast accommodation was that her disability entitled her to receive DLA. The Court of Appeal thought that it could not have been intended that such a case would be covered by section 20 of the DDA.

Knowledge of the disability

Service providers will not normally be in the same position as employers when it comes to assessing whether people they are dealing with have disabilities. There is no reported case-law on this issue. It would appear on a literal interpretation that knowledge of disability is not relevant, but a court might apply a different reasoning when the case comes before it.

The service provider's duty to make reasonable adjustments

While the duty to make reasonable adjustments within the employment provisions is owed to individual employees, the duty on service providers is owed to disabled people at large. Service providers have an on-going anticipatory and evolving duty to consider the accessibility of their services for disabled people generally. Therefore knowledge of an individual's disability is irrelevant in deciding whether the duty applies. It is important to remember, when enforcing rights as a result of a service provider's failure to make reasonable adjustments, that the disabled person must show that the duty was triggered, *i.e.* broadly speaking that it was impossible or unreasonably difficult for disabled people generally (not just the individual) to access the service in question. The person must then show that it was unreasonably difficult or impossible for him or her to access the service in question prior to the burden shifting to the service provider to justify his or her failure on the basis of one of the five fair reasons in section 20 (see p.318 below).

Under section 21 a service provider may have to take reasonable steps to:

- change practices, policies or procedures which make it impossible or unreasonably difficult for disabled people to make use of services,
- provide a reasonable alternative method of making services available to disabled people where a physical feature makes it impossible or unreasonably difficult for disabled people to make use of them, and
- provide an auxiliary aid or service if it would enable (or make it easier for) disabled people to make use of services.

Adjustments are not required to be made, however, where there would be a fundamental alteration in the nature of the service or business provided.

From October 2004 service providers will be required to remove, alter or avoid a physical feature if it makes it impossible or unreasonably difficult for disabled people to access the service.

When is the reasonable adjustment duty triggered?

The duties highlighted above are triggered at different times. In regard to practices, policies and procedures and physical features, the trigger is when it is impossible or unreasonably difficult for disabled people to make use of the services. The DDA does not define what it means by "unreasonably difficult", but the Code of Practice gives guidance as to what factors may be taken into account in determining this. Such matters include whether the time, inconvenience, effort or discomfort entailed in using the service would be considered unreasonable by other people if they had to endure similar difficulties.

Changes to practices, policies and procedures etc. might include, for instance, removal of a "no dogs policy" in order to permit guide dogs on to premises.

The Disability Discrimination (Services and Premises) Regulations (NI) 1999 (the Services and Premises Regulations) highlight the physical features which are subject to the reasonable adjustment duty. These reflect, broadly, those contained in the Employment Regulations. The provision of a temporary ramp might provide a way around steps which prevent the user of a wheelchair accessing a building. In terms of auxiliary aids or services, the duty to provide these is triggered when the aid or service would enable or facilitate disabled people. This might include the provision of information to a blind person on tape, or provision of a sign language interpreter.

What are reasonable steps?

Unlike with the employment provisions, there are no specific examples of reasonable steps given in this part of the DDA. Nor is there any definition of what reasonable steps are. Factors such as the nature and size of the service provider and the nature of the disability will be relevant. Section 21 also fails to specify any particular factors that should be taken into consideration when considering what is reasonable. But the Code lists some factors that might be taken into account. These are not exhaustive, but include:

- the effectiveness of any particular step in overcoming the difficulties,
- the extent to which it is practicable for the service provider to take the step,
- the financial and other costs of making the adjustment,
- the extent of any disruption caused by taking steps,
- the extent of the service provider's financial and other resources,
- the amount of any resources already spent on making adjustments, and
- the availability of financial or other assistance.

The defence of justification

There are five potential grounds of justification, depending on the nature of the discrimination. Additionally, the test contains both a subjective and objective element as confirmed in the case of *Rose v*

Bouchet (1999). The service provider must show that at the time of the alleged act of discrimination he or she was of the opinion that one of the five reasons listed below was satisfied. Once that hurdle is cleared, it is then for the service provider to show that it was reasonable in all circumstances of the case to hold that opinion. The list of justifications is contained in section 20:

- the treatment is necessary in order not to endanger the health or safety of any person,
- the disabled person is incapable of entering into an enforceable agreement, or of giving an informed consent,
- in a case falling within section 19(1)(a) (refusal of a service), the treatment is necessary because the provider of the services would otherwise be unable to provide the services to members of the public,
- in a case falling within section 19(1)(c) or (d) (standard of service or terms of service), the treatment is necessary in order for the provider of services to be able to provide the service to the disabled person or to other members of the public, and
- in a case falling within section 19(1)(d) (terms of service), the difference in the terms on which the services provided to the disabled person and those on which it is provided to other members of the public reflects the greater cost to the provider of services in providing the service to the disabled person.

The service provider need not be an expert on disability, but he or she should take into account all the circumstances, including the information available (and the possibility of getting more advice) and the opinion of the disabled person. The service provider will be judged by what he or she knew (or could reasonably have known), what was done and why it was done. The provisions in section 20 do not require service providers to consider reasonable adjustments prior to seeking to justify less favourable treatment, as is required in the employment provisions of the DDA, but the Act encourages this approach.

Insurance, guarantees and deposits

Special rules apply in these areas, as set out in the Disability Discrimination (Services and Premises) Regulations, (NI) 1996. Where such a service provider, for a disability-related reason, treats a disabled person less favourably than he or she treats (or would treat) someone to whom that reason does not (or would not) apply, this will be unlawful unless the treatment can be justified. The special justifications in such situations are highlighted below.

Regulation 2 deals with insurance services. If the less favourable treatment is based on current information such as actuarial, medical or statistical data relevant to the assessment of risk to be insured and is from a source upon which it is reasonable to rely and the treatment is reasonable, having regard to such information relied upon and any other relevant factors, the justification hurdle will be cleared. Such rules aim to prevent insurers adopting a policy of non-insurance of people with certain disabilities.

Guarantees (which are defined to include any document where a service provider provides for a replacement, repair or refund if the goods are not of a satisfactory quality) are addressed by regulation 5. If a service provider refuses to provide a replacement, repair or refund under a guarantee because of damage related to the disabled person's disability, he or she must be in a position to show that it is reasonable in all the circumstances of the case to refuse such a refund etc. and that the damage is above a level which the guarantee would normally be honoured.

In relation to the return of deposits which are refundable if goods, premises or facilities are returned/left undamaged, if the provider refuses to refund some or all of the deposit for returned goods etc., which have been damaged for a reason relating to the disabled person's disability, such action will be justified (pursuant to reg.6) only if it is reasonable in all the circumstances of the case for the service provider to refuse to repay the deposit in full because the damage is above the level at which the service provider would normally refund the deposit in full. Under section 19(1)(d), service providers cannot justify charging disabled customers higher deposits than non-disabled customers, or indeed require a deposit only from disabled customers.

Property and premises

Those individuals with power to dispose of any premises and persons managing any premises also have obligations under the DDA not to discriminate, unjustifiably, against a disabled person when managing, disposing of or selling property. The provisions do not apply to residential property falling in the small premises exemption (s.23). This applies to a person who takes up to six lodgers in his or her home. Additionally the exemption will apply if the following criteria are met:

- the relevant occupier, *i.e.* the person with the power of disposal, and members of the household, reside in the accommodation occupied by the relevant occupier,
- in addition to this accommodation there is residential accommodation for at least one other household in the property,
- the accommodation for the other household is let (or is available for letting) on a separate tenancy or similar agreement,
- there are not normally more than two households in the property,
- the relevant occupier to residing and intends to continue to reside in the property, and
- the shared accommodation must not be storage accommodation or a means of access.

Private sales of houses are also exempt if the owner/occupier does not sell the house through an estate agent or advertise the property in any way.

There are six forms of discrimination which may apply to those with the power to dispose of or manage premises. They are as follows:
- discriminating in the terms on which they offer to dispose of the premises to a disabled person,
- refusing to sell or let etc. to a disabled person,
- discriminating against a disabled person by way of treatment in relation to any list of persons in need of premises of that description,
- discriminating in the way the manager of the premises permits a disabled person to make use of any benefits or facilities or refuses or deliberately omits to permit the disabled person to make use of such benefits or facilities, or subjecting a disabled person to any other detriment,
- evicting a disabled person or subjecting him or her to any other detriment, and
- withholding a licence or consent for the disposal of premises leased or sub-let to a disabled person.

There is no duty in this context to make reasonable adjustments for people with a disability. Moreover, under section 24, the person with power of disposal or management of premises may be able to justify the less favourable treatment if two hurdles are cleared. First, at the time of the alleged act of discrimination, the person believed that one of the following conditions applied and, second, it was reasonable in all the circumstances of the case to hold that belief:

- the treatment was necessary to avoid a health and safety risk to the disabled person or anyone else,
- the disabled person was incapable of entering into an enforceable agreement or of giving an informed consent, or
- in regard to the access to, or use or refusal of, benefits and facilities, the treatment was necessary in order for the disabled person or other occupiers to use a benefit or facility.

Enforcement and remedies

If a disabled person feels that he or she has been discriminated against regarding access to services or disposal of premises, civil proceedings need to be initiated in the county court. As in industrial tribunals, a county court can order a declaration and damages, including a sum for injury to feelings. There is no power to make recommendations, but the court can order additional remedies that are available in the High Court, including injunctions. Proceedings must be lodged in the county court within six months of the alleged act of discrimination. As in an industrial tribunal, there is no limit on damages for injury to feelings, but the downside of county court proceedings is the possibility of orders for costs being made against the unsuccessful party. There are provisions within the DDA for the establishment of a conciliation service to deal with goods, facilities and services cases. While such a service operates in Great Britain, none has yet been established in Northern Ireland.

Education

The DDA also deals with education. However, the relevant provisions do not apply in Northern Ireland. From September 2002, in Great Britain, the Special Educational Needs and Disability Act 2001 provides rights with regard to the prevention of discrimination against disabled people in their access to education. The Act makes it unlawful to discriminate, again without justification, against disabled people in all aspects of school life. As in other areas of the DDA, there is a duty not to treat disabled people less favourably, without justification, for a reason related to their disability and also a duty to make reasonable adjustments to avoid placing disabled people at a substantial disadvantage. However, the reasonable adjustment duty does not require educational authorities to provide auxiliary aids and services or to make alterations to the physical features of schools. In Northern

Ireland, draft legislation addressing similar issues was the subject of consultation in the summer of 2002 (the Special Educational Needs and Disability Bill). It is anticipated that this legislation will come into force no earlier than September 2004.

Public transport

Under section 19(5) of the DDA, goods, facilities and services, in so far as they apply to the use of any means of transport, are not covered by the Act. Therefore disabled people have no civil remedy if they are unable to access buses, taxis, airplanes or ferries. However, related goods, facilities and services, such as ticket offices, waiting rooms and other public areas in, for example, train stations are subject to the DDA's provisions. Additionally, employees in various transport services will be covered by the Act (subject to the exceptions noted above). The DDA empowers the government to enact new accessibility standards for public transport.

Taxis

The Department of Environment (DoE) has been given power under section 32(1) to make taxi accessibility regulations. The purpose of these would be to ensure disabled people can get into and out of, and travel in, licensed taxis in safety and reasonable comfort. Ultimately the aim is to ensure that taxi drivers recognise their duty to carry disabled passengers. The grant of taxi licences will, eventually, be subject to compliance with such regulations. When eventually issued such regulations will apply only to those taxis which are licensed to stand or ply for hire under the Road Traffic (NI) Order 1981 and which seat no more than eight passengers in addition to the driver.

Additional responsibilities that taxi drivers will assume pursuant to section 36 when regulations are introduced will include:

- carrying a wheelchair user in his or her chair without additional charges,
- carrying the wheelchair in the taxi if the disabled person chooses to sit in a passenger seat,
- taking such necessary steps to ensure that the passenger is carried in safety and reasonable comfort, and
- providing reasonable assistance to disabled passengers in getting into and out of taxis (whether in a wheelchair or not) and in loading and unloading luggage (including a wheelchair if need be).

Sections 37 and 38 already require the drivers of taxis to carry guide and hearing and assistance dogs free of charge. Taxi drivers who cannot comply with such duties on medical grounds can apply to the DoE to be exempted. These provisions came into force in the summer of 2001. Failure to comply is a criminal offence punishable by a fine. It is unclear when the remainder of the taxi related regulations will be made.

Public service vehicles (PSVs)

PSVs are vehicles adapted to carry more than eight passengers (in addition to the driver) and which are in public service. They therefore include buses and coaches offering a public service. Under sections 40–45 of the DDA the DoE has power to make regulations governing access to such vehicles in order to ensure that disabled people can get on and off such vehicles safely and without unreasonable difficulty and travel in safety and reasonable comfort. As with the regulations relating to taxis, breach of the regulations will amount to a criminal offence punishable by a fine. The Public Service Vehicles Accessibility Regulations (NI) 2003 were made on 21 January 2003. Generally speaking new buses and coaches will have to comply with various aspects of these regulations by 31 August 2003.

Rail vehicles

Sections 46 and 47 deal with rail vehicles. In July 2001, the Department for Regional Development made the Rail Accessibility Regulations (NI) 2001. These came into operation in October 2001 and apply to passenger-carrying vehicles using railways that were first brought into use, or belong to a class of vehicle brought into use, after 1998. The principal feature of the regulations is that they seek to secure that it is possible for disabled persons to get on and off "regulated rail vehicles" safely and without unreasonable difficulty and to be carried in such vehicles in safety and in reasonable comfort. Special provision is made for users of wheelchairs to ensure that they can get on and off trains safely and without unreasonable difficulty while remaining in their wheelchairs as well as be carried in such vehicles in safety and reasonable comfort while remaining in their wheelchairs. Exemption regulations permit operators to apply for exemptions. Again, as with PSVs, an operator commits a criminal offence punishable on conviction by a fine if he or she does not comply with the regulations.

Air and water transport

The DDA does not address such forms of transport at all.

Further useful addresses

- Disability Action
  Portside Business Park
  189 Airport Road West
  Belfast BT3 9ED
  tel: 028 9029 7880
  www.disabilityaction.org

Chapter 16

Mental Health

Michael Potter[*]

Many people have a "mental condition", *i.e.* a mental illness, mental disability or other mental condition, which affects the functioning of their mind, brain or personality to a greater or lesser extent. Some of these people, with or without medication, can continue to live fully independent lives, responsible for themselves, families and jobs. But others can be significantly impaired in their daily existence, making it difficult, and at times impossible, to perform ordinary tasks or make basic day-to-day decisions concerning themselves, family or work. People with mental conditions may consequently require assistance, care and treatment. Health and welfare authorities have a legal responsibility to meet this need, commensurate with their available resources and in accordance with the law.

Mental health law provides the regulatory framework within which mental health decision-makers (such as health and welfare authorities) perform the complicated task of striking an appropriate balance between various competing, and often, conflicting obligations, responsibilities, rights and interests, including:

- the health and welfare of the patient,
- the human rights and interests of the patient,
- the health and welfare of the patient's family,
- the safety of the population, and
- available health and social services resources.

The concept of autonomy, or self-government, is central to mental health law. Similarly, human rights law recognises the principle of individual liberty, *i.e.* people have the right and freedom to make decisions about their own lives, *e.g.* as to where they live, who they live

[*] The author acknowledges assistance from Mr Francis Walsh, Chief Executive of the Mental Health Commission for Northern Ireland, and Ms Valerie Martin, from the Office of Care and Protection.

with and what they eat. The weight afforded to an individual's autonomy and civil liberty is informed by a range of factors, including the ability of the person affected to make considered decisions and to be responsible for his or her conduct. Obviously a person's mental condition is pivotal in such assessments. Mental health law must also contemplate the "public interest". For example, the state has a responsibility to protect society from people who have mental conditions which cause them to pose a threat of violence or serious harm to others. Issues such as the civil detention of such persons raise many complicated and controversial legal questions encompassing a variety of human rights concerns.

It is not possible in this chapter to explore every aspect of mental health law in Northern Ireland. The chapter concentrates on those central aspects of the civil legal framework that commonly impact on the lives of persons with mental disorder. The regulatory framework governing mental healthcare in Northern Ireland can be viewed at three levels: (1) European Convention law, (2) domestic law, including legislation and common law, and (3) other relevant standards for care and treatment, specifically, international standards and the Code of Practice issued under the Mental Health (NI) Order 1986.

European Convention law

There are three key provisions within the European Convention on Human Rights that concern people with mental conditions – Articles 3, 5 and 8.

Article 3

Article 3 prohibits torture or inhuman or degrading treatment or punishment in the care and treatment of people with a mental condition, including their medical treatment. In the case of *Herczegfalvy v Austria* (1993) the European Court on Human Rights intimated that treatment which conformed to psychiatric principles, generally accepted at the time, would not contravene Article 3. This is known as the "principle of therapeutic necessity". In particular, the European Court stated that:

> *The position of inferiority and powerlessness which is typical of patients confined in psychiatric hospitals calls for increased vigilance in reviewing whether the Convention has been complied with. While it was for the medical authorities to decide, on the*

basis of the recognised rules of medical science, on the therapeutic methods to be used, if necessary by force, to preserve the physical and mental health of patients who are entirely incapable of deciding for themselves, such patients nevertheless remain under the protection of article 3, whose requirements permit of no derogation. (para.86)

Article 5

Article 5 protects against arbitrary arrest and detention, although it states that it is legal to deny liberty to "persons of unsound mind". The European Court has not provided a definition of the concept "unsound mind". In *Winterwerp v Netherlands* (1979) it said:

This term is not one that can be given a definite interpretation: ... it is a term whose meaning is continually evolving as research in psychiatry progresses, an increasing flexibility in treatment is developing and society's attitude to mental illness changes, in particular so that a greater understanding of the problems of mental patients is becoming more wide-spread. (para.37)

According to the case-law of the European Convention (see *Winterwerp v Netherlands*, 1979, *Ashingdane v UK*, 1985, and *Johnson v UK*, 1999), a number of requirements have to be fulfilled if the detention of a person of unsound mind is to be lawful:

- it must be medically established that the person concerned is of unsound mind,
- the mental disorder must be of a kind or degree warranting compulsory confinement,
- the validity of continued confinement depends upon the persistence of such a disorder, and
- the detention must be in accordance with applicable domestic legal procedure.

The Convention specifically provides for the right of a detained person to challenge the legality of his or her detention. Under Article 5(4):

everyone who is deprived of his liberty by arrest or detention shall be entitled to take proceedings by which the lawfulness of his detention shall be decided speedily by a court and his release ordered if the detention is not lawful.

The rights of a person making such a challenge were circumscribed by the European Court in its decision in *Megyeri v Germany* (1992), where the Court stated that:

> *The judicial proceedings referred to in Article 5(4) need not always be attended by the same guarantees as those required under Article 6(1) for civil or criminal litigation. Nonetheless, it is essential that the person concerned should have access to a court and the opportunity to be heard either in person or, where necessary, through some form of representation. Special procedural safeguards may prove called for in order to protect the interests of persons who, on account of their mental disabilities, are not fully capable of acting for themselves.* (para.22(b)).

Article 8

Finally, Article 8 concerns the right of a person to his or her private and family life, home and correspondence. This obviously applies to people with mental conditions whether they are living at home, in residential accommodation or in a hospital. Article 8(2) permits interference with Article 8(1) rights if it is in accordance with law and:

> *necessary in a democratic society in the interests of public safety, for the prevention of disorder or crime, for the protection of health or morals, or for the protection of the rights and freedoms of others.*

Domestic law

The Mental Health (NI) Order 1986 (the MHO) is the primary domestic legal source. The Order provides, amongst other things, for compulsory admission and detention in hospital, non-consensual treatment, guardianship and the management of a patient's property and affairs. It also makes provision for persons involved in criminal proceedings.

Other relevant statutory provisions include the Health and Personal Social Services (NI) Order 1972. This allows for state intervention in the lives of persons who appear to be at risk or to require care and attention. There is also the Children (NI) Order 1995, which permits state intervention in the lives of children with psychiatric conditions.

Finally, the common law (*i.e.* judge-made law) contains pertinent legal rules concerning the care and treatment of persons with mental conditions, particularly in relation to the non-statutory detention of patients who are incapable of consenting to treatment.

Other relevant law, policy and practice

There are some international legal standards governing the care and treatment of persons with mental conditions. The Principles for the Protection of Persons with Mental Illness and the Improvement of Mental Health Care (the Mental Health Care Principles) were adopted by the UN General Assembly on 17 December 1991 by Resolution 46/119. The Declaration on the Rights of Mentally Retarded Persons was proclaimed by the UN General Assembly on 20 December 1971. It has particular application to persons with conditions variously labelled as mental handicap, mental disability and/or learning difficulties. These international standards are not binding law in any part of the United Kingdom, but it is nevertheless reasonable to expect compliance with them, especially the more recent set, because they represent best international practice.

On a domestic level, pursuant to article 111 of the MHO, a Code of Practice has been issued to provide advice and guidance on good professional practice relating to the procedures prescribed in the Order. A failure to comply with this Code is not itself unlawful but it can be cited as evidence of illegality in any dispute which might arise.

Detention, treatment and consent

Any person can of course be admitted to hospital or receive medical treatment if he or she consents. The law presumes that a person has mental capacity to consent to medical treatment. Whether, in law, a person lacks mental capacity is decided by considering his or her ability to comprehend and retain information relevant to a decision, to appreciate the significance of the decision and to make a considered decision on the basis of such information (*Re C (Refusal of Medical Treatment)*, 1994, *Re MB (Medical Treatment)*, 1997 and *Re B (Consent to Treatment)*, 2002).

Voluntary patients, including in-patients, enjoy the protection of European Convention law, including all of the Article 5 safeguards against arbitrary deprivation of liberty. In *De Wilde, Ooms and Versyp v Belgium* (1971) the European Court stated that:

The right to liberty is too important in a "democratic society" within the meaning of the Convention for a person to lose the benefit of the protection of the Convention for the single reason that he gives himself up to be taken into detention.

As a general rule, mentally competent adults of 18 years and over (*i.e.* of full age) can give or withhold consent in matters concerning their healthcare (s.1(1) of the Age of Majority Act (NI) 1969). However, the law is different for minors (*i.e.* persons under 18 years): it provides separately for minors aged under 16 years and those aged 16 or 17 years.

For a minor aged under 16 years, it is a question of medical judgement as to whether he or she has the mental capacity (*i.e.* sufficient understanding and intelligence) to make a given healthcare decision (*Gillick v West Norfolk and Wisbech Area Health Authority*, 1986). If such a minor is found not to have the required capacity (*i.e.* is Gillick-incompetent), a healthcare decision is made by the parents or a guardian of the minor and a relevant medical practitioner. A parental refusal for medical treatment can be overridden by a court under its *parens patriae* ("parent for the nation") jurisdiction, but only if the court considers the proposed treatment to be within the minor's best interests. The minor's welfare has to be the court's paramount consideration (*Re B (A Minor) (Wardship: Medical Treatment)*, 1981). If a minor aged under 16 years is found to have the required capacity (*i.e.* is Gillick-competent), but refuses to consent to medical care and treatment, the courts can again override the minor's wishes on the ground that the proposed care and treatment is in his or her best interests (*Re R (A Minor) (Wardship: Consent to Treatment)*, 1992).

The Age of Majority Act (NI) 1969 authorises minors aged 16 or 17 years to consent to surgical, medical or dental treatment (s.4). But similar principles apply to these minors as those outlined above in relation to Gillick-incompetent and Gillick-competent minors aged under 16 years (*Re W (A Minor) (Medical Treatment: Court's Jurisdiction)*, 1993).

Hence, court decisions about a minor's mental capacity and ability to consent to treatment are premised upon a range of factors including the minor's age, his or her current and past mental health and the level of personal development, understanding and maturity exhibited by the minor.

Compulsory detention

Persons with mental conditions can be compulsorily detained under both statute law and common law. Compulsory detention under the *MHO* (sometimes referred to as formal detention) comprises of two stages: (1) initial admission for assessment and (2) detention for treatment.

Admission for assessment

A person with a "mental disorder" can be compulsorily admitted to hospital for assessment. If he or she is living in the community, the involuntary admission to hospital can be by an approved social worker or by the nearest relative on the recommendation of a medical practitioner. Mental disorder is broadly defined as "mental illness, mental handicap and any other disorder or disability of mind" (art.3(1) of the MHO). Excluded from the statutory definition of mental disorder are mental conditions caused "by reason only of personality disorder, promiscuity or other immoral conduct, sexual deviancy or dependence on alcohol or drugs" (art.3(2)). More particularly, a person can be admitted for assessment only if he or she is:

- suffering from mental disorder of a nature or degree which warrants his or her detention in a hospital for assessment (or for assessment followed by medical treatment), and
- failing to detain him or her would create a substantial likelihood of serious physical harm to him or her or to other persons (art.4(2)).

The person admitted must be examined on admission by a psychiatrist. If the admission is deemed appropriate, the person can be detained for assessment for up to 14 days (art.9). Under Part IV of the MHO, he or she can be treated without consent (see below).

Provision is also made under the MHO for the compulsory detention of a voluntary in-patient where, for example, he or she tries to leave hospital (art.7). This may occur in the following ways. A medical practitioner who is a hospital staff member can furnish a report to the responsible authority stating his or her opinion that an application to admit a patient for assessment is necessary. Where such an application is made successfully, the person concerned may be detained for up to 48 hours (art.7(2)). Alternatively, a mental health nurse can authorise the detention of a patient for up to six hours in circumstances where the nurse believes an assessment application is necessary but securing the immediate attendance of a medical practitioner for the purpose of furnishing a report under article 7(2) is not practicable (art.7(3)).

Article 10 provides a further safeguard for persons who are discharged from hospital after being assessed as not needing to be detained for treatment. In a range of prescribed circumstances such persons are not obliged to disclose their admission and detention for assessment. They enjoy legal protection and relief against any discriminatory and detrimental treatment based on the fact that they were so admitted and detained (art.10(4)).

Detention for treatment

A patient may be detained for longer than 14 days only if his or her condition falls within the criteria contained in article 12(1) of the MHO, namely:

- the patient is suffering from a mental illness or severe mental impairment of a nature or degree which warrants his or her detention in a hospital for medical treatment, and
- failure to detain the patient would create a substantial likelihood of serious physical harm to him or her or to other persons (art.12(1)(a) and (b)).

A person can be initially detained for treatment for up to six months (art.12(1)) but can be further detained for a second period of up to six months (art.13(1)(a)). Thereafter a patient can be detained for periods of up to one year (art.13(1)(b) and (c)). One safeguard introduced by article 13(4) requires that, once a person has been detained for a year, the authorisation of further detention must be made by two psychiatrists, of whom one must be:

> a person who is not on the staff of the hospital in which the patient is detained and who has not given either the medical recommendation on which the application for assessment in relation to the patient was founded or any medical report in relation to the patient under article 9 or 12(1) (art.13(4)(c)).

The Mental Health Review Tribunal

Any person compulsorily detained under the MHO can make an application to the Mental Health Review Tribunal (the Tribunal), challenging the lawfulness of his or her detention. The Tribunal is composed of three members, namely a legal member, a medical member and a third "lay" member. It normally convenes at the hospital in which the patient is being held, often the Boardroom. Its procedure is governed by the Mental Health Review Tribunal (NI) Rules 1986, which must now be read in conjunction with European Convention law.

A detained patient has the right to representation, including legal representation, before the Tribunal. He or she will often want to consider the merits of obtaining independent psychiatric evidence, particularly if the psychiatrist in charge of his or her care is opposed to his or her discharge. Advice concerning Mental Health Review Tribunal representation can be obtained from a solicitor, the Northern Ireland Human Rights Commission and the Northern Ireland Association for Mental Health. Legal aid may be available too if certain financial conditions are met.

The Tribunal has discretion to direct the discharge of any patient (art.77(1)). It is required to direct the discharge of a patient if it is satisfied that the patient's condition does not fulfil the relevant criteria, namely:

- the patient is not suffering from mental illness or severe mental impairment or from either of those forms of mental disorder of a nature or degree which warrants his or her detention in hospital or for medical treatment, and
- the discharge of the patient would not create a substantial likelihood of serious physical harm to him or her or to other persons (art.77(1) of the MHO).

The Tribunal may also: (a) direct the discharge of a patient on a future date, (b) recommend a patient's leave of absence or his or her transfer to another hospital or into guardianship, and (c) further consider a patient's case if there is non-compliance with such a recommendation (art.77(2)).

In this context the recent decision in *R v Mental Health Review Tribunal, ex parte H* (2001) is important. The English Court of Appeal held that the statutory provision placing the burden of proof on the patient to show why he or she should be released from detention was incompatible with the presumption of innocence protected by Article 6 of the ECHR, which requires the burden of proof to be placed on the authority arguing for continued detention. The Court relied upon the decision of the European Court of Human Rights in *Winterwerp v Netherlands* (1979), where it was stated that an individual "should not be deprived of his liberty unless he has been reliably shown to be of 'unsound mind'" (para.39). Consequently, and pursuant to section 10 of the Human Rights Act 1998, the Mental Health Act 1983 (Remedial) Order 2001 was enacted (coming into force on 26 November 2001) to remove the incompatibility between the relevant provisions of the Mental Health Act 1983 and Article 6 of the European Convention. The 2001 Remedial Order reverses the burden of proof, placing it on the detaining authority, but it does not apply in Northern Ireland. The Mental Health Review Tribunal for Northern Ireland needs to keep the *Ex parte H* decision in mind when adjudicating the lawfulness of detentions under the MHO.

Detention under the Children (NI) Order 1995

Provision is made under the Children (NI) Order 1995 for interventions concerning children who require psychiatric care and treatment. A supervision order can be imposed where a child requires care that his or her parents are unable to provide (art.50). A court can authorise the psychiatric examination of a child subject to a supervision order if it is satisfied, on the evidence of a medical practitioner, that the child may be suffering from a mental condition that requires treatment and that is medically treatable (Sch.3, para.4). A court can also authorise the medical treatment of a child where appropriate (Sch.3, para.5).

Detention under the Health and Personal Social Services (NI) Order 1972

The Health and Personal Social Services (NI) Order 1972 makes provision for state intervention concerning persons who:
- suffer from grave chronic disease or, being aged, infirm or physically incapacitated, are living in insanitary conditions, and
- are unable to devote themselves, or to receive from persons with whom they reside, or from persons living nearby, proper care and attention (art.37).

Such intervention can include the non-consensual removal of such persons to other accommodation where necessary (Sch.6).

A social worker may initiate proceedings to remove a person from his or her place of residence if the social worker reasonably believes that removal is necessary in the interests of the person concerned or to prevent the causing of serious nuisance or injury to a third party. The social worker must initially consult with both the general medical practitioner of the person concerned and a medical officer designated by the health authority. He or she may make a removal application based on the medical certification of the health authority's designated medical officer that such removal is necessary. Thereafter the health authority may apply to the magistrates' court within the jurisdiction where the person resides for an order to remove him or her to a suitable hospital or other place and for his or her detention there for up to three months. The health authority must give the nearest relative of the person concerned three days' notice of its intention to apply to the court for a removal order and it must also inform the person managing the accommodation which is to receive the person that a removal hearing is to take place. At the hearing the health and welfare authority must lead evidence to substantiate its application. The court may also hear evidence from the person concerned and/or his or her nearest known relative, and he or she has the right to be legally represented at such a hearing.

Detention under the common law

Article 127 of the MHO contemplates the hospital admission and treatment of patients outside the statutory framework prescribed under the MHO. The legal basis for informal or non-statutory intervention is found in the common law (*i.e.* judge-made law) principle of necessity, as articulated by the House of Lords in the English case *R v Bournewood Community and Mental Health NHS Trust, ex parte L* (1998). In that case, an autistic and profoundly mentally retarded 48-year-old man, who was incompetent, was admitted to hospital "informally". The psychiatrist considered it unnecessary to admit him under the Mental Health Act 1983 because the man appeared fully compliant and did not resist admission. The lawfulness of the informal admission was challenged by his carers but the House of Lords held that the non-statutory admission of patients who are incapable of providing informed consent, but who do not object to hospital admission, was lawful.

Two judges, however, dissented. Lord Steyn said that the exercise of informal powers deprived the patient of safeguards applying to formal patients. He maintained that:

> *the common law principle of necessity is a useful concept, but it contains none of the safeguards of the Act of 1983. It places*

effective and unqualified control in the hands of the hospital psychiatrist and other healthcare professionals.

He also pointed out that informal detention was not provided for in the Mental Health Act Code of Practice. This Code has subsequently been amended in England and Wales, but no such step has yet been taken in Northern Ireland. It appears that informal detention is lawful if the action is taken to prevent imminent harm and is in the best interests of the person concerned. It is a crisis intervention measure, but whether it is in accord with humane practice and with health professionals' duty of care is still a moot point.

Guardianship

In mental health law, guardianship is an arrangement for people aged 16 or over who suffer from mental illness or have a severe mental handicap and who require supervision in the interests of their welfare. The appointment of a guardian and the establishment of an authoritative framework for working with a patient with a minimum of constraint is intended to help the patient live as independent a life as possible within the community.

A guardianship application can be made by an approved social worker or the nearest relative (art.20). In considering how to discharge his or her statutory duties, a nearest relative is *prima facie* entitled to access relevant documentation, including any medical or welfare recommendations, notwithstanding the patient's right to confidentiality or privacy (*S v Plymouth City Council (C as interested party)*, 2002).

The application must be accompanied by two medical recommendations and a welfare recommendation (art.19(3)); an approved social worker provides the latter. To be received into guardianship, a person must meet two criteria:

- he or she must be suffering from mental illness or severe mental handicap of a nature or degree which warrants his or her reception into guardianship, and
- it must be necessary in the interests of the welfare of the person concerned (art.18(2)).

The guardian, once appointed, has three essential powers:

- to require the patient to reside at a certain place,
- to require the patient to attend for medical treatment, occupation, education or training at specific times and places, and

- to require access to be given at any place where the patient is residing to a doctor, approved social worker or other authorised person.

Guardianship initially lasts for six months but it may be renewed for a further six months and thereafter annually. A person may be discharged by either the medical officer or the authorised social worker. The nearest relative may also discharge the person concerned from guardianship, but this power is subject to the medical and/or welfare officer's agreement (art.24(4)). Finally, a person can be discharged by a Mental Health Review Tribunal (art.77(3)). A tribunal is required to direct the discharge of a patient if it is satisfied that the patient's condition does not fulfil the criteria mentioned above.

Persons involved in criminal proceedings or under sentence

The courts have power to remand to hospital a person charged with or convicted of an imprisonable offence, so that a report can be prepared on his or her mental condition (art.42). A magistrate can make such a hospital remand only if satisfied that the individual concerned committed the offence with which he or she is charged, or if the individual has consented to the exercise of this power (art.42(2)(b)).

A person detained in custody, who is charged with an imprisonable offence for which the sentence is not fixed by law, can be remanded to hospital for treatment prior to sentence as well as before or during his or her trial (art.43). The court must be satisfied on the oral evidence of a psychiatrist who has been appointed under the MHO that the accused or convicted person is suffering from mental illness or severe mental impairment of a nature or degree which warrants his or her detention in hospital for medical treatment. And a court cannot make an order remanding an accused or convicted person to hospital for treatment unless the Department of Health and Social Services and Public Safety has been given an opportunity to make representations in relation to the proposed remand.

A person convicted of an imprisonable offence for which the sentence is not fixed by law can be committed to the care of the Department, if:

- he or she is suffering from mental illness or severe mental impairment of a nature or degree that warrants his or her detention in hospital for medical treatment, and,

- committal for psychiatric care and treatment is the most suitable means of dealing with his or her case (art.44).

This form of sentence is known as a hospital order. A court may restrict a person's discharge from hospital if it finds that such a course is necessary to protect the public from serious harm (art.47). The restriction order can be made with or without a time limit.

A court can place under the guardianship of a health authority, or such other person approved by a health authority, a person convicted of an imprisonable offence for which the sentence is not fixed by law (art.44). This form of sentence, known as a guardianship order, can be issued in similar circumstances to a hospital order, although one key difference is that a guardianship order can be imposed only where the offender is aged 16 or over.

A person charged with a criminal offence may be found to be unfit for trial. Where such a determination is reached, the person concerned is automatically subject to an order which has the same effect as a hospital order together with a restriction order without a time limitation (art.49). Similarly, when a court directs a finding to be recorded to the effect that an accused person is not guilty of the offence charged on the ground of insanity, the person is automatically subject to an order which has the same effect as a hospital order together with a restriction order without a time limitation (art.50).

Powers of the police

Under the MHO the Police Service of Northern Ireland is charged with a number of functions relating to persons with a mental disorder.

Article 130: Removal of persons found in a public place

If a police officer finds a person in a public place who appears to him or her to be suffering from mental disorder and in "immediate need of care or control", the officer may remove that person to a place of safety, "if he thinks it necessary to do so in the interests of that person or for the protection of other persons" (art.130). A person so removed may be detained for 48 hours to allow him or her to be examined by a doctor and interviewed by an approved social worker and to enable any necessary arrangements to be made for his or her care or treatment (art.130). A "place of safety" means any hospital which is willing temporarily to receive such a person, a police station or any other suitable place where the occupier is willing temporarily to receive such persons (art.129(7)). The police officer is obliged to inform both a responsible person residing with the person concerned and, if not the same person, the nearest relative of the person concerned, that he or she has been removed to a place of safety.

Article 129: Intervention by warrant

Article 129 provides authority for a magistrate or Justice of the Peace, on complaint by an officer of a Board or Trust (*e.g.* a social worker), or a constable, (*i.e.* a police officer), to issue a warrant. The issue of a warrant authorises the police, amongst other things, to enter premises, search for a patient and take custody of a patient. The person removed may be detained in a place of safety for up to 48 hours (art.129(5)). The MHO contemplates the issue of a warrant in three main situations:

(a) Admission to hospital

The applicant is authorised to convey the patient to hospital where an application has been completed under the MHO for admission to hospital for assessment. If the applicant finds that it is not reasonably practicable for him or her, or a person authorised by him or her, to fulfil this duty, he or she may request assistance from the police. If there is reasonable cause to believe that a patient is to be found on any premises, the applicant may apply for a warrant under Article 129(4), which authorises a police officer accompanied by a doctor to "enter, if need be by force, the premises and to take and convey the patient to the hospital specified in the application".

(b) Re-taking of a person liable to be detained who is at large

Where an officer of a Board or Trust, or a police officer, has reasonable cause to believe that a patient who has absconded or is at large may be at any premises, a warrant may be obtained authorising a police officer accompanied by a doctor to enter the premises and remove the patient, if need be by force (art.129(2)).

(c) Persons at risk

Where an officer of a Board or Trust, or a police officer, has reasonable cause to believe that a person suffering from mental disorder "has been or is being ill-treated, neglected or kept otherwise than under proper control or being unable to care for himself is living alone", a warrant may be obtained to authorise a police officer, accompanied by a doctor, to enter premises and remove the patient to a place of safety (art.129(1)).

Treatment

The law governing medical treatment of persons with a mental condition is premised upon the concepts of autonomy and mental capacity. In the American case of *Schloendorff v Society of New York Hospital* (1914), Justice Cardozo stated:

Every human being of adult years and sound mind has a right to determine what shall be done with his own body; and a surgeon who performs an operation without his patient's consent commits an assault.

In a similar vein, in the important House of Lords decision in *Re F (Mental Patient: Sterilisation)* (1989), Lord Goff stated "I start with the fundamental principle, now long established, that every person's body is inviolate". Notwithstanding these well recognised statements of legal principle, the MHO provides for the psychiatric treatment of persons with mental disorder, including the non-consensual treatment of competent persons. In civil liberty terms, Part IV of the MHO contains some of the most invasive provisions in Northern Ireland law. They are outlined below.

Treatment under the common law

There is a rebuttable presumption that every adult person has the mental capacity to make an informed decision about whether he or she consents to proposed medical treatment. As outlined above, the legal test for competency focuses on whether a person's capacity is so reduced by his or her mental condition that he or she does not sufficiently understand the nature, purpose and effects of the proposed treatment (*Re C (Refusal of Medical Treatment)*, 1994). In determining whether a person's capacity is so reduced, Lord Justice Butler-Sloss held that a patient is unable to make a decision when he or she:

(a) ...is unable to comprehend and retain the information which is material to the decision, especially as to the likely consequences of having or not having the treatment in question; [and/or]

(b)...is unable to use the information and weigh it in the balance as part of the process of arriving at the decision.

(See also *Re MB (Medical Treatment)*, 1997 and *Re B (Consent to Treatment)*, 2002).

The common law permits the medical treatment of an incompetent person if such treatment is necessary to preserve the life, health or well-being of the patient concerned, and is in his or her best interests (*Re F (Mental Patient: Sterilisation)*, 1989). Medical practitioners are under a legal duty to administer treatment to mentally incompetent patients where such a course is necessary to preserve the patient's health and in the patient's best interests. The treatment will be in the patient's best interests only if it is carried out either to save the patient's life or to ensure improvement or prevent deterioration in his or her physical or mental health (*Re F (Mental Patient: Sterilisation)*, 1989). But such treatment cannot be administered where a legally valid "advance directive" refusing medical treatment exists (*Re T*, 1992).

Ultimately the lawfulness of any proposed medical intervention is a matter for the courts. An interested party may ask the High Court to adjudicate on the lawfulness of proposed treatment. It is standard practice for health authorities to seek judicial approval before undertaking certain operations, particularly those involving the withdrawal of life support, sterilisation and abortion. The Official Solicitor will be appointed to represent the patient in such applications (*Re F (Mental Patient: Sterilisation)*, 1989; *Northern Health and Social Services Board v A and others*, 1994; *Re B (Adult: Refusal of Medical Treatment)*, 2002).

It is questionable whether incompetent patients are adequately protected by the prevailing law. Health authorities are authorised to broadly intervene as outlined above, but there are few legal safeguards to protect the rights of a patient.

Psychiatric treatment and the MHO

Part IV of the MHO makes special provision for the psychiatric treatment of mental disorder. It generally applies to all patients. Articles 64 and 69 apply only to patients liable to be detained and do not apply to patients detained pursuant to Article 7(2) or (3), persons detained under the police powers outlined above or persons subject to guardianship.

As a general rule, persons who are liable to be detained under the MHO may be treated for mental disorder without their consent under the direction of the responsible medical officer, regardless of their mental competency (art.69).   This supersedes the common law provisions governing treatment and consent.   To mitigate this permissive statutory power, safeguards are provided for specified treatments. They are contained in Articles 63, 64 and 66.

Article 63

Article 63 applies to all patients and not only to patients "liable to be detained". It prohibits the performance of operations that destroy brain tissue or its functioning, or the administration of hormone implants to reduce sex drive, unless the patient consents and a second medical opinion certifies that the treatment is appropriate "having regard to the likelihood of the treatment alleviating or preventing a deterioration of the patient's condition" (art.63(2)(b)). The second medical opinion must be provided by a psychiatrist appointed by the Mental Health Commission for Northern Ireland, also known as the Second Opinion Appointed Doctor (SOAD).

Article 64

Article 64 provides for a lower level of protection for the administration of medicines and electro-convulsive therapy (ECT). Such treatment is lawful in three situations:

- where the patient consents, the treatment is lawful only if an authorised psychiatrist certifies that the patient has the mental capacity to consent and has in fact consented to the proposed treatment (art.64(3)(a));
- where the patient is incapable of consenting, an SOAD must certify that the patient is incapable of consenting to the treatment and that the treatment should be given due to the likelihood of it "alleviating or preventing a deterioration of his or her condition" (art.64(3)(b)); and
- where a patient is capable of consenting but has refused to consent, an SOAD must certify that, notwithstanding the patient's refusal to consent, the treatment should be given due to the likelihood of it

"alleviating or preventing a deterioration of his or her condition" (art.64(3)(b)).

The SOAD must reach his or her own independent view of the desirability and propriety of the treatment pursuant to the relevant statutory criteria (*R (Wilkinson) v Broadmoor RMO and others*, 2002). The above safeguards apply before the administration of ECT. However, the safeguards do not become effective in relation to the administration of medicines until a detained patient has received such medicine (by any means) for a period of three months (art.64(1)(b)). This is known as the "three months rule".

Article 66

Article 66 enables a patient who has consented to a treatment under articles 63 or 64 to withdraw his or her consent either before or during a course of treatment or at any point within a treatment plan. Where consent has been withdrawn, the treatment may proceed only where statutory provision for non-consensual treatment exists.

Urgent treatment

In an emergency, safeguards prescribed in articles 63 and 64 may be waived pursuant to article 68. The following treatments may then be administered without the patient's consent or a second opinion:

- surgery affecting brain tissue and the implantation of hormones to reduce sex drive may be administered to all mental patients including informal mental patients; and,
- ECT and medication for psychiatric purposes may be administered to patients liable to be detained subject to the exceptions listed above.

These safeguards may be waived where the administration of treatment is "immediately necessary" for one of the following reasons:

- to save the patient's life,
- to prevent a serious deterioration of the patient's condition, as long as the treatment is not irreversible,
- to alleviate serious suffering by the patient, as long as the operation is not irreversible or hazardous, or
- to prevent the patient from behaving violently or being a danger to him or herself or to others, as long as the operation is not irreversible

or hazardous, and the treatment represents the minimum interference necessary.

As outlined above, a patient can at any time withdraw consent to any treatment governed by articles 63 or 64. However, notwithstanding a patient's withdrawal of consent, a treatment plan may be continued under article 68(2) if the responsible medical officer considers that "the discontinuance of the treatment or of treatment under the plan would cause serious suffering to the patient".

The management of incompetent patients' property and affairs

Where a person becomes unable to look after his or her property and affairs, the law contains a number of mechanisms for substitute decision-making. Health and welfare authorities may receive and hold the money and valuables of patients living in local authority accommodation who are incapable by reason of mental disorder of managing their property or affairs (art.116). A trust is empowered to expend that money or dispose of those valuables for the benefit of the patient (art.116(3)). These authorities may not receive or hold patients' monies or valuables exceeding in the aggregate £5,000 unless they have the permission of the Mental Health Commission for Northern Ireland.

The Department for Social Development can appoint an individual to receive and administer social security benefits that are payable to a person who is "unable for the time being to act", in the absence of the appointment of a controller by the High Court (regs.33-34 of the Social Security (Claims and Payments) Regulations (NI) 1987).

Finally, an individual can create an enduring power of attorney to give an authorised person the power to act on his or her behalf in the event of supervening mental incapacity (Enduring Powers of Attorney (NI) Order 1987). The High Court regulates enduring powers of attorney under a system of registration.

The main statutory framework for intervention in matters concerning a person's property and affairs is found at Part VIII of the MHO. Under this Part, legal responsibility for the management of a person's property and affairs may be removed from him or her only if "after considering medical evidence the court is satisfied that a person is incapable by reason of mental disorder of managing and administering his property and affairs" (art.97(1)). Order 109 of the Rules of the Supreme Court (NI) requires an application to be made to the Office of Care and Protection (an office of the High Court) for the appointment of a controller to deal with the daily management of the patient's financial affairs. Such an application may specify a suitable person who is willing to act as the patient's controller, such as a relative, friend or professional adviser. The Office can direct an Officer of the Court or the Official Solicitor to make such an application if there is no suitable person to do so. Moreover, the requirement to apply in writing may be waived in urgent cases.

In appointing a controller, the Office considers the name stated on the application. Alternatively, where there is no suitable or willing person, the Office may appoint an Officer of the Court or the Official Solicitor. The breadth of a controller's powers are prescribed by the order of appointment (art.101(2)). He or she can be discharged by a court order if the patient dies, if the court is satisfied that the patient is no longer incapable or if discharge is regarded as otherwise expedient.

The appointment of a controller may be bypassed by an aptly named "short procedure"' under Rule 5 of Order 109 of the Rules of the Supreme Court (NI). It is also less costly than the normal procedure. This short procedure may be used if it appears to the court that the patient's property does not exceed £5,000, or if it is otherwise appropriate to proceed under Rule 5 and it is not necessary to appoint a controller for the patient. In such a case, the court can direct an Officer of the Court or some other suitable person to deal with the patient's property and affairs.

The Mental Health Commission for Northern Ireland

The Mental Health Commission for Northern Ireland (the Commission) was established by Part VI of the MHO, to "keep under review the care and treatment of patients including the exercise of the powers and the discharge of the duties conferred by the Order" (art.86(1)). It performs the responsible task of monitoring the care and treatment of persons with mental disorder and it has specific responsibility for ensuring the appropriate and lawful exercise of powers under the MHO.

The duties of the Commission

The Commission's functions are mainly set out in articles 86 and 87 of the MHO. Article 86(2) places specific statutory obligations upon the Commission, namely:

- to inquire into any case where it appears to the Commission that there may be ill-treatment, deficiency in care and treatment or improper detention in hospital or reception into guardianship of any patient, or where the property of any patient may by reason of his or her mental disorder be exposed to loss or damage;
- to visit detained patients;
- to notify the relevant authority where it appears that action is necessary to: (i) prevent ill-treatment, (ii) remedy a deficiency in care or treatment, (iii) end improper detention in hospital, or (iv) prevent or redress loss or damage to property;
- to provide advice to relevant authorities on matters pertaining to the MHO where a matter has been referred to the Commission, and
- to bring matters concerning the welfare of patients to the attention of relevant authorities or persons.

The powers of the Commission

To assist the Commission in the discharge of its above-stated statutory duties, it has various powers, including:

- the power to refer cases to the Mental Health Review Tribunal (see p.332 above),
- the power to visit and examine patients, and
- the power to inspect records relating to the detention and treatment of persons (art.86(3)) – although this power is vested only in a member of the Commission who is a medical practitioner or a medical practitioner appointed by the Commission for that purpose (art.87(2)).

Where the Commission has brought to the attention of a body or person responsible for the care of patients (*e.g.* a Trust or a person carrying on a private hospital, a home for persons in need, a voluntary home or a nursing home) a matter of concern in relation to the care and treatment of patients, the Commission may serve a notice on such a body or person requiring it "to provide to the Commission such information concerning the steps taken or to be taken by that body or person in relation to that case or matter as the Commission may so specify" (art.86(6)). The body or person in question is statutorily obliged to comply with the requirements of such a notice.

Further useful addresses

- Mental Health Commission for Northern Ireland
  Elizabeth House
  116-118 Holywood Road
  Belfast BT4 1NY
  tel: 028 9065 1157

- Mental Health Review Tribunal for Northern Ireland
  Room 112B
  Dundonald House
  Belfast BT4 3SU
  tel: 028 9048 5550

- Mind: The Mental Health Charity
  15-19 Broadway
  Stratford
  London E15 4BQ
  tel: 020 8519 2122
  www.mind.org.uk

- National Schizophrenia Fellowship
  Knockbracken Health Care Park
  Saintfield Road
  Belfast BT8 8BH
  tel: 028 9040 2323

- Northern Ireland Association for Mental Health
  80 University Street
  Belfast BT7 1HE
  tel: 028 9032 8474

- Northern Ireland Human Rights Commission
  Temple Court
  39 North Street
  Belfast BT1 1NA
  tel: 028 9024 3987
  www.nihrc.org

- The Office of Care and Protection
  Royal Courts of Justice
  Chichester Street
  Belfast BT1 3JF
  tel: 028 9023 5111

Family and Sexual Matters

*Rachel Murray**

S ince the coming into force of the Human Rights Act 1998, *HRA*
provisions of the European Convention on Human Rights
(ECHR) have gained increased importance in Northern Ireland's
law.   The two most significant ECHR provisions in the context of
family and sexual matters are Articles 8 and 12:

Article 8

*(1)   Everyone has the right to respect for his private and family life,
his home and his correspondence.*

*(2)   There shall be no interference by a public authority with the
exercise of this right except such as is in accordance with the law
and is necessary in a democratic society in the interests of
national security, public safety or the economic well-being of the
country, for the prevention of disorder or crime, for the
protection of health or morals, or for the protection of the rights
and freedoms of others.*

Article 12

*Men and women of marriageable age have the right to marry and to
found a family, according to the national laws governing the
exercise of this right.*

Article 6 (the right to a fair trial) may also be important with
regard to the procedure used to make decisions in the sphere of family
law.

Under section 75 of the Northern Ireland Act 1998 public
authorities in Northern Ireland are now also required to act with due
regard to the need to promote equality of opportunity between:

- persons of different religious belief, political opinion, racial group,
age, marital status or sexual orientation;
- men and women generally;
- persons with a disability and persons without; and

---

* I would like to thank Lisa Glennon at the Queen's University of Belfast for all
her invaluable help.

- persons with dependents and persons without.

Without prejudice to this requirement, public authorities are also under a duty to have regard for the desirability of promoting good relations among those of different religious or political beliefs or racial groups. As explained in Chapter 11, public bodies have to produce Equality Schemes, to be submitted for the approval of the Equality Commission, and to conduct equality impact assessments of their policies.

Family life *[handwritten: What constitutes Family!!]*

Article 8 of the ECHR provides for the right to private and family life. What constitutes a "family" has been interpreted by the ECHR organs to include not just a married couple's relationship but also a couple living together. The length of the relationship and whether the individuals have shown commitment to each other by, for example, having children together, will be taken into consideration in this regard (*X, Y and UK*, 1997, where a transsexual man, his female partner and their child were held to constitute a family). Article 8 has also been held to provide protection for the "inner circle" (*Niemetz v Germany*, 1992) and for "family ties", so the relationship with a child resulting from a non-married relationship (*Keegan v Ireland*, 1994) and between an unmarried father and his child, even if the father has not lived with the mother or had a great deal of contact with the child (*Soderback v Sweden*, 1999), may also be protected. The European Court of Human Rights has held that family life and the protection of Article 8 cover the relationship between a foster parent and the fostered child (*Frette v France*, 1999) and between adoptive parents and the adopted children (*X v France*, 1986).

[handwritten: Doesn't mean right to create a family] The right to family life is not a right to create a family and does not entail a duty on the state to provide assistance for one parent to look after a child at home (*Andersson and Kullman v Sweden*, 1986).

Marriage

In Northern Ireland's law marriage is "the voluntary union between one man and one woman to the exclusion of all others". The law requires those wishing to marry to be at least 16 years of age and it bars marriage between certain persons who are related to one another (see the Family Law (Miscellaneous Provisions) (NI) Order 1984, art.

18, as amended by the Family Law (NI) Order 1993). Many of the issues surrounding marriage are governed by the Matrimonial Causes (NI) Order 1978, which also confirms, in article 13(1)(e), that marriage can only be between individuals of the opposite sex. Article 12 of the ECHR also provides protection only to marriages between individuals of the opposite sex but it has recently been held to extend to transsexuals (*Goodwin v UK*, 2002) and the House of Lords has declared the English equivalent to article 13(1)(e) to be incompatible with the ECHR (*Bellinger v Bellinger*, 2003).

Although relationships between individuals of the same sex fall under the protection of Article 8, there may not always be a breach in respect of such individuals. So, for example, there was no breach when a male transsexual was not registered as the father of the child of a female partner (*X v UK*, 1997). This may change, as the Convention is seen as a "living instrument" which can be interpreted to reflect views of the time. In *Goodwin v UK* (2002) the European Court of Human Rights said (at para. 90):

> *In the twenty first century the right of transsexuals to personal development and to physical and moral security in the full sense enjoyed by others in society cannot be regarded as a matter of controversy requiring the lapse of time to cast clearer light on the issues involved. In short, the unsatisfactory situation in which post-operative transsexuals live in an intermediate zone as not quite one gender or the other is no longer sustainable.*

In respect of whether prisoners have a right to marry, the UK was held to have violated Article 12 by requiring them to wait until the end of their sentences before getting married (*Hamer v UK*, 1979; *Draper v UK*, 1980). But Article 12 cannot be used to justify conjugal visits in prisons.

In many situations married and unmarried individuals are treated differently by the law in Northern Ireland. This difference in treatment will not amount to discrimination under Article 14 of the ECHR if it can be objectively justified (*McMichael v UK*, 1995). So, for example, different requirements in terms of tax paid by unmarried and married individuals have been considered to be justifiable and not contrary to Article 14 (*Lindsey v UK*, 1986). Likewise, the law on sex discrimination protects married people against discrimination, but not single people.

The Marriage (NI) Order 2003 reforms and simplifies the preliminaries and procedures which have to be complied with for a valid marriage to take place in Northern Ireland.

Divorce, breakdown and separation

Separation and divorce

Breakdown of marriages can be remedied by separation or divorce. Divorce law in Northern Ireland is contained primarily in the Matrimonial Causes (NI) Order 1978 and cases are considered in the county court or High Court, whereas the law on separation is dealt with by the Domestic Proceedings (NI) Order 1980 and cases are heard in the magistrates' court.

Divorce is available in Northern Ireland if it can be shown there is an irretrievable breakdown of the marriage. To do this, the person requesting the divorce (the petitioner) must prove that his or her spouse (the respondent):

- committed adultery,
- behaved in such a manner that it would not be reasonable to expect the petitioner to live with the other spouse,
- deserted the petitioner for at least two years,
- has lived apart from the petitioner for at least two years and the respondent agrees to a divorce, or
- has lived apart from the petitioner for at least five years continually.

Divorce can be applied for only after at least two years of marriage. Legal aid is still available for divorce cases if certain criteria are satisfied.

Although Article 16 of the Universal Declaration of Human Rights does provide for a right to divorce *per se*, this is not found in either Article 8 or Article 12 of the ECHR and that there is no right to divorce has been affirmed by the European Court of Human Rights in *Johnston v Ireland* (1987) and by the High Court in the UK (*Dennis v Dennis*, 2000). The ECHR would appear, however, to require that there is a right to remarry, provided that divorce is available in the national law (*F v Switzerland*, 1987).

Financial provision outside of divorce

The laws in Northern Ireland in respect of breakdown of relationships apply only to married couples and not to cohabitees. Where married couples are separated, one spouse can apply to a magistrates' court for a financial provision order to require payments (either a lump sum or regular "maintenance" payments) to be made by the other spouse. For such an order to be granted either both individuals have to agree or certain conditions have to be satisfied (Domestic Proceedings (NI) Order 1980, arts.3-9, as amended by the Matrimonial and Family Proceedings (NI) Order 1989, arts.12-15). These conditions include that the spouse did not provide reasonable maintenance to the other spouse or child of the family, that the spouse was adulterous or had deserted the other, or that the behaviour of the spouse was so unreasonable that the other could not be expected to live with him or her. When considering whether to grant an order, the magistrate can take into account such issues as the income, financial resources and needs of the parties, their standard of living, their age, the duration of the marriage, the contribution they each made to the family and whatever disabilities they may have.

Financial provision when there is a divorce

When dealing with a divorce petition, a court can make a number of orders (arts.24, 25 and 26 of the Matrimonial Causes (NI) Order 1978, as amended by art.5 of the Matrimonial and Family Proceedings (NI) Order 1989). It can award maintenance pending the hearing of the petition or it can award a financial provision order or a property order after issuing the divorce decree.

In making such decisions, the court will have regard to the welfare of any child of the parties, the income and earning potential of the parties and their respective needs and responsibilities, their standard of living and age, the duration of the marriage, whether either of the parties has any disabilities, the contribution each party may have made to the welfare of the family, their conduct, and any pension that may be available.

Although "possessions" in Article 1 of Protocol 1 of the ECHR (which provides for the right to "peaceful enjoyment of possessions") includes the matrimonial house and pensions, this provision is unlikely to give much protection because of the wide discretion given to states to limit protection in the "public interest". In addition, where transfer of the home is being considered, although Article 8 would require that this is proportionate, such a transfer is likely to be proportionate as long as it was not done arbitrarily.

Article 5 of Protocol 7 to the ECHR provides that:

Spouses shall enjoy equality of rights and responsibilities of a private law character between them, and in their relations with their children, as to marriage, during marriage and in the event of its dissolution. This Article shall not prevent States from taking such measures as are necessary in the interests of the children.

Unfortunately this Protocol has not yet been ratified by the UK, although the Government has been talking about doing so and has recognised that there are inconsistencies in domestic law which it intends to legislate to remove.

In 2001 the Office of Law Reform issued a consultation paper on reforming divorce law in Northern Ireland. The Family Law (Divorce etc.) (NI) Order is in draft form, waiting to be debated as an Order in Council at Westminster or (should devolution be restored) as a Bill in the Northern Ireland Assembly.

Property issues

Where a couple are married, the Matrimonial Causes (NI) Order 1978 provides that, if the family home is in the name of the husband, the wife has no legal interest in the family home unless:

- she can show there was a prior agreement or understanding with the husband,
- she made a financial contribution to buying the home, or
- she made some other indirect financial contribution to buying the home and it was understood that this would create for her an interest in the property.

Bringing up children is not taken to be a sufficient contribution for the wife to gain an interest in the property. In addition, the present situation is that any money given to the wife by the husband for housekeeping purposes remains the property of the husband. The Law Reform Advisory Committee, in its 2001 consultation paper on matrimonial property, argued that this rule did not reflect the reality of life today and recommended that it be changed.

Issues relating to children

These issues are governed by the Children (NI) Order 1995, as amended by the Family Homes and Domestic Violence (NI) Order 1998. For information about the proposed Children's Commissioner and the Guardian *Ad Litem* Agency, see Chapters 2 and 18 respectively.

There are certain presumptions in Northern Ireland's law regarding who is the parent of a child. If the child is resident in Northern Ireland and it is alleged that a particular man was married to the child's mother between the time of conception and the time of birth, and the child is not adopted, it will be presumed that that man is the child's father (s.2 of the Family Law Act (NI) 2001). In addition, if the individual in question is registered as the father, it will be presumed that he is the parent (*Kroon and others v Netherlands*, 1994). Section 3 of the Family Law Act (NI) 2001 also provides for tests to determine parentage in civil proceedings where parentage is at issue. If an individual refuses to take a test of parentage, or if the test proves that he is the father, then there is a presumption of parentage. There is also a power to take samples from the child. There is a question over whether this is fully compatible with the ECHR in cases where the test may not be in the best interests of the child. Forcing a child to take a test may violate Articles 3 and 8 of the ECHR.

Parental responsibility in Northern Ireland is provided automatically to the mother of the child and to the father if married to the mother. Otherwise, the father can acquire parental responsibility by either being registered as the father, applying to the court for a parental responsibility order, making an agreement with the mother, marrying the mother, obtaining a residence order (art.12 of the Children (NI) Order 1995) or being appointed guardian of the child (art.7). The Family Law Act (NI) 2001 amended the Children (NI) Order 1995 and provides in section 1 for parental responsibility for unmarried fathers if there is the consent of the mother. This would seem to satisfy the requirements of Article 8 of the ECHR, which say that an unmarried father should be able to have sufficient opportunity to develop a relationship with his child. However, as the consent of the mother is still required, parental responsibility in such cases is not automatic and therefore does not arise to the same extent as when the man is married to the mother. But this is probably compatible with the ECHR.

The Family Law Act (NI) 2001 also provides for step-parents to apply to the court to have parental responsibility. However, the Act states that such a step-parent cannot then have the power to consent to adoption. In such cases this may amount to a violation of Articles 6 and 8 of the ECHR.

A number of orders can be made by the court in respect of children in family proceedings:

- *Residence order*: This decides who the child will live with and various arrangements concerning that. It can be made in favour of two or more persons not necessarily living together (Children (NI) Order 1995, art.11(4), as amended by the Family Homes and Domestic Violence (NI) Order 1998). Such orders give automatic parental responsibility to the individual to whom they are granted. In making the order the court will consider if the child suffered or is at risk of suffering harm by seeing or hearing ill-treatment of another person.
- *Contact order*: This requires contact to be granted by the person with whom the child is living to another person.
- *Specific issue order*: This deals with particular issues in respect of those who have parental responsibility for the child.
- *Prohibited steps order*: This requires that no action should be taken without the consent of the court, for example, taking the child abroad.

In deciding whether to grant such orders the welfare of the child is the paramount consideration for the court (art.3(1) of the Children (NI) Order 1995). This may conflict with the rights or wishes of the parents or others in the family (*Johansen v Norway*, 1996). Where a national court had decided that a child should be in the custody of the mother because the father was in a homosexual relationship, the European Court of Human Rights held that this amounted to a breach of Articles 8 and 14 (*Salgueiro da Silva Manta v Portugal*, 1999).

Regarding access to children, the ECHR would seem to suggest that a divorced parent who cannot obtain custody of the child should have the right of access and contact with the child (*W v Germany*, 1987). In addition, unmarried fathers who have been in previous contact with their children should then be able to have access to them in compliance with Article 8 (*El Sholz v Germany*, 2000).

Child support issues are governed by the Child Support (NI) Orders 1991 and 1995. The Child Support Agency can ask the single parent for the name of the other parent to enable it to obtain money from that parent. In one case before the European Court of Human Rights no violation of the ECHR was found where payments made under the Child Support Act 1991 were so large that the father was not able to afford the costs necessary to make a visit to the child (*Logan v UK*, 1995).

Adoption

The Adoption (NI) Order 1987 requires that the welfare of the child be the paramount consideration in the adoption process, even if this means going against the wishes of the natural parent. Parents can, however, challenge an application for adoption and adoption has in some cases been found to be a violation of the parents' rights under Article 8 of the ECHR.

In making decisions, the court will consider the safety and welfare of the child and the provision of a stable and harmonious home, as well as the wishes and feelings of the child, depending on his or her age and understanding. Those applying to adopt must be over 21 years of age. A married couple can adopt, as can a single person, and adoption has been permitted to homosexual individuals (*Re W (Adoption: Homosexual Adopter)*, 1997). The fact that adoption does not require the consent of the unmarried father of a child before the court grants an adoption order may breach Articles 6 and 8 of the ECHR. Those who are successful in adopting a child then automatically obtain parental responsibility.

It is important that the procedure by which the adoption process is conducted is in compliance with Article 6 of the ECHR (*Keegan v Ireland*, 1994, where there was held to be a violation of this Article in that the adoption took place without the knowledge or consent of the father). The consent of the child is not required for adoption, which again is arguably a breach of Articles 6 and 8 of the ECHR. The Adoption (Intercountry Aspects) Act (NI) 2001 gives effect to the international Convention on Protection of Children and Co-operation in respect of Intercountry Adoption (the Hague Convention).

Article 12 of the ECHR does not include a right to adopt or a right to create a family (*X v Belgium and Netherlands*, 1974), although Article 8 has been held to apply to the relationship between adopted parents and the child (*X v France*, 1986).

Domestic violence

The Domestic Proceedings (NI) Order 1980, as amended by the Family Homes and Domestic Violence (NI) Order 1998 (which increased the possible remedies and those who could apply for them), provides for a number of orders to be granted by the court to protect against violent persons in the home. These are:

- Occupation orders (art.11 of the Family Homes and Domestic Violence (NI) Order 1998): These replaced the "exclusion order" available under the Domestic Proceedings (NI) Order 1980. Occupation orders can be used for property disputes and they enable the applicant to stay in the home, or to enter the home, and can, amongst other things, prohibit a respondent from occupying it, or exclude him or her from an area around and including the home.

- Non-molestation orders (art.20 of the Family Homes and Domestic Violence (NI) Order 1998): These prohibit one person from "molesting" a child or another person "who is associated with the respondent".

- Matrimonial home rights orders (art.4 of the Family Home and Domestic Violence (NI) Order 1998): To apply for these orders the parties must be married, one spouse must be entitled legally to occupy the home and the other not, and the property in question must be a dwelling-house or intended to be used as the matrimonial home. The order can provide that the spouse in the home has a right not to be evicted or excluded unless the court decides otherwise.

Under article 3 of the Family Homes and Domestic Violence (NI) Order 1998, occupation orders and non-molestation orders are available to co-habitees (defined in the Order as "a man and a woman who are living together as husband and wife") and "associated persons" (those who "live or have lived in the same household, otherwise than merely by reason of one of them being the other's employee, tenant, lodger or boarder") as well as to married couples. Matrimonial home rights orders, on the other hand, are available only to married parties.

If the respondent contravenes an order, he or she commits an offence under article 25 of the Family Homes and Domestic Violence (NI) Order 1998 and can be punished with up to six months' imprisonment. Contravention is also an arrestable offence.

It is possible, depending on the factors taken into account by the court at the time, that evicting a person from his or her home under any of these orders may violate Article 8 of the ECHR (*Wiggins v UK*, 1978) and Article 1 of Protocol 1 (*Sporrong and Lonroth v Sweden*, 1982). However, laws which prohibit individuals from separating from a violent spouse may also violate Article 8 of the ECHR (*Airey v Ireland*, 1979).

Physical punishment of children has been held to be incompatible with the ECHR whether this takes place in state schools, private schools or in the home. Thus, in *A v UK* (1998), where a stepfather had beaten the child, the defence of "reasonable chastisement" (which succeeded in the English court) was held by the European Court of Human Rights not to be sufficient to prevent a violation of Article 3. Not all physical punishment will, however, amount to inhuman or degrading treatment in violation of Article 3. A recent English Court of Appeal decision has said that *A v UK* should lead to an amendment to the law on reasonable chastisement (*R v H (Reasonable Chastisement)*, 2001). The Office of Law Reform is currently consulting on what changes should be made to Northern Ireland's law on physical punishment of children at home. Legislation is expected within the next year or so.

There have been other cases where the failure of a public authority to protect children adequately against severe neglect and abuse by their parents has been held to be in violation of Articles 3 and 8 of the ECHR (*e.g. Z and others v UK*, 2001). In addition, the process by which decisions are made on how children in these situations should be cared for has to comply with Article 6 of the ECHR (*TP and KM v UK*, 2001, where the European Court of Human Rights also held that the removal of a child from her mother on the incorrect grounds that she was being abused by her mother's boyfriend was a violation of Article 8). The right to receive information, protected by Article 10 of the ECHR, may also be at issue. The European organs have held, for example, that an individual held in care should be able to see the files relating to his or her case (*Gaskin v UK*, 1989); see too Chapter 10.

Abortion

Unlike the rest of the United Kingdom, the Abortion Act 1967 does not apply in Northern Ireland, so the law on abortion is governed by the Offences Against the Person Act 1861, the Infant Life Preservation Act 1929 (enabling abortion to preserve the life of the mother) and its interpretation in *R v Bourne* (1938). It is thus an offence for a woman to unlawfully procure her own miscarriage or for someone to assist her in doing so, by the use of poisons, instruments or other things. However, a "lawful" abortion can be carried out if the woman would otherwise be a "physical and mental wreck", or where there is a risk to the life of the woman if the pregnancy were to be continued. Those performing an abortion can claim a defence under section 25 of the Criminal Justice (NI) Act 1945 if they act in good faith to preserve the life of the mother. A woman who is raped, however, cannot lawfully obtain an abortion on that ground alone and the availability of abortion in Northern Ireland is severely limited, with few women being able to find doctors willing to perform the procedure.

Many women wishing for an abortion now travel to England for the operation to be performed (the Northern Ireland Family Planning Association estimated this to be around 1,500 in the year 2000). Some abortions do appear to be carried out in Northern Ireland, but only where there is a serious risk to life or health and only up to five months of pregnancy. In March 2002 the result of a referendum in the Republic of Ireland rejected the government's proposal for imposing further restrictions on the abortion laws there. In July 2003 Kerr J rejected an application by the Family Planning Association for a court order requiring the Minister for Health and Social Services to provide guidance about the circumstances in which abortion may be obtained in Northern Ireland and to investigate whether women are receiving satisfactory termination of pregnancy services here. He said that the current law was not uncertain and that no evidence had been produced to show that the medical profession was incapable of recognising where abortion would be justified. On these grounds he ruled that the existing legal position in Northern Ireland was not incompatible with the ECHR (*Re Family Planning Association of Northern Ireland*, 2003).

Although the European Court of Human Rights has been unwilling to say that there is a right to an abortion under the Convention, cases have indicated that the authorities should not restrict the provision of information to women on how to travel elsewhere to obtain an abortion (*Open Door and Dublin Well Woman v Ireland*, 1992) under Article 10 of the ECHR. Alternatively, the prosecution of an individual campaigning against abortion for distributing leaflets prior to a general election was held to be a violation of Article 10 of the ECHR (*Bowman v UK*, 1998).

Sexual offences

The main legislation in Northern Ireland governing sexual offences still stems from the Victorian era (the Offences Against the Person Act 1861 and the Criminal Law Amendment Act 1885 but more recent amendments have been made by the Children and Young Persons Act (NI) 1968, the Sexual Offences (NI) Order 1978 and the

Homosexual Offences (NI) Order 1982. Further changes are contained in the proposed Criminal Justice (NI) Order 2003.

The age at which it is lawful to consent to sexual intercourse is 17 in Northern Ireland, whereas it is 16 in England and Wales. While it is not an offence for a girl to have sexual intercourse under the age of 17, and while it is possible for her to obtain contraception if she understands the treatment being given, a male having sexual intercourse with her would be acting unlawfully. The Criminal Justice (Children) (NI) Order 1998 provides in article 3 that no-one under the age of 10 can be guilty of any offence. Article 23 also provides that during preliminary investigation proceedings at a magistrates' court for a violent or sexual offence, a child cannot be called as a witness for the prosecution, although his or her statement may be admissible in evidence.

Article 6 of the same Order provides that if the Chief Constable believes someone is a sex offender (*i.e.* a person who has been convicted of a sexual offence under Part I of the Sex Offenders Act 1997, even if found not guilty by insanity or disability, and including a person who has been convicted outside the UK for an offence which is also an offence in the UK) and has reasonable cause to believe an order is necessary to protect the public from serious harm, the Chief Constable can apply to a court for a sexual offender's order. This order can impose prohibitions that are "necessary for the purpose of protecting the public from serious harm from the defendant". It remains in force for a minimum of five years and it is an offence if the individual acts contrary to the order during the specified period.

Rape

Rape is an offence under article 3(1) of the Sexual Offences (NI) Order 1978 and is at present committed if a man (over the age of 14) has unlawful sexual intercourse (defined as penetration of the vagina with a penis) with a woman or girl who did not consent, knowing that, or being reckless as to whether, she did not consent. If the woman is threatened by violence or is mentally vulnerable or drunk, so that she is not in a position to be able to consent, then rape is still committed. The proposed Criminal Justice (NI) Order 2003, by article 23, will remove the statutory presumption that a boy under 14 years of age is incapable of sexual intercourse and so will make it possible to convict such a boy of rape. Article 18 will redefine rape so that men can be recognised as victims just as much as women. It will also confirm in legislation, for the first time in Northern Ireland, the ruling by the House of Lords in 1991 that a wife is not presumed necessarily to have consented to having sex with her husband (*R v R*). Article 19 of the 2003 Order will also decriminalise anal intercourse between consenting heterosexual couples (nearly a decade after it was decriminalised in England and Wales). *In re McR* (2002), Kerr J held that section 62 of the Offences Against the Person Act 1861, in so far as it criminalises consensual anal intercourse between a man and a woman, is incompatible with Article 8 of the European Convention on Human Rights. This was the first, and to date the only, declaration of incompatibility issued in Northern Ireland under the Human Rights Act 1998. Article 19 will redress this anomaly.

The maximum sentence for rape is life imprisonment (s.48 of the Offences Against the Person Act 1861) and for attempted rape it is seven years. The Northern Ireland Court of Appeal has suggested that the minimum sentence for rape should be seven years where the case is contested (*R v McDonald and others*, 1989).

Unlawful sexual intercourse

Section 3(1) of the Criminal Law Amendment Act 1885 makes it an offence for an individual to procure sexual intercourse by threats or intimidation. The victim must be a woman. Similarly, section 3(2) makes it an offence to procure sexual intercourse by fraud and section 3(3) by drugs.

Incest

It is an offence under section 1 of the Punishment of Incest Act 1908 where a man has sexual intercourse with his grand-daughter, daughter, sister or mother, even if there is consent.

Indecency offences

Indecent assault is a crime under sections 52 (if the victim is a female) and 62 (if the victim is a male) of the Offences Against the Person Act 1861. What constitutes "indecency" is measured by what "right minded" persons consider to be so.

It is an offence to commit gross indecency with a child under the age of 14 (s.22 of the Children and Young Persons Act (NI) 1968). There is also the common law offence of outraging public decency, which must take place in public and be capable of being seen by at least two members of the public. Where a man exposes himself to a woman and this is done "wilfully, openly, lewdly and obscenely", there is an offence under section 4 of the Vagrancy Act 1824. In addition, indecent behaviour in a public place is an offence under section 9(1) of the Criminal Justice (Miscellaneous Provisions) Act (NI) 1968.

Homosexuality

In many areas of the law in Northern Ireland individuals who are gay, lesbian or bisexual fail to have the same protection as those who are heterosexual. It is only fairly recently that the law was amended, following a judgment by the European Court of Human Rights in *Dudgeon v UK* (1981), to decriminalise situations where a man over 21 commits buggery or gross indecency with another man in private with consent. By the Criminal Justice and Public Order Act 1994 the age for legal acts of this kind was reduced to 18 and then by the Sexual Offences (Amendment) Act 2000 it was further reduced in Northern Ireland to 17 (and in England to 16).

The highest UK court (the House of Lords) has recognised that a gay partner should be able to succeed to a tenancy on the death of his partner and should be considered as "family" for the purposes of the relevant statute (*Fitzpatrick v Sterling Housing Association Ltd*, 1999).

It is an offence for a man to "procure" another male to commit buggery with a third male (Homosexual Offences (NI) Order 1982, art.7(1)), and "procure" can cover the placing of adverts.

The Offences Against the Person Act 1861, in section 62, provides for an offence of indecent assault on a male. Article 21 of the proposed Criminal Justice (NI) Order 2003 increases the maximum penalty for this to 10 years in prison. A decision by the House of Lords that homosexual sadomasochist acts in private between consenting adults were not lawful (*R v Brown (Anthony)*, 1993) was found by the European Court of Human Rights not to be a violation of Article 8 of the ECHR, because the prohibition of such activities was "necessary in a democratic society...for the protection of health or morals" (*Laskey, Jaggard and Brown v UK*, 1997).

There are no laws prohibiting lesbianism, although indecent assault could be committed if one of the women involved did not consent.

An EU Framework Employment Directive, agreed in 2000 (see Chapter 11), requires states to introduce legislation to make unlawful discrimination in employment and training on the basis of sexual orientation.   The UK government is committed to introducing the necessary legal provisions by December 2003.

Transsexualism

The rights of transsexuals received a great boost when, in two cases from Britain decided in July 2002 (*Goodwin v UK* and *I v UK*), the Grand Chamber of the European Court of Human Rights held that the rights of post-operative transsexuals under Articles 8 and 12 of the ECHR had been broken because their "new" gender had not been officially recognised by the state for the purposes of employment law, pension law and marriage law.   The decisions represent a significant development in the European Court's thinking because in several earlier cases on similar facts it had been unwilling to find any breach of the Convention.   In *Rees v UK* (1985) the Court held that it was not a breach of Article 8 for a transsexual to be unable to alter the gender listed on his or her birth certificate.   In *X, Y and Z v UK* (1997) the Court held that there was no obligation on the authorities to recognise as the father on a child's birth certificate a transsexual (and therefore non-biological) father; the failure to recognise the relationship between the transsexual man and his female partner was not a violation of Article 8 or Article 14.   In *Sheffield and Horsham v UK* (1998) the Court again held that the refusal by the UK authorities to change the birth certificates of two transsexuals was not a violation of Articles 8, 12 or 14 of the ECHR.

It remains to be seen how far the European Court will go in extending transsexuals' rights.   At present, in English law, Article 8 of the ECHR does not make it possible to argue for gender reassignment surgery (*R v NW Lancashire Health Authority, ex parte A, D and G*, 2000), but this may change in the wake of *Goodwin v UK*.   In *Bellenger v Bellenger* (2003) the House of lords has decided that the Matrimonial Causes Act 1973 is incompatible with the ECHR in so far as it requires parties to a marriage to be of different genders at the time of birth rather than at the time of marriage.

The European Court of Justice has held that discriminating against a transsexual in an employment setting is contrary to EU law (*P v S*, 1996).   As a result the Sex Discrimination (Gender Reassignment) Regulations (NI) 1999 were enacted to prevent discrimination on the grounds of gender reassignment in any aspect of employment, including pay, and training (see also Chapter 13).

Further useful Addresses

- Coalition on Sexual Orientation (CoSO)
  2-6 Union Street
  Belfast BT1 2JF
  tel: 028 9031 9030
  www.coso.org.uk

- Family Planning Association Northern Ireland
  113 University Street
  Belfast BT7 1HP
  tel: 028 9032 5488
  www.fpa.org.uk

- Law Centre NI
  124 Donegall Street
  Belfast BT1 2GY
  tel: 028 9024 4401
  www.lawcentreni.org

- The Nexus Institute
  119 University Avenue
  Belfast BT7 1HP
  tel: 028 9032 6803
  (Derry/Londonderry: 028 7126 0566
  Enniskillen: 028 6632 0046
  Portadown: 028 3835 0588)

- Northern Ireland Human Rights Commission
  Temple Court
  39 North Street
  Belfast BT1 1NA
  tel: 028 9024 3987
  www.nihrc.org

- Office of Law Reform
  Lancashire House
  5 Linenhall Street
  Belfast BT2 8AA
  tel: 028 9054 2900
  www.olrni.gov.uk

Chapter 18

Children's Rights

Anne McKeown

This chapter deals with the rights of children to care and justice. Further information on the rights of children in other contexts is provided in Chapters 4, 16, 17 and 19. The international standards most relevant to this chapter are:

- the UN's Convention on the Rights of the Child 1989 (UNCRC),
- the UN's Standard Minimum Rules for the Administration of Juvenile Justice 1985 (known as the Beijing Rules),
- the UN's Declaration of Basic Principles of Justice for Victims of Crime and Abuse of Power 1985 (the Minnesota Declaration),
- the UN's Rules for the Protection of Juveniles Deprived of their Liberty 1990,
- the UN's Guidelines for the Prevention of Juvenile Delinquency 1990 (the Riyadh Guidelines), and of course
- the European Convention on Human Rights (ECHR) 1950.

The Children (NI) Order 1995

The general principles of the UNCRC are substantially reflected in the Children (NI) Order 1995 (the Order), the main legislation relating to the care of children in Northern Ireland. It mirrors the Children Act 1989 in England and Wales. Judicial interpretations of that Act can therefore be expected to be highly persuasive in Northern Ireland. The Department of Health, Social Services and Public Safety (DHSSPS, or the Department) has overall responsibility for implementing crucial aspects of the Order. There are four Health and Social Services Boards, each of which is responsible to the Department for services to children within its area. Several volumes of Guidance on the Order have been published by the Department.

The Health and Personal Social Services (NI) Order 1991, as amended in 1994, enabled the establishment of Health and Social Services Trusts. The legislation allows them to undertake the statutory childcare functions which are the responsibility of Boards. Boards purchase services from the Trusts and may stipulate conditions, but Trusts are entitled and expected to develop their own plans and priorities. In practice it is the Trusts which deliver all services to children. Boards may also purchase services from other sources. These arrangements are currently under review.

The Northern Ireland Assembly has passed the Health and Personal Social Services Act (NI) 2001, which establishes the Northern Ireland Social Care Council and provides for the registration, regulation and training of social care workers, including social workers, whether working in the statutory or voluntary sectors.

Boards, Trusts and the Social Care Council are public authorities and are therefore bound by the Human Rights Act 1998 to act in ways which are compatible with the ECHR. They also have to comply with the duties regarding equality of opportunity and good relations imposed by section 75 of the Northern Ireland Act 1998 (see Chapter 11).

Children in need

The Order gives extensive powers to Boards to avoid children being taken into care, by instead supporting families which are caring for children "in need". Article 17 defines a child as "in need" if:

- he or she is unlikely to achieve or maintain a reasonable standard of health or development without the provision of services,
- his or her health or development is likely to be significantly impaired, or further impaired, without the provision of such services, or
- he or she is disabled.

This definition is open to variable interpretation, particularly in relation to "a reasonable standard of health or development". Elsewhere in the Order the test of "significant harm" requires the comparison of a child's health or development with "that which could reasonably be expected of a similar child" (art.50(3)). If such comparisons were used to distinguish those "in need", this could exclude children who are disadvantaged because of poverty, culture, ethnicity or lack of resources. The Order must, however, be interpreted in such a way as to be compatible with the ECHR and the authority's obligation to promote equality of opportunity.

Duties of Boards in respect of children in need

Article 18 of the Order provides that:

It shall be the general duty of every authority...to safeguard and promote the welfare of children within its area who are in need, and...to promote the upbringing of such children by their families, by providing a range and level of personal social services appropriate to those children's needs.

Services may be provided to the child in need, his or her family, or any member of the family, "if the service is provided with a view to safeguarding and promoting the child's welfare" (art.18(3)). While assistance may be unconditional, authorities may charge for services, having regard to a family's ability to pay. People in receipt of various state benefits are exempt from such charges. Services provided may include "giving assistance in kind or, in exceptional circumstances, in cash" (art.18(6)). The provision is not used in circumstances where an application for social security benefits, loans or grants would be appropriate.

To enable Boards to carry out their functions, specific duties and powers are set out in Schedule 2 to the Order. These include duties to take reasonable steps to identify the extent to which there are children in need within the authority's area, to publish information on services and to ensure this is received by those who might benefit from it. The authority must maintain a register of disabled children and provide services enabling them to lead lives which are as normal as possible. Services should prevent the neglect and abuse of children and authorities should take steps to reduce the need to bring criminal or care proceedings in relation to children. Advice, guidance, counselling and occupational, social, cultural or recreational activities may be provided through family centres or elsewhere. When providing day care facilities and encouraging people to act as foster parents, authorities should consider the racial groups to which children belong. In several instances, the Board must provide such services only to the extent it considers appropriate.

Day care, childminding and other services

Day care is defined (art.19(1)) as "any form of care or supervised activity provided for children during the day." Authorities *must* provide day care for children in need aged five or under who are not yet attending schools, and they *may* provide it for other such children.

Boards (through Trusts) are empowered to provide training, advice, guidance and counselling for day care workers, but are not obliged to do so by the Order.

Authorities *must* provide care and supervised activities outside school hours and during school holidays for school children in need and *may* provide such facilities for any school child. Provision should take account of facilities maintained by others, including district councils or Education and Library Boards.

The range of services provided by Trusts can include day nurseries, playgroups, out of school clubs, holiday schemes, parent and toddler groups, toy libraries, drop-in centres and play-buses. They may also resource community, voluntary and church schemes, such as parents' self-help groups. Bodies whose help is requested, such as Education and Library Boards, are obliged to comply with the request if this is compatible with their own statutory duties. A Health Board, in conjunction with the appropriate district council and Education and Library Boards, must review the total provision of day care, childminding and other services at least once every three years (art.20). In practice, Boards work with a broad range of other agencies to develop Children's Services Plans.

Registration of childminding and day care services

Both childminders and persons wishing to provide day care must first register with the relevant Trust. This register is open to the public. Schools, hospitals, children's homes and nursing homes are exempt from definitions of day care and childminding and are not required to register. Premises where day care is provided on less than six days in any year are also exempt from registration but the person providing care must still notify the relevant Trust in writing before the first occasion when the premises are to be used.

Article 119 of the Children (NI) Order 1995 defines a childminder as a person who looks after children under 12 years of age, for reward, for more than two hours in any day. Exemptions from this definition include parents, relatives, people with parental responsibility, foster parents and nannies. A childminder is not a social care worker as defined in section 2 of the Health and Personal Social Services Act (NI) 2001.

A person may be disqualified from being registered to provide childminding or day care services, because, for example, he or she has been convicted of a prescribed (*e.g.* violent or sexual) offence. No one disqualified from being registered can be employed, or have a financial or management interest, in the provision of day care without disclosing the disqualification to the authority and obtaining its written authorisation. A Board may refuse to register an applicant if that person or any person residing on the premises or employed or likely to be employed on the premises is not "fit to look after" or "be in the proximity of" children under the age of 12 (art.124).

Boards may impose such reasonable requirements on childminders (art.125) and persons providing day care for young children, as they consider appropriate. Currently there is no requirement that such persons hold a relevant childcare qualification. The conditions and requirements which do apply regarding maintenance of premises, food hygiene and so on are set out in the Children (NI) Order Regulations and Guidance, Volume 2. One set of Regulations exempts certain supervised activities from the requirement to register. These include

> *uniformed organisations and religious activities for children, leisure and recreational activities, extra-curricular activities occurring mainly in schools, activities designed to enhance a child's skills and attainments including dancing, sports related activities and education tuition.*

Staff and volunteers

The Department has issued "Our Duty to Care", a set of guidelines on the recruitment, training and selection of all staff or volunteers who work with children. The Department has also extended the remit and use of the Pre-employment Consultancy Service (PECS), which had previously been established following the Kincora sex abuse scandal. PECS provides a vetting service said to "complement" standard recruitment procedures by giving prospective employers access to information thought to have a bearing on prospective employees' or volunteers' suitability. These checks are available to any organisation whenever the post (paid or unpaid) involves substantial access to children and the organisation's recruitment and selection procedures comply with the principles set out in "Our Duty to Care". The Children's Homes Regulations (NI) 1996 oblige certain childcare employers to notify the DHSSPS of any conduct suggesting that a person may not be suitable to work with children.

Part V of the Police Act 1997 is soon to be extended to Northern Ireland. It will then be possible for the police to check a person's name against statutory lists held in England, Wales a. Protection of Children and Vulnerable Adults (NI) C PECS on a statutory basis, provides a new tribunal . against registration and allows courts to make "disqualifi, preventing certain people from working with children. Th, extends the number of organisations required to make r, DHSSPS of people who may be unsuitable to work with chila.   The Order was not yet in force as of 1 March 2003. At the moment appeals against names being added to the PECS list are made to the DHSSPS itself. Complaints regarding the maladministration of the process can be made in the normal way to the Ombudsman; complaints regarding the reasonableness of decisions can be judicially reviewed (see Chapter 2).

Investigation of abuse and neglect

Many professionals can be involved in the protection of children – social workers, police officers, probation workers, medical practitioners, health visitors, nursing staff and teachers. Area Child Protection Committees have been established at Board level to monitor and review the child protection policies of the relevant agencies and to oversee the work of Child Protection Panels (CPP), which operate at Trust level. The CPP's role is to implement policy and to facilitate multidisciplinary working to prevent, investigate and treat child abuse. In practice, social workers and the police will have the key roles in dealing with more serious allegations of child abuse and neglect. The police will be concerned to investigate whether any offence has been committed, while the social workers will focus on the child's welfare and the family's capacity to provide care.

When a child discloses abuse to any professional, that person must report it immediately. Failure to do so may result in disciplinary action or, with the permission of the DPP, the person may be prosecuted for failure to report a crime (Criminal Law Act (NI) 1967, s.5). In circumstances where a Trust (or NSPCC) has reasonable cause to suspect that a child "is suffering or is likely to suffer significant harm", it has a duty to investigate (1995 Order, art.66). An assessment of the needs of the child and family should be undertaken. Where social workers have such concerns about a child's welfare, they should first seek the voluntary co-operation of parents in making an assessment, and may provide services to help the family care for the child. "Harm" is defined as ill-treatment or impairment of health or development, compared with that which could reasonably be expected of a similar child (1995 Order, art.50(3)). Health is defined as physical or mental health, and development as physical, intellectual, emotional, social or behavioural development. "Ill-treatment" includes forms which are not physical.

If there is an allegation that child abuse has occurred, a strategy discussion will normally be held between social workers and police within 24 hours of receiving the referral or discovering the facts. The "Protocol for Joint Investigation by Social Workers and Police Officers of Alleged and Suspected Cases of Child Abuse" will govern the investigation process. The police have established special Child Abuse and Rape Enquiry (CARE) units to deal with cases of child abuse and sexual offences (see also Chapter 17).

Volume 6 of the 1995 Order's Guidance and Regulations states that within 15 days of a formal (social work) investigation being initiated, a child protection case conference should be held to decide whether there is sufficient concern to place the child's name on the Child Protection Register. The updated Guidance is called "Co-operating to Safeguard Children". While the Guidance says that information is shared on a need to know basis, all agencies in contact with the child may, initially, be invited to attend. If it is decided to place the child's name on the register the case will be reviewed in six months' time. Family members, including the alleged abuser and the child under discussion, may also be invited to attend the whole or part of these case conferences. If the alleged abuser is not heard the case conference may be held to have acted unfairly and in breach of natural justice (*R v Norfolk County Council, ex parte M*, 1989). Decisions about who attends a case conference have traditionally been taken by the professionals, but the child and relevant others now have rights to be consulted on how they wish to make their views known and considered, on who attends the case conferences and on the exchange of information between the agencies, where this would affect the person's ECHR rights such as the right to a fair hearing (Art. 6) and the right to private and family life (Art. 8).

On registration of a child, the case conference should set a time limit for the completion of a comprehensive assessment and an initial child protection plan. This plan is a written agreement drawn up with parents and carers. It outlines the roles and expectations of agencies and carers with regard to the child's care and protection. A child may be "de-registered" by a child protection case conference if it is believed that circumstances have changed significantly and the child is no longer at risk. In childcare cases, a person's right to information may be restricted in order to prevent information being disclosed which could place the child at risk (*Re M (A Minor) (Disclosure of Material)*, 1990).

The child's evidence

If a child is interviewed jointly by a police officer from the CARE unit and a social worker, consideration will be given to whether he or she should have a parent, relative or friend present. Normal practice is that a trusted adult will be available to the child in an adjoining room. The need for medical examination and for video-recording of interviews will also be considered. Such recordings may be used in either civil or criminal court proceedings. The Children's Evidence (NI) Order 1995 has inserted provisions into the Police and Criminal Evidence (NI) Order 1989 to allow a video-recording of an interview with a child to be used as the child's evidence-in-chief in criminal proceedings, subject to certain conditions. A Memorandum of Good Practice has been issued by the Northern Ireland Office on how video-recorded interviews should be conducted.

The Children's Evidence (NI) Order 1995 allows for a notice of transfer to be issued by the Director of Public Prosecutions (DPP) if the DPP is satisfied that there is enough evidence to commit a defendant to trial. This enables the case to be heard by the Crown Court without a preliminary hearing in a magistrates' court. There is no appeal against a notice of transfer. At trial, the child's evidence and/or cross-examination may be through a television link so that the alleged victim does not have to see the alleged abuser while giving evidence. The NSPCC provides a young witness support service to children required to give evidence in some Crown Courts. This is expected to be extended to all Crown Courts within the next two years. The absence of a scheme in some courts may be a breach of children's right not to be discriminated against in relation to a fair hearing (Arts.6 and 14 of the ECHR).

The Criminal Evidence (NI) Order 1999 has not yet been implemented. It substantially mirrors aspects of the Youth Justice and Criminal Evidence Act 1999 in England and gives new rights to *all* children under 17 years (and to other vulnerable witnesses) to have special measures taken to protect them when giving evidence. These measures can include screening, live video links, clearing the public from the court, dispensing with wigs and gowns, video-taping the cross-examination and any re-examination of the witness in advance of the trial and allowing the use of aids to communication such as an interpreter or a sign board for persons with a disability. The absence of similar support and protection for young or vulnerable defendants in Northern Ireland may infringe the defendants' ECHR rights in relation to a fair hearing.

Commissioner for Children and Young People

As noted in Chapter 2, a Commissioner for Children and Young People (NI) Order was enacted at Westminster in February 2003. It establishes the office of Commissioner to protect and promote children's rights, advise authorities and challenge them when necessary. There are concerns, however, that the powers available to the Commissioner may not be extensive enough to provide effective mechanisms of redress to children whose rights may have been breached, especially in the criminal justice system.

Physical punishment

The Office of Law Reform has recently published a consultation paper on the physical punishment of children and a debate has taken place in the Assembly. Children's rights groups have led a strong lobby for legal reform to ensure that children are no longer subject to any physical punishment and that an education programme on positive discipline is provided to support parents. However legislation on the matter is still awaited. Meanwhile article 36 of the Education and Libraries (NI) Order 2003 ensures the abolition of corporal punishment even in independent schools in Northern Ireland.

The employment of children

The employment of children is mainly regulated by articles 133-148 of the Children (NI) Order 1995 and the Employment of Children Regulations (NI) 1996. In general, no child under the age of 13 can be employed at all, and no child who is 13 or older can work before 7.00 am or after 7.00 pm or for more than two hours on any one school day (art.135). Nor can a child be employed in street trading or in any occupation likely to be injurious to his or her health or education. But children *can* be licensed by an Education and Library Board to take part in a public performance or (if 13 or older) to train for performances, even of a dangerous nature.

An officer of an Education and Library Board, or a police officer, can be granted a warrant to enter premises to make inquiries concerning a child if there is reasonable cause to believe the regulations are being contravened. Any person employing a child in contravention of the law (or any parent allowing it) can be fined up to £1,000, while any child engaged in street trading can be fined up to £200 (art.147). Employers should notify the appropriate Education and Library Board at least seven days prior to the employment of a child. Parents must consent to the child being employed and a medical practitioner must confirm that the occupation is not likely to be injurious to the life, limb, health or education of the child. Under the Working Time Regulations (NI) 1998 extra health and safety requirements were introduced for the protection of workers who are over the school-leaving age but still under 18.

Children and the civil courts

Article 164(4) of the Children (NI) Order 1995 provides that a juvenile court "sitting for the purpose of exercising any jurisdiction covered by or under [the] Order may be known as a family proceedings court." The Children and Young Persons Act (NI) 1968 continues to apply in respect of the constitution of these courts, *i.e.* they comprise a resident magistrate and two lay panellists. Under the Children (Allocation of Proceedings) Order (NI) 1996, seven family proceedings courts have been established, one in each county court division.

Applications will normally begin in the family proceedings court unless other proceedings in relation to the child are pending in the High Court or the county court. Applications may also be transferred from the family proceedings court to a specialist county court (known as a Care Centre) if the proceedings are exceptionally grave, important or complex. Applications may then be transferred from the Care Centre to the High Court if the issues are considered appropriate for determination in the High Court and it would be in the best interests of the child. Any proceedings which have been transferred may be returned to the original court if the transfer criterion no longer applies. Appeals from a family proceedings court will be to a Care Centre, which for the purposes of the appeal will sit without lay assessors. Where cases have already been transferred to the Care Centre, decisions of that court may be appealed to the High Court and thereafter to the Court of Appeal.

Court orders and child protection

Child's welfare paramount

Article 3 of the Children (NI) Order 1995 requires a court determining any question relating to a child's upbringing to regard the child's welfare as "the paramount consideration". The article provides the court with what has become known as a "welfare checklist". This includes consideration of the child's ascertainable wishes and feelings, his or her physical, emotional and educational needs, the likely effect on the child of any change in circumstances, his or her age, sex, background and other relevant characteristics, the capacity of the child's parents to meet his or her needs, and any harm the child has suffered or is at risk of suffering. The direction that the court "shall not make (any order) unless it considers that to do so would be better for the child than making no order at all" establishes a presumption of non-intervention. The court must also have "regard to the general principle that any delay in determining the question is likely to prejudice the welfare of the child" and so must "draw up a timetable with a view to determining (any) question without delay" (art.11).

Assessment and protection orders

In some situations social workers will be able to ensure the child's safety by persuading the alleged abuser to leave the home. Paragraph 6 of Schedule 2 to the 1995 Order empowers Trusts to provide accommodation for an alleged abuser. Alternatively the "non-accused" parent may apply for a non-molestation order (Family Homes and Domestic Violence (NI) Order 1998, art.20) (see also Chapter 17). A child under 16 years may apply for such an order with leave of the court, which has to be satisfied that he or she has sufficient understanding to make the application.

Trust and NSPCC social workers (Children (NI) Order 1995, art.49) may apply for a child assessment order (art.62) in circumstances where there is insufficient information to be sure that a child is suffering significant harm, but where parents will not co-operate to allow an assessment to be made. Such an order has a maximum duration of seven days and the court directs the type and nature of the assessment to be carried out. A child of sufficient understanding may, however, refuse to undergo any medical, psychiatric or other assessment. For such an assessment the child will remain at home, separated from his or her parents only if this is necessary to comply with court directions, *e.g.* for medical or other interviews.

If a court, hearing an application for a child assessment order, becomes satisfied that there are grounds to make an emergency protection order, it must make this order instead. Any person, moreover, may apply directly to the court for an emergency protection order (art.63). In certain circumstances (*e.g.* at weekends or at night) such an order may be issued by a resident magistrate or member of the juvenile court panel sitting alone. The court will make an emergency order only if satisfied that there is reasonable cause to believe that the child is likely to suffer significant harm if he or she is not removed from the situation (*e.g.* the family home) or does not remain in the situation (*e.g.* in hospital recovering from an injury). These orders last for up to eight days and can be extended for a further seven days. Where the court is satisfied that it would benefit the child, and there is someone to care for him or her, it may include an exclusion requirement in the order, removing a named person rather than the child from the family home. Certain people, including the child and his or her parents, may apply for the discharge of an emergency order after a period of 72 hours, but no appeal can be made against court decisions to make, extend or discharge an order (*Essex County Council v F*, 1993). An emergency order grants parental responsibility to the applicant whilst it is in force. This allows the applicant to take whatever action is necessary to safeguard the child's welfare and comply with DHSSPS requirements.

In practice it will usually be Trust or NSPCC social workers who apply for emergency protection orders. Although such orders allow for the removal of a child from the family home, the applicant is still required to ensure the child has reasonable contact with parents, anyone else who has parental responsibility for him or her, and others, such as people he or she was living with before the order was made. However, the court may restrict such contact if it considers this appropriate (art.63(6)) and may direct that medical, psychiatric and other assessments be made, subject to the right of a child of sufficient understanding to refuse to submit to examination or assessment. The police have powers to take children into police protection for up to 72 hours where a child might otherwise suffer significant harm (art.65). They may also assist in searching premises for a child in need of emergency protection, if the court issues a warrant to this effect.

If there continue to be concerns regarding children subject to child assessment orders, emergency protection orders or police protection, application may be made by Trusts or the NSPCC for a care or supervision order (see below). Alternatively, where concerns about a child's health or development relate to specific matters rather than the parents' general capacity to provide care or control, social workers may seek leave of the court to apply for an order under article 8 of the Children (NI) Order, if the child is under 16 years. Article 8 prohibits the making of residence or contact orders in favour of a Trust, but a "specific issue order" or a "prohibited steps order" can be obtained (see also Chapter 17). A specific issue order can be made if, for example, a child needs treatment, such as a blood transfusion, where parents refuse to consent or cannot be contacted. A prohibited steps order can be made to prevent parents from doing something which could prejudice the child's health or development. Even if social workers apply for a care or supervision order, the court has power to make an article 8 order of its own motion if it believes that this would be the most appropriate course of action.

Care and supervision orders

Where a Trust or the NSPCC apply to the court for a care or supervision order, the court has power to make either order irrespective of the preferred option of the applicant. Decisions to make either order may be made only if the court is satisfied that the child is suffering or likely to suffer significant harm which is attributable to a lack of parental care or to the child being beyond parental control (art.50(2)). The harm the child is experiencing must be current or likely to occur in the future. Events which have happened in the past are relevant to the extent that they might influence present or future conduct.

To ensure that the court's decisions are based on the known facts, the rule that parties to litigation may obtain an expert's report which remains privileged unless the party wishes to rely on it may be overridden in children's cases. All relevant reports should be disclosed. This applies to the Trust (*see R v Hampshire County Council, ex parte K*, 1990) as well as to all other parties in care proceedings (see *Oxfordshire County Council v M*, 1994).

The court may make interim care or supervision orders if satisfied that there are reasonable grounds for believing that the grounds for making a full order exist (art.57(2)). When making an interim care order, the court may exclude a named person from the family home rather than removing the child, provided a parent or other person is able and willing to live there with the child and give care to him or her

(Children (NI) Order 1995, art.57A, inserted by the Family Homes and Domestic Violence (NI) Order 1998). The maximum period of an interim order is, in the first instance, eight weeks. Subsequent orders may be made for maximum periods of four weeks.

Supervision orders have an effect for a period of one year and may be extended to up to three years (Sch.3, para.6). The order can include directions as to psychiatric and medical treatment, with the child's consent. The supervisor may require the child to live at a specified place and to participate in activities. He or she should "advise, assist and befriend the supervised child" (art.54).

The effect of a care order is to give the designated authority parental responsibility for the child, who must be received into its care. The Trust shares parental responsibility with parents and others who already have it. The Trust has, however, power to limit the extent to which any person may exercise his or her parental responsibility for the child in certain circumstances, if this is reasonable for the purposes of promoting the child's welfare. Children in care should normally be allowed contact with parents, guardians and others with whom they resided prior to the order being made. Trusts can apply to the court for permission to refuse contact with any person (art.53) and may refuse contact itself in any case, on an emergency basis, provided the refusal does not last for more than seven days. Parties to care proceedings are invited to comment on arrangements for contact before a care order is made.

No care or supervision order may be made with respect to a child who has reached the age of 17 (or 16, in the case of a child who is married (art.50(4)). Any care or supervision order may be discharged by the court on application of the child or person who has parental responsibility for him or her or the authority designated by the order. Where a care order is discharged the court has power to substitute a supervision order, if it wishes to do so.

Guardians *ad litem*

In almost all of the above public law cases, the court will appoint a guardian *ad litem* who will be under a duty to safeguard the interests of the child. To ensure the independence of the guardian *ad litem*, a separate agency has been established known as the Guardian *ad Litem* Agency, and it has a panel of guardians, who are qualified, experienced social workers. Once appointed, a guardian's role is to investigate all the circumstances of the case and make a report to the court to assist it to take decisions in the best interests of the child. The guardian will consult parents and others as necessary. He or she will also examine the Trust's plans for the child and may make recommendations in respect of these. He or she has a right of access to and copies of any records relevant to the Trust or NSPCC's contact with the child and may present any part of any record as evidence in court. Where the guardian believes that acquiescing to the child's wishes is not in his or her best interests, both the child's view and the guardian's should be reported to the court.

The guardian will appoint a solicitor to act for the child if the court has not already done so and where the child is not of sufficient understanding the guardian will instruct the solicitor on the child's behalf. Article 60 empowers the court to appoint a solicitor for any child whether or not a guardian *ad litem* is appointed, provided a child of sufficient understanding wishes to instruct a solicitor and/or this appears to the court to be in the child's best interests. Solicitors should act on the instructions of a child of sufficient understanding in the normal way. There is no definition in the Order of "sufficient understanding". The principle has, however, been tested in relation to medical decisions. A child of 16 years can consent to medical or other treatment without the consent of a parent or guardian (Age of Majority Act (NI) 1969, s.4). A younger child may do so if he or she fully understands the nature and implications of the proposed treatment (*Gillick* v *West Norfolk and Wisbech Area Health Authority,* 1986). However, a younger child who refuses life-saving treatment may be given such treatment if the High Court in its inherent jurisdiction or anyone with parental responsibility for the child consents to it (R*e W,* 1992). See too Chapter 17.

Accommodation for children

A Trust *must* provide accommodation for children in need whenever the person caring for them is prevented from doing so for whatever reason (art.21(1)(c)) and *may* provide accommodation for any child if it considers that this would safeguard or promote his or her welfare. The Trust should ascertain the child's views, if he or she is able to express them. The Trust does not acquire parental responsibility by providing accommodation. While the child's daily care has been delegated to the Trust (art.5(8)), it cannot take major decisions or continue to care for the child without the consent of a person with parental responsibility. In emergencies, where such persons cannot be contacted or do not consent, *e.g.* to medical treatment, the Trust may seek leave to apply for an article 8 order (see p.378).

Any child found lost or abandoned may also be provided with accommodation, and so an emergency protection order will not be required unless the child is also believed to be at risk of significant harm. A person who has reached the age of 16, but is under 21, may be accommodated by a Trust if his or her welfare "is likely to be seriously prejudiced if it does not provide" such accommodation. When a person of this age group agrees to be accommodated, the Trust need not discharge him or her at the request of a person with parental responsibility.

Looked after children

Regardless of whether a child is accommodated by the Trust or placed by the court on a care order, certain general rules apply (Arrangement for Placement of Children (General) Regulations (NI) 1996). No child should be placed in a children's home before other options such as family placements are considered and all children admitted to care must have a written care plan. Care planning should aim to promote the child's welfare in consultation with the child and family, having regard to their wishes and feelings. Each child's case should be reviewed within two weeks of the child being admitted to care, reviewed again not more than three months later and thereafter every six months (Review of Children's Cases Regulations (NI) 1996, reg.3). If the child is accommodated for only short periods (not more than four weeks in any single period or more than 90 days in any 12 month period) the review will take place within three months of the beginning of the first short period, and six monthly thereafter while the case continues.

Reviews take the form of meetings, which the child, the family and relevant professionals are invited to attend. Children can make their views known in writing, on tape or by other means. A child's religious, linguistic, cultural and ethnic background must be taken into account in making plans for the child.

Fostering

For children whose relatives cannot care for them, foster care is the preferred way of providing care. The Children (NI) Order Regulations and Guidance, Volume 3, "Family Placements and Private

Fostering", govern the recruitment, management and support of foster carers. The Foster Placement (Children) Regulations 1996 regulate the assessment, approval and registration of foster parents. The approving authority must review the foster parent's approval and ensure that his or her home continues to be suitable at least annually. Foster parents should, where possible, be of the same religious persuasion as the child, or must give a written undertaking that the child will be brought up in his or her own religious persuasion (see *Re T*, 2001). The Trust can remove a child from a foster placement immediately if it appears "that continuation of the placement would be detrimental to the welfare of the child" (reg.7). If a child has lived with foster parents for a period of at least three years within the five years before making the application, the foster parent can apply for a residence order in respect of the child (Children (NI) Order 1995, art.9). The foster parent will then have parental responsibility for the child while the residence order remains in force.

The Children (Private Arrangements for Fostering) Regulations (NI) 1996 are the statutory rules which apply to situations where children are placed with foster carers by private agreement with their parents. A foster parent must notify the Trust not less than six weeks before receiving the child, unless he or she was already caring for the child before becoming a foster parent or had to do so in an emergency. In the latter circumstances, the authority should be notified not more than 48 hours after the arrangements begin. A social worker will visit the child within one week of the fostering arrangement beginning and then at intervals of not more than six weeks in the first year, and three monthly in any second or subsequent year. The foster parents and their accommodation will be assessed to ensure that they are suitable and that the child's health and educational needs will be met. The foster parent must notify the Trust of any termination of placement.

Children's homes

The Children (NI) Order Regulations and Guidance, Volume 4, "Residential Care", govern the care of children admitted to children's homes run by Trusts, voluntary societies or private businesses. All voluntary and privately run homes must be registered. These children's homes, and those run by Trusts, will be inspected by officers of the relevant Board's Registration and Inspection Unit. Registration of voluntary or privately run children's homes may be subject to such conditions as the authority thinks fit and will be reviewed annually.

Appeals against decisions of the authority on matters relating to registration can be made to a Registered Homes Tribunal. A person who has been disqualified from fostering a child privately cannot be involved in the management of, employed in or have a financial interest in, a voluntary or privately run home without disclosing this to the Trust and obtaining its written permission to do so.

The Guidance requires children's homes to be adequately staffed to meet the aims and objectives of the Inspection Unit, having regard to the age, sex and characteristics of the children. In maintaining good order and discipline, staff should promote the participation of children in decision-making and take account of the child's age, understanding and competence. The Guidance states that formal (non-physical) sanctions should be used sparingly and, if administered, recorded in a separate logbook. Sanctions specifically prohibited by the regulations include corporal punishment, deprivation of food and drink, restriction or refusal of visits or communications, requiring a child to wear distinctive or inappropriate clothing, withholding medication, intentional deprivation of sleep and intimate physical searches. Staff may refuse a child permission to go out, or require a child to pay for or contribute to the repair or replacement of any items stolen or damaged.

Holding a child is permitted, for instance when leading a child away from destructive or disruptive behaviour by the hand, arm or by means of an arm around his or her shoulder. Holding is distinguished from physical restraint by the degree of force used. Holding would discourage; restraint would prevent an action. Physical restraint is permitted by the Children's Homes Regulations (NI) 1996 to the extent that it is "action immediately necessary to prevent injury to any person or serious damage to property" (also see Criminal Law Act (NI) 1967, s.3 regarding use of reasonable force, discussed in Chapter 3). Afterwards the child should be counselled on why restraint was necessary and be given an opportunity to put his or her side of the story. The residential social worker's line manager should discuss the incident with him or her within 24 hours and a full report should be prepared within 48 hours. The child should also be interviewed by someone not directly connected to the home in question, for example the field social worker. The frequency with which physical control is used should be monitored.

Complaints about the use of restraint can be made under the child protection or complaints procedures. Allegations of assault can be reported to the police in the normal way. Responsible authorities (Trusts, voluntary organisations, and privately run children's homes) are required to have a procedure for considering representations, including complaints, about children's services and to publicise these. The complainant can be the child, a person with parental responsibility or any person considered to have sufficient interest in the welfare of the child. The complaint may be written or oral. Where problems are unresolved, the complaints procedure should be initiated, an investigation should take place and the complainant should be notified of the outcome of the investigation.

Secure accommodation

Article 44 of the 1995 Order and the Children (Secure Accommodation) Regulations (NI) 1996 provide the statutory framework for the restriction of the liberty of children in care.

A child should not be kept in secure accommodation unless he or she "has a history of absconding and is likely to abscond from any other...accommodation" and, if absconding, "is likely to suffer significant harm" or to injure him- or herself or other persons if kept in other accommodation. A child should not continue to have his or her liberty restricted once the criteria cease to apply. The protection of others is, however, considered a valid reason for the continued use of secure accommodation. (art.26(5) and *Re M (A Minor) (Secure Accommodation Order)*, 1995). The 1995 Order and the Regulations must now be interpreted in such a way as to be compatible with Article 5 of the ECHR (the right to liberty and security).

No child under the age of 13 may be placed in secure accommodation without the prior approval of the DHSSPS. Before seeking such approval, Trusts should first discuss the case with the Social Services Inspectorate. Regulation 3 prohibits the use of secure accommodation for children in certain circumstances, including when children are detained under any provision of the Mental Health (NI) Order 1986 or when they are over 16 and are being provided with accommodation under the Trust's discretionary powers. Regulation 6 sets a maximum period of 72 hours, either consecutively or in aggregate in any period of 28 days, for the restriction of a child's liberty without court authority, unless the 72 hour period expires late on a Saturday, a Sunday or a public holiday. In this instance the period will be treated as if it did not expire until 12 noon on the next working day. The maximum period a court may authorise a child to be kept in secure accommodation is three months in the first instance, although on subsequent applications the court may authorise secure accommodation for six months at a time.

No court may exercise its powers to restrict a child's liberty unless the child is legally represented in court, except where a child who has been informed of the right to legal aid, and given the opportunity to do so, has refused or failed to apply for such aid. A guardian *ad litem* should be appointed, unless the court does not consider this necessary to protect the welfare of the child. Article 166 makes provision for appeals against court decisions to authorise or refuse to authorise restriction of a child's liberty. The Trust must also appoint three persons to review the placement within one month of its commencement and thereafter at three monthly intervals.

The child's care should also be reviewed in the normal way in accordance with article 45. Trusts providing secure accommodation must keep records of occasions when the child is locked up alone in any room other than during usual bedtime hours. Secure accommodation is inspected by the relevant Board's Registration and Inspection Unit and the DHSSPS oversees these Units through the Social Services Inspectorate. The Justice (NI) Act 2002 will introduce custody care orders, which allow 10 to 13 year olds found guilty of certain offences to be held in secure accommodation.

Aftercare, advice and assistance

Article 35 of the 1995 Order empowers Trusts to provide advice and assistance to persons who were in various forms of care at any time after reaching their sixteenth birthday and who are still under 21 years of age. Currently, a young person who qualifies for assistance may have been looked after by a Trust, a voluntary organisation, or a registered children's home. Young people who were accommodated for a consecutive period of at least three months by an Education and Library Board, a residential care home, a hospital, any other prescribed accommodation, or who were privately fostered, also qualify, even if the period of three months began before the child reached the age of 16. The Trust *must* provide assistance to young people if they were looked after by the Trust or a voluntary organisation and *may* provide it if the young people were accommodated in the other circumstances described (art.35(4)). The conditions are that the young person must ask the Trust for help of a kind it can give. The Trust must be satisfied that the person needs such help and that the agency or person previously caring for him or her cannot give it. The Trust can make payments and give grants in relation to the young person's employment and education, even if he or she reaches the age of 21 before the course is completed. The Children (Leaving Care) Act (NI) 2002 will provide authorities with additional duties and powers, including duties to assist with continuing education, to appoint personal advisers and to develop pathway plans for children leaving care who are aged 16 or over.

While voluntary organisations and privately run homes do not have a statutory duty to provide aftercare, they must prepare the young person for the time when he or she ceases to be accommodated by them (arts.76(1)(c) and 92(1)(c) respectively). Young people have a right to make complaints in relation to the aftercare provided to them.

Children with a disability

All of the provisions already mentioned in this chapter apply to disabled children as they do to others. By article 2(2) of the 1995 Order a child is defined as disabled if he or she is:

> blind, deaf, or dumb or suffering from mental disorder of any kind or substantially and permanently handicapped by illness, injury or congenital deformity or such other disability as may be prescribed.

(See also art.3 of the Mental Health (NI) Order 1986 for a definition of mental disorder, and Chapter 16 above.) While Trusts must keep a register of disabled children, this is designed to help planning and monitoring services. Parents do not have to agree to their child being registered and provision of services is not dependent upon it. Publications relating to services for children with a disability should take account of the needs of people with communication difficulties.

Some children with a disability will have their needs assessed under the Chronically Sick and Disabled Persons (NI) Act 1978, the Education and Libraries (NI) Order 1986, the Disabled Persons (NI) Act 1989 or other legislation, and Trusts need not make a separate assessment to meet their obligations under the Children (NI) Order 1995.

Trusts have a duty to ensure that the welfare of children being provided with accommodation in a hospital, school, private hospital, residential care or nursing home or by an Education and Library Board is being adequately safeguarded and promoted. Trusts should be notified if the child has been or is intended to be accommodated in such facilities for a period of at least three months.

Article 175 empowers a person authorised by the Trust to enter any residential care home, nursing home or private hospital within the Trust's area for the purpose of ensuring that the child's welfare is safeguarded. There are no such powers in respect of Education and Library Board establishments. The standards to be met by any of these establishments are lower than those required of residential children's homes. In so far as they are used predominately by disabled children, it is possible that the lower standards infringe the disabled child's right under Article 14 of the ECHR not to be discriminated against in relation to enjoyment of the rights to a fair hearing (Art.6) and to a private and family life (Art.8). Public authorities also have a positive duty to promote equality of opportunity regardless of disability (s.75 of the Northern Ireland Act 1998).

Children and criminal justice

The main legislation governing the treatment of children in the criminal justice system is the Criminal Justice (Children) (NI) Order 1998 (CJCO). In this context a child is deemed to be someone who is under the age of 17 (CJCO, art.2), but the Justice (NI) Act 2002, when it is in force, will redefine children for this purpose as persons under the age of 18. The age at which a child can be held criminally responsible is 10.

The youth court

Cases in Northern Ireland's youths courts are heard by a panel of three members, one of whom must be female. The panel consists of two lay members and a legally qualified resident magistrate as chairperson. The two lay members must attend an approved training course.

At present article 4 of the CJCO 1998 obliges the court to:

have regard to (a) the welfare of any child brought before it and (b) the general principle that any delay in dealing with the child is likely to prejudice the child's welfare.

Under the Act of 2002 this article is replaced by section 53, which sets out the aims of the youth justice system. It requires *all* those involved to:

...have regard to the welfare of children affected by the exercise of their functions (and to the general principle that any delay in

dealing with children is likely to prejudice their welfare), with a view (in particular) to furthering their personal, social, and educational development.

Parents may be required to attend court proceedings and can be given the opportunity to give evidence, call witnesses or make a statement. Proceedings are in private, with only a limited number of people entitled to attend. It is an offence to publish or broadcast information which is likely to lead to the identification of a child or young person concerned in court proceedings, unless the court or the Secretary of State dispenses with these restrictions in the interests of justice. The court may direct the exclusion from the court of all those not directly involved in proceedings if the child's evidence relates to matters of an indecent or immoral nature (art.21). These modifications can apply in adult as well as juvenile trials. Article 33 of the CJCO allows a court dealing with an alleged offender to notify social services if it is concerned for a child's welfare, irrespective of whether the child is found guilty.

All courts, including youth courts, are "public authorities" and are therefore required by the Human Rights Act 1998, so far as it is possible to do so, to interpret legislation in such a way as to be compatible with the ECHR.

Arrest and detention

Article 9 of the CJCO 1998 requires children to be detained separately from adults in police stations and says that girls must be under the care of a woman. The powers of the police and army to stop, search, arrest, and question persons aged 10 and over are described in Chapters 3 and 4 above. Children are subject to both ordinary and emergency law in virtually the same way as adults. Children aged 14 and over can have negative inferences drawn from their failure to give evidence in court. However, article 10 of CJCO gives children in police detention an additional right to have a person responsible for their welfare informed as soon as practicable that they have been arrested and why and where they are detained. Social services and the probation service may also be informed if the child is in care or if a supervision or probation order is in force.

Both the Terrorism Act 2000 and the PACE Codes of Practice provide that a child should be cautioned and informed of his or her rights in the presence of an "appropriate adult". This person may be a parent, guardian, relative, social worker or any responsible person over

18 who is not a police officer or someone employed by the Policing Board. The role of the appropriate adult is to advise and assist the child, ensure that he or she understands the questions, is fairly treated and that there is no oppression. He or she may consult privately with the child at any time or may contact a solicitor on the child's behalf, but he or she does not have the right to maintain confidentiality if the child gives him or her information which might assist the police.

Once there is sufficient evidence to charge the child, questioning should cease. The child will be released on bail if he or she, or his or her parent or guardian, enter into a recognisance (*i.e.* a promise to return for trial), with or without someone standing surety. Bail will be refused to a child arrested under warrant, or to a child under 14 arrested without a warrant, only if he or she was arrested for a serious arrestable offence or if detention is believed necessary to protect the public. Bail cannot be granted for a scheduled offence (see Chapter 2) by the police or by a magistrates' or youth court.

In other circumstances, the court may grant the defendant bail and bind him or her over to reappear (Magistrates' Courts (NI) Order 1981, arts.127 and 138) or remand him or her in custody (CJCO 98, art.13). In exceptional circumstances, children aged 16 and younger may be bailed to their parents, but provided with accommodation in a children's home with the consent of the relevant Trust. Seventeen-year-olds may be accommodated in a bail hostel if the court would otherwise be unwilling to agree to bail. This option has tended to be used only in a limited number of cases. A joint police/probation bail information scheme and bail support scheme for persistent young offenders are planned.

A juvenile may be remanded for the purposes of obtaining further information. The CJCO requires that the child then appear before the court every two weeks. Children who are not released on bail may be held in a juvenile justice centre or young offenders centre. The Justice (NI) Act 2002, when in force, will amend the CJCO to allow children under 14 years to be held on remand in secure accommodation. A child aged 15 years or over may be placed in a young offenders centre if the court considers that he or she is likely to injure him- or herself or someone else (CJCO, art.13).

Cautioning, diversion and crime prevention

Informal warnings and formal police cautions can be an effective means of avoiding the need to process offenders through the courts.

For this reason they are usually a preferred option for both children and parents. A caution is given only on an admission of guilt, possibly without legal advice and may be cited later as evidence of a criminal record.

The police's Juvenile Liaison Scheme deals with offenders largely outside the formal criminal justice system. Its purpose is to divert young people away from re-offending. At the time of writing, it is proposed that this scheme will be replaced by the Youth Justice Diversionary Scheme, which will be based on the restorative justice model. Youth Diversion Officers will work in partnership with probation officers, social services, education and voluntary bodies in every District Command Unit. The aims of the scheme include diverting children from the formal criminal justice system and from re-offending. In relation to non-offending behaviour, an officer identifying a child as engaging in activities which he or she believes may place the child at risk of offending will be able to provide that young person with "informed advice". The details of what happened will be recorded and sent to the Youth Diversion Officer, who will maintain a register of such incidents. If three referrals are received within a 12 month period about the same child, the child's parents will be asked to agree to the child being referred to a multi-agency panel to consider what action could be taken or services offered to help the child or his or her family. The informed advice records will be weeded from the system after 12 months, provided no further referrals of this type are received.

If a child commits an offence, he or she will usually receive an "informed warning" or a "restorative caution". The former will be delivered by trained police facilitators and will not require the attendance of the victim. The warning will be recorded and kept for 12 months before being destroyed (or six months for 10 to 13-year-olds), unless further offences take place within that period. A restorative caution will be given in more serious cases and will be delivered through a restorative conferencing process. The child may meet the victim of the crime and any affected members of the community. The caution will be recorded as a criminal record for two-and-a-half years before being destroyed, unless further offences are committed in this period.

If a child has already received two cautions or an informed warning and a restorative caution, then a third offence within the timescale given will result in automatic referral for prosecution. The new Public Prosecution Service for Northern Ireland will be able to refer a child's case to a youth conference co-ordinator, who will then convene a diversionary youth conference, similar to the restorative conference described above. The purpose of this conference will be to make one of the following recommendations:

- that no further action be taken against the child in respect of the offence,
- that proceedings against the child be continued or instituted, or
- that the child be subject to a youth conference plan in respect of the offence.

The child, an appropriate adult (usually the child's parent), a police officer, and a youth conference co-ordinator must be present at the youth conference meetings. The child's legal representative, and the victim of the offence or his or her representative, may also be present. Social workers, probation officers and others may be present in certain circumstances. Others may be invited to attend by the youth conference co-ordinator. Anyone expected to participate in the plan or affected by it must agree to that part of the plan, including the child and a police officer. The youth conference plan is a proposal that the child be required to do certain things. It may require the child to apologise to the victim, to make reparation for the offence to the victim or to the community, to make a payment to replace or repair property, to submit to adult supervision, to perform unpaid work (if 16 years or over), to submit to restrictions on his or her conduct or whereabouts or to submit to treatment for any mental condition or alcohol or drug dependency. The child may be required to follow the plan for up to one year.

Pre-sentencing reports

Magistrates and youth courts have power to adjourn a case after a finding of guilt and before sentence for the purpose of enabling inquiries to be made or of determining the most suitable method of dealing with the case (Magistrates' Courts (NI) Order 1981, art.50). A pre-sentence report, also known as a social enquiry report, regarding the circumstances of any child may be provided by a probation officer or a social worker. Such reports must be obtained by the court before it makes a probation order (if it is to include special conditions), a community services order or a combination of these two orders.

While a court may decide that a pre-sentence report is unnecessary, it must give its reasons in open court. Where a report is not obtained, an appeal court should obtain one or explain why it is unnecessary. Similarly, a report should usually be obtained if a custodial sentence is to be passed. This must always be done in respect of a child under 17, unless the court has information available from a previous report.

Pre-sentence reports should provide information on the child's home circumstances, physical and mental health and "character". They should also include an examination of the child's history of offending and should, where possible, identify the causes of the behaviour, the potential for family support, any risk factors and mitigation and the anticipated impact of the various sentencing options on the child. It is Probation Service policy that the reports are shared with the defendant and/or the defendant's family before the court hearing and any recommendations contained in the report are then explained. Article 34 of the Criminal Justice (NI) Order 1996 obliges courts, other than youth courts, to give a copy of the probation officer's report to the offender or his or her legal representative. If the offender is under 17 years of age and is not legally represented, a copy of the report must be given to his or her parents or guardian.

Non-custodial disposals

Youth and magistrates' courts may not use the words "conviction" and "sentence" in relation to children and young people found guilty of an offence. Instead they must talk of a "finding of guilt" and "disposal". The types of non-custodial disposals available include the following.

(a) *Absolute or conditional discharge.* An absolute discharge means that the child is unconditionally released and has no further liability for the offence for which he or she was found guilty. A conditional discharge has the same effect except that the child must commit no further offence during a specified period, not exceeding three years. Before making either of these orders, the court must be satisfied that it is "inexpedient to inflict punishment", having regard to the nature of the offence and the character of the offender. If a person commits an offence within the period of conditional discharge, the original court or a Crown Court may deal with the offender as if he or she had just been convicted. Ancillary orders for costs, compensation, restitution or disqualification from driving may be made with an absolute or conditional discharge. Parents of a child under 14 who is conditionally discharged may be required to enter into a recognisance for the good behaviour of the child. If the offender is 14 or over, but under the age of 17, either the child or his or her parents may be required to enter into a recognisance (see Criminal Justice (NI) Order 1996 (CJO 1996)).

(b) *Recognisance or binding over.* This is an undertaking to the court that the offender will be of good behaviour for a specified period and that a specified sum will be paid to the court if he or she breaches that undertaking. The maximum period for which a person may be bound over to keep the peace in this way is two years. In addition to or in lieu of any other order, the court may order the parents of a child under 17 to enter into a recognisance as security for the good behaviour of the child (CJCO, art.36).

(c) *A fine.* A court dealing with a juvenile has power to fine his or her parent or guardian. It may be combined with a period of detention or imprisonment or a probation order. The ultimate sanction for not paying the fine is imprisonment. Article 35 of the CJCO places a duty on the parent or guardian to pay fines imposed on children under 16 and allows the court to impose this in respect of older children. Before fixing a fine to be imposed on an offender a court must take account of his or her financial circumstances as well as the seriousness of the offence. To this end, a financial circumstances order may be made obliging the offender to provide the court with the relevant information (CJO 1996, art.30).

(d) *Probation order.* This order can be made in respect of anyone over the age of criminal responsibility (10 years), except for the offence of murder. It requires the person convicted of an offence to be placed under the supervision of a probation officer for a period of not less than six months and not more than three years. Its purposes are to secure the rehabilitation of the offender, to prevent or reduce offending behaviour and to protect the public. Before making a probation order the court must obtain the consent of offenders aged 14 years or over. Schedule 1 to the CJO 1996 allows additional conditions to be included in a probation order. These are:

- that the probationer reside at a specified place for a specified period,

- that he or she attend such approved place as the probation officer may direct, to participate in activities (for not more than 60 days in total),
- that he or she attend a day centre for not more than 60 days,
- that he or she receive medical treatment for a mental condition which requires and is susceptible to treatment, and
- that he or she receive treatment for alcohol dependency which is believed to have contributed to the offence and which requires and is susceptible to treatment.

Amendments to the requirements of a probation order may be made on the application of the probationer or the probation officer to the court. A probation order may not be reduced in length, but it can be discharged or extended (to the maximum of three years).

(e) *A community service order.* Anyone aged 16 or over may, with his or her consent, be made subject to a community service order for an offence punishable with imprisonment or detention, provided the offence in question is not murder. Within 12 months of the order being made, the offender is required to undertake a period of unpaid community work for not less than 40 and not more than 240 hours. The period may be extended on application to the court. Where a community service order is made for two or more offences, the hours of work may run at the same time or one after the other, provided that the total hours worked do not exceed 240 (art.13).

(f) *A combination order.* Offenders aged 16 or over may be subject to a combination order if convicted of an offence punishable with imprisonment or detention (except in cases of murder). The order comprises a probation order *and* a community service order. In this instance the probation order must be for not less than 12 months and not more than 3 years. The community service hours must be not less than 40 and not more than 100 hours. The reason for giving the order must be stated in court and explained to the offender in ordinary language (art.15).

(g) *An attendance centre order.* Children under 17 who are found guilty of an offence punishable in the case of an adult with imprisonment, or who are in default of the payment of any sum of money or in breach of a probation order, may be made subject to an attendance centre order. The child must attend for the designated period, which will not be less than 12 hours (unless, given his or her age and circumstances this seems unreasonable) and not more than 24 hours (CJCO, art.37). The centre provides various educational and other activities and its purpose is diversionary.

(h) *Drug treatment and testing order.* The court may make this order if a person of 17 years or over is convicted of an offence other than murder, if he or she is dependent on or has a propensity to misuse drugs and if that dependency or propensity is such as requires or is susceptible to treatment (CJCO 1998, art.8). The court will explain to the offender in ordinary language the effects of the order but it will make the order only if the offender agrees to comply with it. The order is made for periods of six months to three years, during which time the offender is under the supervision of a probation officer and must submit to drug treatment at a specified hospital by a specified person. The probation officer reports on the offender's progress to the court not less than once per month. The offender may be required to attend this "review hearing." If, however, the court is satisfied with the offender's progress, it may choose to allow subsequent reviews to take place without a hearing. If, at any subsequent review, the court becomes dissatisfied with the offender's progress it may then revert to having review hearings and require the offender to attend.

(i) *Deferment of sentence.* Provided the offender consents, any magistrates' court or Crown Court may defer passing sentence, for up to six months, for the purpose of enabling the court to have regard to the offender's conduct after conviction. However, if in the meantime he or she commits any further offence and is convicted, the court may then pass sentence before the expiration of the period of deferment. A magistrate may not exercise this power where the Crown Court deferred passing a sentence, and the Crown court may not pass a sentence which could not be passed by a magistrates' court, where that court made the deferment (CJO 1996, art.3).

(j) *A suspended sentence.* This disposal differs from a conditional discharge in that there is a specific term of detention, in a young offenders centre, not exceeding two years, which may be activated on the commission of a further offence. Such a sentence should not be passed unless detention would be appropriate without the power to suspend the sentence. The operational period of the suspension may be between one and three years. The sentence may be passed along with a fine or a compensation order. If a further (imprisonable) offence is committed, the court can order the original sentence to take effect, substitute a lesser term, extend the operational period (to expire not later than three years from the date of the suspension) or make no order. This last option is available only if the court is of the opinion that making an order would be unjust in the circumstances (Treatment of Offenders Act (NI) 1968, s.19).

(k) *Sex offender notification requirements.* Section 1 of the Sex Offenders Act 1997 makes sex offenders subject to "notification requirements" if:
- he or she is convicted of a relevant sexual offence,
- he or she has done the act charged but is not guilty by reason of insanity or disability, or
- he or she is cautioned in relation to a relevant sexual offence.

A "notification requirement" is a requirement that an offender notify the police of his or her date of birth, name and home address within 14 days of becoming subject to the requirements. The offender must also notify the police of any changes of name or address within 14 days of the change occurring. This continues for specified periods ranging from five years to indefinitely. Periods of five to 10 years are treated as periods of two-and-a-half to five years for people under 18 years. Failure to provide this information or falsification of information is an offence. A person with parental responsibility will be directed by the court to comply with notification requirements on behalf of any child under 18 years and that person will be liable for any failure to comply.

Breaches of community orders

If a person is in breach of a "community order" (*i.e.* (d) to (h) above), a youth or magistrates' court may impose a fine not exceeding £1,000 or make a community service order or an attendance centre order (if the child is under 17). However, the court may instead decide to revoke the original order and deal with the offender as if he or she had just been convicted, choosing any of the original options open to it. A further offence is not itself a breach of a community order.

New non-custodial orders

There are a number of new disposals which are to become available in the near future:

- *Disqualification order.* The Protection of Children and Vulnerable Adults (NI) Order 2003 will give courts power to make "disqualification orders". These will be available where a person commits a specified violent or sexual offence for which a sentence of 12 months or more has been imposed (whether suspended or otherwise) or a hospital or guardianship order within the meaning of the Mental Health (NI) Order 1986. The disqualified person commits an offence if he or she knowingly applies for, offers to do, accepts or does any work in a "regulated position". This means any work in relation to accommodation, detention, education, training, hospitals and other positions where the person has unsupervised access to children. The Criminal Justice and Court Services Act 2000 provides that a person disqualified in England or Wales is also disqualified in Northern Ireland from occupying regulated positions. The Act also provides that any statutory disqualification or prohibition either here or in Scotland will have effect in England and Wales.

- *Reparation order.* This is an order requiring a child to make reparation for the offence (CJCO, art.36A-36D, inserted by the Justice (NI) Act 2002). It can be made in respect of any child, provided the offence in question is not murder. The child may be directed to undertake work (up to a maximum of 24 hours) for the victim of the crime, for another person affected by it or for the community at large. The work should be completed within six months of the making of the order. The court must acquire a pre-sentence report before making such an order and the victim of the crime, the child and any other person affected by the making of the order must agree to it. The child will be under the supervision of a probation officer, social worker or other designated person. The order cannot be made in conjunction with a custodial sentence, a community service order, a community responsibility order or a combination order. It will be subject to the breach conditions for community orders set out above.

- *Community responsibility order.* This is an order requiring the child to attend a specified place for instruction in citizenship and to carry out a number of hours of practical activities related to the instruction received (CJCO, art.36E–36I, as inserted by the Justice (NI) Act 2002). It will be awardable in respect of any offence other than murder and the total number of hours allocated must be between 20 and 40, at least half of which must be spent receiving instruction on citizenship. The obligations imposed in the order should be completed within six months. The child must consent to the order being made and will be supervised by a probation officer or by a social worker or other designated person. The Order will be subject to the breach conditions for community orders set out above.

- *Youth conference order.* This is an order requiring the child to comply with a youth conference plan. In certain circumstances a court *must* refer a child who has been found guilty of an offence to a youth conference co-ordinator, who will convene a youth conference, and in other circumstances a court *may* do so. The child must agree to participate. The purpose of the conference is to recommend:
    - that the court exercise its powers to deal with the offence,
    - that the child be subject to a youth conference plan, or
    - that the court impose a custodial sentence and subject the child to a youth conference plan in respect of the offence.

As with diversionary youth conferences, the co-ordinator cannot make recommendations unless the child, and any person in relation to whom the child is required to take action, agrees to the taking of the action. Recommendations are in the form of a written report, including details of the proposed plan. The court may order that the youth conference be terminated, on application of the youth conference coordinator, if it is satisfied that it would serve no useful purpose. The order will again be subject to the breach conditions for community orders set out above.

Custodial sentences and remands

Remands

A child or young person may be remanded, by the police, if arrested for a serious offence or in order to protect the public. Children not released will usually be brought to a juvenile justice centre and will appear before a magistrate within 36 hours. The courts may also remand a child but should release him or her on bail unless it is necessary to protect the public and the offence is a violent or sexual offence, or one where an adult would be liable to 14 years' imprisonment on conviction (or 5 years for a scheduled offence). The Justice (NI) Act 2002 provides that 10 to 13-year-olds can be remanded to secure accommodation.

Juvenile justice centres

Courts have power to commit a child or young person to a juvenile justice centre if he or she is found guilty of an offence punishable in the case of an adult with imprisonment (CJCO, art.39). The order will endure for six months unless the court specifies that it must be for longer. It will in any case not exceed two years and will comprise a period of detention in a juvenile justice centre followed by a period of supervision by a probation officer. The child will be in custody for one half of the period of the order. The length of time the child spends in custody will be reduced by any period spent on remand in relation to the case.

If a juvenile breaches a juvenile justice centre order, he or she will be liable to spend 30 days in a centre (with no reduction in the period of supervision) or to a fine not exceeding £200 if under 14 or £1,000 if older. Harbouring or concealing a person sent to a juvenile justice centre is an offence. Anyone escaping from a centre may be arrested without warrant by a police officer or any person authorised by the manager of the centre. The managers of a juvenile justice centre have parental responsibility for detained children and are included in the definition of guardians. The Justice (NI) Act 2002 allows 17-year-olds to be placed in a juvenile justice centre.

The Northern Ireland Office has power to choose which centre a child will be placed in and controls the provision of custodial services through the Youth Justice Agency, which replaced the Juvenile Justice Board early in 2003. At present there are no publicly available criteria for determining a child's placement. All children are initially placed in Lisnevin for assessment. Lisnevin has traditionally provided secure custody for boys and it conforms to the specifications of a grade C prison. It is, however, due to close very soon. Rathgael is the only other juvenile justice centre and it is a more open facility. The

Northern Ireland Office can at any time order the release of a child or his or her transfer from one centre to another.

There is an Independent Representative Scheme in place to allow young people in juvenile justice centres or young offenders centres to complain to an independent person about their treatment. The Scheme is run by the Northern Ireland Association for the Care and Resettlement of Offenders and funded by the government. It has no statutory basis and is dependent on the voluntary co-operation of the manager of the institution concerned. The local Ombudsman in Northern Ireland (see Chapter 2) has no remit to deal with complaints regarding maladministration in the centres.

Custody care orders

The Justice (NI) Act 2002 introduces this new order. It will apply to children aged 10 to 13 years and will operate in the same way and for the same period as a juvenile justice centre order. These children will no longer be placed in a juvenile justice centre but will be placed in secure accommodation for the period of their committal to custody. A child who attains the age of 14 years while in secure accommodation may, if the court has so directed, be transferred to a juvenile justice centre. The court is not bound by article 3 of the Children (NI) Order 1995 (the welfare principle) when making the order. Certain parts of the Children (NI) Order 1995 will, however, apply to the child's care while in custody. The period of supervision stipulated in the order will be under a probation officer.

Young offenders centre

Male offenders aged 17 to 21 years can be committed by court to the young offenders centre at Hydebank, Belfast, but females are committed to the Young Persons Wing at Maghaberry Prison, Lisburn. Both are regulated by the Prison and Young Offenders Centre Rules (NI) 1994. Article 7 of the Treatment of Offenders (NI) Order 1989 restricts the use of young offenders centres to persons aged between 16 and 21 years. The maximum term of imprisonment is four years. As previously mentioned, a 15-year-old may be sent to a young offenders centre if he or she is likely to injure him- or herself or others. However, the Treatment of Offenders Act (NI) 1968, as amended, allows the Secretary of State in certain circumstances to transfer to a young offender's centre young people aged 14 or 15. Likewise, the

Secretary of State may direct that a person under 21 years be transferred from a young offenders centre to prison if a Visiting Committee has reported him or her to be "incorrigible" or a "bad influence" on other inmates (Treatment of Offenders Act (NI) 1968, s.7(1)(b)).

Custody probation orders

A custody probation order may be considered by the court when a sentence of 12 months or more in prison would be justified. The court may direct that the person should serve a custodial sentence, reduced by the time the court believes should be taken into account because the offender will also be supervised by a probation officer on his or her release. The period of supervision must be not less than 12 months and not more than three years (CJO 1996, art.24).

Restrictions on custodial sentences

Article 19 of the CJO 1996 restricts the use of custody to crimes which the court regards as so serious as to justify custody or, in the case of violent or sexual crimes, where custody is necessary to protect the public. The court must state its reasons for giving a custodial sentence unless the offender refuses to consent to a community sentence.

Sexual offences

On sentencing a person in respect of any sexual offence, the courts are empowered to direct that, instead of early discharge through remission, the person must be under the supervision of a probation officer for the whole of the sentence period following release (CJO 1996, art.26).

Sex offender order

Article 6 of the Criminal Justice (NI) Order 1998 provides that the Chief Constable may apply for this civil order, which is not available to the court which sentences an offender, if a person is a sex offender and he or she has, since being convicted, acted in such a manner as to give reasonable cause to believe that an order is necessary to protect the public from serious harm.

A person is deemed a sex offender if he or she meets the criteria for the sex offender notification requirements (see p.396 above) or has been convicted in another country of an offence which would constitute a sexual offence if it had occurred in the UK. On being satisfied that these conditions are met, the court has power to place any prohibition on the defendant if it believes this to be necessary to protect the public from serious harm. A sex offender order has effect for a minimum of five years and can be discharged before then only with the agreement of the defendant and the police. During the period the order is in force, the offender is subject to the notification requirements outlined above (p.396). Failure to comply with the order is punishable by imprisonment, a fine or both.

Grave crimes

Children convicted of any offence punishable in the case of an adult with 14 years in prison or longer (CJCO, art.45(2)) or five years or longer in the case of a terrorism-related offence (Terrorism Act 2000, s.78), may be detained for a specified period in such place and under such conditions as the Secretary of State may direct. Children (under 18) convicted of offences carrying a life sentence may be detained during the pleasure of the Secretary of State (and are known as SOSPs) (CJCO, art. 45(1)). Article 46 allows the Secretary of State to release an offender on licence under such conditions as he or she may direct. The licence may be varied or revoked at any time. The Life Sentences (NI) Order 2001 provides for review of the tariff (*i.e.* the fixed element) of the sentence. See also Chapter 6.

Conclusion

The introduction of the Criminal Justice (NI) Order 1996 and of the Criminal Justice (Children) (NI) Order 1998 in many respects brought the juvenile system more into line with the Beijing Rules and the UNCRC. However, there will continue to be certain aspects of the criminal justice system in Northern Ireland which do not meet these international standards, such as the indeterminate nature of SOSP sentences, the lack of legal representation for children transferred between juvenile justice centres, the failure to provide criteria to govern such transfers and to address actual and potential inequality of treatment on the basis of gender and religion, the low age of criminal responsibility, and the failure to include the best interests principle to underpin the deliberations of courts or agencies working to rehabilitate children who offend. The Justice (NI) Act 2002 was an opportunity to remedy these defects, but unfortunately it was not grasped.

Further useful addresses

- Children's Law Centre
  3rd floor, Philip House
  123-127 York Street
  Belfast BT15 1AB
  tel: 028 9024 5704
  Freephone 080 8808 5678 (Young People's Advice and Information)
  www.childrenslawcentre.org

- Save the Children Fund
  15 Richmond Park
  Finaghy
  Belfast BT10 0HB
  tel: 028 9062 0000
  www.savethechildren.org.uk

- NSPCC
  Divisional Headquarters
  Block One, Jennymount Business Park
  North Derby Street
  Belfast BT15 3HN
  tel: 028 9035 1135
  NSPCC Helpline: 0808 800 5000
  www.nspcc.org.uk

- Barnardo's
  230 Belmont Road
  Belfast BT4 2AW
  tel: 028 9065 8105
  www.barnardos.org.uk

- Child Care (NI)
  216 Belmont Road
  Belfast BT4 2AT
  tel: 028 9065 2713
  www.childcareni.org.uk

- Include Youth
  Alpha House
  3 Rosemary Street
  Belfast BT1 1QA
  tel: 028 9031 1007

- Guardian *Ad Litem* Agency
  Centre House
  79 Chichester Street
  Belfast BT1 4JE
  tel: 028 9031 6550
  www.nigala.n-i.nhs.uk

Chapter 19

Education Rights

Chris Moffat

This chapter describes some of the rights which parents and their children have while the children are of compulsory school age. It does not cover pre-school or third-level education.

The right to education

The Universal Declaration of Human Rights and other international human rights treaties recognise the right to education as both a human right in itself and a means of realising other human rights. The UN's Convention on the Rights of the Child (UNCRC), agreed in 1989, says in Article 29 that the education of a child should be directed to:

- the development of the child's personality, talents and mental and physical abilities to their fullest potential;
- the development of respect for human rights and fundamental freedoms, and for the principles enshrined in the Charter of the UN;
- the development of respect for the child's parents, for his or her own cultural identity, language and values, for the national values of the country in which the child is living and the country from which he or she may originate, and for civilisations different from his or her own;
- the preparation of the child for responsible life in a free society, in the spirit of understanding, peace, tolerance, equality of sexes, and friendship among all peoples, ethnic, national and religious groups and persons of indigenous origin; and
- the development of respect for the natural environment.

The European Convention on Human Rights (the ECHR), now part of the law of Northern Ireland by virtue of the Human Rights Act 1998, lays down the state's responsibility for ensuring educational rights:

No person shall be denied the right to education. In the exercise of any function which it assumes in relation to education and teaching the government shall respect the right of parents to ensure education and teaching for their children in conformity with their religious and philosophical convictions. (Art.2 of Prot.1)

In the case of the UK, the government has expressly limited its duty under Article 2 to "the provision of effective education and training and the avoidance of unreasonable public expenditure".

The UNCRC gives a more positive framework for children's rights, although it is not directly enforceable in the courts of Northern Ireland. It asserts that the basic right to education belongs to the child and that it should be accessible to all on the basis of equality of opportunity (Art.28), that children have the right to have their views taken into account, "the view of the child being given due weight in accordance with the age and maturity of the child" (Art.12) and that for all children, including disabled children, access to education should be effective (Art.23).

Both the ECHR and the UNCRC require that there should be no discrimination in access to education on the grounds of sex, race, colour, language, religion, political or other opinion, national or social origin, association with a national minority, property, birth or other status. However discrimination is permitted where it can be reasonably or objectively justified.

The equality provisions in the Northern Ireland Act 1998 go further than the ECHR. The Department of Education, Education and Library Boards (ELBs) and the Council for Catholic Maintained Schools (CCMS) must all "have due regard to the need to promote equality of opportunity" and "regard to the desirability of promoting good relations between persons of different religious belief, political opinion or racial group" (s.75). In addition, they must not "discriminate or aid or incite another person to discriminate against a person or class of person on the grounds of religion, belief or political opinion" (s.76).

The duty of parents

Parents have a duty to ensure that their children of compulsory school age receive "sufficient full-time education suitable to their age, ability and aptitude, and any special educational needs they have, either by regular attendance at school or otherwise" (art.45 of the Education and Libraries (NI) Order 1986). "Parent" includes a guardian and every person who has actual custody of a child or young person.

In theory parents can discharge their obligation under article 45 by educating their children at home. But the education must be approved by the Department of Education and the local ELB must be satisfied that it is "suitable for the child's age, ability and aptitude, and any special educational needs he or she has" and that attendance is regular. The emphasis is on the suitability of the education rather than on whether it is as good as that which would be received in school. The fact that education at home may result in a conflict between the rights of the child and the rights of parents means that parents will need to consider this option carefully.

School ages

Children are of compulsory school age between 4 or 5 and 16 years. The precise cut-off dates are as follows:
- for children whose fourth birthday occurs before 1 July, compulsory school age is from the following 1 September; children whose birthdays fall after 1 July are deemed not to be of compulsory school age until 1 September of the next year;
- for children whose 16th birthday occurs before 1 July, the upper limit of compulsory school age is at the end of their current school year (art.156 of the Education Reform (NI) Order 1989).

Educational provision

The Department of Education has overall responsibility for the provision of education in Northern Ireland. The five ELBs contribute to planning the provision of schools in their area and must secure "sufficient schools", i.e. "sufficient in number, character and equipment to afford all pupils opportunity for education offering such variety of instruction and training as may be desirable in view of their different ages, abilities and aptitudes" (art.6 of the Education and Libraries (NI) Order 1986). ELBs also have general functions with regard to the administration, maintenance and funding of education and specific functions as an upper tier of management for controlled schools in their area. The CCMS, which was created under the 1989 Order, is a separate representative and co-ordinating body for schools in the Catholic maintained sector.

The 1986 Order provides that pupils should be educated according to the wishes of their parents, so long as this is "compatible with the provision of efficient instruction and training and the avoidance of unreasonable public expenditure" (art.44). There is, however, no agreed definition of "unreasonable public expenditure" or of how parents' wishes should be ascertained. Any proposal to change existing provision of schools which affects educational access, such as the closure of schools, the establishment of, or refusal to establish, new schools (such as Irish-medium or integrated schools) or non-selective education, tends to exacerbate conflicts of interest. Where the courts have intervened (*e.g. In re Cecil*, 1989) they have tended to interpret parents' rights restrictively. For instance, the European Court of Human Rights ruled in 1978 that the refusal to fund integrated schools in Northern Ireland was not in breach of parents' human rights (*X v UK*, 1978).

Over 95% of Catholic pupils attend Catholic maintained schools and a similar proportion of Protestants attend state or controlled schools. The integrated sector caters for less than 5% of pupils. This is complicated by enduring problems of social exclusion in educational structures. Secondary education is selective at an early age, with separate grammar or secondary provision according to pupils' performance in a competitive transfer exam taken during the last year of primary school. Recent proposals (the Burns Review) suggesting that the selection process is not in the best interests of the majority of children and should be abolished and replaced by guided parental choice are still under review.

Broadly speaking, there are seven types of schools in Northern Ireland. These are described below.

Controlled schools

Controlled schools are provided and managed by ELBs. They comprise nursery schools, primary schools, secondary schools (including 18 controlled grammar schools) and special schools. They cater for around 43% of pupils. The controlled sector is meant to provide non-denominational "state" education, but in practice the schools are attended overwhelmingly by Protestant pupils. Boards of governors of controlled primary and secondary schools include members nominated by the Protestant churches (so-called "transferors"). The Transferors Representatives' Council speaks for the four main Protestant churches in the management of controlled schools.

Catholic maintained schools

Catholic maintained schools are provided by the Roman Catholic diocesan authorities. They include nursery, primary and secondary schools as well as some special schools and they provide approximately 38% of school places. Boards of governors include diocesan trustees appointed by the CCMS. No pupil may be refused admission to a voluntary maintained school on religious grounds, but the schools are intended primarily for Catholic pupils. The CCMS represents the Catholic bishops' views on education in Catholic maintained schools, provides support and protection for the ethos of the schools in the sector and appoints and employs teachers.

Voluntary grammar schools

Voluntary grammar schools are provided by self-governing non-denominational or denominational trusts or religious orders. Voluntary grammar schools select pupils on the basis of academic ability and are permitted to charge all pupils annual fees. They provide around one third of post-primary places. Of the 54 voluntary grammar schools, 32 are Catholic and 22 non-Catholic, mainly Protestant and mostly with private "prep" (*i.e.* preparatory) departments. More than half are single-sex. The boards of governors of voluntary grammar schools include a majority of representatives from trustees or denominational authorities, as well as representatives of the Department of Education (or ELBs). The interests of voluntary grammar schools are represented by the Governing Bodies Association.

Grant-maintained integrated and controlled integrated schools

Only 5% of pupils are currently educated in integrated nurseries, primary and secondary schools or colleges. Such schools are required to "attract reasonable numbers of both Protestant and Roman Catholic pupils" (art.66(2) of the Education Reform (NI) Order 1989). Integrated education is not defined any further in the legislation, but the schools try to maintain at least a 60:40 balance between the two main ethno-religious traditions amongst teaching staff and governors as well as pupils. There are two types of integrated school: grant-maintained integrated (GMI) schools, which are self-governing, and controlled integrated schools, which are under the control of ELBs. In both types of school parents have an important role on boards of governors.

Church nominees are, however, not represented as of right on the boards of GMI schools.

Integrated schools are represented by the Northern Ireland Council for Integrated Education (NICIE). It receives funding from the Department of Education to "encourage and promote the development of integrated education" and operates a trust fund to assist new GMI schools. These are eligible for full recurrent funding and capital expenditure (where approved), once they meet prescribed criteria concerning minimum enrolment and admissions numbers. In practice it is government policy to encourage existing non-integrated schools to "transform" to controlled integrated status.

Irish-medium schools

There are currently 23 Irish-medium primary schools (bunscoilleanna) and 3 secondary schools (meanscoilleanna), plus a significant number of nursery and pre-school groups. Irish-medium education is also provided in Irish speaking streams in mainstream schools. As with integrated education, new Irish-medium schools are eligible for full recurrent funding and capital expenditure once they meet prescribed criteria, but they must operate as independent schools until they achieve the required minimum enrolment and admissions numbers. Irish-medium education is represented by Comhairle na Gaelscolaíochta, which receives funding under the 1998 Order to encourage the development of Irish language schools. The Irish-medium Trust Fund, Iontaobhas na Gaelscolaíochta, helps to support their development.

Independent schools

There are a few independent schools providing full-time education outside state control for pupils of compulsory school age. They are not grant-aided and are not required to comply with Education Orders except with respect to human rights standards, registration with the Department and the maintenance of minimum requirements as to premises, accommodation and efficient and suitable instruction having regard to the ages, sexes and abilities of the pupils.

Special schools

ELBs and the CCMS provide a range of separate special schools and special units within mainstream schools for children with special educational needs. They are managed by boards of governors including representatives of parents, teachers and the ELB or trustees.

Educational access

Open enrolment

Open enrolment means parents have the right to state their preference for any grant-maintained school they would like their child to attend (art.9 of the Education (NI) Order 1997). The first and each subsequent preference is taken as a separate application for admission; if it is refused, the next preference is considered to be a first preference.

A school must generally admit a pupil whose parents apply for a place if it has room. The Department of Education determines each school's total enrolment number and admissions number (the maximum first year intake). Schools may not exceed their enrolment and admissions numbers in any school year except to admit a child with a statement of special educational needs or a school attendance order or to comply with a direction of an Appeals Tribunal or the Department of Education.

Schools must draw up admission criteria to be applied where the school is oversubscribed. The regulations stipulate that all children resident in Northern Ireland must be admitted before any non-resident child. Admission criteria must give the order of priority for admission and must not include the fact that the school was the parent's first or higher preference. Specific regulations which apply to different school sectors are explained below.

Nursery schools

Nursery admissions procedures, including admissions to separate nursery schools, nursery units attached to primary schools and voluntary places under the Pre-School Education Expansion Programme (PSEEP) are co-ordinated by ELBs. Shortage of places in some areas may mean only part-time places are available. Some primary school reception classes enrol children when they reach their fourth birthday, but such classes may not exceed 30 children and the government is proposing to restrict the practice.

If nursery schools and units are oversubscribed they must first give priority to those who otherwise do not have a pre-school education place (full-time or part-time) in the following order of priority:

- children from socially disadvantaged circumstances who will be four years old before 1 September in their final pre-school year ("socially disadvantaged" refers to children whose parents are in receipt of income support or income-based jobseeker's allowance and whose application form is endorsed by the Social Security Agency);
- children from socially disadvantaged circumstances who will be three years old before 1 September in their final pre-school year;
- other children who will be four years old before 1 September in their final pre-school year;
- other children who will be three years old before 1 September in their final pre-school year.

Nursery schools or units may apply their own additional published sub-criteria to allocate places if they are still over-subscribed. These may include giving priority to children in their final pre-school year if they have special educational needs (*i.e.* "significantly greater difficulty in learning than the majority of children of their age"), if they live close to the school or if they have a family connection with the school. Parents may appeal to an admissions appeal tribunal against a decision to refuse admission if they think the admission criteria were not correctly applied.

Primary schools

Primary school admissions are co-ordinated by the ELBs. Parents may name up to three preferred schools in order of preference on the standard application form. They should include all the details which they wish to be taken into account concerning their child's application, including written confirmation of any special circumstances, any reasons for the preferred school and details of siblings already attending, etc.

Transport assistance to a grant-aided school may be provided by ELBs if the school is more than two miles from a pupil's normal residence. However assistance may be provided only if a place has been sought and admission refused at all suitable schools in the same category which are within the two mile statutory walking distance.

Boards of governors of primary schools must apply their published criteria to allocate places if they are over-subscribed. The regulations prescribe that primary schools must:
- give priority to children who will have obtained compulsory school age;

- not select pupils by reference to ability, aptitude or performance in a test or examination held by, or on behalf of, the board of governors;
- apply admission criteria to pupils of compulsory and below compulsory school age, including those already enrolled in an "approved" nursery class (but not a reception class) at the preferred school; and
- not admit more that 30 pupils in any P1 to P4 class.

Primary schools' sub-criteria typically include siblings already at the school, children who have attended any attached nursery, children of staff employed at the school, residence in one or more particular parishes connected with the school or in a traditional catchment area, other family links with the school and the distance of the pupil's home from the school. An excess of family and traditional or communal criteria can sometimes discriminate against newcomers to an area and may also result in indirect religious or ethnic discrimination, for instance against Travellers. But under the present system there is no redress for parents and children who may be affected if the published criteria are applied correctly. Governors who are responsible for school admission criteria should, however, be conscious of their wider social responsibilities regarding fairness and social inclusion.

Parents may appeal to an appeal tribunal against a decision to refuse admission if they think the school did not apply, or did not correctly apply, its admission criteria (see p.417 below).

Post-primary schools

Most areas have a selective post-primary school system. Only a small number of areas offer a choice of non-selective or delayed selection schools. Admission to grammar schools is on the basis of ability only, rather than parental preference. Admission to secondary schools or colleges according to ability or aptitude is not permitted. Boards of governors of post-primary schools must draw up the admission criteria to be applied if they are over-subscribed according to the regulations. Admission criteria for both year eight and the sixth form must be published and must be capable of allocating the last available place.

Post-primary admission criteria

In the case of a grammar school, admission criteria must:

- use the results in the transfer procedure tests to admit day pupils in strict order of the grade achieved;
- take account of medical or other problems which may have affected a child's test performance where supported by a medical certificate or other appropriate documentary evidence; and
- in addition, grammar schools may admit boarding pupils without reference to transfer grade, but only so long as the number admitted does not exceed the number of boarders accepted in 1990.

Secondary non-grammar schools' admission criteria must not include:
- provision for selecting pupils by reference to ability or aptitude, except in the case of a school which has been permitted to select some of its pupils by ability or aptitude; or
- performance in any other special test set by an ELB or the Department (*e.g.* for a pupil who has lived abroad).

No post-primary school may include in its admission criteria the outcome of any assessment in Key Stage 2 (KS 2) or information provided by the primary school principal about the pupil's classroom performance, except where there are special circumstances such as illness or family bereavement. Schools may apply any other admission criterion, provided it is not specifically forbidden in the regulations above and is legal (*e.g.* gender in the case of single-sex schools).

When there are vacant places the only grounds on which a child who otherwise meets the criteria may be refused admission is where he or she is not in the normal transfer age group and admission would "prejudice the efficient use of resources", or where a grant-aided grammar school believes it would be "detrimental to the educational interests of the child and it has obtained the approval of the Department to refuse admission" or "the academic ability of the child is not of a standard equivalent to that of the pupils with whom he or she would be taught at the school" (arts.13 and 14 of the Education (NI) Order 1997).

Information about schools and the transfer process is published by the ELBs. Transfer report forms are completed in a parents' interview with the pupil's primary school principal. ELBs advise parents to nominate at least one non-grammar school amongst their preferred schools and they can include schools outside the pupil's current ELB area. The transfer form also provides space for the inclusion of additional details, such as official confirmation of any medical or special circumstances (*i.e.* doctor's or psychologist's report), any reasons for the preferred school and details of siblings already attending, etc.

For many families, the availability of transport assistance will be important in deciding on a post-primary school. This may be provided by ELBs if the school is more than the statutory walking distance (3 miles) from a pupil's normal residence, provided a place has been sought and admission refused at all suitable schools in the same category which are within three miles. "Suitable" means, in the case of secondary schools, controlled, maintained, integrated or Irish-medium and, in the case of grammar schools, denominational or non-denominational. Transport assistance is not available in the case of a preference for a single-sex school. The order in which schools are listed on the transfer report form is the main factor taken into account when transport applications are being assessed. (See also p.439 below.)

Selection tests (the "11 plus")

Pupils' suitability for grammar schools is determined by two sets of test papers administered and marked by the Council for Curriculum, Examinations and Assessment (CCEA). The papers are based on the KS 2 programmes of study in English, maths and science. Marks are aggregated and converted into a single grade with pre-set grade boundaries. Currently these are: Grade A – the top 25% of the entire age group eligible to sit the tests, Grade B1 – the next 5%, Grade B2 – the next 5%, C1 – the next 5%, C2 – the next 5% and Grade D – the rest.

No particular grade can guarantee a child admission to a grammar school. However pupils must take the tests in order to be considered for a place. Pupils in "non-selective" areas must also take part if they want to be considered for a grammar school in another area. Only one attempt at the test is allowed. Pupils may sit it a year "early" or a year "late", but only with the approval of the board of governors of their primary school. Pupils with special educational needs who are not "statemented" (see p.427 below) are advised by ELBs to take the tests if their parents want them to be considered for a grammar school place. A pupil with a statement of special educational needs (SEN) is not intended to take part.

Grammar schools must consider any special circumstances which may have affected performance in the test. If a child's availability for, or performance in, the test is adversely affected by illness or other factors, marks are not adjusted, but a supplementary test may be taken.

Any medical or non-medical factors which may have affected a test performance must be included in the transfer report.

ELBs advise that "educational evidence" to be considered as part of the special circumstances of "a medical or non-medical nature" should be submitted on a specially designed form to be attached to the transfer report. It should include information about the child's performance in P7 class tests in English, maths and science compared with other pupils in the same class, together with the primary principal's comments on academic achievements. The parent and principal must gather this information. Arguably the "special circumstances" provisions tend to favour articulate parents and have helped to undermine confidence in the fairness of the transfer process.

Problems with the transfer test

Transfer test grades are meant to be objective. Apart from "special circumstances" no other factor may be considered in grammar school admissions unless two or more pupils have the same grade. However research has raised serious doubts about grades based on test scores. One estimate suggests that at least 30% of pupils may be assigned the wrong grade in such tests. Performance is influenced by many factors other than a pupil's ability or aptitude, such as social background or quality of teaching or whether pupils have received private coaching.

Parents can query the grade awarded to their child and can ask their primary principal to request remarking. However they cannot challenge the validity of inferences about their child's "ability" or the weighting and standardisation factors which affect the validity of a particular grading. A judicial review, to be successful, would require the test to be shown to be unreasonable. Parents might arguably complain to the Department of Education or the Equality Commission that the test discriminates against those with disadvantaged backgrounds and is a breach of the Department's new duty to promote equality of opportunity (s.75 of the Northern Ireland Act 1998).

Other admission criteria

Other admission criteria apply only when non-grammar schools are over-subscribed or when a grammar school must distinguish between pupils with the "same" grade. There is no requirement that they should be fair or even relevant, but they must be applied correctly and consistently as published. Grammar schools may give priority to former "prep" department pupils, or to pupils with family or traditional connections with the school. Some admission criteria typically used by oversubscribed secondary schools include priority for pupils whose siblings currently or previously attended the school, for pupils coming from traditional contributory or parish primary schools, for pupils living in a more or less well-defined catchment area, or for children of current or past members of staff. Examples of other admission criteria which are currently used include priority to pupils with other family links with the school, the behavioural report from the previous school, the family's distance from school, the parents' support for the aims of the school and (in an integrated school) having a balance of Protestant and Catholic pupils.

Arguably some of these criteria may discriminate on the grounds of religion, but it is not clear that they would be seen as contravening the equality provisions of the Northern Ireland Act where a school can show that it is respecting parental preference as required by the legislation. Other selection criteria may indirectly discriminate on social, ethnic or other grounds. One group of parents argued that priority for pupils from certain rural primary schools in a secondary school's admission criteria prejudiced the admission chances of pupils from a much nearer urban estate (*In re Moore*, 1996). Their case was rejected at the Court of Appeal under the legislation then in force.

Admissions Appeal Tribunal

Once published, criteria must be applied in an unambiguous and procedurally fair way. Parents who are dissatisfied with the refusal of a school to admit their child may appeal to an appeal tribunal (art.15 of the Education (NI) Order 1997), but only on the grounds that the school did not apply, or incorrectly applied, its admission criteria and the child would otherwise have been admitted to the school.

Appeals must be made in writing to the tribunal. Parents must be given an opportunity to appear and to make written and oral representations on their own behalf. No new information may be considered in an appeal. If the tribunal finds in favour of the appeal, it must direct the board of governors of the school to admit the child even if this means the school will exceed its admissions and enrolment number.

Judicial review

Parents who are dissatisfied with the decision of an appeal tribunal, or who believe that a school's admission criteria are not in accordance with the regulations, may seek a judicial review in the High Court (see Chapter 2). A child in such a case is generally eligible for legal aid. A difficulty is that a judicial review can reverse a decision of a tribunal only if it can be shown that the tribunal considered inappropriate (or did not consider appropriate) evidence or that no reasonable authority could have made the decision in question. Even if a judicial review finds in favour of a complainant, the High Court can reverse an appeal tribunal decision only if a proper application of the criteria would actually have resulted in admission.

The transfer procedure and inequality of opportunity

Arguably the current selection procedure is contrary to the government's duty to have due regard to the need to promote equality of opportunity under the Northern Ireland Act 1998. The Burns Review on selection (2001) proposed abolition of the transfer test and its replacement by "guided parental choice". However the Burns proposals might still fail to promote equality of opportunity if there is no substantial effort to reduce differences between different types of schools. A greater emphasis on parental choice might also reduce the opportunity for pupils' voices to be heard in selection decisions.

The curriculum

Common standards of teaching and learning across all schools regardless of type are essential for equality of opportunity. The 1989 Order lays down a minimum legally required curriculum for every registered pupil of compulsory school age in grant-aided primary and secondary schools. All schools have a duty to provide "a balanced and broadly based curriculum which promotes the spiritual, moral, cultural, intellectual and physical development of pupils, and thereby prepares them for the opportunities, responsibilities and experiences of adult life" (art.4(2)). Under the ECHR the curriculum should be presented in an "objective, critical and pluralistic manner" (*Kjeldsen, Busk Madsen and Petersen v Denmark*, 1976).

Currently the Northern Ireland curriculum is under review and it is likely in due course to become more flexible and less prescriptive. The curriculum in force at the time of writing must include provision for religious education and for "areas of study" made up of "contributory subjects" including English, maths, science and technology (science only at primary level), environment and society, creative and expressive studies, and language studies (in second level schools only, except in Irish-medium schools).

The curriculum for each listed contributory subject must cover "programmes of study" (*i.e.* what is required to be taught) and the "attainment targets" (*i.e.* what pupils are expected to know). The school career is divided into four Key Stages: KS 1 for the first four years of primary school, KS 2 for the last three years of primary school, KS 3 for the first three years of secondary school and KS 4 for the last two years of compulsory schooling. Pupils are assessed at the end of each Key Stage.

All schools are required to promote, wholly or mainly through the teaching of contributory subjects and religious education, the attainment of objectives in the following educational themes: Information Technology, Education for Mutual Understanding, Cultural Heritage, Health Education, Economic Awareness and Careers Education (secondary schools only). Following the current review of the curriculum, specific timetabled subjects (Personal Development, Citizenship and Education for Employability) are likely to replace some of these "cross-curricular themes".

Since 2000 there has been increased flexibility for pupils at KS 4 to study vocational subjects not included in the statutory curriculum. KS 4 pupils are permitted to take part in work-related learning either in the workplace or in a college of further education (FE), provided it comprises not more than 40% of a pupil's total KS 4 programme and is offered in partnership with a recognised training organisation or FE college. To permit this the Department of Education has extended an existing provision to "disallow" parts of the statutory curriculum with respect to any pupil or group of pupils for "development work". However such "learning programmes" must be "agreed with each pupil in the context of a career interview" before the end of the school year "when the child and parents are able to make an informed choice." If a problem arises parents can complain to the principal and board of governors, then to the Curriculum Complaints Tribunal (see p.423 below).

Assessment and examinations

The CCEA draws up the curriculum and organises assessment and examinations on behalf of the Department of Education. School "league tables" are no longer published in Northern Ireland, but statutory assessment information is used for school target-setting and for reporting attainment levels to parents.

An eight-level scale is used for measuring attainment over the 12 years of compulsory schooling and the expected level pupils ought to have achieved at the end of each Key Stage. There is also a statutory baseline assessment of P1 pupils during their first school year. At KS 1 and KS 2 pupils are assessed holistically in class by teachers in English and maths. At KS 3 (14 years) pupils are assessed both by their teachers and in standardised tests in English, maths and science.

A problem with these assessment procedures is their tendency to reinforce indirect gender, ethnic and possibly other forms of discrimination. Parents and students should always question pre-emptive judgements about a student's expected development from one level or Key Stage to another in assessment decisions.

GCSE examinations

The CCEA is the regulatory body for GCSE and other external examinations in Northern Ireland and is responsible for scrutinising procedures to ensure that standards are maintained. Schools must enter pupils for approved public examinations unless there are educational reasons for not doing so, but they are permitted to recover "wasted examination fees" from the parent if any pupil "fails without good reason to meet any examination requirement for that syllabus" (art.84 of the Education (NI) Order 1998).

Pupils have a right of appeal if they believe they have been unfairly graded, but they cannot appeal in person. Appeals for a paper to be remarked must be made by the principal of their school or college to the appropriate examination board. If the pupil and principal are not satisfied a further complaint can be made to the examination board and they can see the pupil's examination scripts. If necessary the school principal may appeal to the examination body's appeal committee. A final appeal may be made to the Examination Appeals Board but only in relation to the examination board's procedures, not the grade awarded. For further information, see the Examination Appeals Board website: *www.theeab.org.uk*.

Religious education

All schools, including special schools, must provide for both religious education and collective worship. This must be so arranged that: "(a) the school shall be open to pupils of all religious denominations for instruction other than religious education and (b) no pupil shall be excluded directly or indirectly from the other advantages which the school affords" (art.21(4) of the Education and Libraries (NI) Order 1986). Ministers of religion of any denomination must be given reasonable access to pupils in order to give religious education, provided parents do not object. Parents can insist that the child be excused from any religion education classes and collective worship and if necessary withdrawn from school for reasonable periods (art.21(5)). Voluntary grammar, Catholic maintained and integrated schools may determine their own provision for collective worship and denominational instruction.

Religious education must be in accordance with any core syllabus specified by the Department of Education. This "core syllabus" is one prepared in consultation with the four main churches in Northern Ireland. In addition, in controlled schools (other than controlled integrated schools) religious education must be undenominational, *i.e.* it must be "based upon the Holy Scriptures according to some authoritative version thereof but excluding instruction as to any tenet distinctive of any particular religious denomination", and collective worship must "not be distinctive of any particular religious denomination" (art.21(2) of the 1986 Order). Parents who have a problem with arrangements for religious education or collective worship should take it up with the principal or write to the board of governors. If the problem is not resolved they can complain to the Curriculum Complaints Tribunal (see p.423).

Variations or exemptions from the curriculum

Boards of governors of grant-aided schools have a statutory duty to deliver the statutory curriculum to all pupils and may vary this only where the Department of Education permits the curriculum to be modified or suspended to allow development work or experiments (art.14), where regulations require it (art.15), where a pupil has a statement of special educational needs which specifies exemption from or modification (art.16) or where a temporary exception is required for an individual pupil (art.17).

Requests for variations in the curriculum by schools could increase as a result of recent Departmental moves to encourage more flexible programmes for KS 4 pupils. A temporary exemption from the curriculum may arise where a pupil's health is affecting his or her ability to learn or where a pupil needs to be assessed by the ELB with a view to making a statement of educational needs. In such cases the principal may direct that for an "operative period" (not more than six months) the curriculum, assessment procedures and educational themes may be modified or not applied.

Where parents are concerned about the situation, they may appeal to the board of governors of the school. If they are still not satisfied they can appeal to the Curriculum Complaints Tribunal or, if their child has a statement of special educational needs, to the Special Educational Needs Tribunal.

School records and reports

Each year, on 30 June or as soon as reasonably practicable, all grant-aided schools must provide parents with information about pupils' achievements. They must provide brief particulars of achievements in subjects which form part of the pupil's curriculum, the level of attainment in any statutorily assessed compulsory subject and the result of any public examination for which the pupil was prepared by the school. They must also provide, not later than 30 September, the summative record of the achievements of a pupil who is leaving school at the end of KS 2, finishing KS 4 or leaving school in the sixth form. In addition, except at the end of KS 2, any school to which the pupil seeks admission may request to see the record.

Access to records

Individual pupils' assessments must not be made available to persons or bodies other than the parents concerned and the Department, except in specified circumstances. Parents (and pupils over the age of 11) have a right to see any "formative record" ("formal record of a pupil's academic attainments, his or her other skills, talents and abilities and his or her educational progress"), but only after making a request in writing to the school. If a parent or pupil regards the record as inaccurate and gives notice in writing, he or she may amend or correct it. The written notice of complaint must be appended to the record and subsequently treated as part of it. A complaint about a refusal to disclose or amend records should be lodged with the school's board of governors.

Reports requested by an educational welfare officer, social worker, probation officer, prospective employer or college do not require schools to disclose any of the following information regarding a pupil:

- details about home circumstances or religious denomination,
- the results of a pupil's attainment assessments,
- reports for the purposes of juvenile or magistrates' courts,
- statements of special educational needs,
- educational records covered by the Data Protection Act 1984,
- information which in the opinion of "holders" would harm the physical, mental or emotional condition of the pupil or any other person to whom it relates, and
- the contents of references to employers, universities or colleges.

Curriculum complaints

In theory, parents who are concerned about the way an ELB or the board of governors of a school is discharging its duties in relation to the curriculum or assessment, religious education, access to information or any related matter, can apply in writing to the Curriculum Complaints Tribunal (art.33 of the Education Reform (NI) Order1989). In practice, information about the Curriculum Complaints Tribunals is not published and it is not clear that the statutory complaints procedure is used to any great extent. The statutory complaints procedure does, however, remain one possible means by which parents might be able to ensure that statutory commitments, including more recent equality provisions, are adhered to.

Children with special educational needs

The principles which underlie current special needs provision were established by the Warnock Report (1978). Approximately 20% of all children are considered to require special educational provision at some time during their lives, although only 2% of pupils may be in special schools. Pupils with special educational needs should thus as far as possible be educated in mainstream schools and special educational needs policy should be guided by the principle of promoting the abilities and potential of all.

A child has "special educational needs" (SEN) if he or she has "a learning difficulty which calls for special educational provision to be made for him or her". A "learning difficulty" means a child "has significantly greater difficulty in learning than the majority of children of his (sic) age, or has a disability which prevents or hinders him from making use of educational facilities of a kind generally provided at ordinary schools for children of his age" (art.3 of the Education (NI) Order 1996). Any special educational needs of a child whose first language is not English must be considered in the light of his or her own cultural and community background.

Under proposed new Special Educational Needs and Disability legislation (SEND) a duty will be imposed on schools and ELBs not to treat disabled pupils "less favourably without justification for a reason which is related to their disability". A disabled pupil for these purposes will be as defined as in the Disability Discrimination Act 1995, namely someone who has "a physical or mental impairment which has a substantial and long term adverse effect on his ability to carry out normal day-to-day activities." (See also Chapter 15.)

The duty of ELBs

Article 6 of the Education (NI) Order 1996 requires that an ELB must "determine and keep under review their policy in relation to special educational provision" and "the arrangements made by it for special educational provision." It must identify and assess any child between the ages of two and 19 who has, or probably has, special educational needs. It must determine the special educational provision called for by any learning difficulty the child has. Where a health and social service authority knows of such a child below compulsory school age, it must inform the child's parents and notify the ELB. In the case of a child under two the ELB must first obtain the parents' consent before proceeding with a statutory assessment.

An ELB must make special educational provision for all children who have special educational needs. It must ensure the following conditions are satisfied for a child for whom a statement of special educational needs is maintained who is to be educated in an ordinary school:

- the child receives the special educational provision which his or her learning difficulty calls for,
- efficient education is provided for the children with whom he or she will be educated, and

- the efficient use of resources (art.7(2)(b)).

Under the proposed SEND legislation incompatibility with these requirements, and specifically with the efficient education of other children, will be deemed to exist only where the ELB can show that there are "no reasonable steps" they can take to facilitate inclusion in an ordinary school. Once in an ordinary school the child must be included in the activities of the school "together with the other children", provided that this is "reasonably practicable".

Special educational provision

Separate specialist provision remains an option for children whose needs require it and whose parents want it for them. Within mainstream schools special provision may range from receiving extra help or support within the classroom of an ordinary school to attending special units or classes within a mainstream school or attending a special school, part-time, daily or on a residential basis. Special schools catering for specific identified needs are usually smaller and often cater for the whole age range (nursery to 16+).

An ELB may make special educational provision otherwise than in a grant-aided school and other than in Northern Ireland if the needs of the child require it and the arrangements are compatible with "the efficient use of resources" (art.10). It may pay fees and any reasonable maintenance and travelling expenses for the child and any person accompanying him or her (art.11).

Under the proposed new SEND provisions ELBs will have a duty to make arrangements for providing information on SEN matters to parents in their area and for publicising the services available.

The Code of Practice

The Code of Practice on the Identification and Assessment of Special Educational Needs sets out the responsibilities of ELBs and of all grant-aided schools with respect to SEN. It prescribes the duties of boards of governors to keep policy under review and to report annually to parents. It defines the specific duties to pupils with special educational needs (SEN) whether statemented or not, of principals, special educational needs co-ordinators (SENCOs) and teachers. All policies must have regard to the Code of Practice which prescribes a five-stage strategy:

- Stage 1: The teacher identifies or registers a concern about a child's SEN and notifies the school's Special Educational Needs Co-ordinator (SENCO) and the child's parents.
- Stage 2: The school's SENCO and the child's teacher, in consultation with the parents, draw up an individual education plan with targets and dates for action and review.
- Stage 3: Teachers and the SENCO review the education plan and are supported by ELB specialists and resources.
- Stage 4: The child is referred to the ELB for a statutory assessment.
- Stage 5: The ELB decides whether a statement of SEN is needed.

Statutory assessment and statements

Assessment for SEN should be carried out within six months, unless the ELB thinks it is not necessary. Parents must be notified when the child will be formally assessed and provided with information on the procedure the ELB will follow, including the name of an ELB officer from whom further information may be obtained and their right to make representations and submit written evidence within a period of not less than 29 days from the date of the notice. Further provisions under the proposed SEND legislation will strengthen parents' rights to be given appropriate and timely notice of all decisions.

The ELB must seek parental, medical, psychological and educational advice and consult the child's school principal and teacher. Parents have the right to be consulted at all stages and may be present at an examination connected with the assessment of their child. Professionals may also wish to talk to the child unaccompanied. The child should be encouraged to contribute to the assessment.

The whole process should take no more than 18 weeks. An ELB does not have to make a statement, but it must notify the parents if it decides not to, setting out the reasons and including copies of any advice received. If parents are dissatisfied they have a legal right to appeal to the Special Educational Needs Tribunal (see below). After the introduction of the new SEND proposals, parents will have the alternative of referring the matter to a new independent conciliation body.

Provision for non-statemented children

Most children with special educational needs are not statemented. School budgets include an element specifically for special educational needs and boards of governors must publish a special educational needs policy in their annual report. Where a child with non-statemented special educational needs attends an ordinary school, the school must use its best endeavours to ensure that:

- the special educational provision which the child's learning difficulty calls for is made,
- those needs are made known to all who are likely to teach the child, and
- the teachers in the school are aware of the importance of identifying and providing for pupils who have special educational needs.

The Special Needs Co-ordinator (SENCO) and class teacher must draw up an individual education plan for any child at Stage 2 (see above). Parents should be fully consulted. If they are not consulted or are not happy with the arrangements they can make a formal request that their child's educational needs be assessed. This can help clarify any concerns about shortcomings in provision made by the school. They have a right to appeal to the SEN Tribunal if refused. In future, under the new SEND proposals, they will also be entitled to appeal to the Tribunal if they believe their child has been discriminated against unfairly.

Provision for statemented children

A "statement" is a legally binding document which sets out the SEN a child has and what provision an ELB intends to make to meet those needs. It includes six parts, the most important of which are:

- Part 2: the educational needs identified in the assessment,
- Part 3: the special help to be provided,
- Part 4: the name of the school the child will attend or other arrangements (but this is not inserted until a final draft is agreed with the parents),
- Part 5: any non-educational needs (*e.g.* physiotherapy), and
- Part 6: the support to be provided to meet the needs listed in Part 5.

Parents must be allowed to comment on a preliminary draft of the statement without the name of a school inserted in Part 4. They must be shown all the formal advice and evidence used to reach a decision. They have 15 days to consider and respond to the first draft before a further meeting is held to discuss final matters. They should examine carefully any support suggested under Part 5. (Seemingly non-educational support may in practice turn out to be of crucial educational importance.) The ELB may name a school (or under the proposed SEND legislation, it may only be required to specify a type of school if it considers the parents have made suitable alternative arrangements). Parents have a further 15 days to respond.

Once a statement has been made, it is the responsibility of the ELB to ensure that the board of governors of any school in which the child is placed makes the necessary special educational provision. Statements must be reviewed at least every 12 months at a meeting with parents. The most important review meetings are those where the child would normally be due to move school (from nursery to primary, or from primary to secondary) or after age 14 when a "transition plan" for the child's move to further or higher education and adult life will be agreed.

Parents need to be closely involved in any review decisions. They may request a different grant-aided school to be substituted. If they do not agree with the school or ELB about what is proposed for their child and cannot resolve the matter, they have a right to appeal to the Special Educational Needs Tribunal. (When the proposed SEND legislation is implemented after 2003, they may alternatively be able to refer, without prejudice, to a proposed new independent conciliation body.)

The Special Educational Needs Tribunal

A parent of a child with an SEN statement, who does not agree with what is proposed, has a right of appeal to the SEN Tribunal. (An independent conciliation service to be established under the new SEND proposals will also be available to parents.) An appeal can be against any aspect of the statement except (under current legislation) aspects referring to non-educational support. The ELB will not in future be permitted to vary provision until an appeal is heard. It is also possible to appeal if:

- an ELB turns down a request to change a school named in the statement (so long as it is a grant-aided school and the child's statement has been maintained by the ELB for at least a year),
- the child has a statement but an ELB turns down a request to re-assess (so long as it has not made a new assessment for at least six months),
- an ELB decides not to maintain a child's statement any longer, or
- after a re-assessment an ELB decides not to amend the statement.

Currently it is not possible to appeal against some decisions, such as those listed below, but future SEND proposals will strengthen parents' right to make representations regarding some of these matters:

- a refusal to assess a child if the parents themselves did not request it,
- a refusal to name an independent school,
- a decision not to amend a statement after an annual review,
- the way an assessment was carried out or the length of time it took,
- the way an ELB is proposing to provide the support specified in a statement,
- the level of funding being provided, or
- the way a school is meeting the child's needs.

If the problem is one which cannot be appealed to the Tribunal parents should talk to the school or contact the Independent Panel for Special Educational Advice (IPSEA). If it is not possible to reach agreement it may be possible to complain to the Department of Education.

Appeals to the Tribunal must be made in writing no later than two months after the ELB makes its decision. The Tribunal may determine an appeal without a hearing if the parents and the ELB agree in writing, otherwise there is an oral hearing. Parents have a right to represent themselves or use a representative at the hearing. Both the parents and the ELB will be able to give written and oral evidence and call up to two witnesses. Parents may be entitled to some legal aid but this may not cover the cost of any independent psychologists or other expert witnesses. Psychologists employed by the ELB involved in the case are contractually barred from giving expert advice against their own authority. However expert advice can be sought from psychologists and other experts employed by other ELBs.

Article 12 of the UNCRC asserts the right of the child who is capable of forming his or her own views "to express those views on any matter affecting him or her" in accordance with his or her age and maturity. The Tribunal chair should allow parents to bring their child to the hearing to give his or her views but under current legislation may not allow him or her to stay for the whole time. The child's participation should be encouraged where possible, if necessary through a video or recorded contribution.

The decision of a Tribunal can be appealed to the High Court on a point of law (rather than an issue of fact) by either the parent or the ELB. The appeal must be lodged within 21 days of the notice of the

Tribunal's decision. Access to legal aid is assessed on the parents' income.

Problems in challenging a statement

Problems can most frequently arise if parents want a statement to specify a particular school or type of treatment for their child which may be costly and only available privately. Article 7(2) of the 1996 Order gives them a right to express a preference for a particular school. But the European Court of Human Rights ruled that a refusal to provide a child with a place in a particular school or type of school is not a breach of the child's right to education under the ECHR. Moreover, where educational authorities provide alternatives they are permitted to take account of financial constraints in determining how a child's needs are to be met. In such circumstances parents who want a place at a particular independent school or a particular form of treatment will need to convince the ELB or, if necessary, the Tribunal or court, that their preference is an "efficient use of resources". Future SEN decisions, however, are likely to be influenced by a recent clarification of the law: ELBs are not now automatically exempt from a duty of care or vicarious liability for any damage which can be attributed to negligence in dealing with children with special educational needs (*Phelps v Hillingdon LBC*, 2000).

Complaints to the Department and the Ombudsman

If the ELB fails to implement an SEN Tribunal decision, parents can complain to the Department of Education under article 101 of the 1989 Order. If parents exhaust the option with either the ELB or Department and still feel they have a complaint, they can contact the Ombudsman (freephone 0800 343424). For further information contact your local ELB, the Children's Law Centre or Disability Action.

Treatment at school

Under the Human Rights Act 1998 schools may impose reasonable disciplinary measures. They must also provide a safe working environment for pupils, teachers and others in the school and promote discipline and good behaviour (the Education (NI) Order 1998 and the Health and Safety at Work (NI) Order 1978). The Education and Libraries (NI) Order 2003 extends the duty of schools to promote the welfare of pupils and to take specific measures to protect children from abuse. For the first time it also requires schools to consult pupils about disciplinary and good behaviour policies.

Discipline policy

The 1998 Order requires the board of governors of grant-aided schools to have specific policies designed to promote good pupil behaviour. There must be a written statement of general principles regarding disciplinary matters to which the principal will have regard in determining school rules and behaviour policies. A copy of the policy should be available to parents of all pupils. The policy may be underwritten by a home/school contract signed by parents and pupils (although this has no legal standing).

The school's discipline policy should include procedures for identifying and dealing with misbehaviour. Serious cases should require a more rigorous process for investigating and identifying the alleged perpetrator. Schools must respect the right of a pupil to rebut any allegations and the process of investigation must conform to agreed standards in conducting searches, recording evidence and dealing with witnesses. Failure to follow written procedures may open the school to the charge of acting unreasonably in law.

Anti-bullying policies

Bullying is defined as "deliberately hurtful behaviour, repeated over a period of time, where it is difficult for the victim to defend him or herself". It may involve verbal or physical abuse, teasing or ridicule, offensive letters, graffiti, or e-mails, or interfering with, or stealing, property. Bullying contravenes a pupil's right to protection from violence and inhuman or degrading treatment (Art.3 of the ECHR) and may also undermine his or her right to education (Art.2 of Prot. 1).

Schools have a duty to tackle bullying. An anti-bullying policy must be part of a school's disciplinary policy but may also be part of a preventive "whole-school" strategy. A policy should include a named person to whom any pupil or parent who has a concern about bullying may report the matter.

Where a school has a "whole school, no-blame" policy, or perhaps a peer mediation programme, the issues to be dealt with by such programmes (*e.g.* falling out between friends, name-calling, etc.) and those which must be referred to a teacher responsible for discipline must be agreed in advance. A designated teacher or peer mediation team will take time to listen to the disputants to understand what has happened and how they feel. A meeting with both sides may be arranged to find out if they can agree a solution. No-one is interrogated or punished but whoever is involved is required to understand how hurtful the behaviour has been and why it is important to try to put it right by agreed procedures.

Where bullying has not been resolved satisfactorily parents should speak to the principal. A victim of bullying has a right to know that his or her concerns are being dealt with properly, that the disciplinary policy is being implemented and that appropriate sanctions as well as behaviour monitoring plans are applied to the perpetrator. In very serious and persistent cases it may be appropriate for parents to contact the police. Further immediate advice can be obtained from NSPCC, Childline or the Children's Law Centre.

Physical punishment

Corporal punishment has been deemed to be inhuman or degrading treatment under the ECHR. Article 36 of the Education and Libraries (NI) Order 2003 makes it unlawful for a member of school staff (*i.e.* a teacher or any person who works at the school, whether for payment or not, who has lawful control or charge of a child) to give corporal punishment to a child for whom education is provided in any grant-aided school or whose education otherwise than at school is provided for by an ELB under article 86 of the 1986 Order. Corporal punishment is defined as "doing anything for the purpose of punishing a child (whether or not there are other reasons for doing it) which, apart from any justification, would constitute battery". Any teacher who uses physical force against a pupil may be open to criminal charges. However, in extreme situations, actions taken by a member of staff may not be deemed to be corporal punishment if done for reasons that include averting an immediate danger of personal injury to, or an immediate danger to the property of any person (including the child).

Disciplinary sanctions

Disciplinary sanctions intended to be used must have been made generally known to parents in the written disciplinary policy (art.5 of the 1998 Order). Any punishment must be reasonable in all the circumstances and proportionate to the misbehaviour and to the pupil's age and any special educational needs or religious requirements affecting him or her. In the case of detention, parents have a right to be told of the reason and given 24 hours' notice in writing before it takes place. Punishments which humiliate or ostracise pupils may be considered inhuman or degrading under the ECHR and punishments which discriminate on any ground (*e.g.* gender, race or religion) which cannot be objectively justified may also contravene the Sex Discrimination (NI) Order 1976, the Race Relations (NI) Order 1997 or section 76 of the Northern Ireland Act 1998.

If parents feel that their child has been unjustly or unreasonably punished, they should initially arrange to meet the school principal to discuss their concerns. If they are still not satisfied they should write to the chairperson of the governors or to the Department of Education. Legal advice should be sought from an advice centre.

Exclusion from school

Temporary or permanent exclusion from school is not on its own a breach of Article 2 of Protocol 1 to the ECHR, but it may be if it denies a pupil access to education elsewhere or the right to due process and a fair hearing. Each ELB, the governors of voluntary and integrated schools and the CCMS must have a scheme in place in relation to the suspension or expulsion of pupils. For further details see the Schools (Suspension and Expulsion of Pupils) Regulations (NI) 1995, as amended.

Temporary exclusion – suspension

An initial suspension should not exceed five school days and no pupil should be excluded for more than 45 days in any school year. The length of suspension should accord with the offence and must take individual circumstances into account. Parents must be notified immediately and told of the period of the suspension – pupils cannot just be sent home. Parents must be requested to meet the principal to discuss the matter and the ELB, the chairperson of the board of governors and, in the case of a Catholic maintained school, the local diocesan office of CCMS must also be informed.

Some points to raise at the meeting with the principal are:
- Clarify exactly why the child is being suspended (English statutory guidance precludes exclusion for minor misdemeanours such as

failure to do homework, poor attendance, pregnancy or not wearing school uniform).

- Is there any doubt that the child did what is claimed?
- Have alternative ways of improving behaviour been tried or have they been discussed with the SENCO (see p.426)?
- If the child does have SEN, is there an individual educational plan which could be amended, instead of suspension?
- What arrangements will be made to get work set and marked? (Even if suspension is implemented the school remains responsible for the pupil's education).

Any undertakings parents are asked to give about their child's future conduct should be put in writing to avoid any misunderstanding.

There is no statutory right of appeal against a decision to suspend (as with expulsion), however if parents are not satisfied they should ask for it to be reviewed. In the case of a controlled school, they should write to the chief education officer of the ELB, in the case of a Catholic maintained school to the director of the CCMS, and in the case of a voluntary or grant-maintained integrated school to the chairperson of the board of governors. If parents believe that the ELB or board of governors has acted unreasonably, they can complain to the Department of Education.

Permanent exclusion – expulsion

A pupil may be expelled from school only after serving a period of suspension and only after consultation about the matter has taken place between the principal, the parents and the chief executive of the ELB, the board of governors or the director of the CCMS and someone authorised by the director. Following a principal's recommendation to expel, a final decision is taken, in the case of a controlled school, by the ELB on the advice of a sub-committee, and in the case of Catholic maintained, voluntary and grant-maintained schools, by the board of governors.

Expulsion can disrupt a child's education badly. A suitable alternative school may be difficult to find and other alternatives, particularly for year 11 and 12 pupils, may be limited educationally. Before a decision to expel is taken a meeting must be held by the principal so that both the educational authorities and the family can consider the future education of the pupil. The precise form of the pre-expulsion meeting is not defined in the legislation, but in accordance with the UNCRC (Art.12) the pupil should have an opportunity to be heard.

Some points which can be raised at the meeting with the principal in addition to those listed above concerning suspension are:

- Have the child's age, health and personal issues been considered? Are there problems with bullying, discrimination, or racial, religious or sexual harassment which could be helped by support from an agency outside school?
- Should an SEN assessment or re-assessment be asked for instead of expulsion? Could the school cope if it received extra help from the ELB?
- Should a temporary period in a referral unit where pupils can get extra specialised support be considered?
- If there is no alternative to expulsion will the school help to get work marked and supervised for any exams?

Parents should consider carefully any suggestion that they should withdraw their child and transfer to another school to avoid the stigma of expulsion on the pupil's record. If parents feel this would unjustly deny them the opportunity of challenging the grounds for expulsion they can complain to the Department of Education under article 101 of the Education and Libraries (NI) Order 1986, as amended.

Appealing against expulsion

Parents can appeal to an appeal tribunal (art.49 of the Education (NI) Order 1993) if they feel the expulsion procedure was not followed properly or was unreasonable. Written notice of the right to appeal must be given to the parents immediately by the principal. ELBs must make arrangements "without delay" for appeal against a decision to expel a pupil from a grant-aided school in its area. Parents can complain if this does not happen.

The tribunal consists of three or five members and may not include staff of the school involved. A parent or pupil (if 18 or over) may make written representations to, and appear before, the tribunal and may be accompanied by a friend or legal representative, but there is no general recognition of a pupil's right to be heard. The tribunal will also hear representations from a member of the board of governors or ELB.

The tribunal must have regard all the circumstances of the case and in particular any representations made by the parent, pupil, expelling authority or ELB, whether the expulsion procedure was properly followed and the interests of other pupils and teachers in the school .

If parents believe that no reasonable authority could have made the decision reached by the tribunal they can seek a judicial review (see Chapter 2).

Education otherwise than at school (EOTAS)

If a pupil is expelled an ELB has the power to direct another specified grant-aided school within a reasonable distance from the child's home to admit the child, provided it is not one from which he or she has already been suspended or expelled. A school which has a vacant place may refuse admission to a pupil on the grounds of "prejudice to the efficient use of resources", but an ELB can appeal against this to the Department of Education.

ELBs must produce a statement setting out the arrangements made or proposed for assisting schools to deal with general or individual behavioural problems and for assisting children with behavioural difficulties to find places at suitable schools (art.6 of the Education (NI) Order 1998). In some cases home tuition may be provided.   However this is often very limited and may not be appropriate for pupils with behavioural difficulties. Arguably, unless it is the only option (for instance in the case of illness) it could amount to a breach of the right to education under Article 2 of Protocol 1 to the ECHR.

Some ELBs provide pupil referral units for older post-primary age pupils whose behaviour and attendance is too disruptive for schools to manage.   Department of Education guidance states that all such placements should ensure that the young person receives a curriculum of basic skills and opportunities for suitable work experience, with courses which lead to accredited qualifications. Parents should seek advice from a Citizens' Advice Bureau or the Children's Law Centre if they are concerned about their child's position.

Attendance at school

Regular school attendance is seen as both a measure of school effectiveness and of parents' compliance with their obligation to ensure their child receives a suitable education. Absenteeism is increasingly recognised as a risk to educational progress which schools should try to minimise. Schools must keep a register of pupils' attendance and a school can legally authorise absence only in the following instances:

- sickness (medical certificate required) or other unavoidable cause (such as a wedding or religious day of observance, for which permission must be obtained),
- there is an absence of arrangements for transporting the child to the nearest "suitable school" and he or she is outside the statutory walking distance (or there is some transport but the child still has to walk this distance),
- the child is employed on work experience, or
- the parent can prove that he or she is engaged in a trade or business which requires him or her to travel and the child has attended school as regularly as the trade or business permitted and for at least 100 days during the last 12 months (art.48 of the 1986 Order).

Persistent absence

Schools must inform the ELB if a pupil does not attend regularly and has no reasonable excuse. Regular attendance is not defined, but education welfare officers consider absence to be serious if it is above 25%. Schools themselves have no legal means of dealing with unauthorised absence but they can encourage better attendance by investigating the reason for unexplained absences, by providing additional support for pupils and by maintaining regular contact with parents.

ELBs can seek legal enforcement of school attendance if parents may be at fault. The first step is a school attendance order (art.27 of the 1996 Order). More serious cases are likely to involve an educational supervision order (ESO).

School attendance orders

An ELB may serve a written notice requiring a parent to satisfy it within 14 days that a child is receiving a suitable education and it may send an education welfare officer to the home to investigate. If the parents cannot satisfy the ELB and it is believed to be expedient that the child should attend school, the ELB must give 14 days' notice to the parents of its intention to serve a school attendance order on the parents requiring the pupil to become a registered pupil at a named school. Parents may within the time limit of the notice apply for the child to be admitted to another grant-aided or independent school. There is no provision for the child's views to be sought.

A school attendance order must continue in force, unless amended by the ELB, for as long as the child is of compulsory school age or would normally leave the specified school. Parents may apply for the order to be revoked if arrangements have been made for suitable education otherwise than at school. If this is refused they can appeal to the Department of Education.

Education supervision orders

Where a child is a registered pupil at a school but does not attend regularly (or is the subject of a school attendance order which is not being complied with), the ELB can seek an education supervision order at the family proceedings court (art.55 of the Children (NI) Order 1995). This has the effect of transferring to the ELB the duty and rights of the parents to secure the child's education.

When making an order the court has a duty to consider the child's welfare as paramount (art.3). An education supervisor is appointed to "advise, assist and befriend the child and to give directions to the child and his or her parents" in a way that will (in the opinion of the supervisor) secure that he or she is properly educated. The supervisor must first "ascertain the wishes and feelings of the child and his or her parents, including their wishes about where the child is to be educated" and "give due consideration, having regard to the child's age and understanding" to such wishes. Directions might include requiring the parents to escort the child to school or keeping the supervisor informed of any change of the child's address (especially if an older child might abscond from home). Parents are guilty of an offence if they fail to comply, unless they can show that the direction was unreasonable or that they took all reasonable steps to comply. An ESO is initially made for one year. It may be extended (up to three years) provided this is done three months prior to the date of expiry.

The child, his or her parents or the ELB may apply to a court to discharge an ESO if it is established that he or she is receiving a suitable education. An ELB may apply for a discharge if it believes an ESO has failed. The court may then direct social services to investigate the child's circumstances. This may result in a care order, which removes the child from the care of his or her parents (see Chapter 18).

Financial considerations

Grant-aided schools may not charge fees or ask parents to pay for or supply books, instruments, equipment or transport required in the statutory curriculum or an approved public examination syllabus. Voluntary grammar schools are an exception and most charge an annual capital fee. All schools may, however, charge for optional extra activities which are additional to the statutory curriculum (*e.g.* music, sports or additional non-compulsory academic subjects which take place wholly or mainly outside school), entry fees for non-required public examinations and board and lodging for residential field trips. Parents on income support or jobseeker's allowance should have costs remitted. Parents can be asked to contribute to school funds provided it is clear that contributions are not obligatory and that pupils will not be treated differently as a result.

Transport assistance

ELBs must make the arrangements considered necessary for the provision of transport, or otherwise or as the Department may direct, for the purposes of facilitating the attendance of pupils at a grant-aided school. They must draw up and publish schemes on the provision of home to school transport. Free transport is provided for pupils attending special schools and for those whose statement of special educational needs requires it and may also be provided where there is a short-term medical or health need.

Assistance with transport may be provided for those who have sought and been refused a place at a "suitable" school or FE college within statutory walking distance from their home, *i.e.* more than two miles from the nearest "suitable" school for a primary pupil or more than three miles from the nearest "suitable" post-primary school (see p. 415 above). To be eligible for transport assistance pupils must first have applied to all schools in the same category that are within walking distance before a preference is expressed for a school which is outside this distance.

Pupils are able to use existing transport services provided by ELBs but additional services are not required to be provided. Transport assistance may include passes for public transport or a contribution to petrol expenses for parents who can drive children to school. ELBs may in some circumstances be under an obligation to provide transport assistance for pupils who live within the statutory walking distance if it is considered "necessary" (Circular 1996/41), for instance, because of the duration or safety of the journey.

Parents who are concerned about the decision of an ELB regarding transport should take it up with the ELB in the first instance. If they are still dissatisfied they may complain to the Department of Education under article 101 of the Education and Libraries (NI) Order 1986, as amended.

School uniforms and PE kit grants

ELBs may give assistance towards the cost of a school uniform and PE kit for special and post-primary school pupils (PE kit only for further education) if parents are on income support or jobseeker's allowance. A separate application on a form obtained from ELB offices has to be made each year.

Education maintenance allowance

Educational maintenance allowance is a mandatory means-tested benefit to assist with the cost of remaining at school beyond the minimum compulsory school leaving age (16 years). The amount is graduated according to the parents' income. A separate application must be made for each child each year. Payment is subject to satisfactory school attendance.

School meals

Midday meals are available in all grant-aided schools and free meals are provided to pupils whose parents are in receipt of income support or jobseeker's allowance. An application form endorsed by the Social Security Agency must be completed and sent to the ELB headquarters as soon as entitlement arises; free meals cannot be provided until official confirmation is received.

Taking matters further

If parents or pupils have a problem or complaint about the education provided in their school it may be simply a question of finding out who to complain to and what remedies are available. Despite the increasing range of responsibilities of schools and educational authorities, however, it is often difficult to establish that duties imposed by educational legislation correspond clearly to substantive and specific educational rights.

It is usually always best to try to get things sorted out with the member of staff concerned or to raise the issue with the child's form tutor, pastoral year head or principal. Some schools may have a specific complaints procedure which should be followed. If the principal does not solve the problem it can be taken up with the board of governors. Parents can approach governors about any school issue and have a right to be told governors' names and addresses. A letter to the chairperson of the governors will put a complaint formally on record. It is important to keep copies of all correspondence.

Appeal to a Complaints Tribunal

If a complaint is not satisfactorily dealt with within the school by the board of governors, the next step will depend on the school sector involved and the type of complaint. As noted already in this chapter, ELBs are responsible for establishing independent tribunals to hear complaints from all school sectors in three main areas: admissions, expulsions and the curriculum. There is also a Northern Ireland-wide Special Educational Needs Tribunal which has different rules of operation and a legally qualified chair.

ELB complaints tribunals are meant to give parents an opportunity to argue in a non-legal context that a school or ELB has not applied the rules or procedures properly. Parents may appear at the tribunal and present evidence and may be accompanied by a friend or be represented. Tribunals may generally only consider whether a school acted reasonably and legally and followed the correct procedures. Where there are special procedures for appeal or complaint these must be exhausted before taking a complaint further.

Complaint to the Department of Education

If an ELB or board of governors fails to comply with any direction of an appeal tribunal, or the matter is not resolved by a tribunal, and for matters not specifically dealt with by one of the complaints tribunals above, parents may complain to the Department of Education under article 101 of the 1986 Order, as amended by article 158 of the Education Reform (NI) Order 1989, if they think the school or another educational body has behaved "unreasonably" or failed in their duties. A complaint can also be about ELBs, CCMS and the

CCEA.   If the Department is satisfied that there has been an unreasonable exercise of a power or duty it must give directions to remedy the complaint.   However this procedure is very rarely used and it can take up to six months or more.   Parents can ask their MLA to help with a complaint to the Department of Education.

Judicial review

Parents who are dissatisfied with the decision of an appeal tribunal, the Department of Education or the board of governors of a school, and who believe that such a body has acted illegally, unreasonably or unfairly in not following the proper procedure, may seek a judicial review in the High Court.   However it is essential that a judicial review is taken promptly (and certainly within three months) and it is necessary to be legally represented.   Some drawbacks with pursuing an application for judicial review are that generally the court can reverse a decision only if it can be shown that the ELB or Department in question considered inappropriate (or did not consider appropriate) evidence or that no reasonable authority could have made the decision in question.   Even if a judicial review finds in favour of a complainant, the High Court may not necessarily reverse a decision or order any remedy, such as the admission of a child who has been refused a place.

Further useful addresses

- Department of Education
  Rathgael House
  43 Balloo Road
  Bangor
  Co Down BT19 7PR
  tel: 028 9127 9279
  www.deni.gov.uk

- Belfast Education and Library Board
  40 Academy Street
  Belfast BT1 2NQ
  tel: 028 9056 4000
  www.belb.org.uk

- North Eastern Education and Library Board
  County Hall
  182 Galgorm Road
  Ballymena
  Co Antrim BT42 1HN
  tel: 028 2565 3333
  www.neelb.org.uk

- South Eastern Education and Library Board
  Grahamsbridge Road
  Dundonald
  Belfast BT16 2HS
  tel: 028 9056 6200
  www.seelb.org.uk

- Southern Education and Library Board
  3 Charlemont Place
  The Mall
  Armagh
  Co Armagh BT61 9AX
  tel: 028 3751 2200
  www.selb.org

- Western Education and Library Board
  1 Hospital Road
  Omagh
  Co. Tyrone BT79 0AW
  tel: 028 8241 1411
  www.welbni.org

- Council for Curriculum, Examinations and Assessment
  Clarendon Dock
  29 Clarendon Road
  Belfast BT1 3BG
  tel: 028 9026 1200
  www.ccea.org.uk

- Special Educational Needs Tribunal
  Albany House
  73-75 Great Victoria Street
  Belfast BT2 7AA
  tel: 028 9032 2894

- Independent Panel for Special Education Advice
  Graham House
  Saintfield Road
  Belfast BT8 8BH
  tel: 028 9070 5654

- Educational Guidance Service for Adults
  4th floor, 40 Linenhall Street
  Belfast BT2 8BA
  tel: 028 9024 4274
  www.egsa.org.uk

- The Children's Law Centre
  3rd floor, Philip House
  123-137 York Street
  Belfast BT15 1AB
  tel: 028 9024 5704
  Freephone 0808 808 5678 (Young People's Advice and Information)
  www.childrenslawcentre.org

- NSPCC
  Jennymount Court
  North Derby Street
  Belfast BT15 3HN
  Freephone 0800 800 500
  www.nspcc.org.uk

- Disability Action
  Portside Business Park
  189 Airport Road West
  Belfast BT3 9ED
  tel: 028 9029 7880
  www.disabilityaction.org

Chapter 20

Employment Rights

Mark Reid [*]

There has been extensive legal intervention in employment relations in Northern Ireland for many years. For convenience, the resulting laws, whether made by Parliament or by judges, can be divided into two categories. This chapter covers both, though the main focus is on the first.

- Individual employment law is concerned with the rights and obligations flowing from the terms of the contract between an employee and an employer. In recent years employees have been given the protection of a "floor" of employment rights, which can be improved upon by negotiation with an employer.
- Collective employment law is primarily concerned with the regulation of the bargaining relationships between trade unions and employers or employers' associations.

For an account of employment law with particular reference to religious or political belief, gender, ethnic origin, or disability see Chapters 12-15 respectively.

Employment law and the legal system

The introduction of substantial employment rights for employees has also resulted in the creation of specialised judicial bodies:

- The industrial tribunals are established under the Industrial Tribunals (NI) Order 1996. They deal mainly with individual employment matters such as unfair dismissal, redundancy, trade union rights, maternity rights and sex discrimination. They are intended to provide cheap, quick and informal methods of hearing complaints, but in many cases, due to the complexity of the legislation, the reality is different. Legal aid is not available for tribunal hearings but it is possible to utilise the "green form" scheme (see Chapter 2),

---

[*] Much of the material in this chapter derives from that produced for the third edition of this handbook by Richard Steele.

whereby subsidised advice and assistance can be obtained from a solicitor in advance of a hearing. Appeals are available on a point of law to the Court of Appeal.

- The Fair Employment Tribunal, which now exists under the Fair Employment and Treatment (NI) Order 1998, hears complaints of discrimination on grounds of religious belief or political opinion (see Chapter 12) and is constituted in the same way as industrial tribunals.
- The Industrial Court is established by the Industrial Relations (NI) Order 1992 and acts as an arbitration body. Its role has been greatly enhanced as a result of its being given the power to determine issues relating to the recognition of trade unions following implementation of the Employment Relations (NI) Order 1999.

The relevant government department responsible for employment legislation and policy is the Department for Employment and Learning (DEL), but responsibility for certain employment functions has been devolved to various statutory bodies:

- The Labour Relations Agency (LRA), now established by the Industrial Relations (NI) Order 1992, has the duty to promote the improvement of industrial relations, in particular by attempting to settle trade disputes. It mainly provides advisory, conciliation, mediation and arbitration services.
- The Health and Safety Executive Northern Ireland was established by the Health and Safety at Work (NI) Order 1978. It reviews health, safety and welfare in connection with work and the control of dangerous substances. Together with district councils it has responsibility for the enforcement of safety laws.
- The post of Certification Officer was established by the Industrial Relations (NI) Order 1992. The Certification Officer has duties in respect of trade unions and employers' associations.
- The Equality Commission for Northern Ireland can provide assistance to individuals who have been discriminated against in the workplace in certain circumstances (see Chapter 11).

Contracts of employment

The great majority of employment rights which can be adjudicated upon by an industrial tribunal are limited to employees. An employee is defined in article 3 of the Employment Rights (NI) Order 1996 (the 1996 Order) as an "individual who has entered into or works under a contract of employment." Case-law has expanded the understanding of the definition of "employee". Essentially there are certain fundamental conditions which must be satisfied:

- the individual must agree to provide work personally; a substitute cannot be nominated;
- there must be mutuality of obligation between the employer and employee; if there is no obligation on an individual to turn up to work, or if he or she is engaged on a "casual as required" basis, he or she will not be an employee; and
- the individual worker must be subject to the overall control of the employer.

If these three conditions are satisfied it is then necessary to look at other elements of the working relationship, for instance who provides equipment to carry out the work. It should be noted that just because a person is described as self-employed and pays tax and national insurance on a self-employed basis, this does not necessarily preclude that person from being an employee.

While many of the rights specified in the 1996 Order are limited to an individual who is an "employee", for instance the right to claim unfair dismissal or a redundancy payment, some other rights can be claimed by a "worker." For instance, a "worker" is protected under the provisions relating to unauthorised deductions from wages. Many of the rights provided as a result of EC Directives are also provided to "workers". Whilst the definition of "worker" includes an employee, it is also wider. It covers almost all contracts to perform work other than that carried out on a self-employed basis.

The basis of an employment relationship is the law of contract. A contract is formed when an employer makes a job offer to a potential employee and that offer is accepted. The terms of the contract define the rights and duties of both parties. These terms are normally a mixture of express, implied, statutory and incorporated terms:

- Express terms, which may be written or oral, are those actually agreed by the employer and employee.
- Implied terms may exist by the operation of custom and practice in an industry or be terms necessary to make the contract of employment work.
- Statutory terms are those implied into a contract by an Act of Parliament, such as the Equal Pay Act (NI) 1970 (see Chapter 13).
- Incorporated terms are those agreed by collective bargaining between a trade union and an employer and incorporated into the

contracts of employment of each employee covered by the collective agreement.

The courts have held that certain implied terms are basic to every contract of employment. The most important of these are:

- that an employee will obey all lawful and reasonable orders, take reasonable care in his or her work, not wilfully disrupt the employer's business and be honest; and
- that an employer will pay agreed wages, take reasonable care for the employee's safety and health, not require an employee to do illegal acts and not act in a manner likely to destroy the relationship of trust or confidence.

Illegal contracts

Contracts which are unlawful (*e.g.* to commit a crime) or contrary to public policy (*e.g.*, to pay a prostitute) are unenforceable.

Likewise, whilst a contract may be capable of being performed lawfully, if it is carried out unlawfully then it will not be enforceable. The most common illegal contract is that which involves a fraud on the Inland Revenue due to the failure to pay tax or national insurance. An individual who has evaded tax will not be able to claim unfair dismissal or breach of contract. However he or she will still be able to claim sex discrimination (and presumably the other types of discrimination also) – see *Hall v Woolston Hall Leisure Limited* (2000).

Written statements of terms

Often there is no formal written contract, making it difficult to ascertain what terms have been agreed between the parties. For this reason Part III of the 1996 Order provides that an employee who is to be employed for more than one month must be provided with a written statement of employment particulars not later than two months after the beginning of employment.

This statement is not automatically a contract of employment and is indeed often only what the employer believes has been agreed with the employee. It is, however, good evidence of what might be contained in the contract of employment.

The following particulars must be given in a single document:
- the names of the employer and employee;

- the date when any period of continuous employment began (taking into account any employment with a previous employer which counts);
- the scale or rate of pay or the method of calculating pay;
- the intervals at which wages are to be paid (*e.g.* weekly or monthly);
- the hours of work;
- entitlement to holidays, including public holidays, holiday pay and entitlement to accrued holiday pay on the termination of employment;
- the title of the job or a brief description of the work; and
- the place of work.

The employer must also provide the following information, although this can be given in instalments:
- the length of notice which the employee has to give or receive to end the contract of employment;
- if the employment is not intended to be permanent, the period for which it is expected to continue or, if it is for a fixed-term, the date when it is to end;
- any collective agreements which directly affect the terms and conditions of employment; and
- other details if the employee is required to work outside the UK in respect of pay, the currency in which he or she is to be paid and how long he or she has to work outside the UK.

The employer also has to provide details of the terms and conditions relating to the following matters, although these can be referred to in a document which is reasonably accessible to the employee:
- incapacity for work due to sickness or injury, including any provision for sick pay; and
- pensions and pension schemes.

The employer also has to provide a note in the statement of employment particulars either specifying grievance procedures or referring to a document where these can be reasonably accessed. Only employers who employ more than 20 employees have to provide details in relation to disciplinary procedures (though this exemption is expected to be repealed in Northern Ireland during 2003). If there are no provisions in the contract about any of the above matters, this must be stated in the statement of employment particulars.

Where there is a change in any of the particulars, the employer must give the employee a written statement containing particulars of the change at the earliest opportunity and in any event not later than one month after the change in question.

If the particulars are not provided, the employee can complain to an industrial tribunal. The tribunal has no power to award compensation but it can declare what the particulars which should have been given are. The complaint can be brought by the employee at any time while still working for the employer or within three months of the employment ending.

Part-time workers

The Part-Time Workers (Prevention of Less Favourable Treatment) Regulations (NI) 2000 make less favourable treatment of a part-time worker in comparison with a comparable full-time worker unlawful if there is no objective reason to justify it.

A worker who considers that the employer has treated him or her less favourably can request a written statement giving particulars of the reasons for the treatment. The worker is entitled to be provided with the employer's statement within 21 days.

An adverse inference can be drawn by an industrial tribunal from a failure to provide a written statement or if the statement is evasive or equivocal. A complaint in respect of unfavourable treatment or failure to provide a written statement can be made to an industrial tribunal within three months of the treatment or failure respectively.

Fixed-term workers

The Fixed-Term Employees (Prevention of Less Favourable Treatment) Regulations (NI) 2002 make less favourable treatment of fixed-term employees compared with comparable permanent employees on the grounds of their fixed-term status unlawful, again unless there is an objective reason to justify such treatment.

A fixed-term employee has the right not to be treated less favourably as regards the terms of the contract or by being subjected to any other detriment by any act or deliberate failure to act on the part of the employer.

A fixed-term employee who feels less favourably treated than a comparable permanent employee may submit a request in writing to the employer for a written statement of the reasons for the treatment. The employer must provide such a statement within 21 days of the request. Failure to provide a statement or an evasive or equivocal reply can lead the tribunal to draw an adverse inference if proceedings are subsequently issued. A complaint of less favourable treatment can be made to an industrial tribunal within three months of the treatment.

The Regulations also provide that, where a fixed-term employee who has been continuously employed on fixed-term contracts for four years or more is re-engaged on a fixed-term contract, the new contract will be regarded as a permanent contract unless the renewal on a fixed-term basis was objectively justified.

Minimum guaranteed rights

Itemised pay statements

Under Part III of the Employment Rights (NI) Order 1996 employees must be given an itemised pay statement every time they are paid. The statement must specify the gross and net wages payable, the amounts of any fixed or variable deductions and, where parts of the net wage are paid in different ways, the amount and method of each part payment.

If an employee does not get an itemised pay statement or disputes the content of the statement, he or she can complain to an industrial tribunal. If unnotified deductions have been made, the tribunal can order the employer to repay the amounts for the 13 weeks prior to the claim.

The minimum wage

The National Minimum Wage Act 1998 and the National Minimum Wage Regulations 1999 brought into force the National Minimum Wage (NMW). The Department of Trade and Industry has produced a booklet entitled "A Detailed Guide to the National Minimum Wage". The Northern Ireland Association of Citizens' Advice Bureaux, in partnership with the Inland Revenue, has set up an advice line (tel: 0845 6500207) to deal with inquiries and complaints in respect of the NMW.

The main rates from 1 October 2002 are as follows:
- workers aged 18-21 are entitled to £3.60 per hour (£3.80 from October 2003);

- workers aged 22 or over in the first six months of employment and doing accredited training are entitled to £3.60 per hour (£3.80 from October 2003); and
- workers aged 22 and over are entitled to £4.20 per hour (£4.50 from October 2003).

Home workers and agency workers are entitled to the NMW. However, certain groups are excluded, *e.g.* prisoners, voluntary workers, workers under 18, workers under 26 employed on the first 12 months of an apprenticeship and apprentices under 19.

An employer must keep records for a three year period which are sufficient to establish that a worker is being paid at least the NMW. A worker who has reasonable grounds for believing that he or she is not being paid the NMW is entitled to have access to and a copy of records within 14 days of a written request. If the worker is refused access he or she can complain to an industrial tribunal within three months of the refusal.

Workers who are not paid their entitlement to the NMW can make a claim for unlawful deductions from wages in the industrial tribunal or sue for breach of contract in the civil courts. The Inland Revenue also has powers to issue an enforcement notice where there has been a failure to pay NMW and to pursue claims in an industrial tribunal on behalf of a worker. It is a criminal offence to fail to pay the NMW or to falsify or fail to keep NMW records.

A worker subjected to a detriment or an employee dismissed due to action taken with a view to securing the benefit of any rights under the NMW can complain to an industrial tribunal. A dismissal in such circumstances will be treated as automatically unfair and no qualifying period of service is required to bring a claim for unfair dismissal.

Deductions from wages

Part IV of the Employment Rights (NI) Order 1996 provides that an employer must not make any deduction from the wages of any worker, or receive payments from the worker, unless the deduction or payment is authorised by statute or by a relevant provision in the worker's contract, or agreed in writing in advance by the worker.

The legislation gives additional special protection to workers in retail employment.

A worker may complain to an industrial tribunal about unlawful wage deductions, provided he or she does so within three months of the deduction being made.

Guarantee payments

Part V of the Employment Rights (NI) Order 1996 provides that employees who have been employed for one month or more may be entitled to certain guarantee payments from their employer if they are laid off or put on short-time working. However, an employee will lose the right to payment if he or she refuses an offer of suitable alternative employment, if there is no work because of a trade dispute involving the employer or an associated employer, or if the employee does not comply with the reasonable requirement of the employer to be available for work. The right to guarantee payments is currently limited to a maximum of £17 a day (which is expected to rise in 2003) and will be paid for up to five days in any three-month period. An employee who does not receive the appropriate payment can apply to an industrial tribunal within three months of the day for which he or she was not paid.

Payment when suspended on medical grounds

There are certain types of employment in Northern Ireland, such as work with lead, paint and chemicals, which are covered by health and safety regulations allowing an employee to be suspended for medical reasons. A list of these regulations can be found in Part VIII of the Employment Rights (NI) Order 1996. The Order provides that an employee who has been suspended under these regulations and who has been continuously employed for one month or more is entitled to receive a normal week's pay for a maximum of 26 weeks. However, an employee will not be entitled to such payment if he or she is incapable of work due to illness or disablement, unreasonably refuses an offer from the employer of suitable alternative work or does not comply with the reasonable requirements of the employer to be available for work.

Hours of work

The Working Time Regulations (NI) 1998 (the WT Regulations) were introduced to implement an EC Working Time Directive which lays down minimum conditions relating to weekly working time, rest entitlements and annual leave and makes special provisions for working hours and health assessments in relation to night workers. The WT Regulations also implement certain aspects of the EC Young Workers Directive relating to adolescent workers (*i.e.* above the minimum school leaving age but under 18). The information in this section relates only to adult workers.

The main entitlements and limits referred to in the WT Regulations provide the following for adult workers:

- a limit on the average weekly working time of 48 hours for each seven days;
- a limit on the average length of night work to eight hours in every 24 hour period;
- a limit on actual length of night work to eight hours in every 24 hour period where work involves special hazards or heavy physical or mental strain;
- a limit on assigning a worker to night work unless an opportunity of a free health assessment has been granted;
- a free health assessment at regular intervals for a night worker;
- adequate rest breaks where the organisation of work is such as to put the health and safety of a worker at risk, in particular because the work is monotonous or the work rate is predetermined;
- a daily rest period of 11 consecutive hours in each 24 hour period;
- an uninterrupted weekly rest period of not less than 24 hours in each seven day period;
- an entitlement to an (unpaid) rest break of 20 minutes where the working day is more than six hours; and
- a right to four weeks' paid annual leave.

Enforcement of the above (except the last four rights) is the responsibility of the local council or the Health and Safety Executive. Broadly speaking, local councils are responsible for offices, catering services, hotels, sports and retail premises. The Health and Safety Executive is the enforcing agency for building and construction sites, colleges, schools, hospitals, quarries, fairgrounds and broadcasting studios. For details see the Health and Safety Executive (Enforcing Authority) Regulations (NI) 1999. A failure to comply with any requirements which a local council or the Health and Safety Executive are responsible for is a criminal offence, punishable by a fine.

In relation to the last four rights listed above, a worker may present a complaint to an industrial tribunal where the employer has refused to permit the worker to exercise the rights. This must be done within three months of the breach.

A worker also has the right not to be subjected to a detriment and dismissal of an employee will be automatically unfair if it is for a reason connected with rights and entitlements under the WT Regulations. An employee does not require any length of service to present a claim.

Exclusions and modifications

The WT Regulations do not currently apply at all to persons involved in:

- air, rail, road, sea, inland water ways and lake transport;
- sea fishing;
- other work at sea; or
- the activities of doctors in training.

However, DEL has announced that it is introducing amending regulations to implement EC Directive 2000/34 to cover all non-mobile workers in the excluded sectors and off-shore and railway workers.

It is possible for workers to sign a written agreement to opt out of the 48-hour weekly maximum. The agreement to opt out can be ended by the worker giving notice in writing. The length of the notice required cannot be a period less than seven days or more than three months.

Workers whose working time is not measured or pre-determined or determined by the workers themselves on account of the specific characteristics of their job are excluded from the limit on the average working week and from requirements as to daily and weekly rest periods, breaks and hours of work for night workers. Such workers may be:

- management executives or other persons with autonomous decision-taking powers;
- family workers; or
- workers officiating at religious ceremonies in churches and religious communities.

Workers employed as domestic servants in a private household are excluded from the provisions relating to the 48-hour week, length of night work, health assessments, transfer to day work and breaks for monotonous work.

A collective agreement or a work-force agreement may modify or exclude the provisions on daily and weekly rest periods, breaks and hours of work for night workers. In such cases, if a worker is required to work during what would otherwise be a rest period, the employer is under a duty wherever possible to allow the worker to take an equivalent period of compensatory rest. In exceptional cases where this is not possible, the employer is under a duty only to afford the worker such protection as may be appropriate in order to safeguard the worker's health and safety.

Sunday working

The Shops (Sunday Trading etc.) (NI) Order 1997 provides for the rights of shop workers in relation to Sunday working. The legislation applies to two different types of workers: "protected shop workers" and "opted-out shop workers".

A protected shop worker is an individual who was employed as a shop worker before 4 December 1997 who was not required under contract to work on a Sunday. A protected shop worker cannot now be required to work on a Sunday unless he or she has given the employer a signed opting-in notice expressly stating that there is no objection from the worker to Sunday working.

An opted-out shop worker is an individual who has at any stage provided his or her employer with an opted-out notice. An opted-out notice is a notice signed and dated by the shop worker stating that he or she objects to Sunday working. It takes effect three months after the notice is given to the employer.

A shop worker who is subjected to a detriment or dismissed for asserting rights in relation to Sunday working can complain to an industrial tribunal within three months of the detriment or dismissal.

Whistleblowing

The Public Interest Disclosure (NI) Order 1998 inserts provisions into the 1996 Order which seek to protect workers who disclose information relating to wrongdoing. Workers have a right not to suffer detriment in employment and employees have a right not to be unfairly dismissed for making protected disclosures. Such a dismissal will be automatically unfair and not subject to a qualifying period of continuous employment.

A qualifying disclosure

A qualifying disclosure is information which, in the reasonable belief of the worker making the disclosure, tends to show one or more of the following:

- that a criminal offence has been committed or is likely to be committed;
- that a person has failed, is failing or is likely to fail to comply with any legal obligation to which he or she is subject (*e.g.* a breach of the contract of employment: *Parkins v Sodexho* (2002);
- that a miscarriage of justice has occurred, is occurring or is likely to occur;
- that the health or safety of any individual has been, is being or is likely to be endangered;
- that the environment has been, is being or is likely to be damaged, or
- that information tending to show any matter falling within any one of the above is being or is likely to be deliberately concealed.

To be a "protected" disclosure, the qualifying disclosure must be made to the worker's employer, to a government Minister (if the employer is a body appointed by statute), during the course of obtaining legal advice or to any other "prescribed" person (see the Public Interest Disclosure (Prescribed Persons) Order (NI) 1999).

Right to be accompanied at disciplinary and grievance hearings

Articles 12–17 of the Employment Relations (NI) Order 1999 make provision for a worker to be accompanied by a fellow worker or a trade union official at a disciplinary or a grievance hearing. Where the chosen companion is not available, the employer must postpone the hearing to an alternative time proposed by the worker (provided the alternative time is reasonable and falls within five working days).

A worker is protected against being subjected to a detriment and dismissal is automatically unfair if the reason for detriment or dismissal is because the employee sought to exercise the rights of accompaniment or postponement or to accompany a fellow worker as a companion. No qualifying period of continuous service is required to claim unfair dismissal in these circumstances.

Stakeholder pensions

An employer who employs five people or more must provide access to a stakeholder pension scheme unless access to a suitable personal or occupational pension scheme is already being offered. The employer does not have to contribute to the stakeholder pension scheme, but does have to ensure that there is at least one registered stakeholder pension scheme which offers membership to all relevant employees.

The employer does not have to provide access to the scheme for employees whose earnings are below the national insurance lower earnings limit (£77 per week from April 2003) or who are unable to join the scheme because they are under 18 or within five years of the scheme's normal retirement age.

The Occupational Pensions Regulatory Authority (OPRA) (tel: 01273 627600) is responsible for regulating and registering stakeholder pension schemes and regulating whether employers offer access and follow the rules for paying employee contributions to the scheme providers

Maternity rights

Maternity leave

Under changes introduced as a result of the Employment (NI) Order 2002, a woman whose baby is expected on or after 6 April 2003 will benefit from new leave rights. The length of ordinary maternity leave will be increased from 18 to 26 weeks regardless of how long she has worked for her employer. A woman who has completed 26 weeks continuous service with her employer by the 15th week before her expected week of confinement (EWC) will be able to take additional maternity leave. Additional maternity leave will start immediately after ordinary maternity leave and continue for a further 26 weeks.

A pregnant employee will be required to notify her employer of her intention to take maternity leave by the 15th week before her EWC, unless this is not reasonably practicable. She will need to tell her employer that she is pregnant, the week her baby is expected to be born and when she wants her maternity leave to start. She can change her mind about when she wants to start her leave provided she tells her employer at least 28 days in advance (unless this is not reasonably practicable).

On receipt of a woman's notification an employer must respond to the employee within 28 days. The employer has to write to the employee setting out the date on which the employer expects her to return to work if she takes her full entitlement to maternity leave. A woman who intends to return to work at the end of her full maternity leave entitlement does not have to give any further notification to her employer. To return to work before the end of her maternity leave an employee will have to give her employer 28 days' notice of the date she wants to return to work.

The earliest date at which maternity leave can start is the beginning of the 11th week before the baby is due. If a woman is absent from work for a pregnancy related illness during the four weeks before the start of her EWC her maternity leave will start automatically. In addition, an employee entitled to maternity leave must not work or be permitted to work by her employer during the period of two weeks beginning with the date of her confinement.

During the 26 weeks of ordinary maternity leave the employee continues to be employed and to benefit from the normal terms and conditions of employment other than the term or condition relating to remuneration. During additional maternity leave the employee will continue to benefit from certain contractual terms.

A woman returning from ordinary maternity leave is entitled to return to the same job, under the same terms and conditions as if she had not been absent. An employee entitled to additional maternity leave has a right to return to the same job as she was employed in before her absence or, where not reasonably practicable, to a job with at least the same terms and conditions as her old position, and of an equivalent or better status. In the case of additional maternity leave the position varies where an employee works for a company employing five employees or less.

Dismissal of a woman on grounds of redundancy is automatically unfair if the employer has failed to offer her a suitable alternative vacancy. It is unlawful to subject a woman to a detriment and dismissal is automatically unfair if it is for a reason connected to her pregnancy or the fact that she has given birth or sought to avail of maternity leave. However, if the employer employs less than six employees there will not be an automatically unfair dismissal if it is not reasonably practicable for the employer either to allow the woman to return to the same job or to offer her a suitable alternative job. This may, however, amount to an ordinary unfair dismissal if the employee has been employed for at least a year.

Maternity pay

A woman who is entitled to Statutory Maternity Pay (SMP) or Maternity Allowance (MA) and whose EWC begins on or after 6 April 2003 is able to receive SMP or MA for 26 weeks.

A woman continuously employed for 26 weeks by the same employer by the 15th week before the EWC who has average weekly earnings of at least the lower earnings limit (£77 from April 2003) may be eligible for SMP. From 6 April 2003, a woman who qualifies for SMP will be entitled to SMP at 90% of average weekly earnings for the first six weeks of the pay period from her employer. Thereafter she will be entitled to a standard rate of SMP from her employer of £100 per week (or 90% of the woman's average weekly earnings if this is less than £100 per week).

A woman who does not qualify for SMP who has earned on average £30 per week in the 66 weeks up to the EWC and has been employed for 26 of those weeks may qualify for MA. If a woman qualifies for MA she will receive £100 per week (or 90% of her average weekly earnings if this is less than £100).

Risk assessment for mothers

The Management of Health and Safety at Work Regulations (NI) 2000 place specific obligations on employers to carry out a risk assessment of work undertaken by women of child-bearing age or a new or expectant mother where she may be exposed to any process, working condition or physical, chemical or biological agent which could give rise to risks to the health or safety of the woman or the baby. Where an employer is notified that a woman employee is pregnant, has given birth within the previous six months or is breast-feeding, the employer must again undertake a review of the current risk assessments for those tasks undertaken by the women in order to identify potential risk. If necessary, preventive or protective measures must be put in place and the employee informed of the contents of the assessment and the measures taken. If it is not possible to avoid the risk, the employer is required to alter the woman's working conditions or, if this is not practicable, to take action to find suitable alternative employment or to place the woman on paid leave for as long as is necessary to protect her safety or health or that of her baby.

Paternity leave and pay

From 6 April 2003 provisions made under the Employment (NI) Order 2002 will enable a person who has or expects to have responsibility for a child's upbringing and who is the biological father of the child or the mother's husband or partner to take paternity leave. To qualify such a person will have to be continuously employed by his or her employer for 26 weeks leading into the 15th week before the baby is due. The paternity leave must be taken within 56 days of the actual date of birth of the child. Only one period of paternity leave is available regardless of whether more than one child is born as a result of the same pregnancy. The paternity leave can be up to two consecutive weeks.

To avail of paternity leave an employee is required to inform the employer of his or her intention to take paternity leave by the 15th week before the baby is expected, unless this is not reasonably practicable. At the same time the employee will need to tell the employer the week the baby is due, whether s/he wishes to take one or two weeks' leave and when s/he wants the leave to start. An employee will be able to change his or her mind about the date on which s/he wants the leave to start, provided that s/he tells his employer at least 28 days in advance, unless this is not reasonably practicable.

An employee who has average weekly earnings above the lower earnings limit for national insurance purposes (£77 per week from April 2003) may qualify for statutory paternity pay, which is £100 per week or 90% of average weekly earnings if this is less than £100 (*i.e.* the same rate as the standard rate of SMP).

Adoption leave and pay

Adoption leave will be available to an employee where an approved adoption agency notifies the employee of a match with a child on or after the 6 April 2003. To qualify the employee will have to have continuously worked for the employer for 26 weeks leading into the week in which he or she is notified of being matched with a child for an adoption. Adoption leave and pay will not be available in circumstances where a child is not newly matched for adoption, for example, when a step-parent is adopting a partner's child.

An employee will be entitled to up to 26 weeks' ordinary adoption leave followed by up to 26 weeks' additional adoption leave. Only one period of leave will be available regardless of whether more than one child is placed for adoption as part of the same arrangement. An individual can choose to start leave from the date of the child's placement or from a fixed date which can be up to 14 days before the expected date of placement.

Adoption leave and pay will be available to only one member of a couple where a couple adopt jointly. The couple may choose which partner takes adoption leave. The other member of a couple who adopts may be entitled to paternity leave and pay.

Statutory adoption pay is payable for up to 26 weeks at the same rate as the standard rate for SMP (£100 per week or 90% of average weekly earnings if this is less than £100). It will be paid only to an employee who has average weekly earnings above the lower earnings limit for national insurance contributions (£77 from April 2003).

An employee will be required to inform the employer of the intention to take adoption leave within seven days of being notified by an adoption agency that he or she has been matched with a child for adoption, unless this is not reasonably practicable. The employee will also have to tell the employer when the child is expected to be placed with the employee and when he or she wants adoption leave to start. An employee will be able to change his or her mind about the date on which he or she wants leave to start, provided the employer is told at least 28 days in advance, unless this is not reasonably practicable. The employee will also have to tell the employer the date he or she expects any payments of statutory adoption pay to start at least 28 days in advance, unless again this is not reasonably practicable.

An employer will have to respond to an employee's notification of leave within 28 days. An employer will need to write to the employee setting out the date on which the employee is expected to return to work if the full entitlement to adoption leave is taken.

An employee who intends to return to work at the end of full adoption leave does not have to give any further notification to his or her employer. An employee who wants to return to work before the end of adoption leave must give 28 days' notice of the date he or she intends to return.

During ordinary adoption leave, an employee will be entitled to the benefit of normal terms and conditions of employment, except for terms relating to wages or salary. During additional adoption leave, the employment contract continues and some contractual benefits and obligations will remain in force, similar to the position regarding maternity leave (see above).

Right to sick pay

Statutory Sick Pay ("SSP") is payable by an employer to an employee for up to 28 weeks at a rate of £64.35 per week from April 2003. Employees must earn at least the lower earnings limit for national insurance contribution liability (£77 from April 2003) and be ill for a period of four days or more in a row.

If the employee is sick for less than four days no SSP is payable. SSP is not payable for the first three days. After this period SSP is only payable for qualifying days.

To claim SSP the employee must notify the employer of his or her illness. Whilst an employer can set a time limit for notification, the employer cannot insist on notification being given personally or more than once in every seven days. Unless otherwise agreed, that notification should be given in writing. If the employer has not set any time limit for notification, the default time limit is that the employee should inform the employer by the seventh calendar day following the first qualifying day.

For the first seven days of absence self-certification is sufficient. After the first seven calendar days of sickness the employer may require the employee to supply medical evidence in the form of a doctor's statement. If notification is not given on time, the employer can still pay SSP if the employer accepts there was good cause for late notification. If the employer withholds SSP the employee can ask the employer for a written statement which explains why SSP is not being paid for the days in question. The employee can then ask the Inland Revenue for a decision on whether SSP is payable. This must be done within six months of the earliest day for which SSP is in dispute.

SSP will not be payable if the employee:

- is over the age of 65 on the first day of sickness;
- is no longer sick;
- has average weekly earnings less than the lower earnings limit (£77 per week from April 2003);
- has become sick within 57 days of having previously received a number of social security benefits;
- has had 28 weeks SSP from the employer (or from a former employer where the last day in which SSP was paid by the former employer was within 8 weeks of the current period of incapacity);
- has become pregnant and goes off sick during the maternity pay period;

- has done no work for the employer under the contract of employment;
- is in legal custody on the first day of incapacity for work; or
- has reached the end of the contract of employment (unless it can be shown that the employer ended the contract to avoid paying SSP).

The Fixed-Term (Prevention of Less Favourable Treatment) Regulations (NI) 2002 have removed the bar on employees being entitled to statutory sick pay where the contract was for a fixed period of three months or less.

Time off

Trade union activities

An employee who is a trade union member or representative is entitled to unpaid time off work to take part in activities of that trade union.

Time off for dependents

Article 85A of the 1996 Order provides that an employee can take a reasonable amount of (unpaid) time off during working hours if this is necessary:

- to provide assistance on an occasion when a dependent falls ill, gives birth or is injured or assaulted;
- to make arrangements for the provision of care for a dependent who is ill or injured;
- in consequence of the death of a dependent;
- because of the unexpected disruption or termination of arrangements for the care of a dependent, or
- to deal with an incident which involves a child of the employee and which occurs unexpectedly in a period during which an educational establishment which the child attends is responsible for that child.

An employee must tell the employer the reason for his or her absence as soon as is reasonably practicable (and, if able to, tell the employer before the absence how long the absence is expected to last).

In this context "dependent" means a child, a parent or a person who lives in the same household as the employee, otherwise than by reason of being an employee, tenant, lodger or boarder. For the purposes of the first two bullet points above, dependent also includes anyone who reasonably relies on the employee either for assistance on an occasion when the person falls ill, is injured or is assaulted, or to make arrangements for the provision of care in the event of illness or injury. For the purposes of the fourth bullet point, dependent includes any person who reasonably relies on the employee to make arrangements for the provision of care.

Flexible working

From 6 April 2003, the Employment (NI) Order 2002 makes provision for parents of children aged under six or of disabled children aged under 18 to have the right to apply to work flexibly. To qualify an employee must have worked with the employer continuously for 26 weeks at the date the application is made and have or expect to have responsibility for a child's upbringing and be making the application so as to be able to care for the child.

The initial onus will be on the employee to make an application in writing to the employer. Only one application can be made per year. Within 28 days the employer should arrange to meet with the employee to explore the desired work pattern in depth and to consider alternatives. The employer will then be expected to write within 14 days of the date of the meeting either agreeing to a new work pattern and a start date or to provide clear business grounds as to why the application cannot be accepted. An employee who is dissatisfied with the decision will then have a right to appeal in writing within 14 days. A further meeting should be held within 14 days to consider the appeal. The appeal decision should then be given to the employee in writing within 14 days.

It should be noted that there is no automatic right to be allowed to work flexibly. An employee can go to an industrial tribunal only in specific circumstances such as the failure to follow the procedural requirements or where the employer's decision to refuse the request is made on the basis of incorrect facts.

Parental leave

Part III of the Maternity and Parental Leave etc. Regulations (NI) 1999 entitles an employee who has been continuously employed by an employer for at least a year and who has or expects to have responsibility for a child to be absent from work on parental leave. An employee is entitled to 13 weeks' leave in respect of any individual child (or 18 weeks if the child is entitled to disability living allowance). In the absence of contractual entitlements which operate by reference to a collective or workforce agreement, default provisions governing the mechanics of parental leave will apply. However, under the default provisions no more than four weeks' leave can be taken in respect of one child in any leave period.

Parental leave may normally be taken only up to the child's fifth birthday or, if the child is entitled to disability living allowance, up to the child's 18th birthday. Leave may be taken only in blocks of a week, unless it is taken in respect of a child who is entitled to disability living allowance.

Under the default provisions the employee must give 21 days' notice to the employer before leave is to commence, specifying the dates leave is to begin and end. The employer may postpone leave (other than leave to be taken when the child is born when the correct notice has been given) only if the employer considers that the operation of the business would be unduly disrupted if the employee took leave during the period requested. To validly postpone leave, the employer must give the employee notice not more than seven days after receiving the employee's notice and the employer's notice must specify a date which is within six months and has been determined by the employer after consultation with the employee.

Paid time off

An employee has rights to paid time off during working hours:

- to carry out certain duties, activities and training if he or she is an official of an independent trade union;
- to perform duties as a Justice of the Peace, or as a member of a district council, statutory tribunal, relevant prison visiting authority, specified health body (*e.g.* a Health and Social Services Trust) or relevant education body (*e.g.* an Education and Library Board);
- to perform duties or undergo relevant training as a trustee of an occupational pension scheme;
- to perform functions or undergo training in relation to being an employee representative for the purposes of collective redundancies or in respect of the transfer of undertakings legislation; or
- to look for work, or arrange training, if employed for two years or more and under notice of redundancy.

Health and safety at work

Health and safety standards in employment are regulated by both judge-made law and by a wide range of legislation. Under the judge-made law, employers have a general duty to take reasonable care for the safety and health of their employees. As regards legislation, in addition to specific health and safety provisions giving protection in, for instance, factories and offices, employees receive health and safety protection under the Health and Safety at Work (NI) Order 1978.

General duties of employers

Article 4 of the 1978 Order specifies that it is the duty of every employer to ensure, so far as is reasonably practicable, the health, safety and welfare at work of all employees. This means, amongst other things, and as far as is reasonably practicable:

- providing plant and systems of work which are safe and without risks to health;
- ensuring safety in connection with the use, handling, storage and transport of articles and substances; and
- providing such information, instruction, training and supervision as is necessary to ensure the health and safety at work of the employees.

An employer must prepare, and when appropriate revise, a written statement of general policy with respect to the health and safety at work of the employees and bring it and any revisions to the notice of the employees (unless there are fewer than six).

Risk assessment and prevention

The Management of Health and Safety at Work Regulations (NI) 2000 require employers to carry out risk assessments to identify health and safety risks. If more than four people are employed the assessment must be recorded. A person within the employer's business can carry out the risk assessment.

Under the Reporting of Injuries, Diseases, and Dangerous Occurrences Regulations (NI) 1997 an employer is obliged to report either to the Health and Safety Executive or to a local council and to keep records of certain matters. This relates mainly to deaths or major injuries connected with work, an accident at work which results in an injury which lasts for more than three days, reportable work related diseases and other dangerous occurrences.

The Safety Representatives and Safety Committee Regulations (NI) 1979 require employers to recognise safety representatives appointed by recognised trade unions and to consult with them. He or she can investigate potential hazards and dangerous occurrences at the workplace, investigate complaints and make representations to the employer.

In circumstances where employees are not represented by union-appointed safety representatives, the Health and Safety (Consultation with Employees) Regulations (NI) 1996 apply. The employer must consult either with the employees directly or with employee representatives on health and safety matters.

Other duties

In addition to the general duties owed by an employer to the employees, the 1978 Order stipulates the duties of employers and the self-employed to non-employees, the duties of persons concerned with premises to persons other than their employees, and the duties of manufacturers as regards articles and substances for use at work. It is also the duty of every employee to take reasonable care for the health and safety of anyone who may be affected by the employee's acts or omissions at work.

Employment protection in health and safety cases

An employee has the right not to be subjected to a detriment and a dismissal will be automatically unfair if the reason for dismissal is because of the employee:

- carrying out activities after being designated by the employer to prevent or reduce risks to health and safety at work;
- performing functions as a representative of workers on health and safety matters or as a member of a safety committee;
- bringing to the employer's attention circumstances connected with work which he or she reasonably believed were potentially harmful to health and safety;
- leaving or proposing to leave or refusing to return to a dangerous part of the workplace while the danger persisted in circumstances of danger which the employee reasonably believed to be serious and imminent and which could not reasonably be averted by the employee; or

- taking or proposing to take appropriate steps to protect him- or herself or other persons from danger in circumstances of danger which the employee reasonably believed to be serious and imminent.

Termination of employment

Notice to terminate employment

A contract of employment can specify how much notice is to be provided to terminate the contract. It is lawful for an employee to accept pay in lieu of notice. Whilst a contract can provide for longer periods of notice, it cannot provide for a shorter period than the minimum period specified in article 118 of the 1996 Order. The minimum period of notice to be given by an employer to an employee (except in cases of dismissal for gross misconduct, where no notice at all is required to be given) is as follows:

Length of Service	Minimum Notice
Less than one month	No minimum
More than one month but less than two years	One week
Two years	Two weeks
More than two years	One week for each complete year worked (up to 12)

Wrongful dismissal

If an employer dismisses an employee and fails to provide notice in accordance with the contract or statutory notice provisions, the employee may be able to claim damages for wrongful dismissal.

Breach of contract claims can be brought in an industrial tribunal provided the contract is connected with employment and the employment has ended. A claim for breach of contract must be brought within three months of termination of the contract. An employer may counterclaim against the employee within six weeks of receiving a copy of the employee's claim. The value of the employer's counter-claim may be worth substantially more than the employee's claim.

The maximum award a tribunal can make in a breach of contract claim is £25,000. Claims can also be brought in the ordinary civil courts (such as the county court or High Court) for breach of contract, and the time limit then is six years from the date of the breach of contract. An employee will not usually be permitted to pursue a claim in the ordinary courts after losing a case before an industrial tribunal.

Statement of reasons for dismissal

Article 124 of the 1996 Order enables an employee to be provided with a written statement giving particulars of the reasons for dismissal. The employee is normally entitled to a written statement only if he or she has been employed for one year at the date of dismissal and has requested the statement. Where the statement is requested it must be provided within 14 days. An employee who is dismissed whilst pregnant or during maternity leave is automatically entitled to a written statement without having to request it and irrespective of how long she has actually been employed.

If the employer fails to provide a written statement or if the reasons are inadequate or untrue a tribunal can award up to two weeks' pay and make a declaration as to what it finds the employer's reasons were for dismissing the employee. The tribunal can consider such a complaint only if it is presented at the same time as a complaint of unfair dismissal.

Unfair dismissal

Article 126 of the 1996 Order provides that an employee has the right not be unfairly dismissed. If an industrial tribunal finds that an employee has been unfairly dismissed it can order reinstatement, re-engagement (to another suitable job) or compensation.

The onus is on the employee to show that a dismissal has occurred. A dismissal takes place when the employer terminates the contract of employment, when a fixed-term contract ends or when the employee is constructively dismissed. A constructive dismissal takes place where an employee terminates a contract of employment by reason of the employer's conduct. It is not enough to show that the employer has acted unreasonably: the employee must actually show that the employer has acted in fundamental breach of the contract of employment. An example of such a breach may be where the employer reduces pay without consent.

To claim unfair dismissal an employee normally needs to have been continuously employed by the employer for one year.

The onus of showing the reason for dismissal is on the employer. The employer must satisfy the tribunal that the employee was dismissed for a reason specified in article 130 of the 1996 Order, *i.e.* incapability, misconduct, redundancy or because the employee could not continue to work in the position held without contravention of a statutory provision or for some other substantial reason.

In the event that the employer is unable to show that the employee has been dismissed for one of these reasons, the dismissal will be unfair. If the employer does show that the employee has been dismissed for one of the above reasons, the industrial tribunal will then determine whether the dismissal is fair or unfair. Among the factors to be taken into account by the tribunal are the size and administrative resources of the employer's undertaking. The tribunal will also assess whether the employer's decision to dismiss fell within the band of reasonable responses which a reasonable employer might have adopted. In cases of dismissal for misconduct, the industrial tribunal may take into account the Code of Practice on Disciplinary and Grievance Procedures issued by the Labour Relations Agency, which came into effect on 1 December 2002.

Automatically unfair dismissals

Dismissal of an employee for certain specified reasons is automatically unfair. In such circumstances the tribunal will not have to look into the reasonableness or otherwise of the dismissal. Selection of an employee for redundancy on the same grounds may also make the dismissal automatically unfair. Likewise, for certain dismissals an employee will not require any length of qualifying employment and upper age limits which apply to prevent employees claiming unfair dismissal will not apply. The dismissals in question in this paragraph are as follows:

- dismissal for maternity related reasons, including the fact that the employee took maternity leave, parental leave, time off under the dependents' provisions, paternity leave or adoption leave;
- dismissal for health and safety related reasons;
- dismissal for performing a role as a trustee of a pension scheme or as an employee representative;
- dismissal of a shop worker in connection with Sunday working;
- dismissal in relation to rights under the Working Time Regulations (NI) 1998;

- dismissal for asserting rights under the National Minimum Wage Act 1998;
- dismissal in respect of protected public interest disclosures;
- dismissal in relation to the right to be accompanied at disciplinary and grievance hearings;
- dismissal for asserting rights as a part-time worker;
- dismissal due to enforcing rights under the Tax Credits Act 2002;
- dismissal for asserting rights as a fixed-term worker;
- dismissal for asserting statutory rights conferred under the 1996 Order or the rights in relation to statutory minimum notice, deductions from pay, union activities and time off; and
- dismissal for trade union membership or activities.

Redundancy

The law takes two approaches to redundancy:
- it requires employers to inform and consult representatives of employees before redundancies are implemented, and
- it provides for compensation to be paid to employees made redundant.

Consultation on redundancies

Part XIII of the Employment Rights (NI) Order 1996 provides that if an employer proposes to dismiss as redundant 20 or more employees at one establishment within a period of 90 days or less, the employer must consult all persons who are appropriate representatives of any of the employees who may be dismissed. Appropriate representatives of employees are employee representatives elected by them, representatives of independent trade unions recognised by the employer or, where there are both employee representatives and trade union representatives, the employer may choose which group to consult.

Consultation must begin in good time. If more than 100 employees are to be made redundant within 90 days, consultations must take place at least 90 days before the first dismissal. Otherwise consultation must take place at least 30 days before the first dismissal takes effect. The consultation must take place with a view to reaching agreement with the employee representatives.

The employer must disclose the following information in writing to trade union representatives:
- the reasons for the proposed dismissals,

- the numbers and descriptions of workers affected,
- the total number of employees of such description employed,
- the proposed method of selecting employees for dismissal,
- the proposed method of carrying out the dismissals, and
- the proposed method of calculating redundancy payments.

If an employer does not comply with the above requirements, a complaint can be made by the appropriate trade union to an industrial tribunal. If the tribunal upholds the complaint it may order the employer to pay wages to redundant or potentially redundant employees for a specified period.

Redundancy payments

An employee employed for two years or more who is made redundant may be entitled to a redundancy payment. Only an employee dismissed because the employer has ceased to or intends to cease to carry on business or because the requirements of the business to carry out work of a particular kind have diminished will be treated as redundant.

The amount of the redundancy payment is based upon the employee's age, length of continuous employment and gross average wage. A redundant employee is entitled to:

- one-and-a-half week's pay for each year of employment between the age of 41 and normal retirement age;
- one week' pay for each year of employment between the ages of 22 and 40; and
- half a week's pay for each year of employment between the ages of 18 and 21.

The maximum number of years to be taken into account in calculating a redundancy payment is 20 and the maximum amount of a week's pay allowed in calculating a statutory redundancy payment is £250 (expected to rise during 2003 to £260). Thus the current maximum payment is £7,500 (*i.e.* 20 years (when aged over 41) x 1.5 x £250).

For each month that an employee exceeds 64, the redundancy payment is reduced by one-twelfth.

Trade union law

A trade union is defined by article 3 of the Industrial Relations (NI) Order 1992 (the 1992 Order) as an organisation which consists:

- of workers of one or more description and has as its principal purpose the regulation of relations between workers and employers or employers' associations, or
- wholly or mainly of an affiliated or constituent group of such organisations or their representatives.

The basis of a trade union's right to exist is the Industrial Relations (NI) Order 1992, and by article 3 of this Order they can sue and be sued in their own name. Even though a trade union is in law an "unincorporated association", any judgment, order or award may be enforced against it as if it were a public company.

The 1992 Order distinguishes between independent unions and others. A union is independent if it is not under the control of an employer or a group of employers and is not liable to interference arising out of the provision of financial or other support which tends towards such control. Only independent trade unions are accorded statutory rights concerning disclosure of information and consultation.

A certain degree of protection and some enforceable rights have been given to employees concerning trade union membership.

Dismissal

Article 136 of the Employment Rights (NI) Order 1996 provides that an employee can complain of unfair dismissal if he or she is dismissed:

- for being, or proposing to become, a member of an independent trade union;
- for taking part at "an appropriate time" in the activities of an independent trade union; an "appropriate time" means time which is either outside working hours or during working hours if the employer has given consent; or
- for non-membership of a trade union.

Victimisation

An employee who has not been dismissed but who has been victimised for trade union membership or activity or for non-membership of a trade union can also complain to an industrial tribunal within three months.

Trade union recognition

A trade union is entitled to seek recognition under the provisions of Schedule 1A to the Trade Union and Labour Relations (NI) Order 1995 to be entitled to conduct collective bargaining in respect of negotiations relating to pay, hours, holidays and additional matters agreed between the union and employer. An employer can expressly or impliedly agree to recognise a trade union voluntarily. If an employer rejects or fails to respond to a trade union's request for recognition within 10 days, or if recognition has not been granted within 20 days of negotiations commencing, an application can be made to the Industrial Court. The Industrial Court is obliged to take various steps under a strict timetable upon receipt of an application for union recognition. It has published a useful document entitled "Northern Ireland Guidance booklet on Trade Union Recognition and Derecognition" (2001).

A worker subjected to a detriment or an employee who is dismissed can complain to an industrial tribunal if the reason for detriment or dismissal is because the worker:

- acted with a view to obtaining or preventing recognition of a union by the employer;
- indicated that he or she supported or did not support recognition of a union by the employer;
- acted with a view to securing or preventing the ending of bargaining arrangements;
- indicated that he or she supported or did not support the ending of bargaining arrangements;
- influenced or sought to influence the way in which votes were to be cast by other workers in a ballot;
- influenced or sought to influence other workers to vote or to abstain from voting in such a ballot;
- voted in a ballot; or
- proposed to do, failed to do, or proposed to decline to do, any of the things referred to above.

Such a dismissal will be automatically unfair and no qualifying period to claim unfair dismissal will apply.

Collective bargaining and legal rights for unions

The normal method of negotiation between trade unions and employers or employers' associations is by way of collective bargaining. By article 26 of the 1992 Order collective agreements are conclusively presumed not to have been intended by the parties to be legally enforceable, unless the agreement is in writing and contains a provision which states that the parties intended the agreement to be a legally enforceable contract. In practice, collective agreements are not enforceable. But certain terms of collective agreements, such as wage rates and holiday entitlement, are incorporated into an individual's contract of employment and can be agreed by an individual employee and his or her employer.

The 1992 Order says it is the duty of every employer, if requested to do so, to disclose information about his or her undertaking to the representatives of any trade union for the purposes of collective bargaining. A complaint of failure to disclose information can be referred to the LRA, which will attempt conciliation. If this fails, the matter may be referred by the LRA to the Industrial Court, which may make a declaration stipulating a period within which disclosure is to be made. If the information is still not forthcoming, a further complaint may be made via the LRA to the Industrial Court, which may then order that the contracts of the employees specified in the claim should include the specified terms and conditions.

If an employer recognises an independent trade union for collective bargaining purposes, consultation must take place with such union representatives in advance of 20 or more redundancies or in advance of a transfer of an undertaking. Alternatively, an employer may consult with representatives of the employees (see p.473 above). In respect of health and safety, the employer must recognise union-appointed safety representatives. Only in the absence of such representatives may an employer consult employees or their representative on health and safety matters (see p.468 above). Enforcement of a failure to consult is by way of complaint to an industrial tribunal.

Trade union administration

Part II of the Trade Union and Labour Relations (NI) Order 1995 (the 1995 Order) concerns trade union administration and adds to the requirements placed on trade unions by Part II of the 1992 Order.

Unions are required to compile and maintain a register of the names and addresses of their members. A union must inform its members and the Certification Officer about the conduct of its financial affairs. The Certification Officer has power to direct a trade union to produce documents relating to its financial affairs and to appoint inspectors to investigate the financial affairs of a union.

Trade union elections

Part III of the 1995 Order concerns trade union elections. It applies to trade unions with their head office located in Northern Ireland and it complements existing requirements placed on trade unions with their head office based in Great Britain. A trade union must ensure that every member of its executive committee has been elected to that position by secret postal ballot within the previous five years, although this provision does not apply to union employees who are within five years of retirement age. A union is required to appoint a qualified independent person to scrutinise and report on the conduct of such elections. Where it is contended that a trade union has not complied with the above requirements, an application may be made to the Certification Officer.

Rights of trade union members

Part IV of the 1995 Order concerns the rights of trade union members. Article 29 establishes a right of union members to a ballot before industrial action is taken.

Articles 31-34 establish a right not to be unjustifiably disciplined. Types of conduct in respect of which discipline is considered unjustifiable include:

- failure to participate in, or conduct indicating opposition to, industrial action, and
- alleging that a union official has acted contrary to union rules or unlawfully.

The Order provides that an employer may not deduct union subscriptions from a worker's wages under check-off arrangements unless the worker has authorised such deductions in writing within the previous three years. Where it is alleged that an employer has made an unauthorised deduction, a complaint may be made to a tribunal.

Trade union political funds

Part V of the 1995 Order relates to the political funds of Northern Ireland trade unions. Similar provisions apply to unions with their head office located in Great Britain. It provides that union funds must not be used for political objectives unless approved by a secret ballot of union members, which is to be held at least every 10 years. Funds paid in furtherance of political objectives must be paid from a separate political fund. Union members who do not contribute to the political fund must not be disadvantaged and may complain to the Certification Officer if they consider this to be the case. The political objectives for which funds must be paid from the political fund are:

- the contribution to the funds of a political party;
- the provision of any service by a political party;
- the selection of a candidate for political office;
- the holding of any meeting by, or on behalf of, a political party; and
- the production, publication or distribution of any literature, document, film, sound recording or advertisement, the main purpose of which is to persuade people to vote for a political party.

A complaint may be made to the Certification Officer that a union has not conducted a ballot in accordance with the system approved by the Certification Officer.

Industrial action

Part VIII of the 1995 Order consolidates and reforms the legal liability of trade unions and their members when engaged in industrial action. Article 97 provides that an act done by a person in contemplation or furtherance of a trade dispute shall be protected from some forms of liability in the law of tort. On the other hand, article 102 removes immunity from action in tort for secondary industrial action (*i.e.* industrial action by workers whose employer is not a party to the trade dispute to which the action relates).

Articles 104-117 stipulate the balloting procedures that must be followed before lawful industrial action may be undertaken. A code of practice was issued in December 2002 by the Department for Employment and Learning regarding "Industrial Action Ballots and Notice to Employers". Article 104 of the 1995 Order provides that a call by a trade union to take industrial action will not be protected unless the industrial action has the support of a ballot.

In order for industrial action to be protected from certain tort claims, article 118 provides that the union must, not later than seven days before the industrial action is intended to start, give written notice to the employer of those employees whom the union envisages will take part in the action. The notice must indicate whether the action will be continuous or discontinuous, and state when the action is intended to start (if it is continuous) or the days on which it is intended to take place (if it is discontinuous).

Dismissal of striking workers

An employee dismissed while taking unofficial industrial action will not normally be able to claim unfair dismissal. However, it will be unfair to dismiss an employee because he or she is taking protected industrial action, unless the industrial action lasts for more than eight weeks and the employer has taken such procedural steps as are reasonable to try to resolve the dispute. Such a dismissal can be brought to an industrial tribunal regardless of the employee's length of service or age. A complaint of unfair dismissal may also be taken by an individual taking protected industrial action if the employer dismisses some but not others taking industrial action or offers re-engagement to an employee dismissed while taking part in industrial action within three months of dismissal but not to all those dismissed.

Liability to pay compensation

A union may be held responsible for the actions of its officials (so-called "vicarious" liability). It is for the courts to decide whether a union is liable for the acts of its members or officials in respect of wrongs such as negligence or nuisance. In respect of the economic wrongs mentioned above, a union will be vicariously liable only for specified unlawful actions which are authorised or endorsed by a "responsible person", defined by article 21 of the Industrial Relations (NI) Order 1992.

If found liable in court proceedings a union can be ordered to pay damages, the size of the award often depending on the size of the union's membership.

Picketing

There is no general right to picket. As with trade disputes, an immunity is conferred, this time by article 98 of the 1995 Order, which provides that it shall be lawful for a person to picket:

- at or near his or her own place of work, or
- if he or she is an official of a trade union, at or near the place of work of a member of that union whom he or she is accompanying and representing.

The picketing must be for the purpose of peacefully obtaining or communicating information, or peacefully persuading any person to work or abstain from working. In addition, if a person works at more than one place, or at a place where it is impracticable to picket, he or she is entitled to picket any premises of the employer from which he or she works or from which his or her work is administered.

Pickets can easily fall foul of both the criminal and civil law. For instance, they may be liable to criminal charges for obstruction of the highway or of the police, intimidation or contravention of the Public Order (NI) Order 1987 in respect of meetings and marches (see Chapter 8). They may also be liable to a civil action for trespass or nuisance.

Further useful addresses

- Labour Relations Agency
  2-8 Gordon Street   and   3 Foyle Street
  Belfast BT2 2LG   Derry/Londonderry BT48 6AL
  tel: 028 9032 1442   tel: 028 7126 4681

- Health and Safety Executive for Northern Ireland
  83 Ladas Drive
  Belfast BT6 9FJ
  tel: 028 9024 3249

- Office of Industrial Tribunals and the Fair Employment Tribunal
  Long Bridge House
  Waring Street
  Belfast BT1 2DY
  tel: 028 9032 7666

- Industrial Court
  Room 203, Adelaide House
  39-49 Adelaide Street
  Belfast BT2 8FD
  tel: 028 9025 7687

- Certification Officer for Northern Ireland
  2-8 Gordon Street
  Belfast BT1 2LG
  tel: 028 9023 7773

Chapter 21

Housing Rights

Sharon Geary[*]

There are three main types of housing tenure in Northern Ireland: owner-occupied (75%), public rented (20%) and private rented (5%) (Department for Social Development, Northern Ireland Housing Statistics 2001-2002). Housing is regulated by the Department for Social Development (DSD) and the Social Development Committee of the Northern Ireland Assembly advises the Department on issues of policy, scrutinises Departmental proposals and suggests amendments to proposed legislation. When the Assembly was suspended in October 2002 a Housing Bill was in the process of being passed. It has since been enacted at Westminster as the Housing (NI) Order 2003 (hereafter called the 2003 Order). However, the 2003 Order does not take effect immediately as a series of commencement orders are required to phase it in.

Owner occupation

Purchasing a home

Purchasing a house is one of the biggest financial undertakings any individual will ever make. It is therefore important to seek advice from a reputable mortgage adviser and to borrow only from a lender who complies with the "Mortgage Code" and is a member of a recognised complaints scheme, such as the Banking Ombudsman, the Building Societies Ombudsman or the Mortgage Code Arbitration Scheme.

A mortgage adviser or lender should be able to provide information on the following areas prior to a person making a final decision to buy a house:

---

[*] The author is grateful to her colleagues at Housing Rights Service for their assistance with this chapter.

- the repayment method (*i.e.* the type of mortgage) and the repayment period,
- the type of interest rate,
- how much future repayments, after any fixed or discounted period, might be,
- whether an insurance service has to be taken with the mortgage and, if so, whether the insurance must be arranged by the lender or intermediary, and
- the costs and fees which might be involved with the mortgage, *e.g.* valuation fees, arrangement fees, legal fees, early redemption fees and high percentage lending fees.

When mortgage intermediaries are arranging loans they must state whether the lender is paying them a fee for introducing the mortgage and whether they usually arrange mortgages from a number of selected lenders or from the market as a whole.

Mortgage repayments

Failure to maintain mortgage payments will normally mean that the lender has the right to pursue an action for repossession, though generally only after following the due process of the law through the court system. Anyone struggling to maintain mortgage payments should seek advice at an early stage from Housing Rights Service, a Citizens' Advice Bureau or another independent advice agency. An adviser can mediate between the borrower and the lender to produce a realistic plan to deal with the arrears.

Even if repossession proceedings have been initiated it is not too late to liaise with the lender to try to resolve the matter. Repossession proceedings are heard in the Chancery Division of the High Court. The Court may decide to adjourn the hearing, make a suspended order (which enables the debtor to abide by the proposal accepted or determined by the court), make a suspended order by consent (if a further default occurs the debtor must then accept that a possession order will be served) or issue a possession order.

A person who loses his or her home as a result of mortgage arrears can apply for rehousing in the public rented sector and may qualify for assistance under the homelessness legislation (see p.510 below).

Rates

The rates payable on a domestic property are determined by reference to its Net Annual Value (NAV), as assessed by the Valuation and Lands Agency, multiplied by the combined rate, that is, the sum of the regional rate for Northern Ireland and the district rate. If an owner-occupier is in receipt of income support or income-based jobseeker's allowance or is on a low income, he or she may be entitled to claim housing benefit, which will help with the payment of rates.

Insurance

There are four main forms of insurance associated with purchasing a house. These are buildings insurance (insuring the structure of the house against damage), contents insurance (insuring the contents of the house against damage and theft), payment protection insurance (insuring the payment of a mortgage if there is a loss of earnings) and life insurance (insuring the mortgage costs in the event of the borrower dying). All insurance policies have different restrictions on them and therefore it is always important to know exactly what type of a policy is being entered into and what it covers.

Planning permission and repairs

Home owners can carry out improvements or extension work to their home subject to building control and planning permission. This is largely governed by the Planning (NI) Order 1991. Planning permission is required for any development of land and for a change in the use of land. Further details are provided in Chapter 23.

Home owners are responsible for any repairs or improvements to their property unless the work needed is as a result of the negligence of another person, in which case legal proceedings should be taken against that person. The owner's liabilities to other persons are governed by the Defective Premises (NI) Order 1975.

If the defect relates to grant-aided work, the Housing Executive's approval of the work when paying out the grant is no guarantee that the work was carried out properly. The Executive may be guilty of maladministration, but it is not legally liable to pay compensation to any present or future owners. However, a surveyor employed by a lender cannot generally escape liability for any negligent failure to recognise what should have been apparent if he or she had used reasonable care and skill.

The Defective Premises (NI) Order 1975 imposes a duty on anyone carrying out work on a dwelling to ensure that the work done is of a professional standard and that the dwelling is fit for habitation when completed (art.3). The Order is intended to prevent vendors of land and builders of houses from being exempt from any claim for negligence made by subsequent purchasers. It also makes a vendor or lessor of land or buildings liable for any negligent action or inaction before the sale or lease (art.5). Liability may be excluded in respect of dwellings which are already covered by a scheme approved for that purpose by the DSD (art.4). This exclusion relates to building schemes such as those controlled by the National House Building Registration Council; these actually provide *greater* safeguards to purchasers and occupiers than is provided by the Order.

Under the Housing (NI) Order 1986, if the DSD decides that a property, purchased from the Housing Executive or a Registered Housing Association (RHA), is defective because of its design or construction, the owner can apply to the Housing Executive for compensation to reinstate the dwelling or, in serious cases, to buy it back. Where repurchase occurs the occupier may be eligible to be granted a secure tenancy of the dwelling or alternative suitable accommodation.

Financial assistance

A home owner may be able to obtain grants from the Housing Executive for works to be carried out. At present those available are renovation grants, replacement grants, disabled facilities grants, minor works assistance grants, common parts grants, repairs grants or houses in multiple occupation grants. An award will depend upon the type of work to be carried out, the NAV of the property and the financial circumstances of the owner. Further information is available from the Housing Executive or Housing Rights Service. (Under the 2003 Order the current mandatory Home Improvement Grants Scheme will be replaced with a largely discretionary scheme.)

Financial assistance for the cost of repairs and improvements may also be obtainable from the social fund Department of the DSD by applying for one of the following:

- *Community care grant* – This may be awarded for minor repairs and improvements intended to meet needs connected with community care. It does not have to be repaid.

- *Crisis loan* – This may be awarded for minor repairs and improvements intended to meet urgent short-term needs. It has to be repaid.
- *Budgeting loan* – This may be awarded to meet the intermittent expenses for improvements, maintenance and security of the home. It too has to be repaid.

All of the above social fund awards are discretionary. An award will depend on the applicant's financial situation. When making a decision on an application a social fund officer must have regard to the nature, extent and urgency of the need, the social fund budget and whether the need could be met elsewhere, such as by the Housing Executive.

Owner-occupiers who are in receipt of social security benefits and need help to keep their home warm may be eligible for grants through the Warm Homes Scheme (see p.508 below).

The Housing Support (NI) Order 2002 provides a new fund, administered by the Northern Ireland Housing Executive, for funding the costs associated with providing housing support services for vulnerable people in supported accommodation.

Disposal of property

Under normal circumstances selling a property is a fairly straightforward process, achieved most easily through retaining the services of an estate agent and solicitor. However, the process becomes more complicated when the sale is due to relationship breakdown, arrears or some other property dispute. In all cases it is important to take legal advice at the earliest opportunity.

Owners who find it difficult to sell their homes because of civil disturbances may benefit from the "SPED" (Special Purchase of Evacuated Dwellings) Scheme. The SPED Scheme allows the Housing Executive to purchase a house which cannot be sold because of its location and closeness to civil disturbances or in cases where the owner-occupier has been intimidated out of the home without first being able to sell the property. A person in this situation should contact Housing Rights Service, a Citizens' Advice Bureau, an independent advice centre or a solicitor.

Public rented sector housing

Most public rented housing (around 124,000 dwellings) is owned and managed by the Housing Executive, which was established in 1971. Registered Housing Associations (RHAs) own and manage some 26,000 dwellings and in recent years the building of public housing has increasingly become the role of those Associations. Under section 75 of the Northern Ireland Act 1998 the Housing Executive is required to carry out its functions, powers and duties with due regard for the need to promote equality of opportunity. At present RHAs are not similarly obliged, but it is envisaged that they will be in the near future.

The Housing Selection Scheme

In Northern Ireland those wishing to access public rented housing from the Housing Executive or a RHA (so-called "social landlords") are assessed and awarded points in accordance with the Housing Selection Scheme. Under this Scheme, accommodation is allocated according to assessed housing need. It covers all applicants for public housing, including those to whom the Housing Executive owes a duty under the homelessness legislation (see p.509 below), as well as current tenants who are seeking a transfer to alternative accommodation. Applicants are placed on a waiting list.

A person is entitled to apply for housing under the Selection Scheme provided that:

- he or she is owed a statutory duty under the Housing (NI) Order 1988, *i.e.* is a "Full Duty Applicant" (see p.488), or
- he or she is nominated through the National Mobility (HOMES) Scheme and wishes to move to Northern Ireland from public housing elsewhere in the UK, or
- he or she meets the requirements as to age (generally the age limit is 18 years) and has a connection with Northern Ireland (*i.e.* is, or was, "ordinarily or habitually or normally" resident in Northern Ireland, or is employed, or seeking employment, in Northern Ireland, or has a "substantial connection" with Northern Ireland because of other circumstances, such as family support or educational purposes).

Ranking applicants

Under the Selection Scheme applicants are awarded points and ranked on the waiting list in descending order. Individuals with complex needs, whose agreed accommodation option is housing with care, are an exception to this assessment process and are placed on an administrative list without reference to points. Points are awarded on a cumulative basis, unless otherwise stated, under the following four categories:

- *Intimidation* – Where a person is homeless by virtue of racial, sectarian or terrorist intimidation.
- *Insecurity of tenure* – Where a person has been assessed as a "Full Duty Applicant", or is homeless but is not a "Full Duty Applicant", or is residing in temporary accommodation for six months or more.
- *Housing conditions* – Where people are sharing accommodation, or are living in overcrowded conditions, or with a lack of amenities or disrepair, or have been in urgent housing need for some time.
- *Health and social well-being* – Where people are assessed as regards "functionality" (their mobility around the home), support and care needs, social needs and complex needs.

Once assessed and pointed, applicants are placed on a waiting list, which is then used by all participating social landlords to allocate accommodation. The general rule is that properties are offered to those with the highest points. Each applicant is entitled to three *reasonable* offers of accommodation. When considering what is reasonable, consideration must be given to the specific needs of the applicant or the household and in particular the size and condition of the accommodation and the suitability of its location and features.

Tenancy agreements

Each tenant is given a standard tenancy agreement, which is a legal document setting out the terms and conditions of the occupation of the premises. A tenant is entitled to a copy of the tenancy agreement (art.38(3) of the Housing (NI) Order 1983, hereafter called the 1983 Order). The tenant should also be given a copy of the Tenant's Handbook, which outlines the rights and duties of both the tenant and the Housing Executive or RHA. In the case of RHAs, tenancy agreements will vary between Associations. However, the tenancy agreement should state that the Association is registered with the DSD and define clearly the landlord's statutory responsibility for internal decorations and repairs.

Tenants' rights

In general, tenants of the Housing Executive and RHAs have security of tenure and enjoy a series of statutory rights. The 2003 Order makes a number of amendments to the 1983 Order which affect security of tenure, tenants' rights and grounds for repossession. In particular, the 2003 Order enables social landlords to adopt an introductory tenancy regime, *i.e.* all new tenancies will be non-secure and for a trial period of one year, after which the tenancy will become secure unless the landlord has taken an action for repossession. The main provisions of the "Tenants Charter", introduced under the 1983 Order, apply to both RHAs and the Housing Executive. The 1983 Order states that secure tenants have the following rights:

- the right to succession (art.26),
- the right to security of tenure (art.27),
- the right to take in lodgers (art.30(1)),
- the right to sublet part of the accommodation, with permission (art. 30(2)),
- the right to assignment (*i.e.* to sell) (art. 32),
- the right to exchange accommodation with another tenant, with permission (art.32(1)),
- the right to improve the accommodation, with permission (art.34),
- the right to information (arts.38 and 39), and
- the right to consultation (art.40).

Introductory tenants will have:
- the right to repair,
- the right to information,
- the right to consultation,
- the right to succession, and
- the right to assignment.

Under Schedule 3 to the 1983 Order a tenancy may be ended by the Housing Executive or RHA only through a court order for repossession, unless the property has been abandoned. At present there are 12 statutory grounds for repossession (one of which is numbered 5a). In grounds 1 to 6 the court must be satisfied that an order for possession is reasonable, in ground 7 there must be alternative accommodation available for the tenant and in grounds 8 to 11 both conditions must be met. Ground 9 applies only to RHAs. The grounds for repossession are as follows:

1. non-payment of rent or the breach of another obligation,
2. causing a nuisance or annoyance to neighbours or using the premises for illegal or immoral purposes,
3. allowing the condition of the property to deteriorate or failing to remove a lodger responsible for such deterioration,
4. allowing the condition of any relevant furniture to deteriorate or failing to remove a lodger responsible for such deterioration,
5. inducing the landlord to grant the tenancy by knowingly or recklessly making a false statement,
5a where a secure tenant has paid a fee in respect of an assignment of a tenancy,
6. where a tenant fails to return to his or her original property after having been decanted for works to be carried out,
7. where the landlord needs to do demolition or reconstruction work, within a reasonable time, and cannot do so without obtaining possession,
8. where a house designed for a disabled person is now occupied by someone who is not disabled and the dwelling is required again for a disabled person,
9. where a RHA dwelling is usually let to a person who finds it difficult to have his or her housing needs met, *e.g.* through having special needs, and the current occupant is not such a person and the dwelling is required again for such a person,
10. where the accommodation is for a person with special needs and the current occupant does not have those needs and the dwelling is required again for a person with special needs, and
11. where there is under-occupation of a house of which the tenancy was obtained through "statutory succession" (see below) by a member of the previous tenant's family, other than the spouse.

The 2003 Order extends the grounds for possession for nuisance or annoyance to neighbours as well as for possession of a tenancy induced by false statement. It also introduces a new ground of domestic violence.

The right to succession

According to article 26 of the 1983 Order a person is entitled to succeed to a tenancy if he or she resided in the property as his or her principal home at the time of the tenant's death, and he or she is either the tenant's spouse or a member of the tenant's family and resided with the tenant prior to the tenant's death for a period of at least 12 months. The landlord has a legal obligation to allow only one succession. Therefore, a legal succession cannot occur if the deceased was him- or herself a legal successor. (Under the 2003 Order the successor to an introductory tenancy will become an introductory tenant.)

The Housing Executive's policy also allows succession to a Housing Executive tenancy in the following instances:

- where a person has been living with the deceased for one year as his or her partner,
- where a person gave up a tenancy or licence or sold his or her own home in order to live with and care for the tenant who has died,
- where a person has taken responsibility for the deceased tenant's dependents, or
- where the Executive's Director of Client Services considers that there are exceptional circumstances.

The right to assignment

Generally, tenants will need to seek consent from their landlord if they want to assign (*i.e.* pass on) their tenancy to another person. Article 32(1) of the 1983 Order allows for a tenancy (including a new introductory tenancy as introduced under the 2003 Order) to be assigned in the following circumstances:

- where the assignment is made as a result of a court order under the Matrimonial Causes (NI) Order 1978, or
- where the assignment is to a person who would have succeeded to the tenancy had the tenant died before the assignment took place (*i.e.* under the right to succession, as explained above).

In addition to the statutory rules, Housing Executive policy states that it has a discretion to allow an assignment to a Housing Executive tenancy in exceptional circumstances, *e.g.* where it is no longer practicable for an existing tenant to continue to act as such or the tenant leaves and someone else takes responsibility for the tenant's dependent children. RHAs will have their own policies on this matter.

The right to exchange

Article 32(1) of the 1983 Order, as amended, confers a right on a secure tenant to exchange accommodation with another secure tenant, subject to the written consent of the landlord. Consent can be withheld only on the following grounds (Sch. 7 to the Housing (NI) Order 1986):

- if there is a court order for possession of the secure tenancy,
- if possession proceedings have been started against the tenant or proposed assignee,
- if the accommodation is bigger than required for the proposed assignee,
- if the accommodation does not meet the needs of the proposed assignee,
- if the accommodation has been adapted to meet the needs of a physically disabled person and the proposed assignee is not such a person,
- if the landlord is a RHA which lets accommodation for persons whose circumstances make it especially difficult to access housing and the proposed assignee is not such a person, or
- if the accommodation is one of a group of dwellings providing housing for people with special needs and a service is provided for the occupants, *e.g.* a warden.

(There is no legal provision enabling introductory tenants to exchange properties).

The right to transfer

A transfer occurs when a tenant moves from one property to another let by a social landlord. This is not a legal right but is allowed under Housing Executive and RHA policy. Transfer applicants are assessed by their existing landlord, given points and ranked in a similar way to general applicants. In addition, transfer applicants may be awarded points for under-occupation. To be eligible for a transfer tenants must meet all the following access criteria (although the criteria must be waived where the tenant is a "Full Duty Applicant"):

- they must have held a secure tenancy for two years,
- they must owe less than four weeks' rent,
- the current property must be in good repair, and
- there must have been no serious breach of the tenancy conditions.

In exceptional circumstances a tenant may be transferred, at the discretion of the Housing Manager, without reference to points.

The right to buy

Most Housing Executive tenants have a right to buy the house in which they reside under the House Sales Scheme, which was introduced by the Housing (NI) Order 1992. But certain properties are exempt from the scheme. At present RHA tenants do not have a statutory right to buy their home although each Association operates a voluntary policy in this regard. However, the 2003 Order will require all RHAs to operate a house sales scheme for secure tenants.

Rent

A tenancy agreement obliges the tenant, *i.e.* the person whose name appears on the tenancy agreement, to pay the agreed weekly or monthly rent when due. Where there is more than one tenant each tenant will be jointly and severally liable for payment of the rent. The total amount payable for a Housing Executive property consists of rent and rates. The Housing Executive will calculate the rent by awarding points to a property, based on its size, age and facilities. Each point has a monetary value. The DSD sets the level of rates. Generally, the rent and rates will increase every year. If the tenant wishes to query the level of rent he or she should contact the local Housing Executive District Office.

In the case of RHAs, each Association will have its own policy in relation to setting rents. The Housing (NI) Order 1992 removed the power of the Department of the Environment (now the DSD) to set rents and allowed RHAs to determine their own rents. Consequently, tenancies which existed before the 16 September 1992 have "protected" rents fixed by the DSD whereas the rent for tenancies after the 16 September 1992 are determined by the individual RHA.

Failure to pay rent is a breach of the tenancy agreement which can lead to the granting of a possession order by a court and the tenant losing his or her home. Any overcharging as a result of the landlord's mistake is recoverable by the tenant, but the landlord cannot generally recover any undercharging. If a tenant is unable to pay the rent because his or her income is insufficient, advice should be sought immediately from Housing Rights Service, a Citizens' Advice Bureau or another independent advice centre.

Arrears

Each RHA will have its own policy on rent arrears, although it must always use the due process of the law. The tenant should therefore check with the Association in question.

The Housing Executive has a proactive policy on the management and recovery of rent arrears. The action taken by the Housing Executive will depend on the type and level of arrears in question. If a voluntary agreement is unobtainable or unworkable the Housing Executive will examine the compulsory options for recovery, *i.e.* deductions from benefits, "clawback" from payments the tenant is due to receive (such as redecoration allowance, home loss and disturbance payments, or compensation payments) or court action. A tenant who gets income support, working families' tax credit or housing benefit can apply to the District Housing Manager, on grounds of financial hardship, to have no deductions made from redecoration or self-help repair allowances, but these are the only types of payment which qualify for such relief.

Under the Social Security Claims and Payments Regulations (NI) 1988, where the tenant owes six weeks' rent, the Housing Executive can apply to the DSD to have payments deducted directly from the tenant's social security benefits. Direct payments can be made from income support, jobseeker's allowance, incapacity benefit, severe disablement allowance, widowed mother's allowance, widow's pension and retirement pension. Where applicable, the Housing Executive will pursue eviction.

Repairs and improvements

The tenancy agreement will highlight the repairing obligations for the landlord and tenant. In the case of Housing Executive tenancies, the Executive is responsible for such external repairs as garden paths, walls, fences and gates, replacement of dustbins every five years and wheelie bins every seven years (unless they are still in good condition). Tenants are responsible for the care and upkeep of gardens, hedges and the cleaning of gutters. As regards internal repairs, the Housing Executive is responsible for electrical wiring, electrical appliances installed by the Housing Executive, pipes, radiators and fittings, window frames and sashes and letter-boxes. The tenant is responsible for internal decoration, electrical appliances not installed by the Housing Executive, tap washers, internal door hinges, locks and handles and replacement of broken glass (unless caused by riot damage and reported to the police). The District Manager has the discretion to have the Housing Executive carry out repairs which are normally the responsibility of the tenant if the tenant is elderly and/or disabled or in financial hardship. A tenant should report any repairs to the local district office by writing, telephoning or calling in. A tenant should receive an acknowledgement within three days of reporting the repair and this will indicate if it is considered to be an emergency, urgent or routine. If the Housing Executive fails to carry out an emergency or urgent repair within the specified time limit, *i.e.* 24 hours for emergency repairs and four working days for urgent repairs, a tenant may be entitled to compensation under the Right to Repair Scheme. (The 2003 Order will make this a statutory scheme for secure tenants and gives the DSD the power to extend the Right to Repair Scheme to introductory tenants.) A tenant also has the option of using the Housing Executive's Self Help Scheme, whereby he or she can carry out certain works, with the written permission of the Housing Executive, and then claim back the money for the repair.

In the case of tenancies with RHAs, according to the "Tenant's Guarantee", issued under the Housing (NI) Order 1992, Associations must provide all tenants, at the commencement of their tenancy, with information outlining, amongst other things, the responsibility for repairs, the methods for reporting repairs, how long it should take for a repair to be carried out and what to do if an RHA fails to meet its repairing obligations. Under the Right to Repair Scheme, a tenant may be entitled to compensation if the RHA fails to meet its published response target for repairs.

Public health repairs

All tenants, irrespective of the terms of their tenancy agreement, can take advantage of the Public Health (Ireland) Act 1878, which makes district councils responsible for ensuring that a statutory nuisance is remedied where:

- premises are in such a state as to be a nuisance or prejudicial to health (*R v Bristol City Council, ex parte Everett*, 1999),
- any pool, ditch, gutter, watercourse or drain is in such a state as to be a nuisance or prejudicial to health,
- any accumulation or deposit is a nuisance or prejudicial to health,
- any animal is so kept as to be a nuisance or prejudicial to health, or

▪ any house or part of a house is so overcrowded as to be dangerous or prejudicial to the health of inmates, whether or not members of the same family.

Where a tenant wishes to pursue a complaint of this nature he or she should do so through the Environmental Health Department of the local district council.

Improvements

Under article 34 of the Housing (NI) Order 1983 (as amended by the 2003 Order) a Housing Executive tenant has the right to carry out certain improvements, providing that written consent is given. At the end of a tenancy the Housing Executive may make a payment of compensation in respect of an improvement carried out by the tenant. (The 2003 Order will make this a statutory right.)

In 2001 the DSD introduced a "Model Scheme for a Right to Compensation" for RHA tenants who carry out improvements to their home. Each Association operates its own scheme based on the model. Compensation is generally available only to secure tenants where the improvement has materially added to the property and the Association has given written consent. At the end of a tenancy the Association may award compensation to the tenant for improvements carried out.

Redevelopment

Under the Housing (NI) Order 1981 and the Local Government Act (NI) 1970 the Housing Executive has statutory powers to propose redevelopment areas, the purpose of which is to improve the living conditions of people residing in unfit dwellings. The Executive will identify houses which are unfit, dangerous or injurious to the health of occupants in the area and provide plans for redevelopment. When a redevelopment scheme is submitted to the DSD it is accompanied by an application for a vesting order to acquire all property in the area. An official of the Environmental Health Department will then carry out a survey of the area to determine if the area needs redeveloped.

Under article 47 of the Housing (NI) Order 1981 the Housing Executive can declare a redevelopment area if the survey shows that at least one-third of the houses in the area are either unfit for human habitation (see p.505) or, by reason of their bad arrangement, or the narrowness or bad arrangement of the streets, dangerous or injurious to the health of the inhabitants of the area, provided (in both cases) that the most satisfactory course of action is to redevelop the area as a whole. The Housing Executive can also apply to vest property in an area on behalf of a RHA.

If there are any objections to a proposed redevelopment the DSD must hold a public inquiry to examine the objections, unless they are considered to be frivolous or vexatious or are withdrawn. For more about public inquiries see Chapter 23.

Compensation

There are several types of compensation available to those who lose their homes as a result of redevelopment, including:

- *Home loss payments*: Owner-occupiers must have been in legal ownership of the property at the date of vesting and tenants must have occupied the property as their principal home for at least one year prior to being displaced.
- *Disturbance payments*: Claimants must have been in legal possession of their home as either an owner-occupier or a tenant at the time when the notice of application for a vesting order was made. Any dispute as to the amount can be referred to the Lands Tribunal for Northern Ireland.
- *Market value*: Owner-occupiers will be offered the market value of their home. Any dispute can be referred to the Lands Tribunal.
- *Injurious affection*: If some of the claimant's land is acquired for redevelopment and the remaining land is reduced in value the claimant may, under the Land Compensation (NI) Order 1982, recover compensation for the reduction in value of the retained land.

The duty to rehouse

Legal occupiers in a redevelopment area are entitled to be rehoused in existing Housing Executive or RHA property, or in one of the new houses in the redevelopment area. Applicants for rehousing are given points according to their housing need and, in addition, awarded "Management Transfer" status, *i.e.* there is a discretion to rehouse without reference to their points level. In exceptional circumstances, dwellings can be purchased for families in redevelopment areas where suitable accommodation is not available within the existing housing stock. Each household will be entitled to three reasonable offers of accommodation. Where these are refused the Housing Executive may initiate legal action for possession. Where legal action has commenced and a decree for possession granted, the

Housing Executive will make one further reasonable offer to prevent the family becoming homeless.

Having "vested" an area, the Housing Executive or RHA becomes responsible for repairs and maintenance of the properties, although major repairs to houses in proposed redevelopment areas will not be undertaken. Minor repairs will be carried out depending on how soon redevelopment is due to take place.

Squatting

"Squatting" occurs when a person enters and occupies premises without the permission of the owner or when a person who previously entered a property unlawfully has since been given permission to occupy (in this instance the person is still an illegal occupant). Both the entering and occupying of a property without the owner's permission are criminal offences under the Criminal Justice (NI) Order 1986.

In the case of Housing Executive property the squatter will be asked to leave voluntarily. Failure to do so will result in a warning letter being sent, giving the squatter seven days to vacate the premises and threatening legal action if he or she remains beyond that time. All squatters should request a homelessness assessment at the earliest opportunity.

The owner can re-enter the property, but will commit a criminal offence if he or she uses, or threatens, force against another person or property. However, the illegal eviction and harassment provisions of the Rent (NI) Order 1978 do not protect squatters. The owner of the property can also take both criminal and civil legal action. Criminal proceedings are usually initiated in a magistrates' court. Once a squatter has been convicted of an offence under the Criminal Justice (NI) Order 1986 the Resident Magistrate can grant a possession order for the premises and also fine and/or imprison the squatter. If the squatter has used force or threatened violence he or she may also be prosecuted under the Protection of the Person and Property Act (NI) 1969.

Where a squatter fails to comply with a possession order, the eviction will be implemented through the Enforcement of Judgements Office (see Chapter 2). The owner can also apply to the High Court under Order 113 of the Rules of the Supreme Court (NI) for summary possession proceedings. Under civil law the squatter is liable to compensate the owner for the amount which the owner would have received for the property had it been lawfully occupied.

A squatter can be issued with a "use and occupation" book requiring the squatter to make periodic payments – the equivalent of rent – with a covering letter making it clear that a tenancy is not being granted (*McCann v NIHE*, 1979). The squatter will remain a trespasser and will have no right, for example, to have repairs carried out, although under the Occupiers' Liability (NI) Order 1986 he or she does have some rights in relation to injuries sustained as a result of disrepair (*McGhee v NIHE*, 1983).

Complaints

Housing Executive tenants who are dissatisfied with the work or decision-making of the Housing Executive can make a formal complaint through the internal complaints procedure. The tenant should first contact the Area Manager, who should respond within 15 working days. If the tenant is still dissatisfied he or she can contact the Chief Executive, who should also respond within 15 working days. If a tenant is unhappy with the outcome of the complaints procedure he or she may ask the Commissioner for Complaints to investigate the complaint (see Chapter 2).

RHAs must have policies and procedures in place to deal with complaints. A tenant who is dissatisfied with the way in which his or her complaint is dealt with may submit a complaint to the DSD. A RHA tenant has a final means of redress through writing to his or her Member of the Legislative Assembly asking that person to refer the complaint to the Assembly Ombudsman. The 2003 Order provides that the Commissioner for Complaints should deal with complaints against RHAs.

Private rented sector housing

Private rented sector tenancies are those for which the landlord is not the Housing Executive or a RHA. They can either be controlled under the Rent (NI) Order 1978 (hereafter called the Rent Order) or uncontrolled. The type of tenancy held will have implications for rent, repairs and security of tenure.

Controlled tenancies

The letting history of a property, together with its Net Annual Valuation (NAV) in 1978 and prior to the beginning of the current tenancy, will help to indicate if the tenancy is controlled or not. A tenancy will be assumed to be controlled unless the contrary can be shown, with the onus resting on the landlord to prove that the property is not controlled. Controlled tenancies can be sub-divided into three specific groups:

- *Restricted tenancy:* This is a controlled tenancy which has had a restricted rent certificate issued (or deemed to have been issued) by a district council. Restricted tenancies have their rents restricted to the amount payable before the introduction of the Rent Order (1 October 1978). This is normally £1 per week plus rates. The properties are usually small terraced houses, built before World War I, and are often in need of repair or modernisation.
- *Regulated tenancy:* These properties are usually of a better standard than restricted properties and if a landlord carries out the proper procedures a rent similar to that charged for a Housing Executive property can be levied. The district council will issue a regulated rent certificate if it is satisfied that the property complies with the regulated tenancy standards.
- *Protected shorthold tenancies:* Shorthold tenancies, introduced by the Housing (NI) Order 1983, are a type of controlled tenancy which are subject to a time limit at the end of which the landlord is entitled to obtain vacant possession through the courts. They are not very common, but can occur where there is a new letting of a restricted or regulated tenancy.

Uncontrolled tenancies

Tenancies not controlled by the Rent Order are known as uncontrolled tenancies (or sometimes as unprotected tenancies) and are governed by private contracts. The tenancy can either be for a fixed-term, *e.g.* one year, or can be periodic running from week to week or month to month. The terms and conditions of the tenancy are therefore agreed entirely between the landlord and tenant and should be set out in the tenancy agreement. However, a tenancy agreement cannot override the basic rights of all private sector tenants (see below).

Tenancy agreements

A tenancy agreement (in law it is called a lease) is a legal contract between a landlord and tenant which binds both parties. Prospective tenants should ensure that they agree to the terms of the agreement before signing it and should look out for key terms such as the amount of rent and when it is payable, the length of the tenancy, the repairing obligations, the amount and purpose of any deposit, the landlord's right to enter premises and whether there are any restrictions on the use of the property, such as keeping pets or lodgers.

Implied terms

In the absence of a written tenancy agreement, or in the case of an inadequate one which fails to set out the tenancy terms sufficiently, the law allows certain terms to be implied. In this instance sections 41 and 42 of the Landlord and Tenant Law Amendment Act (Ireland) 1860 (known by lawyers as "Deasy's Act") assume that the landlord will ensure that the tenant will have quiet and peaceful enjoyment of the premises, that, if furnished, the accommodation is fit for human habitation, that the common parts of the premises will be kept in repair, that any premises let in the course of their construction will be built with proper materials in a workmanlike manner and that any charges for services will be fair and reasonable. Likewise, it is assumed, unless the tenancy agreement states otherwise, that the tenant will pay rent and rates, keep the premises in good condition and repair and give up possession of the premises at the end of the lease.

Unfair terms

The Unfair Terms in Consumer Contracts Regulations 1999 apply to tenancy agreements and aim to ensure that the terms contained in any contract will be fair to the tenant. Any terms considered to be unfair will be unenforceable if they are detrimental to the tenant (*London Borough of Camden v McBride*, 1999). Terms also have to be written in plain and intelligible language. Agreements which are deemed to be unfair will not be binding.

Private tenants' rights

All private tenants, whether controlled or uncontrolled, have certain basic rights which a tenancy agreement cannot override. Any attempt to do so will be unenforceable and may even be illegal. The basic rights for all private tenants are:

- *The right to a rent book*: Article 38 of the Rent Order and the Rent Book Regulations (NI) 1983 require a landlord to supply a tenant with a rent book, which must include the address of the landlord, the amount of rent and rates payable and the amount and description of any other payment(s) the landlord requires the tenant to make. Private tenants should also be informed of their right to claim housing benefit.

- *Freedom from harassment and illegal eviction:* There are both criminal and civil remedies for harassment or illegal eviction. Articles 54-56 of the Rent Order set out the rights of private tenants in this respect.   Local councils have the powers to investigate allegations and prosecute offenders. Harassment can include cutting off the electricity or water supply, verbal abuse, entering without permission, changing locks, starting building work without notice, interfering with possessions, theft, threatening behaviour or continually telephoning or calling at abnormal hours. There must be an intention to make the tenant vacate the premises, give up a right (such as the right to claim housing benefit) or not pursue a remedy (such as seeking repairs through the public health procedures). Illegal eviction occurs when a tenant is deprived of the occupation of all or part of the tenancy without due process of law.

- *The right to due process of law*: In order to evict a tenant, a landlord must obtain an order for possession from a court and have it enforced through the Enforcement of Judgments Office (see Chapter 2).

- *The right to notice to quit*: A landlord and tenant are each required to serve a notice to quit of at least four weeks. The exception to this is in the case of a fixed-term tenancy.

Security of tenure in controlled tenancies

Restricted and regulated tenancies provide security of tenure. Consequently, a landlord must show grounds for repossession in order to obtain a court order. These grounds are set out in Schedule 4 to the Rent Order. There are 10 discretionary grounds on which a court *may* grant possession:

- where there has been non-payment of rent or a breach of the tenancy agreement,

- where those residing in the dwelling have caused a nuisance or have used the dwelling for immoral purposes,
- where damage has been caused to the property,
- where damage has been caused to furniture provided,
- where the tenant has given notice to quit and the landlord has arranged another agreement for which vacant possession is required,
- where the tenant has sub-let the house,
- where the tenant held the tenancy as an employee of the landlord and the landlord now requires the dwelling house for a new employee,
- where the landlord needs possession of the dwelling in order to live in it,
- where the tenant has sub-let part of the house at an excessive rent, and
- where the house is on agricultural land which the landlord wishes to sell.

The Rent Order also sets out eight mandatory grounds where a court *must* grant an order for possession to the landlord:

- where the landlord originally occupied the dwelling and, prior to the tenancy, notified the tenant that he or she might in future wish to live there again,
- where, prior to the tenancy, the landlord notified the tenant that he or she intended to seek possession of the dwelling house on retiring from employment,
- where the property was originally intended for occupation by a minister of religion or missionary and it is now required for this purpose,
- where the property was originally intended for occupation by an agricultural worker employed by the landlord,
- where there has been an agricultural letting in certain circumstances and two farms are to be amalgamated,
- where the landlord wants to recover possession of an agricultural letting in certain circumstances when the tenant is not, and has never been, an employee of the landlord,
- where the term of a protected shorthold tenancy has expired and the landlord has served a valid notice to quit, and
- where the landlord was a member of the armed forces at the time the dwelling was let and, prior to the commencement of the tenancy, notified the tenant that he or she might in future seek possession of the dwelling house in order to live there.

Most controlled tenancies can be ended by the tenant giving four weeks' notice to quit.

Security of tenure in uncontrolled tenancies

Those living in uncontrolled tenancies have security of tenure only for the term of the tenancy agreement. The landlord and tenant of a fixed-term tenancy need not give any period of notice once the tenancy has reached the end of its agreed period. However, a landlord must always apply to the court for a possession order and use the official court enforcement procedure in order to evict a tenant. Where there is a periodic tenancy, four weeks' notice to quit must be given.

Rents

The Rent Order fixes the rent that can be charged for a restricted or regulated tenancy. A landlord or tenant may apply to the DSD to register a regulated rent. Registering a rent is a means of increasing the rent beyond the 1978 level. The rent charged for a restricted tenancy will be the amount which was payable immediately prior to the implementation of the Rent Order. This is usually £1 per week, excluding rates, and will not increase unless the landlord applies to the district council for a regulated rent certificate and then registers the rent as regulated with the DSD. If a tenant pays more rent than the landlord is legally entitled to charge he or she can claim back up to two years' overpaid rent.

Where a tenancy is classified as regulated the rent is registered with the DSD, although the Housing (NI) Order 2003 transfers this function to the Housing Executive. The landlord or tenant can appeal the rent level by applying to a rent assessment committee.

For a letting to qualify as a shorthold tenancy the rent must be registered with the DSD no later than 28 days after the tenancy commences. A tenant is required to pay the registered rent and cannot be charged more than this amount.

Rents in the uncontrolled sector will normally be fixed for the period of the lease, *e.g.* one year. If a tenant stays on at the end of the fixed-term the tenancy becomes periodic (often referred to as "from month to month") and a new rent level can be set. If a lease is for more than one year the agreement may contain a clause allowing the landlord to review the rent level at fixed intervals, *e.g.* on a yearly basis. There are additional considerations for uncontrolled tenants:

- *Deposits:* These are generally used as security against damage, theft or rent arrears.
- *Rent in advance*: A landlord or agent will often request the first month's rent to be paid at the start of the tenancy, generally in addition to a deposit.
- *Letting fee*: This is a fee often demanded by agents in respect of their administration costs. It is illegal to require this fee to be paid by tenants.
- *Key money*: This is a payment to a landlord, agent or former tenant for their granting or handing over the tenancy of the property being let. It is illegal to ask a prospective tenant for key money and any payment made in these situations would be recoverable.
- *Guarantors*: Some landlords or agents may request prospective tenants to provide a guarantor, *i.e.* someone who guarantees to make payments should the tenant fail to do so.

Repairs

The repairing obligations of landlords and tenants will depend on whether the tenancy is controlled or uncontrolled. However, all tenants generally have the right to have repairs which are a danger to health or safety carried out under the Public Health (Ireland) Act 1878 (see p.495). District councils have a responsibility under this legislation to ensure that a statutory nuisance is remedied.

Unfit houses

A house is unfit for human habitation if it fails to meet one or more of the following standards set out in article 46 of the Housing (NI) Order 1981 as amended by article 90 of the Housing (NI) Order 1992:

- be structurally stable,
- be free from serious disrepair,
- be free from dampness prejudicial to the health of the occupants,
- have adequate provision for lighting, heating and ventilation,
- have an adequate piped supply of wholesome water,
- provide satisfactory facilities in the house for the preparation and cooking of food, including a sink with hot water,
- have a suitably located toilet for the exclusive use of the occupants,
- have a suitably located bath or shower and wash-hand basin for exclusive use by the occupants, each with a satisfactory supply of hot and cold water, and

- have an effective system for the draining of foul, waste and surface water.

If a dwelling is unfit the Housing Executive may serve a repair notice, make a closing order or make a demolition order. The Housing (NI) Order 2003 enables the Housing Executive to introduce "Deferred Action Notices", which can be served on any unfit property where, in the Executive's opinion, remedial action would not be the best course of action. Furthermore, a tenant in these circumstances will be entitled to additional points under the Housing Selection Scheme. If a restricted tenancy is considered to be unfit, it may be possible for the tenant to be re-housed by the Housing Executive.

Defective premises

The Defective Premises (Landlord's Liability) Act (NI) 2001, which came into effect on 2 July 2002, extends the duty of care on landlords of residential premises to prevent defects from causing personal injury or damage to possessions. It widens the duty of care to all persons who might be reasonably expected to be affected by defects in the state of a landlord's premises. Furthermore, the duty of care applies not only if the landlord knows of the defect but also if he or she ought to have known of it in all the circumstances.

Repairs in controlled tenancies

Restricted tenants have few repairing rights. Unless the tenancy agreement states otherwise, restricted tenants can normally insist upon only "public health" type repairs (see p.495). In a regulated tenancy, responsibility for repairs will depend on what is set out in the tenancy agreement or (by default) in the Rent Order. This states that the landlord is responsible for the structure and exterior of the dwelling whereas the tenant is legally responsible for taking proper care of the premises.

Should the landlord of a regulated tenancy default on his or her repairing obligations, the tenant can apply to the Environmental Health Department of the local district council to inspect the property. If the Environmental Health Officer confirms that the landlord has broken his or her repairing duties, the council will issue a certificate of disrepair. Failure to comply with such a certificate can result in a court appearance, with an order being issued requiring the repairs to be carried out within a specific period of time.

Repairs in uncontrolled tenancies

In uncontrolled tenancies repairing obligations are normally set out in the tenancy agreement. Where there is no tenancy agreement, tenants can generally only use the statutory nuisance and unfitness procedures (see p.505). All landlords and tenants are entitled to take private legal action where a repairing obligation has been breached. A tenant may also be able to use self-help, which allows a tenant to carry out the repair work for which the landlord is responsible and offset the cost against the rent due to the landlord. Tenants must seek specialist advice if wishing to pursue this course of action, as the landlord may decide to end the tenancy as a result.

Home improvement grants

Under the Housing (NI) Order 1992 grant aid may be available to a private rented sector tenant, owner-occupier or landlord to carry out improvements and/or repairs to a property. The Housing Executive administers the Home Improvement Grants Scheme. The 2003 Order replaces the minor works assistance grant with home repair assistance, whereby the Housing Executive will provide a grant or materials to help with works to repair, adapt or improve a property and will make repair grants available only to properties in the private rented sector. The 2003 Order will also replace the current mandatory scheme with a largely discretionary scheme. The following grants are currently available (the first five are means-tested, but the rest are not):

- *Renovation grants:* These are aimed at bringing properties up to the appropriate fitness standard. They are available to owner-occupiers, private landlords (except of houses in multiple occupation – see below) and tenants.
- *Replacement grants:* These are given where the property does not meet the fitness standard and renovation would not be the best course of action. They are available to owner-occupiers and to landlords.
- *Disabled facilities grants:* These facilitate making a disabled person's home more accessible and are available to owner-occupiers, landlords and tenants (except Housing Executive tenants).
- *Common parts grants:* These are discretionary grants aimed at improving the common parts of a building containing one or more flats. They are available to landlords and tenants.
- *Houses in multiple occupation grants:* These bring such homes up to normal fitness standard. They are normally discretionary but if the

work is required to comply with a statutory notice they are mandatory. They are available to landlords who are owners of the property.

Non-means tested grants

- *Minor works assistance grants:* These are discretionary grants to help those on low incomes to carry out minor essential improvements to their homes. They are available to owner-occupiers and tenants.
- *Repair grants:* These are mandatory grants to meet the cost of carrying out repairs required after the issuing of a statutory notice. They are available to owner-occupiers, landlords, agents and tenants.

Energy efficiency

The Warm Homes Scheme was introduced in July 2001 and provides grants to both owner-occupiers and private rented sector tenants in receipt of social security benefits who need help to keep their homes warm. A maximum of £750 is available to households to implement energy efficiency measures, such as loft insulation, draught proofing and hot water tank jackets. Under the Warm Homes Plus Scheme a maximum grant of £2,700 is available to anyone over 60 and in receipt of benefit, for such measures as converting existing solid fuel heating or Economy 7 to oil or gas heating and repairs to existing heating systems.

Houses in multiple occupation (HMOs)

In Northern Ireland up to 30,000 people live in houses let in multiple occupation (HMOs). HMOs are defined in the Housing (NI) Order 1992 as houses which are "occupied by persons who do not form a single household." The 2003 Order amends this definition. Articles 75-87 of the Housing (NI) Order 1992 empowers the Housing Executive to set and enforce standards requiring repairs and maintenance work to be carried out in HMOs and also to ensure the installation of fire safety features. The Order enables the Executive:

- to serve an overcrowding notice,
- to ensure the dwelling is occupied in accordance with proper standards of management,
- to issue a notice specifying work needing to be carried out to make the property fit for human habitation,

- to ensure adequate means of fire escape and other adequate fire precautions,
- to fix occupancy limits, and
- to ensure works are carried out.

The Housing Executive has several options available to it in situations where the necessary standards are not satisfied. If the house is not fit for human habitation and/or lacks adequate amenities, including means of escape from fire and other fire precautions, the Housing Executive will serve a statutory repair notice on the owner or manager of the house. If the owner or manager does not comply with the notice the Housing Executive will take action through the courts, which may result in a fine being imposed on the landlord. As a last resort the Housing Executive may carry out the work and charge the landlord for the costs. A grant may be available to assist in meeting the cost of the works (see p.485).

Voluntary licensing scheme

In September 2001 the Housing Executive introduced a voluntary licensing scheme for HMOs with the aim of promoting better standards in the HMO sector. A landlord can obtain a three-year licence if his or her property satisfies the Housing Executive's standards, *e.g.* as regards fire safety and management. The register is open to the public for inspection. The 2003 Order will require the Housing Executive to produce a compulsory scheme. Under the new scheme registration will be for a period of five years.

Homelessness

The Housing (NI) Order 1988 (hereafter called the 1988 Order) requires the Housing Executive to provide assistance to those who are homeless or threatened with homelessness and stipulates the duties of the Housing Executive when dealing with homeless persons. The Housing Executive's statistics reveal that in 2001-2002 14,164 households presented as homeless. The level of assistance granted will depend on whether the person in question is homeless, in priority need and not intentionally homeless. Where a person qualifies under these three "tests" they will be awarded "Full Duty Applicant" status and will, at present, be made an offer of permanent accommodation. The 2003 Order makes a number of amendments to the 1988 legislation, which may affect the level of assistance provided.

The "homelessness" test

Under article 3 of the 1988 Order there are three definitions of homelessness.

- *Actual homelessness*: Where a person has no accommodation in Northern Ireland. (The 2003 Order amends this to "no accommodation in the UK or elsewhere.")
- *Deemed homelessness:* Where it is not "reasonable" for a person to continue to occupy accommodation, *e.g.* because of serious overcrowding, a threat of violence or a danger to health.
- *Threatened with homelessness*: Where it is likely that a person will become homeless within 28 days from the date on which he or she gives written notice to the Housing Executive, either as a result of having received a valid notice to quit or because of being subjected to possession proceedings.

The "priority need" test

Under article 5 a person will be in priority need if he or she or a member of his or her household falls within one of the following categories:
- is pregnant,
- has dependent children,
- is in fear of or subject to violence,
- has lost his or her home due to fire, flood or other disaster,
- is vulnerable as a result of old age, mental or physical disability or other special reason, or
- is a person aged 16-21 at risk of sexual or financial exploitation.

The "intentionality" test

Under article 6 a person must show that he or she did not contribute to the loss of his or her last legal settled address (not including temporary accommodation) by some deliberate act or failure to act, when that address would have been available and continued occupation would have been reasonable. (The 2003 Order introduces an additional intentionality test which will examine collusion between the person applying as homeless and the person who had been accommodating him or her.)

The duties of the Housing Executive

The level of assistance owed to a person will depend on the decision as to his or her homelessness, priority need and intentionality:

- *If a person is found to be not homeless or threatened with homelessness*, the Housing Executive's duty to make further inquiries comes to an end. In practice, however, verbal and/or written guidance on finding accommodation is usually provided.
- *If a person is found to be homeless but not in priority need*, the duty to make further inquiries ends there. The Housing Executive is nevertheless legally required to provide the applicant with advice and assistance on how to obtain accommodation.
- *If a person is found to be homeless and in priority need*, the Housing Executive has a statutory duty to provide temporary accommodation while it carries out further inquiries, if required, into the reasons for the person's homelessness.
- *If a person is found to be intentionally homeless and in priority need*, temporary accommodation must be provided for a period of time to allow him or her reasonable opportunity to find alternative housing. This is normally a period of up to 28 days or until the outcome of any appeal. The Housing Executive must also provide advice and assistance on rehousing options.
- *If a person is found to be unintentionally homeless and in priority need* (*i.e.* passes all three tests above), he or she will be awarded "Full Duty Applicant" status. This will entitle the person to 70 points under the Housing Selection Scheme and may also trigger the award of additional points under the other assessment categories. If permanent housing is not immediately available, the Housing Executive must provide suitable temporary accommodation until the person can be rehoused permanently.

Irrespective of the outcome of their homelessness assessment, all applicants should be assessed under the Housing Selection Scheme (see p.487).

Challenging a decision

The Housing Executive must provide the applicant with written notification of the homelessness decision in his or her case, together with reasons. The applicant can then lodge an appeal through the Housing Executive's internal appeals system or, where the person wishes to challenge the level of points awarded under the Housing

Selection Scheme, he or she must use the internal complaints procedure (see p.499).

Internal appeal system

The Housing Executive's internal appeal procedure has two stages. A letter of appeal should first be sent to the appropriate Area Manager who should, in normal circumstances, give his or her decision in writing within 15 working days (and advice about the second stage appeal). If the applicant is still dissatisfied, he or she can submit a further letter of appeal to the Director of Housing and Regeneration of the Housing Executive, who should give his or her decision in writing, again within 15 working days.

As the actions of the Housing Executive with regard to homelessness applications are governed by statute, the applicant may challenge the Housing Executive's decision by judicial review in the High Court (see Chapter 2).

Further useful addresses

- Housing Rights Service
  Middleton House
  4th Floor, 10-12 High Street
  Belfast BT1 2BA
  tel: 028 9024 5640
  www.housing-rights.org.uk

- Northern Ireland Housing Executive,
  The Housing Centre
  2 Adelaide Street
  Belfast BT2 8GA
  tel: 028 9024 0588
  www.nihe.gov.uk

- Homeless Advice Centre
  32-36 Great Victoria Street
  Belfast BT2 7BA
  tel: 028 9031 7000

- Department for Social Development Housing Association Branch
  Churchill House
  Victoria Square
  Belfast BT1 4SD
  tel: 028 9056 9100

- Eaga Partnership Ltd (Warm Homes Scheme)
  Freepost BE2107
  Dungannon
  Co. Tyrone BT70 5BR
  tel: 0800 181 667
  www.eaga.co.uk

- Lands Tribunal for Northern Ireland
  Royal Courts of Justice
  Chichester Street
  Belfast BT1 3JJ
  tel: 028 9032 7703

- The Financial Ombudsman Service
  South Quay Plaza
  183 Marsh Wall
  London E14 9SR
  tel: 0845 080 1800
  www.financial-ombudsman.org.uk

- Rates Collection Agency
  Oxford House
  49 – 55 Chichester Street
  Belfast BT1 4HH
  tel: 028 9025 2113
  www.ratecollectionagencyni.gov.uk

- Valuation and Lands Agency
  Queen's Court
  56 – 66 Upper Queen Street
  Belfast BT1 6FD
  tel: 028 9025 0700
  www.vla.nics.gov.uk

Chapter 22

Social Security Rights

Eileen Evason

This chapter provides a very general overview of entitlement under the benefits system in Northern Ireland. As a preliminary to the discussion of individual benefits, three observations can be made.

First, although European law has had some effects at the margins of the benefits system through the Equal Treatment Directive (see Chapter 13), in essence the rights people enjoy with regard to the social security system hinge largely on what the government thinks these should be. Few effects are so far discernible as a result of the Human Rights Act 1998. This context helps to account for the way in which the government has been able to substantially modify provision over the past two decades. This has occurred despite the popular perception that the payment of national insurance contributions produces some kind of contractual relationship between the individual and the state. In practice, national insurance benefits have been reduced in value, made less accessible or abolished altogether in much the same way as has occurred in other parts of the social security system. In essence, national insurance contributions are more appropriately regarded as a tax.

Second, benefits systems are not neutral. They reflect the contexts in which they operate and the priorities and perspectives which dominate policy as a whole at a given point in time. Between 1979 and 1997 the objectives of the government were four fold. A prime concern was to cut costs, so many benefits were reduced in their worth, made more difficult to get or simply abolished altogether. A further concern was to shift costs by, for example, transferring the cost of the first 28 weeks of sickness to employers. A third element in the strategy was to ensure that unemployed workers were willing to accept whatever work was on offer in a deregulated, flexible labour market, thereby explaining many of the changes made to provision for the unemployed. Finally, successive Conservative governments sought to "encourage" a move away from statutory provision to reliance on the private market. This was most evident in pensions policy.

The election of a Labour government has brought some change but much continuity. The dismantling of the benefits provided under the national insurance scheme has continued, although there has been no commensurate reduction in national insurance contributions. There has been a heavy emphasis on rebuilding the welfare state around paid employment (with little regard for the unpaid work done largely by women), with New Deals of varying severity for different claimant groups and the national minimum wage. More positively, there has been the emphasis on tackling child poverty, with improvements in child benefit and means-tested help for those with children in and outside employment.

Third, as a result of the amendments to benefits that have taken place, together with other policy changes, the balance within the social security system has shifted markedly. In essence, social security systems may offer benefits in three main ways. Benefits may be universal – *i.e.* detached from contribution conditions but not dependent on means or income, *e.g.* child benefit. Benefits may be on a contributory basis – *i.e.* paid as of right without a means test if contribution and other conditions are fulfilled. Finally, benefits may be payable only to those satisfying a test of means as well as other conditions.

The Beveridge model of the 1940s, imperfectly executed though it was, envisaged national insurance as the centrepiece of provision, with the role of the social security system being primarily to support those outside the labour market for one reason or another. In consequence of the strategy outlined above, however, support from the benefits system increasingly means reliance on means-tested benefits, with all the difficulties provision of this kind entails. There are the take up and poverty trap problems and the system deters effort and thrift. Additionally, means-tested benefits for those in poorly paid work in the labour market have been of increasing significance in the drive to encourage the unemployed and lone parents to accept whatever employment is available. Indeed, for these groups policy discussions on the benefits system revolve purely and simply around the effectiveness of the structure in achieving this objective rather than on the extent to which provision meets need or prevents poverty. This, perhaps more than anything else, sums up the very fundamental changes that have occurred over the past 20 years and helps to explain why a set of provisions which may be thought to be primarily about assisting those in difficulty so frequently seems ill designed for this purpose.

Unemployment

Provision for this group has been cut and amended on an ongoing basis since 1980, culminating in the introduction of the jobseeker's allowance (JSA) in October 1996. JSA replaced unemployment benefit – the national insurance benefit for the unemployed – and the means-tested assistance formerly available to the unemployed under the income support scheme (see below). JSA, in fact, consists of two benefits.

Contribution-based JSA

Receipt of this depends on claimants satisfying contribution conditions as well as meeting all the tests outlined below. Put briefly, claimants must have actually paid class 1 contributions to the value of 25 times the lowest possible contribution in one of the two tax years preceding the year of the claim. Additionally, claimants must have paid or been credited with contributions to the value of 50 times the lowest possible contribution in both of the two years preceding the claim. These are exactly the same as the contribution conditions for the former unemployment benefit, but satisfying them does not attract the same level of support.

Contribution-based JSA is payable only for six months, whereas unemployment benefit was payable for one year. Contribution-based JSA is payable at two rates, with claimants aged 18-24 being entitled, at the current (2003-2004) weekly rates, to £43.25 and those aged 25 and over to £54.65. Unemployment benefit made no such distinction. The payment of varying amounts with no variation in contribution conditions is a significant change in practice.

In line with the former unemployment benefit, no additions are payable for dependent children. However, whereas claimants of unemployment benefit received additions for adult dependents, *i.e.* partners with no or limited earnings, contribution-based JSA consists of an allowance for the claimant only. This represents a substantial cut and taken as a whole this benefit may be considered to be a very poor return for contributions paid. Finally, it should be noted that contribution-based JSA will be reduced pound for pound by any earnings over £5 obtained from part-time work (there are some exceptions to this). The pound for pound deduction also applies to occupational or personal pensions of over £50 a week.

Income-based JSA

The inadequacy of contribution-based JSA means that many unemployed people will also need to claim this means-tested benefit at the outset of their claim. This is also the only source of support available when entitlement to contribution-based JSA is exhausted or where there is no entitlement in the first place because the claimant cannot meet the contribution conditions. The amount of benefit payable is assessed in the same way as for income support (see below). It should be noted that claimants with partners working 24 hours a week or more are excluded from this benefit regardless of the actual income of the couple.

Other conditions

For both contribution-based and income-based JSA, claimants must also comply with a number of other conditions. One of these is that they must not be working for more than 16 hours a week. There are four others.

a) Claimants must be capable of work

This is not a new provision but the test of incapacity introduced for incapacity benefit in 1995 (see below) necessitates further consideration of it. Regulations provide that persons deemed capable of work for incapacity benefit *must* be accepted as such for JSA. The problem remains, however, that persons with very remote chances of securing employment may be decanted from incapacity benefit to JSA and, whilst some concessions are made to such persons, they may find it difficult to satisfy all of the conditions attached to this benefit.

b) Claimants must be available for employment

In essence, claimants must be ready to take any job immediately unless, for example, they have caring responsibilities, in which case they must be available for work on 48 hours' notice or have been allowed a period of up to 13 weeks to look for work in their usual employment. It is important to emphasise that it is irrelevant whether work is or is not available or likely to be available.

c) Claimants must be actively seeking work

Benefit is payable only for each week when claimants are actively seeking work and claimants can be required at any point to provide details of steps taken in the previous week to secure work. "Steps" include activities such as making written or oral applications for jobs and preparing a c.v. It would appear that two steps each week are sufficient to meet this condition.

d) Claimants must have a current jobseeker's agreement in force

The agreement sets out the steps the claimant will take to find work and is signed by both the claimant and officer. If either decline to sign, no benefit is payable. Where claimants are unhappy with the contents of the agreement they can ask for it to be referred to a decision-maker and, if they are still dissatisfied, to a different decision-maker. From this point claimants may appeal to a tribunal and, on a point of law, to a Social Security Commissioner. As claimants run the risk of losing benefit for significant periods if they enter into disputes over jobseeker's agreements, the value of these procedures in practice is debatable and claimants have little real option but to agree to whatever the officer considers appropriate.

Sanctions

Claimants may be refused benefit for varying periods. They may lose JSA for between one and 26 weeks if it is decided that they lost their previous employment as a result of misconduct or leaving it without just cause. Claimants may also be sanctioned for two or four weeks if they fail to comply with a direction from an officer telling them to take some specific action to secure work or to enhance their chances of finding work. Claimants will be sanctioned for two or four weeks if they fail to take up a place on a training scheme and from one to 26 weeks if they fail to take up a job notified to them. Claimants can ask for these decisions to be reviewed and may appeal to a tribunal and, on a point of law, to a Social Security Commissioner. Sanctioned claimants on income-based JSA may apply for hardship payments. Where claimants are sanctioned the period for which this applies is deducted from the 26 week period of entitlement to contribution-based JSA. Sanctioned claimants may therefore find their entitlement to this is wiped out altogether, despite the contributions they have already paid.

Sickness and disability

Provision for these contingencies consists of a number of benefits which can be grouped into four main categories. First, some benefits (statutory sick pay and incapacity benefit) have the function of providing a weekly income for persons incapable of work as a result of sickness or disability. Second, some benefits (attendance allowance and disability living allowance) are intended to provide assistance with the extra costs which those with disabilities may incur. Third, the benefits system makes some provision for people suffering disability as a result of industrial injury. Fourth, there is some provision for informal carers – people, normally relatives, who give unpaid support to persons with disabilities in the community.

Statutory sick pay and incapacity benefit

Statutory sick pay (SSP) is administered by employers. Prior to 1994 employers recovered the bulk of the cost incurred by deducting the amounts paid from their national insurance liability. This arrangement was in recognition of the fact that SSP was substituting for sickness benefit (now short term incapacity benefit) under the national insurance scheme. Now, however, the entire cost normally falls on the employer. This is clearly likely to make it more difficult for those with disabilities to secure work in the first place and employers may be reluctant to operate a provision whereby the state gives rights to individuals but makes no contribution to the resulting costs.

The current weekly rate of SSP is £64.35. There are no additions for dependents. The benefit is payable for the first 28 weeks of sickness, after which claimants may transfer to incapacity benefit (see below). Employees may receive additional support depending on their contract of employment, but as a basic minimum employees are entitled to SSP unless their earnings are below £77.00 a week or they are on contracts of under three months. It is not lawful for employers to employ people on a series of short-term contracts to evade their liability to pay SSP. Cases of dispute can be referred to the Inland Revenue, with a subsequent appeal to the tax appeal commissioner. Employees not entitled to SSP should claim incapacity benefit.

Incapacity benefit replaced sickness and invalidity benefit in April 1995. In essence, the new arrangements deliver lower benefits which, in consequence of the new test of incapacity for work (see below), are more difficult to obtain. Receipt of incapacity benefit depends on claimants satisfying contribution conditions.   Claimants must have actually paid class 1 or 2 contributions equal to 25 times the lowest possible in one of the three tax years preceding the year of the claim, and paid or been credited with 50 times this amount in each of the two tax years preceding the year of the claim. Persons incapable of work as a result of industrial injury were formerly exempt from these conditions but this concession was withdrawn in April 1995. Incapacity benefit consists of three elements:

- *Short term incapacity benefit.* This is payable for the first 28 weeks of sickness in cases where there is no entitlement to SSP. The current rate is £54.40. No additions are payable for dependent children and a significant saving has been made by the provisions which restrict the addition for an adult dependent (£33.65) to cases where the partner is over 60 or caring for dependent children.

- *Short term incapacity benefit at the higher rate.* Previously claimants transferred after 28 weeks of sickness to the broader and more adequate benefit for long term sickness – invalidity benefit. Now, after 28 weeks, unless they are terminally ill or on the highest rate of the care component of disability living allowance (see below), claimants move on to another short-term benefit which is payable at a higher rate for 24 weeks. At present the rate is £64.35. The addition for an adult dependent (£33.65) is again payable only where the dependent is over 60 or caring for children. Additions for dependent children are, however, payable with this benefit. Apart from the limited provision for adult dependents, further savings have been made by making this benefit taxable.

- *Long term incapacity benefit.* This is payable after one year. The current rate is £72.15 for the claimant plus, if applicable, £43.15 for an adult dependent, plus additions for child dependents. The benefit differs from invalidity benefit, which it replaced in a number of ways. No addition is payable from the state earnings related pension scheme. The age addition is payable only where incapacity occurs before the age of 45: £15.15 is payable where incapacity occurs before the age of 35 and £7.60 where the onset of incapacity occurs between the ages of 35 and 44. Unlike invalidity benefit this benefit is taxable and it is payable only up to the state retirement age – 65 for men and 60 for women. Where claimants are in receipt of occupational or personal pensions of over £85 a week, benefits can be reduced by half of the excess.

The "own work" and personal capability assessment

For the first 28 weeks of incapacity the test of incapacity for work for persons who have an "own occupation" is whether they can do their normal job – *i.e.* a job they worked in for at least 16 hours a week for more than eight weeks in the 21 weeks preceding the claim. Persons without an "own occupation" must satisfy the personal capability assessment, which also applies to all claimants after 28 weeks of incapacity unless they are in an exempt category. Those exempt include, for example, persons certified by the Benefits Agency Medical Services as suffering from a severe learning disability or severe mental illness.

The personal capability assessment differs from the previous arrangements in various ways. Formerly the test of incapacity related to actual work. Was there a job – regardless of its availability – that this person was fit to do? Consideration could also be given to the reasonableness of expecting the claimant to do such a job. By contrast, the personal capability assessment relates to functional capacity. Claimants complete questionnaires which cover a range of activities, such as walking up and down stairs. For each activity there is a list of descriptors – statements which describe the varying extent to which people may be able to cope with the activity in question. The claimant is then examined by an examining medical officer – not his or her own GP – and this officer's report goes to a decision-maker for a decision. In essence, points are awarded on the basis of what the claimant can and cannot do. For example, being unable to walk up and down a flight of 12 stairs without holding on to something and taking a rest attracts seven points. Claimants are deemed to be incapable of work if they obtain 15 points from the physical disabilities list of activities or 10 points from the mental disabilities list or 15 from both lists combined, with a minimum of six from the mental disabilities list.

The upshot of all of this is that it is quite possible for a person to have difficulties with a number of activities, which when taken together make it highly unlikely that he or she could obtain and hold down any job, but which produce only 14 points so that the person is deemed capable of work. Claimants have a right of appeal to a tribunal and heavy use is being made of this to challenge the number of points awarded.

Industrial injuries benefits

There are no contribution conditions for these benefits but any accident which has occurred must have arisen out of, and in the course of, employment. In the case of disease the claimant can claim only if he or she has one of a list of prescribed diseases and has worked in a specified employment which has caused the disease. The case-law on this is extensive and, perhaps for this more than any other part of the benefits system, claimants wishing to appeal should contact a reputable advice centre if their trades union cannot assist.

For industrially injured claimants unable to work, SSP and incapacity benefits are payable on the same conditions as for other claimants. Additionally, disablement benefit is payable 15 weeks after the accident or onset of the disease, regardless of whether the claimant is at work or not. The amount of disablement benefit depends on the degree of disablement. In the majority of cases nothing will be paid if the condition is assessed at less than 14%. Otherwise weekly disablement benefit varies from £23.36 to £116.80. In addition, claimants may receive constant attendance allowance if their disablement is assessed at 100%, if they require constant attendance and if they claim within three months. Persons getting this allowance may also qualify for exceptionally severe disablement allowance.

A matter of some concern to the industrially injured is the recovery of benefits claimed as a result of accident or disease from compensation awards. The provisions introduced in 1989 were very harsh in that the total amount of compensation awarded was held to be available for the recovery of benefits, although awards under £2,500 were ignored altogether. In consequence of changes to the legislation, awards in respect of an accident, injury or disease after the 6 October 1997 are treated differently. Amounts awarded for pain or distress are now outside the recovery process, but the £2,500 exemption has been abolished.

Attendance allowance

Attendance allowance is paid to those who are aged 65 or over and so severely disabled (physically or mentally) that during the day they need frequent attention in connection with bodily functions or continual supervision in order to avoid danger to themselves or others, or during the night they require prolonged or repeated attention in connection with bodily functions or need someone else to be awake for prolonged periods "to watch over " them. At current weekly rates, £57.20 is paid if care or supervision is needed day *and* night and £38.30 if the need is for the day *or* night. There are also residence conditions to be satisfied and benefit cannot be paid until the need has lasted for six months (except in the case of the terminally ill). Persons in hospital or other publicly provided accommodation lose their entitlement after four weeks.

This benefit is the subject of some confusion. It is paid to the person who needs care, not to the carer, and receipt hinges on the need for care or supervision rather than on the existence of specified persons caring and the specific illness the person has. There are no contribution conditions and the means of the person are irrelevant. A major point to note is that attendance allowance is normally disregarded in the assessment of income support and housing benefit. It is therefore a real addition to resources.

Disability living allowance (DLA)

DLA is for persons under 65. Because it is more generous than attendance allowance (which is paid to people aged 65 or over), provisions to assist the disabled now appear to discriminate on the basis of age.

DLA consists of two components – care and mobility – and claimants may qualify for either or both. The care component is payable at three rates. The highest rate (£57.20) is for persons requiring care or supervision both day *and* night. The middle rate (£38.30) is payable to those needing care or supervision day *or* night. The lower rate (£15.15) is payable to persons requiring care for a significant part of the day or unable to cook a main meal. Persons under 16 cannot qualify under the cooking condition.

The mobility component is payable at two rates. The higher rate (£39.95) is for persons unable or virtually unable to walk, persons who are both deaf and blind, the severely mentally impaired with severe behavioural problems, and double amputees. The lower rate (£15.15) is for those able to walk but requiring guidance or supervision. Children can qualify for the higher rate from the age of three and the lower rate from the age of five.

Carer's allowance

Although it has been estimated that people, normally women, who provide care for the sick and disabled in our society save the state roughly £20 billion per year, carer's allowance represents the only significant recognition of the costs they incur and the service they provide. Benefit currently amounts to £43.15 a week. Additions for dependents may be payable. The main conditions governing receipt are that claimants must be caring for someone in receipt of attendance allowance or the middle or higher rate of the DLA care component, the task must take up 35 hours a week or more, and the claimant must not be gainfully employed (*i.e.* earning over £75.00 a week) or in full-time education (*i.e.* where class based or supervised study amounts to 21 hours a week or more).

Prior to 1986, married women were excluded from receipt of this benefit, a restriction found to be contrary to the European Union's Equal Treatment Directive. Whilst the removal of this discriminatory provision has helped some persons, the gains have not been as much as expected because of provisions governing the interaction between this and other benefits. Under the overlapping benefits regulations, carer's allowance cannot be paid on top of another principal benefit, such as widowed mother's allowance. Thus removal of the age barrier, so that persons over 65 can now claim, will assist few as elderly carers will have state pensions. In addition, carer's allowance cannot be paid if the carer is a dependent of a person in receipt of any benefit which includes an addition for the carer as a dependent. Thus, a woman caring for a relative whilst her own husband is on incapacity benefit and claiming for her as a dependent will not be entitled to the allowance. Finally carer's allowance counts as a resource in the assessment of entitlement to means-tested benefits. However, where the allowance is deducted from income support or housing benefit, claimants are partially compensated by the carer's premium.

Lone parents and bereavement benefits

For lone parents other than widows, the main options are child benefit and means-tested benefits. In April 1998 child benefit at the special rate was abolished for new claimants and those becoming lone parents after that date receive child benefit on the same basis as other families – currently £16.05 for first or eldest child and £10.75 for each other child. Lone parents not in employment (*i.e.* working less than 16 hours per week) can claim income support if their resources are below the prescribed levels.

Lone parents who are able to secure employment may also have their income increased through child tax credit and working tax credit and housing benefit (see below). It should be noted that lone parents on income support may have their benefit reduced for three years for failure to cooperate with the Child Support Agency (see Chapter 18). At the end of this period a further three year penalty may be imposed on the lone parent.

With regard to widowed persons, benefits were restructured in April 2001. Ostensibly the new provisions are gender neutral, as payments can now be made to men as well as women. In practice, however, as access depends on the late spouse's contribution record and women are more likely to have incomplete records, the gains for widowers are likely to be limited. Provision consists of three elements. First, there is the bereavement payment of £2,000, provided national insurance and other conditions are met. This is not payable where someone qualifies for the widowed parent's allowance – the second element in provision. This is a weekly payment which, in essence, is payable for as long as the claimant has at least one child qualifying for child benefit. The third element in provision is the bereavement allowance. Whilst the bereavement payment and widowed parent's allowance are fairly similar to preceding provisions, the bereavement allowance represents a major change. In effect, the widow's pension, which was formerly payable to widows on or after the age of 45 and up to retirement age, has been abolished, although widows already in receipt of the benefit prior to 9 April 2001 will continue to receive it. Women (and men) aged 45 or over who are bereaved after this date are entitled – provided other conditions are met – to a weekly payment (currently £77.45) for up to one year only. This is a substantial cut in provision of which many couples may be unaware.

Pensioners

A central aim of the Pensions Act 1975 was that, as far as possible, everyone would be entitled to a basic pension plus an earnings-related pension either from their employer or from the state. Legislation in 1986, however, sought to reduce the commitment of the state and expand the role of the private market by reducing the adequacy of SERPS (the state earnings-related pension scheme) and encouraging membership of company pension schemes and greater reliance on personal pensions. The logic of this approach is clearly open to question in the light of episodes such as the Maxwell scandal and the mis-selling of personal pensions.

The current structure of pensions provision is as follows. All of these bits and pieces add up to less than might be expected, hence many pensioners have to rely on income support and housing benefit as well.

- Provided contribution conditions are fulfilled, a category A pension is payable (current rate £77.45 per week). Payment of the pension is not conditional on retirement and there is no earnings rule. The full basic rate is payable only after contributions have been paid or credited for 90% of working life and it is a source of considerable surprise to many pensioners that their entitlement after 50 years of contributions is so little. The main reason for this is the decision in 1980 to uprate long-term benefits in line only with *prices*. This has resulted in the basic category A pension falling steadily as a percentage of average *wages*.
- Category B pensions (£46.35) are paid to married women relying for their entitlement on their husband's contributions. The category B pension is not payable until the husband claims his category A pension. Many married women now have some entitlement to a category A pension as well as the category B pension. However only one – the higher – can be paid. Married women with entitlement in their own right to category A pension of less than £46.35 therefore gain nothing from this.
- Category D pensions (£46.35) are non-contributory and are paid to pensioners who are over 80 years of age and have no other pension or a pension below the category D level.
- Beyond the basic pension, claimants may be entitled to graduated retirement benefit under the 1961-75 state scheme. Normally, however, the amounts involved are trifling. Those retiring after April 1979 may have entitlement under SERPS, introduced in 1975, except for periods when they were in occupational pension schemes or personal pensions and contracted out of SERPS.

It can be noted that the election of a Labour government in 1997 has not altered pension provision dramatically. The basic state pension is to continue to wither away, although means-tested help for pensioners has been made more generous and a winter fuel allowance for persons aged 60 and over has been introduced. SERPS has been abolished and, in the continuing drive to privatisation, it is hoped that people on modest earnings will make provision for themselves via the new stakeholders pensions – a re-packaged form of personal pensions offered by insurance companies. SERPS has been replaced by a new state second pension for, for example, people on very low wages, but this will not mature fully until 2050.

Means-tested benefits: income support

Income support is known as the minimum income guarantee if the claimant is a pensioner.

Because benefits available as of right are inadequate in many respects, income support is of great importance. Income support assists those not in full-time (*i.e.* at least 16 hours per week) employment and without partners in full-time employment, excluding the unemployed who claim JSA (see p.517). Persons with savings or assets of more than £8,000 (£12,000 for people aged 60 or over) are also excluded. Benefit consists of the difference between resources (minus any "disregards" the claimant is entitled to) and the prescribed applicable amounts. Resources include earnings and most benefits paid to the claimant and his or her partner (excluding attendance allowance, DLA and housing benefit). Capital between £3,000 and £8,000 (£6,000 and £12,000 for people aged 60 or over) is assumed to generate a weekly income of £1 for each block of £250. The applicable amounts consist of three elements.

- First, a basic personal allowance, for example £85.75 for a couple.
- Second, for certain categories of claimants set additions are made known as "premia".
- Third, help with some types of housing costs (notably mortgage interest payments) may be paid. For help with rent and rates, income support claimants must make a separate claim for housing benefit (see below).

The scheme has given rise to a number of difficulties. To begin with, the basic allowance for single people under 25 is very low at £43.25 and certainly insufficient for them to live independently in the community. In addition, there is now no provision for increasing the weekly benefit of claimants with special needs (*e.g.* the cost of a special diet or extra heating). The premia which have been substituted for these provisions are not always sufficient to cover such special needs. Moreover, claimants who might previously have been able to claim help with such needs will not always happen to fall into a category attracting a premium. A further difficulty is that "single payments" (lump sums for exceptional items of expenditure) have been replaced by the social fund (see below).

Finally, a major source of current difficulty relates to the substantial cuts that have been made in the assistance claimants many receive with mortgage payments. Unless claimants are in an exempt category, claimants with mortgages taken out after September 1995 receive no help for the first 39 weeks of the claim. Up to various limits, assistance with mortgage interest payments at a standard rate is payable after this. With regard to mortgages obtained before October 1995, claimants receive no help for the first eight weeks of the claim, 50% of the costs for the next 18 weeks and 100% of such costs after this (again up to varying limits). The amount payable will be reduced if there are non-dependents in the household or costs are deemed unreasonable. In essence, despite the policy of encouraging home ownership, owner-occupiers may receive very little assistance, and are expected to take out insurance policies to meet their housing costs when their circumstances change and they have difficulty meeting their costs

The social fund

The social fund came fully into operation in April 1988 and replaced not just single payments but also maternity and death grants. It provides two sets of assistance.

- Under the non-discretionary part of the scheme, persons on income support, disabled persons tax credit, income-based JSA or working families tax credit (see below) can claim a maternity expenses payment of £500. The same groups, plus persons on housing benefit, may be able to claim help with funeral expenses. Small amounts known as cold weather payments are also payable in very restricted circumstances.
- Under the discretionary part of the scheme, persons on income support may be awarded budgeting loans, crisis loans and community care grants.

Budgeting loans can be given for occasional, exceptional items of expenditure. Crisis loans may be obtained in cases of emergency or disaster. However all loans will be recovered by direct deductions, at source, from claimants' benefits. Moreover, claimants may be refused a loan if they are deemed to be too poor and indebted to be able to repay it. Also, because the system is cash limited, a decision-maker may refuse to assist because to do so would mean exceeding the budget. For such claimants there is now no statutory safety net and an application to a charitable organisation may be the only option open to them.

Community care grants are payable to persons moving out of institutionalised care and to vulnerable groups in the community such as older persons, people with a disability and families under stress. The guidance and directions to social fund officers are very restrictive. Claimants can ask for the decision to be reviewed, but they have no right of appeal to independent social security appeal tribunals.

Housing benefit

Housing benefit is payable to those on low incomes (those with capital exceeding £16,000 are excluded altogether) and provides assistance with rent and rates to public and private sector tenants and owner-occupiers. For income support claimants, benefit equals maximum housing benefit minus non-dependent contributions. For others the assessment of entitlement is again a complex process.

The first stage is to calculate the maximum housing benefit (MHB), *i.e.* the most that could be paid. MHB consists of rent and/or rates, less any deductions for non-dependents. In plainer English, this means that, if claimants, for example, have grown-up sons and daughters in the household, those persons are assumed to be contributing specified amounts towards housing costs regardless of whether or not they can or wish to do so.

The second stage is to calculate the claimant's "applicable amounts", *i.e.* his or her needs according, with some minor variations, to the income support rates. If income is below the applicable amount, benefit equals the MHB. If income is above the applicable amount, a percentage (65% for rent and 20% for rates) of the difference between income and the applicable amount is deducted from the MHB and the housing benefit equals whatever remains. For present purposes income means net wages (minus any "disregards" to which there is entitlement) and most benefits apart from attendance allowance and DLA.

A number of points can be made about this benefit. First, the tapers, *i.e.* the rate at which benefit is cut if income is above the applicable amounts, are much harsher than prior to 1988. Persons on very low incomes can find that they are considered too affluent to receive housing benefit.   Additionally, over the past 10 years substantial changes have been made to curtail the assistance given to private sector tenants. The maximum housing benefit for persons aged under 25 is now normally restricted to the amount payable for a room in a shared house – regardless of the accommodation occupied. Beyond this the regulations have been amended so that private sector tenants generally are less likely to have their full rent covered.

Tax credits and the pension credit

In April 2003 government introduced two new provisions – child tax credit (CTC) and working tax credit (WTC). The working families tax credit has been abolished for new claimants.   It should be emphasised that, despite the use of the work "tax" and the fact that CTC and WTC are administered by the Inland Revenue, these are means-tested benefits which do not affect people's liability for tax in any way.

CTC is payable to families, regardless of whether parents are in work or not and including students, where there is at least one child aged under 16 (or between 16 and 18 and in relevant education). CTC replaces the tax allowance for children known as the children's tax credit and the allowances for children formerly payable for children with a range of benefits such as working families tax credit and income support. It is estimated that about 90% of families will quality for some help under CTC and the scope of the benefit derives, in part, from the fact that it is compensating families for the loss of a tax allowance. This has not been made clear in the advertising campaign to encourage people to claim CTC but taxpayers should be aware that they must claim CTC to recover the amount lost with the withdrawal of children's tax credit.

Working tax credit is a means-tested benefit for those on low wages – there is no longer a requirement that the claimant have dependent children. To quality for WTC a person must be in full-time work.   This means 16 hours a week or more where the person has responsibility for a child or the person has a mental or physical disability which puts them at a disadvantage in securing employment and they are in receipt of a disability benefit. In other cases persons must be aged over 25 and in employment for at least 30 hours a week.

Claimants may receive either or both of these benefits. The first stage is to calculate all of the elements for which the claimant qualifies. For example, the child element is £27.75 per child and the childcare element consists of 70% of costs up to £135 where only one child is being cared for by a formal carer such as registered childminder. The next stage is to establish the annual income – current or previous year depending on circumstances – of the claimant. This figure is then compared with the appropriate threshold figure. If income is less than the threshold then the claimant is entitled to maximum tax credits, i.e. the total amount worked out in the first stage of the calculation. If income is above the threshold, 37% of the difference between income and the threshold is deducted from the total worked out at stage one of the calculation and claimants receive what remains.

Families are likely to need considerable help getting to grips with this but can find out more from the Inland Revenue website – *www. inlandrevenue.gov.uk.*

The pension credit is to be introduced in October 2003. This will consist of two elements. The first element will be the guaranteed credit. This is simply a new label for the minimum income guarantee and will bridge the gap – if there is one – between claimants' resources and their applicable amounts. The second element will be the savings credit. This will be a benefit based on the amounts people have by way of small earnings or private pensions. Thus, for example, a person with a full basic state pension and a private pension of £10 will receive £6 by way of savings credit. Claimants may get either or both elements. For help with the pension credit the best course is to direct people to their local CAB or independent advice centre.

Further useful addresses

- Child Poverty Action Group
  4th floor, 1-5 Bath Street,
  London EC1V 9PY
  tel: 020 7405 5942
  www.cpag.org.uk

- Law Centre (Northern Ireland)   and   Western Area Office
  124 Donegall Street   9 Clarendon Street
  Belfast BT1 2GY   Derry/Londonderry
  tel: 028 9024 4401   BT48 7EP
  www.lawcentreni.org   tel: 028 7126 2433

Chapter 23

Environmental Rights

Neil Faris

A bewildering mass of environmental law and regulation now faces the individual seeking a legal solution or legal help for an environmental problem. But there are several ways in which anyone can use the law to make an effective contribution in environmental decision-making. This chapter aims to set out some of the legal tools that can be used and offers some suggestions as to how the individual may make the most effective use of them. In addition, the Human Rights Act 1998 and the human rights provisions of the Northern Ireland Act 1998 are beginning to make themselves felt in matters concerning the environment and this chapter considers these too.

The right to environmental information

It probably all starts with information: without knowledge you cannot be an effective participant in the debate on any environmental issue. Through European Union (EU) law any individual now has the right to request environmental information from any government department, district council or other public body. The right extends to obtaining the information from any other person or body who is carrying out any functions of public administration or who has public responsibilities for the environment. Accordingly, the now privatised companies which provide utility services, such as NIE plc, may be obliged to provide on request environmental information relating to their public functions. This would not extend, however, to information held by NIE or any of its subsidiary companies not relating to the public supply of electricity.

At international level the Aarhus Convention was adopted on 25 June 1998 by a wider group of European states than those in the EU. It entered into force on 30 October 2001. It provides for three pillars: access to information, public participation and access to justice in environmental matters. The UK Government has still to ratify the

Convention and to introduce the necessary regulations. As will be seen below, a consultation process is under way. In addition the EU has issued a new Directive 2003/4/EC on Public Access to Environmental Information.

The previous law was set out in Council Directive 90/313/EEC on Freedom of Access to Information on the Environment. This became directly part of the law in Northern Ireland through the Environmental Information Regulations (NI) 1993. As a result, anyone is entitled to information or data held by the government and other public bodies relating to the state of water or air, flora or fauna, soil or any natural site or land and any activities which may adversely affect such natural environments.

The Regulations specify that the government or public body concerned may impose a reasonable charge for providing the information, but must deal with the request within a period of at most two months. The Regulations do not specify a standard charge, but any charges must not be set at such a level to be in effect a barrier to access.

Note, however, that no-one has the right under these Regulations to obtain confidential information. Nevertheless, the courts have held that they will tend to favour the disclosure of information under the Regulations. Note also that material such as consultants' reports, which may have been commissioned by the government or other public bodies, is possibly not covered by the Regulations as it may not properly be regarded as "information" but rather as advice to the government department or other public body. However, we will see below that much advisory material may in fact be obtainable where it forms part of an "environmental impact assessment" of a particular project or development.

Furthermore, the 1993 Regulations do not really provide any satisfactory remedy for the individual who faces a refusal of his or her request for environmental information. Certainly, such refusal could form the grounds for a judicial review application, but this is a cumbersome, time-consuming and expensive means of litigation. It may be justified in particular circumstances, but legal advice should be taken.

At the date of publication of this book the government has just completed a public consultation on proposals for new environmental information regulations. It is proposed to broaden the definition of "environmental information" and of "public authorities" and to make new provisions on matters such as time limits, charging and exceptions to the regulations. The government would intend that the new regulations would enable it to ratify the Aarhus Convention (see above) and put it in a position to be in compliance with the new EU Directive. Further details may be obtained from the Environmental Policy Division of the Department of the Environment (NI).

Planning permission

The development of property often gives cause for concern about the impact on the environment. The next section examines in that context the important procedures of environmental impact assessment. But first we need to explain the circumstances in which planning permission is required. Planning law is detailed and complex and this section does not attempt to cover all the ground.

Under article 12 of the Planning (NI) Order 1991, planning permission is required for the carrying out of any "development" of land. Article 11(1) defines development as:

The carrying out of building, engineering, mining or other operations in, on, over or under land, or the making of any material change in use of any buildings or other land.

Article 11(3) identifies a number of actions concerning buildings or land which are expressly "development". The first is sub-division of a dwelling house. The second is deposit of waste on land. The third is the display of advertisements on any external part of a building which is not normally used for that purpose. In all three cases the actions are treated as involving a material change in the use of that part of the building.

Article 11(2) of the 1991 Order provides, in turn, for a number of circumstances which are not "development". The first is maintenance of the interior of a building, including works of improvement or other alteration which affect only the interior or which do not materially affect the external appearance of the building. However, the interior of a building as well as its exterior may be specifically protected if it is a listed building, *i.e.* a building of special architectural or historic interest under article 42 of the 1991 Order. The maintenance of services by a district council or statutory undertaker providing services such as water, sewerage, electricity or gas is not development where the works are for the purpose of inspecting, repairing or renewing mains, pipes, cables or other apparatus, including the breaking open of any street or other land for that purpose.

Use of buildings or land for "incidental purposes" is not development. This is the case so long as the incidental use becomes subordinate to the main use of the property. Of course if you have a dog or other domestic pet in your house, that can legally be described as an "incidental use" of your house. But if you keep 40 dogs in your house it may be found that this is no longer an incidental use. It could be that your predominant use of the property is as a dog pound and no longer a domestic dwelling house.

The use of land for agriculture and forestry is not development for the purposes of the 1991 Order. This may cause problems when what is thought in ordinary language to be undesirable development in the countryside does not constitute development for the purposes of the 1991 Order. Note, however, that some such agricultural and forestry development on a large scale may require environmental impact assessment even though it does not require planning permission.

There are quite detailed rules about changes of use of commercial property. Some changes of use, such as change of a bookshop to a clothes shop, would not be a material change of use and so would not require planning permission. Other changes of use *are* material and do require planning permission: for instance the change of a shop to an office. The detailed rules on this are contained in the Planning (Use Classes) Order (NI) 1989, as amended.

Environmental impact assessments

While all "development" (as described above) requires planning permission, major development of land requires in addition environmental impact assessment before planning permission will be granted. So if you are faced with a major development in your neighbourhood you should immediately ask to see the "environmental statement". This is a document which the developer must prepare and submit in connection with the necessary application for planning permission or other statutory permission required for major projects. It is required for major projects by virtue of the Environmental Impact Assessment Directives of the EU (85/337/EEC, as amended by Directive 97/11/EEC). These have been implemented in Northern Ireland law, for projects where planning permission is required, by the Planning (Environmental Impact Assessment) Regulations (NI) 1999.

Note there can be important projects which do not require an application for planning permission, such as forest planting, harbour works, drainage and roadworks. Such projects may still require environmental impact assessment and environmental campaigners should be alerted to that possibility. So in such cases you should ask for the environmental statement.

Of course it is not every project which requires environmental impact assessment: the Directive and the Regulations set out categories of projects. The first category is for works likely to have a major impact upon the environment – in these cases an environmental impact assessment is always required. The second category is where the requirement for an assessment is discretionary – in these cases it is a matter for the government to assess whether such an assessment is required. The government must do this according to criteria set out in the Regulations, such as the scale, nature and location of the project. So it is possible for objectors to challenge any decision not to call for an environmental impact assessment and objectors should press the Planning Service to explain and justify any such decision.

Where environmental impact assessment is required the developer of the project is required to produce the environmental statement. The statement should assess all of the likely significant environmental impacts of the proposal upon the environment. In the case of most large projects, environmental consultants and other experts will be hired by the developer. They will produce apparently comprehensive reports on the various environmental aspects of the project. These reports, in the form of the environmental statement, will be submitted (in a planning case) together with the planning application and will be available for consultation or purchase by the public. This will become an invaluable reference source for any objector to the proposal.

Environmental impact assessment should not be thought of as solely a paper-based exercise. Before beginning the assessment the consultants engaged by the developer should "scope" the project. This entails assessing what are *likely* to be the environmental impacts of the project. For this purpose the consultants should engage in preliminary consultation with the relevant government departments and other public bodies, including, for instance, the local district council. However, such scoping may also require consultation with relevant environmental NGOs, such as the Royal Society for the Protection of Birds or the National Trust, in appropriate cases. Consultation may also be required with local residents and other interest groups, for the obvious reason that local people will have direct and personal knowledge of their local environment.

Often local people and environmental campaigners will have a natural hostility to a proposed development. They will feel disinclined to co-operate with the developer or the developer's representatives, such as the consultants carrying out the environmental impact assessment. Everyone has to make his or her own decision and strategy in a campaign of opposition to any project. However, working with the developer's consultants for the purpose of improving the environmental impact assessment does not necessarily mean that those who are so engaged are collaborating with the developer in the project itself. Properly carried out, an environmental impact assessment is not "for" or "against" a particular project. It should be what it says it is: an assessment of the environmental impact of the project which helps all concerned to assess whether or not the project should go ahead. The environmental statement should also help to identify ways in which the environmental effects of a project may be ameliorated. In effect the project should then be permitted to proceed only in a modified form. In addition, those who participate fully in the process will of course come to understand the project all the more thoroughly. By co-operating with the developer's consultants they will inevitably be in a better position to obtain all important information. Armed with that, they will be in a better position to make cogent opposition at later stages.

It is also important to understand that the environmental assessment does not begin and end with the production of the environmental statement by the developer. After the developer has submitted the environmental statement, Planning Service (in a planning case) then engages in a further widespread consultation exercise. For instance, in the case of the planning application for a major landfill site at Magheramorne in County Antrim some years ago, the Planning Service obtained the views of over 30 consultees on the developer's environmental statement. Consultation was carried out with different divisions of government, the relevant district councils and other public bodies, such as Northern Ireland Railways and the Northern Ireland Tourist Board. All of their consultation responses were gathered together by the Planning Service and submitted to the ensuing planning inquiry. All of this information formed an extremely helpful volume of evidence and information for the objectors to the proposal.

At this stage, armed with this information and with other knowledge and advice (particularly local knowledge), the objectors themselves should not miss the opportunity to make representations to the Planning Service that the environmental statement is, or parts of it are, insufficient or inadequate. This can be an extremely effective weapon in the hands of objectors to stymie or at least delay a project. The objectors should seek to demonstrate to the Planning Service that further environmental information is required from the developer on the basis of the environmental statement so far produced. At this stage the objectors should make a detailed and focused critique of elements of the environmental statement. This is not the place for general declarations against the project, but more detailed criticisms at this stage may well pay dividends. Of course, sometimes objectors are reluctant to show their hand and hope to save their best points for maximum use at any subsequent inquiry. That is a matter of tactics in each case. Note, however, that it is not every project that goes to an inquiry.

Planning inquiries

Where the Department of the Environment considers that a planning application involves a substantial departure from a local development plan or would affect a substantial section of the community, it may apply article 31 of the Planning (NI) Order 1991 to the application. Under article 31(2) the Department may ask the Planning Appeals Commission to make a recommendation with regard to the planning application. The Planning Appeals Commission will appoint one of the members of the Commission, acting as an inspector, to hold a public planning inquiry into the matter. This is publicly advertised and objectors to the proposal are entitled to make representations and participate in the hearing. Sometimes these hearings can be extensive and long-running events and can attract considerable interest, including representations from environmental NGOs as well as local residents' groups and other objectors. The Planning Appeals Commission will make arrangements for the holding of the hearing either in its own offices in Great Victoria Street in Belfast or in other appropriate venues such as the local district council offices or a leisure centre in the locality concerned.

Crucially, however, such a planning inquiry does not finally decide the issue of whether or not planning permission should be granted. After the inquiry has finished the inspector holding it will consider all the submissions and evidence and will submit a report to the Board of the Planning Appeals Commission. The Commission will then make a corporate decision to accept or reject the report of the inspector who held the hearing. That decision then becomes the recommendation of the Planning Appeals Commission. This is submitted, together with the inspector's report, to the Department of the Environment, which will, sometimes after a considerable period of time, issue the final decision in the matter. There is no right of appeal at such final stage, although either the applicant for the planning permission or any objector may consider their rights to apply for judicial review.

Objectors' tactics

It can be seen from all of the above that objecting to works which affect the environment can be a lengthy and elaborate process. If you are an objector you should always bear in mind your ultimate goal. This is to achieve final success in the decision to be issued by the Department of the Environment. Often objectors can mislead themselves as to the actual strength of their best points. So testing them at an early stage with the developer may show weaknesses or points which the objectors should address further. In addition, developers and their professional advisers may then feel compelled to show something more of their case in response. Ultimately the exchange of information between the parties is to the general public good and benefit of the environment, which should be everyone's ultimate goal.

Thus there can be little doubt that, intelligently used, the environmental impact assessment process is a powerful weapon in the hands of objectors to a project to ensure at least that all the environmental impacts are properly assessed and addressed before the project is allowed to proceed. As already indicated, if it appears that a major project is going ahead without environmental impact assessment, objectors should be alert to their right to challenge this.

This is not an area where experts should be allowed total dominance. In the case of the Magheramorne Landfill Inquiry, local people from Magheramorne and the Islandmagee area played a key, and perhaps in the end decisive, part in the successful opposition to that planning application. Local knowledge is very important: objectors cannot expect to succeed on mere emotion or on absolute commitment alone.

The Habitats Directive

The Habitats Directive (its full title is the Directive 92/43/EEC on the Conservation of Natural Habitats and of Wild Fauna and Flora is also a key piece of environmental protection legislation. It has been implemented in Northern Ireland by the Conservation (Natural

Habitats, etc.) Regulations (NI) 1995. The Directive and the Regulations apply to specified species of wild animals and plants and to the network of European protected sites (including those in Northern Ireland) known as Natura 2000. In Northern Ireland these consist of Special Areas of Conservation (SAC) under the Habitats Directive and Special Protection Areas (SPA) under the Birds Directive (79/409/EEC). The 1995 Regulations provide that a landowner or developer must not carry out specified development in cases to which the Regulations apply without first serving nine months' notice in writing on the Department of the Environment. Where the site is an SAC or SPA, the work must not proceed without the consent of the Department.

Furthermore, and this is particularly important for objectors, developments which will adversely affect the integrity of a protected site are forbidden even if the land being developed is itself outside the protected area. This is specifically provided for in Article 6 of the Habitats Directive. A development (wherever it is situate) may proceed only if an assessment of the implication for any protected conservation site shows that the integrity of the protected site will not be adversely affected. If the assessment shows a negative effect the development may proceed only if there is no alternative solution and if there are imperative reasons of overriding public interest, including those of a social or economic nature. In cases where there is a priority habitat, the permission of the European Commission must be obtained.

In effect, then, the burden of proof shifts in these cases. Under the ordinary principles of planning law a developer who has applied for planning permission is entitled to the grant of planning permission unless the Planning Service can show reasons – "material considerations" they are called in law – why the permission should not be granted. However, where a site is protected under the Habitats Directive it is up to the developer to establish that there will be no negative effect created by the development on the integrity of the protected site.

In the case of the Magheramorne Landfill Inquiry the quarry was not itself protected. However, about 1.5 kilometres away in Larne Lough was the protected site of Swan Island, which was the habitat of a small colony of roseate terns. These are protected under the Birds Directive. The evidence of the Royal Society for the Protection of Birds was that the landfill site would attract gulls, which would then be likely to predate upon Swan Island and its fragile colony of roseate terns. Thus the development proposal was likely to have an adverse effect upon a protected site. The Director of the Countryside and Wildlife Division of the Environment Service himself gave evidence against the application on this particular point. In his report the inspector held that, although the developer was proposing gull control measures, any additional presence from gulls could upset what appeared to be a delicate balance for the survival of the colony of terns on Swan Island. He concluded that a planning condition (as had been suggested by the developer) to impose bird control measures at the landfill site at all times would not be sufficient to remove the suggested adverse affect. No other measures were suggested which would do so. Ultimately, this decision was upheld by the Department of the Environment for Northern Ireland. Accordingly planning permission for the development was refused.

This highlights the importance of the Habitats Directive in such circumstances.   The Planning Service of the Department of the Environment for Northern Ireland has published details of the implementation of the Habitats Directive in a planning policy statement on Planning and Nature Conservation (PPS 2). This shows the sites protected in Northern Ireland at the time of publication of the Statement.   Accordingly, anyone objecting to a proposal for developments should obtain this booklet and consider it carefully. Note that the list of sites in Annex 3 of PPS 2 is now a little out of date.

The relevance of human rights

As is explained in Chapter 1 of this book, the Human Rights Act 1998 and the human rights provisions of the Northern Ireland Act 1998 have incorporated into the law of Northern Ireland many of the provisions of the European Convention on Human Rights. Sometimes it is mistakenly alleged that the European Convention concerns only civil and political rights and does not provide for social and economic rights or for environmental rights. However, the Convention should be thought of as a "living instrument". Certainly, when the Convention was drafted at the end of the 1940s, in the aftermath of the Second World War, environmental rights were probably not at the forefront of anyone's mind. Nevertheless, there have been significant decisions and judgments under the Convention since then on environmental issues.

The right to property

Note first of all the potential application of Article 1 of Protocol 1 of the European Convention, which provides some protection for property rights. The case-law establishes that "property" is to be given a wide meaning in this Article. This provision can be used by victims of environmental damage when their property rights have been infringed. It may also be used by businesses if they are able to argue that their property rights are infringed by the disproportionate application of environmental regulations. But the right in Article 1 is heavily qualified by the sphere of action allowed to governments under paragraph 2 of the Article. So in effect there is quite a high hurdle for claimants to get over if they are to succeed against government. The most dramatic impact of Article 1 of Protocol 1 (taken together with Article 6 of the Convention, which protects the right to a fair trial), may be in relation to third party rights (see p.546 below).

The right to private and family life

Article 8 of the Convention, which protects the right to private and family life, has been interpreted by the Court in Strasbourg in ways which were probably never in the contemplation of the original drafters of the Convention. In particular it has been employed in several cases to indicate that states do have a duty of environmental protection.

The most striking recent example is *Hatton and others v UK* (2003). Here the applicants, being residents near Heathrow Airport, challenged the government's policy in permitting night flights (albeit with restrictions) to and from Heathrow. At the first hearing the challenge succeeded under Articles 8 and 13 (the right to an effective remedy). With regard to Article 8 the Court held that the modest steps (as they described them) taken by the government with respect to restrictions on night flights were not capable of constituting the "measures necessary to protect" the applicants' position. The Court held that the government had failed to strike a fair balance between the UK's economic well-being and the applicants' effective enjoyment of their right to respect for their homes and their private and family lives. The Court also held there was no effective remedy under UK law, as the remedy of judicial review would not have been sufficient in the circumstances.

However, on appeal (to the "Grand Chamber" of the Court) the decision under Article 8 was overruled. But the Grand Chamber did acknowledge that, while there was no explicit right in the Convention to a clean and quiet environment, where an individual is directly and seriously affected by noise and pollution an issue may arise under Article 8. It was held that this may apply where the pollution is directly caused by the state and also where state responsibility arises from the failure of the state properly to regulate private industry. In such circumstances the Court may assess the substantive merits of the government's decision to ensure it is compatible with Article 8. The Court may also scrutinise the decision-making process to ensure that due weight has been accorded to the interests of the individual.

In the circumstances the Grand Chamber held that the UK government's decisions regarding the night flights at Heathrow did meet these tests. But the judgment has lessons for the government: it must be in a position to show that it has properly evaluated the conflicting rights. The case is also important for objectors: in dealing with government you should not be slow to assert your right that the decision being taken must on its merits respect the terms of Article 8. In addition it must be shown that the decision-making process gives fair weight to the interests of individuals who may be directly and seriously affected.

In *S v France* (1990) it was held that Article 8 applied to the circumstances where a nuclear power station was built some 300 metres from the applicant's home. However, it was also held that the French government had satisfied its obligations by the payment of some monetary compensation to the applicant. A case in which the applicant succeeded was *Lopez Ostra v Spain* (1994), where Mrs Ostra complained that a waste treatment plant had been built some 12 metres from her home and had not been properly regulated or controlled by the Spanish government. Mrs Ostra's daughter in particular became ill because of toxic fumes from the plant. The Spanish government was held liable, even though it was not itself responsible for the operation of the plant, because of its inadequate regulatory regime which failed to protect the applicant's home and private and family life. That was perhaps a case where there was a gross failure of regulatory control on the part of the state. Nevertheless, it is again significant as an example of where further intervention by the courts may occur.

In *Guerra v Italy* (1998) the Italian government was held liable for a breach of Article 8 for failing to take action with regard to a chemical plant which was a high risk operation. The European Court of Human Rights held that the plant's location close to private homes meant that there should be adequate information provided about the potential risks of the operation to the private and family lives of the home-owners. The applicant could not show direct injuries arising from the action (or inaction) of the regulators with regard to the chemical plant, despite a long-term history of problems there. (This is always a problem for plaintiffs in environmental litigation.) But the European Court still held that the failure of the (local) government to give the residents essential information to enable them to assess the risks was a breach of Article 8. In Northern Ireland, as already explained, the public does already have a right to obtain *on request* environmental information, under the Environmental Information Regulations (NI) 1993. The *Guerra* decision implies that there is a positive duty on the government to issue information to people likely to be affected by an environmental problem. A minority of the judges in the *Guerra* case went even further and held that failure to provide information to people could constitute a breach of Article 2 (the right to life) if information were withheld about circumstances which could present a real risk of danger to health and physical integrity.

However, some words of caution. The *Guerra* case involved circumstances which in Northern Ireland could amount to maladministration on the part of the government and perhaps therefore the Ombudsman would have intervened (see Chapter 2). A court may not be so anxious to hold against the government where, although there is a problem, the government has been shown to have taken some action when the blame begins to fly after a disaster. Courts will in each case conduct a *balancing* exercise. In Article 8 of the Convention, as in other Articles, paragraph 1 confers the right but paragraph 2 then qualifies it in some ways. The government is able to rely on considerations such as national security, public safety, the economic well-being of the country and the protection of health or morals, provided its actions were in pursuit of a legitimate aim, the interference corresponded to a pressing social need and it was proportionate to the aim pursued. These are not necessarily factors which a defendant could rely upon in common law litigation over trespass or nuisance. So plaintiffs should pause for thought before rushing in with a human rights claim.

The right to a fair hearing

Article 6 of the European Convention on Human Rights protects the right to a fair hearing. Paragraph 1 provides:

In the determination of his civil rights and obligations or of any criminal charge against him, everyone is entitled to a fair and public hearing within a reasonable time by an independent and impartial tribunal established by law. Judgment shall be pronounced publicly but the press and public may be excluded from all or part of the trial in the interests of morals, public order or national security in a democratic society, where the interests of juveniles or the protection of the private life of the parties so require, or to the extent strictly necessary in the opinion of the court in special circumstances where publicity would prejudice the interests of justice.

In the case-law of the European Court of Human Rights, how far does this right extend? Certainly, it has been held to apply to the decisions and determinations of many other decision-making bodies as well as courts. On the other hand, there are limitations such as where the decision to be made is held to be a matter of expert or technical evaluation or determination rather than a matter requiring judicial judgment.

The House of Lords has recently considered this issue in a series of cases in England involving the exercise of planning and vesting powers (the so-called *Alconbury* cases). It held that a government Minister can be both a policy maker and a decision taker, provided the courts have jurisdiction to conduct a judicial review of the lawfulness and fairness of the decision. This process complies with Article 6 even though the court cannot rehear the matter or substitute its own view on the facts. The House of Lords in *Alconbury* was quite firm in holding that it was central to parliamentary democracy that Ministers accountable to Parliament should take these decisions rather than the courts. In our increasingly regulated world this is a particularly important point, as many regulatory bodies may be making daily decisions relating to the civil rights and obligations of business. The key question is, are these decisions "determinations" for the purposes of Article 6?

Alconbury suggests that the government's decision-making powers have survived their first major human rights challenge, but Article 6 is still important in controlling many of the procedures of decision taking. As has been explained, an applicant for planning permission, who receives a refusal of permission, may appeal to the Planning Appeals Commission. There is, first, the question whether the Planning Appeals Commission is fully independent of government in accordance with Article 6 of the European Convention. That apart, what is the position of the objectors where property rights (in the wide sense of Article 1 of Protocol 1) may be infringed by the grant of planning permission? An objector may make representations to the Planning Service when the application is being considered; but if the application is granted the objector has no right of appeal. It is likely that this will now be challenged in the courts. Indeed, there is currently a judgment expected from the High Court in Belfast on this issue.

Further recent case-law from England (in the summer of 2002) indicates that where resolution of "primary fact" is required the courts will incline to look for procedures akin to the conventional mechanisms for finding fact: cross-examination, access to documents and a strictly independent decision-maker. If procedures of that kind are not available at the first stage the courts will look to see how far they are given by any appeal or review system. (The procedures of judicial review may not be sufficient for this purpose.) But when the matter involves the application of judgment or the issue of discretion (especially involving policy issues and the interests of others) the courts may be satisfied, for the purposes of Article 6, with a form of inquisition at first instance in which the decision-maker is more an expert than the judge. In such cases the remedy of judicial review may be regarded as satisfactory for the second stage.

In *In re Stewart* (2003) the procedures of the Planning Appeals Commission with regard to appeals were under scrutiny, with particular regard to the position of third party objectors. Mr Justice Gillen held that the "informal procedure" adopted by the Planning Appeals Commission met the criteria of Article 6. The Court of Appeal agreed but commented that there could be circumstances where the need to establish the correct facts in a conflict of evidence, or to test the validity of certain types of evidence, would indicate that an informal hearing might not be sufficient to satisfy Article 6. The Court of Appeal also held that it would only be in an extreme case that an objector might be able to mount a legal challenge that the proposed development would affect private and family rights under Article 8 or property rights under Article 1 of Protocol 1.

In any event, everyone in the regulatory business needs to be armed with information about at least the following guarantees conferred by Article 6:
- access to the courts,
- protection against self-incrimination,
- presumption of innocence,
- equality of arms,

- delay, and
- independence and impartiality of adjudicators.

Many of these guarantees are by no means new to our legal system, as they are already incorporated within the common law principle of natural justice. However, they have been re-invigorated and given new dimensions by Article 6. In the *Alconbury* cases (p.545 above) the House of Lords held that neither the Minister nor the planning inspectors could be considered truly independent or impartial when they were taking planning decisions, but their powers were not liable to a human rights challenge so long as the courts had jurisdiction over the lawfulness and fairness of their decisions.

In any case where the decision-making body does have full jurisdiction (such as a court or tribunal), questions concerning independence and impartiality cannot be side-stepped in this way. In such cases there are issues as to the manner of appointment and terms of reference of the persons sitting in the bodies concerned. It may also be relevant to consider who has the power to remove or re-appoint the judges or tribunal members. The real question in those instances may be not what is the likelihood of the individual with such jurisdiction actually showing any bias in favour of the government, but the perception that this could be the case. If there is such perception then there may be a breach of Article 6, notwithstanding that the individual adjudicator may be proceeding with every propriety. The position of the Planning Appeals Commission in this regard is still not absolutely clear. It is significant that the power to appoint Commissioners has been moved from the Department of the Environment (NI) to the Office of the First Minister and Deputy First Minister.

There is a separate question as to the impartiality of judges. This would have been a novel question before the Human Rights Act 1998, but the legislation now gives the judiciary increased powers of intervention to decide whether or not particular government action is proportionate in any circumstance. If there is litigation about whether a planning decision was properly proportionate, could a question be asked about the judge's impartiality if he or she has "conservationist" sympathies, manifested perhaps through membership of the Ulster Architectural Heritage Society?

The Lord Chief Justice of Northern Ireland, Sir Robert Carswell, has alluded to the issues that may arise on "such compulsory focus on human rights and international conventions…" He delivered a paper on *Human Rights and the Rule of Law* at the Fifth Conference of the

World Police Medical Officers in Clinical Forensic Medicine in Vancouver, Canada, in August 1999. This was subsequently published in the Journal of Forensic Medicine in 1999. In his paper he suggested:

> *[This impact] may be mirrored in the process of selection of judges and their accountability. Will the public want to look at the record of judges on the Bench or the recorded actions and statements of candidates for appointment? In the English tradition, to which in my jurisdiction we strongly adhere, nothing but merit is taken into account in the appointment of a judge, in the sense of his ability to discharge the judicial function better than any of the persons being considered for appointment. Political affiliations are left out of account and it is assumed in the famous phrase used of a candidate for appointment to the bench in Victorian times, that he has the politics of an equity draftsman. I fear there may be a growing demand for changes in appointment procedures for judges, though I do claim the right to wonder what this will achieve apart from deterring some of the best practitioners from letting their names go forward.*

Judicial review

This is not the case for a detailed review of the procedures for applying for judicial review. More is said about the remedy in Chapter 2. The central point to remember for those who wish to challenge environmental or planning decisions is the need to act quickly. As soon as a decision is issued, an objector must proceed almost immediately with an application to the High Court if a challenge is to be made. The Rules of Court state that the application must be made "promptly" *and* within three months of the decision being challenged. The High Court has a discretion to allow for a longer period in suitable circumstances, but it may also refuse an application even within the three months period if it holds that the objector has not moved sufficiently promptly. This is especially likely to be the case where another party, such as a property developer, has obtained planning permission. That developer is entitled to proceed with the development on the basis of the planning permission unless an immediate challenge by way of judicial review is made. Accordingly, the High Court will be distinctly unsympathetic to any objector who is not able to bring the matter to court immediately. In a planning judicial review there is a rule of thumb that any application must be lodged in court within six weeks of the date of the decision in question. However, do not rely even on the possibility of a six-week period. As soon as you think you may possibly have a judicial review, go immediately to your lawyer.

Furthermore, judicial review is not a means of appealing against a decision with which you disagree, even if there are good grounds for disagreeing with the decision. Judicial review will be successful only if the court is satisfied that there has been a material departure from proper procedures or if the decision is so manifestly unreasonable that no reasonable decision-maker could have come to it. Of course, there is a new emphasis on human rights because of the Human Rights Act 1998 and the human rights provisions of the Northern Ireland Act 1998. Accordingly, the courts have somewhat extended the grounds on which they will allow judicial review so as to include instances where there is an established breach of the human rights legislation. However, the judges are acting quite cautiously in this area. Objectors should certainly not expect any automatic human rights remedy from the courts. There are many injustices which are not human rights violations.

There have been some significant judicial review successes by objectors to planning decisions, as in cases involving major supermarket sites. But it is noticeable that many of these successful applications were made by other commercial interests, who were well enough resourced to mount a full-blown challenge. This is not to deny the importance of the judicial review remedy for those on the other side of the environmental and planning fence. Certainly, leading NGOs such as the Friends of the Earth, the RSPB and the National Trust have the expertise and resources to mount judicial review challenges in appropriate cases.

As already indicated, if an individual objector considers there may be grounds for challenge he or she should immediately seek legal advice. If possible this should be even before the decision is actually made. With legal help there may be opportunities to persuade the decision-maker to change course. If such efforts are not successful then at least the lawyers will be in a better position to advise the objector as to how to move promptly forward with the judicial review application as soon as a decision is made. In reality it is sadly all too often too late if lawyers are first called in only after the disputed decision has been made.

Practical tips for objectors

It may be useful to conclude with some practical tips for objectors who face the challenge of wishing to oppose a major new development which they believe will have adverse environmental consequences for them, their families or their neighbourhood. Often the forces ranged against the objector appear almost insurmountable. In the case, for instance, of a major planning application, the applicant for the planning permission is likely to be a well-financed property developer or a large corporation. The applicant will have an array of expert help from lawyers, architects, engineers and planning and environmental consultants. The developer of any major development will have produced a large and impressive environmental statement which will certainly *appear* to deal with all environmental issues. They will indicate that they have the resources and commitment to go through the sometimes lengthy planning inquiry process.

The objector or objecting group, in contrast, is likely to have little resources and perhaps little experience of dealing with matters of this type. Such "ordinary people" may also, unfortunately, have little or no access to the relevant legal and other professional advice. Consequently the objectors' reaction may either be to entirely give up the game altogether or else to concentrate solely on activities such as street protests, publicity and perhaps other forms of direct action. Certainly, within the law, local objectors do need to raise local support and assistance from further afield. So a publicity and consciousness raising campaign is essential. The next stage, as indicated earlier, is information gathering. Much of this can be done by lay people, with expert help and guidance where necessary. But this stage does take time and patience. The objectors should try to choose from their active supporters those who have expertise or at least a likely aptitude for dealing with officialdom.

Sometimes objectors are disheartened because the developer's side has an eminent Queen's Counsel appearing at the relevant inquiry. The objectors then feel that they must also obtain similar representation to achieve success. Almost certainly an experienced barrister is the best professional advocate for a client if the client can afford the professional fees, which are likely to be very large especially in the case of a long running inquiry. Nevertheless, the best use will only be made of such advocacy if the ground work has been thoroughly prepared in advance.

One option is to concentrate professional help on a particular "big issue". The other issues can then be handled at the inquiry by the objectors themselves. Sometimes this can be quite effective. In almost every case it is worthwhile to take preliminary legal and other professional advice at an early stage. This need not be expensive for preliminary professional views. Such initial advice can be extremely helpful in assisting the objectors to best plan their case and make best use of resources. Those objecting to a proposal need, as much as the developer of a project, an overall strategy from the earliest opportunity. This strategy should involve consideration of what resources are available to the objectors and how such resources can be best employed. Almost certainly substantial fundraising will be necessary, but a local community may have access to some voluntary help, for instance from recently retired professional people in the neighbourhood. Some organisational help, or at least advice, may be available from organisations such as the Environmental Law Foundation. Local NGOs, such as Friends of the Earth (NI), may themselves wish to take up the case and will at least be willing to provide helpful information. The strategy can then be developed with assistance such as this to build up the information available to the group through intelligent use of environmental rights such as the right to information, the environmental impact assessment process and the Habitats Directive.

By these means the group can begin to position itself so that the professional consultants acting for the developer begin to react to its (reasonable) position. Sometimes also objectors can be tempted to "wage war" on the planning officials and other civil servants and to treat them as "the enemy". This comes from inexperience or frustration. The Planning Service should at least now provide full access to documents under their "Open File" policy. By these means, for instance, sometimes the developer can be required to provide further environmental information and the planning process can be delayed until that it is produced. This can certainly be a very time-consuming process for the objectors as well as for the developer. There is a temptation for the objector group to lose patience with the process. However in reality it is unlikely there will be any knock-out blow; rather it will be the persistent attention to detail that is likely to gain progress for the objector group.

Further useful addresses

- The Environment and Heritage Service
  Department of the Environment (NI)
  Calvert House
  High Street
  Belfast BT1 1FY
  tel: 028 9054 6533
  Water Pollution Hotline 0800 807060
  www.ehsni.gov.uk

- Environmental Policy Division
  Department of the Environment (NI)
  River House
  48 High Street
  Belfast BT1 2AW
  tel: 028 9025 1300
  www.doeni.gov.uk

- The Planning Service
  Department of the Environment (NI)
  Clarence Court
  Adelaide Street
  Belfast BT2 8GB
  tel: 028 9054 0540
  www.doeni.gov.uk/planning

- The Planning Appeals Commission
  Park House
  87-91 Great Victoria Street
  Belfast BT2 7AG
  tel: 028 9024 4710
  www.pacni.goc.uk

- Arena Network Northern Ireland
  c/o Business in the Community NI
  770 Upper Newtownards Road
  Belfast BT16 0UL
  tel: 028 9041 0410
  www.greentriangle.org

- Department of the Environment, Food and Rural Affairs
  Ergon House
  17 Smith Square
  London SN1P 3JR
  tel: DEFRA Helpline 084 5933 5577
  www.defra.gov.uk

- The Environment Agency
  Rio House
  Waterside Drive
  Aztec West
  Almonsbury
  Bristol BS32 4UD
  tel: 01454 624400
  www.environment-agency.gov.uk

- Environmental Law Foundation
  Suite 309
  16 Baldwins Gardens
  London EC1N 7RJ
  tel: 020 7404 1030
  www.elflaw.org

- Friends of the Earth (NI)
  7 Donegall Street Place
  Belfast BT1 2FN
  tel: 028 9023 3488
  www.foe.co.uk

- Northern Ireland Environment Link
  77 Botanic Avenue
  Belfast BT7 1JL
  tel: 028 9031 4944
  www.niel.demon.co.uk

- European Commission Office
  Windsor House
  9-15 Bedford Street
  Belfast BT2 7EG
  tel: 028 9024 0708
  www.europa.eu.int

Further Reading

Books on international human rights law

P R Ghandhi, *Blackstone's International Human Rights Documents*, Oxford University Press, Oxford, 3rd ed., 2002

Rebecca Wallace and Kenneth Dale-Risk, *International Human Rights: Text and Materials*, Sweet and Maxwell, London, 2nd ed., 2001

Gudmundur Alfredson et al, *International Human Rights Monitoring Mechanisms*, Martinus Nijhoff, The Hague, 2001

D J Harris, M O'Boyle and C Warbrick, *Law of the European Convention on Human Rights*, Butterworths, London, 2nd ed., 2003

Clare Ovey and Robin White, *Jacobs and White: European Convention on Human Rights*, Oxford University Press, Oxford, 3rd ed., 2002

Keir Starmer, *European Human Rights Law*, Legal Action Group, London, 1999

Philip Leach, *Taking a Case to the European Court of Human Rights*, Blackstone Press, London, 2001

Philip Alston (ed.), *Promoting Human Rights Through Bills of Rights: Comparative Perspectives*, Oxford University Press, Oxford, 1999

Books on rights and liberties in the United Kingdom

Les Allamby, *Rights in Progress: A guide to the European Convention on Human Rights and the Human Rights Act*, Law Centre (NI), Belfast, 2002

Richard Clayton and Hugh Tomlinson, *The Law of Human Rights*, Oxford University Press, Oxford, 2000, and *Second Supplement*, 2003

David Feldman, *Civil Liberties and Human Rights in England and Wales*, Oxford University Press, Oxford, 2nd ed., 2002

Helen Fenwick, *Civil Liberties and Human Rights*, Cavendish Publishing, London, 3rd ed., 2002

Philip Plowden and Kevin Kerrigan, *Advocacy and Human Rights: Using the Convention in Courts and Tribunals*, Cavendish Publishing, London, 2002

Edwin Shorts and Clare de Than, *Human Rights Law in the United Kingdom*, Sweet and Maxwell, London, 2001

Peter Duffy, Jack Beatson and Stephen Grosz, *Human Rights: The 1998 Act and the European Convention*, Sweet & Maxwell, London, 1999

John Wadham and Helen Mountfield, *Blackstone's Guide to the Human Rights Act 1998*, Blackstone Press Ltd., London, 2nd ed., 2000

Richard Stone, Textbook on Civil Liberties and Human Rights, Blackstone Press, London, 4th ed., 2002

Noel Whitty, Thérèse Murphy, and Stephen Livingstone, *Civil Liberties Law: The Human Rights Era*, Butterworths, London, 2001

Victims, Police Powers and Prisoners

Brice Dickson, *The Legal System of Northern Ireland*, SLS Legal Publications, Belfast, 4th ed., 2001

Northern Ireland Criminal Justice Review Group, *Review of the Criminal Justice System in Northern Ireland,* The Stationery Office, London, 2000

Ben Emmerson and Andrew Ashworth, *Human Rights and Criminal Justice*, Sweet and Maxwell, London, 2001

Clive Walker, *Blackstone's Guide to the Anti-Terrorism Legislation*, Oxford University Press, Oxford, 2002

Michael Zander, *The Police and Criminal Evidence Act 1984*, Sweet and Maxwell, London, 4th ed., 2003

Mary O'Rawe and Linda Moore, "Accountability and Police Complaints in Northern Ireland: Leaving the Past Behind?" in Andrew Goldsmith and C. Lewis (eds.), *Civilian Oversight of Policing: Governance, Democracy and Human Rights*, Hart Publishing, Oxford, 2000, pp.259-293

Stephen Livingstone, Tim Owen and Alison Macdonald, *Prison Law: Text and Materials*, Clarendon Press, Oxford, 3rd ed., 2003

Committee on the Administration of Justice, *A Guide to Prisoners' Rights and Prison Law in Northern Ireland,* Belfast, 1998

Immigration, Marches, Free Speech and Information

Nicholas Blake and Laurie Fransman, *Immigration, Nationality and Asylum under the Human Rights Act 1998*, Butterworths, London, 1999

Joint Council for the Welfare of Immigrants, *Immigration, Nationality and Refugee Law Handbook*, London, 2002

Michael Hamilton, Neil Jarman and **Dominic Bryan**, *Parades, Protests and Policing: A Human Rights Framework*, Northern Ireland Human Rights Commission, Belfast, 2001
Northern Ireland Office, *Report of the Review of the Parades Commission and Public Processions (NI) Act 1998* (the Quigley Report), Belfast, 2002
Andrew Nicol, Gavin Millar and **Andrew Sharland**, *Media Law and Human Rights*, Blackstone Press, London, 2001
Iain Cameron, *National Security and the European Convention on Human Rights*, Kluwer, The Hague, 2000
Rosemary Jay and **Angus Hamilton**, *Data Protection Law and Practice*, Sweet and Maxwell, London, 1999
Madeleine Colvin, *Developing Key Privacy Rights*, Hart Publishing, Oxford, 2002

Equality and Discrimination

Committee on the Administration of Justice and Unison, *Equality and Human Rights: The Equality Provisions of the Good Friday Agreement and the Northern Ireland Act*, Belfast, 1999
Equality Commission for Northern Ireland, *Guide to the Statutory Duties*, Belfast, 2000
Equality Commission for Northern Ireland, *Section 75 of the Northern Ireland Act 1998: Practical guidance on equality impact assessment*, Belfast, 2000
Equality Coalition, *Section 75: Next Steps – Screening and Impact Assessment,* Belfast, 2001
Bob Hepple, Mary Coussey, and **Tufyal Choudhury**, *Equality: A new framework,* Hart Publishing, Oxford, 2000
Christopher McCrudden, *Mainstreaming Equality in the Governance of Northern Ireland*, (1999) 22 *Fordham International Law Journal* 1696
Northern Ireland Affairs Committee, *Operation of the Fair Employment (NI) Act 1989: Ten Years On*, Vol. 1, session 1998-1999, London
Sandra Fredman, *Discrimination Law*, Clarendon Press, Oxford, 2003
Brian Doyle, *Disability Discrimination: Law and Practice*, Jordan Publishing, Bristol, 2003
Richard Jones, *Mental Health Act Manual*, Sweet and Maxwell, London, 8th ed., 2003

Isabel Manley and Avrom Sherr (eds.), *Advising Clients with HIV and AIDS*, Butterworths, London, 2000

Northern Ireland Human Rights Commission, *Enhancing the Rights of Lesbian, Gay and Bisexual People in Northern Ireland*, Belfast, 2001

Maura McCallion, *Enhancing the Rights of Older People in Northern Ireland*, Northern Ireland Human Rights Commission, Belfast, 2001

Family, Children and Education

S Leech and R Young, "Marriage, Divorce and Ancillary Relief under the Human Rights Act 1998: An Introduction", [2001] 3 *European Human Rights Law Review* 300-311

Heather Swindells, Andrew Neaves, Martine Kushner and Rupert Skilbeck, *Family Law and the Human Rights Act 1998*, Jordan Publishing, Bristol, 1999

Kerry O'Halloran, *Family Law in Northern Ireland*, Gill and Macmillan, Dublin, 1997

Office of Law Reform, *Divorce in Northern Ireland: A Better Way Forward*, Belfast, 1999

Northern Ireland Human Rights Commission, *In Our Care: Promoting the Rights of Children in Custody*, Belfast, 2002

Ursula Kilkelly, *The Child and the European Convention on Human Rights*, Dartmouth Publishing Ltd., Aldershot, 1999

Rachel Hodgkin and Peter Newell, *Implementation Handbook for the Convention on the Rights of the Child*, UNICEF, New York, revised ed., 2002

Save the Children Fund and Children's Law Centre, *Getting It Right? The State of Children's Rights in Northern Ireland at the end of the 20th Century*, Belfast, 1999

Children's Law Centre, *Information Pack*, Belfast, 2002

Laura Lundy, *Education Law, Policy and Practice in Northern Ireland*, SLS Legal Publications (NI), Belfast, 2000.

Employment, Housing, Social Security and the Environment

Robin Allen and Rachel Crasnow, *Employment Law and Human Rights*, Oxford University Press, Oxford, 2002

Peter Wallington (ed.), *Butterworths Employment Law Handbook*, Butterworths, London, 11th ed., 2003

Housing Rights Service, *Housing Rights Manual*, Belfast, loose-leaf, regularly

Sharon Turner (ed.), *The Implementation of EC Environmental Law in Northern Ireland*, SLS Legal Publications (NI), Belfast, 2000

Sharon Turner and Karen Morrow, *Northern Ireland Environmental Law*, Gill and Macmillan, Dublin, 1997

Arena Network (NI) and Cleaver Fulton Rankin (Solicitors), *The Green Triangle: Law Business and the Environment*, Belfast, 1997

J A Dowling, *Northern Ireland Planning Law*, Gill and Macmillan, Dublin, 1995

Table of Legislation and Treaties

(Page references are at the end of each entry, in italics)

Table of Cases

(Page references are at the end of each entry, in italics)

Index

children disability
immigration
privacy
social security
equality
discrimination
detainees prisoners
employment
police powers
mental health

1873285345

£9.50
Published by
The Committee on the Administration of Justice